"The call we made in *Our Common Future*, back in 1987, is even more relevant today. Having a coherent resource like the *Encyclopedia of Sustainability*, written by experts yet addressed to students and general readers, is a vital step, because it will support education, enable productive debate, and encourage informed public participation as we join, again and again, in the effort to transform our common future."

—**Gro Harlem Brundtland,** chair of the World Commission
on Environment and Development and three-time prime minister of Norway

"This is undoubtedly the most important and readable reference on sustainability of our time."

—**Jim MacNeill**, Secretary-General of the Brundtland Commission
and chief architect and lead author of *Our Common Future* (1984–1987)

"Sustainability is one of the most important concepts of the 21st century yet remains elusive in implementation. This set of authoritative volumes provides an 'operator's manual' for the long-term sustainability of the human enterprise on planet Earth."

—**Will Steffen**, executive director of The Australian
National University Climate Change Institute

"The *Berkshire Encyclopedia of Sustainability* makes a timely and unique contribution to understanding and professionalizing the concept of sustainability to which Rio +20 is dedicated."

—**Maurice Strong**, former Secretary General of the 1992 UN
Conference on Environment and Development (Rio Earth Summit)

"Sustainability will be the defining discipline of the 21st century. Making sense of the sprawling body of sustainability knowledge and insights—to help make it available for a growing audience—is a massive challenge. Berkshire's *Encyclopedia of Sustainability* has risen to that challenge with flair, imagination and commanding authority."

—**Jonathon Porritt**, founder/director, forumforthefuture.org

"The Enlightenment of the 18th century had its famous encyclopedia that catalyzed dramatic improvements in science, society, and governance . . . the dawning Ecological Enlightenment of the 21st century now has its encyclopedia to light the way forward to a durable and decent future for humankind . . . a compass for a long, perilous journey through an unknown territory."

—**David W. Orr**, Oberlin College, author of *Hope is an
Imperative* and *Down to the Wire: Confronting Climate Collapse*

"The 21st century will be the age of sustainability or bust. As the journey becomes imperative, there is no better *vade mecum* than the *Berkshire Encyclopedia of Sustainability*—informative, lively, and comprehensive in its scope."

—**Isabel Hilton**, editor, chinadialogue.net

"It's past time for proponents of sustainability to move beyond empty slogans and baby steps. Everyone who is ready to get serious will profit from this robust, comprehensive, diverse collection of cutting edge thinking from some of the smartest members of our species."

—**Denis Hayes**, principal organizer of the first
Earth Day, and president of the Bullitt Foundation

BERKSHIRE
ENCYCLOPEDIA OF SUSTAINABILITY
VOLUME 10

THE FUTURE OF SUSTAINABILITY

© 2012 by Berkshire Publishing Group LLC

Digital editions

The *Berkshire Encyclopedia of Sustainability* is available through most major ebook and database services (please check with them for pricing). Special print/digital bundle pricing is also available in cooperation with Credo Reference; contact Berkshire Publishing (info@berkshirepublishing.com) for details.

For information, contact:
Berkshire Publishing Group LLC
122 Castle Street
Great Barrington, Massachusetts 01230-1506 USA
info@berkshirepublishing.com
Tel + 1 413 528 0206
Fax + 1 413 541 0076

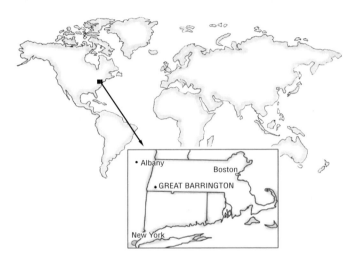

Library of Congress Cataloging-in-Publication Data

Berkshire encyclopedia of sustainability: / The future of sustainability, edited by Ray C. Anderson, et al.
   v. cm.
   Includes bibliographical references and index.
   Contents: vol. 10:. The Future f Sustainability —
   ISBN 978-1-933782-63-8 (vol. 10 print : alk. paper)
   1. Environmental quality—Encyclopedias.   2. Environmental protection—Encyclopedias.   3. Sustainable development—Encyclopedias.
I. Ray C. Anderson, et al.

Berkshire encyclopedia of sustainability (10 volumes) / edited by Ray Anderson et al.
   10 v. cm.
   Includes bibliographical references and index.
   ISBN 978-1-933782-01-0 (10 volumes : alk. paper) — 978-1-933782-00-3 (10 volumes e-book) — ISBN 978-1-933782-15-7 (vol. 1 print : alk. paper) — ISBN 978-1-933782-57-7 (vol. 1 e-book) — ISBN 978-1-933782-13-3 (vol. 2 print : alk. paper) — ISBN 978-1-933782-55-3 (vol. 2 e-book) — ISBN 978-1-933782-14-0 (vol. 3 print : alk. paper) — ISBN 978-1-933782-56-0 (vol. 3 e-book) — ISBN 978-1-933782-12-6 (vol. 4 print : alk. paper) — ISBN 978-1-933782-54-6 (vol. 4 e-book) — ISBN 978-1-933782-16-4 (vol. 5 print : alk. paper) — ISBN 978-1-933782-09-6 (vol. 5 e-book) — ISBN 978-1-933782-40-9 (vol. 6 print : alk. paper) — ISBN 978-0-9770159-0-0 (vol. 6 e-book) — ISBN 978-1-933782-69-0 (vol. 7 print : alk. paper) — ISBN 978-1-933782-72-0 (vol. 7 e-book) — ISBN 978-1-933782-18-8 (vol. 8 print : alk. paper) — ISBN 978-1-933782-73-7 (vol. 8 e-book) — ISBN 978-1-933782-19-5 (vol. 9 print : alk. paper) — ISBN 978-1-933782-74-4 (vol. 9 e-book) — ISBN 978-1-933782-63-8 (vol. 10 print : alk. paper) — ISBN 978-1-933782-75-1 (vol. 10 e-book)
   1. Environmental quality—Encyclopedias.   2. Environmental protection—Encyclopedias.   3. Sustainable development—Encyclopedias.
I. Anderson, Ray, et al.
   HC79.E5B4576   2010
   338.9'2703—dc22   2009035114

Image Credits

The illustrations used in this volume come from many sources. There are photographs provided by Berkshire Publishing's staff and friends, by authors, and from archival sources. All known sources and copyright holders have been credited.

Front cover photo, of fireflies (*Pyractomena borealis*) on an Iowa prairie, by Carl Kurtz.

Inset cover photo, as well as the image for the volume introduction, directory of sustainability programs, and index, is of red poppies on the terrace of the Berkshire Publishing Group office, Great Barrington, Massachusetts, USA. Photo by Karen Christensen.

Engraving illustrations of plants and insects by Maria Sibylla Merian (1647–1717); illustration of dragonfly in the Introduction by Lydia Umney.

Photos used at the beginning of each section:

A. *Mushroom mountain, Xishuangbanna Tropical Botanical Garden, Yunnan, China.* Photo by TAKANO Takenaka Kohei.

B. *Church with grass roof, Hof, Iceland.* Photo by Amy Siever.

C. *Sakura trees lining a river in winter, Sabae City, Japan.* Photo by Amanda Prigge.

D. *Rhinoceros cave painting, Chauvet Caves, southern France.* Photo by Inocybe.

E. *Sakura blossoms at twilight, Sabae City, Japan.* Photo by Amanda Prigge.

F. *Crab in a fish market in Echizen, Japan.* Photo by Amanda Prigge.

G. *Tea plantation in west Sumatra, Indonesia.* Photo by TAKANO Takenaka Kohei.

L. *Dahlia, Butchart Gardens, Victoria Island, British Columbia, Canada.* Photo by Ellie Johnston.

M. *Boy on a horse in Mongolia.* Photo by TAKANO Takenaka Kohei.

N. *Bromeliad flower, St. Croix, US Virgin Islands.* Photo by Anna Myers.

P. *Hibiscus flower, St. Croix, US Virgin Islands.* Photo by Anna Myers.

S. *The* Viking Lady, *a fuel cell–powered ship.* Photo printed by permission of Eidesvik.

V. *Sunflowers in the Cotswold Hills, United Kingdom.* Photo by Amy Siever.

W. *Jökulsárlón glacial lagoon, southern Iceland.* Photo by Bill Siever.

Berkshire Encyclopedia of Sustainability

Contents

List of Entries and Contributors in Volume 10

About the *Berkshire Encyclopedia of Sustainability*

The following section contains material relating to all ten volumes of the *Berkshire Encyclopedia of Sustainability*:

- a dedication and introduction to the entire series;
- a list of topics listed alphabetically, from "Accounting" to "Zero Waste";
- a Reader's Guide, in which the articles are divided up by topic ("Agriculture and Food," "Cities and the Built Environment," "Energy," etc.).

Following the articles themselves, we've included an appendix of sustainability-related programs and materials for students and teachers, followed by a Master Bibliography of all books, websites, and journals that have been cited at least three times in the *Encyclopedia of Sustainability*. (We've also included a list of the most cited works.) This is followed by a list of the over 900 contributors to the set. Lastly, the volume ends with an index to volume 10 as well as a Master Index of all ten volumes.

We encourage readers who are interested in further resources, and commenting on what they've read, to visit TheSustainabilityProject.com.

Dedication

It's been a special joy to see the commitment to the future shown by our authors and editors, and a few of them have, during the time we have worked together on the *Berkshire Encyclopedia of Sustainability*, shown their commitment and hopefulness in a most tangible way, by becoming parents.

Four of these babies were born to volume editors: Leo Miguel Dougherty; Zingwei Zhao, born to Jingjing Liu while work was being done on the volume she was editing (volume 7); Simeon Jacob Jackson Jenkins; and Ameya Pellissery. Many babies were born to our contributors: Bethany Ling; Emily Abigail Thomas and Lindsay Christine Thomas; Anastasia Gennet Sayre; Emilia Grace Nevada Allison-Biber; Gianna Melosi McDonald; Logan Beck; Iver Rock Brinkman; James Van Alen Trumbull; Elias Finn Newton; Benjamin Victor Moscoso; Hazel Anne Thrasher and Lucy Elizabeth Thrasher; Quincy Santana Newman; Ellis Chappells Dummer; Maya Maria Waldmann; Luigi Notarnicola; Peter Burnell; Lucas Viviani Lima; Savannah Nelson and Summer Nelson; Ryder Henley-Grieve; Ian Gutknecht; Aleksandra Elisa Pattberg; Tristan Shai Humby; Zeyong (Lerry) Lu; Marilena Tassielli; Ansel Peter Ricci; Isabella Vogiatzakis; Noah Jonathan Sommer; Torsten Peterson Gordon; and Shrey Lal. Author Melissa Rock is expecting a baby (name as yet unknown) in October of this year.

Several of our contributors became new grandparents while we working on the series, as well, and we welcome these children, as well: Anderson Olufimihan Aderibigbe; Caroline Suzanne Boyd; João Vicente Drummond; Daniel Karakashov; Mattia and Alessandro Negri; and Sebastian and Celeste Ellis.

We dedicate this work, the 10-volume *Berkshire Encyclopedia of Sustainability*, to these children, as representatives of the newest generation on Planet Earth. They inherit many challenges, but will also have great opportunity to shape a new future for humankind, and we intend this publication, as it evolves, to play a role in the changes ahead.

At the same time, we think of those who are no longer with us: Ray Anderson, for one, whose last words to us provided inspiration during the final year of work on the encyclopedia. In his last email to us, he said, "I'm very impressed with the progress you have made and wish you good luck and a wind at your back." Ray has done much to give all of us the wind we need to do the work that lies ahead. Steve De Gruchy, who contributed an article on sustainable development to volume 1, tragically drowned at the age of 48 while vacationing in his native South Africa with his family. Neil Whitehead, who wrote on Amazonia in volume 8, died at the age of 56 after battling an illness. Jon M. Van Dyke, who wrote on international law in volume 3, died at the age of 68 while attending a conference in Australia. While she was not a direct contributor to this encyclopedia, the political scientist Elinor Ostrom, whose work on sharing common resources won her the Nobel Prize for economics (despite the fact that she was not an economist), died during production of this final volume at the age of 78; her work and sense of humor inspired us and many of our contributors. Many of our contributors have lost loved ones over the last four years, all of whom will be sorely missed.

Lastly, we'd like to dedicate this series to Rachel Carson (1907–1964), the marine biologist and author whose work galvanized the public and governments around the world and is frequently credited as having started the modern environmental movement. Carson wrote *Silent Spring* while suffering from cancer, knowing that she had a limited time to live. Her words remind us to enjoy the beauties of the natural world and that we, too, are inseparably part of it:

For me it was one of the loveliest of the summer's hours, and all the details will remain in my memory: that blue September sky, the sounds of the wind in the spruces and surf on the rocks, the gulls busy with their foraging, alighting with deliberate grace, the distant views of Griffith Head and Todd's Point, today so clearly etched, though once half seen in swirling fog. But most of all I shall remember the monarchs, that unhurried westward drift of one small winged form after another, each drawn by some invisible force. . . .

But it occurred to me this afternoon, remembering, that it had been a happy spectacle, that we had felt no sadness when we spoke of the fact that there would be no return. And rightly—for when any living thing has come to the end of its life cycle we accept that end as natural.

For the monarch, that cycle is measured in a known span of months. For ourselves, the measure is something else, the span of which we cannot know. But the thought is the same: when that intangible cycle has run its course it is a natural and not unhappy thing that a life comes to an end.

Rachel Carson, *Letters*, 10 September, 1963

Silent Spring was published 50 years ago, and has inspired us and those who contributed, directly or indirectly, to the *Encyclopedia of Sustainability*, and in her honor we wish to all who turn to this work something that Carson experienced throughout her life and shared in her writing: a sense of wonder.

Marine biologist Rachel Carson (1907–1964), author of Silent Spring, *in 1944. Her book was very controversial at the time of its publication in 1962; it is widely credited with starting the worldwide environmental movement. We dedicate the* Encyclopedia of Sustainability *to* her legacy.

Introduction to the *Berkshire Encyclopedia of Sustainability*

Much of the *Berkshire Encyclopedia of Sustainability* is devoted to issues of design. From the architecture that we live and work in to the infrastructure that allows us to get around in the world, design dictates how we live, whether we realize it or not. Although this encyclopedia is not specifically a work on design, "good" or "bad" design informs everything that has anything to do with sustainability.

Although many people say that *sustainability* is a difficult term to define, one thing that is clear is that there are various facets of the world around us that need to be better designed: our buildings (homes and offices) need to do more with less; we need infrastructure to make it easier for people to ride bicycles and trains to work; we need food to feed the world without damaging natural support systems. Our energy infrastructure needs to be redesigned to favor (and allow) using less energy in a less polluting fashion, so that people around the world can have access to good, nutritious food that does not ruin the environment in the process of being grown and moved to their dinner plates. Whether we take this upon ourselves or let our governments take the helm is a matter of great debate, all over the world.

Observation of the natural world has always informed and contributed to human design and aesthetics, even in cases where designers have chosen to create forms deliberately and sometimes aggressively "against" nature. In the modern world, human designs—and here a darker, more calculated meaning can underlie that term—impact the sustainability of our environment through a variety of areas and fields: product design, building design, town and regional planning, manufacturing and data management systems, and more. It is all of this that has driven the writing of this entire encyclopedia; to set out in ten volumes the intricate and often complex interplay between design and sustainability. Indeed can we "design" for

sustainability given that this inevitably requires foresight? Sustainability is about the future (the focus of volume 10) as well as the present and past, but accurately predicting trends and designing a transport system or town with the goal of addressing any issues that we think may arise is a challenge, and we often have managed to get it wrong.

No one has said that sustainability is easy to achieve, or even to define. This could be simply because many people are not familiar with the three pillars of sustainability: economic, environmental, and social, any one of which collapses without the support of the other two. Social sustainability and economic sustainability are both dependent on the sustainable and equitable use of nature and the environment. Put one way, we have to live within environmental limits, which we are not doing. Put another way, sustainability is about living equitably within the non-negotiable laws of thermodynamics, chemistry, and ecological interaction.

Design Challenges

Two design challenges confronted us with this massive, ten-volume project. Thoughts about our coverage came first: how should we ensure that design innovation and the ramifications of industrial and product design were fully explored in our different volumes? Our "appearance"—the surface of design—came next: what should an *Encyclopedia of Sustainability* look like? To our minds a print encyclopedia should be, in the words of the English polymath William Morris, both beautiful and useful. In other Berkshire encyclopedias we made photographs not only an essential element of the design but a supplementary teaching tool.

For the *Encyclopedia of Sustainability,* however, we were starting a series with one rather abstract subject, "spirit" and ethics, and two others, business and law, that don't easily lend themselves to visual enhancement. Although we used twenty-one different photographic images—one per letter group of entries—to enhance the title pages of the articles, photographs would not effectively add to the intellectual content of these first volumes. So we decided to use decorative elements with a "message." Our inspiration came from scientific illustration, which, in the days before photography was in widespread use, conveyed to the general public an essential part of the discoveries being made about the natural world. Scientists were artists and artists were scientists—seeing the world afresh in a concerted effort to understand it and to organize knowledge about it. (This is similar to what happened in anatomical studies: drawing the human body was an essential part of understanding how it worked.) For volume 1 of this series, *The Spirit of Sustainability*, we chose natural history as our theme: drawings (of a beetle, moth, ladybug, and dragonfly, as seen on the right) by Lydia Umney as well as other illustrations (creatures of the air and flora) from the archives of the Library of Congress and the New York Public Library. Subsequent volumes have featured other illustrations on relevant themes.

Our cover photograph by Carl Kurtz shows fireflies (*Pyractomena borealis*) on the Iowa prairie. We selected this image for the *Encyclopedia of Sustainability* because it so vividly presents the beauty of a restored habitat—not a necessarily exciting or dramatic habitat, at least to the casual observer, but one that is nevertheless lovely and rich—and because it speaks volumes about the diverse life that exists on our planet. It also has symbolic resonance. The myriad points of light remind us that a sustainable future is within reach.

A Black Belt in Sustainability

Everyone tells us that publishing ten volumes on sustainability is a triumph. It is certainly a major accomplishment, especially for a relatively new publishing house like Berkshire. We are conscious, however, of how much more there is to do, and while we explain how our small team—with the very large team of authors and editors with whom we have been so exceptionally engaged—created this publication, we will provide a look at the things to come, some already in progress, and others for the longer term.

Much of our attention is on making this project as international as possible. As final brushstrokes were being put on the *Encyclopedia of Sustainability* we learned that

another of our publications, the *Berkshire Encyclopedia of World History*, second edition, would be only the third major English language reference work ever to be translated into Chinese—following in the footsteps of *Encyclopaedia Britannica* (founded in 1768) and *Science and Civilisation in China*, published (starting in 1955) by Cambridge University Press and the life project of sinologist Joseph Needham; the latter massive work was an inspiration for our own *Encyclopedia of China*. This seemed appropriate because we also hope to see the *Encyclopedia of Sustainability* in Chinese, and much of our work on China has been inspired by the knowledge that cooperation on environmental issues is the key to our common future.

"Our common future" is a phrase that has echoed throughout work on this project. It is the title of the Brundtland Report as published in 1987, and it has been our guiding principle: What do we need to know and understand in order to have, all of us who share planet Earth, the future we want for ourselves, our children, and our grandchildren?

As we reflect on what we have accomplished, we cannot help thinking about what lies ahead, and how much more is needed from us, how much more there is to learn and share, and quickly. This situation is rather like that of someone who has spent years training in martial arts, aiming to wear a black belt, who actually becomes a "black belt," only to find that that's not how it works, once one "arrives." The black belt, *shodan*, is simply a marker that you've learned the basics. It is a new beginning. The learning goes on. That is what this encyclopedia is: a beginning, a starting point.

It is the work of a community of nearly a thousand experts, who have worked with Berkshire to create a work that defines the field more than anything else that exists. The first six volumes provide coverage of all the core topics, while the next three focus on sustainability in different regions, and the final volume is a collection of major essays on the future of sustainability. This is truly a groundbreaking interdisciplinary resource created to allow us to transform our common future.

The Encyclopedia's Coverage

Think of these nearly nine hundred articles in ten volumes as a collection of precisely tuned review articles. They provide complete but compact coverage of issues that

Gro Harlem Brundtland, chair of the World Commission on Environment and Development and three-time prime minister of Norway. The Brundtland Report, commonly known as Our Common Future, *remains one of the most influential publications on sustainability of all time.*

students, faculty, businesspeople, and civic leaders are eager to learn about, from sustainability in the pharmaceutical and health care industries to nanotechnology and the environmental repercussions of free trade.

This series represents a critical mass of short (with the exception of volume 10, whose essays are longer), well-organized, expert-written material that is simply not available from other sources. The collection itself creates a frame of reference that makes it easier to get a handle on complex issues quickly. A unique global network of experts was created in the process of creating this series: experts in the fields of business, law, ecosystem and resource management, environmental history, ethics and philosophy, and many more. These experts have, often for the first time, put their research into layperson's language, to be as accessible as possible to as large an audience as possible.

Many social and economic issues are dependent on environmental sustainability—poverty, literacy, and human rights, to name a few—and we have included articles about them. But we have tried to avoid suggesting that all problems are equal or that all must be solved at once. Too often, reports on sustainability read like a laundry list of problems, small and large, recent and as old as humanity. By not prioritizing them, or organizing them in terms of immediate impact or some logical process of change, well-meaning environmentalists and even world leaders can leave the public feeling that the situation is irredeemable.

Our fundamental premise, as we've created this work, is that the human impact on the natural world is profound and highly problematic in terms of our own future, but that change is possible, that humans are inventive and adaptable, that natural systems are resilient, and that abundance as well as scarcity is a characteristic of the world we live in. We sought to be realistic but not pessimistic, and we sought to see change as more likely to be motivated by visionary thinking and creativity than by scolding or doomsaying.

Not all our editors or authors will agree with us, or with one another, and that too is part of the value of the *Encyclopedia of Sustainability*. In fact, we will make the debates and controversies of sustainability a core part of TheSustainabilityProject.com, which brings together all the content found in the *Encyclopedia of Sustainability* along with a great deal of new material, especially that geared to teaching and training.

As we developed the ten volumes of the *Encyclopedia of Sustainability*, we have become increasingly aware of the importance of community-building and leadership. This includes the work of environmental thinkers and activists who have made a difference by inspiring others, creating coalitions that have changed the world (we think of Lois Gibbs at Three Mile Island; Rachel Carson's book *Silent Spring*, published fifty years ago; Wangari Muta Maathai's founding of the Green Belt movement in Africa; or the Brazilian anti-logging activist Chico Mendez, murdered for his activities; and of Ray Anderson, our guiding light and guardian angel: more on him in the Project Background section below).

The knowledge community of nearly a thousand authors whose work you find here represents a much larger community of historians, sociologists, and scientists of all sorts—past and present—who have labored to understand the world we live in and how we affect it, and how we can make ourselves, and generations to come, at home on Earth. We were particularly glad to include historian David Christian's article "Collective Learning" in volume 10 because that is precisely what the *Encyclopedia of Sustainability* was designed to encourage and support, in the classroom as well as in the boardroom.

Project Background

The *Encyclopedia of Sustainability* was first intended to be four volumes published in 2007. It turned out to be ten volumes published in 2012, and the expansion began over a lunch at the Cosmos Club in Washington, DC, when one of our *Encyclopedia of World Environmental History* (Routledge, 2003) authors (Marty Reuss, who contributed the article "Dams and Reservoirs" to volume 4 of the *Encyclopedia of Sustainability*) argued that the topic deserved more space and more time. There is no written record of that conversation, because no business is allowed at the Cosmos Club, but Marty and Berkshire's publisher, Karen Christensen, immediately sketched a possible ten volumes. That outline has been almost exactly followed, and we have, as Marty suggested then, designed the work so each volume can be used (and purchased) separately.

The *Encyclopedia of Sustainability* also has origins in Beijing because of an introduction to C. S. Kiang, a formerly US-based physicist, then head of an institute at Peking University. He invited Karen Christensen to meet him in Atlanta and took her to meet industrialist-turned-environmental-activist Ray Anderson at his offices in the headquarters of the multi-million-dollar modular carpet manufacturer Interface, Inc. That was their only meeting, and Ray is not alive today to be presented with the entire set that bears his name along with those of hundreds of others—many of them people who were inspired by his work, his vision, his speeches and books, and by his commitment to building a sustainable business and to articulating a fresh way to look at the role of business and businesspeople.

Karen presented him with a few past titles and explained the goals of the project. Ray pointed out the piles of books on the floor in front of the expanse of windows in his spacious office and said that he was prepared to lend his services as an advisor to the *Encyclopedia of Sustainability*. Ray then introduced Chris Laszlo as a potential editor for the volume on business, and continued to be a warm supporter until only weeks before his death in August of 2011.

His leadership extended far beyond his own company and industry. His books, especially the latest, *Confessions of a Radical Industrialist* (St. Martin's Press, 2009), will continue to inspire, and Ray's influence will continue to be felt through the work of all the people he has encouraged, supported, and instructed.

When the Library of Congress insisted on having a single editor listed first on every volume—even though each volume has a separate set of editors—we realized that if we listed the general advisory board, his name would appear first. We wrote to explain, and he graciously agreed that we could use his name. The *Encyclopedia of Sustainability* is thus listed as Anderson et al., and we could not be more proud. His vote of confidence and trust means a great deal

Publisher Karen Christensen of Berkshire Publishing (front row, fourth from left) with students from Peking University.

to Berkshire and to the other people who have worked on the encyclopedia.

Ray's graciousness and humor were clear that day in Atlanta. Karen feels even more grateful today that he recognized the educational importance of this great work. In his last email, Ray said, "I'm very impressed with the progress you have made and wish you good luck and a wind at your back." Ray has done much to give all of us at Berkshire the wind we have needed to do the work required to get this monumental work finished.

When we began, there were publishing colleagues who didn't even understand the title of this encyclopedia. "What's sustainability?" one asked. As we publish the final volume in 2012, that question seems inconceivable. Today, there is a growing emphasis on local and sustainable production. Everything claims to be "local" and "sustainable." The ubiquity of the term *sustainability* gives more importance to this effort to explain what it really means.

That, in itself, was an issue. The question as to what sustainability is has long been asked and, to be frank, the answers are often vague and "flexible." Hence was it really a suitable title? We spent weeks arguing with the Library of Congress about how to classify the *Berkshire Encyclopedia of Sustainability*. The Library's catalogers initially classified it with titles on sustainable development. We wrote many emails explaining that our focus was environmental sustainability, which meant that it needed to be under "sustainability" or at least "environment." The Library of Congress is the authority, and

Ray C. Anderson (1934–2011), industrialist-turned-environmental activist and general editor of the Encyclopedia of Sustainability.

hated to admit to making a mistake in classification, but we eventually prevailed; the description on our copyright page now is "Environmental quality—Encyclopedias; Environmental protection—Encyclopedias; Sustainable development—Encyclopedias." To us, this was a sign of how early we were in designating a major work with this title.

Encyclopedias generally have boring titles, for good reason—titles should be solid, clear, unmistakable landmarks. An "Encyclopedia of Environmental Issues" would be the "right" title, it seemed. But that awkward title did not convey the spirit of the project. The word *sustainability* came to mind. At first we dismissed it as too vague, too ephemeral, too much an insider term. But it shouldn't be a word known only to the initiated, we thought. Sustainability is a concept everyone can grasp, and indeed we can go further by arguing that it is a concept that everyone has to grasp: otherwise the human race is in trouble. Although sustainability is often equated with doomsaying, and such negative connotations do not necessarily help when attempting to promote the concept, there is nonetheless an inevitable limit set by the fact that we have only one Earth, and we all have to live on it.

When no other sufficient title came to mind, we made our early announcements with the *Berkshire Encyclopedia of Sustainability* as the tentative title, and somehow it stuck despite concerns, questions, and comments from our widening network. Dan Vasey, who has contributed to several volumes of the *Encyclopedia of Sustainability* and is one of the editors of volumes 4 and 10, expressed a worry echoed by others, that *sustainability* seems to mean entirely different things to different people. Some people asked whether the term was itself sustainable—meaning that ideas and terms sometimes surge then fade, and an encyclopedia should not peg itself to an idea that is not well established. Is "sustainability" a flash in the pan, they asked, an idea that will be seen as "so 2009"? Or is it a major societal shift, like the Industrial Revolution, that needs to be documented? We would say that sustainability is here to stay, whether we like it or not. It is unlike any other societal shift in that it demands a consideration for both the future and for the now. It is thus truly timeless, and indeed can hardly be said to be new. While the word *sustainability* may be a relatively new invention, people have been thinking about their future for as long as the human race has existed. We may have extended that horizon from the next meal to the next generations, but the essence is the same.

Dan also pointed out a fundamental problem inherent in the encyclopedia format, which "by segregating interconnected subjects," he wrote,

. . . makes sustainability look easier than it is. The concern extends to my own recent contribution, "Agriculture" [in volume 1]. I tried to be holistic, and the word limits allowed me to consider population, urban sprawl, and phosphorus resources, but the best I could do on energy was to note reliance on fossil fuels and pressures from biofuel production. If I were to take full account of those and other trends and proposals—that we allocate metal and cement to wind, solar, and hydro; use the generated power to run tractors and fertilizer factories; grow the cloth that now comes from petroleum; achieve consumer equity—and then draw a flow chart of competing resource demands, the result would look and sound less sanguine.

An editor for volume 2, Peter Whitehouse, commented on the need to make connections from volume to volume:

In medicine there is a tendency to compartmentalize ethics and hence marginalize moral conversations. *Business*, like *ethics*, is a word signifying a set of concepts and practices. "Natural capitalism," for example, is only a start at looking how we account for the world's resources. Developing "sustainable value" is a key approach but the values underlying that creation are key.

We faced a similar dilemma with the *Encyclopedia of World History*. One of its editors, and now a mainstay Berkshire author, David Christian (who also contributed to the final volume of the *Encyclopedia of Sustainability*), began our first conversation by saying that an encyclopedia went against the basic premise of the *Encyclopedia of World History*, that everything is connected.

Karen Christensen recently wrote in *Library Journal*, "I've come to see the encyclopedia as the Greeks did: 'a complete course of instruction in all parts of knowledge' (*Encyclopaedia Britannica*, 1911 ed.), providing crisp short-form content that is perfect for our fast-paced world and for students who want information at a touch." This sums up our goal for the *Berkshire Encyclopedia of Sustainability*.

Fortunately, our hundreds of authors seem now to agree that the term *sustainability* is sufficiently broad and inclusive, that it provides a way to identify, appreciate, and measure change, and that it makes connections between environmental issues and other global challenges.

Early on we thought we should address the need for an authoritative and comprehensive guide to environmental solutions. We sought comprehensive coverage, including science and technology, agriculture and consumer product design, community development and financial markets. We believed early-stage solutions, assessed with proper academic rigor, merited coverage in the encyclopedia and that we should carefully develop and assess definitions of *sustainability* and other key terms using collaborative tools. We further prioritized the place of international and cross-cultural differences.

The need for an international approach was obvious at Berkshire because Karen is also an environmental author (with titles ranging from *Home Ecology* [1989] to *The Armchair Environmentalist* [2008]). One of her priorities as a publisher has been to include environmental topics in all Berkshire publications; this sustainability encyclopedia is the culmination of a growing interest in environmental issues at Berkshire that began with Karen's early books and developed through early Berkshire publications and the growing relationship with environmental history.

The *Encyclopedia of Sustainability* includes environmental history, but its focus is on the present, and many of its authors are scientists specializing in a vast array of ecological and technological aspects of environmental management. We have been able to create an interdisciplinary network of scholars working on sustainability and brought in people outside academia who are actively contributing to the development of tools and knowledge. That's really the role we have as publishers of major international reference projects: creating networks, assembling the expertise of these networks into comprehensive and balanced resources, and sustaining the networks and communications for ongoing collaboration.

Organizing Sustainability

But what exactly does the *Encyclopedia of Sustainability* include, and why is it organized the way it is? In 2004 Berkshire Publishing distributed a survey among librarians; we asked them to list the subjects they'd most like to see covered in newly published works. Our list was expansive—Asian studies; China/Chinese history and culture; Latino studies; environmental issues; international relations; personal relations and communications; primary text resources; religion and society; sports; technology and society; terrorism and global security; world history; world theater, dance, and music—and included a number of topics that coincided with Berkshire projects already or soon to be under way. Although environmental issues were not as central to public discourse in 2004 as they are in 2012, the librarians put "environmental issues" at the top of the list. We at Berkshire were surprised. A lot of reference material on environmental issues appeared to be quite good. Why then would librarians be asking for more?

We came to the conclusion that existing books often did a great job of explaining the problems—species loss, air pollution, climate change, toxic chemicals in our homes—but included very little about solutions. We needed to develop instead a project about solutions, about a green future.

Although we originally scheduled *The Spirit of Sustainability* as volume 3, and later as volume 2, in the end it took final shape more quickly than the others (due in large part to the diligence and networking of editor Willis Jenkins) and became volume 1. Some might see this as providential. Functioning in many ways as an introduction to the whole project, volume 1 focuses not solely on religious beliefs and the environment, an important area of increasing influence in the real world, but on the underlying values and perspectives that shape how human society approaches environmental problems and searches for solutions.

In mapping out topics and organizing the volumes of the *Berkshire Encyclopedia of Sustainability*, we set out to (1) increase general knowledge of sustainability; (2) provide subject-specific coverage that is not readily accessible outside the scientific or academic community; and (3) connect current research with the political, professional, and personal opportunities available to individuals and organizations. Our goals are also revolutionary and far-reaching. We want to help individuals, policy makers, and businesses change the world for the better. Nothing less is acceptable to us. This may be seen by some as ambitious, but we see it as a necessity. We are not making pronouncements about the right path or indeed paths to follow. Rather we are bringing together the best thinking and using the tool kit of a global encyclopedia publisher to organize and integrate information from different areas of study (water conservation, alternative energy, ecosystems, and consumer products, for instance) into an abundance of short-form material that will be widely useful.

Coverage in the Regional Volumes

The basic coverage within the regional volumes (7–9) follows a similar pattern: each volume contains a core group of articles on such general topics as agriculture, energy issues, education, fisheries, e-waste, agriculture, and environmental law and justice. Each volume also has a handful of entries on the environmental history of representative nations and regions as well as portraits of specific cities in each region. In our coverage of cities we tried to focus on those cities that are "obvious" choices because of their progressive city planning and activism—cities like Stockholm and Vancouver come to mind—as well as lesser-known sustainability pioneers such as Curitiba, Brazil, and Auckland, New Zealand. We also wanted to include cities such as Las Vegas and Phoenix, infamous for their unsustainability, in part to find out what people are doing, against the odds, to lessen those cities' impact on the environment. Finally, because sustainability is approached differently in different parts of the world, each volume has articles specific to each region: women's roles in development in India, anti-desertification strategies in Africa, mining in Australia, and the environmental consequences of the North American Free Trade Agreement in that continent.

A Wide-Angle View of Sustainability

By gathering the work of so many experts, we also experienced something about how ideas move from the societal fringes to common acceptance. This shift is something blogs and newspaper articles can't capture, but an encyclopedia can. In effect, we have taken a wide-angle snapshot here of something in an almost continual state of change, but the big picture—the panoply of ideas evolving to meet a complex, fast-changing, far-ranging set of global issues—is one we need to see clearly. Otherwise it's just too difficult for those working in one part of an environmental field (whether ecosystems management, urban design, or bioremediation of toxic waste) to make broad connections and forge new collaborations. Our aim is to make it easier for a high school teacher, a financial manager, or a global executive, for example, to understand more easily the issues most relevant to their work and to the students, citizens, shareholders, and customers for whom they are responsible.

We had seen too many cases where people weren't basing decisions on measurable impact and weren't weighing options in a rational way. Public policy on environmental issues is insufficiently grounded in empirical evidence, and sometimes environmentalism comes across as a kind of religious faith to be adopted and adhered to no matter what. We were also concerned about making this project something that people on different sides of various environmental issues (such as nuclear energy), in different countries, can trust. In the years we have been working on this, the problem of trust has become much more important, particularly in (but certainly not limited to) the United States: skepticism about certain scientific findings—including climate change and even the theory of evolution, fundamental to so much modern science—among the public. Including so much on measurements and indicators (volume 6) is a clear statement of how important it is to us that people be able to back up proposals for change.

One challenge in those early days was with authors not used to providing hard data to support their ideas. We took a stand against the popular idea of "thought leadership" by insisting that authors provide data to back up their thoughts and to provide real-life examples and countering points of view. This approach—practical, research-based, and balanced—was not universally admired. But we soon discovered that there were many experts who were delighted to contribute to a work that was not advocating any one particular viewpoint. Take nuclear power, an always-contentious topic that is covered—strictly in an unbiased fashion—in the following articles:

• "Energy Industries—Nuclear" (volume 2) discusses how nuclear power can (perhaps) be made safer and more cost effective;
• "Chernobyl" (volume 3) discusses the world's deadliest nuclear disaster;
• "New Zealand Nuclear Free Zone, Disarmament, and Arms Control Act" (volume 3) discusses how New Zealand risked its Cold War–era strategic partnership with the United States by banning all nuclear vessels from its waters;
• "Thorium" and "Uranium" (volume 4) are two articles that discuss the use, history, and future of two elements vital to every kind of nuclear usage, from peaceful energy generation to nuclear weapons;

• "Energy Industries—Nuclear" (volume 7, covering China, India, and East Asia) discusses the nuclear power industries in these nations, especially important given the tsunami that devastated Japan's northeast coast and (perhaps) the future of its nuclear industry along with it;
• "Nuclear Power" (volume 10), a historical view of the subject, as well as a look forward to the industry's possible futures.

Notably lacking from these pages, readers will find, is a message saying that nuclear power is "good" or "bad." There are legitimate arguments on both sides of the nuclear question, and readers need to understand that. Similarly, we strove for a neutral treatment of the role of corporations and the private sector in the push for sustainability. Many people share our desire to go beyond advocacy and blanket criticisms to look at different points of view and will appreciate the objective tone found in these pages.

To be sure, there are those who will say we have not gone far enough—that the problems facing the planet are so serious and so catastrophic that extreme measures are required. Most people don't see things that way, however. Most citizens, throughout history, have ignored big dangers because they are immersed in all the practical complications of making a living, raising children, and doing the myriad things that make up our personal and social worlds. A call to action is the role of activists; regulating destructive activities is the role of governments. Our role is to inform, educate, and encourage readers to think—not necessarily to tell them what to think.

Others may see us as too "green," too committed to environmental issues, to which we say: this is an *Encyclopedia of Sustainability*, and we firmly believe that environmental sustainability (or, to be more specific, lack of sustainability) is the single most important issue facing humanity today and into the future. This is evidenced by our commitment to assembling this ten-volume series. Again, we want to avoid telling people what to think: there are many potential paths to reaching the ultimate goal of a more sustainable world.

How to Use the *Encyclopedia of Sustainability*

An encyclopedia like this one is a circle of knowledge, and it is designed, even in print, to be used as part of an ongoing education in classrooms, in professional development and training courses, as well as for writing papers and reports. More than one person—including a customer service staffer at Berkshire—has told us that they "want to read the whole thing." This is daunting—the entire *Encyclopedia of Sustainability* is nearly five thousand pages—but it also makes sense, in the sense that you have here an educational resource that is unmatched, and broken up into parts that are easy to read, coherent in themselves as well as useful in conjunction with other articles in the same and in other volumes.

The articles in the *Encyclopedia of Sustainability* were written by experts using the latest research and, in many cases, their own research and analysis. Further, the writing is accessible and jargon-free. The articles have been peer reviewed, revised by the author as necessary, and copyedited to Berkshire standards (as set out in our *Berkshire Manual of Style for International Publishing*). They are comparable to journal articles in quality, though written and edited for a general readership. They are an ideal introduction to unfamiliar topics and provide an excellent start for student and professional research.

Some of the volumes—notably *The Law and Politics of Sustainability*, *The Business of Sustainability*, and *Measurements, Indicators, and Research Methods for Sustainability*—will be used as textbooks, and courses could be designed around them, where they do not already exist. (Berkshire will be gathering and developing course syllabi for inclusion in TheSustainablityProject.com.)

These articles can be used as supplementary course readers. There are a wide variety of ways that this can work. Copies can be made directly from the print volumes. Berkshire allows free use of up to ten copies of no more than two articles (per course or program), and more extensive use can be granted for a fee either directly from Berkshire or through the Copyright Clearance Center website. Teachers at institutions with an online subscription to separate volumes or the entire work—available through all major digital library vendors worldwide—can assign a selection of articles. It is also possible to download individual articles directly from Berkshire, with permission fees based on type of institution and number of students. (Please refer to the copyright page for more details.)

Instructors can also create their own books, for students to purchase through the university bookstore, by visiting AcademicPub.com and choosing from the full range of *Encyclopedia of Sustainability* articles. Berkshire is creating a range of article collections, too, under the "Berkshire Essentials" list. The following topics have been planned and more will follow:

- Design and Sustainability
- Environmental Law and Sustainability
- Industrial Ecology and Sustainability
- Energy Industries and Sustainability
- Business Strategies, Management, and Sustainability
- Finance, Investment, and Sustainability
- Religion and Sustainability
- Ecosystem Services and Sustainability

The Reader's Guides found at the beginning of volumes 1–9 of the *Encyclopedia of Sustainability* allow users to see quickly what the related articles are. (Volume 10 has a master Reader's Guide, on pages L–LXXIII, with all articles in all ten volumes divided by category; volume 10 does not have a separate guide because of the relatively small number of articles.) For example, someone looking up "Social Issues" in *The Law and Politics of Sustainability* will find the following topics (among others): "Armed Conflict and the Environment"; "Bhopal Disaster"; "Chernobyl"; "Eco-Terrorism"; "Education, Environmental Law"; "Fair Trade"; "Grassroots Environmental Movements"; "Intergenerational Equity"; "Justice, Environmental"; and "Love Canal."

Cross references after each article also point the reader to articles in that volume that they may also find of interest. And in the final volume there is a Master Index that lists all the places in the *Encyclopedia of Sustainability*, by volume, where one might find mention of, for example, genetically modified organisms (another increasingly important topic).

Volume 10: *The Future of Sustainability*

Volume 10 is, in more ways than one, the culmination of years of work and presented us with tough decisions. The aforementioned Dan Vasey, author of "Agriculture" in volume 1, asked early on: "How wide a range of views do you plan to include in volume 10? The writers who most often use the word *sustainability* cluster in a middle ground. Will you also include prominent environmentalists who say the world can at best support a billion bicycling vegetarians? What about believers in limitless growth, free markets, resource substitutability, cold fusion, hot fusion, breeder reactors, desalinization, lunar mines, hydroponics, and super-photosynthesizing algae?" (It should be noted that all of these topics have been at least touched on throughout the pages of the *Encyclopedia of Sustainability*.)

The Future of Sustainability, the tenth and final volume of the *Berkshire Encyclopedia of Sustainability*, brings together

PUBLISHING SUSTAINABLY

At Berkshire we always ask ourselves how we can run our business in a way that will help preserve and even restore the planet. Publishing an encyclopedia devoted entirely to the idea (and the practice) of sustainability makes the challenge even more immediate. Using a "green" printer like Thomson-Shore and choosing the right paper, as we did for the *Encyclopedia of China* (and are doing for the *Encyclopedia of Sustainability)*, is only a first step. Submitting each volume for an Eco-Audit (found on page VI of this volume) sponsored by The Green Press Initiative, a nonprofit organization with a mission to help those in the publishing industry conserve natural resources, is a second.

Many in the industry believe that depending more and more on the electronic world is a planet-friendly move. But reading and publishing online—as well as the virtually paperless editorial processes gradually adopted by sustainability-savvy publishers (Berkshire included)—are not carbon-free activities: data centers consume vast quantities of resources to keep the arrays of servers on which we depend running smoothly, twenty-four hours a day; e-waste and rare earth mineral extraction are other undesirable side effects of the paperless revolution. After chairing the first Green Data Centres conference in London in 2008, publisher Karen Christensen came to realize that in some ways publishing on paper is a better choice than e-publishing. (Berkshire is doing both, trying to improve and streamline its digital and "hard copy" procedures.) Books that last because of the paper they are printed on and endure because of the words they contain fulfill an important component of sustainability—the production of quality goods with a long life. Berkshire hopes to offset its carbon footprint (at least somewhat) by the knowledge that readers gain from the pages herein. Other factors besides the physical printing of books contribute significantly to the carbon footprint industry-wide—for one, the supply chain and shipping methods by which books get to distributors and, finally, to customers, are extremely inefficient and costly. (Volume 2, *The Business of Sustainability*, offers a substantial contribution to this discussion.) We are learning about our subject as we live it, and we have the privilege of being able to tap the expertise of an extraordinary roster of global sustainability experts and professionals.

essays from a group of renowned scholars and well-known environmental thinkers, many of whom contributed either as authors or editors (or both) to previous volumes in the series. Some of the world's more crucial topics are considered in terms of the future of humanity and its relationship with the natural world: aging and world population; the future of nuclear energy; cities, energy, agriculture, water, food security, mobility, and migration; the role of higher education; and the concept, unique to our species, of collective learning. This is where the reader will find the big issues: where the idea of "progress" has brought us (and will bring us) as a species, and how to view the Earth's changing climate from the larger perspective of "big history." The volume concludes with a resource guide for teaching materials at several levels, a directory of leading undergraduate- and graduate-level programs in sustainability, and the comprehensive combined index of the ten-volume set mentioned earlier.

We did not include some articles we initially hoped to have: Economic Growth, the Internet (the epitome of a "moving target"), Space, Data Storage, Global Governance, and a general future-oriented discussion of smart energy. Business and religion had had whole volumes devoted to them. We focused instead on concepts such as "Property Rights" and "Progress" that have big implications for choices in the years ahead. Space is to some extent covered in "Geoengineering," renewable energy in "Energy Efficiency." There is plenty more to be covered; in every volume, we have had to do without topics we would have loved to include; such is life. But this is where technology can help: in the post-print SustainabilityProject.com, we will be able to feature interactive material as well as including articles that we were not able to include in the first print edition.

Many of the topics in the final volume are more future-oriented takes on topics already covered in previous volumes: "Water," "Mobility," "Shipping," and "Population," among others. In some respects, however, authors throughout the entire set have had an eye to the future; after all, that is essentially what sustainability is. In much the same way, many of the articles in *The Future of Sustainability* provide a fresh historic perspective on issues of utmost importance. It's impossible to think of future possibilities of technology, or cities of the future, without understanding how far we've come as a species. "Anthropocene Epoch," "Climate Change and Big History," "Design and Architecture," "Progress," "Population," and "Collective Learning" all discuss human habitations and origins, from the Chauvet Caves of southern France to our unique abilities to learn. David Christian writes in "Collective Learning":

> First, the adjective *collective* is important. There are limits to what an isolated individual can learn. . . . Human brains are indeed larger than those of our closest relatives, chimpanzees. But the roughly threefold difference in brain capacity is not enough to account for the much greater differences between the cumulative, diverse, and highly changeable historical trajectory of *Homo sapiens* and the relatively stable historical trajectories of all other species. Nor have humans gotten any brainier. . . . What distinguishes us from all other species is that we can share information rapidly, efficiently, and precisely, creating a large and growing stock of information that we share collectively. In principle, this stock of information can grow without limit.

It has become fairly obvious from the world's political landscape that getting people to agree on things is not easy, especially when national pride and natural resources are at stake. It is thus evident that if we want to "save the planet," we must use our abilities to learn collectively to generate a renewed sense of community. As Karen Christensen writes in her article on that topic,

> A renewed sense of community . . . is part of every scenario for a sustainable future. While not everyone espousing sustainability agrees that "degrowth" is essential . . . many talk about a world in which progress is no longer measured by economic or gross domestic product growth, but by levels of well-being and happiness, and by the well-being of the natural world.

We invite the readers of these books to join in this collective endeavor: it is, after all, "our common future" that is at stake. And most of all: enjoy!

Acknowledgments

The entire *Encyclopedia of Sustainability* has a galaxy of advisors, including Ray Anderson, the founder and CEO of Interface, Inc. and author of *Confessions of a Radical Industrialist*. Other longtime friends and advisors include Christine Loh, CEO of Civic Exchange and founder of Hong Kong Human Rights Monitor; we are thrilled to hear that Loh was recently named Hong Kong's Under Secretary for the Environment, and wish her the best of luck at her new post; Lester Brown, founder of the Worldwatch Institute and the Earth Policy Institute; and Ashok Khosla, president of the International Union for Conservation of Nature.

In addition, every volume has a group of editors and associate editors who have helped us to shape the list, recommend authors, and review articles. We are especially grateful to Ian Spellerberg of Lincoln University, Daniel Vasey of Divine Word College (emeritus), and Mark Anderson of the University of Maine for their help and advice in developing *The Future of Sustainability*.

Volume Editors

Sara G. Beavis, *The Australian National University*

Klaus Bosselmann, *University of Auckland*

Karen Christensen, *Berkshire Publishing Group*

Robin Kundis Craig, *University of Utah*

Michael L. Dougherty, *Illinois State University*

Daniel Fogel, *Wake Forest University*

Sarah Fredericks, *University of North Texas*

Sam Geall, *chinadialogue*

Tirso Gonzales, *University of British Columbia Okanagan*

Lisa M. Butler Harrington, *Kansas State University*

Willis Jenkins, *Yale University*

Louis Kotzé, *North-West University*

Chris Laszlo, *Case Western Reserve University*

Jingjing Liu, *Vermont Law School*

Stephen Morse, *University of Surrey*

John Copeland Nagle, *University of Notre Dame*

Bruce Pardy, *Queen's University*

Sony Pellissery, *Institute of Rural Management, Anand*

J. B. Ruhl, *Vanderbilt University Law School*

Oswald Schmitz, *Yale University*

Lei Shen, *Chinese Academy of Sciences*

William Smith, *Wake Forest University*

Ian Spellerberg, *Lincoln University*

Shirley Thompson, *University of Manitoba*

Daniel Vasey, *Divine Word College*

Gernot Wagner, *Environmental Defense Fund*

Peter Whitehouse, *Case Western Reserve University*

Associate Editors

E. N. Anderson, *University of California, Riverside*

Whitney Bauman, *Florida International University*

Ricardo Braun, *Centre for Environmental Analysis (Nasa), Brazil*

Joel Campbell, *Troy University*

Norman Christensen Jr., *Duke University*

Irina Krasnova, *Moscow State Academy of Law*

Joanna I. Lewis, *Georgetown University*

Muhammad Aurang Zeb Mughal, *Durham University*

Fred Nelson, *Maliasili Initiatives Ltd.*

Janet Neuman, *Lewis and Clark College*

Anthony O'Connor, *University College London*

Maria Proto, *University of Salerno*

Fabienne Quilleré-Majzoub, *IODE—University of Rennes 1*

Mark Wilson, *Northumbria University*

Patricia Wouters, *University of Dundee*

Editorial/Advisory Board

Ray C. Anderson, *Interface, Inc.*

Lester R. Brown, *Earth Policy Institute*

Eric Freyfogle, *University of Illinois, Urbana-Champaign*

Luis Gomez-Echeverri, *United Nations Development Programme*

John Grim, *Yale University*

Brent Haddad, *University of California, Santa Cruz*

Daniel M. Kammen, *University of California, Berkeley*

Ashok Khosla, *International Union for Conservation of Nature*

Christine Loh, *Civic Exchange, Hong Kong; Under Secretary for the Environment, Hong Kong*

Cheryl Oakes, *Duke University*

Mary Evelyn Tucker, *Yale University*

Others who helped with Volume 10 by reviewing articles, advising us on the educational material that follows the articles, or otherwise sharing their expertise:

John Elkinton, *VolansVentures, Ltd.*

Billie Turner, *Arizona State University*

Bo Poulsen, *Aalborg University*

Michael Sims, *independent scholar, Eugene, Oregon*

Roger W. Eardley-Pryor, *University of California, Santa Barbara*

Christopher Ling, *Royal Roads University*

Orin Gelderloos, *University of Michigan*

Mark B. Milstein, *Cornell University*

Marco A. Janssen, *Arizona State University*

David Christian, *Macquarie University; Ewha Womans University*

Mark Anderson, *University of Maine*

Catherine P. MacKenzie, *University of Cambridge*

Debra Rowe, *US Partnership for Education for Sustainable Development*

Claude Comtois, *Université de Montréal*

Kate Sherren, *Dalhousie University*

Kerry Shephard, *University of Otago*

Julie Newman, *Yale Office of Sustainability*

Nicola Acutt, *independent scholar, San Francisco*

Yu Wenxuan, *China University of Political Science and Law*

Berkshire Publishing is extremely grateful to all of these people, as well as to many others who do not appear on this list, for their help and advice with the Encyclopedia of Sustainability.

Combined List of Entries from the Ten Volumes of the *Encyclopedia of Sustainability*

The following is a list of all of the articles that appear in the ten volumes of the *Berkshire Encyclopedia of Sustainability*, followed by the volume or volumes that the article appears in. Please note that some topics, such as "Agriculture," appear in more than one volume. Please refer to the series page that appears on page VI for the names of the volumes. Following this section is a Reader's Guide, on pages L–LXXIII, in which the articles are divided up by topic (e.g., "Agriculture and Food," "Cities and the Built Environment," "Energy").

A

Accounting (Vol. 2)

Activism, Judicial (Vol. 7)

Activism—Nongovernmental Organizations (NGOs) (Vol. 2)

Adaptive Resource Management (ARM) (Vol. 5)

Administrative Law (Vol. 5)

Advertising (Vol. 6)

Afghanistan (Vol. 9)

Africa, Central (Vol. 9)

Africa, East (Vol. 9)

Africa, Southern (Vol. 9)

Africa, Western (Vol. 9)

African Diasporan Religions (Vol. 1)

African Union (AU) (Vol. 9)

Agenda 21 (Vols. 1, 6)

Aging (Vol. 10)

Agrarianism (Vol. 1)

Agricultural Innovation (Vol. 10)

Agricultural Intensification (Vol. 5)

Agriculture (Vols. 1, 2)

Agriculture (China and Southeast Asia) (Vol. 7)

Agriculture—Developing World (Vol. 4)

Municipalities (Vol. 2)

Murray–Darling River Basin (Vol. 8)

Mutualism (Vol. 5)

N

Nairobi, Kenya (Vol. 9)

Nanotechnology (Vols. 4, 7)

Nanotechnology Legislation (Vol. 3)

National Environmental Accounting (Vol. 6)

National Environmental Policy Act (Vol. 3)

National Pollution Survey (China) (Vol. 7)

National Religious Partnership for the Environment (Vol. 1)

Natural Capital (Vols. 5, 10)

Natural Capitalism (Vol. 2)

Natural Gas (Vol. 4)

Natural Resource Economics (Vol. 4)

Natural Resources Law (Vols. 3, 4)

Natural Step Framework, The (TNSF) (Vol. 2)

Nature (Vol. 1)

Nature Religions and Animism (Vol. 1)

New Age Spirituality (Vol. 1)

New Ecological Paradigm (NEP) Scale (Vol. 6)

New Orleans, United States (Vol. 8)

New York City, United States (Vol. 8)

New Zealand (Vol. 8)

New Zealand Nuclear Free Zone, Disarmament, and Arms Control Act (Vol. 3)

Nickel (Vol. 4)

Nile River (Vol. 9)

Nitrogen (Vol. 4)

Nitrogen Saturation (Vol. 5)

Nongovernmental Organizations (NGOs) (Vol. 7)

Nonprofit Organizations, Environmental (Vol. 1)

Nonviolence (Vol. 1)

North American Free Trade Agreement (NAFTA) (Vol. 8)

Northwest Passage (Vol. 8)

Petroleum (Vol. 4)

Pharmaceutical Industry (Vol. 2)

Phoenix, United States (Vol. 8)

Phosphorus (Vol. 4)

Pilgrimage (Vol. 1)

Place (Vol. 1)

Plant-Animal Interactions (Vol. 5)

Platinum Group Metals (Vol. 4)

Poaching (Vol. 4)

Politics (Vol. 1)

Polluter Pays Principle (Vol. 3)

Pollution, Nonpoint Source (Vol. 5)

Pollution, Point Source (Vol. 5)

Population (Vols. 1, 10)

Population Dynamics (Vol. 5)

Population Indicators (Vol. 6)

Potassium (Vol. 4)

Poverty (Vols. 1, 2)

Pragmatism (Vol. 1)

Precautionary Principle (Vols. 1, 3)

Principle-Based Regulation (Vol. 3)

Process Thought (Vol. 1)

Product-Service Systems (PSSs) (Vol. 2)

Progress (Vol. 10)

Property and Construction Industry (Vol. 2)

Property and Possessions (Vol. 1)

Property Rights (Vol. 10)

Property Rights (China) (Vol. 7)

Public Health (Vol. 7)

Public Transportation (Vol. 2)

Public–Private Partnerships (Vols. 2, 7)

Public–Private Partnerships (Africa) (Vol. 9)

Public Transportation (Vols. 7, 8)

Q

Quantitative vs. Qualitative Studies (Vol. 6)

R

Racism (Vol. 1)

Rain Gardens (Vol. 5)

Reader's Guide to the *Berkshire Encyclopedia of Sustainability*

The following is a list of articles in the ten volumes of the *Berkshire Encyclopedia of Sustainability*, divided by category. The names of the volumes follow each entry; please note that many topics appear in more than one category, and some topics appear in more than one volume; in the latter case, the focus of the article is different depending on which volume it appears in. For instance, "E-Waste" appears in volumes 7, 8, and 9; the different articles focus on e-waste in China, India, and East and Southeast Asia; the Americas and Oceania; and Afro-Eurasia, respectively. Please refer to the series page that appears on page VI for the names of the volumes that appear after each article title.

AGRICULTURE AND FOOD ARTICLES

Agrarianism (Vol. 1)

Agricultural Innovation (Vol. 10)

Agricultural Intensification (Vol. 5)

Agriculture (Vols. 1, 2)

Agriculture (China and Southeast Asia) (Vol. 7)

Agriculture—Developing World (Vol. 4)

Agriculture—Genetically Engineered Crops (Vol. 4)

Agriculture—Organic and Biodynamic (Vol. 4)

Agriculture, Small-Scale (Vol. 9)

Agriculture (South Asia) (Vol. 7)

Agriculture, Tropical (the Americas) (Vol. 8)

Agroecology (Vol. 5)

Alfalfa (Vol. 4)

Animal Husbandry (Vol. 4)

Bushmeat (Vol. 4)

Cacao (Vol. 4)

Coffee (Vol. 4)

Cotton (Vol. 4)

Desertification (Vol. 5)

Desertification (Africa) (Vol. 9)

Dung (Vol. 4)

Fast Food Industry (Vol. 2)

Fertilizers (Vol. 4)

Fiber Crops (Vol. 4)

Fish (Vol. 4)

Fisheries (Vols. 9, 10)

Fisheries (China) (Vol. 7)

("Agriculture and Food" articles continue on the next page)

("Agriculture and Food" articles, continued from p. L)

Food, Frozen (Vol. 4)

Food in History (Vol. 4)

Food Security (Vols. 4, 10)

Food, Value-Added (Vol. 4)

Genetically Modified Organisms Legislation

Grains (Vol. 4)

Grasslands (Vol. 4)

Green Revolution (Vol. 4)

Guano (Vol. 4)

Honeybees (Vol. 4)

Insects—Beneficial (Vol. 4)

Insects—Pests (Vol. 4)

Local Food Movements (Vol. 4)

Malnutrition (Vol. 4)

Manure, Animal (Vol. 4)

Manure, Human (Vol. 4)

Nitrogen (Vol. 4)

Permaculture (Vol. 5)

Pest Management, Integrated (IPM) (Vol. 4)

Phosphorus (Vol. 4)

Potassium (Vol. 4)

Ranching (Vol. 4)

Rice (Vol. 4)

Root Crops (Vol. 4)

Soil (Vol. 4)

Soil Conservation (Vol. 5)

Soybeans (Vol. 4)

Sugarcane (Vol. 4)

Tea (Vol. 4)

Urban Agriculture (Vol. 5)

CITIES AND THE BUILT ENVIRONMENT ARTICLES

Architecture (Vols. 1, 8, 9)

Auckland, New Zealand (Vol. 8)

Beijing, China (Vol. 7)

Bogotá, Colombia (Vol. 8)

Brownfield Redevelopment (Vol. 5)

Building Rating Systems, Green (Vol. 6)

Building Standards, Green (Vol. 2)

Buildings and Infrastructure (Vol. 10)

Cairo, Egypt (Vol. 9)

Cape Town, South Africa (Vol. 9)

Cement Industry (Vol. 2)

Chennai, India (Vol. 7)

Cities and the Biosphere (Vol. 10)

Cities—Overview (Vol. 7)

Curitiba, Brazil (Vol. 8)

Delhi, India (Vol. 7)

Design and Architecture (Vol. 10)

Detroit, United States (Vol. 8)

Development, Urban (Vol. 2)

("Cities and the Built Environment" articles continue on the next page)

Climate Change and Air Pollution Articles

("Climate Change and Air Pollution" articles continue on the next page)

("Climate Change and Air Pollution" articles, continued from p. LII)

Anthropocene Epoch (Vol. 10)

Cap-and-Trade Legislation (Vol. 2)

Carbon Capture and Sequestration (Vol. 4)

Carbon Footprint (Vol. 6)

Clean Air Act (Vol. 3)

Climate Change (Vol. 1)

Climate Change and Big History (Vol. 10)

Climate Change Disclosure (Vol. 2)

Climate Change Disclosure—Legal Framework (Vol. 3)

Climate Change Migration (India) (Vol. 7)

Climate Change Mitigation (Vol. 3)

Climate Change Mitigation Initiatives (China) (Vol. 7)

Climate Change Refugees (Africa) (Vol. 9)

Coastal Management (Vol. 5)

Convention on Long-Range Transboundary Air Pollution (Vol. 3)

Copenhagen Climate Change Conference 2009 (Vol. 3)

Earth Charter (Vol. 1)

Global Climate Change (Vol. 5)

Greenhouse Gases (Vol. 4)

International Law (Vol. 3)

Kyoto Protocol (Vol. 3)

Montreal Protocol on Substances That Deplete the Ozone Layer (Vol. 3)

Northwest Passage (Vol. 8)

Reducing Emissions from Deforestation and Forest Degradation (REDD) (Vol. 6)

Regulatory Compliance (Vol. 6)

Remote Sensing (Vol. 6)

Rio Earth Summit (UN Conference on Environment and Development) (Vol. 8)

Trail Smelter Arbitration (*United States v. Canada*) (Vol. 3)

United Nations Global Compact (Vol. 2)

United Nations—Overview of Conventions and Agreements (Vol. 3)

COUNTRIES AND REGIONS ARTICLES

Afghanistan (Vol. 9)

Africa, Central (Vol. 9)

Africa, East (Vol. 9)

Africa, Southern (Vol. 9)

Africa, Western (Vol. 9)

African Union (AU) (Vol. 9)

Amazonia (Vol. 8)

Association of Southeast Asian Nations (ASEAN) (Vol. 7)

Australia (Vol. 8)

("Countries and Regions" articles continue on the next page)

DEVELOPMENT AND PLANNING ARTICLES

("Development and Planning" articles continue on the next page)

("Development and Planning" articles, continued from p. LIV)

Development, Sustainable—Overview of Laws and Commissions (Vol. 3)

Development, Urban (Vol. 2)

Fencing (Vol. 5)

Five-Year Plans (Vol. 7)

Framework for Strategic Sustainable Development (FSSD) (Vol. 6)

Global Trade (Vol. 10)

Globalization (Vol. 1)

Green Belt Movement (Vol. 1)

Greenbelts (Vol. 4)

Land Use—Regulation and Zoning (Vol. 3)

Landscape Architecture (Vol. 5)

Landscape Planning, Large-Scale (Vol. 5)

The Limits to Growth (Vol. 6)

Local Food Movements (Vol. 4)

Local Living Economies (Vol. 2)

Microfinance (Vols. 7, 9)

Millennium Development Goals (Vols. 1, 6)

Natural Capitalism (Vol. 2)

Place (Vol. 1)

Property and Construction Industry (Vol. 2)

Public–Private Partnerships (Vols. 2, 7)

Public–Private Partnerships (Africa) (Vol. 9)

Public Transportation (Vol. 2, 7, 8)

Regional Planning (Vol. 6)

Rewilding (Vol. 5)

Rio Earth Summit (UN Conference on Environment and Development) (Vol. 8)

Road Ecology (Vol. 5)

Rural Development (Vols. 7, 9)

Rural Development (the Americas) (Vol. 8)

Rural Livelihoods (Vol. 7)

Smart Growth (Vol. 2)

Sustainable Livelihood Analysis (SLA) (Vol. 6)

Triple Bottom Line (Vols. 2, 6)

Urbanization (Vol. 8)

Urbanization (Africa) (Vol. 9)

Urbanization (Europe) (Vol. 9)

Urbanization (Western Asia and Northern Africa) (Vol. 9)

White Revolution of India (Vol. 7)

World Bank (Vols. 1, 9)

ECOLOGY ARTICLES

Adaptive Resource Management (ARM) (Vol. 5)

Best Management Practices (BMPs) (Vol. 5)

Biodiversity (Vols. 1, 5)

Biodiversity Conservation (Vol. 9)

("Ecology" articles continue on the next page)

("Ecology" articles, continued from p. LV)

("Ecology" articles continue on the next page)

("Ecology" articles, continued from p. LVI)

Marine Ecosystems Health (Vol. 8)

Marine Protected Areas (MPAs) (Vol. 5)

Microbial Ecosystem Processes (Vol. 5)

Mutualism (Vol. 5)

Nitrogen Saturation (Vol. 5)

Nutrient and Biogeochemical Cycling (Vol. 5)

Ocean Acidification—Management (Vol. 5)

Ocean Resource Management (Vol. 5)

Outbreak Species (Vol. 5)

Plant-Animal Interactions (Vol. 5)

Pollution, Nonpoint Source (Vol. 5)

Pollution, Point Source (Vol. 5)

Population Dynamics (Vol. 5)

Rain Gardens (Vol. 5)

Reforestation (Vol. 5)

Reforestation and Afforestation (Southeast Asia) (Vol. 7)

Refugia (Vol. 5)

Regime Shifts (Vol. 5)

Resilience (Vol. 5)

Restoration (Vol. 1)

Rewilding (Vol. 5)

Road Ecology (Vol. 5)

Succession (Vol. 5)

Safe Minimum Standard (SMS) (Vol. 5)

Shifting Baselines Syndrome (Vol. 5)

Silent Spring (Vol. 3)

Species Reintroduction (Vol. 5)

Stormwater Management (Vol. 5)

Strategic Environmental Assessment (SEA) (Vol. 6)

Tree Planting (Vol. 5)

ECONOMICS, BUSINESS, AND INDUSTRY ARTICLES

Accounting (Vol. 2)

Advertising (Vol. 6)

Airline Industry (Vol. 2)

Automobile Industry (Vol. 2)

Automobiles and Personal Transportation (Vol. 7)

Base of the Pyramid (Vol. 2)

Business Reporting Methods (Vol. 6)

Cement Industry (Vol. 2)

Climate Change Disclosure (Vol. 2)

Corporate Accountability (Vol. 8)

Corporate Accountability (Africa) (Vol. 9)

Corporate Accountability (China) (Vol. 7)

Corporate Citizenship (Vol. 2)

CSR and CSR 2.0 (Vol. 2)

Ecological Economics (Vol. 2)

Economics (Vol. 1)

Economics, Steady State (Vol. 10)

Ecosystem Services (Vols. 2, 5)

("Economics, Business, and Industry" articles continue on the next page)

("Economics, Business, and Industry" articles continue on the next page)

("Economics, Business, and Industry" articles, continued from p. LVIII)

Shipping (Vol. 10)

Shipping and Freight (Vol. 9)

Shipping and Freight Indicators (Vol. 6)

Smart Growth (Vol. 2)

Social Enterprise (Vol. 2)

Sporting Goods Industry (Vol. 2)

Stakeholder Theory (Vol. 2)

Steel Industry (Vols. 2, 7)

Supply Chain Analysis (Vol. 6)

Supply Chain Management (Vol. 2)

Sustainable Value Creation (Vol. 2)

Taxes, Green. (*See* Green Taxes)

Telecommunications Industry (Vol. 2)

Textiles Industry (Vol. 2)

Tourism (Vol. 4)

Transparency (Vol. 2)

Travel and Tourism Industry (Vols. 2, 8, 9)

Triple Bottom Line (Vols. 2, 6)

True Cost Economics (Vol. 2)

World Bank (Vols. 1, 9)

ENERGY ARTICLES

Algae (Vol. 4)

Bioenergy and Biofuels (Vol. 4)

Coal (Vol. 4)

Dam Removal (Vol. 5)

Dams and Reservoirs (Vol. 4)

Energy (Vol. 1)

Energy Conservation Incentives (Vol. 3)

Energy Efficiency (Vols. 2, 8, 10)

Energy Efficiency Measurement (Vol. 6)

Energy Industries—Bioenergy (Vol. 2)

Energy Industries—Coal (Vol. 2)

Energy Industries—Geothermal (Vol. 2)

Energy Industries—Hydroelectric (Vol. 2)

Energy Industries—Hydrogen and Fuel Cells (Vol. 2)

Energy Industries—Natural Gas (Vol. 2)

Energy Industries—Nuclear (Vols. 2, 7)

Energy Industries—Oil (Vol. 2)

Energy Industries—Overview of Renewables (Vol. 2)

Energy Industries—Renewables (China) (Vol. 7)

Energy Industries—Renewables (India) (Vol. 7)

Energy Industries—Solar (Vol. 2)

Energy Industries—Wave and Tidal (Vol. 2)

Energy Industries—Wind (Vol. 2)

Energy Labeling (Vol. 6)

Energy Security (East Asia) (Vol. 7)

Energy Security (Europe) (Vol. 9)

Energy Subsidies (Vol. 3)

("Energy" articles continue on the next page)

("Geographic Features" articles continue on the next page)

("Laws, Conventions, and Politics" articles continue on the next page)

("*Laws, Conventions, and Politics*" articles, continued from p. LXI)

("*Laws, Conventions, and Politics*" articles continue on the next page)

("Laws, Conventions, and Politics" articles, continued from p. LXII)

MEASUREMENTS, INDICATORS, AND RESEARCH METHODS ARTICLES

("Measurements, Indicators, and Research Methods" articles continue on the next page)

("Measurements, Indicators, and Research Methods" articles continued from p. LXIV)

National Environmental Accounting (Vol. 6)

New Ecological Paradigm (NEP) Scale (Vol. 6)

Ocean Acidification—Measurement (Vol. 6)

Organic and Consumer Labels (Vol. 6)

Participatory Action Research (Vol. 6)

Performance Metrics (Vol. 2)

Population Indicators (Vol. 6)

Quantitative vs. Qualitative Studies (Vol. 6)

Remote Sensing (Vol. 6)

Risk Assessment (Vol. 6)

Shifting Baselines Syndrome (Vol. 5)

Social Life Cycle Assessment (S-LCA) (Vol. 6)

Social Network Analysis (SNA) (Vol. 6)

Species Barcoding (Vol. 6)

Sustainability Science (Vol. 6)

Systems Thinking (Vol. 6)

Taxation Indicators, Green (Vol. 6)

Transdisciplinary Research (Vol. 6)

Tree Rings as Environmental Indicators (Vol. 6)

Sustainability Theory (Vol. 1)

Sustainable Livelihood Analysis (SLA) (Vol. 6)

University Indicators (Vol. 6)

NATURAL RESOURCES AND WASTE ARTICLES

Alfalfa (Vol. 4)

Algae (Vol. 4)

Aluminum (Vol. 4)

Animals (Vol. 1)

Bamboo (Vol. 4)

Bioenergy and Biofuels (Vol. 4)

Bushmeat (Vol. 4)

Cacao (Vol. 4)

Chromium (Vol. 4)

Coal (Vol. 4)

Coffee (Vol. 4)

Coltan (Vol. 4)

Conflict Minerals (Vols. 4, 9)

Copper (Vol. 4)

Cotton (Vol. 4)

Dung (Vol. 4)

Fiber Crops (Vol. 4)

Fish (Vol. 4)

Fish Hatcheries (Vol. 5)

Fisheries (Vols. 9, 10)

Fisheries (China) (Vol. 7)

Fisheries Management (Vol. 5)

Forest Management (Vols. 5, 8)

Forest Management Industry (Vol. 2)

Forest Products—Non-Timber (Vol. 4)

("Natural Resources and Waste" articles continue on the next page)

("Natural Resources and Waste" articles continue on the next page)

("Natural Resources and Waste" articles, continued from p. LXVI)

Recycling (Vol. 4)

Remanufacturing (Vol. 2)

Rice (Vol. 4)

Rivers (Vol. 4)

Root Crops (Vol. 4)

Rubber (Vol. 4)

Salt (Vol. 4)

Sands and Silica (Vol. 4)

Shale Gas Extraction (Vol. 5)

Silver (Vol. 4)

Soil (Vol. 4)

Soil Conservation (Vol. 5)

Solar Energy (Vol. 4)

Soybeans (Vol. 4)

Sugarcane (Vol. 4)

Sulfur (Vol. 4)

Svalbard Global Seed Vault (Vol. 9)

Tea (Vol. 4)

Thorium (Vol. 4)

Three Gorges Dam (Vol. 7)

Tin (Vol. 4)

Titanium (Vol. 4)

Traditional Chinese Medicine (TCM) (Vol. 7)

Tragedy of the Commons, The (Vol. 1)

Tree Planting (Vol. 5)

Uranium (Vol. 4)

Waste (Vol. 1)

Waste—Engineering Aspects (Vol. 10)

Waste Management (Vols. 4, 5)

Waste Shipment Law (Vol. 3)

Waste—Social Aspects (Vol. 10)

Wetlands (Vol. 4)

Wilderness (Vol. 1)

Wilderness Areas (Vol. 5)

Wind Energy (Vol. 4)

Zero Waste (Vol. 2)

RELIGIONS, BELIEFS, AND PHILOSOPHY ARTICLES

African Diasporan Religions (Vol. 1)

Agrarianism (Vol. 1)

Anthropic Principle (Vol. 1)

Anthropocentrism (Vol. 1)

Anthroposophy (Vol. 1)

Bahá'í (Vol. 1)

Beauty (Vol. 1)

Biocentrism (Vol. 1)

Bioethics (Vol. 1)

Biophilia (Vol. 1)

Buddhism (Vol. 1)

Christianity—Anabaptist (Vol. 1)

Christianity—Eastern Orthodox (Vol. 1)

Christianity—Evangelical and Pentecostal (Vol. 1)

("Religions, Beliefs, and Philosophy" articles continue on the next page)

("Religions, Beliefs, and Philosophy" articles continue on the next page)

("*Religions, Beliefs, and Philosophy*" articles, continued from p. LXVIII)

National Religious Partnership for the Environment (Vol. 1)

Nature (Vol. 1)

Nature Religions and Animism (Vol. 1)

New Age Spirituality (Vol. 1)

Nonviolence (Vol. 1)

Order and Harmony (Vol. 1)

Pacific Island Environmental Philosophy (Vol. 8)

Paganism and Neopaganism (Vol. 1)

Pilgrimage (Vol. 1)

Place (Vol. 1)

Pragmatism (Vol. 1)

Process Thought (Vol. 1)

Religions (Vol. 7)

Responsibility (Vol. 1)

Sacrament (Vol. 1)

Sacred Texts (Vol. 1)

Sacrifice (Vol. 1)

Science, Religion, and Ecology (Vol. 1)

Shamanism (Vol. 1)

Shinto (Vol. 1)

Sikhism (Vol. 1)

Simplicity and Asceticism (Vol. 1)

Sin and Evil (Vol. 1)

Spirit and Spirituality (Vol. 1)

Stewardship (Vol. 1)

Subsistence (Vol. 1)

Theocentrism (Vol. 1)

Time (Vol. 1)

Traditional Knowledge (China) (Vol. 7)

Traditional Knowledge (India) (Vol. 7)

Unitarianism and Unitarian Universalism (Vol. 1)

The Universe Story (Vol. 1)

Utilitarianism (Vol. 1)

Values (Vols. 1, 10)

Vegetarianism (Vol. 1)

Virtues and Vices (Vol. 1)

Weak vs. Strong Sustainability Debate (Vols. 3, 6)

White's Thesis (Vol. 1)

Wisdom Traditions (Vol. 1)

Wise Use Movement (Vols. 1, 4)

World Constitutionalism (Vol. 3)

World Religions and Ecology (Vol. 1)

SCIENCE, DESIGN, AND TECHNOLOGY ARTICLES

Architecture (Vols. 1, 8, 9)

Biomimicry (Vol. 2)

Carbon Capture and Sequestration (Vol. 4)

Chemistry, Green (Vol. 2)

Coltan (Vol. 4)

("*Science, Design, and Technology*" articles continue on the next page)

(*"Science, Design, and Technology"* articles, continued from p. LXIX)

SOCIAL ISSUES AND EDUCATION ARTICLES

(*"Social Issues and Education"* articles continue on the next page)

("Social Issues and Education" articles, continued from p. LXX)

Consumer Behavior (Vol. 2)

Consumerism (Vol. 7)

Corporate Citizenship (Vol. 2)

CSR and CSR 2.0 (Vol. 2)

Culture (Vol. 1)

Desertification (Vol. 5)

Desertification (Africa) (Vol. 9)

Diet and Nutrition (Vol. 9)

Disaster Risk Management (Vol. 9)

Drug Production and Trade (Vol. 4)

Earth Day (Vol. 1)

Eco-Terrorism (Vol. 3)

Ecocentrism (Vol. 1)

Ecology, Cultural (Vol. 1)

Ecology, Social (Vol. 1)

Ecotourism (Vols. 4, 7, 9)

Ecotourism (the Americas) (Vol. 8)

Ecovillages (Vols. 1, 8)

Education (Vol. 1)

Education, Business (Vol. 2)

Education, Environmental (Vol. 9)

Education, Environmental (China) (Vol. 7)

Education, Environmental (India) (Vol. 7)

Education, Environmental (Japan) (Vol. 7)

Education, Environmental Law (Vol. 3)

Education, Female (Vol. 7)

Education, Higher (Vols. 2, 10)

Education, Higher (Africa) (Vol. 9)

Feminist Thought (Vol. 1)

Free Trade (Vols. 2, 3)

Fundamentalism (Vol. 1)

Future (Vol. 1)

Future Generations (Vol. 1)

Gender Equality (Vols. 7, 8)

Grassroots Environmental Movements (Vol. 3)

Green Belt Movement (Vol. 1)

Gross National Happiness (Vol. 6)

Health, Public and Environmental (Vol. 2)

Human Ecology (Vol. 5)

$I = P \times A \times T$ Equation (Vol. 6)

Immigrants and Refugees (Vol. 9)

Intellectual Property Rights (Vol. 6)

Intergenerational Equity (Vol. 3)

Investment, Socially Responsible (SRI) (Vol. 2)

Justice (Vol. 1)

Justice, Environmental (Vol. 3)

Labor (Vols. 7, 8)

Language (Vol. 1)

Local Living Economies (Vol. 2)

Local Solutions to Global Problems (Vol. 10)

("Social Issues and Education" articles continue on the next page)

("*Social Issues and Education*" articles, continued from p. LXXI)

TRANSPORTATION, MOBILITY, AND SHIPPING ARTICLES

("*Transportation, Mobility, and Shipping*" articles continue on the next page)

(*"Transportation, Mobility, and Shipping" articles, continued from p. LXXII*)

(*"Water and Fisheries" articles continue on the next page*)

(*"Water and Fisheries" articles, continued from p. LXXIII*)

Aging

No simple relationship exists between aging populations and the environment, although improvements in medicine and living conditions have resulted in greater life expectancy throughout the world, and thus a larger population. The global population of older persons is growing at 2.6 percent per year; the share of people aged 65 and over in the world will soon exceed that of children under 5 for the first time in history. Some demographers estimate that by 2050 more than 25 percent of people will be older than 60 years of age. Global communities and governments will need to acknowledge the problems associated with aging populations, including provision of services for health and caretaking.

Human beings—their sheer numbers, where they are, how they live, and what needs they have—are at the center of the sustainability concerns as proclaimed in Principle 1 of the Rio Declaration on Environment and Development (UNEP 1992). The number and age of people on Earth are not exactly known, but various estimates exist. According to the United Nations' projections, the world population reached 7 billion in October 2011, or according to the estimates of the US Census Bureau, this happened in March 2012 (Goodkind 2011). No simple relationship exists between population size and the planet, except that the Earth has physical and biophysical limits that determine the existence of land, water, air, forests, and other resources. The larger the human population is, the bigger its impact on these resources, not only in terms of resource availability for humans but also as habitat for other species and the natural environment. The rapid growth of the number of people on Earth, estimated to be at a rate above 1 percent in 2011, or 2.4 persons added every second (US CIA 2012), has been an intense topic in sustainability debates. This growth creates challenges about how this population could continue to be fed; what other needs it has; how much, and what, these people are going to be consuming and where they will do so; and how this growth will affect the planet.

Demographers, the scientists who study population trends, however, are expressing different types of concerns. They relate to the fact that the global population is aging overall. In the last sixty years, the median age of the world's population (the point below which half of the people are younger and above which half of the people are older) has increased by more than 5 years, from 23.6 in 1950 (*The Economist* 2003) to 28.7 in 2010 (US Census Bureau 2012).

This major demographic change is related to two main global trends: first, people live longer due to decreasing mortality rates; and second, people have fewer children because of reduced fertility rates. The world's life expectancy at birth (an indicator representing the average number of years a person can expect to live if the conditions at the time of birth continue throughout this person's lifetime) has increased dramatically from 50 years in 1979 to 68 years in 2011 (US Census Bureau 2012); it has increased by 21 years since 1950 (UN 2009; US CIA 2012). On the other hand, the globe's total fertility rate (the number of births per woman) has decreased from 5.9 in 1979 to 2.4 in 2011 (US Census Bureau 2012). From a sustainability point of view, both of these trends are positive. The fact that people live longer means that living conditions have improved overall; these conditions include advances in medicine, health care, food production, housing, sanitation, education, and reduction in violent conflicts, among other positive changes associated with development. The continuingly decreasing fertility rates, on the other hand, allow demographers and policy makers to expect the size of global population to stabilize sometime in the future. Stabilization is unlikely to happen before 2100, however, when scientists project the global population to reach 10 billion if fertility levels of all countries converge to replacement level (the average number of live births per woman needed to maintain the population) (UN 2011).

Despite these global trends, significant differences occur between regions, and population growth is uneven with a big gap of survival prospects between rich and poor (UN 2012a). Some countries have very slow and even negative population growth, while others are still growing fast because of the relatively high shares of young people, not far from childhood themselves, who are having children of their own. As a result, in the future, scientists expect an increasing share of the world's population to reside in the developing world. On the other hand, the developed world is already experiencing the true effects of population aging, namely, an increasing share of people aged 60 years and over, which, in many places, is already more than 20 percent (UN 2012b). A population is considered aging when the respective shares of people over age 60 and 65 exceed the 10 and 7 percent thresholds (UN 2002).

The global population of older persons is growing at 2.6 percent per year (UN 2009). The share of people aged 65 and over in the world will soon exceed that of children under 5 for the first time in history, and by 2050, some demographers estimate that more than 25 percent of people will be older than 60 years of age (Wells 2012). The actual numbers of old people are also dramatically increasing. In 2012, 562 million people in the world were 65 and older, and scientists project this number to increase to 1.56 billion by 2050 (US Census Bureau 2012). Global communities and governments, therefore, need to be aware of all aspects of population aging, including provision of services and living conditions for all age groups, as well as understanding how population aging affects sustainability. "As people live longer and have fewer children, family structures are transformed, leaving older people with fewer options for care" (National Institute on Aging et al. 2007, 3). Scientists also have concerns about what this aging population means for the planet's environmental health. The reality of old age is becoming a challenge for the baby boomers (those born in the population rise following World War II) in the West, as well as for Asian countries, such as China, India, Indonesia, Japan, and Thailand.

The United Nations 2009 Report describes population aging as unprecedented—without a parallel in the history of humanity; pervasive—affecting nearly all countries; profound—having major implications for all facets of human life, as well as for sustainability; and enduring—the trends of aging witnessed today have remained unchanged since the 1950s and are likely to persist (UN 2009). Considering the implications of an aging population on the social, economic, and environmental aspects of sustainability, it is important to understand not only the historical, current, and future patterns of population aging, but also the regional dynamics and demographic differences and what they mean for the economy, society, and the planet's ecology. Demographers analyze the changes in the demographic profiles. Economists and policy makers ask whether older people typically use more or fewer natural resources than younger people and what financial challenges an aging population brings. Meanwhile, the community is concerned about whether government and society can provide adequate services for the old, to guarantee that they live and enjoy happy and productive lives. Environmentalists and ecologists are unsure about how this aging population will affect the habitat for other species, as well as the other global phenomena of climate change, biodiversity loss, nitrogen fixation in the soil, stratospheric ozone depletion, ocean acidification, phosphorus cycle, and changes in land use and water use (Pearce 2010). All these communities are discussing the many scenarios, projections, and forecasts, making calls for adequate policy making as well as individual action to counter the impacts of the unique phenomenon of population aging on the planet's sustainability.

Aging Population

Reductions in birth and death rates are creating a fundamental change in the age structure, and people are living longer. Scientists project the global population's median age to reach 37.1 by 2050, a further increase by 8.4 years from its 2010 level. They also estimate that shares of old people will increase significantly. (See table 1 on page 4.) Because women tend to live longer (the 2011 life expectancy for women was 69.73 years compared to 65.59 years for men, according to US CIA 2012), scientists also expect the sex ratio (the number of men per 100 women) to change for the entire global population, resulting in more women than men by 2050—another first in the history of humanity.

The aging population is an important issue for not only developed countries; emerging and developing countries also face the aging pressure. The matter of aging is therefore a global issue. In its essence, global aging is a story of human success and triumph in areas of endeavor, such as medicine, public health, economic development, and education (National Institute on Aging et al. 2007). It also requires the human race to demonstrate creativity and ingenuity of the same scale, however, to handle successfully the implications aging creates.

The majority of the developed countries already have to manage their changing demography, including declining working-age populations and issues such as

TABLE 1. Estimates of Future Global Population Aging

	2010	2020	2030	2040	2050
Total Population	6.9 billion	7.6 billion	8.3 billion	8.9 billion	9.3 billion
Sex ratio*	101.4	101.2	100.7	100.1	99.5
Median age	28.7	31.2	33.6	35.5	37.1
Growth rate of the decade ending (%)	1.2	1.06	0.86	0.68	0.53
Population over 60	772 million	1.04 billion	1.4 billion	1.7 billion	2.08 billion
−Share in total population (%)	11.2	13.7	16.9	19.6	22.2
−Sex ratio	84	84.2	84.4	84.1	84.4
Population over 65	534 million	729 million	998 million	1.3 billion	1.6 billion
−Share in total population (%)	7.8	9.6	12	14.7	16.7
−Sex ratio	84.2	80.5	80.2	80.4	80.3
Population over 85	42 million	65 million	92 million	151 million	224 million
−Share in total population (%)	0.6	0.9	1.1	1.7	2.4
−Sex ratio	48.5	51.7	52.5	53.2	52.9

Source: Calculated from US Census Bureau (2012). These figures have been rounded off from the Census Bureau estimates.

Note: Sex ratio is the number of men per 100 women.

retirement age, pensions, superannuation and social insurance systems, housing, health care, and transportation, as well as recreation within the context of people living longer lives. Life expectancy at birth in 2011, for example, reached 83.91 years in Japan, 79.76 for the European Union, and 78.49 for the United States (US CIA 2012). The oldest age group, those above 85, is the fastest growing section of many national populations (National Institute on Aging et al. 2007). Many countries believe that the demands of their aging populations are stretching their resources, and their policy responses vastly differ. Australia, for example, has no legal age of compulsory retirement, and the 2004 Age Discrimination Act protects the old if they wish to remain in the labor force. Mandatory retirement is similarly unlawful in the United States. Because these countries need a larger labor force, they welcome migrants as well as increased participation from all age groups. Being able to remain in the workforce also keeps people engaged and active, and many enjoy healthy and meaningful longer lives. Most of the European countries, on the other hand, have a strictly legislated retirement age at which employers can terminate or deny employment. This age varies by country (68 in the United Kingdom, 67 in Norway and Germany, 65 in France and Sweden, 60 in Italy), is constantly debated

by policy makers, and often gives rise to public concern and political preferences.

Different population aging levels occur worldwide, but many Asian countries also already have a shrinking labor force. This smaller workforce negatively affects the region's economic prosperity. The challenges of population aging in developing countries are different from those in developed countries, because developing countries' populations are aging quickly due to their historical patterns of growth. Although populations in developed countries are overall older than populations in developing countries, the latter are aging much faster than the former.

The Asia Pacific Region overall is aging more quickly than other places that have low- and middle-income countries, faster than was previously the case with Europe and North America. Japan has experienced dramatically decreased fertility rates, below replacement level, and it took only 26 years (from 1970 to 1996) for its population aged over 65 to increase from 7 percent to 14 percent, compared to 73 years for Australia (from 1938 to 2011) (National Institute on Aging et al. 2007). Because of a range of historical factors, poorer medical conditions, lower education, and political governance, countries like Cambodia, Laos, and Pakistan still have relatively high fertility and mortality rates with relatively low longevity; however, the situation in Singapore and Thailand is the reverse (Wong and Yeoh 2003).

A major contributor to population aging in Asia is China, whose unique historical circumstances have accelerated this process, significantly and artificially. It took Australia 100 years of industrialization and development to reach the current life expectancy of over 82 years (ABS 2012), but reaching this expectancy is likely to happen much faster in China. This country managed to achieve an increase from 71 years to 75 years of life expectancy within one decade (between 1999 and 2011), something that took Australia 23 years (between 1960 and 1983) (World Bank 2012). Since 2000, however, China's population has started to show signs of population aging, with its share of people over 65 expected to reach 14 percent within 26 years. In comparison with Japan, which underwent a similarly fast transition, many commentators state that China is getting older before it is becoming richer. China's one-child policy has reinforced its unique aging population momentum, which is continuously contributing to the global aging population. According to China's Ministry of Civil Affairs, the number of people above 60 is likely to increase from 185 million (14 percent) in 2011 to 480 million (33 percent) by 2050, with a small share of the country's labor force covered by pension systems (*China Daily* 2012). The share of the working-age population consequently will be decreasing significantly.

India is another looming challenge for the Asia-Pacific Region. Its population size is projected to overtake that of China by 2025 (US Census Bureau 2012). Although India's population is not yet classified as aging (its share of people over 60 is 8.5 percent and over 65 is 5.6 percent in 2012), this situation is likely to change soon, namely, by 2020, according to US Census Bureau (2012) projections. By 2050, scientists expect India's population over 60 to be greater than the total 2012 US population (PRB 2012). Again, this profound shift will bring a plethora of social, economic, and environmental challenges to the country itself and to the world.

The sharp decline in the world's fertility, a contributing factor to population aging, is also determined by a range of socioeconomic factors directly linked to the status of women, namely, women's higher levels of education, income, and labor force participation, and a higher age of marriage. On the other hand, with the improvement of public health and medical care, the mortality rates of older people have been falling worldwide. With continuing economic development, the world's life expectancy at birth is expected to increase further, which is a positive outcome but will definitely challenge the health and social security systems in many developing societies. The pension requirements are becoming difficult to provide, not only for developing countries, but also for rich countries such as the United States and the United Kingdom (Blackburn 2006). Lower fertility and mortality and longer life expectancy make both developed and developing countries' populations age sooner. By the mid-twenty-first century, aging will be the most significant transformation of all the population changes, and it will significantly affect global sustainability.

Sustainability Implications of an Aging Population

According to the Royal Society (2012, 4), there is no doubt that "the combination of increasing global population and increasing overall material consumption has implications for a finite planet." What is still uncertain is how population aging affects this finite planet. There are several important considerations.

Younger Age Brackets

Statistical data from countries of the European Union, Australia, China, and Japan show that the age group below 30 is the lowest consuming age bracket based on total household expenditure estimates (e.g., Eurostat 2011; Lee and Mason 2012; Martins, Yusuf, and Swanson 2012; Ying and Yao 2006). This bracket is also where the median age of the global population (28.7 years) currently sits.

The age groups between 31 and 59 are associated with significantly higher consumption patterns. As the global population ages and more people get out of poverty, society will feel more and more strongly the global implications from the consumption of unsustainable products. Society needs a significant shift in preferences and an acknowledgment that the planet could not support further expansion in biophysically uncontrolled human behavior. Such a transformation has to happen first where the bulk of unsustainable consumption is as indicated, for example, by levels of per capita carbon dioxide emissions, due to high energy, transport, and meat consumption (Raphaely and Marinova 2012), among other factors.

Older Age Brackets

The age group of 60 and above generally represents much weaker consumers; in some cases, their household expenditures drop to half of those of the previous age groups. The nature of the products and services they use, however, changes. For example, in the rapidly aging US population, older persons use more residential energy than the younger generations (Tonn and Eisenberg 2007), and if this energy is largely sourced from fossil fuels, their ecological footprint is likely to be high.

On the other hand, mounting evidence—for example, a Global Trends study of twenty-eight markets (Ipsos 2011)—suggests that older people care more about the environment than the younger consumers do; older people do more recycling, prefer greener products and organic food, and behave generally in a more sustainable way. This behavior indicates that when older people are given a choice, with the wisdom of their lived experiences, they opt for the more environmentally friendly options. With their preferences as consumers and as role models, they can also influence the availability and marketing of green products and a broader sustainable behavior.

In a narrow sense, people can regard population aging as a challenge for achieving socioeconomic and environmental goals (Guo, Marinova, and Jia 2011). Sustainability is about arable land, water, and other limited natural resources being available for current and future generations, and the more people the planet supports, including older people, the higher the demand on these resources. Moreover, the relatively lower share of younger people will have to face the increasing social and economic pressures from the large growing aging population. These pressures include demand for health care and medical services, but also include consequences from the ecological deterioration the activities of these same aging people caused during their working lives, including the impacts of climate change. Both health-care demands and ecological decline have significant financial implications, require serious consideration, and need resolution. Increasing ecological problems such as air, land, and water pollution, insufficient land for housing, and decreased outdoor activities can cause problems affecting human health. The world must face an aging population in the severity of a deteriorating ecological environment, which could lead to further social predicaments.

Like the young, older people need a sound environment for their well-being, such as public open spaces and parks, fresh air, and clean drinking water. The availability of land, however, is shrinking in most urban areas, and significant difficulties are arising from global freshwater scarcity and water pollution in many countries (UNEP 2012).

Another example relates to current modes of transportation, which not only increasingly contribute to air pollution with the constantly rising numbers of vehicles on the road, but also are not easily adaptable for the old to use. The issues of the expanding aging population are even worse with climate change and weather extremes, such as heat waves, droughts, or floods. Solving global environmental issues, such as greenhouse gas emissions and air and water pollution, will add more stress in addressing population-aging issues.

Furthermore, aging populations challenge a society's ability to achieve socioeconomic sustainability. A range of contributing factors exists. A high concentration of older people in urban areas will add more pressure on local governments to provide land, public transport, and infrastructure for aging citizens. Preventative health education, health care for the aging, disability services, and social security costs will affect expenditure on the resources already competing for ecological conservation.

In the future, many countries will have to face a large older population and the unavoidable socioeconomic and environmental impacts the aging population may bring. Most seriously, health-care services will be more in demand as societies tackle global warming, a complicated problem that is believed to have negative effects on human health. Each country, therefore, but also the international societies, will have to invest more resources and human capital to guarantee a good quality of life for aging persons. Making a transition toward better health-care and pension systems is a major component of the government strategies for addressing the challenges triggered by both the quickly growing global population-aging and environmental pressures.

Policy Recommendations

When planning for the future, governments and policy makers must pay attention to the age-specific changes occurring in their countries. Despite the overall population-aging trend, the issues they need to manage vary.

In many countries, the first baby boomers have become elderly residents now, people who did not experience higher personal savings rates when they were in their forties and fifties (National Institute on Aging et al. 2007). Governments must take urgent and effective actions to maintain the quality of life for these baby boomers. Fortunately, in the developed regions of the world, technology plays a strong role in the current and future provision for a country's older citizens. For example, in Australia, services such as Telehealth and Telecare use innovative solutions for providing primary care, and the Internet is assisting with social connection (Wells 2012). This technology reduces the need to travel and relieves the pressure on hospitals, which are some of the largest energy consumers, emitting 918 megajoules (MJ) of energy, or 224 kilograms (kg) of carbon dioxide equivalents per square meter (CO_2e/m^2) per annum (Department of Health 2010), compared to 200 MJ/m^2 or 49 kg CO_2e/m^2 in residential dwellings (Department of the Environment, Water, Heritage and the Arts 2008).

Although the proportion of older persons is higher in developed countries, their number is increasingly larger in developing countries. Large numbers of older people in the poor part of the world, such as in Africa and some regions of China, are still struggling for their basic needs. Meanwhile, the rapid shrinking of the working-age population has challenged the younger generations' traditional role in taking care of the elderly. Promoting healthy and positive aging therefore becomes an uneasy task for governments. Societies should encourage private institutions and caregivers to support homecare as a good option to avoid a collapse in the care of older citizens. As an essential aspect of human development, older people deserve to enjoy a positive and productive longevity. Education on promoting healthier lifestyles and using new technology can play a great role in achieving this goal (UN 2012a and 2012b).

From a global perspective, as the population ages, international communities should try to achieve more balanced life expectancies levels and encourage cooperation between developed and developing countries to boost efforts for aged care and accommodate extra funds, such as in education on preventing diseases and conducting research on medical services. In particular, battling noncommunicable diseases, which cause more than 80 percent of all deaths among the population aged 60 years and older (UN 2012b), deserves special attention. In addition, communities should take measures to control air and water pollution to reduce related diseases elderly people suffer with the purpose of lowering medical costs and reducing mortality (PRB 2010). The global trend of aging will continue, and younger generations will come under more pressure to support the elderly in the future. An urgent need therefore exists to boost efforts and distribute more financial assets to enhance social support mechanisms for providing better homecare and health care for the aging population.

On the other hand, the older generation can offer wisdom, knowledge, and experience that young people do not have. If in good health and retired or working part-time, older people have more time and are more involved with voluntary, philanthropic, and not-for-profit organizations; they also work in the community and for the environment. For example, in Australia, studies found the gross value of volunteering to be equivalent to the amount the government spends on all aged care services, and this contribution is estimated at around 7 percent of GDP (Healy 2004). "Far from being net receivers of help and support, older people are, in fact, net providers, at least up to the age of 75 years" (Healy 2004, ix). They assist with childcare; perform house chores; provide financial, practical, and emotional support to family and friends; and assist community groups and charities. They have strong networks and engage passionately with environmental and social justice issues.

People in each human generation have a habit of basing their assessments and practices on how things were when they were young. Global research has shown that many ecosystems have declined by as much as 90 percent from their historical conditions, but people's notion of sustainability is based on what they remember or have personally experienced (Jackson, Alexander, and Sala 2011). People living longer helps preserve the memories of that distant time, and these recollections speak on behalf of people themselves, other people who are no longer alive, but also on behalf of the planet. Encouraging such continuous intergenerational social communications is another important area of policy recommendations.

Outlook

Whether global population size will become stable, and when, the differences between countries and regions in terms of population aging, but also in relation to population consumption and environmental impact, are likely to remain for the foreseeable future. In the search for sustainability solutions, it is important to identify the subsections of the global population that are contributing the most to environmental degradation and those that are most vulnerable to its consequences (IIASA 2012). As development has proved so far, economic, social, political, and environmental factors drive demographic changes. Education is a powerful factor in solving the problems of population size because "well educated people tend to live longer healthier lives, are more able to choose the number of children they have and are more resilient to, and capable of, change" (The Royal Society 2012, 5).

Changing the patterns of population consumption appears to be much more difficult. Food is an excellent example of this point. All estimates of the contribution of the livestock industry to global greenhouse gas emissions show that this sector has a large impact (between 18 percent, according to FAO 2006, and 51 percent, according to Goodland and Anhang 2009). What are considered to be the right nutritional choices in a situation of food scarcity (such as in developing countries) are not necessarily correct when there is an abundance of food alternatives (such as in the developed world). For the world to become more sustainable, people need to preserve its resources while continually improving the living standards for its aging population. Achieving sustainability also requires constant reassessment of human behavior and human needs, as well as food and other choices made in our daily lives. People are at the core of the sustainability concerns, but people can also be part of the solution (O'Neill 2010).

Population aging is probably the most powerful manifestation of human sustainability, but humanity must also show that this sustainability does not come at the expense of the sustainability of other species and the ecological well-being of the planet.

Dora MARINOVA and Xiumei GUO
Curtin University

See also Collective Learning; Community; Education, Higher; Mobility; Population; Progress; Values

FURTHER READING

Australian Bureau of Statistics (ABS). (2012). 1367.0: State and territory statistical indicators. Canberra: Australian Government.

Blackburn, Robin. (2006). The global pension crisis: From grey capitalism to responsible accumulation. *Politics & Society, 34*(2), 135–186.

China Daily. (2012, May 18). State to boost efforts for rural elderly care. Retrieved July 18, 2012, from http://www.chinadaily.com.cn/china/2012-05/18/content_15325393.htm

Department of the Environment, Water, Heritage and the Arts. (2008). Energy use in the Australian residential sector, 1986–2020. Canberra: Commonwealth of Australia.

Department of Health. (2010). Energy consumption and carbon emissions of hospitals: An analysis by functional end use. Retrieved July 17, 2012, from http://docs.health.vic.gov.au/docs/doc/922468712 EDE0624CA2579400076F1DA/$FILE/energy-carbon.pdf

The Economist. (2003, March 6). Median age of the population. Retrieved July 16, 2012, from http://www.economist.com/node/1622427

Eurostat. (2011). Household consumption expenditure. Retrieved July 16, 2012, from http://epp.eurostat.ec.europa.eu/statistics_explained/index.php/Household_consumption_expenditure

Food and Agriculture Organization (FAO) of the United Nations. (2006). Livestock's long shadow: Environmental issues and options. Retrieved July 24, 2012, from http://www.fao.org/docrep/010/a0701e/a0701e00.HTM

Goodkind, Daniel. (2011). The world population at 7 billion. Retrieved July 16, 2012, from http://blogs.census.gov/2011/10/31/the-world-population-at-7-billion/

Goodland, Robert, & Anhang, Jeff. (2009). Livestock and climate change. Retrieved July 17, 2012, from http://www.worldwatch.org/node/6294

Guo, Xiumei; Marinova, Dora; & Jia, Ruiyue. (2011, December 12–16). Population ageing and the ecology in China: Towards a balanced developmental strategy model (pp. 1680–1686). Perth, Australia: 19th International Congress on Modelling and Simulation.

Healy, Judith. (2004). The benefits of an ageing population. The Australia Institute. Retrieved July 24, 2012, from http://www.tai.org.au/documents/dp_fulltext/DP63.pdf

International Institute for Applied Systems Analysis (IIASA). (2012). Demographic challenges for sustainable development: The Laxenburg Declaration on Population and Sustainable Development. Retrieved July 17, 2012, from http://www.iiasa.ac.at/Research/POP/Laxenburg%20Declaration%20on%20Population%20and%20Development.html

Ipsos. (2011, April 7). Synovate unveils results from Inaugural Global Green Habits Study. Retrieved July 17, 2012, from http://www.ipsos-na.com/news-polls/pressrelease.aspx?id=5481

Jackson, Jeremy B. C.; Alexander, Karen E.; & Sala, Enric. (Eds.). (2011). *Shifting baselines: The past and the future of ocean fisheries.* Washington, DC: Island Press.

Lee, Ronald, & Mason, Andrew. (2012, March). India's aging population. *Today's Research on Aging, 25,* 1–6. Retrieved July 17, 2012, from http://www.prb.org/pdf12/TodaysResearchAging25.pdf

Martins, Jo M.; Yusuf, Farhat; & Swanson, David A. (2011). *Consumer demographics and behaviour: Markets are people.* (The Springer series on demographic methods and population analysis 30). Dordrecht, The Netherlands: Springer Science+Business.

National Institute on Aging; National Institutes of Health; United States Department of Health and Human Services; & United States Department of State. (2007). Why population aging matters: A global perspective. Retrieved July 16, 2012, from http://www.nia.nih.gov/sites/default/files/WPAM.pdf

O'Neill, Brian C. (2010). Climate change and population growth. In Laurie Mazur (Ed.), *A pivotal moment: Population, justice, and the environmental challenge* (pp. 81–94). Washington, DC, & Covelo, CA: Island Press.

Pearce, Fred. (2010, February 27). Earth's nine lives: How much further can we push the planetary life-support systems that keep us safe? *New Scientist, 205*(2749), 30–35.

Population Reference Bureau (PRB). (2010). China's rapidly aging population. *Today's Research on Aging, 20,* 1–5. Retrieved July 17, 2012, from http://www.prb.org/pdf10/TodaysResearchAging20.pdf

Population Reference Bureau (PRB). (2012, March). India's aging population. *Today's Research on Aging, 25,* 1–6. Retrieved July 17, 2012, from http://www.prb.org/TodaysResearch.aspx

Raphaely, Talia, & Marinova, Dora. (2012). Flexitarianism: A more moral dietary option. *International Journal of Sustainable Society* (forthcoming).

The Royal Society. (2012). *People and the planet: Summary and recommendations* (Report 01a/12). London: The Royal Society Science Policy Centre.

Tonn, Bruce, & Eisenberg, Joel. (2007). The aging US population and residential energy demand. *Energy Policy, 35*(1), 743–745.

United Nations (UN). (2002). World population ageing: 1950–2050. Retrieved July 24, 2012, from http://www.un.org/esa/population/publications/worldageing19502050/

United Nations (UN). (2009). World population ageing (ESA/P/WP/212). Department of Economic and Social Affairs, Population Division. Retrieved July 16, 2012, from http://www.un.org/esa/population/publications/WPA2009/WPA2009_WorkingPaper.pdf

United Nations (UN). (2011). World population to reach 10 billion by 2100 if fertility in all countries converges to replacement level. (United Nations Press Release). Retrieved July 16, 2012, from http://www.ciesin.columbia.edu/binaries/web/global/news/2011/pressrelease-worldpopproj.pdf

United Nations (UN). (2012a). Towards global equity in longevity (Population facts, No 2012/2). Department of Economics and

Social Affairs, Population Division. Retrieved July 18, 2012, from http://www.un.org/esa/population/

United Nations (UN). (2012b). Population ageing and the non-communicable diseases (Population facts, No 2012/1). Department of Economics and Social Affairs, Population Division. Retrieved July 18, 2012, from http://www.un.org/esa/population/

United Nations Environment Programme (UNEP). (1992). Rio Declaration on Environment and Development. Retrieved July 16, 2012, from http://www.unep.org/Documents.Multilingual/Default.asp?documentid=78&articleid=1163

United Nations Environment Programme (UNEP). (2012). Measuring water use in a green economy. Retrieved July 18, 2012, from http://www.unep.org/resourcepanel/Portals/24102/Measuring_Water.pdf

United States (US) Census Bureau. (2012). International programs: International data base. Retrieved July 16, 2012, from http://www.census.gov/population/international/data/idb/information Gateway.php

United States Central Intelligence Agency (US CIA). (2012). *The world factbook*. Retrieved July 16, 2012, from https://www.cia.gov/library/publications/the-world-factbook/geos/xx.html

Wells, Yvonne. (2012, April 7). Inclusion vital for a healthy ageing population. Retrieved July 16, 2012, from http://theconversation.edu.au/inclusion-vital-for-a-healthy-ageing-population-5969

Wong, Theresa, & Yeoh, Brenda S. A. (2003). Fertility and the family: An overview of pro-natalist population in Singapore (Asian Metacentre research paper series, no.12). Retrieved July 18, 2012, from http://www.populationasia.org/Publications/RP/AMCRP12.pdf

World Bank. (2012). Life expectancy at birth, total years. Retrieved July 17, 2012, from http://wikiposit.org/w?filter=Economics/World%20Bank/By%20Indicator/Health/Life%20expectancy%20at%20birth,%20total%20years/

Ying, Bin, & Yao, Rui. (2006). Consumption patterns of Chinese elders: Evidence from a survey in Wuhan, China. *Journal of Family and Economic Issues, 27*, 702–714.

Agricultural Innovation

Perennial plants growing in species mixtures are an essential component of nature's ecosystems; they build the soil that humanity depends on. Essentially all of the high-yield crops that feed humanity, however—including rice, wheat, corn (maize), soybeans, and peanuts—are currently annuals. Perennialization has the potential to extend—vastly—the productive life of soils. Since the 1980s, scientists at The Land Institute, in the United States, have been developing herbaceous perennial grains with deep root structures that can survive the winter and stay in the soil year after year. These perennial crops have the potential to cut down on agricultural energy use, keep carbon in the ground, reduce harmful runoff, prevent biodiversity loss, and seem certain to be more resilient to climate change. The institute proposes a "50-Year Farm Bill" to gradually institutionalize the perennialization of agriculture.

Agriculture needs new strategies that emphasize efficient nutrient use in order to lower production costs and minimize negative environmental effects. Today, the best soils on the best landscapes are already being farmed, so much of the future expansion of agriculture will be onto marginal lands, with a high risk of irreversible soil degradation. Expensive chemical, energy, and equipment inputs will thus become less effective and much less affordable. Moving toward perennialization of cropland now growing annual grains, however, has the potential to extend the productive life of soils from hundreds to thousands of years.

The sooner successful agricultural alternatives become available, the more land can be saved from degradation. A vision for the future is predicated on the need to end the ecological damage to agricultural land associated with grain production—damage such as soil erosion, poisoning by pesticides, and biodiversity loss. The most cost-effective way to do this—and stay fed—is to perennialize the landscape. Although this article focuses on the situation in the United States, the type of agricultural innovation proposed here—as well as innovations developed by other researchers—can be adapted for use in other parts of the world as well.

The record-setting drought—worse than the Dust Bowl, in the 1930s—that struck a vast area of the United States' Midwest in the summer of 2012 shows the danger of dependence on annual crops, such as corn, that are more water-dependent than are perennial crops with their deep, year-round root systems. Prices for a large array of commodities, from meat products and dairy to packaged cereals and plastics based on plant matter, are expected to spike worldwide as a result of this drought.

The current agricultural system in practice in the United States and throughout much of the world is not sustainable. Since the 1980s, scientists at The Land Institute, a group in the United States whose stated purpose is to "develop an agricultural system with the ecological stability of the prairie and a grain yield comparable to that from annual crops" (The Land Institute 2012), are among many worldwide who are trying to combat this trend. The Land Institute's work is the subject of this article, although it should be noted that the institute is one of many working toward the goal of a more sustainable agricultural system.

The scientists at The Land Institute have been developing herbaceous perennial grains to be grown in mixed-species polycultures. The result is crops with deep root structures that can survive the winter and stay in the soil year after year. This not only reduces the need to crop, turn, and plant seeds each year—the largest energy input in agriculture—but it also keeps carbon in the ground, reduces harmful runoff by eliminating tilling, and prevents biodiversity loss by restoring prairie systems.

The Land Institute's first farmer-ready crops will be available on a limited scale by the early 2020s, but many people believe that it is time for the government of the United States (and, by extension, global governments) to come up with a plan to start the transition toward a sustainable agricultural future. The Land Institute advocates that the current five-year plans of the US Department of Agriculture (USDA) be used as mileposts in what the institute calls a 50-Year Farm Bill. (See figure 1 below.)

The transition of agriculture from an extractive to a renewable economy in the foreseeable future can be realistically imagined. There is little doubt that the agricultural transition can be made fast enough to stay ahead of the adjustments that will be imposed by climate change and the end of the fossil-fuel era. If we humans can keep ourselves fed without destroying the planet in the process, we'll have a chance to solve our other problems.

The fifty-year plan's key concepts are:

- Current US agricultural production is renowned for its ability to feed the nation and alleviate food shortages in other parts of the world. That production, however, comes with significant and increasing threats to biodiversity and ecosystem function, and is increasingly at risk from drought, flooding, and other climate change–related calamities.

- Those threats—such as soil and wind erosion, nutrient depletion, salinization and toxic buildup in soils, water depletion, and harmful runoff—stem primarily from the production of annual grains, including rice, wheat, and corn (maize).

- Perennial plants can solve many of the problems perpetuated by annual grains while maintaining agricultural production, but more research is required.

- US agriculture is guided by five-year farm bills and heavily entrenched subsidies. A 50-Year Farm Bill based on the transition to perennial agriculture would move the United States toward sustainable agricultural production.

- Perennial agriculture could be a model for parts of the world with more serious agricultural production problems than those in the United States (one example among many being the cotton-growing regions surrounding the Aral Sea in Central Asia; the sea is a fraction of its former size after disastrous Soviet-era irrigation programs diverted water to water-thirsty cotton crops).

The Trouble with Agriculture

Across the farmlands of the world, climate change overshadows an ecological and cultural crisis of unequaled scale: soil erosion, loss of wild biodiversity, poisoned land

Figure 1. Proposed Timeline for the 50-Year Farm Bill

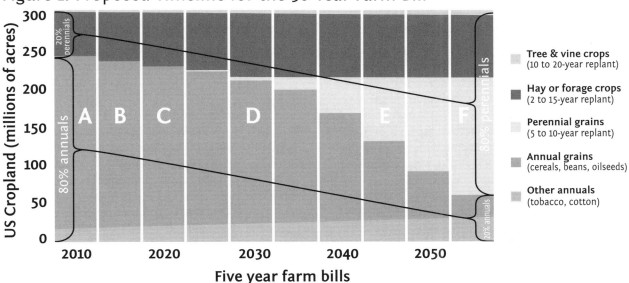

Source: The Land Institute.

Note: 1 acre = .4 hectare

Figure 1 shows a plan to perennialize crops incrementally:

A. 2010: Hay or grazing operations will continue as they exist. Preparations for subsidy changes begin.

B. 2015: Subsidies become incentive to substitute perennial grass in rotations for feed grain in meat, egg, and milk production.

C. 2020: The first perennial wheat will be farmer-ready for limited planting.

D. 2030: Educate farmers and consumers about new perennial grain crops.

E. 2045: New perennial grain varieties will be ready for expanded geographical range. Also potential for grazing and hay.

and water, salinization, expanding dead zones, and the demise of rural communities. The Millennium Ecosystem Assessment (MEA) concludes that agriculture is the "largest threat to biodiversity and ecosystem function of any single human activity" (Cassman and Wood 2005). Up to 40 percent of global croplands are experiencing soil erosion, reduced fertility, or overgrazing (Wood, Sebastian, and Scherr 2000). It is likely that agricultural land worldwide will expand in the coming decades as the human population increases to 8, 10, or even 15 billion people. The same thing exacerbating climate change helps drive the agricultural crisis: cheap fossil fuel.

In the United States, commodity subsidies that focus on getting the most out of each parcel of land—an industrial model that much of the world wants to imitate—continue to promote an increasingly unsustainable agricultural economy. Over the past century, the number of farms in the United States has declined as the average farm size has increased. At the same time, the number of commodities per farm—such as corn, wheat, barley, soybeans, alfalfa, tobacco, potatoes, pigs, and chickens—has decreased from an average of five to just one (Dimitri, Effland, and Conklin 2005). As stated before, agriculture in the United States is guided by five-year farm bills and heavily entrenched subsidies. Export policy, where agricultural products from the United States are heavily subsidized so as to encourage export to other countries, is designed to offset the nation's balance-of-payments deficit, which includes the purchase of foreign oil.

A long-term, conserving vision will counteract these trends. Five-year farm bills should be mileposts in a fifty-year journey to end the degradation of agricultural capital. Where to begin?

The United States is a big country, and its ecological mosaic is daunting. The soils of the upper Midwest are deep and rich in nutrients from the Pleistocene era's scouring ice and watered by moisture blown from the Gulf of Mexico. But soil erosion, nitrogen fertilizer, and pesticides have seriously degraded this gift of good land, the best contiguous stretch in the world. In California, rich valleys and reliable snow pack in a Mediterranean environment lessen the problem of soil erosion. But that region is negatively affected by spraying, salinization, and loss of farmland to sprawl.

This inventory could continue, but the point is that each region has its own problems and opportunities. It must be acknowledged that all successful corrections will be local, and play to an often-overlooked point: the decline of fossil fuels will require more farmers on the land. Cultural and ecological adaptations thereby become one subject.

Looking broadly (and again, this can be applied to other nations), the USDA and the secretary of agriculture need to see that the first order of business should be to prevent soils from eroding and declining in quality—they are the source of most of the nutrients that feed the country. If soils are protected, the water falling on them can be protected and properly used on its trip to the atmosphere, ocean, or aquifer. The United States has about 162 million hectares of cropland, with around 14.6 million hectares placed in the Conservation Reserve Program (Pollack and Perez 2007; USDA 2007). The US secretary of agriculture must look at the aggregate use of these croplands. At any one time, 80 percent of that land grows annual crops. The other 20 percent is in perennials, such as pastures or hay, although, to be clear, sometimes in a rotation with annuals such as corn or sorghum.

Such an overview quickly draws attention to the core of what might be called "the problem of agriculture": essentially all of the high-yield crops that feed humanity—including rice, wheat, corn, soybeans, and peanuts—are annuals. With the cropping of annuals, alive just part of the year and weakly rooted even then, comes more loss of precious soil, nutrients, and water.

The problem of agriculture involves more than its mainly annual condition. Another important liability is growing crops in vast, unnatural monocultures. This makes harvest easy, but there is *only one kind* of root architecture in any given field; the living roots are not there year-round and therefore manage nutrients and water poorly. Waste of both is the rule.

The trouble with agriculture is not a recent development. Soil erosion and soil salting brought down civilizations long before the industrial and chemical era. Why the crisis now? Simply, a surge in human population—which has more than doubled from about 3.3 billion in 1965 to just over 7 billion as of 2012—with land lost to sprawl and the remainder used far more intensively, as well as the accumulation of large dead zones in the world's oceans.

The Alternative

What is the alternative scenario? Prudence requires looking first to nature, the ultimate source of food and production, no matter how independent humankind feels it has become. Looking at all the natural land ecosystems within the ecosphere, from alpine meadows to rainforests, it can be seen that mixtures of perennial plants rule (Chiras and Reganold 2004). Annuals are opportunists that sprout, reproduce, throw seeds, and die, whereas perennials hold on for the long haul, protect the soil, and manage nutrients and water to a fine degree. In this regard, perennials are superior to annuals, whether in polyculture or monoculture. The Land Institute's long-standing mission has been to perennialize major crops, such as wheat, sorghum, and sunflower, and to domesticate a few wild perennial species to produce food like their annual analogs. The use of biotechnology in agriculture allows plants to exhibit desired characteristics (be they higher yield, drought resistance, or, in this case,

TABLE 1. A 50-Year Vision

Five-year farm bills address:	• Exports
	• Commodities
	• Subsidies
	• Some soil conservation measures
	• Food programs
A **"50-Year Farm Bill"** would use the five-year bills as mileposts, adding larger, more-sustainable goals to existing programs:	• Protect soil from erosion
	• Cut fossil-fuel dependence to zero
	• Sequester carbon
	• Reduce toxins in soil and water
	• Manage nitrogen carefully
	• Reduce dead zones
	• Cut wasteful water use
	• Preserve or rebuild farm communities
	• Protect soil from erosion

Source: The Land Institute 2010, "A Fifty-Year Farm Bill."

perennialism) that they would not otherwise exhibit. The goal is to grow them in mixtures according to what the landscape requires. With the pre-agricultural ecosystem as the standard, The Land Institute is attempting to bring as many processes of the wild to the farm as possible, below as well as above the surface.

Because these perennial crops will not be ready for the farmer on any appreciable scale for another quarter-century, the landscape must be perennialized in other ways in the meantime. The Land Institute proposes as a first step to increase the number of pastures and have fewer livestock in the feedlot by phasing out subsidies for production-oriented grain commodities. That changes the emphasis to saving the soil and allowing water to improve instead of extra meat or corn sugar.

In California and elsewhere across the mosaic, where soil erosion is less serious, perennials are superior for managing nutrients and water (Randall and Mulla 2001). Species mixtures can form barriers to insect outbreaks and disease epidemics. So nature's example can be referred to no matter where the landscape. Perennialization would start what the US economic and social critic, author, and farmer Wendell Berry calls a "conversation with nature," which begins with three questions: "What is here? What will nature permit us to do here? [And w]hat will nature help us do here?" (Berry 1987, 146).

A Fifty-Year Plan for Change

The five-year plans in use by the USDA are mainly instruments for protecting the failing agricultural system. They address exports as well as commodity subsidies that focus on yield per land, subsidies, food programs,

and some soil measures. The Land Institute suggests that the five-year increments be used to build a radically different type of agriculture: a fifty-year vision of perennial, low-impact agriculture. (See table 1 above.)

In the short term, the fifty-year plan will encourage farmers to increase the use of perennial grasses and legumes in crop rotations. This will help protect soils and reduce the need for fertilizer, while preparing farms for the use of perennial grains.

Pastures and perennial forage crops are already available in permanent stands and rotations. The Land Institute proposes incentives that would maintain the present perennial hectares and increase their presence in rotations. When perennial grains become available, they will require no financial subsidy, since they will represent a compelling alternative.

As more of the land is switched to perennial agriculture, and with the fifty years of concerted investment in research, education, and incentives envisaged in the plan, perennial crops can be expected to increase from 20 to 80 percent of the agricultural land.

US agriculture is widely used as a model for the rest of the world. Although a US perennial program would not solve all agricultural problems, it could be helpful around the world, in that some perennialized grains could be planted elsewhere and techniques developed to perennialize US agriculture could be applied to native plants in other countries. US expertise could be exported much as it is today, to help with the sustainability problems of agriculture globally. In other words, the same approach to improving agriculture that led to the worldwide Green Revolution, a program that increased the yield in developing countries but eventually proved to be environmentally unsustainable, could lead to a sustainable ecological agriculture.

The Heart of the Plan: The Plants

Breeding perenniality into a broad spectrum of grain crops will take time. Even so, prototypes have thrived for several years in Kansas (Cox et al. 2006). As the prototype yields increase, perennials will replace their annual relatives—one prototype may be ready by 2022. Initially, these crops will be released on a limited scale, and researchers will work with farmers on agronomic problems, such as seeding density and planting time, as they arise.

Wheat

Wheat has been hybridized with several different perennial species to produce viable, fertile offspring. Thousands of such plants have already been produced. Many rounds of crossing, testing, and selection will be necessary before perennial wheat varieties are available for use on the farm. So far, genetically diverse populations of Kernza have been established using parental strains from the USDA and other sources. In 2009, 12 hectares were harvested and an additional 51 hectares were planted. The overall nutritional quality is superior to that of annual wheat.

Grain Sorghum

Grain sorghum is a drought-hardy feed grain in North America and a staple human food crop in Asia and Africa, where it provides reliable harvests in places where hunger is always a threat. It can be hybridized with the perennial species *Sorghum halepense*. Large plant populations have been produced from hundreds of such hybrids, and perennial strains have been selected with seed size and grain yields up to 50 percent of those of annual grain sorghum.

Illinois Bundleflower

Illinois bundleflower, *Desmanthus illinoiensis*, is a native prairie legume that fixes atmospheric nitrogen and produces abundant, protein-rich seed. It is one of the strongest candidates for domestication as a crop. This plant is seen as a partial substitute for the soybean. A large collection of bundleflower seed from a wide geographical area has been assembled and integrated into a breeding program.

Sunflower

Sunflower is another annual crop that has been hybridized with perennial species in its genus, including *Helianthus maximiliani*, *H. rigidus*, and *H. tuberosus* (commonly known as Jerusalem artichoke). Breeding work has turned out strong perennial plants. Genetic stabilization will improve their seed production.

Rice

Upland fields of annual rice are highly vulnerable to erosion, yet millions of people in Asia depend on them. In the 1990s, the International Rice Research Institute achieved significant progress toward breeding a perennial upland rice using crosses between the annual *Oryza sativa* and two wild perennial species, *Oryza rufipogon* and *O. longistaminata* (Sacks, Roxas, and Sta. Cruz 2003). When the project was terminated in 2001, the breeding and genetic populations were transferred to the Yunnan Academy of Agricultural Sciences in southwestern China, where work has continued with funding support from The Land Institute. The focus is now on the more difficult work with the distantly related *O. longistaminata*, which, when crossed with rice, produces plants with underground stems called rhizomes (Cox et al. 2002). In recent breakthroughs, a small number of perennial plants with good seed production have been produced.

Corn and Soybeans

Corn and soybeans are two species that, more than any other crop, need to be perennialized. Corn is a top carbohydrate producer, typically grown on more than 28 million hectares annually (USDA 2007). Until soybean land use increased, corn caused the greatest amount of soil erosion in the

United States. It will be a challenge to perennialize this crop, but serious consideration is being given to doing so by exploring two main paths. (1) Genes could be obtained from a few distant relatives of corn that are in the genus *Tripsicum*. All are perennial and at least one is winter-hardy. (2) The other, more likely route would be to cross corn with two much closer perennial relatives. Unfortunately, both species, *Zea perennis* and *Z. diploperennis,* are tropical and thus not winter-hardy. Further research is necessary before traditional corn can be replaced.

Several Australian species of the soybean genus *Glycine* are perennial; they are difficult to breed with soybean but are potential targets for direct domestication, without crossing with soybean. Exploration into perennializing soybeans has been very limited. Work is being done to make Illinois bundleflower a satisfying substitute.

Mimicking Natural Ecosystems

To mimic a natural ecosystem will require some degree of crop diversity, and there is potential for many more perennial grains, including rosinseed, eastern gamagrass, chickpea, millet, flax, and a range of native plants. Researchers have elected not to wait until perennial grain crops are fully developed in order to gain experience with the ecological context in which they will grow. The Land Institute has established long-term ecological plots of close analogs in which to compare methods of perennial crop management. Their perennial-grain prototypes, including Kernza and bundleflower, allow them to initiate long-term ecological and production research in these plots. For other crops they are forced to use analogs, but eventually true perennial grain mixtures will replace them. Additionally, ongoing studies of natural ecosystems, such as tallgrass prairie, provide insight into the functioning of natural plant communities.

Outlook

Essentially all of nature's ecosystems feature perennial plants growing in species mixtures, systems that build soil. Agriculture reversed that process nearly everywhere by substituting annual monocultures. As a result, ecosystem services—including soil fertility—have been degraded. Most land available for new production is of marginal quality that declines quickly. The resulting biodiversity loss gets deserved attention; but soil erosion is less mentioned and addressed.

Perennialization of the cropland now growing grains has the potential to extend the productive life of soils from the current tens or hundreds of years to thousands or tens of thousands. New perennial crops, like their wild relatives, seem certain to be more resilient to climate change. They will surely increase the sequestration of carbon, as well as reduce the land runoff that creates coastal dead zones and affects fisheries, and will maintain the quality of scarce surface and ground water. Food security will improve.

It will not be easy to overturn decades of policy and centuries of turning to annuals. There are entrenched interests that can slow change, but the social stability and ecological sustainability resulting from secure perennial food supplies make the fight worthwhile. Long-term strategies like the 50-Year Farm Bill will buy time to confront the intersecting issues of climate, population, water, and biodiversity.

Wes JACKSON and Wendell BERRY
The Land Institute

This article was adapted by the editors from the authors' article, "The 50-Year Farm Bill," which originally appeared in the online journal *Solutions* (Volume 1, Issue 3: pages 28–35, 7 July 2010). Adapted with kind permission of *Solutions*. The original article is available online at http://www.thesolutionsjournal.com/print/649.

The original article was written with indispensable assistance from Land Institute scientists Stan Cox, Lee DeHaan, David Van Tassell, Jerry Glover, and Cindy Cox. Wendell Berry, Joan Jackson, Fred Kirschenmann, and Ken Warren provided editorial help. Joe Roman, Jack Fairweather, Tess Croner, James Dewar, Arjun Heimsath, and B. B. Mishra gave valuable reviews and assistance.

See also Energy Efficiency; Food Security; Local Solutions to Global Problems; Population; Progress; Water

FURTHER READING

Berry, Wendell. (1987). *Home economics: Fourteen essays.* New York: North Point Press.

Cassman, Kenneth G., & Wood, Stanley. (2005). Cultivated systems. In Rashid Hassan, Robert Scholes & Neville Ash (Eds.), *Ecosystems and human well-being: Current state and trends: Vol. 1* (pp. 745–794). Washington, DC: Island Press. Retrieved June 1, 2012, from http://www.maweb.org/documents/document.295.aspx.pdf

Chiras, Daniel D., & Reganold, John P. (2004). *Natural resource conservation: Management for a sustainable future* (9th ed.). Upper Saddle River, NJ: Prentice Hall.

Cox, Thomas S., et al. (2002). Breeding perennial grain crops. *Critical Reviews in Plant Sciences, 21,* 59–91.

Cox, Thomas S.; Glover, Jerry D.; Van Tassel, David L.; Cox, Cindy M.; & DeHann, Lee R. (2006). Prospects for developing perennial grain crops. *BioScience, 56,* 649–659. Retrieved June 1, 2012, from http://www.landinstitute.org/pages/Bioscience_PerennialGrains.pdf

Dimitri, Carolyn; Effland, Anne; & Conklin, Neilson. (2005). The 20th century transformation of US agriculture and farm policy. *US Department of Agriculture, Economic Information Bulletin, 3*, 1–14. Retrieved June 1, 2012, from http://www.ers.usda.gov/publications/EIB3/EIB3.pdf

The Land Institute. (2012). Introduction and mission. Retrieved June 1, 2012, from http://www.landinstitute.org/vnews/display.v/SEC/About%20Us

Pollack, Susan, & Perez, Agnes. (2007). Fruit and tree nuts situation and outlook yearbook 2007. Washington, DC: USDA. Retrieved May 31, 2012, from www.ers.usda.gov/publications/FTS/2007/Yearbook/FTS2007.pdf

Randall, Gyles W., & Mulla, David J. (2001). Nitrate nitrogen in surface waters as influenced by climatic conditions and agricultural practices. *Journal of Environmental Quality, 30*, 337–344.

Sacks, Erik J.; Roxas, Jose P.; & Sta. Cruz, Maria Teresa. (2003). Developing perennial upland rice I: Field performance of *Oryza sativa/O. rufipogon* F_1, F_4 and BC_1F_4 progeny. *Crop Science, 43*, 120–128.

United States Department of Agriculture (USDA) National Agricultural Statistic Service. (2007). Agricultural statistics 2007. Washington, DC: USDA. Retrieved June 1, 2012, from http://www.nass.usda.gov/Publications/Ag_Statistics/2007/2007.pdf

Wood, Stanley; Sebastian, Kate; & Scherr, Sara J. (2000). Pilot analysis of global ecosystems: Agroecosystems. Washington, DC: International Food Policy Research Institute and World Resources Institute.

Anthropocene Epoch

Humankind has become a global geological force in its own right, but the notion that we might have become the dominant force for change in the biosphere—the relatively small sliver of the Earth's crust that supports life—crystallized only in the last two decades of the twentieth century. Many scholars now argue that in the last two centuries we have in fact entered a new geological epoch, the "Anthropocene," a turbulent period of exceptional and unpredictable change. What is the evidence for such a claim? And what is its significance for discussions of sustainability?

The geological time chart—a system for dating events in the Earth's history based on rock stratification—contains several different types of time periods. The largest are the *eons*, such as the Phanerozoic, the era of large organisms, which covers the last 540 million years. The next largest are the *eras*, such as the Cenozoic, the era of mammals, which covers the last 66 million years. Eras, in turn, can be divided into *periods*, such as the Quaternary, which covers the last two million years. And finally, periods are subdivided into *epochs*. The last and shortest of the epochs is the Holocene, which includes the 11,500 years since the end of the last ice age, a period of unusual climatic stability. In his book *The Holocene: An Environmental History*, the British geographer Neil Roberts provides a fine, readable history of the Holocene epoch that can help put the new idea of the Anthropocene into perspective (Roberts 1998). A number of scholars have begun to argue that the Holocene has ended, because in the last two centuries we have entered a new epoch, the "Anthropocene," a turbulent period of exceptional and unpredictable change. The defining feature of the Anthropocene is the transformative role played by our own species, *Homo sapiens*. For most modern humans,

increasing human control over the biosphere (the relatively thin sliver of the Earth's crust that supports life) has meant a vast improvement in living standards; improved nutrition, housing, and health care; better communications; and faster transportation. But in the last fifty years it has also become apparent that these gains may have come at a considerable cost.

In its modern form, the idea of an "Anthropocene epoch" is generally attributed to the Dutch climatologist Paul Crutzen. According to one account, at a conference around the early 2000s he became increasingly frustrated by claims that we still were living in the Holocene epoch and finally could not resist saying, "We're no longer in the Holocene. We are in the Anthropocene." The idea of a distinct Anthropocene epoch immediately attracted attention, and today Crutzen is widely regarded as the term's originator (Kolbert 2011).

Although it began recently on geological timescales, the Anthropocene is noteworthy even on the huge timescales of planetary history, because it marks the first time in the almost 4-billion-year history of life on Earth that a single species has played the leading role in shaping the biosphere. We are also changing things very very fast. There have been occasions when whole groups of organisms, such as the first bacteria capable of photosynthesis, have had a transformative impact on the biosphere (the first photosynthesizers began pumping oxygen into the atmosphere) or periods in which particular organisms had a significant impact on regional environments. But never before has a single species had the power to transform the entire biosphere on the time scale of just a few centuries. As the authors of a recent paper put it, "The term Anthropocene suggests: (i) that the Earth is now moving out of its current epoch, called the Holocene, and (ii) that human activity is largely responsible for this exit from the Holocene, that is, that humankind has become a global geological force in its own right" (Steffen et al. 2011, 843).

The idea of the Anthropocene is not just of interest to geologists or paleontologists. It should also interest historians and anthropologists because of the central role it assigns to our own species, *Homo sapiens*. The idea offers a powerful lens through which to view human history and to consider what it is that makes our species so distinctive. Historians may also find the idea valuable because it suggests a new and more precise way of thinking about the epoch of human history generally described, with deliberate vagueness, as "modernity." But the idea of the Anthropocene should be of particular interest to the emerging global-change community, specialists from many different backgrounds who study our rapidly increasing impacts on the biosphere. (For a concise history of this scholarly community, see Robin and Steffen 2007.) Crutzen himself has described the idea as "a warning to the world" (Kolbert 2011).

The Evolution of an Idea

The idea that human beings are playing a transformative role in the biosphere is not entirely novel. It is present to some degree in religious traditions, including Christianity, that see human beings as masters of the Earth. As a scientific idea, its seeds are present in the pioneering work of the early US environmentalist George Perkins Marsh, who wrote in the middle of the nineteenth century (Marsh 1864/2005; Guha 2000; McNeill 2003; Christian 2011). The late-nineteenth-century Italian geologist Antonio Stoppani wrote of an "Anthropozoic era," arguing that humanity had become a "new telluric force which in power and universality may be compared to the greater forces of Earth." In the 1890s the Swedish scientist Svante Arrhenius argued that human emissions of carbon might eventually transform global climates. In the 1920s, the French philosophers Pierre Teilhard de Chardin and Edouard le Roy and the Russian geochemist Vladimir Vernadsky built on the British geologist Eduard Seuss's notion of a biosphere by proposing the idea of a *noosphere*, a realm dominated by human thought and activity (Steffen et al. 2011, 844; Crutzen and Stoermer 2000).

But not until the appearance of modern environmental movements in the second half of the twentieth century did such ideas get a broader airing. Late-twentieth-century environmental movements and scholarship were driven largely by a growing awareness of the rapidly increasing scale of human impacts. But the notion that we might have become the *dominant* force for change in the biosphere crystallized only in the last two decades of the twentieth century. The US biologist Eugene Stoermer began to use the term *Anthropocene* informally in the 1980s, while the US journalist Andrew Revkin argued in a 1992 book that we might be entering an entirely new age, and suggested it might be named the "Anthropocene" (Steffen et al. 2011, 843).

Current use of the term *Anthropocene* dates from a short article published in 2000 by Paul Crutzen (best known for his Nobel Prize–winning work on ozone depletion) and Eugene F. Stoermer in the *Newsletter of the International Geosphere-Biosphere Programme*. After describing earlier versions of their idea, and listing some of the evidence for increasing human impacts on the biosphere, they wrote:

> Considering these and many other major and still growing impacts of human activities on Earth and atmosphere, and at all, including global, scales, it seems to us more than appropriate to emphasize the central role of mankind in geology and ecology by proposing to use the term "anthropocene" for the current geological epoch. The impacts of current human activities will continue over long periods. (Crutzen and Stoermer 2000)

In 2002 Crutzen proposed the idea slightly more formally in *Nature*:

> For the past three centuries, the effects of humans on the global environment have escalated. Because of these anthropogenic emissions of carbon dioxide, global climate may depart significantly from natural behaviour for many millennia to come. It seems appropriate to assign the term "Anthropocene" to the present, in many ways human-dominated, geological epoch, supplementing the Holocene—the warm period of the past 10–12 millennia. The Anthropocene could be said to have started in the latter part of the eighteenth century when analyses of air trapped in polar ice showed the beginning of growing global concentrations of carbon dioxide and methane. This date also happens to coincide with James Watt's design of the steam engine in 1784. (Crutzen 2002)

Since 2002 many geologists, paleontologists, and scholars within the global-change community have taken up the idea of the Anthropocene, and reports on it have begun to appear in the press—in articles in the *Economist*, the *New York Times*, the *National Geographic*, and elsewhere (Kolbert 2011; Economist 2011; Revkin 2011). Within the Subcommission on Quaternary Stratigraphy, the body that formally decides on divisions between different eras within the Quaternary period, an Anthropocene Working Group has been formed to consider whether the notion of an

Anthropocene epoch should be formally recognized. In 2009, a proposal for formal recognition of the new epoch, co-authored by more than twenty prominent geologists, was published in the journal of the Geological Society of America (Zalasiewicz et al. 2009). In March 2012, the idea of the Anthropocene was at the center of discussions at the four-day Planet under Pressure conference held in London (Planet under Pressure 2012a and 2012b).

Evidence for a New Geological Epoch

Although the Anthropocene epoch and the changes associated with it may seem recent, they are the culmination of processes that go back to the beginnings of human history. Our technological precocity as a species was apparent, already, in the artistic and technological skills evident at archaeological sites such as Blombos cave in South Africa. Here, almost 100,000 years ago, humans learned how to use shellfish, developed sophisticated palettes of colors, and carved intricate patterns on ocher rocks. (See Scarre 2005 for a superb, up-to-date collection of essays on the earliest phases of human history.) Sophisticated paint-making kits have been found at Blombos cave, dating back almost 100,000 years (Henshilwood et al. 2011). But our remarkable technological creativity as a species was displayed even more spectacularly in the global migrations, which, from about 60,000 years ago, took small groups of humans to all of the world's continents except for Antarctica. Each migration required new strategies and technologies to deal with unfamiliar climates, plants, animals, and physical environments. The extinctions of many species of megafauna that appear to have accompanied these migrations are a reminder that even early in our history, human technological creativity threatened other species, including our closest relatives, the few surviving species of hominids. The technological revolutions that have created the Anthropocene epoch in the last two centuries represent a sharp acceleration in processes that are as old as *Homo sapiens*.

The evidence that we have entered a very different geological epoch is extensive and varied. In his 2002 article in *Nature*, Paul Crutzen listed some of the more important kinds of evidence (Crutzen 2002):

- a tenfold increase in human numbers since 1700
- rapid growth in the number of human domesticates, leading to a significant increase in methane production
- direct human exploitation of up to 50 percent of the Earth's surface
- a sharp decline in the area occupied by tropical forests, which has accelerated species extinctions and reduced the ability of the biosphere to absorb carbon dioxide
- increasing human control of water flows, including human control of over 50 percent of all freshwater
- human removal of between 25 percent and 35 percent of primary production in ocean fisheries
- a sixteenfold increase in human energy use since 1900, which has doubled emissions of sulfur dioxide
- the amount of nitrogen fixed through the manufacture of fertilizers now exceeds the amount fixed in natural ecosystems
- human emissions of nitric oxide through the burning of fossil fuels and biofuels also exceed natural emissions
- increasing concentrations of carbon dioxide and methane respectively by 30 percent and 100 percent over pre-industrial levels

Directly or indirectly, the thread that unites these changes is the dynamism of societies and economies based on the rapidly increasing use of fossil fuels. Earlier human societies had access to limited reserves of energy, derived from recently captured solar energy. That energy was tapped either as wind or water power (as solar energy pumped the two great fluids of the atmosphere and the hydrosphere) or in the form of foods and fuel energy from plants (solar energy captured through photosynthesis) or through the food and energy supplied by domesticated animals and slaves (which represented solar energy captured by plants and recaptured by animals and humans higher up the food chain). All these sources of energy derived from solar energy that was captured within recent decades or centuries. In contrast, fossil fuels—coal, oil, and natural gas—represent flows of solar energy captured and buried over several hundred million years. So the technologies that allowed human societies to exploit these fuels efficiently and cheaply, beginning with the improved James Watt steam engine, multiplied available energy supplies by several orders of magnitude. In the 200 years since 1800 it is estimated that human energy use has increased by at least forty times, and today at least 85 percent of human energy supplies come from fossil fuels (Steffen, Crutzen, and McNeill 2007, 616).

With the help of this seemingly inexhaustible supply of energy, humans found they could mobilize and control the resources of the biosphere on unimaginable scales. Fertilizers such as guano could be transported around the world, as could the increasing supplies of produce whose production these fertilizers made possible. Agricultural production and the clearing of land and forests could be undertaken on industrial scales and at industrial speeds. Enough energy was available to allow the synthesis of thousands of new chemicals on industrial scales—including the artificial fertilizers that have transformed agriculture, made by fixing atmospheric nitrogen in ammonia through the Haber-Bosch process. Massive fossil fuel–powered earth movers and transporters helped divert

Figure 1. Increasing Energy Use in the Modern Era, 1850–2000

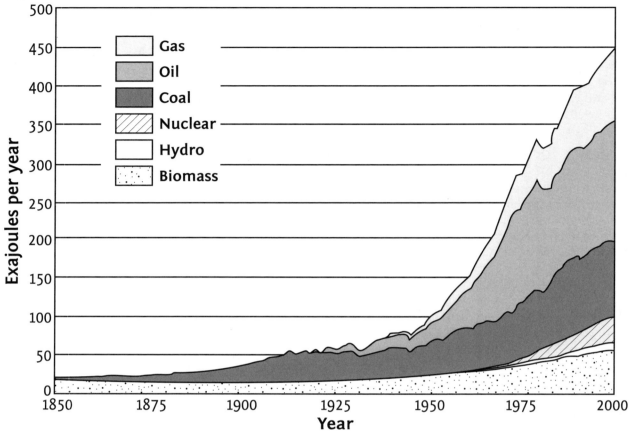

Source: Adapted by Berkshire Publishing Group from Alfred Crosby, *Children of the Sun: A History of Humanity's Unappeasable Appetite for Energy* (2006), page 162. New York: Norton.

Figure 1 shows human energy consumption as measured in exajoules during the years 1850–2000. A joule is the power required to produce one watt for one second; an exajoule is a million million million joules.

rivers and build the vast dams that supplied drinking water to growing cities, irrigated farms, and produced cheap electricity, while cheap fossil fuel–powered pumps drew up the freshwater stores of aquifers around the world. Supported by these unprecedented energy and resource flows, human populations rose from 1 billion to almost 7 billion in 200 years, while global production of goods and services increased by at least fifty times (Steffen et al. 2011).

The vast increase in human control of biospheric resources has become particularly apparent since the middle of the twentieth century when, after a period of slower growth and destructive global wars, growth took off faster than ever before, driven in part by war-time innovations such as nuclear power and computers. The sharp acceleration after 1950 marks a second phase in the Anthropocene. The acceleration is evident from the following graph of energy use, taken from a 2007 book by Alfred Crosby titled *Children of the Sun: A History of Humanity's Unappeasable Appetite for Energy.* (See figure 1 above.) But it is also evident in many other changes shown in a series of graphs from a 2007 article on the Anthropocene by Will Steffen, Paul Crutzen, and John McNeill titled "The Anthropocene: Are Humans Now Overwhelming the Great Forces of Nature?" (See figure 2 on page 21.)

The changes made possible directly or indirectly by the fossil fuels revolution explain why our species now plays such a decisive role in the biosphere and why so many scholars date the Anthropocene epoch to the Industrial Revolution and the invention of an improved steam engine. Whereas premodern farmers and manufacturers could, and did, transform local or regional ecosystems, never before did humans have a transformative impact on the biosphere as a whole. Although some authors, such as the aforementioned George Perkins Marsh, understood that human environmental impacts were rising sharply even in the nineteenth century, it was not until the

Figure 2. Acceleration of the Human Enterprise from 1750 to 2000

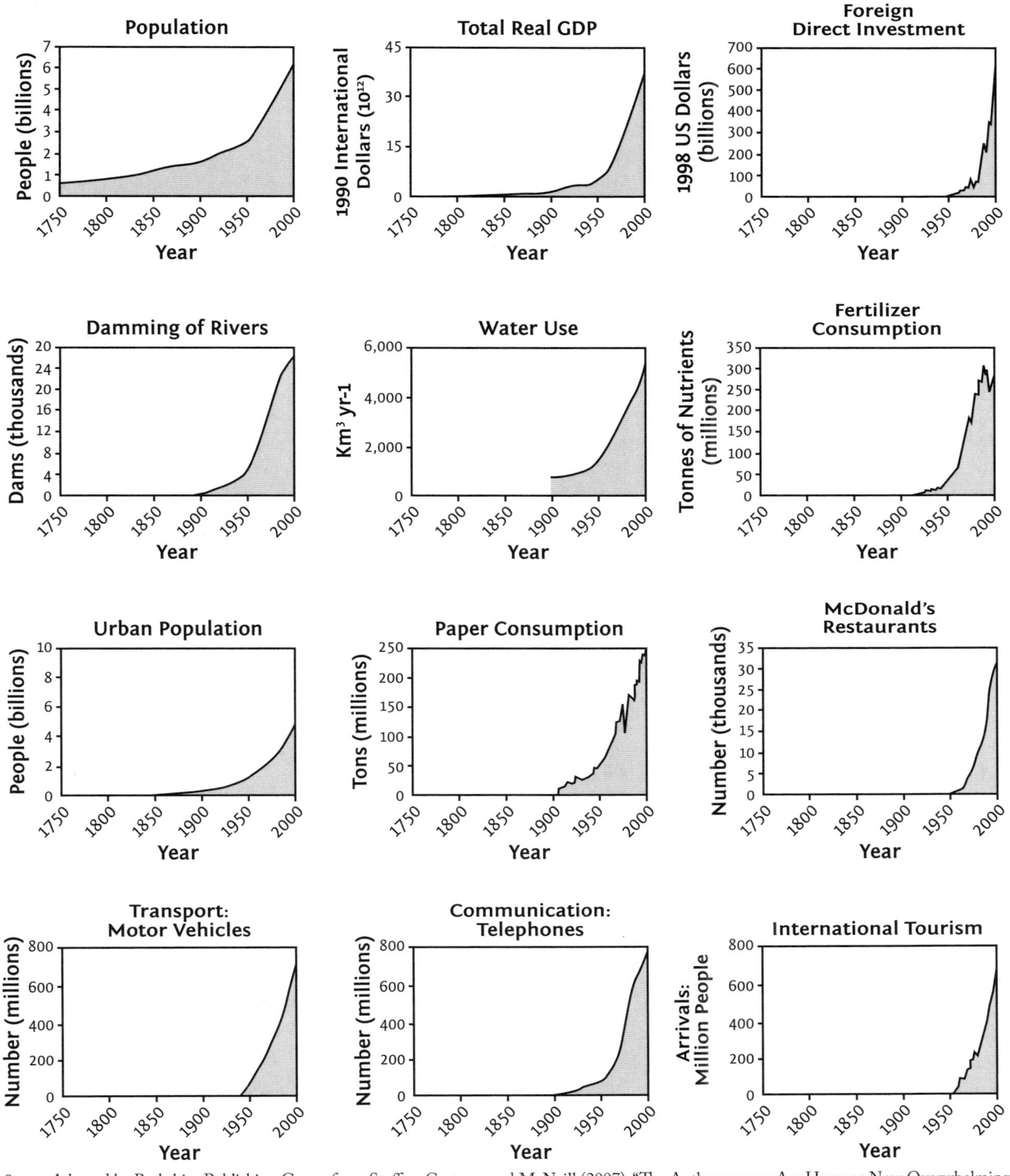

Source: Adapted by Berkshire Publishing Group from Steffen, Crutzen, and McNeill (2007), "The Anthropocene: Are Humans Now Overwhelming the Great Forces of Nature?" AMBIO, 36(8), page 617. Original image © Springer-Verlag Berlin Heidelberg, 2005.

Technological developments from the late eighteenth century on gave humans the ability to exploit fossil fuels cheaply and efficiently, greatly increasing available energy supplies. This in turn has allowed us to mobilize and control the resources of the biosphere on previously unimaginable scales, particularly since 1950, when a period of great acceleration in the human enterprise began.

second half of the twentieth century that it became clear that we had become a planet-changing species. As the US historian John McNeill puts it in *Something New Under the Sun,* his environmental history of the twentieth century, "The human race, without intending anything of the sort, has undertaken a gigantic uncontrolled experiment on the Earth" (2000, 4).

The scale of these changes is apparent in all key sectors of the biosphere.

- *The Atmosphere:* The burning of fossil fuels has significantly raised levels of greenhouse gases such as carbon dioxide (CO_2) and methane. Indeed, we have no evidence of any natural process that has ever released carbon dioxide into the atmosphere as rapidly as modern human society. Pre-industrial levels of CO_2 fluctuated between 200 and 300 parts per million (ppm). As of 2012, they have reached almost 400 ppm. Evidence from ice cores shows that this level is higher than at any time in the last 800,000 years, and perhaps higher than any time in the last 3 million years (Haywood et al. 2011, 934). There is growing evidence that this change is raising global temperatures, transforming climates across the world, and causing a significant rise in sea levels as oceans expand and ice sheets melt. The stability of CO_2 ensures that, once it is in the atmosphere, such changes will take many centuries to reverse. Less predictable, but perhaps more worrying, is the possibility that there may be dangerous tipping points beyond which climate could change very fast indeed. Could warming of the tundra lead to sudden releases of methane, speeding up global warming? Could the Gulf Stream, whose warm currents maintain the temperate climates of northwestern Europe, switch direction once more—as it has in the past—driving Europe into a new ice age? As the US climate scientist Wally Broecker of Columbia University puts it: "The climate is an angry beast, and we are poking it with a stick" (Lynas 2011).
- *The Oceans:* The burning of fossil fuels is also altering that other global fluid, the hydrosphere. Absorption of CO_2 in the world's oceans is temporarily slowing the rise in atmospheric CO_2. But it is simultaneously increasing acidity levels in the oceans (so far by 0.1 pH units), which will impact coral systems and the many other marine organisms that produce chalk to make their shells or skeletons (Zalasiewicz and Freedman 2009, 6).
- *The Land:* Through construction, mining, dam construction, and agriculture, humans are now moving many more times the amount of soil than is normally shifted by nonhuman processes such as erosion (Zalasiewicz and Freedman 2009, 5). As one study concludes: "At present, even were human populations to decline substantially or use of land become far more efficient, the current global extent, duration, type, and intensity of human transformation of ecosystems have already irreversibly altered the terrestrial biosphere at levels sufficient to leave an unambiguous geological record differing substantially from that of the Holocene or any prior epoch" (Ellis 2011, 1010).
- *Biodiversity:* Rates of extinction are approaching levels seen only during the greatest mass extinctions of the last 600 million years. By some estimates rates of extinction are between one hundred and one thousand times the background level for the last few million years. The primary causes are overfishing of the oceans and human transformation of the land, the latter of which is destroying or breaking up habitats. Other human activities, such as the disposal of plastics, waste products, and other pollutants in the oceans, are important contributory factors.
- *Natural Cycles:* The burning of fossil fuels has transformed the carbon cycle by pumping back into the atmosphere in just a century carbon that was buried over several hundred million years. Meanwhile, the burning of fossil fuels and the manufacture of artificial fertilizers are converting vast amounts of nitrogen into more reactive forms, and doing so at a speed and on a scale that can no longer be managed by the natural nitrogen cycle (Steffen, Crutzen, and McNeill 2007, 617).
- *Genetic Engineering:* Driven by advances in the life sciences, synthetic biology has enabled us to start manipulating living organisms genetically. Some claim we are close to redesigning our own species.
- *Nuclear Power:* One of the most spectacular measures of increasing human power within the biosphere is the evolution of nuclear weapons, which have given humans the power, in principle, to destroy much of the biosphere in just a few hours.

A recent attempt to identify when such changes crossed dangerous thresholds concludes that in three areas—carbon dioxide levels, flows of nitrogen, and rates of extinctions—we have already moved well beyond safe "planetary boundaries" (Rockström et al. 2009).

Significance

Such changes raise profound questions about the nature and future of our own species. What explains the fact that we seem to be the first species in the almost 4-billion-year history of life on Earth to have exercised such powers? From the perspective of the Anthropocene, it is tempting to say that these powers define us as a species.

Why are humans so endlessly (and perhaps dangerously) creative? At present, the best answer seems to be that human language itself crossed a tipping point that allowed information to be exchanged so efficiently and with such precision that it could be stored securely within the collective memory and could therefore accumulate from generation to generation. Unlike other species, where innovations seem to evaporate as easily as they appear, humans seem capable of storing enough information with sufficient security that over time there is a net gain in the information available to entire communities. That increasing stock of information is the ultimate source of humanity's increasing control over the biosphere (Christian 2004 and 2010). As Will Steffen, Paul Crutzen, and John McNeill put it, "[S]poken and then . . . written language [promoted] communication and transfer of knowledge within and between generations of humans, efficient accumulation of knowledge, and social learning over many thousands of years in an impressive catalytic process, involving many human brains and their discoveries and innovations. This power is minimal in other species" (Steffen, Crutzen, and McNeill 2007, 614).

If this hypothesis is correct, it suggests that something like the Anthropocene era was predictable as soon as there appeared a species capable of communicating precisely enough to accumulate information over multiple generations. That, in turn, suggests that we are probably the first such species in the history of our planet, because any earlier species with such powers would have left paleontological traces as clear as those we will undoubtedly leave to future generations. There is a wonderful discussion of the traces we may leave behind to future paleontologists in *The Earth after Us: What Legacy Will Humans Leave in the Rocks?* by the British geologist Jan Zalasiewicz (2009).

What Is to Be Done?

As Paul Crutzen has argued, the idea of the Anthropocene is also a call to action because it points to many dangers that need to be tackled soon if human societies are to avoid serious—and perhaps catastrophic—changes in coming decades. If the science behind the notion of an Anthropocene epoch is correct, it follows that it would be foolish for human societies to continue evolving on their current path of "business as usual."

The problem is partly a matter of speed. Human-induced changes, both within human societies and in the biosphere as a whole, are now proceeding so fast that natural processes cannot keep up with them. Carbon and nitrogen cannot be recycled fast enough, freshwater cannot be replenished fast enough, fish stocks cannot recover fast enough, and some changes, such as species extinctions, allow no second chances. We humans also struggle to keep track of the many changes we are causing. Computer models offer interesting and promising scenarios, but the truth is that the speed and complexity of change makes reliable prediction extremely difficult. But the dangers are also a matter of scale. The sheer amount of earth, nitrogen, carbon dioxide, water, and novel chemicals being forced through natural cycles makes it difficult to tell how the various, interlinked systems of the biosphere will respond. Human activity is pushing the biosphere as a whole into uncharted territory.

The terrifying pace and scale of change in the Anthropocene suggests that it would be prudent to slow those changes that are having the greatest impacts on the biosphere. This would be wise not because we *know* where change is leading, but because we do *not* know where it is leading. Slowing down means reducing the scale on which greenhouse gases, new anthropogenic chemicals, and other pollutants are released into the atmosphere, reducing the scale of fisheries and freshwater use, and slowing human population growth. It does *not* mean slowing the pace of technological change because new technologies, including more sustainable forms of energy production and recycling, may play a crucial role in reducing human impacts on the biosphere. Nor does slowing down necessarily mean giving up on the many gains in welfare that are the most positive side of the Anthropocene era.

But the idea of the Anthropocene does seem to suggest the need for rapid, thoughtful, and perhaps fundamental change in the ways that human societies exploit the biosphere. Will the same process of collective learning that explains our power as a species also help us ensure that future generations do not pay too high a price for the many gains in human welfare that have accompanied the Anthropocene epoch?

David CHRISTIAN
*Macquarie University; WCU Professor,
Ewha Womans University, Seoul*

See also Agricultural Innovation; Climate Change and Big History; Collective Learning; Population; Progress

FURTHER READING

Christian, David. (2004). *Maps of time: An introduction to big history.* Berkeley & Los Angeles: University of California Press.

Christian, David. (2010). The return of universal history. *History and Theory, 49*(4), 6–27.

Christian, David. (2011). World environmental history. In Jerry Bentley (Ed.), *The Oxford handbook of world history* (pp. 125–142). Oxford, UK, & New York: Oxford University Press.

Crosby, Alfred. (2006). *Children of the sun: A history of humanity's unappeasable appetite for energy.* New York: Norton.

Crutzen, Paul J. (2002). Geology of mankind: The Anthropocene. *Nature, 415,* 23. Retrieved April 25, 2012, from http://www.nature.com/nature/journal/v415/n6867/full/415023a.html

Crutzen, Paul J., & Stoermer, Eugene F. (2000, May). The Anthropocene. *International Geosphere-Biosphere Programme (IGBP) Newsletter 41*. Retrieved March 17, 2012, from http://www3.mpch-mainz.mpg.de/~air/anthropocene/

Economist. (2011, May 26). The Anthropocene: A man-made world. Retrieved April 25, 2012, from http://www.economist.com/node/18741749

Ellis, Erle C. (2011). Anthropogenic transformation of the terrestrial biosphere. *Philosophical Transactions Royal Society A*, *369*(1938), 1010–1035.

Guha, Ramachandra. (2000). *Environmentalism: A global history*. New York: Longman.

Haywood, Alan M., et al. (2011). Are there pre-Quaternary geological analogues for a future greenhouse warming? *Philosophical Transactions of the Royal Society A*, *369*(1938), 933–956.

Henshilwood, Christopher S., et al. (2011). A 100,000-year-old ochre processing workshop at Blombos Cave, South Africa. *Science*, *334*(6053), 219–222.

Kolbert, Elizabeth. (2011, March). Enter the Anthropocene: The age of man. *National Geographic Magazine*. Retrieved April 25, 2012, from http://ngm.nationalgeographic.com/2011/03/age-of-man/kolbert-text

Lynas, Mark. (2011). *The God species: How humans really can save the planet*. London: Fourth Estate.

Marsh, George Perkins. (1864/2005). *Man and nature: Or, physical geography as modified by human action*. David Lowenthal (Ed.). Cambridge, MA: Harvard University Press.

McNeill, John R. (2000). *Something new under the sun: An environmental history of the twentieth-century world*. New York & London: Norton.

McNeill, John R. (2003). Observations on the nature and culture of environmental history. *History and Theory*, *42*(4), 5–43.

Planet under Pressure. (2012a). Homepage. Retrieved April 25, 2012, from http://www.planetunderpressure2012.net/

Planet under Pressure. (2012b). State of the planet declaration. Retrieved April 25, 2012, from http://www.planetunderpressure2012.net/pdf/state_of_planet_declaration.pdf

Revkin, Andrew C. (2011, May 11). Confronting the Anthropocene. *New York Times*. Retrieved April 25, 2012, from http://dotEarth.blogs.nytimes.com/2011/05/11/confronting-the-anthropocene/

Roberts, Neil. (1998). *The Holocene: An environmental history* (2nd ed.). Oxford, UK: Blackwell.

Robin, Libby, & Steffen, Will. (2007). History for the Anthropocene. *History Compass*, *5*(5), 1694–1719.

Rockström, Johan, et al. (2009, September 24). A safe operating space for humanity. *Nature*, *461*(7263), 472–475.

Ruddiman, William. (2005). *Plows, plagues, and petroleum: How humans took control of climate*. Princeton, NJ: Princeton University Press.

Scarre, Christopher. (Ed.). (2005). *The human past: World prehistory and the development of human societies*. London: Thames and Hudson.

Steffen, Will. (2010). *Will Steffen: The Anthropocene* [Video]. TEDxCanberra (Producer). Retrieved April 25, 2012, from http://www.youtube.com/watch?v=ABZjlfhN0EQ&feature=player_embedded

Steffen, Will; Crutzen, Paul J.; & McNeill, John R. (2007). The Anthropocene: Are humans now overwhelming the great forces of nature? *AMBIO*, *36*(8), 614–621. Retrieved April 25, 2012, from http://allenpress.com/pdf/ambi-36-08-06_614..621.pdf

Steffen, Will; Grinevald, Jacques; Crutzen, Paul; & McNeill, John. (2011). The Anthropocene: Conceptual and historical perspectives. *Philosophical Transactions of the Royal Society A*, *369*(1938), 842–867.

Welcome to the Anthropocene. (n.d.). Homepage. Retrieved April 25, 2012, from http://www.anthropocene.info/en/home

Zalasiewicz, Jan, & Freedman, Kim. (2009). *The Earth after us: What legacy will humans leave in the rocks?* Oxford, UK: Oxford University Press.

Zalasiewicz, Jan, et al. (2009, February). Are we now living in the Anthropocene? *Geological Society of America*, *18*(2), 4–8.

Buildings and Infrastructure

Many conventional buildings and infrastructures are not sustainable. There is a need to fundamentally rethink how buildings interact with the natural environment in order to create functional, efficient, and healthy spaces. The challenges of sustainable building encompass many elements such as energy use, land use, water, materials, emissions, waste generation, and air quality. By understanding natural processes and their interactions with human needs, designers can create buildings that are conducive to environmental and social well-being.

The built environment is designed to meet basic material needs for shelter, comfort, hygiene, and sanitation that are vital for human health, productivity, and well-being. Meeting these needs is a key element of sustainable development as defined by the Brundtland Commission in its report *Our Common Future* (1987), but buildings can also generate many negative impacts (Burnett 2007). Living standards and material consumption practices associated with the built environment now exceed basic needs, surpass global ecological capacity, and disregard long-term sustainability for future generations (Næss 2001). In industrialized societies, buildings and the movement of people between them together account for two-thirds of the energy consumed (Foster 2011).

Consideration of the wider life cycle environmental impacts of building construction and consumption reveals a multitude of unsustainable practices. In the United States, buildings account for 36 percent of total energy use, 30 percent of greenhouse gas emissions, 30 percent of raw materials use, 30 percent of waste output, and 12 percent of potable water consumption (US EPA 2011). High consumption standards associated with building

design and urban lifestyles also set the norms to which newly industrialized societies aspire.

To secure available resources for future generations, burgeoning consumption loads associated with the built environment need to be urgently addressed. Since the 1980s, there has been a policy focus on green buildings and sustainable construction practices. While conventional building design concerns focus on the provision of economy, durability, utility, and comfort, the sustainable building agenda expands this list. Sustainable buildings should minimize environmental impacts through resource efficiency and conservation, but should also provide healthy environments for people and have a positive impact on local culture and urban life (Williams and Lindsay 2007). Building designers, architects, and engineers have responded to this challenge with many different sustainable building prototypes. Some have drawn upon high-tech futuristic visions to inspire intelligent and iconic green buildings featuring smart controls for environmental management. Others have looked to past traditions of culturally specific vernacular architecture (i.e., the indigenous building style of a place or people) or passive designs that adapt naturally to the dynamics of local environments for inspiration. These various blueprints for sustainable building each imply fundamentally different socio-technical trajectories that will simultaneously shape the future of the built environment.

Faced with increased energy demands and resource shortages, many infrastructures in both the developed and developing world are failing to deliver even a basic level of service. Formal housing stock in developing countries is inadequate for the needs of a rapidly expanding urban population. Water, energy, sewage, and solid waste systems are already stretched well beyond their limits. Aside from social and environmental considerations, there is also an important economic driver for sustainable buildings as costs associated with heating, water, and sewerage provision continue to rise. A World Bank report on the projected demand for infrastructure services in developing countries suggested that annual investment and maintenance costs could total more than US$450 billion per annum if services are to meet demand (Fay and Yepes 2003).

Developed societies are not immune to the disruptive effects of infrastructure breakdown. In 2003, blackouts in parts of Canada and the United States affected 50 million people, while power cuts in Italy and France during the summer of the same year were associated with increased energy demand for air conditioning (Trentmann 2009). Across the world, many infrastructure networks are at or close to their capacity at times of peak demand, creating significant problems for long-term resilience, health, and security as well as for ecological sustainability. These combined challenges make buildings and infrastructures a compelling and vital topic.

Changing Ideas

The realization that many conventional building forms are not sustainable is not new (John, Clements-Croome, and Jeronimidis 2005). Traditionally, buildings in hotter climates (e.g., in the southern United States) were designed to maximize shade and incorporate features such as verandas for natural cooling, thus minimizing energy usage. In the 1950s, these features began to be excluded as an increasing number of US homes and commercial buildings were constructed as autonomous units with internal mechanized heating, cooling, and ventilation systems that were no longer integrated with the outdoor environment but served to exclude it (Cooper 1998). This "environmental fortress" mentality of building modernization, which was normalized with the support of the heating, ventilation, and air conditioning (HVAC) industry, rapidly became a template for building practices in the United States and has since proliferated worldwide, driving up building energy use.

In the 1970s, many architects were critical of new building designs that sought to exclude nature rather than embrace and use it (Fitch 1972; Heschong 1979). Through the 1980s and 1990s, there was continued support for alternative greener architecture and technologies, which would conserve energy, minimize resource use, and work with rather than against the climate (Seyfang 2010). Current adaptive-design debates further address the need to fundamentally rethink how buildings interact with the natural environment in order to create delightful as well as functional and efficient spaces (John,

Clements-Croome, and Jeronimidis 2005). These more recent discussions about contemporary nature-building interactions also propose employing technologies in smarter new ways, such as using adaptive controls or intelligent building materials that can mimic natural processes.

Building designs throughout history have also reflected changing cultural ideas about what is conducive to human comfort and productivity. A preference in North America today is for detached family homes with private gardens rather than more compact forms of living. Unfortunately, this requirement for individual space has collectively manifested into the reality of urban sprawl, where extensive systems of roads, automobiles, water pipes, and sanitation networks are required to support resource-intensive suburban lifestyles (Bartuska 2007). Such forms of decentralized and individualized living have been widely criticized for neglecting and being wasteful of other positive urban sustainability features such as spaces for community interaction. This rejection of suburbia has led contemporary advocates of sustainable urbanism to support more compact and denser building forms.

Dense city cores can also produce negative environmental and social impacts through the concentration of people and resource use, but they can also achieve economies and efficiencies of scale through the centralization of infrastructure and provide other positive sustainability features such as concentrated social and cultural facilities. It is argued that many of the world's most vibrant and attractive cities have commendable public transportation systems and provide walkable, bikeable, and livable communities that play an important role in supporting a large number of people. Investigations have shown that city dwellers commute much less by car and have lower space heating needs, with correspondingly lower energy use and lower emissions than suburban dwellers (Næss 2001). Tall buildings or skyscrapers with iconic green features that are often conceived as part of a compact city model can also have an important visual and cultural role with relation to promoting sustainable urbanization (Tavernor 2007).

An alternative development model has addressed the importance of community-based "ecovillages," where development is scaled to locally available resources and around neighborhood provision of water, sewage, and energy services. Critics of lower-density, more dispersed eco-communities as a model for sustainability point out that this would require an unrealistic expectation of change in people's lifestyles and in the current orientation toward urbanization. Community-led initiatives for sustainable urbanization that comprise more low-tech solutions that use off-grid renewable energy, water, and waste have also been seen as strategic green niches with the potential for adaptation to more mainstream settings (Seyfang 2010).

Regional Dynamics and Global Convergence

The challenges of sustainable building and infrastructure vary between different world regions and encompass many heterogeneous elements such as energy use, land use, water, materials, emissions, waste generation, and air quality. Globally, buildings are believed to be directly and indirectly responsible for approximately 30 percent of total greenhouse gas emissions (OECD 2002). In 2005, 27 percent of the United Kingdom's carbon dioxide emissions were attributed to heating, lighting, and running domestic buildings, with this figure expected to rise as demand for new housing stock and technologies, including air conditioning, increase (Ravetz 2008). In the European Union, construction and demolition wastes from the building industry account for one-fourth of waste generation (OECD 2002). In the United States, estimates of the magnitude of this construction waste stream have typically ranged from 10 percent to 30 percent of municipal solid waste generation (OECD 2002). As of 2012, however, a relatively small proportion of wastes has been recycled or reused.

In the industrialized world, concerns predominantly focus on how to curtail unsustainable growth in building stock and associated resource consumption, as well as on how to reduce the environmental impact of existing, older building stock. In many European countries there is increased demand for new housing (this includes an estimated 3 million new homes for the United Kingdom alone by 2020) (Seyfang 2010). Making sure that these new homes are built to more sustainable and efficient standards is a priority.

An equally pressing issue in many European countries, however, is how to retrofit older buildings, which make up a large proportion of the overall building stock. It has been estimated that up to 75 percent of dwellings in the United Kingdom that will exist in 2050 have already been constructed and that the energy-efficiency performance of much of this existing stock is generally low (Ravetz 2008). In most of the industrialized world,

improvements in the resource efficiency of buildings have been reported. In the United Kingdom, the energy efficiency of homes has been steadily increasing over the last decade (Ravetz 2008). Improved efficiencies, however, continue to be offset by more resource-intensive lifestyles and consumption standards.

In Europe and the United States, there has been a common trend: a decrease in the number of occupants per dwelling (this includes more single-family households), while the average size of dwellings has simultaneously increased. In some Nordic countries, the size of building stock compared to population size is among the highest in the world; Norwegians and Danes have twice as much floor space in 2000 as they did only thirty years earlier, and they have 70 percent more floor space than in Japanese homes (Næss 2001). In the United States, growth in floor area per inhabitant has been steady and significant in the post–World War II period in both residential and nonresidential buildings. Since 1950, the average size of a new single-family US home has more than doubled, from an average size of about 102 square meters in the 1940s to 217 square meters in 2002 (Wilson and Boehland 2005). As house size increases, so too do the environmental impacts associated with buildings and development: resource consumption increases, the land area affected by development grows, stormwater runoff increases as impermeable surface area increases, and energy use rises. In 1975, 46 percent of new US houses had central air conditioning, but by 2002, 87 percent had been equipped with it (Wilson and Boehland 2005).

Challenges of rapid urbanization in the newly industrialized economies of Asia and in the developing world create a different scale of challenge in terms of upgrading building stock and infrastructures to accommodate urban population growth. Evaluations of changing consumption patterns in Asia forecast major impacts from increased demand for energy and buildings (Zhao, Liu, and Dong 2008).

In China, energy consumption in the building sector accounts for approximately 25 percent of the nation's total energy use (Jiang and Tovey 2010). Since the construction boom of the 1990s, China has experienced a steady growth in total building stock, and more than one-half of China's estimated urban residential building and commercial building stock constructed by 2015 will have been constructed after the year 2000 (Zhu and Lin 2004). The rapid development of Beijing's residential building system in the first decade of the 2000s has become a major ecological pressure for urban sustainable building development. A study of material and energy flows associated with urban residential building systems in Beijing between 1949 and 2008 found that the amount of building wastes generated from 2004 to 2008 accounted for 52.2 percent of the total wastes generated between 1949 to 2008 (Hu et al. 2010). Building energy consumption is accordingly increasing year after year. By the end of the year 2000, it was estimated that only 0.5 percent of the total building floor area in China complied with energy-efficiency design standards. Most new buildings were also still consuming huge amounts of energy. In 2004, it was reported that residential buildings in Beijing consumed 50–100 percent more energy for space heating as compared to buildings in similar cold climates in Western Europe or North America and still provided far less comfort (Zhu and Lin 2004).

Another major concern (on a global scale) is what the consequences will be if consumers in countries like China and India aspire to reach the same consumption levels and standards as European or US societies. The number of airtight buildings equipped with air conditioning units and the corresponding levels of energy consumption from residential and commercial buildings have both increased markedly in China since 1990 because of rapid economic growth and urbanization. The ratio of household air conditioners owned for every one hundred families in southern China has increased at a ratio of 20 percent with the rapid development of the building industry since the 1990s and the improvement in people's living standards (Zhu and Lin 2004). The increase in the number of air conditioners in India has already been associated with increasing rates of blackouts (Wilhite 2008).

Different Approaches

Emergent forms of green buildings appear to offer an impressive array of sustainability features that fulfill requirements for environmental, economic, and social sustainability. These include energy efficiency, water recycling, use of recycled construction materials, composting systems, use of local supply chains, accessibility to public transport, interconnected outdoor spaces, and secure and adaptable spaces. The meaning and practice of sustainable building, however, is the subject of much contestation between architects, policy makers, and the public (Guy 2011). In reviewing different interpretations of sustainable design, a number of coexisting approaches can be identified. Each of these green building approaches is rooted in a different conceptualization of the built environment, its purpose, and the role of different actors—including designers and users—in shaping it.

In Europe and the United States, the need to reduce the energy and resource intensity of buildings while maintaining comfort levels and quality of life has been a central concern since the energy crisis of the 1970s. The dominant approach since this time has been on improving the technical efficiency of building stock. This has included the retrofitting of conventional buildings with greener technologies that have various levels of sophistication—ranging from fitting compact fluorescent light bulbs, low-flow water fixtures, smart energy meters, and/or solar panels. A high-profile example is the retrofitting of the Empire State Building, which has been transformed into a more energy-efficient structure at a cost of US$550 million and is the tallest Leadership in Energy and Environmental Design (LEED) building in the United States (Dailey 2011). The changes (e.g., completed installation of the lighting has been slated for September 2012) are expected to reduce the building's energy consumption by more than 38 percent.

The approach used to improve the resource efficiency of technologies, materials, and processes within the built environment since the 1990s has become a holistic one. From a life cycle perspective, sustainability is a process rather than a goal, with sustainable buildings seen as "an outcome of a design which focuses on increasing the efficiency of resource use—energy, water, and materials—while reducing building impacts on human health and the environment during the building life cycle, through better location, design, construction, operation, maintenance, and removal" (Kamana and Escultura 2011, 725). Later interpretations of a building life cycle approach have also recognized the importance of social and cultural interaction, where the sustainability of the building life cycle and performance is dependent on the extent to which it achieves its role as a combined physical, social, economic, and cultural asset (Ravetz 2008).

Other models of sustainable innovation have evolved less from a resource-based techno-engineering approach as from the socio-ecological traditions in adaptive urban design and green architecture, where buildings are conceptualized in connection to the local environments in which they are embedded. Proponents of passive design suggest that resource demands can be minimized by natural means, such as using the mass and orientation of the building to capture sunlight, fresh air, and rainwater (Clements-Croome 2011). A European study found that passive homes can offer extended living comfort with only 15–20 percent of the space-heating demand of conventional new buildings, while the extra costs of this standard represent only about 10 percent of the total building costs (Schneiders and Hermelink 2006). By understanding natural processes and their interactions with human needs, designers can create buildings that are functional, productive, and conducive to accomplishing wider environmental and social well-being.

Application of such ideals can be generated at many different scales. There are plentiful examples of individual buildings or small-scale sustainable communities that have employed passive design features to take advantage of natural variations in climate, such as cool breezes for ventilation and shading from the sun, that minimize their environmental impact through better resource use. For example, the Hockerton Housing Project is a development of five self-sufficient earth-sheltered homes in the United Kingdom, which uses a passive solar-heating system (van Vliet, Chappells, and Shove 2005). An example of contemporary design embracing vernacular traditions on a grander scale is the planned Masdar City in Abu Dhabi, a high-density, carbon neutral, and zero waste community. The starting point for this design included consideration of traditional settlements in the region, which inspired designs based on narrow streets that are oriented to maximize shade and buildings and public spaces with fountains, greenery, and wind towers to encourage cooling air currents and minimize energy use (Foster 2011). Approaches rooted in achieving techno-efficiency and those that promote the incorporation of nature into design have also come together in the context of debates about intelligent buildings, where a new range of smart-control technologies and materials can take inspiration from and mimic nature to produce sustainable innovation (Clements-Croome 2011). Within such a model, a central concern is to ensure that buildings, while technologically advanced, are flexible vis-à-vis the local climate and adaptive to users' needs.

The approaches so far reviewed do not presume any radical rethinking of how the current unsustainable design and use of built environments is culturally specified and defined. An acknowledged measure of the success of a building design is whether it is "fit for purpose" (John, Clements-Croome, and Jeronimidis 2005). From a sociocultural perspective, however, the "purpose" of built environments is itself negotiable. Historically different designs of workplaces and homes represent responses to changing cultural and social norms and to values that concern the relative importance of aspects such as efficiency, domesticity, security, and productivity. Following this reasoning, if some of these life goals were reprioritized, then more sustainable ways of organizing the built environment might be envisaged. Once normal features of homes in the southern United States, such as verandas and porches, were valued because they produced a space for relaxation and social interaction, thus embracing certain ideals of domesticity and community. In the context of global warming, a question that has been reconsidered is how to reincorporate usable outdoor spaces into building design as a way of restoring balance in relation to comfort, refreshment, relaxation, and social interaction as well as reducing the dependence on air conditioning (Cox 2010). Debates about sustainable cities in the twenty-first century have also highlighted the positive benefits of greenery, such as plants and trees, as a recreational and aesthetic resource for urban dwellers and workers and as a form of natural shading and cooling for buildings.

Performance and Barriers to Innovation

The array of sustainable design aspects and technologies now being incorporated in the built environment is impressive, but numerous studies have pointed out that sustainable buildings have as yet failed to reach their full potential. Green buildings still represent only a small proportion of the existing building stock, and innovative sustainable design is the exception rather than the rule in most regions. In England, for example, the government has supported an agenda for sustainable building for well over a decade, but recent reviews suggest that, as a proportion of building stock, the number of sustainable buildings is still actually very small (Williams and Lindsay 2007). Improvements in resource efficiency and sustainable construction are supported through various UK building regulations, but research evidence shows that sustainability objectives and building regulations are not always enforced, with the majority of new housing projects having few distinct sustainability features such as water recycling systems, bicycle storage systems, or adaptable housing layouts (Williams and Lindsay 2007). In response to this evidence, it has been argued that more stringent building regulations and planning policies are needed to normalize sustainability as part of routine building practice rather than to regard it as only a niche, novel, or add-on development choice.

Although the Chinese government has initiated policies to reduce energy intensity, industrialization and urbanization are likely to keep the country on a course of rapidly rising energy demand. In 2004, China's government launched a vigorous program to reverse the trend of rising national energy intensity and to reduce intensity by 20 percent over the period 2006–2010 (Andrews-Speed 2009). Buildings are a priority target for government policies because of the large amount of energy used to heat or cool them, with some city governments raising the permitted levels of summer temperatures in public buildings and offices in order to reduce the demand for air conditioning (Andrews-Speed 2009). Since 2007, attempts have also been made by China's government to strengthen existing building codes and to encourage the retrofitting of older buildings as a way of curbing wasteful and energy-inefficient construction practices. It has been reported, however, that many Chinese construction companies lack guidelines and training for energy-efficient building design and construction. Energy use per square meter in Chinese buildings is still (in 2012) much lower than in OECD countries, but it is anticipated that this is almost certain to change as rising social expectations result in a desire for higher indoor temperatures in winter and lower temperatures in summer (Yoshino et al. 2006; Andrews-Speed 2009).

Building environmental assessment methods (BEAMs) emerged in the 1990s to provide some way to measure the environmental performance of buildings, and more than twenty such tools are now in use worldwide (Burnett 2007). These include the international assessment tool BREEAM (the Building Research Establishment Environmental Assessment Method), used mostly in the United Kingdom and some other European countries, and the LEED evaluation tool, mostly used in the United States but also adapted to some Asian countries. Most assessment tools focus on the energy consumption and environmental load of buildings over their lifetime and the extent to which the building and its engineering systems meet the needs of users and operators. One review of building assessment tools found that these provide a measure of environmental performance and raise awareness within the industry of criteria other than cost, but that the range of assessment tools available makes it difficult to compare performance standards (Burnett 2007). Additionally, BEAMs are generally undertaken on a voluntary basis and are often seen as an additional requirement rather than exemplary practice such that other financial pressures may overcome the need to achieve a high level of environmental performance.

Limitations in how current assessment tools conceptualize and delineate the built environment have also been noted. Usually, the boundaries of the assessment are circumscribed by the building site and adjacent properties rather than by addressing wider urban planning issues, although criteria on some external impacts may also be included (e.g., greenhouse gas emissions, water pollution, waste, and noise). As the Italian architecture and urban planning scholars Emilia Conte and Valeria

Monno argue (2012), building-evaluation systems rarely consider the multiple dimensions of sustainability and are overwhelmed by a prevailing building-centric approach, which emphasizes an environmental perspective and where the technological content of the building emerges as the most important factor affecting sustainability. This approach, they suggest, ignores integration between buildings and the urban context in which they are situated. Buildings are not isolated from other buildings, infrastructures or urban space, neighborhood or community, and sustainability assessments need to account for the wider socio-ecological functioning of the built environment as a whole, not as aggregated parts (Conte and Monno 2012). A more systemic urban scale approach might incorporate planning legislation, local community and climate, public-transport accessibility, and the availability of outdoor space in determining the in situ suitability of a building.

The complexity of the built environment, which encompasses many interacting systems, makes sustainable transformation a difficult task. Remodeling buildings and infrastructure requires interaction between urban planners, building design professionals, facilities managers, utilities, and users. It necessitates an understanding of the multiple, systemic, interacting scales at which nature, buildings, technologies, and urban landscapes intersect and interact. Socio-technical studies have proved useful in addressing the systems and processes involved in the construction and use of sustainable buildings and the barriers to sustainable design these can construct (Rohracher 2001). From these contributions we have learned that better integration of technological design with building use and a system-oriented approach that reconnects supply-side and demand-side elements of buildings can be fruitful for overcoming barriers to sustainable design.

The inertia of the construction industry is a potential institutional barrier to sustainable building on the supply and/or production side. It has been suggested that factors such as immobility, complexity, durability, or costliness have resulted in a preference for standard mass-produced buildings, rather than sustainable buildings, which have more specialist and high-priced requirements (Rohracher 2001). Some building professionals have expressed the belief that sustainable building is more expensive than standard building practice and that this acts as a disincentive to client innovation. In a study of the design of thermal-comfort systems for UK office buildings, the researchers Heather Chappells and Elizabeth Shove (2005) found that clients' concerns over cost, status, and comfort often outweighed sustainable innovation. Other studies suggest that sustainable building can be financially profitable but that there has been little incentive in the building industry to promote the positive features of such developments (van Hal 2007). Barriers to the transfer of practices between green builders and mainstream building providers are seen to encompass ideological, cultural, social, political, and ethical factors as well as economic and technical ones (Seyfang 2010). Innovative community-led solutions have, therefore, proven difficult to enact within mainstream structures and systems (van Vliet, Chappells, and Shove 2005), and consequently the opportunity to learn from these examples and broaden their scope has been limited. In this context, stronger policy and regulatory support for innovation is also seen as a prerequisite for the development of a sustainable building practice.

On the demand side, it is important to consider how people actually use buildings and to what extent buildings are designed to meet the cultural values and needs of different users. Feedback studies of sustainable buildings suggest that these can deliver comfort and environmental performance. A worldwide study of users' perceptions of thermal comfort conditions in thirty-six exemplary sustainable commercial and institutional buildings found that there was a good degree of satisfaction with thermal comfort conditions overall, when compared to users' perceptions in a set of more conventional buildings (Baird and Field 2012). It has also been found that use and acceptance of sustainable buildings is informed by the way user needs are negotiated and taken into account in the design of infrastructure systems (Rohracher and Ornetzeder 2002). In much conventional building practice, user needs have often been considered only after the crucial design stages have been completed, and consequently many buildings have failed to deliver either comfortable or sustainable environments. Feedback studies have consistently demonstrated that users value having an active role in building design and benefit from a degree of control over their environment (Cole et al. 2008).

Future Scenarios

There will probably be no consensus on a model of universal best environmental practice for sustainable buildings because heterogeneous urban-design strategies currently coexist (Guy 2011). A review of existing trajectories of sustainable building innovation identifies three scenarios in which sustainable buildings and infrastructure appear to be emerging. These represent coexisting pathways, and the hybridization of ideas across each is likely; but they help to identify the dominant trajectories that are currently favored as *the* model for sustainable-building practice. Additionally, these scenarios are enacted across a range of different scales (from retrofitting existing buildings to redesigning entire urban communities and, finally, to transforming culture). (See table 1 below.)

A prerequisite for more inclusive sustainable design is for policy makers to evaluate which discourses of sustainability currently inform building frameworks and performance evaluations and which are excluded. Numerous measures to evaluate the environmental performance of buildings are (often) rooted in a techno-engineering

TABLE 1. Scenarios for Sustainable Building

Scenario	Building Logic	User Role	Exemplar
Techno-engineering	Decrease resource intensity through intelligent buildings and technologies	Partly delegated to interactive smart controls, with user input in design	Iconic green building design and retrofitting
Socio-ecological adaptation	Integration of buildings with local environments	Opportunities for user adaptation and control through life of building	Passively designed homes and updated vernacular building/city forms
Socio-cultural transformation	Redefine what buildings are for and how they connect to wider urban culture	User habits may need to change to adapt to new sustainable needs	Changed context of building use—interacting indoor/outdoor spaces or homeworking (i.e., telecommuting)

Source: author.

model of sustainable design, which may undermine those that draw more on adaptive socio-ecological or socio-cultural traditions of vernacular design.

We also need to anticipate how future changes in climate, lifestyles, technologies, and habits may emerge and how these will create new challenges for these various scenarios of building and infrastructure design. Following the lead of the British researcher Joe Ravetz (2008), we might ask, with relation to proposed retrofit planning, how far the current building stock will be fit for purpose in 2050. It would be unrealistic and unwise to take for granted that prevailing lifestyles and consumption habits will stay the same. The term *rebound effect* has long been used to describe behavioral or other systemic responses to the introduction of new technologies that can produce less than anticipated resource savings, such as increasing the size of family homes driven by fuel efficiencies in home-heating technologies. Similarly, perceived heat energy savings from installing insulation or double glazing may be offset by a new need for more cooling as buildings become too hot in summer. Changing climatic conditions, including increased peak summer temperatures, may create significant further demand for air conditioning; and there is evidence that this is already occurring even in traditionally cooler climates.

Despite persistent advice on the need to conserve energy, many consumers still aspire to new living arrangements—such as conservatories that are mechanically heated or patio heating—that run counter to energy-saving advice (Ravetz 2008). With relation to socio-ecological adaptation, many buildings designed and constructed during the twentieth century have been difficult to adapt to new uses, and the long-lived nature of these buildings is problematic for sustainability. A priority will be to create future adaptable buildings that can respond to changing climatic and cultural conditions, not ones that are fixed into an unsustainable trajectory of resource use (OECD 2002). An example of innovation of this type is to be found in Dutch housing developments, which are being built to anticipate the localized problem of future flooding related to climatic change (Guy 2011).

The need to connect social practices and lifestyles to the design and development of buildings is another consideration. Societies are increasingly mobile, and new living-working arrangements of that mobile society could be used to create niches for the sustainable use of buildings, but we should also expect and anticipate unintended consequences. "Homeworking" (i.e., telecommuting) has often been associated with reduced travel and fuel needs, but it has been noted that the costs linked to non-work-related commuting trips and household-energy needs may counteract the benefit of those reduced needs, such that recorded energy savings from telecommuting are actually quite small (Marvin 1997).

Outlook

Buildings and infrastructures represent the single most important elements in achieving the wider vision of sustainable urban design; they are responsible for a vast proportion of material and resources consumption and for the production of wastes. Achieving future sustainability in these sectors requires an integrated approach that views buildings and infrastructures in the context of a wider urban system. Buildings are often a response to individual client demands and not part of an integrated urban design encompassing transformations in city planning.

Achieving sustainable building goals may also require changes in social and cultural community beliefs about the role of the built environment as a means of security, comfort, or shelter. It is clear that achieving a sustainable built environment within all scenarios will require a long-term vision and a *system-oriented* approach to addressing technological, economic, environmental, cultural, and social challenges in sustainability. Understanding the multiplicity of players involved in reconstructing the urban built environment, including communities of building practitioners, design professionals and users, and the divergent visions and meanings of sustainability they carry with them is another vital consideration in determining how future trajectories will evolve.

Heather CHAPPELLS
Dalhousie University and Saint Mary's University

See also Cities and the Biosphere; Community; Design and Architecture; Energy Efficiency; Waste—Engineering Aspects; Waste—Social Aspects; Water

FURTHER READING

Andrews-Speed, Philip. (2009). China's ongoing energy efficiency drive: Origins, progress and prospects. *Energy Policy, 37*(4), 1331–1344.

Baird, George, & Field, Carmeny. (2012, February). Thermal comfort conditions in sustainable buildings: Results of a worldwide survey of users' perceptions. *Renewable Energy.* doi: 10.1016/j.renene.2012.01.069

Bartuska, Tom J. (2007). The built environment: Definition and scope. In Wendy R. McClure & Tom J. Bartuska (Eds.), *The built environment: A collaborative inquiry into design and planning* (2nd ed., pp. 3–14). Hoboken, NJ: John Wiley & Sons.

Burnett, John. (2007). City buildings: Eco-labels and shades of green. *Landscape and Urban Planning, 83*(1), 29–38.

Chappells, Heather, & Shove, Elizabeth. (2005). Debating the future of comfort: Environmental sustainability, energy consumption and the indoor environment. *Building Research and Information, 33*(1), 32–40.

Clements-Croome, Derek. (2011). Sustainable intelligent buildings for people: A review. *Intelligent Buildings International, 3*(2), 67–86.

Cole, Raymond J.; Robinson, John; Brown, Zosia; & O'Shea, Meg. (2008). Re-contextualizing the notion of comfort. *Building Research and Information, 36*(4), 323–336.

Conte, Emilia, & Monno, Valeria. (2012). Beyond the buildingcentric approach: A vision for integrated evaluation of sustainable buildings. *Environmental Impact Assessment Review, 34,* 31–40.

Cooper, Gail. (1998). *Air-conditioning America: Engineers and the controlled environment, 1900–1960.* Baltimore: Johns Hopkins University Press.

Cox, Stan. (2010). *Losing our cool: Uncomfortable truths about our air-conditioned world.* New York: New Press.

Dailey, Jessica. (2011). Empire State Building achieves gold LEED certification. Retrieved May 6, 2012, from http://inhabitat.com/nyc/empire-state-building-achieves-leed-gold-certification/

Department for Communities and Local Government (DCLG). (2007). *Building a greener future: Policy statement.* London: The Stationery Office.

Fay, Marianne, & Yepes, Tito. (2003). *Investing in infrastructure: What is needed from 2000 to 2010?* (World Bank research working paper 3102). Washington, DC: World Bank.

Fitch, James Marston. (1972). *American building: The environmental forces that shape it.* Boston: Houghton Mifflin Company.

Foster, Norman. (2011, September 5). Building a sustainable future. *The Telegraph.* Retrieved May 5, 2012, from http://www.telegraph.co.uk/sponsored/earth/the-age-of-energy/8741595/Norman-Foster-on-building-a-sustainable-future.html

Guy, Simon. (2011). Designing fluid futures: Hybrid transitions to sustainable architectures. *Environmental Innovation and Societal Transitions, 1*(1), 140–145.

Heschong, Lisa. (1979). *Thermal delight in architecture.* Cambridge, MA: MIT Press.

Hu, Dan, et al. (2010). Input, stocks and output flows of urban residential building system in Beijing city, China from 1949 to 2008. *Resources, Conservation and Recycling, 54*(12), 1177–1188.

Jiang, Ping, & Tovey, Keith. (2010). Overcoming barriers to implementation of carbon reduction strategies in large commercial buildings in China. *Building and Environment, 45*(4), 856–864.

John, Godfaurd; Clements-Croome, Derek; & Jeronimidis, George. (2005). Sustainable building solutions: A review of lessons from the natural world. *Building and Environment, 40*(3), 319–328.

Kamana, Chandra Prakash, & Escultura, Edgardo E. (2011). Building green to attain sustainability. *International Journal of Earth Sciences and Engineering, 4*(4), 725–729.

Marvin, Simon. (1997). Environmental flows: Telecommunications and the dematerialization of cities. *Futures, 29*(1), 47–65.

Næss, Petter. (2001). Urban planning and sustainable development. *European Planning Studies, 9*(4), 503–524.

Organisation for Economic Co-operation and Development (OECD). (2002). *Design of sustainable building policies: Scope for improvement and barriers.* Paris: Working Party on National Environmental Policy, OECD.

Ravetz, Joe. (2008). State of the stock: What do we know about existing buildings and their future prospects. *Energy Policy, 36*(12), 4462–4470.

Rohracher, Harold. (2001). Managing the technological transition to sustainable construction of buildings: A socio-technical perspective. *Technology Analysis and Strategic Management, 13*(1), 147–150.

Rohracher, Harold, & Ornetzeder, Michael. (2002). Green buildings in context: Improving social learning processes between users and producers. *Built Environment, 28*(1), 73–84.

Schneiders, Jurgen, & Hermelink, Andreas. (2006). CEPHEUS results: Measurements and occupants' satisfaction provide evidence for passive houses being an option for sustainable building. *Energy Policy, 34*(2), 151–171.

Seyfang, Gill. (2010). Community action for sustainable housing: Building a low-carbon future. *Energy Policy, 38*(12), 7624–7633.

Tavernor, Robert. (2007). Visual and cultural sustainability: The impact of tall buildings on London. *Landscape and Urban Planning, 83*(1), 2–12.

Trentmann, Frank. (2009). Disruption in normal: Blackouts, breakdowns and the elasticity of everyday life. In Elizabeth Shove, Frank Trentman & Richard Wilk (Eds.), *Time, consumption and everyday life* (pp.67–84). Oxford, UK: Berg.

United States Environmental Protection Agency (US EPA). (2011). EPA green buildings. Retrieved May 5, 2012, from http://www.epa.gov/oaintrnt/projects/

van Hal, J. D. M. (2007). A labeling system as a stepping stone for incentives related to the profitability of sustainable housing. *Journal of Housing and the Built Environment, 22*(4), 393–408.

van Vliet, Bas; Chappells, Heather; & Shove, Elizabeth. (2005). *Infrastructures of consumption: Environmental innovation in the utility industries.* London: Earthscan.

Wilhite, Harold. (2008). Consumption and the transformation of everyday life: A view from south India. Basingstoke, UK: Palgrave Macmillan.

Williams, Katie, & Lindsay, Morag. (2007). The extent and nature of sustainable building in England: An analysis of progress. *Planning Theory and Practice, 8*(1), 31–49.

Wilson, Alex, & Boehland, Jessica. (2005). Small is beautiful: US house size, resource use, and the environment. Retrieved May 5, 2012, from http://www.greenbiz.com/news/2005/07/12/small-beautiful-us-house-size-resource-use-and-environment

Yoshino, Hiroshi, et al. (2006). Indoor thermal environment and energy saving for urban residential buildings in China. *Energy and Buildings, 38*(11), 1308–1319.

Zhao, Jingzhu; Liu, Hongpeng; & Dong, Rencai. (2008). Sustainable urban development: Policy framework for sustainable consumption and production. *International Journal of Sustainable Development and World Ecology, 15*(4), 318–325.

Zhu, Yingxin, & Lin, Borong. (2004). Sustainable housing and urban construction in China. *Energy and Buildings, 36*(12), 1287–1297.

Berkshire's authors and editors welcome questions, comments, and corrections. Send your emails about the *Berkshire Encyclopedia of Sustainability* in general or this volume in particular to: sustainability.updates@berkshirepublishing.com

Cities and the Biosphere

Cities are a type of socio-ecological system that has an expanding range of connections with nature's ecologies. As of 2012, most of these connections produce environmental damage: to mention just two cases, greenhouse gases pollute the atmosphere and felled trees contribute to desertification. The carbon footprint of urbanites, therefore, is enormous. Can we begin to use these connections to produce positive outcomes—outcomes that allow cities to contribute to environmental sustainability? The complex systemic and multi-scalar capacities of cities have massive potential for a broad range of positive connections with nature's ecologies.

The city is a key scale for implementing a broad range of environmentally sound policies and a site for struggles over the environmental quality of life for different socioeconomic classes (e.g., Satterthwaite et al. 2007; Redclift 2009; Van Veenhuizen and Danso 2007). Cities can help address air, noise, and water pollution, even when the policies involved may originate at the national or regional level. Thousands of cities worldwide, in fact, have initiated their own de facto environmental policies to the point of violating national law, not because of idealism, but because they have been compelled to do so. In contrast, national governments are far more removed from the immediate catastrophic potentials of poisoned air and floods and have been slow to act.

The current phase of economic globalization, which puts direct pressures onto cities, has sharpened further the acuteness of environmental challenges at the urban level. One example of these pressures is the global corporate demand for the extreme type of built environment Dubai epitomizes. The other side of this situation is the sharply increased demand for inputs, transport, and infrastructure for mobility—the enormous demand for wood, cement,

nonrenewable energy, air transport, trucking, shipping, and so on. A second element influenced by the current global corporate economy is the World Trade Organization's subordination of environmental standards to what are presented as "requisites" for "free" global trade and proprietary "rights" (e.g., Gupta 2004; Mgbeogi 2006). Finally, privatization and deregulation reduce the government's role, especially at the national level, and hence weaken its mandatory powers over environmental standards.

These urban conditions, some negative, some positive, will become increasingly critical for policy matters not only for cities, but also at regional, national, and global levels. The city is one of the strategic sites where most of the questions about environmental sustainability become visible and concrete.

A Multi-scalar Ecological Urban Analysis

The city is a strategic space for the direct and brutal confrontation between enormously destructive forces that harm the environment and increasingly acute needs that support environmental viability. Much of what we keep describing as global environmental challenges becomes tangible and urgent in cities. Cities likely will need to implement and enforce international and national standards at the urban scale. The urban scale has limits, however, especially in the Global South, where local governments have limited funds. This scale is one at which societies can achieve many specific goals, however. (See figure 1 on page 37.) Local authorities are in a strong position to pursue the goals of sustainable development in their roles as direct or indirect providers of services; regulators, leaders, and partners; and mobilizers of community resources. Each urban

Figure 1. The Nested Scales of Urban Impacts on the Biosphere

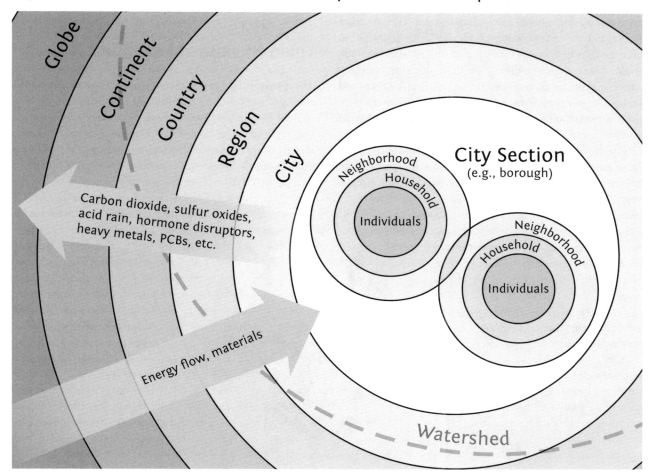

Source: Berkshire Publishing.

Figure 1 shows the interconnectivity of the world from the largest scale to the scale of the individual, with watersheds showing across regions. Energy and materials—which release carbon dioxide, sulfur oxides, acid rain, hormone disruptors, heavy metals, PCBs, and other poisons that are often shipped from developed countries to developing countries—flow into the city. Each urban combination of elements is unique, as is the way it fits within local and regional ecosystems.

combination of elements is unique, as is the way it fits within local and regional ecosystems. From this specificity comes place-based knowledge that can be scaled up and contribute to the understanding of global conditions. The case of ozone holes illustrates this scale-up. The damage occurs at the microlevel of cars, households, factories, and buildings, but its full impact becomes visible and measurable only over the North and South poles, where there are no cars and buildings.

City-related ecological conditions operate on a diversity of geographic scales. Cities incorporate a range of scales on which a given ecological condition functions, and in that sense, cities make visible the fact itself of scaling. Further, cities make the multi-scalar properties of ecological systems present and recognizable to their residents. Developing and strengthening this urban capacity to make these properties visible will become increasingly critical for policy matters,

not only for cities, but also at regional, national, and global levels. For the majority of those who write about environmental regulation in, and of, cities, the strategic scale is the local one (Habitat II, Local Agenda 21). Others have long argued that the ecological regulation of cities can no longer be separated from wider questions of global governance (Low and Gleeson, 2001). This is also a long-standing position in general, nonurban analyses of the "economy and the environment" (e.g., Etsy and Ivanova 2005).

A debate gathering heat, beginning in the 1990s and remaining unresolved as of 2012, pits the global against the local, or vice versa, as the most strategic scale for action. The British sociologist Michael Redclift (1996) argued that society cannot manage the environment at the global level. Global problems result from the aggregation of production and consumption, much of which is concentrated within the world's urban centers. Redclift maintains that achieving sustainability at the local level must come first. He argues that the flurry of international agreements and agencies are international structures for managing the environment, and they bear little or no relationship to the processes transforming the environment. Not everyone agrees. The British environmental expert David Satterthwaite (1999) thus has long argued that we need global responsibilities, but these require international agreements. Nicholas Low, professor of Environmental Planning at the University of Melbourne (2000), adds that a global system of corporate relationships exists in which city administrations are increasingly a part. This complex cross-border system increasingly is responsible for the health and destruction of the planet. Today's development processes bring into focus the question of environmental justice at the global level, a question that, if asked in the early industrial era, would have been heard at the national level.

One key aspect of such an effort is to understand the biosphere's capacities to provide "nature's services," or "ecosystem services," which factory-made chemicals provide today: for instance, instead of controlling pests with pesticides, we would diversify the species in the cultivated land to ensure a balance. We have forgotten the knowledge about how a mix of species can ensure a balance that handles predators. Rotating crops according to the season is a long-standing example worldwide. We must relearn by using particular forms of scientific knowledge that help us understand what the biosphere can do. This replacement in itself would reduce the role and power of major corporate actors, such as pesticide manufacturers; each farm and each garden would be a center for managing a balanced distribution of species.

Greening our cities would mean that all households, neighborhoods, and firms would need to be part of the effort, thereby making of each of these an active contributor to environmental sustainability. Cities are complex systems and can wire this decentralizing of greening efforts into the urban fabric itself. This integration could balance the growth of inequality that became wired into the urban fabric when certain types of economic growth took off in the 1980s. Greening our cities, the necessity of confronting the environmental catastrophe, can force

growing participation by all and push toward developing a new politics.

Environmental Inequalities

The possibility that greening might have distributive social effects adds to its importance, because environmental destruction is likely to add sharply to the inequality between poor and rich. Low-income settlements absorb more of the environmental damage than wealthy settlements do, even when the latter are far more destructive of the environment (Satterthwaite et al. 2007). The evidence shows that the decline of health because of global environmental change (including climate change) is predicted to be far greater in poor African populations than in European populations. Several factors are at work, from regional variations in the impact and types of climate change, to differences in existing levels of heat and food stress.

This trend also cuts across the high-income/low-income country divide. For instance, data on Los Angeles, California (United States), which is in many ways a rich city, show a sharp climate gap (Morello-Frosch et al. 2009). African Americans in Los Angeles are twice as likely as other city residents to die during heat waves, and families living below the poverty line are less likely to have access to air conditioning or cars to escape the heat. Five of the smoggiest cities in California have the highest concentrations of people of color and low-income residents; these communities are projected to have the largest increases in smog associated with climate change. Low-income and minority families spend more of their income than most others in the United States do on food, electricity, and water—as much as 25 percent of total family income.

This unequal distribution of the costs of environmental damage is also evident in studies about who will be the environmental refugees of the near future, when rising water levels and desertification worsen. Estimates of the numbers of migrants and projections of future numbers vary, but clearly, there will be many, and mostly the poor will have to flee for refuge. The estimates range from 25 to 50 million by the year 2010 to almost 700 million by 2050; the International Organization for Migration (IOM) takes the middle road with an estimate of 200 million environmentally induced migrants by 2050 (IIED 2007, 17–25). A sea-level rise of 1 meter could affect 23.5 million people and reduce agricultural lands by 1.5 million hectares in the Ganges, Mekong, and Nile river deltas; a sea-level rise of 2 meters would impact an additional 10.8 million people and reduce agricultural lands by an additional 969,000 hectares.

These numbers point to a disturbing landscape of massive threats and sharp inequalities in the intensity of these threats for different areas and income groups.

Cities at the Heart of Our Environmental Future

The massive processes of urbanization under way in the early twenty-first century are inevitably at the center of the environmental future. Humankind increasingly is present in the planet through cities and vast urban agglomerations; it mediates its relation to the various stocks and flows of environmental capital through its urban presence. The urban hinterland—the surrounding area or region from which a city draws much of the resources it needs—is today a global hinterland. As the global economy expands, we have raised our capacity to annex growing portions of the world to support a limited number of industries and places.

Major cities have become distinct socio-ecological systems with planetary reach, going well beyond urban space. Massive population growth in cities and the consumption patterns of rich countries have combined with the sharpening of profit seeking by agribusiness to disrupt older, balanced ways of producing food. Traditional rural economies and their long-standing cultural adaptation to biological diversity ensured that the biosphere could replenish the land with needed nutrients. Humankind no longer allows the land to do so and, in fact, kills some of its nutrients with excess pesticides. In addition, rural populations increasingly are forced to consume goods, including food, the industrial economy produces, and this economy is much less sensitive to biological diversity. Food has become a commodity not to satisfy a basic need but designed to make a profit. The rural condition has evolved into a new system of social relations, one that supports monocrops rather than biodiversity and embraces the pecuniary nexus (financial connections) rather than community and meaningful interpersonal relationships. These developments all signal that the urban condition is a major factor in rural areas as well. It all amounts to a radical transformation in the relation between humankind and the rest of the planet.

Urbanization, an enormously distinctive presence, is changing, directly and indirectly, a growing range of nature's ecosystems, from the climate to species diversity. Urbanization is leading to the formation of new environmental conditions—heat islands, ozone holes, desertification, and water pollution. Urbanization and industrialization have made humankind the major consumer of all significant ecosystems. A set of global ecological conditions never seen before is the result.

Are these global ecological conditions, however, the result of urban agglomeration and density? Or are they the result of the specific subtypes of urban systems humankind has developed to handle transport, waste disposal, building, heating and cooling, food provision, and the industrial process through which we extract, grow, make, package, distribute, and dispose of all the foods, services, and materials we use?

It is, doubtless, the latter—the specific urban systems humankind has made. One of the outstanding features among a range of major cities in the early twenty-first century is their sharp differences in environmental sustainability. These differences result from diverse government policies, economic bases, cultures of daily life, and so on. European cities generally are far more engaged with environmental sustainability than are US cities, and the poor megacities of both the poor and rich worlds face a particularly big challenge.

Urbanization is inevitably going to alter the biosphere—cement covering land and water is just one simple element. But it need not be as damaging as it is now. Beyond the city itself, rural areas have adopted environmentally harmful production processes largely oriented to the urban demand for food. Until fifty years ago, or a hundred years in some regions, rural areas primarily had environmentally sustainable economic practices, such as crop rotation, and did not use chemicals to fertilize soil and control insects. Further, extreme capitalism has made the rural poor, especially in the Global South, so poor as of the early twenty-first century that, for the first time, many are also engaging in environmentally destructive practices, notably practices leading to desertification; thus very poor rural settlements are often pushed to live at the edge of inhospitable lands, such as deserts, where gathering wood for cooking means taking the few frail trees that prevent further desertification.

Delegating to the Biosphere

Beyond the differences among cities are a few foundational elements that dominate how we do things and are at the heart of what we need to address. One of these is the rupture in the energy and material flux through the human economy—in other words, what we use and need returns in altered form as pollution and waste to the ecosphere. Humans disrupt the biosphere's ongoing cycle whereby, for example, rain or an animal's death replenishes the Earth with needed nutrients. This disrupting of continuous cycles occurs in nearly all economic sectors, from urban to rural. The cities, however, are where it takes on its most complex interactions and cumulative effects. This situation makes cities a source of most of the environmental damage and some of the most intractable conditions feeding the damage. The complexity of cities, however, also is part of the solution. Some cities are doing a great deal to maximize the flow through—with waste recycling the most familiar case.

An important concept to heal the rupture in how energy and material flow through the human economy is to use humankind's inventive skill and technology to redesign the manufacture processes. Users would return products, such as computers, lawn mowers, automobiles, and appliances, to the manufacturer when they no longer function. Manufacturers who saw the same parts returning to the input stream likely would find new solutions to make the objects work in the same way, but with different parts and processes. Another foundational element is that human-made chemicals have replaced far too many of nature's balancing processes, thereby further disrupting nature's cycles. Delegating back to nature would encourage ecologically sound practices. A familiar case that illustrates this dynamic is biodiversity in agriculture—crop rotation is one way of achieving what destructive chemical fertilizers and pest-killing poisons now do.

Multiple ways are possible to use nature for what destructive industrial goods do (see Sassen and Dotan 2011). It has taken science, however, to reconnect us to this knowledge. Industrialized societies buried these practices, along with the knowledge. For instance, we now know that certain bacteria that can live in cement can neutralize the carbon dioxide emissions of buildings—extremely important because buildings account for well over half of all such emissions worldwide (Jonkers 2007). One dramatic technology being developed is self-healing bacterial concrete. In this technology, bacteria living within concrete structures seal cracks and reduce the permeability of concrete surfaces by depositing dense layers of calcium carbonate and other minerals. Several groups have demonstrated the feasibility of this approach. This technology is still under development, but it promises to reduce energy and materials needed to maintain human infrastructures. Buildings thus would more closely model the self-sustaining, homeostatic (having balance among elements) physical structures found in nature. Furthermore, this technology is not expensive, except for high-rise buildings. Residents in most residential areas, notably low-income ones, could implement this

change themselves, thereby contributing to employment and civic engagement. In major office districts, the matter changes, because major firms would need to handle the height.

Another example is using certain types of algae to clean up chemically contaminated water and ground. The problems of concentrated contaminants are a major issue in cities due to extremely high population densities. Landfill waste that human activity generates becomes a dangerous pollutant, a source of greenhouse emissions, and a terminal break in many natural cycles. The development of landfill bioreactors (devices using living organisms to synthesize useful substances or break down harmful ones) is one way of using nature for the cleanup. Landfill bioreactors accelerate waste decomposition by improving conditions for aerobic or anaerobic biological processes. This result is paired with the capture of by-products, such as carbon dioxide and methane, released in these processes, which produce a fuel known as "landfill gas" (LFG). This process both reduces the uncontrolled diffusion of greenhouse gases and provides a concentrated fuel source; it also makes possible the use of carbon dioxide for carbon sequestration (carbon dioxide removal) and fuel generation. These are just two examples. There are many more.

There is, however, a second course of action: fighting the power and profit logics that have organized environmentally destructive economies and societies.

The Complexity and Global Projection of Cities

Humankind cannot reduce the question of urban sustainability to modest interventions that leave the major economic systems untouched. Although in some environmental domains (e.g., protecting the habitat of an endangered species), simply acting on scientific knowledge can produce considerable advances, this is not the case when dealing with cities, multinationals, or society at large. Nonscientific elements, such as political will, are a crucial part of the picture: questions of power, poverty and inequality, ideology, and cultural preferences must be addressed. Policy and proactive engagement are critical dimensions for environmental sustainability, whether they involve asking people to recycle garbage or demanding accountability from major global corporations known to have environmentally damaging production processes.

The spaces where damage occurs often differ from the sites where responsibility for the damage lies (such as the headquarters of mining corporations) and where society should demand accountability. A crucial issue is the massive investment around the world promoting large projects that damage the environment. Deforestation, mining, and construction of massive dams are perhaps among the best-known cases. The scale and the increasingly global and private character of these investments suggest that citizens, governments, and nongovernmental organizations (NGOs) all lack the power to alter these investment patterns. Tactics are available, however, most notably in global cities, which should be seen as structural platforms for acting and contesting these powerful corporate actors (Sassen 2005). A firm may have hundreds of mines across the world, but its headquarters are likely to be in one or a few major cities, where it is far easier to confront the firm than in hundreds of often isolated production sites.

The geography of economic globalization is strategic rather than all-encompassing, especially when it comes to the managing, coordinating, servicing, and financing of global economic operations. About seventy-five cities worldwide contain just about all the headquarters of globally operating firms. The strategic nature is significant for regulating and governing the global economy. The network of global cities is a strategic geography where the density of economic transactions and top-level management functions come together and constitute a concentrated space of global decision making.

This strategic geography also is available for demanding accountability from major corporate headquarters about the environmental damage they have produced. It is precisely because the global economic system is characterized by enormous concentration of power in a limited number of large multinational corporations (about 300,000 MNCs compared to millions and millions of small firms) and global financial markets that makes for concentrated rather than widely dispersed sites for accountability and for demanding changes in investment criteria. Engaging the headquarters actually is easier than engaging the thousands of mines and factories in often remote and militarized sites or the millions of worldwide service outlets of such global firms. Direct engagement with the headquarters of global firms benefits from the recognition, among consumers, politicians, and the media, of an environmental crisis. Because the global economy needs a growing number of global cities, not just one perfect imperial capital, these cities are a key space for countries around the world to engage global firms. The common though erroneous idea that cities compete with each other, however, has kept urban leaderships from collaborating to contest the claims of powerful global firms.

Specific networks of cities are natural platforms for cross-border city alliances that can confront the demands of global firms. Dealing with the headquarters of large firms, of course, leaves out millions of independent small local firms responsible for considerable environmental damage, but national regulations and local activism are more likely to control these.

One major obstacle in much of the effort to promote environmental sustainability is the absence of a strong recognition of the local level in interstate policy discussions and negotiations. Important here is that attaining major or minor recognition in global governance framings brings the focus on a level—cities—that helps make visible the limitations of existing climate governance framings. Every major city, regardless of country, would become a complex space for the implementation of processes that actually cut environmental damage rather than shift it around as is the case in carbon trading, still the preferred way for national governments.

Shortcomings in the Climate Change Governance Framework

Neither the Kyoto Protocol (KP; protocol aimed at fighting global warming) nor the United Nations Framework Convention on Climate Change (UNFCCC, or the Convention) contains specific references to local government or city-level actions to meet the Protocol commitments. A few references allude to local-level involvement, with Article 10 in the Kyoto Protocol recognizing that regional programs may be relevant to improve the quality of local emission factors. The latest UN Climate Conference (COP15) did not advance matters much, even though the addition of a Local Government Climate Change initiative did introduce some local issues into some of the debates and briefings.

Although neither the KP nor UNFCCC considers any role for cities or local governments, local governments have, in fact, established and built up financial and fiscal incentives, local knowledge and education, and other municipal frameworks for action through the actual practical obligations and opportunities that municipal-level governments encounter. Based on their legal responsibility and jurisdiction, local governments have developed targets and regulations; in this work, they have tended to exceed national and state jurisdictional obligations. In view of the failure to recognize cities at the international climate negotiations, the Local Government Climate Roadmap (a consortium of global municipal partnerships) has focused on this failure from 2007 onward. One basic premise in this effort is that including the local government level would ensure that the full chain of governance, from national to local, would be involved in the implementation of a climate agreement.

Further, and very illuminating about a specific urban structural condition, some of these local initiatives go back to the 1980s and 1990s, when major cities, notably Los Angeles, California, and Tokyo, implemented clean-air ordinances, not because their leaderships were particularly enlightened, but because public-health reasons compelled them. The global initiative Cities for Climate Protection, developed by the ICLEI Local Governments for Sustainability network (founded in 1990 as the International Council for Local Environmental Initiatives), has been active as far back as 1993; the initiative included mostly results-based, quantified, and concrete local climate actions, launched long before the Convention and KP for national governments came into force (see ICLEI's Climate Program). Local governments have held Municipal Leadership Summits in 1993, 1995, 1997, 2005, and 2012, parallel to the official Conference of Parties (COP) meetings of national governments. As a result, the Local Government and Municipal Authority Constituency (LGMA) has built upon its role as one of the first NGO constituencies acting as observer to the official international climate negotiations process (or UNFCCC).

These interactions have led to an increasing recognition of a role for local governments and authorities, particularly regarding discussions on reducing emissions from deforestation and forest degradation in developing countries and the Nairobi work program on adaptation within the new and emerging concepts of the international climate negotiations. An extensive set of studies shows that cities and metro regions can make a large difference in reducing global environmental damage; it focuses mostly on greenhouse gas emissions (GHG). The international level, however, whether the Kyoto Protocol or the post-2012 UNFCCC negotiations, fails formally when it comes to recognizing this potential, nor is this potential built into draft agreements. Localizing the discourse on mitigation and adaptation, including in its international financing options, would involve both a bottom-up—information from local level—and a top-down understanding of how existing protocols and post-2012 agreements could integrate cities.

Ultimately, however, there is a need to go well beyond these governance frameworks, and cities make this need visible and urgent. Simply redistributing carbon emissions is not enough, nor are mitigation and adaptation directives enough. The process needs to bring in the knowledge that diverse natural sciences have accumulated, including practical applications, to address the major environmental challenges.

At the city level, using this knowledge is a far more specific and interactive effort than the more top-down modes of national policy. Further, it will entail an internationalism derived from the many different countries that are leaders in these scientific discoveries and innovations. This internationalism, however, will run through localities, each locality having its own political and social cultures for implementing change. Finally, capturing the complexity of cities in their multi-scalar and multi-ecological composition will permit many more implementation channels than just about any other level, whether national, international, or suburban. These additional channels should, in turn, allow us to go well beyond adaptation and mitigation as currently understood.

Outlook

Two issues stand out as strategic. One is the use of science and technology in ways that could lead to multiplying the positive articulations between cities and the biosphere. This step is merely one in a trajectory that should aim at fully using the complexity of cities—their multi-scalar and ecological features. We may not be close to such a full use, but a mobilization is beginning in that direction. Urban experts and scientists should succeed at connecting far more, which might enable us to move much faster on this potential.

A second strategic element concerns the city as a social and power system—with laws, extreme inequalities, and vast concentrations of power. Urban complexity and diversity are further augmented by the fact that implementing environmental measures that go beyond current modest mitigation and adaptation efforts will require engaging the legal systems and profit logics that underlie and enable many of the environmentally damaging aspects of our societies. Any advance toward environmental sustainability necessarily is implicated in these systems and logics. The actual features of these systems vary across countries and across the North-South divide. In some of the other environmental domains, it is possible to confine the discussion to scientific knowledge, but this is not the case when dealing with cities.

Nonscientific elements are a crucial part of the picture. Questions of power, political will, values, beliefs, poverty and inequality, ideology and cultural preferences, and impact of purchasing power are all part of the question and the answer. One major dynamic of the current era is globalization and the spread of markets to more and more institutional realms. Questions of policy and proactive engagement possibilities have become a critical dimension of treatments of urban sustainability, whether they involve asking people to support garbage recycling or demanding accountability from major global corporations that are known to have environmentally damaging production processes.

Saskia SASSEN

Columbia University

See also Buildings and Infrastructure; Climate Change and Big History; Collective Thinking; Community; Design and Architecture; Local Solutions to Global Problems; Migration; Mobility; Population; Waste—Engineering Aspects; Waste—Social Aspects

FURTHER READING

Beddoe, Rachel, et al. (2009). Overcoming systemic roadblocks to sustainability: The evolutionary redesign of worldviews, institutions, and technologies. *Proceedings of the National Academy of Sciences, 106*(8), 2483–2489.

Daly, Herman E. (1977). *Steady-state economics: The economics of biophysical equilibrium and moral growth*. San Francisco: W. H. Freeman and Company.

Daly, Herman E., & Farley, Joshua. (2003). *Ecological economics: Principles and applications*. Washington, DC: Island Press.

Dietz, Thomas; Rosa, Eugene A.; & York, Richard. (2009). Environmentally efficient well-being: Rethinking sustainability as the relationship between human well-being and environmental impacts. *Human Ecology Review, 16*(1), 114–123.

Etsy, Daniel C., & Ivanova, Maria. (2005). Globalisation and environmental protection: A global governance perspective. In Frank Wijen, et al. (Eds.), *A Handbook of globalisation and environmental policy: National government interventions in a global arena*. Cheltenham, UK: Edward Elgar.

Huq, Saleemul; Kovats, Sari; Reid, Hannah; & Satterthwaite, David. (2007). Special issue: Reducing the risk to cities from disasters and climate change. *Environment and Urbanization, 19*(1). Retrieved May 30, 2012, from http://eau.sagepub.com/content/vol19/issue1/

Garcia, J.; Mujeriego, R.; & Hernández-Mariné, M. (2000). High rate algal pond operating strategies for urban wastewater nitrogen removal. *Journal of Applied Phycology, 12*, 331–339.

Girardet, Herbert. (2008). *Cities people planet: Urban development and climate change* (2nd ed.). Amsterdam: Amsterdam: John Wiley & Sons.

Gund Institute for Ecological Economics, University of Vermont. (2009). Homepage. Retrieved May 30, 2012, from http://www.uvm.edu/giee/

Gupta, Anil K. (2004). *WIPO-UNEP study on the role of intellectual property rights in the sharing of benefits arising from the use of biological resources and associated traditional knowledge*. Geneva: World Intellectual Property Organization & United Nations Environment Programme.

International Institute for Environment and Development (IIED). (2007). Adapting to climate change in urban areas. Retrieved July 18, 2012, from http://pubs.iied.org/pdfs/10549IIED.pdf

Jonkers, Henk M. (2007). Self healing concrete: A biological approach. In Sybrand van der Zwagg (Ed.), *Self healing materials: An alternative approach to 20 centuries of materials science* (pp. 195–204). New York: Springer.

Low, Nicholas P., & Gleeson, Brendan. (Eds.). (2001). *Governing for the environment: Global problems, ethics and democracy*. Basingstoke, UK: Palgrave Publishers Ltd.

Mgbeogi, Ikechi. (2006). *Biopiracy: Patents, plants, and indigenous knowledge*. Vancouver, Canada: University of British Columbia Press.

Morello-Frosch, Rachel; Pastor, Manuel; Sadd, James; & Shonkoff, Seth B. (2009). The climate gap: Inequalities in how climate change hurts Americans & how to close the gap. Los Angeles: University of Southern California program for environmental and regional equity. Retrieved May 30, 2012, from http://college.usc.edu/geography/ESPE/documents/The_Climate_Gap_Full_Report_FINAL.pdf

Porter, John; Costanza, Robert; Sandhu, Harpinder; Sigsgaard, Lene; & Wratten, Steve. (2009). The value of producing food, energy, and ecosystem services within an agro-ecosystem. *Ambio, 38*(4), 186–193.

Redclift, Michael. (1996). *Wasted: Counting the costs of global consumption*. London: Earthscan.

Redclift, Michael. (2009). The environment and carbon dependence: Landscapes of sustainability and materiality. *Current sociology, 57*(3), 369–387.

Rees, William E. (1992). Ecological footprints and appropriated carrying capacity: What urban economics leaves out. *Environment and Urbanization, 4*(2), 121–130.

Rees, William E. (2006). Ecological footprints and bio-capacity: Essential elements in sustainability assessment. In Jo Dewulf & Herman Van Langenhove (Eds.), *Renewables-based technology: Sustainability assessment* (pp. 143–158). Chichester, UK: John Wiley and Sons.

Reuveny, Rafael. (2008). Ecomigration and violent conflict: Case studies and public policy implications. *Human Ecology, 36*, 1–13.

Sassen, Saskia. (2001). *The global city* (2nd ed.). Princeton, NJ: Princeton University Press.

Sassen, Saskia. (2005). The ecology of global economic power: Changing investment practices to promote environmental sustainability. *Journal of International Affairs, 58*(2), 11–33.

Sassen, Saskia. (Ed.). (2006). Human settlement and the environment. *Encyclopedia of life support systems (EOLSS). Encyclopedia of the environment: Vol. 14*. Oxford, UK: EOLSS & UNESCO.

Sassen, Saskia. (2008). *Territory, authority, rights: From medieval to global assemblages*. Princeton, NJ: Princeton University Press.

Sassen, Saskia, & Dotan, Natan. (2011). Delegating, not returning, to the biosphere: How to use the multi-scalar and ecological properties of cities. *Global Environmental Change, 21*(3), 823–834.

Satterthwaite, David. (1999). *The Earthscan reader in sustainable cities*. London: Earthscan.

Satterthwaite, David, et al. (2007). Adapting to climate change in urban areas: The possibilities and constraints in low- and middle-income nations. (Human settlements discussion paper series). London: IIED. Retrieved May 30, 2012, from http://www.iied.org/pubs/pdfs/10549IIED.pdf

Schulze, P. C. (1994). Cost-benefit analyses and environmental policy. *Ecological Economics, 9*(3), 197–199.

Van Veenhuizen, R., & Danso, G. (2007). Profitability and sustainability of urban and peri-urban agriculture. Rome: Food and Agriculture Organization of the United Nations. Retrieved June 21, 2012, from http://www.ruaf.org/node/2295

Warner, Koko; Ehrhart, Charles; de Sherbinin, Alex; Adamo, Susana; & Chai-Onn, Tricia. (2009). In search of shelter: Mapping the effects of climate change on human migration and displacement. CARE international. Retrieved May 30, 2012, from http://www.gsdrc.org/go/display&type=Document&id=3905

Climate Change and Big History

Skepticism about climate change is a major barrier to action, and education provides the best counterbalance to it. More than scientific knowledge is required, however: we will also need knowledge from the social sciences and humanities, along with a genuinely global perspective, and a sense of multiple timescales. The idea of "big history" integrates the history of humans and the Earth into the narrative of the universe's creation, providing the best possible perspective from which to understand the environmental challenges of our "Anthropocene" era.

The outcome of two major international conferences on climate change, the United Nations 2011 summit in Durban, South Africa, and the Rio+ 20 conference in June 2012, seems to have been little more than a number of agreements to keep talking. At the Durban conference, participants agreed "to launch a process to develop a protocol" (UNFCCC 2011). Even that outcome was a surprise to some, but the chances of limiting global warming to an increased 2°C over the next century (a level beyond which many argue that radical and unpredictable changes become likely) are vanishing fast (Rockström 2009). Lack of understanding of environmental issues is an education problem and requires an education solution.

A major barrier to effective international action is skepticism about climate change in the United States, the richest and most powerful country in the world, and the country with the largest scientific establishment and the largest number of Nobel Prize winners. This skepticism baffles many. It is true that powerful interests have conducted a well-funded and skillfully managed campaign of disinformation, efficiently exploiting every

loophole or ambiguity in the discussions about climate change. But their success also depends on ignorance—on the fact that not enough people have enough understanding of the science to see through bad arguments.

Do we need more science education? Not necessarily, because understanding environmental issues requires some familiarity with the social sciences and humanities as well as the natural sciences: it requires a global perspective and also a sense of how the environment changes at many different timescales. Today, few school syllabi help develop these perspectives, but such perspectives lie at the heart of a new approach to education known as *big history*.

What Is Big History?

Big history integrates human history and the planet's history into the narrative of the universe's creation (IBHA n.d.; Christian 2004). The Web site of the International Big History Association states that big history seeks to "understand the integrated history of the Cosmos, Earth, Life, and Humanity, using the best available empirical evidence and scholarly methods" (IBHA n.d.). College-level courses in big history have been taught for more than twenty years, mainly in the United States, but also in Australia, the Netherlands, Russia, Egypt, South Korea, and elsewhere.

A typical big history course surveys the past on multiple scales. It begins by describing the origins of our universe 13.7 billion years ago in which cosmologists call "the big bang." Then it describes the emergence of more complex entities as the simple early universe (made up of little more than hydrogen and helium atoms and lots of energy) began to generate increasingly complex phenomena. In the course taught at San Diego State University and Macquarie University by the Australian historian David Christian (a pioneer in teaching big history), the creation of stars and galaxies (the first large, complex objects) is discussed next, and then the creation of new elements in dying stars. Those new elements generated new forms of matter, including those from which the first planets and solar systems were built. The creation of our own solar system, around 4.5 billion years ago, and the evolution of planet Earth are examined next; then the discussion turns to the origins and evolution of life on Earth and the coevolution of life and the planet within the biosphere. Finally, the course surveys the evolution of our own strange species, tracking how the exceptional efficiency of human languages enabled us to share and accumulate new information in quite unique ways. This capacity to share information through "collective learning" helps explain our accelerating technological creativity over more than 100,000 years and our rapid path from being just one more primate species to being the dominant species on the planet. Big history provides the best possible perspective from which to understand the distinctive features of the "Anthropocene" era, the first era in 4 billion years in which a single species has dominated change in the biosphere (Crutzen 2002; Steffen, Crutzen, and McNeill 2007).

When Christian first taught big history more than twenty years ago, the course ended in the present day. Most students found that the course validated the large questions about life, the Earth, and the universe that they desperately wanted to explore and that most university courses seemed to ignore. But for precisely this reason, they wanted to discuss where the story was going: they wanted to talk about the future. Christian was soon persuaded that a discussion of trends extending over millions or even billions of years cannot stop on a dime, and, with a colleague in biology, he began lecturing on the future. This turned out to be one of the most exciting parts of the course because the questions were so urgent. Are current extinction rates comparable to those of the five major extinction events of the past? Will a 2°C increase in average global temperatures make a difference? Are capitalism and sustainability compatible? Will we run out of cheap energy or will new technologies allow sustained (and sustainable) growth? The lectures made clear that there were no firm answers to such questions, but provided a context within which students could explore the problems and look at some options.

What Is the Big History Project?

Today, big history courses are being taught in at least fifty college-level institutions. With the support of the billionaire philanthropist Bill Gates, a team of professionals is also building an online syllabus in big history for high schools (for more information, see Big History Project 2011). In September 2011, five schools in the United States started testing the syllabus, and in February 2012, two Australian schools started a second pilot program. Up to fifty schools will take part in a second round of test runs beginning in September 2012. Then, in the middle of 2013, after the syllabus in big history has been thoroughly crash tested, it will be made available to everyone freely. All the materials will be available online. The hope is that within ten years schools in many different countries will be teaching at least one big history course. In November 2011, Christian described the big history project for an audience of teachers from around the world; he was approached by teachers from at least fifteen different countries who said they would love to teach big history.

Big History as Origin Story

In the past, origin stories lay at the heart of education systems. Big history courses use the best of modern scientific scholarship in the sciences and humanities, linking them in a single, coherent, and universal story about how everything around us was created. This means that big history courses can play the educational role once played by traditional origin stories. Like all origin stories, big history uses the best available knowledge to construct an evolutionary map of the entire universe, onto which individuals and societies can map themselves. Such stories empower students intellectually by giving them an overview within which they can situate themselves, their home communities, and everything they know. Origin stories offer a view from the mountaintop: that view may lack detail, but it shows how different landscapes fit together, and that perspective can transform how you see your home landscapes. Their absence from modern education is anomalous and disastrous, because it leaves students without compass or sketch map in the vast tsunami of information available on the Internet. Big history aims to correct this pedagogical blunder.

Big History and the Environment

Big history courses will be particularly valuable in informing students about the global challenges that the planet faces. Three aspects of big history are particularly relevant: (1) big history studies the past at multiple scales;

(2) it teaches interdisciplinarity by leading students seamlessly from cosmology to geology to biology and human history; and (3) big history is global and holistic, so it can help students see humanity as a global species facing global problems requiring global solutions. Each of these perspectives can contribute powerfully to environmental understanding.

Scale

Many environmental issues, from mass extinctions to climate change, can be understood only when studied at multiple scales, from a few months or years to hundreds of millions of years. Understanding that our oxygen-dominated climate was created over the course of billions of years as photosynthesizers pumped oxygen into the atmosphere is critical to understanding the major drivers of climate change. Students of big history, like students of geology or cosmology, have to stretch their imaginations to the point where they really do understand the difference between a hundred years and a billion years.

When it comes to the study of human history, big history can expand on the broad perspectives of world history. Big history considers the past at such huge scales that it can attempt, as more conventional types of history cannot, to understand the trajectory of the biosphere as a whole, and to see human history as part of that larger trajectory. It therefore provides a natural framework for the type of world history that will be needed increasingly in a world facing challenges, from the threat of nuclear war to that of ecological collapse and climate change, challenges that cannot be tackled nation by nation. Big history provides a natural framework for the construction of a modern history of humanity that places issues such as climate change within an appropriate context.

Within that framework, human history as a whole divides naturally into three main eras: the foraging era (the Paleolithic era, up to c. 10,000 years ago), the agrarian era (dominated by agrarian societies and continuing until just a few centuries ago), and the modern era. (The emergence of a possible fourth era marked by humanity's impacts on the biosphere, called the Anthropocene, is the subject of another article in this volume.) Human impacts on the biosphere were mostly local during the Paleolithic era, although our Paleolithic ancestors may have had a significant impact on animals (by contributing to the extinction of many species of megafauna) and plants (by firing the land and transforming the distribution of plant species). In the agrarian era, humans began to have significant impacts on the atmosphere by reducing forest cover and introducing paddy rice farming (which increased atmospheric levels of the major greenhouse gases, carbon dioxide and methane) and through metallurgy, which raised lead levels. (Evidence for higher lead levels is present in Greenland ice cores [Ruddiman 2005].) But of course the largest impacts of all have appeared in the shortest of these periods, since the Industrial Revolution, when humans began to use fossil fuels on a large scale.

To understand such a periodization it is vital to feel comfortable moving between different temporal scales. Big history helps students move easily between these and even larger scales and grasp the critical differences between different scales. Of the three major eras of human history, for example, the first is by far the longest, lasting for more than 95 percent of the time that humans have lived on Earth, whereas the modern era is the shortest, lasting roughly a quarter of a millennium. Perhaps 12 percent of the roughly 100 billion humans who have ever lived, lived during the foraging era, while 68 percent lived in the agrarian era, and 20 percent in the modern era.

Interdisciplinarity

Many environmental issues cross multiple disciplines, meaning that looking for solutions will require multidisciplinary research efforts. It is necessary, first, to have some grasp of the core sciences: how do climatologists study past climates? What can we tell about climate fluctuations on scales of hundreds of millions of years? How do natural cycles of elements such as carbon and nitrogen work, and how are anthropogenic processes affecting them? What processes drive global climates? But it is also necessary to understand something of the economics of industries from timber extraction to power generation, and also to understand the astonishing history of increasing global energy use since the Industrial Revolution. Finally, it is important to understand the politics of global and national negotiations over carbon emissions or debates over the reality and extent of climate change. The politics may turn out to be particularly important as it is becoming increasingly clear that even where solutions to global warming are scientifically well understood, global political processes may be incapable of introducing them in a timely manner.

As the Australian climate scientist Will Steffen says, "Climate change is like no other environmental problem that humanity has ever faced. . . . Perhaps no other problem—environmental or otherwise—facing society requires such a strong interdisciplinary knowledge base to tackle; research to support effective policy-making and other actions must cut across the full range of natural sciences, social sciences (including economics), and humanities" (Steffen 2011, 21).

An example of research that crosses these disciplinary borders is IHOPE (Integrated History and Future of People on Earth), a research project that is building a detailed account of interactions between humans and the environment over several hundred thousand years (IHOPE n.d.). Like IHOPE, big history will help students become comfortable with the idea of moving easily between different disciplines, because the conventional big history syllabus already does this, more or less seamlessly.

Global Thinking

Environmental issues cannot be understood in isolation. Climate change, acidification of oceans, high rates of extinction, and deforestation are all linked and have to be seen as expressions of a single phenomenon: the astonishing technological creativity of our species that has culminated in the Anthropocene epoch. To solve these problems, we must understand what links these issues, and we will need a global approach because they cross national borders. Again, Will Steffen puts it well: "Climate change is truly global in that it is centered around the two great fluids—the atmosphere and the ocean—that transport material and energy around the planet" (Steffen 2011, 22).

Solutions to global problems will also require some sense of global citizenship, a sense of shared humanity across the world. Because courses in big history encounter humans first as a global species rather than as a cluster of national "tribes," big history provides a natural introduction to such a global perspective. For this reason, education in big history might help create a world in which negotiators at summits on major global challenges will bring with them not just the national perspectives of their governments, but also the large-scale, interdisciplinary, and global perspectives of big history. The chances of success will surely be greater than they are today.

Comments from one student of big history hint at the transformative power of the big history perspective: "When I was first asked to consider my role in the universe four months ago . . . I do not think I fully realized there was even a living community around me, never mind an Earth full of other humans and an entire universe beyond. . . . But after this long, incredible voyage of exploration . . . I have a newfound sense of what the universe is. I have learned . . . that we are all part of the Global Future, and I can make a difference in my life as well as the lives of others. . . . My role is now to change my ways and respect this beautiful planet that granted us life, and to get others to join me" (Rodrigue 2011, 77).

David Christian
*Macquarie University; WCU Professor,
Ewha Womans University, Seoul*

This article is an adaptation by the author of an article that originally appeared in March of 2012 in Volume 3, Issue 3 of the online journal *Solutions*. Adapted with kind permission of *Solutions*. The original article, titled "Big History for the Era of Climate Change," is available at http://www.thesolutionsjournal.com/node/1066\.

See also Anthropocene Epoch; Economics, Steady State; Education, Higher; Local Solutions to Global Problems; Progress; Values

FURTHER READING
Big History Project. (2011). Homepage. Retrieved July 26, 2012, from www.bighistoryproject.com
Christian, David. (2004). *Maps of time: An introduction to big history.* Berkeley and Los Angeles: University of California Press.
Crutzen, Paul J. (2002). Geology of mankind: The Anthropocene. *Nature, 415,* 23.

Integrated History and Future of People on Earth (IHOPE). (n.d.). Homepage. Retrieved May 29, 2012, from http://www.nceas.ucsb.edu/featured/costanza

International Big History Association (IBHA). (n.d.). Homepage. Retrieved May 18, 2012, from www.ibhanet.org

Rodrigue, Barry H. (2011). The evolution of macro-history in the United States. In Leonid E. Grinin, Andrey V. Korotayev & Barry H. Rodrigue (Eds.), *Evolution: A big history perspective* (pp. 71–81). Volgograd, Russia: Uchitel Publishing House.

Rockström, Johan. (2009, September 24). A safe operating space for humanity. *Nature, 461,* 472–475.

Ruddiman, William F. (2005). *Plows, plagues, and petroleum: How humans took control of climate.* Princeton, NJ: Princeton University Press.

Steffen, Will. (2011). A truly complex and diabolical policy problem. In John S. Dryzek, Richard B. Norgaard & David Schlosberg (Eds.), *The Oxford handbook of climate change and society* (pp. 21–37). Oxford, UK: Oxford University Press.

Steffen, Will; Crutzen, Paul J.; & McNeill, John R. (2007). The Anthropocene: Are humans now overwhelming the great forces of nature? *AMBIO, 36*(8), 614–621.

United Nations Framework Convention on Climate Change (UNFCCC). (2011). Establishment of an ad hoc working group on the Durban Platform for Enhanced Action. Retrieved May 18, 2012, from http://unfccc.int/files/meetings/durban_nov_2011/decisions/application/pdf/cop17_durbanplatform.pdf

Collective Learning

Collective learning is the ability to share information so efficiently that the ideas of individuals can be stored within the collective memory of communities and can accumulate through generations. The appearance of a species capable of collective learning marks a tipping point in the history of the biosphere, after which the very rules of change begin to change. Humans are the only species capable of sharing information with such efficiency that cultural change begins to swamp genetic change. Collective learning counts as a defining feature of our species, because it explains our astonishing technological precocity and the dominant, and perhaps dangerous, role we play in the biosphere.

The term *collective learning* is used here for an idea that appears under different names in different disciplines (Christian 2004, 2010). Near synonyms include *culture* or *social learning* (Richerson and Boyd 2005). Although their meanings overlap, there are subtle but important differences between these terms. *Collective learning* is defined here as the ability of a species to share information so efficiently and so precisely that learning takes place not just at the level of the individual, but also at the level of the community and the species.

The human species has crossed a fundamental tipping point in communicative efficiency, so that information can keep accumulating without any apparent limits at the level of the whole species. Already by the eighteenth century, the Scottish philosopher Adam Ferguson had grasped the importance of our capacity for collective learning: "In other classes of animals, the individual advances from infancy to age or maturity; and he attains, in the compass of a single life, to all the perfection his nature can reach: but, in the human kind, the species has a progress as well

as the individual; they build in every subsequent age on foundations formerly laid" (Ferguson 1767, sec. 1).

Why Is Collective Learning Important?

Properly understood, collective learning is an idea of profound importance because it helps explain what makes our species, *Homo sapiens*, unique in the history of the biosphere. Collective learning explains why we are the only species in almost 4 billion years to have a history of long-term change. It explains the distinctive nature of change in human history as the idea of natural selection explains the distinctive forms of change we see in biological history. The idea of collective learning helps explain the remarkable and terrifying power we wield today, and why to many scholars human activities seem to threaten humanity and perhaps much of the biosphere. As the Dutch climatologist Paul Crutzen has argued, we now have become so powerful that, for better or worse, we are the dominant force for change in the biosphere, a species capable of transforming the climate, the oceans, the rivers, and the landscapes of an entire planet. That is why he argues that we have entered a new geological era: the "Anthropocene," or the era dominated by human beings (Crutzen 2002; Steffen, Crutzen, and McNeill 2008).

Like natural selection, the idea of collective learning may seem simple, but it, too, contains important and subtle nuances.

First, the adjective *collective* is important. There are limits to what an isolated individual can learn, whether the individual is a human or a member of any other intelligent species. Human brains are indeed larger than those of our closest relatives, chimpanzees. But the roughly threefold difference in brain capacity is not enough to account for the much greater differences between the cumulative, diverse, and highly changeable historical trajectory of *Homo sapiens* and the relatively stable historical trajectories of all other species. Nor have humans gotten any brainier. We have no evidence that individuals today can store more information in their brains than our Paleolithic ancestors could, even if we may be better at accessing the vast stores of information that exist outside our individual brains. What distinguishes us from all other species is that we can share information rapidly, efficiently, and precisely, creating a large and growing stock of information that we share collectively. In principle, this stock of information can grow without limit. As the Canadian psychologist Merlin Donald puts it, "The key to understanding the human intellect is not so much the design of the individual brain as the synergy of many brains" (Donald 2001, xiii).

The second important nuance is contained in the notion of a "threshold" or "tipping point" in communicative efficiency. In a limited sense, many species are capable of collective learning. They have languages and can share information, so they can be said to have "cultures." Primatologists know that different communities of primates vary slightly in their technologies and behaviors. Some chimp communities, for example, use sticks to extract termites from termite mounds, in a practice known to primatologists as "termiting," and it seems clear that young chimps learn these culturally specific behaviors from their elders (Goodall 1990). So it makes sense to talk of different communities having different cultures and to presume the existence among many primates of some form of social learning.

But the notion of social learning blurs a critical distinction. Some information does indeed circulate within the collective memory of primate communities and other intelligent species, but it circulates so inefficiently, so slowly, and with so many leaks that gains are eventually canceled by losses. That is why the behaviors of other intelligent species do not appear to change in fundamental ways on scales of centuries or millennia. We have no evidence that chimp technologies have improved significantly over time. Nor is there any evidence of sustained accumulation of cultural or technological information in any species apart from ourselves. Indeed, if there had

been such a species, its existence surely would show up in evidence that the species had expanded its range and transformed its environment.

In what follows, the phrase *social learning* refers to cultural sharing in general, and the word *culture* refers to the products of that sharing. The phrase *collective learning* is confined to social learning that operates so powerfully that learning begins to accumulate without clear limits. Defined in this way, collective learning is unique to our species and should be considered as a defining feature of *Homo sapiens*.

In short, collective learning is social learning that has crossed a tipping point beyond which culture does not merely exist; it evolves, changes, and gains increasing power. The tipping point can be found where new and more powerful forms of communication emerge, allowing such efficient sharing of information that more information accumulates in the collective memory than is lost through misunderstanding, forgetfulness, "leakiness," or simple chaos. The difference between either side of the threshold may seem small, a matter, perhaps, of minor rearrangements in the brain. Perhaps, as the US linguist Noam Chomsky suggests, it is grammar that explains the critical increment in efficiency. Or, as the US anthropologist Terrence Deacon has argued, it may have been the ability to use language symbolically (Deacon 1997). However we explain it, the crossing of this threshold in communicative efficiency was an event of profound significance in the history of our planet. It is what physicists might describe as a "phase change": a small change in some parameter that proves transformative. Imagine water flowing into a tub and out through a drain. For a time, the water level will remain steady, but if the flow increases, there will come a tipping point when water begins to flow in faster than it flows out. Suddenly, the water level will start to rise, and it will keep rising, without clear limits, as long as the high flow is maintained. Where previously there was stasis, now there is change. The difference, though small, is transformative.

There are powerful reasons for thinking that our species may be the first in the history of the biosphere to have crossed this important threshold. Once a species begins accumulating cultural information, there is no limit to the process, so in principle, information can accumulate until such a species acquires powers that are dangerous both to itself and to its environment. Eventually, such a species will start transforming its home planet. This is why the notion of collective learning may have much to tell us about the Anthropocene era.

Species of such power should show up in the archaeological record, as our species certainly will, on scales of millions or even hundreds of millions of years (Zalasiewicz 2009). Yet we have no evidence that such a species has ever existed before us. Furthermore, as we move back a few hundred million years in paleontological time, the size of the largest brains diminishes and the likelihood of such a species having existed fades to nothing. So there are good reasons to think that we are the first species capable of collective learning in the 4-billion-year history of Earth.

The existence of a threshold also suggests that at any one time there is likely to be only one such species on the planet. This is because collective learning unleashes mechanisms of change so much faster than those of natural selection that they will close off all opportunities for other species to evolve down similar pathways. This is apparent in today's world, in which human numbers are rapidly increasing, while our closest relatives, some of the most intelligent species on the planet, are close to extinction. The ecological principle of "competitive exclusion" explains why two nearly identical species can never share the same niche; in a zero-sum competition, tiny differences ensure that one species will drive out the other. So it explains why, even if Neanderthals crossed the same linguistic threshold as our ancestors, and at about the same time, only one of these species was likely to survive, particularly as both species may have been expanding the niches they occupied. Our propensity to keep widening our niche may also explain why we seem to have driven so many other species to extinction, beginning with our closest relatives.

The idea of collective learning helps explain why we are unique on scales of billions of years, and why humans alone have a history of sustained, long-term change. It also explains the technological precocity that has created the world of the Anthropocene and that may be threatening the sustainability of the biosphere as a whole.

Collective Learning and the Trajectory of Human History

This discussion may seem to imply that collective learning has generated a steady trickle of cultural and technological change throughout human history. But of course that is not quite right. The pace and nature of change has varied enormously in different eras of human history and in different environments. On occasion, after wars, or natural or ecological or epidemiological disasters, there also have been periods of regression, when information was lost faster than it was found, even if the long trend has undoubtedly been toward sustained and accelerating cultural accumulation.

So how does collective learning work in detail? How has it shaped human history in different eras and different environments? Why are cultural and technological changes so fast today; and why were they so slow in the Paleolithic era? As such questions suggest, the idea of collective learning can generate some rich historical research agendas. The following sections sketch some of the more important principles that explain why collective learning operates in different ways and with differing effects in different environments.

Feedback Cycles and Accelerating Change

Perhaps the most important general principle about the workings of collective learning is that it generates many positive feedback loops. Collective learning feeds on itself. An obvious example is when new technologies, such as writing, printing, or the Internet, improve the efficiency of information sharing and storage, so as to increase the power of collective learning in general. Multiple feedback loops explain why the long trends in human history, whether of population growth, control of biospheric resources, or cultural accumulation, have accelerated over the course of human history, culminating in the frenetic changes of today. To understand how these feedback mechanisms work, it may help to begin by describing how collective learning worked in the relatively simple communities of our Paleolithic ancestors.

Collective Learning in Paleolithic Societies

The archaeological record shows that, by modern standards, change was glacially slow in the Paleolithic era. Most anthropologists agree that our species appeared between 100,000 and 200,000 years ago (Scarre 2005). If collective learning is what makes our species so distinctive, it makes sense to equate the origin of our species with the beginning of collective learning. But identifying the earliest evidence of collective learning is difficult. Human communities were small, and if technologies were accumulating, they did so slowly—so slowly that change may be almost undetectable from the available archaeological evidence. Signs of growing technological diversity might be one indication that local cultural accumulation was driving different communities along divergent cultural pathways, but detecting such diversity is difficult. If collective learning depends, however, on improved forms of communication, then it may be worth looking for evidence of new, perhaps symbolic, forms of communication. That makes early evidence of symbolic activities, such as the use of ocher (an iron ore used as a pigment, presumably to paint bodies or objects), highly significant (McBrearty and Brooks 2000). The US anthropologists Sally McBrearty and Alison Brooks offer tentative evidence both for technological innovation such as hafting (or adding a handle to a tool or weapon) and symbolic activity (such as the use of ocher) from African sites that are 200,000 years old. By 100,000 years ago, evidence of both kinds is more common and more reliable. Sites such as Blombos cave in South Africa, which dates to almost 100,000 years ago, make it all but certain that by then collective learning was under way and generating considerable cultural and technological creativity.

But of course, cultural accumulation would have been slow in the small and relatively homogenous communities of the Paleolithic. In foraging communities, ideas were exchanged by small groups with broadly similar experiences. Their size and homogeneity limited possibilities for interesting cultural synergies. This may explain the slow pace of change in the Paleolithic era. Nevertheless, even in this period change was extremely rapid compared to the biological realm, where change is driven by genetic rather than cultural evolution. Only in comparison with today's world does technological change appear slow in the Paleolithic era of human history. The piecemeal migrations that took modern humans to all continents apart from Antarctica by 15,000 years ago depended on constant innovation, as communities learned how to exploit new environments and new plant and animal species and to deal with extreme climatic conditions, such as those of northern and eastern Siberia. (See figure 1 below.)

Figure 1. Behavioral Innovations of the Middle Stone Age in Africa

Images		
Beads		
Microliths		
Notational Pieces (incised)*		
Mining		
Barbed Points		
Bone Tools		
Fishing		
Long Distance Exchange		
Shellfishing		
Points		
Pigment Processing		
Grindstones		
Blades		

Thousand years ago 20 30 40 50 80 70 80 90 100 110 120 130 140 150 160 170 180 190 200 210 220 230 240 250 260 270 280

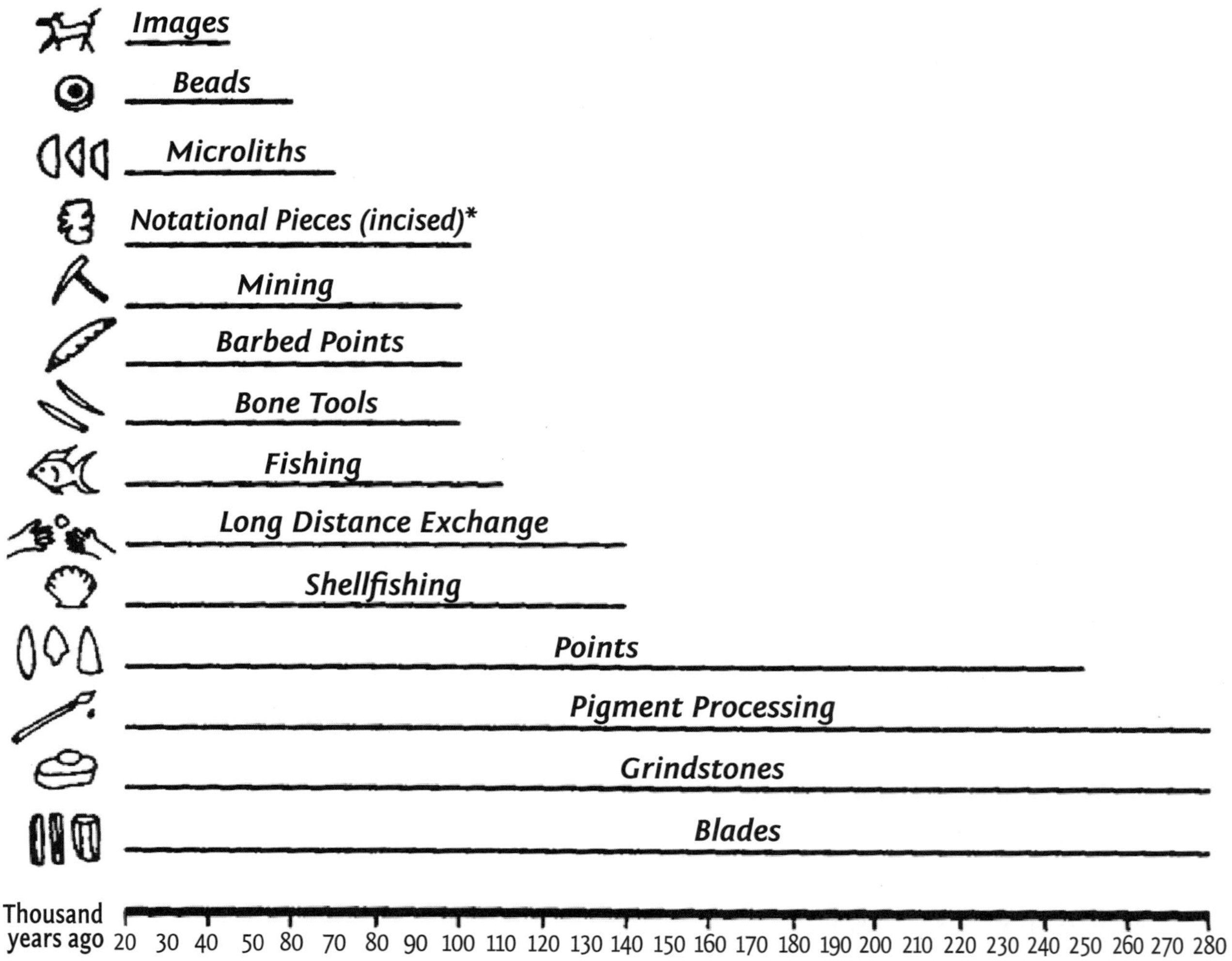

Source: McBrearty and Brooks (2000, 530).

*Note: "Notational pieces (incised)" refers to carved pieces of bone, stone, and red ocher.

Figure 1 shows the evolution of various implements and other innovations throughout the Middle Stone Age in African history, from the development of blades (c. 160,000 years ago) to the relatively recent appearance of images (c. 20,000 years ago).

Agriculture and Collective Learning

Agriculture, which appeared about 11,000 years ago, transformed the workings of collective learning and generated powerful new synergies. Agriculture consisted of a suite of technologies that diverted more of the products of photosynthesis toward our own species by altering environments in order to eliminate species we cannot use ("pests" or "weeds") and to favor the growth of species we can use ("domesticates"). As a result, humans began to commandeer more and more of the energy and resources of the biosphere, and human populations (and those of their domesticates) began to increase. (See figure 2 below.)

The new synergies were powerful. Larger communities meant more people sharing more information. The impact of greater numbers was not just additive; it was exponential. The mathematics is simple. In a group of three people, three distinct links are possible, but in a group of four, six links are possible, in a group of ten, forty five links are possible, and in general, the number of possible links in a group of n people is proportional not to n but to $n \times (n - 1)/2$. (With large numbers, this is close to half of n^2.) More people does not just mean more information sharing, but *lots* more sharing. Population increase alone thus multiplied the potential synergy of collective learning in agricultural societies.

Agricultural communities were also more diverse than foraging communities because surpluses began to support nonfarming groups, encouraging a growing division of both labor and knowledge. Specialization distilled and concentrated expert knowledge in different sectors of society, filing it within distinct groups. This

Figure 2. Human Population Growth since 100,000 Years before Present (in millions)

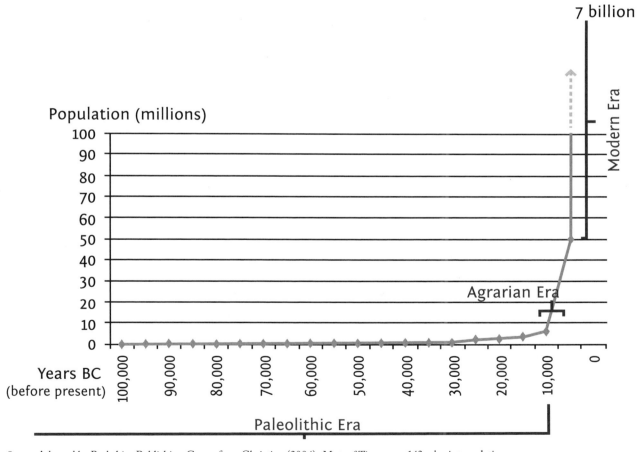

Source: Adapted by Berkshire Publishing Group from Christian (2004), *Maps of Time*, page 143, plus interpolation.

Note: The human population has increased from 6.3 billion to 7 billion since the publication of the original figure in 2004.

There has been a sharp spike in the global population since around 11,000 years ago, when the spread of agriculture diverted more of the products of photosynthesis toward our own species. The use of agriculture alters environments in order to eliminate species we cannot use (so-called weeds) and favors the growth of species we can use (e.g., wheat or tomatoes). The population continues to rise, passing 7 billion people in early 2012.

process significantly increased the total stock of available information. Markets also encouraged exchanges of goods and information between scattered communities. In all these ways, agriculture created new synergies and new feedback mechanisms within expanding networks of collective learning.

For all these reasons, it should be no surprise to find that the pace of technological change accelerated after the appearance of agriculture. Accelerating technological change increased human control over the resources of the biosphere, which encouraged further population growth, creating a new feedback loop of extraordinary power. As it spread, agriculture generated larger and more diverse communities, which stimulated technological change, which allowed the emergence of even larger and more diverse communities over several thousand years. The impact of these feedback loops is apparent from any attempt to calculate human population growth over thousands of years.

Increasingly diverse communities and a division of labor and knowledge also made for more complex social structures and ensured that different groups would have differential access to information. As a general rule, those best connected within networks of information exchange were those with the greatest power. They were, in the familiar cliché, "better connected." Traders, city dwellers, and elite groups tended to be better connected than peasants and that meant they had better access to the information filed away within particular specialist groups. This emerging hierarchy of connectedness and access to information may help explain the development of hierarchies of power, prestige, and wealth within agrarian societies.

Networks of collective learning share important properties with networks in general. Since the middle of the twentieth century, mathematicians, economists, computer programmers, biochemists, and specialists in many other fields have realized that networks are ubiquitous, and they share common features, whether they consist of reactions within a living cell or servers on the Internet. Networks are much more than the sum of their parts; they are active forces, and their topologies and evolutionary rules shape how they work.

Networks have two main components: points and links. Mathematicians call the points *nodes* and the links *edges*, while they commonly refer to entire networks as *graphs*. One of the most important properties of networks is that variations in the connectedness of different nodes may affect the efficiency with which the entire network is connected. If most nodes are connected only to close neighbors, there are many "degrees of separation," so that getting from one random node to another can take a long time. (This is surely a plausible description of a world of small peasant communities.) But add a few random long-distance connections, perhaps a few itinerant peddlers or migratory workers, and then add markets, cities, and rulers, and suddenly everything changes. Now the best-connected nodes create information peaks from which information can move more efficiently to other parts of the network. Then, as the US physicist Mark Newman and the Australian physicist Duncan Watts have shown, the network seems to shrink as the number of steps between any two nodes is suddenly reduced.

> Let's say we have a population of 1,000 people with 10 friends each and no "random" friends. That is, everyone's friends are drawn only from a strictly defined social circle. Then the average degree of separation is 50; in other words, on average it will take 50 hops to get from one randomly selected person to another. But if we now say that 25 percent of everyone's friends are random, that is, drawn from outside their normal social circle, then the average degree of separation drops dramatically to 3.6. (Beinhocker 2007, 146)

These general principles suggest that the diverse and hierarchical structures of complex societies must have greatly enhanced the synergies of collective learning.

Collective Learning in Agrarian Civilizations

Agrarian civilizations magnified the power and scope of collective learning in many ways. Cities developed trading links reaching over hundreds or even thousands of miles. Eventually, those links extended beyond the borders of particular regions until, by 4,000 years ago, Eurasian networks of exchange began to span the entire continent, sharing technologies such as horse riding and bronze making and goods such as silk and jade (Christian 2000). As links of various kinds developed over larger and larger distances, the number and diversity of information exchanges increased until, 800 years ago, there emerged in the Mongol Empire, a polity reaching from Korea to the Mediterranean.

Similar changes also occurred in other parts of the world, but at different speeds. In Australia, there were no agricultural communities when European colonizers arrived in the eighteenth century. Nevertheless, there was plenty of cultural and technological change, and change was accelerating in recent millennia in ways that are reminiscent of the "affluent foragers" that lived in southwest Asia in the Fertile Crescent, just before the appearance of agriculture. Populations increased in favored regions, some groups became more sedentary, and new technologies appeared.

In the Americas, agriculture appeared several thousand years later than in the core agrarian regions of

Afro-Eurasia, but it generated similar changes. Despite the lack of any clear links with Afro-Eurasia, farming communities, cities, states, writing systems, monumental architecture, and extensive networks of exchange appeared. But with smaller populations and fewer metropolitan centers than in Afro-Eurasia, networks of exchange in the Americas were smaller and less diverse, and collective learning operated less powerfully. For example, there is little evidence of significant links between the major agrarian civilizations of Mesoamerica and the Andes. When the Americas and Afro-Eurasia came into contact after 1492, these differences mattered. The technologies of metallurgy and gunpowder making and horse riding, which had not evolved in the more limited networks of the Americas, gave European invaders significant military advantages. Even more important were the epidemiological networks through which diseases, like information, had been exchanged in Afro-Eurasia over large areas. Afro-European colonizers brought to the Americas hardened immune systems, while Americans, whose exchange networks had exposed them to fewer diseases, succumbed in millions to Afro-Eurasian diseases, such as smallpox.

So it really did matter if collective learning operated within large, populous, diverse, and dynamic networks or within networks that were smaller and less varied. These differences had a profound impact on the pace and nature of change in different regions and different eras.

Collective Learning and the Modern World

The linking of local networks into a single global system of information exchange in recent centuries has created larger, more diverse, and more efficient networks of exchange than ever before in human history. Their evolution may help explain the extraordinary acceleration in the pace of change in the modern era, as crops, livestock, and commodities began to travel across the entire world, along with new technologies such as the trilogy of gunpowder, paper, and the compass, inherited by European societies from China. For a time, European societies, which sat at the center of the first global networks of exchange, benefited disproportionately from these global flows of information and ideas. Since 1800, railways, steamships, the telegraph, the telephone, the radio, automobiles, air travel, and the Internet have magnified the efficiency and power of modern networks of collective learning by many orders of magnitude.

Today, highly efficient global networks of collective learning are generating a tsunami of new information that threatens to overwhelm us while it accelerates change in general. The astonishing power of modern networks helps explain the rapid increase in the ecological power of our species during the last two centuries and the fact that our species has sharply increased its control over the resources and the energy of the biosphere, particularly since learning how to exploit the energy of fossil fuels. Not surprisingly, as our species has commandeered more resources, more energy, and more ecological space, other species have suffered.

Collective Learning and the Future

The idea of collective learning can help us make sense of the large trajectories of human history, with their many accelerating trends. Indeed, the idea of collective learning is so powerful that it has something of the power of a paradigm, in the sense made famous by the US historian of science Thomas Kuhn (1970). That is to say, it has the potential to help coordinate the research of scholars working in many different humanities disciplines.

Can the idea of collective learning also help us think more clearly about the future? If the ideas described above are correct, they suggest that our astonishing technological precocity arises from our very nature as a species. Something like today's Anthropocene era was predictable as soon as the first humans crossed the threshold in communicative efficiency that switched on the engine of collective learning. Although many different factors may have shaped the timing, pace, and geography of change, the general—and accelerating—trend of collective learning can be traced all the way back to our species' origins. As a species, we cannot help being creative and innovative, even if some of our innovations, such as the increasing use of fossil fuels or the creation of nuclear weapons, may pose grave threats to our future. The challenges we face today are no accident of history.

This may seem a pessimistic conclusion, suggesting that the dangers of today's world are inherent in our nature as a species and that we are, therefore, doomed to self-destruction. But the notion of collective learning also points to more optimistic conclusions. If the dangers and challenges of today's world are products of our capacity to learn collectively, so too is our ability to find and implement appropriate solutions. Rather than winding back the technological clock, we will need to *use* our creativity in more disciplined ways in the future, to develop technologies that are more sustainable, to build political and social relationships that enhance global collaboration and collective learning, and to redefine our understanding of a good life and a good society in ways that allow a more durable relationship with the biosphere as a whole. These are all tasks that will depend on exploiting to the full the powerful synergies we see in today's interconnected world, in which 7 billion individuals are linked, more or less in real time, within a single global network of collective learning.

Our collective intellectual power as a species is surely increasing as fast as the scale of the military, ecological, and resource problems that we face. Far from disowning our remarkable creativity, we need to direct it in new ways. This conclusion suggests the profound importance of education, of communications, of science, of effective collaboration—in short, of all the skills humans will need to fully exploit our remarkable capacity for collective learning.

David Christian

Macquarie University; WCU Professor,
Ewha Womans University, Seoul

See also Agricultural Innovation; Anthropocene Epoch; Community; Education, Higher; Global Trade; Local Solutions to Global Problems; Migration; Progress

FURTHER READING

Barabasi, Albert-Laszlo. (2002). *Linked: The new science of networks.* Cambridge, MA: Perseus Publishing.

Beinhocker, Eric. (2007). *The origin of wealth.* Boston: Harvard Business School Press.

Christian, David. (2000). Silk roads or steppe roads? The silk roads in world history. *Journal of World History, 11*(1), 1–26.

Christian, David. (2004). *Maps of time: An introduction to big history.* Berkeley & Los Angeles: University of California Press.

Christian, David. (2010). The return of universal history. *History and Theory, 49,* 5–26.

Crutzen, Paul. (2002). The Anthropocene. *Nature, 415,* 23.

Deacon, Terrence W. (1997). *The symbolic species: The co-evolution of language and the brain.* Harmondsworth, UK: Penguin.

Donald, Merlin. (2001). *A mind so rare: The evolution of human consciousness.* New York & London: W. W. Norton & Co.

Ferguson, Adam. (1767). An essay on the history of civil society. Retrieved January 18, 2012, from http://socserv.mcmaster.ca/econ/ugcm/3113/ferguson/civil1

Goodall, Jane. (1990). *Through a window: My thirty years with the chimpanzees of Gombe.* Boston: Houghton Mifflin.

Kuhn, Thomas S. (1970). *The structure of scientific revolutions* (2nd ed.). Chicago: University of Chicago Press.

McBrearty, Sally, & Brooks, Alison S. (2000). The revolution that wasn't: A new interpretation of the origin of modern human behavior. *Journal of Human Evolution, 39*(5), 453–563.

Richerson, Peter J., & Boyd, Robert. (2005). *Not by genes alone: How culture transformed human evolution.* Chicago & London: University of Chicago Press.

Scarre, Chris. (Ed.). (2005). *The human past: World prehistory and the development of human societies.* London: Thames and Hudson.

Steffen, Will; Crutzen, Paul J.; & McNeill, John R. (2008). The Anthropocene: Are humans now overwhelming the great forces of nature? *Ambio, 36*(8), 614–621.

Swain, Tony. (1993). *A place for strangers: Towards a history of Australian Aboriginal being,* Cambridge, UK: Cambridge University Press.

Zalasiewicz, Jan. (2009). *The Earth after us: What legacy will humans leave in the rocks?* Oxford, UK: Oxford University Press.

Community

Almost everyone is in favor of "community" as a con-cept, even when their activities tend to damage or diminish it in reality. The belief that community is essential to sustainability is also enduring, even though over recent decades, television, the Internet, social mobility, and globalization have almost completely changed traditional notions of community life. While the idea of "living locally" gained prominence at the beginning of the twenty-first century, more effort is needed to develop a modern, global replacement for the traditional forms of real-life community. Three aspects of community are particularly important to our think-ing about a sustainable future: social cooperation; small-scale resource management and production; and human connection as a source of happiness and well-being.

The instinct to create community is so powerful that humans can create communities under even the most adverse conditions, such as prisons or labor camps. Some would argue that the various environmental challenges that the planet faces count as such an "adverse condition," and that the need for community to counter these chal-lenges is therefore more urgent than ever. Ironically, this burgeoning need comes at a time when real community is in danger of becoming a thing of the past.

Community is directly relevant to sustainability in several ways: close personal ties create practical options for sustainable living; a sense of community provides per-sonal satisfactions that can make a less resource-intensive way of life more attractive; online connections can be powerful tools for influencing government and business, as well as for sharing information and supporting people's efforts to adopt practices that are less polluting or resource-intensive.

There is a huge body of research on what community is and how membership in communities is essential to individual health and happiness as well as the health of human society, but there are diametrically opposed views about the relative value of online and face-to-face com-munities, and debate about how to balance an urban future with the focus on self-sufficient, rural communi-ties that has long been part of environmentalists' vision of "the good life."

The Evolution of Communities

The modern study of community generally dates back to the work of German sociologist Ferdinand Tönnies (1855–1936) and the French sociologist Émile Durkheim (1858–1917), who examined the social changes brought about by the Industrial Revolution, setting forth the basic dichotomy between community (*Gemeinschaft*)—the traditional, warm, intimate village community—and society (*Gesellschaft*)—the colder, more perfunctory con-nections of industrial urban society. This trend continued and accelerated, with the development of new technolo-gies, and forms of communication and transportation. In the twenty-first century, for the first time in human his-tory, people in the urban, developed world can (and often do) manage to live without cordial relations with their neighbors. A whole panoply of modern institutions make it possible to earn a living among people with whom one does not live and to secure essential services by paying fees to other strangers or specialist acquaintances who can be replaced, if necessary, by strangers—something that would have been inconceivable until quite recently in human history.

Communities linking people who never actually meet have existed for a very long time; many individuals have had identities that allow them to claim membership of a remote or even global community. A prime example is that of Islam, a religion that quickly spread across Asia and Africa. Muslims had a strong sense of belonging to one community, the *ummah*. The sense of warmth and kinship has been supported by a remarkable similarity in rituals and the almost universal use of Arabic as the language of prayer.

Modern technologies have, of course, made such "virtual" communities much more common. Technology enables us to do things without direct human interaction if we so desire. The invention of the telephone, followed by that of television and home video players, followed by the increasingly widespread use of the Internet, all have allowed people to stay at home while still being entertained. As a result, people no longer know their neighbors as they once did, and, in the developed world in many places, it has become rare to see children playing in the street (especially without adult supervision). Informal hospitality at home is, for many, a thing of the past.

Indeed, online social networking platforms allow us to "connect" to far more people (even strangers) than was possible before, and we have an endless variety of ways to reach out to people we know or know slightly, and even to strangers. There has been a steep decline in the number of confidants that people say they talk to about important personal matters, however, and those who do depend on online communities exhibit a surprisingly high level of depression and loneliness. Research on the psychological and cognitive effects of exclusively online interaction is in its early days, but there is discussion in the business world of young people's inability to handle conflict and show empathy. One topic that is getting attention is the "Dunbar number" proposed by the UK anthropologist and specialist in primate behavior, Robin Dunbar: there is a limit to the real social relationships possible for human beings—150 people seems to be an agreed-on average—which has bearing on virtual communities' effectiveness at actually building community.

The First Step: Defining Community

We use the word "community" casually, and inconsistently, without the precision of similar terminology used for ecological communities and ecosystems. A more exact understanding of how human communities work is essential to planning a sustainable future. In the same way that scientists can monitor the Earth's changing climate by measuring such things as subtle changes in ice cores and tree rings around the world, the ability to measure what community *is*, and what a functioning community can *do*, is of the utmost importance to the pursuit of sustainability.

Community is famously hard to define. The workings of human community have challenged scholars and philosophers for centuries. A 1955 article by the US sociologist George A. Hillery gave ninety-four definitions of community, and summed up with this: "community consists of persons in social interaction within a geographic area and having one or more additional common ties" (1982, 15). In the twenty-first century, though, geography has ceased to be a defining characteristic of community. "Communities" are often created online, or are so widely diffused that the members' common geography might be a continent, in the case of the European Union (which had its beginnings with the European Coal and Steel Community, founded, in part, to prevent future war), or even the entire planet.

The editors of the *Encyclopedia of Community* wrote that "communities are the human webs that provide us with emotional and practical security, and a sense of continuity through shared memory. They give us a sense of purpose. They are a primary source of happiness in good times, and essential sources of support and solace during bad times" (Christensen et al. 2004, xiii). A more precise (though by no means limiting) definition is that a community is any informal, extended group of unrelated people who share common location, common heritage or beliefs, common interests, or a common purpose.

This confusion about what makes up a community is to be expected. Social and technological changes—the growth of online interaction at the expense of in-person connections, for example—are altering our ideas about, and our experience of, community. For environmentalists, the search for community presents conflicting choices. On the one hand, the idea of living and eating "locally" has become a mantra for individuals and even for corporations. On the other hand, global environmental problems—including but not limited to climate change—require us to act globally, and even those who lead major environmental organizations often do massive amounts of traveling and often lack local community ties. Some argue that the lack of a sense of community is why it remains so difficult to get individuals and nations to make changes even when they acknowledge that the way things are being done results in environmental damage. This raises the question: is the global community of all humans simply too large to generate strong feelings of membership?

The global community has made the pursuit of community infinitely more complicated than it was in the past. Traditional communities were highly practical. They evolved to meet economic and security needs as well as to provide social and emotional support. One of the challenges for community builders today is that these aspects of life have become compartmentalized. Trying to promote sustainability programs when the participants have no other enduring economic or social ties can be difficult because "sustainability" is not simply an interest or hobby around which a loose association can be formed.

The Next Step: Restoring Community

A renewed sense of community—whatever that looks like—is part of every scenario for a sustainable future. While not everyone espousing sustainability agrees that "degrowth" (a reduction in consumption by people in developed countries) is essential—indeed, degrowth cuts against the grain of the entire capitalist system as we currently understand it—many talk about a world in which progress is no longer measured by economic or gross domestic product (GDP) growth, but by levels of well-being and happiness, and by the well-being of the natural world.

The word community is also employed in the fields of ecology and ecosystem management. This article focuses on human communities, with the understanding that they are part of larger ecological communities—or ecosystems—whether they are rural, suburban, or urban areas. Environmental science has some useful concepts to add to our understanding of community. Foremost is the concept of "resilience," which is how much change or disturbance an ecosystem (or a human community) can tolerate. Sometimes "small changes to a system may have disproportionately large consequences, and vice versa" (Allen, Garmestani, and Sundstrom 2011).

Human communities can also experience what ecologists call "regime shifts": large-scale, sudden, and enduring changes in the structure and function of a natural system. A "failed state" is one example of a regime shift in human systems, at the national scale. Rural ghost towns, with only a handful of elderly residents remaining, and crime-ridden urban neighborhoods are two local-level examples. Sustainability is virtually impossible within communities that are experiencing social breakdown of this kind.

In thinking of community, it may be useful to think of topsoil, the foundation of life on Earth. Topsoil is what plants need to flourish and flower, and all forms of terrestrial life depend on it. Community is the topsoil in which we human beings grow and flourish. Community, like topsoil, is a complex, living system in which old and new become inextricably mixed; both need constant replenishing as well as time to develop.

And the problem with community is the same as that faced by those whose work is restoring natural ecosystems. An ecosystem may be, says evolutionary biologist Olivia Judson (2009), "a Humpty Dumpty community: if it disintegrates, you cannot rebuild it from its parts. In other words, the ability to reconstitute the community depends on species that are no longer there."

This is why community building is so difficult. Like topsoil, it is made up of myriad parts. The loss of one or two keystone species may make it impossible to revive, leaving behind the community equivalent of a Dust Bowl, bereft of topsoil.

But community building may be a bit easier than, say, prairie restoration, a painstaking process that takes years. We can take advantage of our species' capacity to react quickly and its exceptional adaptability to make social repairs in relatively short periods of time, once the dynamics of a particular place and people have been understood.

Three Key Aspects of Community

While we are busy figuring out what, exactly, community is, and how we can restore lost communities, it is important to keep goals in mind so that we are aware of our aim. Three aspects of community are particularly important to our thinking about a sustainable future: social cooperation, what is called "bridging social capital"; practical matters vital to the environment; and happiness and well-being.

Bridging Social Capital

First, the creation of what is known as "bridging" social capital is required to obtain the agreement and cooperation of large numbers of people who have different priorities and points of view. To make changes at the local, regional, national, and international levels, environmentalists need ways to promote a sense of a collective vision and awareness that all humans share a common future. Particularly important is the need for environmentalists to be able to communicate with people outside of their own community so that they are not "preaching to the choir." Social capital is a way to describe the value gained from interpersonal relationships, such as business contacts, and friendships. Bridging social capital is developed between people who do not naturally share a close affinity with one another; bonding social capital is a way to describe warmer, more intimate connections.

This is vitally important because human beings' relationships with one another have profound and long lasting consequences for the biosphere (i.e., the relatively thin part of the Earth's crust that supports life). War, for example—the opposite of building social capital—produces devastating effects on the environment. Many of the international disputes we see, and the lack of consensus on how to respond to climate change, emanate from different understandings of mutual responsibility, which makes any discussion of community—and our mutual rights and responsibilities—so important. Individual rights and self-fulfillment are central to modern ideas about what comprises an ideal society and about democratic governance, but when discussing a sustainable future we almost always talk about the importance of collective endeavor.

Cooperation: Bridging and Bonding

People today are more connected technologically, but less connected practically and emotionally than in the past. People are able, because of technology and outsourced services, to do anything and everything without help from their neighbors, whereas for most of human history our very survival depended on good relations with our neighbors. Surveys show that a majority of us do not even know our neighbors' names or faces, let alone feel comfortable borrowing something from them or inviting them for a meal. This has been borne out by a wide variety of studies, but research on loneliness in a highly networked world has barely begun.

The Danger of Reinforcing Existing Beliefs

An even greater risk, especially for those focused on online communities, is the ease with which people associate only with those who share the same opinions, i.e., they are not bridging social capital. Technology, in fact, reinforces this. Google's algorithms, for instance, allow that, over time, the search results for someone with conservative political beliefs—say, someone who believes that climate change science is a left-wing plot—will be different from the results of the same search conducted by someone who has other beliefs (Halpern 2011). The results simply reinforce existing beliefs. Instead of broadening our thinking through access to the vast trove of information available online, we may end up more polarized than ever. In terms of human bonding this may be fine—people like to spend time with those who share their values—but it is a disastrous approach if our aim is to cooperate, and compromise, in order to solve environmental challenges.

"Social Norming"

We are social animals with an innate need to belong, and our natural tendency is to join the crowd. But we have other instincts, too. We will compete for scarce resources and protect our children and relations. Many of us also have a powerful need to compete and win. Most people want affirmation that they, as an individual, matter. All of these natural tendencies can lead to environmental degradation—as we build more and bigger buildings, buy more and bigger cars, and use material wealth to display our status and power; advertising has an enormous role to play in this. But these natural tendencies can also be used to promote behavior that has less impact on the natural environment. "Social norming" is a fancy way of saying that people are affected by the behavior of those around them and that attitude can be used to considerable effect. As an example, the "Don't Mess with Texas" campaign targeted young, macho Texan men and was tremendously helpful in getting people in Texas to stop littering in that state.

While social norming uses information to encourage positive behaviors, "nudges" (a term common in behavioral economics and sociology) influence behavior by offering things differently: for instance, the option to ride a bicycle or take public transport rather than taking a car. Energy companies, for example, now report how your electricity use compares to that of your neighbors. This takes advantage of the human desire to conform—and might set up some desirable competition, too.

Real-Life Environmental Matters: Including Localism

The second key aspect of community building is that community has bearing on real-life environmental matters. Traditional, real-life, face-to-face, place-based communities and virtual communities are both enabled by modern telecommunications, and have become essential to sustainability. While membership in a national or international environmental organization or participation in an email list is not sufficient, neither is the idea that we should all live in small rural communities realistic. A sustainable future requires us to balance the rural ideal with urban reality (or the urban ideal with the rural reality, if that is the case), and to restructure the suburban in-between.

Living Lighter by Living Locally

A big part of this second aspect, the "real-life" value of community, is the idea of localism. The words "local" and "sustainable" are often paired up in advertisements and marketing campaigns; and "local" is now used on nationally distributed products because, especially since the worldwide economic downturn of 2008, the term has come to have such desirable connotations. The idea that locally produced goods are desirable from an environmental standpoint has a much longer history, and this is closely linked with the idea that small communities producing their own food and energy offer the most desirable way to live. Whether these small communities can be sustained in the long term is a matter of debate. The US evolutionist David Sloan Wilson, for example, argues that cultural evolution works at the group level as well as at the individual level. In the same way that species evolve over time, with some surviving and some not, "sustainable communities" are those that will survive selection pressures over time.

The Worldwatch report, *State of the World 2012*, connects living locally with "degrowth":

> By realigning economic priorities, the degrowth movement seeks to improve individual well-being, strengthen community resilience, and restore the planet's ecological systems. Reducing overall consumption is a primary way to achieve degrowth. This involves shrinking home sizes, living in walkable and bikeable neighborhoods, eating less and lower on the food chain, and generally owning less stuff.

There are a wide variety of ways that "living locally" is being practiced in the twenty-first century. Community gardens have sprung up in many neighborhoods, urban and rural, in part as a defense against rising food prices, but also as a place to learn gardening tips from others and, generally, to socialize. Locally sourced food as well as other products and manufactured goods reduce transportation costs and climate change impact, may allow for more efficient recycling or the composting of waste, and can also reduce storage costs.

Energy can be generated locally, in individual homes, and in towns and regions. Stockholm has one of the lowest rates of carbon-dioxide release in the world, in part because of innovative district-wide (not individual) heating/cooling systems.

Even water supplies can be locally sourced and managed. Countries like Oman, Morocco, Algeria, Syria, Iraq, and Iran are reviving an ancient method of desert irrigation called *qanats* (underground water tunnels that bring water to the surface using only gravity), which originated some 3,000 years ago in the Achaemenid (Persian) Empire.

Happiness and the Search for the Good Life

The third key aspect of community is that it is necessary that we develop a vision for the future in which our sense of community becomes a source of happiness and well-being, not just a comfort in the event of disaster and decline. Again, this relates to an improved environment. A fully functioning community can make access to many things that are good for human health and well-being—three examples being nutritious food, good air, and exercise—more possible.

There is a significant effort underway to create a science of happiness that can translate into economic theory and economic statistics. Authors Robert and Edward Skidelsky point out, however, that "people overestimate the long-term happiness they will derive from consumption goods and underestimate the satisfactions of leisure, education, friendship and other intangibles" (2012, 106).

The search for community is closely tied to a search for what the Greeks called "the good life," a term that was used as the title of a book inspiring the 1960s "back-to-the-land" movement and as the title of a British sitcom about suburban homesteading. For the ancient Greeks, the question of how to achieve the good life (*eudaimonia*)—which included the notions of virtue as well as happiness and well-being was of great importance. The philosophy of natural law defined the good life as that which resulted from living in harmony with nature. This ideal—living in harmony with nature's limits or boundaries as well as with other human beings—is one that continues to influence environmentalists, sometimes overtly and sometimes subconsciously. The challenge, however, is converting that ideal into a program of action and implementation that will work in the real world.

This problem has always plagued intellectuals who tend to romanticize country living (more prominent in places such as Great Britain, the United States, and Russia; less so in France, where intellectuals have most commonly celebrated strictly city living). Nathaniel Hawthorne and Margaret Fuller, for example, were associated with the short-lived Brook Farm Commune in Massachusetts, which was part of a larger nineteenth century movement of intellectuals trying to make a life in the countryside. Their idea was to grow vegetables during the day and talk about poetry and ideas all evening. Unfortunately, participants found that growing vegetables all day didn't leave them much energy for pursuits of the mind.

The Importance of Place

Although humans have migrated around the planet for at least 60,000 years, most people have, until the twenty-first century, lived out their entire lives within a very small circle, a familiar place in which they were born, raised children, and died. This constancy created a powerful connection to a particular place and region, and therefore a concern about the land's ability to support future generations. This connection with place is particularly important, even today, in certain cultures. The concept of *laojia*, which has roots in China's history as an agrarian society, remains an important aspect of social identity for Chinese people, even for those overseas. A person's *laojia* isn't necessarily linked to where they grew up and went to school. The word translates as "old home" and means where a person's family came from—the ancestral village. Early Chinese immigrants to the United States would save and carefully wrap the bones of those who died there, until they could be carried back to the village for burial.

It is easy to see how "place" matters in the way we live even when we live in unfamiliar environments: humans gravitate to places that seem like home, and create new "home" places with remarkable speed. Migratory hunters and gatherers—people who might be mistaken for being "placeless"—tell stories about the places where they wander. We have favorite chairs, favorite tables, favorite spots in a park, and even favorite spots in parking lots. This need to plant ourselves and to come back to a familiar spot is in our genes, an inclination sorely tested in the modern, impersonal, transient, urban environments in which more and more people live. Creating places that meet humans' emotional and psychological needs is one of the challenges facing planners today.

City Planning

The relationship between sustainability and community can be explained in many ways, but the questions that arise are quite simple: What should we be doing to create the kind of beneficial communities that will make sustainable living possible? How can a sense of community reduce our impact on the natural world?

Social reformers and, more recently, environmentalists have seen sustainable communities as taking us closer to nature, an approach that can be seen in the US historian, sociologist, and literary critic Lewis Mumford's ecological regionalism in the 1920s; the "back to the land" ethos of the 1960s (set out most clearly by Scott and Helen Nearing, authors of *The Good Life*) and the eco-village

movement, which began in the mid-1990s; and in calls for rural smallholding and local self-sufficiency. More recently, there has been a pro-city perspective, with economists and planners (such as those associated with the "New Urbanism" movement) claiming that an urban future is also a "green" future because people who live in cities are less dependent on cars, have smaller homes, and use resources more efficiently. There is a huge body of research devoted to the question of whether urban or rural living is more inherently "sustainable," but rising urbanization is a fact of life that few people expect to change, even in the event of environmental disaster.

In addition to Lewis Mumford, another great writer on the city in the twentieth century was Jane Jacobs, a US writer and activist who eventually moved to Canada. While European "greens" admired both, Mumford's ideas, promulgated through more recent writers, have had the greatest influence on environmentalists (as well as on city planners). Jacobs was highly critical of the arrogance of those who thought they should determine how people ought to live, and while Mumford and his cohort were proponents of the "garden city" and of planned communities, Jacobs was enthusiastic about casual street life and the kind of informal village-like relationships that she believed naturally develop when people live near one another.

Planners start with ideas about how humans should be organized, and hope that a real sense of community will arise within the structures they create. Unfortunately, they often get it wrong. Parks and green spaces have gone unused. Urban renewal projects have created areas where, subsequently, crime has become rife. Planners today have specific goals for sustainability and they face the same risks of failure if they try to impose change without previously getting the support of existing communities.

City life needs to be transformed if it is to be sustainable in social and economic terms, as well as in terms of environmental impact. In some parts of the United Kingdom, for example, abandoned buildings abound, whereas in other areas there is not sufficient affordable housing stock. But people want to be where jobs exist, where there are activities of interest going on, where their friends and family live, and where they have roots. While governments (such as the Chinese and Soviet governments) may attempt to move people according to the exigencies of the government, even free people will stay in places that are dangerous and polluted because social connections take precedence, at least in the short term, over considerations of physical well-being.

Third Places

Some foresighted planners—and even well-known Seattle property developer Ron Sher—are alert to the importance of what sociologist Ray Oldenburg calls "third places," the informal places—not home and not work—where people have, throughout history, gathered to talk, joke, gossip, and play games. Third places include the village green, the town water pump, markets, teahouses and coffee shops, pubs and bars, barber shops and hairdressing salons. They are in decline all over the world but at the same time are being recreated—because they matter to us. Oldenburg, a sociologist at the University of West Florida and author of *The Great Good Place*, says that the focus of his work is conversation, something of considerable importance in social capital terms, and also a source of pleasure and comfort. The idea of comfortable surroundings that encourage human interaction is part of New Urbanism, too, and those concerned about sustainability will find many practical ideas for transforming urban, suburban, and rural environments in the work of innovative planners. For example, in *City Comforts: How to Build an Urban Village*, David Sucher puts considerable focus on making the places we live walkable.

They follow Jane Jacobs, too, in understanding that economic activity is not a negative—to be divorced from our home and social lives—and work to encourage diverse commercial enterprise. Bringing jobs closer to where people live is a way to improve quality of life and to reduce fossil fuel use, another way in which community, economics, and sustainability are entwined.

Economics and Human Behavior

Community and economics are intricately linked; much of economics deals with how communities relate, both to each other and to the rest of the world, natural and otherwise. We generally see the natural world as what is described as "public goods." There is little incentive for an individual to avoid using or polluting them, and there is much incentive to "free ride"—that is, to take advantage of anything available. A strong sense of community—whether in real life or online—can change this. The US political economist Elinor Ostrom (1933–2012) received a Nobel Prize for her research into ways in which people collaborate to protect collective goods—countering the idea that there will always be a tragedy of the commons. (The "tragedy of the commons" is the idea made famous by the US ecologist Garrett Hardin in a 1968 *Science* article of that name that individuals don't have the economic incentive to want to conserve shared resources such as fisheries, because if one person doesn't use the resource, someone else will.)

The "share" economy—services such as City Bikes, Zipcars, home exchange, and couch surfing, all of which allow people to share services with those near and far, after (it is hoped) careful vetting—is booming. It seems that access to information about other people (even though it means a loss of privacy) creates trust among strangers, creating, in the process, a new form of community.

Public Awareness vs. Inaction

Most human beings are subject to economic pressures and conscious of social status, and make choices based on convenience, personal status, and their need to belong rather than on what is best for the environment or subsequent generations. Environmentalists often are surprised and dismayed—although economists may not be—when public awareness does not lead to immediate and significant changes in behavior. For example, a survey of residents of eight Chinese cities where low-carbon education programs had been launched found that although most people were aware of the "green" programs in their city, very few people did anything about changing their personal habits to be less carbon-intensive (Zhang and Wang 2012). A study of what sociologists call "human factors"—psychological needs, physiological drives, and the human interconnections we call community—can thus help us to design better community-based approaches to sustainability.

A Norwegian study found, ironically, that people who see themselves as "green" are more likely to indulge in long-distance, carbon-intensive holidays because they feel virtuous about their everyday lifestyle choices (CICERO 2011). Similarly, improvements in fuel efficiency lead to more driving. Economic psychologists call this behavior "licensing."

Community and Individualism

There are barriers to community in modern beliefs and values, and in the current economic system. In the 1990s, a German-Israeli-US sociologist named Amitai Etzioni attracted considerable attention with his writing about the political philosophy known as "communitarianism:" his premise was that the increasing focus on the rights of individuals and on "good" as it is defined by each individual—basic to liberal democracy—had led to a diminution of our sense of responsibility for one another. This had implications for politics and was relevant to the environmental agenda at a time when NIMBYism ("not in my backyard" syndrome) was interfering with the ability of local and state governments to install renewable energy projects.

To some, the term "community" sounds too much like "communism." This has bearing when, for example, people and governments accuse the United Nations—the original community of nations—of infringing on their nation's sovereign rights. This is particularly true in the United States, where there is deep-seated distrust among many people of the UN's Agenda 21, which promotes, among other issues, energy conservation and anti-sprawl initiatives that activists consider a breach of their property rights.

Some scholars, such as the US philosopher Bryan Norton, have asserted that Western culture works against community by focusing economic theory on the individual: an economy that uses rising incomes as a measure of wellbeing works against traditional notions of community. In many modern societies, an over-emphasis on mobility (at the expense of community) means that if someone loses his or her job, another job (or one with a higher wage) may well be available somewhere else, so that person needs to move to experience that higher income and/or employment. The effect of this is shorter residence times in any one place, serial careers, and the idea that housing is a financial asset rather than a home. All of these factors clearly work against community.

The Dangers of Community and the Appeal of Disaster

All too often, the most successful efforts at community-wide change come about when there is a threat that affects everyone: war, for example, or natural disasters (earthquakes, tsunamis, hurricanes, cyclones), or some kind of pollution that not only affects health but also property values—in many cases the rich are able to insulate themselves from harm, which makes it far less likely that long-term changes will be made to promote sustainability.

Unfortunately, the communities that develop in response to a threat can be insular, and/or hostile to anyone who is outside the group, and antagonistic to anything that might impinge on the group's members even if it appears to offer benefits to the wider society. Community can be dangerous. The ultimate example of bonding social capital is that of a terrorist cell or a cult.

Nationalism and other created forms of solidarity can lead to the perception of those outside the group as dangerous, even not truly human, thus justifying behavior that would never be accepted inside the community. Communities are nested, and overlapping: any single community is part of many others, except in the case of extremists, who try to withdraw entirely from the world.

Another community-related danger facing environmentalists is the appeal of real or potential disaster. Indeed, disasters can and do lead to a renewed sense of community. Blackouts and power cuts get neighbors talking to one another and people often seem nostalgic about those periods in which they learned to help and depend on those close at hand. After the terrorist attacks in New York on 11 September 2001, politicians as well as citizens talked about the increased sense of community. The UK's prime minister, Tony Blair, gave what became known as his "power of community" speech. The social consequences of Hurricane Katrina striking the southern United States were not exclusively sinister ones such as looting (although that did occur); there were positive ones as well, detailed in Rebecca Solnit's *A Paradise Built in Hell: The Extraordinary Communities That Arise in Disaster*. Solnit also discussed the 1906 San Francisco earthquake and says that "people were for the most part calm and cheerful, and many survived the earthquake with gratitude and generosity" (2009, 15).

Popular dystopian and apocalyptic films are full of examples of communities arising during a disaster—in the face of zombie and alien invasions, for example, which often unite strangers and even people normally hostile to one another. Some environmentalists anticipated the threat of a complete computer network breakdown at Y2K—the transition from 1999 to 2000—as positive. They created a "spotty" (i.e., not full-fledged) millennial movement—which was not simply survivalist but approached those religions that hope for radical transformation through disaster.

This tendency to come together during disaster, and the implicit desire for community, can be seen in writings about peak oil and climate change: some argue that only disaster will inspire a majority of human beings to make the changes required for our global population to live sustainably. But as appealing as redemption through disaster may be, millennialism (i.e., utopianism based on the destruction of the current world) is a fatalistic approach to the future. Inasmuch as community is one of the benefits people perceive in an apocalyptic disaster, those working towards a sustainable future ought to be focusing on the myriad ways we have to build community here and now.

By doing so, both online and off-line communities can promote the kind of contentment and well-being that will moderate consumerism—thereby reducing pressure on the planet—and also find far better ways to cooperate on pressing issues such as climate change, resource equity, and population, among others.

Community and a Sustainable Future

William H. McNeill, world historian and author of the 1964 National Book Award for history winner for *The Rise of the West: A History of the Human Community*, concludes in the recent book he co-authored with his son J. R. McNeill, *The Human Web: A Bird's Eye View of World History*, that our future depends on finding new kinds of communities to replace those of the past:

> Either the gap between cities and villages will somehow be bridged by renegotiating the terms of symbiosis, and/or differently constructed primary communities will arise to counteract the tangled anonymity of urban life. Religious sects and congregations are the principal candidates for this role. But communities of belief must somehow insulate themselves from unbelievers, and that introduces frictions, or active hostilities, into the cosmopolitan web. How then sustain the web and also make room for life-sustaining primary communities?
>
> Ironically, therefore, to preserve what we have, we and our successors must change our ways by learning to live simultaneously in a cosmopolitan web and in various and diverse primary communities. How to reconcile such opposites is the capital question for our time and probably will be for a long time to come (McNeill and McNeill 2003, 326–327).

This call to live both globally and locally is the challenge of sustainability for every one of us, because our physical and psychological well-being depends on the emotional bonds we are able to form with one another. Three approaches seem particularly promising. They are not radical, and they do not pit one group against another: for example, the "1 percent" versus the "99 percent"— terms that became widely known during the recent Occupy Wall Street movement—or developed versus developing countries.

First, we need to focus on "bridging" activities that create bonds (and social capital) between people who are different from one another. This is what organized meetings of stakeholders—all who will be affected by a new development or regulation—are designed to do. Town and regional planners have a more formal process of sequential meetings and discussions, called *charettes*,

which aim to build support across social groups by bringing everyone into the planning process. Bridging social capital is created by those ordinary human activities that bring together people from different social and economic classes such as parent-teacher associations (PTAs), pick-up basketball games, block parties, and volunteer associations. Studies show that in communities where people have overlapping ties, social friction is much reduced: even if they disagree over a school issue, they play on the same softball team or go to the same church, and come to know each other in multiple dimensions and have opportunities to talk both informally and regularly. This creates the social capital that gives people an incentive to look at environmental issues from other people's points of view and to work together at finding solutions.

Second, we need to recognize that face-to-face relationships are different in essence from exclusively online connections. Sustainability is a real-world challenge, and as valuable as online communications may be, change has to take place in the physical world, and within the particular domains that human beings share. Face-to-face relationships provide satisfactions that we cannot get via cable and WiFi, and connection with the physical world—whether alone or collectively— is also a primary source of satisfaction to human beings. A sustainable future will become more likely when we find ways to get out on the sidewalks, into coffee houses, and in the woods or on the beach with other people.

Understanding community and relishing its complexities (rather than trying to reduce it to a simple formula) is going to help us find a balance between individualism and the common good.

Finally, we need to explore the ways in which community can satisfy needs and desires, offering sustainable satisfactions—and happiness. In the various efforts to redefine our measures of progress, and once certain basic and vital needs are met, most of what matters to people is generated through their relationships with others. Human health is closely linked to the quality of relationships—the sense of community—people have. By valuing our connections more, and becoming more comfortable with the give and take of today's complex, global relationships and with the differences of perspective that make life interesting, we can find common ground. "What unites us is greater than what divides us," says William H. McNeill, and our search for community will make a sustainable future possible.

Karen CHRISTENSEN
Berkshire Publishing Group

See also Aging; Buildings and Infrastructure; Cities and the Biosphere; Collective Learning; Design and

Architecture; Economics, Steady State; Local Solutions to Global Problems; Migration; Mobility; Progress; Property Rights

FURTHER READING

Alexander, Christopher, et al. (1977). *A pattern language: Towns, buildings, construction.* Oxford, UK: Oxford University Press.

Allen, Craig R.; Garmestani, Ahjond S.; & Sundstrom, Shana M. (2011). Resilience. In Robin Kundis Craig, John Copeland Nagle, Bruce Pardy, Oswald J. Schmitz, & William K. Smith (Eds.), *Berkshire encyclopedia of sustainability: Vol. 5. Ecosystem management and sustainability* (pp. 335–339). Great Barrington, MA: Berkshire Publishing Group.

Brown, Lester R. (2003). *Plan B: Rescuing a planet under stress and a civilization in trouble.* New York: W. W. Norton & Company.

Center for International Climate and Environmental Research-Oslo (CICERO). (2011). Green families not so eco-friendly after all. Retrieved December 5, 2011, from http://www.cicero.uio.no/webnews/index_e.aspx?id=11523

Christakis, Nicholas A., & Fowler, James H. (2009). *Connected: The surprising power of our social networks and how they shape our lives.* New York: Little, Brown and Company.

Christensen, Karen, et al. (Eds.). (2004). *Encyclopedia of community.* Great Barrington, MA: Berkshire Publishing Group.

Etzioni, Amitai. (2003). *Communitarianism. The spirit of community: Rights, responsibilities, and the communitarian agenda.* New York: Crown Publishing.

Grubbs, Morris Allen. (Ed.). (2007). Conversations with Wendell Berry. Jackson: University Press of Mississippi.

Halpern, Sue. (2011, June 23). Mind control & the internet. *The New York Review of Books.* Retrieved September 11, 2012, from http://www.nybooks.com/articles/archives/2011/jun/23/mind-control-and-internet/?pagination=false

Hardin, Garrett. (1968, December 13). The tragedy of the commons. *Science, 162*(3859), 1243–1248. Retrieved September 11, 2012, from http://www.cs.wright.edu/~swang/cs409/Hardin.pdf

Hillery, George A., Jr. (1982). *A research odyssey: Developing and testing a community theory.* New Brunswick, NJ: Transaction Inc.

James, Sarah, & Lahti, Torbjörn. *The Natural Step for communities: How cities and towns can change to sustainable practices.* Gabriola Island, Canada: New Society Publishers.

Judson, Olivia. (2009, August 11). Humpty Dumpty and the ghosts. *The New York Times.* Retrieved September 11, 2012, from http://opinionator.blogs.nytimes.com/2009/08/11/humpty-dumpty-and-the-ghosts/

Latouche, Serge. (2004). Degrowth economics. *Le Monde diplomatique* (English edition). Retrieved September 11, 2012, from http://mondediplo.com/2004/11/14latouche

Lax, Rick. (2012, March 2). Dunbar's Number kicked my ass in Facebook friends experiment. Retrieved September 11, 2012, from http://www.wired.com/underwire/2012/03/dunbars-number-facebook/

Luccarelli, Mark (1997). *Lewis Mumford and the ecological region: The politics of planning.* New York: Guildford Press.

Marche, Stephen. (2012, May). Is Facebook making us lonely? *The Atlantic.* Retrieved September 11, 2012, from http://www.theatlantic.com/magazine/archive/2012/05/is-facebook-making-us-lonely/308930/

McNeill, J. R., & McNeill, William H. (2003). *The human web: A bird's-eye view of world history.* New York: W. W. Norton & Company.

McNeill, William H. (1997). *Keeping together in time: Dance and drill in human history.* London: Harvard University Press.

Nearing, Scott, & Nearing, Helen. (1990). *The good life: Helen and Scott Nearing's sixty years of self-sufficient living.* New York: Schocken Books Inc.

Nordhoff, Charles. (2008). Communistic societies of the United States: Harmony, Oneida, the Shakers, and others. St. Petersburg, FL: Red and Black Publishers.

Oldenburg, Ray. (1999). *The great good place: Cafes, coffee shops, bookstores, bars, hair salons, and other hangouts at the heart of a community.* New York: Marlowe & Company.

Ostrom, Elinor. (1990). *Governing the commons: The evolution of institutions for collective action (Political economy of institutions and decisions).* Cambridge, UK: Cambridge University Press.

Putnam, Robert. *Bowling alone: The collapse and revival of American community.* New York: Simon & Schuster.

Sale, Kirkpatrick. (1980). *Human scale.* New York: Coward, McCann & Geoghegan.

Skidelsky, Robert, & Skidelsky, Edward. (2012). *How much is enough? Money and the good life.* New York: Other Press.

Solnit, Rebecca. (2009). *A paradise built in hell: The extraordinary communities that arise in disaster.* New York: Penguin Books.

Sucher, David. (2003). *City comforts: How to build an urban village.* Seattle, WA: City Comforts Inc.

Tönnies, Ferdinand. (2002). *Community and society* (Charles P. Loomis, Trans.). Devon, UK: Courier Dover Publications.

Worldwatch Institute. (2012). State of the world 2012: Moving toward sustainable prosperity. Washington, DC: Worldwatch Institute.

Zhang Chun, & Wang Haotong. (2012, August 3). Eco pilots find habits hard to change. *chinadialogue.* Retrieved September 11, 2012, from http://www.chinadialogue.net/article/show/single/en/5056

Design and Architecture

Design and architecture are at a critical juncture. Both fields must transition from "business as usual" to a more place-based approach that reduces environmental destruction and adds to what enlightened business calls "the triple bottom line," where economy, ecology, and social equity all support one another. Sustainable design ideas promote an infrastructure that mimics how the natural world works: rather than spending money to design and build sewage-treatment plants that remove organic matter from wastewater, for instance, designers should let marshes do this work naturally. Designers looking to natural systems to discover equivalents useful in designing a built environment must absorb an extremely large field of potential information. Architects and designers are only at the beginning of the learning curve.

Technological advances and production drive the modern age. These enterprises often measure success by profitability instead of environmental impacts or long-term effects. The "business as usual" philosophy, where businesses erect a poorly designed building with an eye on low construction costs (such as inferior materials and low-quality construction) for the sake of a higher profit margin while they ignore its impact on the environment or the inhabitants, needs amending.

Modern society is reaching a point called The Great Turning, a phrase coined by the US eco-philosopher Joanna Macy to describe the shift from an industrial-growth society to a life-sustaining civilization. E. F. Schumacher, the German-British author of *Small Is Beautiful* and *Guide for the Perplexed*, put it this way:

> Can we rely on it that a "turning around" will be accomplished by enough people quickly enough to save the modern world? This question is often asked. But whatever answer is given to it will mislead. The answer "yes" would lead to complacency; the answer "no" to despair. It's desirable to leave these perplexities behind us and get down to work. (Schumacher 1978, 154)

In discussing twenty-first-century design, the three Rs—restoration, regeneration, and resiliency—mean integrating building design within a larger context of community design and the integral ecological design of food, water, energy, and recycling systems at every scale. The US architect Frank Lloyd Wright once said, "The heart is the first feature of working minds." Just as we always should remember to make nature's flows and cycles integral to what we design, we always should remember that we are nature. Today's designers need to imprint this idea into their awareness. The interactions between the natural world and built environments are far too complex to lend themselves to simple metrics such as the term *sustainability* suggests.

Planning for the Long Term

Modern ways of thinking have difficulty stretching beyond more than a couple of generations, which complicates making changes and planning on such a long-term scale. In pre-modern times, compared to post-industrial times, this type of challenge was nonexistent because humans' ability to affect the environment was limited. The German filmmaker Werner Herzog's 2010 documentary, *Cave of Forgotten Dreams*, is the story of the Chauvet Caves in southern France (pictured in the image above by the French photographer Inocybe). These dwellings, discovered in 1994, were home to humans 30,000 years ago. The beautiful charcoal animal drawings that cover their walls span 20,000 years. It is daunting to imagine that 700 generations of humans used these ritual spaces. The Industrial Age is 200 years old, or only seven generations of humans. In that time, we have transformed the entire living Earth in drastic and dire ways that threaten our future.

The most fundamental problem that affects everything now was the leap toward a modern world 300 years ago. The European view of early science and philosophy, that our bodies and minds were separate entities and that we humans were separate from and above nature, fueled this leap. The twentieth century began with an event in the then-emerging world of modern science that few are aware of: the battle between the Physicalists and the Vitalists in the German universities. The Physicalists maintained that only phenomena they could physically scrutinize and measure were legitimate objects of scientific study, while the Vitalists maintained that beyond the strictly measurable physical world were vital forces beyond physical/material description. Physicalist materialist science won, and students had to take an oath in blood, swearing to uphold the Physicalist ideology. This ideology has led us to a modern world in which the destruction of the natural world is justified in the name of progress for the human world.

Battling Rigid Instability: How to Adapt

Norms in a society may change over time. Change becomes more difficult as a society builds infrastructure around widely accepted norms, such as on which side of the road to drive. The more embedded the infrastructure, the more difficult it is for a regime shift to take place. In the case of design and architecture, the norm is the idea that cheap, conventional, poorly constructed buildings are desirable because they make their builders money and, thus, the theory goes, save their occupants money, too.

Our society—that of the developed world—appears to be in a condition of rigid instability. Buildings are a sum of their parts, from the materials used to the laws regulating how they may be built. Major institutions—government and politics, the economy, the media, education, and health care—all affect the built environment and influence people's attitudes toward it. These complicated institutions also resist change, thus creating instability.

Scale is part of the problem. These institutions, whether on a national or global scale, are too large and cumbersome, each lacking accountability or transparency. The institutions known as nation-states, particularly those countries covering large parts of continents, such as the United States, China, and Russia, are especially vulnerable to rigid instability.

Jared Diamond's book *Collapse*, Charles Mann's *1491*, and Amy Chua's *Day of Empire* are works that tell the story of great societies throughout history that collapsed because their rigid belief structures could not adapt to new challenges. Through their rigid denial, they overshot their ecological base. Rigid structures, both mental and physical, are unstable because they do not adapt easily to change. The two changes that will most severely impact how we live are the fact that the world is running out of easily extractable oil—the lifeblood of our economy and way of life—and the global climate meltdown this dependence on oil produces. We do not yet have an alternative economic base to replace the dependence on oil, or an ecological plan to handle the fallout. We need to design and create resilient communities. Resilience is generally defined as the ability to spring back, rebound, or return to an original form after having been compressed or stretched or to recover from illness, depression, or adversity; it also can refer to the ability of entire ecosystems to recover from change or abuse. It requires a certain amount of flexibility, which governmental policies, cultural attitudes, and design applications worldwide currently lack.

Modernist Architecture, and a Return to Reality

Architecture is design within which people live and work. The importance of well-designed architecture cannot be stressed enough. Poorly designed architecture enables rigid instability because of the large and (generally) permanent nature of buildings. Architecture has been contributing to rigid instability for some time. The birth of the Modernist architecture movement at the beginning of the twentieth century enthusiastically embraced a philosophy of ignoring the qualities of place in favor of bold new form statements based on the technologies of glass, steel, and concrete and the availability of cheap fossil fuels and electricity to heat and light this new international style. It reflected the hopeful optimism of a European generation of architects after World War I to replace the imperial architecture of the old order with a more socially and regionally equalizing architecture based on technological advances. In the post-World War II world, Modernism spread everywhere, but the social and human values its founders held were often sacrificed to the dogma of modern style, regardless of the qualities of place or function.

Bringing place—and, with it, reality—back to architecture and design is vital, for many reasons. Some architecture schools already have programs that involve practical and innovative hands-on design and construction by students, such as the Annual Solar Decathlon competition sponsored by the US Department of Energy, where engineering students compete to build innovative, energy-efficient houses powered by the sun. Some organizations provide design services to the vast majority of the world's population, which is off the radar of many architects. We must integrate what these organizations do and how they work into a design education that is less insulated from the reality of how most of the world lives. We need to downsize the scale of things to a manageable level where people can come together to solve common problems creatively and help each other. We need to redesign for the human scale of local community.

Integrating design into early education is a way to start. California schools have started programs to inspire the next generation of designers and architects by integrating eco-literacy, the understanding of the interaction of natural systems, into the regular classwork. Students in kindergarten through twelfth grade are responsible for tending vegetable gardens on school grounds, combining lessons in ecology, nature, and math. The students learn how to plan and cultivate these gardens, which contribute to the cafeteria menu, and they compost the food scraps; in an interesting role reversal, they share this knowledge with their parents, who then share their children's classroom activities with their friends, family, and co-workers. High school students learn how to do professional-level ecological surveys and mappings of sites, such as analyzing potential impacts of activities like construction or chemical use on watersheds. (See for example the curricula of Ross School in East Hampton, New York, and San Domenico School in San Anselmo, California.)

Prohibiting Common Sense

Sustainability is one of the big buzzwords of the twenty-first century, and not just in architecture. How can we build more sustainably, though? In the United States, unfortunately, government and special interests contribute significantly to the problem of rigid instability. Often, the people who have the most to gain from a rule change are the ones who write the new rule. The state of California, for instance, passed new rules for septic fields, rules that the engineers whose business it is to design and build these fields had written. Regulation may protect corporate interests at the expense of what is best for the environment or the infrastructure itself; that may mean allowing the use of cheaper, hazardous

materials or inadequate seepage prevention, practices that may be illegal otherwise if drafted through the lens of environmental and health concerns. Regulation often results in laws that prohibit common sense.

In many suburbs, ordinances prohibit drying clothes on an outdoor clothesline or raising chickens. In Oak Park, Michigan, a family was cited for growing vegetables on their front lawn. There, the local ordinance permits "only grass." Oak Park dropped the charges in July 2011 as media coverage and worldwide support attracted negative publicity. Canada has had similar occurrences: a man in Lantzville, British Columbia, was charged with zoning violations when he transformed a one-hectare dilapidated lot into a small farm (Tuttle 2011). In Toronto, Ontario, the Traffic Planning Department cited a family for having a front-yard garden. As worldwide support for the family grew, the department dropped charges and the city changed the ordinances to allow front-yard gardens (Vanderlinden 2011).

Most obstructive to ecologically intelligent design are the code barriers. These include codes that prohibit the use of recycled materials, including straw bale and rammed earth, as well as graywater reuse (which reuses 50 percent or more of household water), composting toilets, and many new building-system products. Codes are necessary; think of the horrific consequences of the 2010 earthquake in Haiti. Although the earthquake was a relatively minor 7.0 on the Richter scale, poor building codes and a lack of industrial development and infrastructure meant the quake was infinitely more destructive to life and property than it would have been had it hit a similarly quake-prone place like California (Koprowski 2010). If we are going to design our way out of the problems we have created, however, we must conceive codes that allow for experimentation with new techniques and methods while still providing for safe buildings.

The US designer Art Ludwig, of Oasis Design, points out the following key issues to consider:

- The culture of regulators and policy makers is grounded in the belief that the current system delivers the safest buildings in the world. Yet awareness of emerging risks due to climate chaos, toxics, and other causes is nearly nonexistent. While historical risks (such as nuclear annihilation or foreign invasion) have lessened, emerging risks that existing regulations fail to cover have more than doubled.

- The action some builders are taking to make buildings more "green" functions more as a diversion than as a remedy. Industry interests (such as the aforementioned engineer-drafted septic regulations) have effectively captured large portions of the regulatory apparatus and are managing it for maximum profit.
- Unpermitted centers for research on sustainability in building and infrastructure have been the source of "deep green" innovation for years, but tight regulation dramatically lessens their productivity, even as their innovation is needed more than ever. (For instance, it took years to get approval for straw-bale construction and graywater reuse.)

The architecture business increasingly is corporate and serves corporate interests. While every architecture office's sales pitch markets "sustainability," "green," and LEED gold medals (the US Green Building Council's widespread and popular Leadership in Energy and Environmental Design program), many ignore the more basic questions of whether a new building's design and uses are part of the solution or part of the problem. How great an impact the USGBC's LEED rating system has had on the reduction of fossil fuel energy use in buildings is questionable, as is how much it has reduced pollution or increased indoor air quality. The system is based on design criteria and calculations, rather than on measuring a completed project's actual performance. Until post-occupancy evaluation of actual building performance becomes the standard for learning from built examples, LEED appears as little more than a marketing tool. The USGBC needs to LEEP beyond LEED. (LEEP stands for Leadership in Energy and Environmental Performance, a proposed rating program for performance over the life of a building [Bartlett 2012].)

Beyond LEED, we can set the bar higher, toward "regenerative" or "living" buildings. Regenerative buildings go further than simply reducing resource and energy use; they produce all of their own energy, emit no carbon dioxide, recycle all their water and wastes, incorporate some food production and green roofs in their buildings and site design, and eclipse being "carbon neutral" by absorbing carbon dioxide emissions from the surrounding environment. Regenerative buildings largely eliminate the need for expensive heating, ventilation, and cooling (HVAC) systems through design that fits climate, place, and site. By restoring natural systems to health and productivity, these buildings regenerate the sites where they are located. Regenerative buildings promote eco-literacy by teaching the understanding of natural systems and their interactions.

Integrating Design and the Environment

Scientists have searched long for a unified approach to the design of systems—both built and natural—that integrates scales ranging from the molecular to the global. Science has confirmed the Gaia hypothesis developed by the British atmospheric scientist James Lovelock and the US microbiologist Lynn Margulis; the hypothesis states that Earth is a single, living, self-regulating organism composed of interconnected life forms that cooperate to maintain ecological balance. This hypothesis is in contrast to the neo-Darwinian thesis—that life is based around competition and survival of the fittest. Nature's geometry is fractal (having a similar, repeating pattern) at every scale, from our galaxy to the geometry of air and water movement, from global weather systems to the spiral whirl spinning down our shower drains. If we are to include ecological concerns within design, we must discover ways to integrate design processes across multiple levels of scale.

Part of the problem of how to integrate design with ecological concerns is that we know that we need to change our systems, but we do not really know where to start. The US systems analyst Donella Meadows wrote a famous paper in 1999 called "Leverage Points to Intervene in a System." She ranks twelve leverage points from least to most effective and indicates that most people think the highest point of leverage to change a system (which could be a corporation, a city, a person's body, or an entire ecosystem) are numbers such as costs, profits, subsidies, taxes, and standards. For instance, to reform our fossil fuels–dependent society, it seems logical to start with the heavily subsidized oil industry, which enjoys an unnatural advantage over renewable energy. Numbers are the most clearly perceived points, but because they rarely change behaviors, they have little long-term effect. (Continuing with the same fossil fuels analogy, oil is subsidized because a large part of our society evidently wants it to be.) The most important leverage points in changing a system are the most difficult to alter: "the mindset or paradigm out of which the system—its goals, structure, rules, delays, parameters—arises" and "the power to transcend paradigms" (Meadows 1999, 3). In other words, the place to start questioning how to change the way we design our buildings (or how we get around) is to question our fundamental definition of what is architecture or mobility. To do that, we need to examine how we think about the way we approach design problems.

Modern culture has thrived through the development of our left-brain capacity to reduce all problems to finite, rational-solution algorithms. The design problems we face, however, consist of multidimensional, complex systems issues that cross traditional disciplines and knowledge sets. We need to develop entire new mind-sets, ways of working together, and ways of communicating across mind-sets, tossing away old habits and inventing new collaborative processes to overcome today's isolated mentalities. We need to shift our focus from the solitary interdisciplinary approach to a more cooperative one: a metadisciplinary, integrated whole systems approach.

Mimicking the Natural World

One way to transition to this integrated whole systems approach is to study nature. What nature does to combat instability in a particular environment involves an integrated or linked diversity in which flows and cycles connect many species, at all scales. Sustainability is all about processes that are built upon a complex, interlinked diversity. We can apply the same criteria to guiding the design of buildings and cities. From this overall principle of linked diversity, we can articulate design principles and strategy for each of the three Es: ecology, economy, and equity (not to be confused with the aforementioned three Rs: restoration, regeneration, and resiliency). Through the application of principles and strategies, we can create a new ethics and a new aesthetics for civilization into the next millennium.

The design principle is to promote a design of infrastructure that mimics how the natural world works. For example, we spend billions of dollars to design and build sewage-treatment plants that remove organic matter from wastewater—precisely the process a marsh does. We could restore wetlands, which reduce flooding and serve to purify wastewater, at costs far lower than conventional sewage-treatment plants. Another obvious example is buildings. If we thought of buildings as organisms rather than as objects, we could design buildings that generate their own energy from the sun on site, reprocess their wastes, and use plant materials on walls and the roof to absorb carbon dioxide and pump out oxygen.

If we are going to reverse the present alarming decline in the planet's health, changes in how, what, and why we build play a key role in determining the human and planetary future. The five principles of ecological design are: (1) know that the best solutions start from paying attention to the unique qualities of place; (2) trace the direct and indirect environmental costs of design decisions using environmental accounting; (3) mimic nature's processes in design, so that the design fits nature; (4) honor every voice in the design process; (5) and make nature visible through design to transform both makers and users (Van der Ryn and Cowan 1996).

Designers looking to natural systems to discover equivalents useful in designing a built environment must absorb an extremely large field of potential information. In the field of architecture and design, we are only at the beginning of the learning curve, shifting the guiding metaphor from thinking of buildings as static machines or pieces of sculpture to conceptualizing them as dynamic living systems that are the essence of nature.

A new ecologically designed home would not be built of virgin wood but of materials reclaimed and remanufactured from the waste stream. A climate-responsive design and energy-efficient equipment would reduce the home's energy demand. It may produce part of its energy from the ambient environment. It could recycle its water and wastes, and occupants may eat from lower on the food chain or grow some of their own foods. The design of the neighborhood and community would reduce automobile use. The different players in this design drama—land developers, local government agencies, material producers, builders, and consumers—are probably unaware of the metabolic chaos their decisions unleash. ("Metabolic" here refers to processes that allow organisms to function and sustain life, such as highly efficient intake of energy and nutrients and the efficient elimination of wastes.) We are only in the first stages of being able to translate ecological thinking into design tools that allow us to trace metabolic effects through the system. Today, not many incentives are available for doing so, because government regulations and our economic system tend to ignore the relationship between self-interest and common interest or the relationships among three types of capital: financial, human, and natural. (Capital often is broken down further into five forms of capital: natural, human, economic, social, and physical.) Smart design decision making should consider the complex interaction of these forms of capital.

When we begin to design buildings from the point of view of metabolism, we move to three important strategies: integrated life cycle costing, decarbonization, and dematerialization. Integrated life cycle costing establishes the value of the building over time, both as a whole and for its particular components. Replacing movable furnishings does not seriously interrupt a building's use, while replacing an HVAC system does. Integrating mechanical systems with natural systems—such as combining daylight with artificial lighting or natural ventilation with mechanical ventilation—may be one way to design redundancy into our buildings, extending useful life and reducing metabolism. (*Redundancy* here refers to the mechanical systems used on a backup basis; the word has a positive connotation in this definition.)

Decarbonizing and Dematerialization

Reducing the throughput of carbon in buildings (i.e., the amount of carbon that enters and leaves buildings) is critical to coping with the growing problem of global warming. The obvious measures include energy efficiency and climate-responsive design. The latter, if taken seriously, would have the effect of outlawing our current "big box" building footprints, which cannot function without massive energy-intensive HVAC and lighting systems. Less obvious and more intriguing is to design buildings with built-in carbon sinks, such as a second skin of living materials that absorb carbon dioxide and other toxins. As thirty- and forty-year-old glass and metal walls wear out, a double skin of energy-producing, heat-absorbing, high-performance glazing and an outer skin of carbon-dioxide-absorbing plants could replace them. As parts of the urban fabric wear out, forests could replace them. Decarbonizing strategies such as these would give true meaning to "greening the city."

Dematerialization—doing more with less by substituting design intelligence for brute force and "stuff"—has been around a long time. By the early 1800s, the speed of human travel had not advanced in thousands of years, not since the domestication of the horse. Now travel and communication have not only sped up almost infinitely, but they also require vastly fewer resources per unit of service. We can pinpoint our location through handheld global positioning system (GPS) equipment weighing very little. Per-unit computing power has fallen from tonnes per gigabyte, as in thirty-year-old mainframe computers with vacuum-tube circuits, to fractions of a gram in today's miniaturized silicon-microchip circuits. These are examples of dematerialization and miniaturization through design. The building sector has had its share of visionaries preaching design through dematerialization, ephemeralization, and miniaturization. Among the most important was the US mathematician, architect, and futurist Buckminster Fuller, who, in the 1950s, was thinking about buildings as ecological systems. Fuller, in his book *Nine Chains to the Moon*, coined the term *ephemeralization* as the ability of technological advancement to do more and more with less

and less until eventually it could do everything with nothing.

To some extent, intelligent design may reduce the initial input of materials in the building, but the key to dematerialization in buildings is likely to revolve around design for reuse and remanufacture. Modern materials—plastics, aluminum, steel, and composites—tend to have high embodied energy, in that it takes a lot of energy and raw material to produce them. If they are deliberately designed for reuse and remanufacture, their initial metabolism and footprint is extended over many lives.

Natural Design over Monumentality

In architecture, monumentality is most often confused with substance. Any object, sufficiently enlarged in size, becomes architecture. The US sculptor Claes Oldenburg, sensing that our symbols today lie in the realm of the human-made, has shown with his giant sculptures of badminton shuttlecocks and spoons that we may elevate any common object to monument simply by puffing up its scale. Unfortunately, our leading architects, whose ego and belief in bigness may outweigh their common sense, have largely succumbed to this false dream. Bigness also often is confused with complexity. Structures that termites construct with their own feces, however, incorporate a highly sophisticated means of climactic adaptation and circulation unequaled by today's mammoth megastructures. The problem is that while we have mastered many aspects of the physical sciences, the design of the built environment does not consider the complexity of life support, the delicate web of ecosystemic processes that make a place livable.

Architecture exists to symbolize the power of centralized bureaucracy, technology, and economics; in short, "progress." It has no process to consider the complexity, richness, and diversity of life. Only one architecture is thus worth trying to master, and that is architecture connected to life processes, or what we can call natural design. During the industrial era, the connection between the design and construction of buildings and nature's processes and ecology was lost. With the widespread adoption of air conditioning after World War II and the development in the United States of a national freeway system, buildings lost connection to place. Air conditioning meant architects and engineers could ignore factors such as local climate and the orientation, size, and floor-plate dimensions of buildings, as well as the scale and context of existing buildings and communities. Up until the 1970s, electricity was so cheap that architects simply did not consider the cost of replacing daylight with electric light or the cost of cooling buildings with electricity rather than with properly oriented operable windows and other natural cooling devices.

Twenty-first-century architecture mainly has provided the settings and armature for the techno-fantasies of modern industrial culture. Modern architecture has glorified humanity over nature, and organization and technology over humanity. Progress created the illusion that humanity and our machines were no longer dependent on nature. Human will and intelligence were expected to reshape Earth into a limitless cornucopia. Architecture was called into service by this new game. Design became a process of abstracting reality into numbers and relationships. What we call "progress" is paid for from an Earth savings account that will be empty in a few short decades. Every aspect of our modern industrial urbanized way of life is dependent on hydrocarbons—a gift from the steamy jungles of many millions of years ago. Architects, engineers, and planners, until recently, have taken these energy sources largely for granted. The archetypal environments of the fossil fuel age—massive cities and high-rise buildings—will soon be as obsolete as the dinosaurs that roamed the forests now turned to oil.

The continuing base for an advanced post-progress civilization is the ability of diverse natural ecosystems to capture and fix solar radiation into usable forms of energy. An advanced society centered on a stable solar economy will combine a highly developed scientific understanding with a liberating technology. We need to look in a more integrative way at how we orchestrate everything that makes up a life-support system—not just shelter and the habitable environment, but food, energy, waste, and every part of the system. We need to consider what happens to the waste that buildings generate, as well as the energy involved in creating and maintaining our buildings.

The socially conscious architect is in a schizophrenic place, however. As technicians, architects serve processes and purposes that often destroy and inhibit the organic and natural designs that should be their goals. Two important books in recent years illustrate the point through the authors' personal, sometimes agonizing, experience. In *Freedom to Build* by the British architect John F. C. Turner, a group of US housing experts involved in various low-cost housing projects, in the United States and abroad, reach a consensus that the housing projects of architects and bureaucrats are seldom as workable and economic as what people can do for themselves using the same resources. The Egyptian architect Hassan Fathy, in *Architecture for the Poor*, recounts his long experience with trying to reestablish "Earth architecture" (such as mud bricks or rammed earth) in Egypt, in the end to be defeated by the housing bureaucracy that favors more "advanced" Western ways.

Architecture is a business that serves corporate interests and the state, yet its underlying themes still maintain its connection to the humanistic, nature-centered power of the individual artist-creator. The deaths of the great makers of the modern movement—Walter Adolph Georg Gropius, Le Corbusier (the professional name of Charles-Édouard Jeanneret), Ludwig Mies van der Rohe (known for the idiom "less is more"), and Frank Lloyd Wright—and the failure of the international architectural establishment to produce anyone of their stature has tended to leave the profession and its training grounds in the university schools of architecture without any powerful figures to represent a happy marriage of humanistic idealism and technological prowess. The US architect Bernard Rudofsky's *Architecture without Architects* popularized architecture's source in indigenous, organic habitation that pre-industrial cultures habitually produced. Imitation misses the point, however. Reproducing Mediterranean fishing villages or Northern California wood barns as stage sets for vacations with good taste is style without substance. To extol the virtues of Las Vegas or Los Angeles as expressions of "popular" design is cynically to ignore the powerful political and economic interests who are the real authors of these landscapes. The point is so obvious that it is hard to keep hold of it: consistency, beauty, naturalness, and order in architecture are not attributes of form alone; they are simply expressions of values, a way of life, and a process. Any assessment of form is always an assessment of culture and value. Architecture is a mirror of the society that creates it; how we, in turn, assess that architecture reflects our own values.

We have seen the pattern all over the world: pleasing, effective, and economical indigenous habitat skills and processes destroyed and replaced with mass sterility. Architects, no matter how well intentioned, are almost inevitably agents for destruction of natural process wherever they encounter it. How could it be otherwise, when Western technology, centralization, economics, and progress are the gods that must be served?

A trend is rising in Northern California, among other places, of people designing and building their own homes. Although many who have built their own houses are architecturally trained, most are not. The most inspiring, beautiful, and practical places reflect the order, integrity, skills, energy, knowledge, and imagination—in short, the life space—of their builders. Architectural training seems to have little to do with the results. Indeed, many architect-builders feel they have had to unlearn most of the fixed images they so assiduously developed over the years. Knowledge of details, drawing visualization, and engineering are the skills of most value; all those pretty pictures in the magazines and volumes on spatial concepts are harmful to practical creation.

As a species, we first developed tools to modify the natural environment to enhance our chances for survival. Architecture grows out of this primary physiological and biological need, which other requirements have overshadowed in time. In the short space of a few hundred years, our tools, monstrously swollen by a fossil fuel diet, threaten to overwhelm our sensibility and nature's capacity to heal herself from our exploitation. The way out is not a way back, but the recognition that we should apply our tool- and symbol-making skills to adapting to, not controlling and thereby destroying, the ecosystems in which all life is embedded. For several hundred years, we assumed it possible to enhance civilization and our lives by harnessing the energy of sunlight that fell on the Earth some millions of years ago. We had the dream, and it is close to an end.

The Future

In cities, suburbs, and the countryside, a new culture can design and live a way of life where the requirements of habitat (shelter, sustenance, sociability) are intimately related to managing the land and its resources, conserving and enhancing the natural ecosystem. Natural design focuses on the design of techniques appropriate to small-scale, stable, self-replenishing systems in which human living space and work space, food and energy production, and the natural ecosystem are designed as a single directly connected system. A naturally designed environment will:

- use up fewer nonrenewable resources;
- rely more on "income" energy from sun, wind, water, and organic sources;
- provide its inhabitants with a closer contact with natural cycles, whether in the city or country;
- involve inhabitants directly in providing for many of their own needs;
- be in harmony with its natural surroundings;
- blur the distinction between production and consumption, work, play, and learning; and
- strive for aesthetic, emotional, and spiritual satisfaction.

No humanly designed system can ever achieve the organization that natural systems have evolved over millions of years. We must remember, though, that integral design has as much to do with process as it has to do with realized form. Process and shape must be analogous, although we do tend to think of houses built with natural materials, such as earth, stone, or unsawn wood, as being more natural than those built with industrial materials, such as glass, steel, or concrete. Integral design applies the lessons of the biology and ecology of the natural systems to the design of environments for people. This emerging kind of integration of architecture and biology, dubbed "bio-tecture" or "eco-tecture," is in its infancy, although we can already begin to identify principles and patterns.

A consequence of several generations of ignoring commonsense climate-responsive design is that the training of architects and engineers for several generations simply ignored time-tested natural climate design approaches. "Bioclimatics," learning how to design to reduce energy and resource use by understanding climate and natural environmental factors, did not come back into architectural and building-engineering education until recently.

We humans are no different from the 700 generations of humans who lived in those French caves 30,000 years ago. We were designed to thrive in a natural world. Our wiring is designed to respond quickly to immediate threats, not to longer-term change. It is interesting that what the English poet Robert Graves called "mechanarchy" swept the world in the early twentieth century, when art moved from a genteel realist tradition to a much more primitive expression, as in the work of Pablo Picasso, whose bulls seem to be channeling the Chauvet caves. All our material comforts and technology, coupled with an overload of demands on our time and neural pathways, mean that we are less adjusted, perhaps, to our overstressed lives than the cave people were to their lives. Could it be that while the tentacles of the powerful, centrally organized scientific and mechanically structured world destroys the living world and its complexity beyond today's science, it is also destroying our very humanity?

Our evolution as a species is not complete. The design of the human brain suggests that we are capable of greater good and greater wisdom if we can evolve the collective cultural forms that encourage all of us to realize our full potential as humans and as part of the larger flow of life. The world we live in today is changing in crucial ways that are challenging and frightening but full of positive opportunities. If we fear change, we respond through denial, escapism, and passivity. If we face change positively, with passion and hope, we just might realize our dreams of healthy buildings, healthy communities, and children who are eco-literate and truly engaged in learning.

Sim VAN DER RYN
Ecological Design Collaborative

See also Buildings and Infrastructure; Cities and the Biosphere; Collective Thinking; Community; Energy Efficiency; Local Solutions to Global Problems; Mobility; Values

FURTHER READING

Bartlett, Dave. (2012, June 7). Enabling buildings to "LEEP" forward. Retrieved August 9, 2012, from http://www.environmentalleader.com/2012/06/07/enabling-buildings-to-leep-forward/

Chua, Amy. (2007). *Day of empire: How hyperpowers rise to global dominance—And why they fall.* New York: Doubleday.

Diamond, Jared. (2004). *Collapse: How societies choose to fail or succeed.* New York: Viking Adult.

Fathy, Hassan. (2000). *Architecture for the poor: An experiment in rural Egypt.* Chicago: University of Chicago Press.

Herzog, Werner. (2010). *Cave of forgotten dreams* (Documentary).

Koprowski, Gene J. (2010, January 15). Is California due for a big earthquake? Retrieved August 20, 2012, from http://www.foxnews.com/scitech/2010/01/15/america-big-earthquake/

Macy, Joanna. (2012). Center for ecoliteracy: The Great Turning. Retrieved August 2, 2012, from http://www.ecoliteracy.org/essays/great-turning

Mann, Charles. (2005). *1491: New revelations of the Americas before Columbus.* New York: Knopf.

Meadows, Donella H. (1999). Leverage points: Places to intervene in a system. Hartland, VT: The Sustainability Institute.

Rudofsky, Bernard. (1987). *Architecture without architects: A short introduction to non-pedigreed architecture.* Albuquerque: University of New Mexico Press.

Schumacher, E. F. (1978). *Guide for the perplexed.* New York: Harper & Row.

Sightline Institute. (n.d.). Homepage. Retrieved August 8, 2012, from http://www.sightline.org/

Turner, John F. C. (1972). *Freedom to build: Dweller control of the housing process.* New York: Macmillan Publishers.

Tuttle, Brad. (2011, July 15). Charges dropped against woman for front yard vegetable garden. Retrieved August 20, 2012, from http://moneyland.time.com/2011/07/15/charges-dropped-against-woman-for-front-yard-vegetable-garden/

United States Department of Energy (US DOE). (2011). Solar decathlon. Retrieved August 2, 2012, from http://www.solardecathlon.gov/competition.html

Van der Ryn, Sim. (2013). *Empathic design.* Washington, DC: Island Press.

Van der Ryn, Sim, & Cowan, Stuart. (1996). *Ecological design.* Washington, DC: Island Press.

Vanderlinden, Colleen. (2011, July 14). Toronto changing ordinance; Will allow front yard vegetable gardens. Retrieved August 20, 2012, from http://www.treehugger.com/green-food/toronto-changing-ordinance-will-allow-front-yard-vegetable-gardens.html

Economics, Steady State

The "steady state" economy is rooted in the nineteenth-century economic theory of John Stuart Mill. Little used until after World War II, the idea is a foundational concept in sustainability science. It can be considered an intellectual fabric with strands from classical economics to neo-Malthusianism, including growth limits, ecological economics, and degrowth. Whether a steady state economy is desirable and achievable remains an unanswered question for sustainability science.

The "steady state" economy (also called the "stationary state" economy) is a 150-year-old economic concept that became central to debates over the meaning of sustainability or sustainable development in the twentieth century. There are several views on what the steady state actually would be, as well as on the process of economic and social change that might lead to it, and whether or not it is even a desirable vision of a sustainable society relevant for the twenty-first century. Many of the debates about the steady state economy are fundamentally the same as debates about sustainability in general.

The steady state concept is rooted in nineteenth-century classical economic theory and is most clearly formulated in a short section in John Stuart Mill's *Principles of Political Economy*. There has not been a clear development of Mill's thought into a modern vision of the steady state. Rather, there are multiple strands of intellectual development that sometimes, but not always, borrow from one another.

The idea comes up in standard economic theory and the neo-Malthusianism of the mid-twentieth century, the return to the ideas of the British scholar T. Robert Malthus that human populations tend to grow faster than food supplies, resulting in a population controlled by famine, disease, or conflict. Steady state economy is central to the Romanian-US economist Nicholas Georgescu-Roegen's

application of the entropy law to economic processes and to the emergence of the limits-to-growth argument in the early 1970s. (Entropy is a concept taken from the sub-discipline of physics called thermodynamics. A basic definition of entropy is the process whereby energy moves from a state of being able to do work—a state of high organization termed "low entropy"—to a state of being unable to do work—a state of lower organization termed "high entropy." Entropy is roughly synonymous with lack of organization.) It is embraced by the US ecological economist Herman Daly and thus is basic to the development of the discipline of ecological economics. There are elements of the steady state within the sustainable development paradigm, and it leads logically to its most radical form, sustainable degrowth. Nonetheless, there remain unanswered questions as to how a steady state economy might be achieved, whether it is still relevant in today's economic environment, and whether it is a desirable part of the sustainability paradigm.

John Stuart Mill

John Stuart Mill introduced the idea of the steady state economy idea in 1848 in a section of Book IV of his *Principles of Political Economy*. The section "Of the Stationary State" was a reaction to the work of other classical economists such as Adam Smith and T. Robert Malthus. Mill questioned the imperative of progress by asking about the end of development and by asserting that "the increase in wealth is not boundless," an early expression of what would come to be known as the limits-to-growth argument.

Mill rejected the contention by other classical economists that the end of progress must result in dire or depressing consequences. He made several claims for the stationary state, first by not assuming that an increase in human population was inevitable. He did acknowledge that if the population was always increasing, then economic growth was necessary to avoid degrading the poorest of those in society; he did not think that growth was required in order for the poor to share in the benefits of society, which they could and must do. He advocated instead a redistribution of wealth and shared access to the paths to decent income. His vision was that "the best state for human nature is that in which, while no one is poor, no one desires to be richer, nor has any reason to fear being thrust back by the efforts of others to push themselves forward."

So a stationary population and shared benefits of the economy (he called this "equality of fortunes") were central to Mill's stationary state. In today's terminology, he was essentially making a quality-of-life argument for the stationary state. A stationary population results in a population density that allows for solitude, "and solitude in the presence of natural beauty and grandeur, is the cradle of thoughts and aspirations which are not only good for the individual, but which society could ill do without." A stationary population, therefore, is necessary for a stationary state economy.

Mill also made the distinction between growth and development that would become important to twentieth-century proponents of the steady state economy, particularly Herman Daly. In Mill's words, "It is scarcely necessary to remark that a stationary condition of capital and population implies no stationary state of human improvement. There would be as much scope as ever for all kinds of mental culture, and moral and social progress."

Mill's stationary state ideas were little used for nearly a century, until the post–World War II era.

Early Uses of the Concept

The theories of growth that dominated early twentieth-century neoclassical economics did not dispense with Mill's steady or stationary concepts, but the ideas were used in a technical sense, exemplified by the US economist Paul Samuelson's (1943) writings at midcentury. The stationary economy was considered as some kind of equilibrium condition that needed to be understood in terms of capital formation and depreciation, interest rates, and the business cycle. The steady state was in no sense a normative concept as used by Mill before and others afterward.

More significant to the emergence of the steady state economy idea was a neo-Malthusian concern for population growth in the post–World War II era. The US ecologist William Vogt (1948), the US conservationist Fairfield Osborn (1948), and others suggested that the Malthusian trap of geometric growth in population

versus arithmetic growth in food supply was a model for understanding the changes facing the world after the cataclysm of World War II. The links between a steady state economy and a stationary population became accepted truths for the neo-Malthusians. As Vogt (1948, 284–288) said, "By excessive breeding and abuse of the land, mankind has backed itself into an ecological trap. . . . [U]nless, in short, man readjusts his way of living, in its fullest sense, to the imperatives imposed by the *limited* resources of his environment—we may as well give up all hope of continuing civilized life." Neo-Malthusian thinking continued into the 1960s, particularly in the writings of the US biologist Paul Ehrlich (1968).

Vogt, Osborn, and others planted the seeds that grew into several different but intertwined strains of steady state economics in the 1960s and 1970s. These included limits to growth, Georgescu-Roegen's application of entropy to economic processes, and Daly's explicit steady state economics.

The Limits-to-Growth Controversy

In the post–World War II era, the emphasis in the industrial nations of the world was to continue economic growth. The reconstruction of Western Europe and Japan, the development of the first Green Revolution, and the formation of the Organisation for Economic Co-operation and Development were all part of a growth-oriented public policy. The fears of the neo-Malthusians were addressed and rejected. In the United States, Resources for the Future (RFF) was founded to research the potential constraints on growth from resource scarcity. In a seminal work from RFF, the researchers Howard Barnett and Chandler Morse concluded that generally declining real prices of natural resources indicated the power of technological change and resource substitution to prevent any specific resource scarcity. "Advances in fundamental science have made it possible to take advantage of the uniformity of energy/matter—a uniformity that makes it feasible, without preassignable limit, to escape the quantitative constraints imposed by the character of the earth's crust" (1963, 11). Barnett and Morse's conclusions reflected the growing dominance of the neoclassical paradigm in the economics profession. In this perspective, the neo-Malthusians were characterized as being just as wrong as Malthus was in his predictions about population growth and food supply.

Yet in the 1960s, there were multiple challenges to the neoclassical model. For example, the US economist Kenneth Boulding used a space-age metaphor to express the idea of limits when he introduced the metaphor of the Earth as a spaceship. Boulding (1966) argued that the standard model of an open economy (he called it a "cowboy" economy) failed to reflect the reality of the limits to the natural system within which the economy as a social system functions. His proposed alternative was a closed or "spaceman" economy where stocks are maintained but throughput (output or production) is minimized. Although Boulding did not call this a steady state economy, he clearly challenged the assumptions of the standard neoclassical growth model.

Despite the challenges by Boulding and others, Barnett and Morse expressed the dominant worldview in Western industrial societies until the publication in 1972 of *The Limits to Growth* (Meadows et al. 1972). This report on computer modeling of the "world system" was sponsored by the Club of Rome, an international group of private citizens brought together by the Italian industrialist Aurelio Peccei and the Scottish scientist Alexander King in 1968 to stimulate international thinking on long-term issues. The project they sponsored at the Massachusetts Institute of Technology developed a systems dynamic model of the world system to test the growth assumptions of the standard economic model.

The results showed that the world system is characterized by resource constraints either in terms of availability of natural resources as inputs or of limits on the pollution-assimilative capacities of the natural environment. Growth then would inevitably lead to "overshoot and collapse." The authors argued that their findings necessitated an equilibrium state. "Thus the most basic definition of the state of global equilibrium is that population and capital are essentially stable, with the forces tending to increase or decrease them in a carefully controlled balance" (Meadows et al. 1972, 171).

Numerous neoclassical economists attacked the limits-to-growth findings, most often based on the contention that Meadows's team had ignored the role of prices in markets to stimulate technical innovation and input substitution (Cole et al. 1973). The book spawned a wide public debate about growth. For example, the American Academy of Arts and Sciences dedicated a whole issue of its journal *Daedalus* to the "No-Growth Society."

Concurrent with the limits-to-growth modeling effort, a few economists began to critique the growth models that had dominated their profession. Two are notable in the evolution of steady state economics: Nicholas Georgescu-Roegen and Herman Daly.

Nicholas Georgescu-Roegen and Herman Daly

The two late-twentieth-century economists most closely associated with the idea of a steady state economy were Nicholas Georgescu-Roegen and Herman Daly. Georgescu-Roegen was a Romanian mathematician and economist whose contributions set the stage for a full development of the steady state economy idea. He argued that economists had limited their analysis in the traditional circular flow model of the economy and ignored the obvious fact that economic processes take place in a larger biophysical realm. The boundaries between the economy and the "material world" are relevant to understanding fundamental economic processes. (See figure 1 on page 81). His profound contribution was to make clear the relevance of the laws of thermodynamics to economics processes, particularly the second law, or entropy law. Once people saw economic processes as essentially ones that converted low-entropy energy to high-entropy energy, they understood that growth had to be limited. Production and consumption of goods and services inevitably lead to the conversion of low-entropy energy to high-entropy energy—a process that physicists assure us cannot continue indefinitely.

Placing the economy within this larger system, which both neoclassical and Marxist economists had failed to do, changed the understanding of what was possible. The economy was constrained by the laws of physics, and those laws could no longer be ignored. Georgescu-Roegen's approach challenged the basic understanding of capital in economic growth models, which treated natural and manufactured capital as substitutes with few or no limits on the degree the economy could replace natural capital with manufactured capital. A prime example of this is the Cobb-Douglas production function, a central analytical tool in the neoclassical canon, which makes

Figure 1. Expansion of Economists' Circular Flow Model Implicit in the Work of Nicholas Georgescu-Roegen

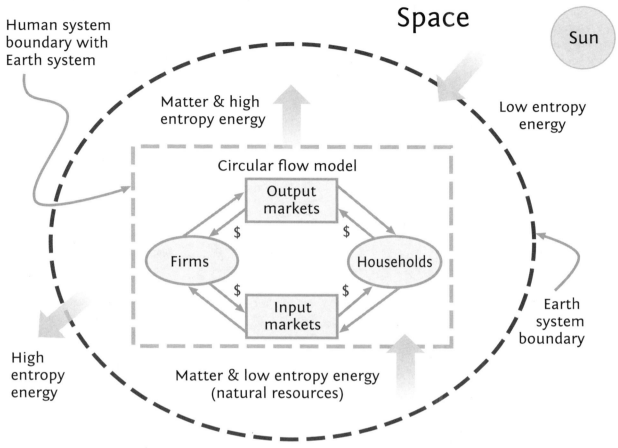

Source: Adapted from Daly (1980, 20), fig. I.2.

There are biophysical constraints on the economy. The boundaries between the economy and the "material world"—the world's oceans, forests, atmosphere, etc.—are relevant to understanding fundamental economic processes, which are, essentially, activities that convert low-entropy energy to high-entropy energy. Sustainability requires that the economy function in ways that account for the biophysical constraints imposed by the larger system within which it is nested.

explicit this fungibility of different types of capital. The price system stimulates technical improvements in the efficiency of manufactured capital, allowing it to replace natural resources in the production function. Georgescu-Roegen's argument was that more often than not, natural capital and manufactured capital complement each other. Furthermore, because production inevitably transforms low-entropy energy, the most basic form of natural capital, growth must be limited. His magnum opus was *The Entropy Law and the Economic Process,* a book more appreciated outside of the discipline of economics than within it (Daly 1995).

Georgescu-Roegen did not embrace the term *steady state economy* in his writings. That became the domain of his student, Herman Daly. Daly studied with Georgescu-Roegen at Vanderbilt University, but later their visions of the appropriate way to think of the possible end states diverged. Daly became the central proponent of the

steady state economy, while Georgescu-Roegen questioned it on the same basis that he questioned the growth paradigm of neoclassical economists.

Daly wrote more forcefully and in more detail on the steady state than anyone else. The idea first showed in his 1968 article, "On Economics as a Life Science." He used biological and ecological analogies to posit a more complete model of the economic process, showing clearly the influence of his mentor, Georgescu-Roegen. Daly's writings on the steady state economy demonstrate a breadth and depth of scholarship both within economics and beyond its narrow disciplinary confines. Ecology, physics, ethics, and evolutionary biology were all brought to bear on the problems of defining the steady state economy. For him, the idea was part of a Kuhnian paradigm shift that was essential for economics to remain relevant as a discipline. The US historian and philosopher Thomas Kuhn (1970) argued that science progresses when the prevailing paradigm in a discipline no longer functions to adequately explain observations by scientists. This necessitates development of a new paradigm, a change that Daly saw to be needed in economics.

For Daly, the need for a steady state economy came from two conflicting ideas. First, the neoclassical growth paradigm assumed that "good" (*welfare* in economist's terminology) comes from both an increase in capital, especially manufactured capital (a stock), and from an increase in income produced with that capital (a flow). Second (which reflects his desire to ground economics in biophysical realities), the Earth "approximates a steady-state open system" and thus nature imposes "an inescapable general scarcity" (Daly 1980, 17, 19). These two ideas represented an irreconcilable internal contradiction in neoclassical economics, demanding a new paradigm—the steady state economy.

The steady state would of necessity have a constant stock of capital and a constant population. But this alone was not sufficient. The capital stock must be durable so that there is a low rate of throughput in the system, an idea similar to Boulding's spaceship economy metaphor. Here Daly showed his grounding in the Georgescu-Roegen concern for the relevance of entropy to the economic process. Daly acknowledged that the limits on throughput can occur on the input side (scarcity of resources) or on the output side (limited capacity for the environment to assimilate used matter and energy).

The obvious problem of this system is that those least well off materially cannot be offered higher incomes through growth, the idea of the growth paradigm being that a rising tide lifts all boats. Physical wealth would be a zero-sum game. This means that "the important issue of the steady state will be distribution, not production" (Daly 1980, 21).

Harking back to Mill again, Daly emphasized the need to see economic well-being as rooted in development rather than growth. There is perhaps no stronger critique of the neoclassical paradigm than when he says, "Paradoxically, growth economics has been both too materialistic and not materialistic enough. In ignoring the ultimate means and the laws of thermodynamics, it has been insufficiently materialistic. In ignoring the Ultimate End and ethics, it has been too materialistic"

(1980, 10). This idea that we can still develop even when there is no more growth is the most important feature of the steady state economy. In this, Daly reflected the thinking of Mill. Yet the possibility of development without growth challenged one of the central tenets of neoclassical economic theory—that well-being (welfare) is measured by willingness to pay for goods and services, and that there is no limit to human desires for additional consumption. Daly rejected the idea that for humans more is always preferred over less.

Daly clearly drew on Georgescu-Roegen by direct reference and in the fundamental importance to his arguments of the finite nature of resources, particularly low-entropy energy. Georgescu-Roegen, however, did not embrace the steady state economy. He came to believe that the entropy law makes even the steady state unachievable and calls it a "topical mirage." He pondered, "Perhaps the destiny of man is to have a short, but fiery, exciting and extravagant life rather than a long, uneventful and vegetative existence. Let other species—the amoebas, for example—which have no spiritual ambitions inherit an earth still bathed in plenty of sunshine" (Georgescu-Roegen 1975, 379).

For many, the steady state economy is related to the principles of sustainable development from the Brundtland Report, the title commonly given to the final report of the World Commission on Environment and Development (1987). While some used the term "sustainable development," others referred to "sustainable growth." Daly called "sustainable growth" an oxymoron, arguing that growth is not sustainable because it implies increase in capital stock, population, or both. The steady state economy sits in the middle between growth models, with the optimism of neoclassical or sustainable growth on one side and the pessimism of Georgescu-Roegen on the other. We thus have three fundamentally different views of what is possible and desirable, reflecting multiple tensions around ideas of growth.

Is the Concept Still Relevant?

The steady state economy concept, in any of its manifestations, is fundamentally opposed to the dominant paradigm in contemporary economic thinking. The normative application of the neoclassical mode is sometimes referred to as neoliberalism. While there are multiple debates within the neoliberal school of economics, its general normative approach favors freer trade among nations, flexible labor markets, freer migration, global financial integration to enhance capital flows, and intellectual property protections. The underlying assumption of this school is that economic growth is the solution to poverty, unemployment, and income inequality, captured in the aphorism "a rising tide lifts all boats."

This viewpoint is evident in the responses to the global financial crises in the first decade of the twenty-first century. National fiscal and monetary policies as well as global trade policies continued to focus on stimulating overall economic growth as measured by traditional metrics like real (inflation-adjusted) gross domestic product per capita. Public policy was clearly dominated by this approach, and few politicians at local or national levels embraced the steady state economy idea. This might bring into question whether the steady state concept is still relevant in a world recovering from a global recession in the business cycle nearly as large as the Great Depression following 1929.

Advocates of the steady state economy argue for a paradigm shift in economics. They reject many of the underlying assumptions of the neoliberal economic thinking and make different assumptions. Three of the important assumptions follow:

- There are biophysical constraints on the economy that must be recognized. (See figure 1 on page 81.) Economic growth as reflected in material throughput therefore cannot continue indefinitely.
- Inequalities in the distribution of income, wealth, and other benefits of economic production are relevant to human well-being, and therefore distributional questions cannot be ignored by advocating for more growth. Utilitarianism is not accepted to be an ethically acceptable approach to measuring welfare changes.
- Human well-being is not just a function of money income, and all values are not captured by individual willingness to pay for goods or services.

It is clear that these assumptions about normative elements of economic theory have not penetrated mainstream economic thinking and were not part of the public policy response to global economic stresses at the beginning of the twenty-first century. A paradigm shift has not occurred yet in economics. There are, however, signs of growing debate among economists that suggest that elements of the steady state economy may well be relevant for the new century.

The normative assumptions of the steady state vision show up in surprising places, indicating that elements of the concept continue to shape debates about economic policy. For example, the idea of biophysical limits on economic activity has taken hold with one of the world's largest traders in currency, Tullett Prebon. The research director for the firm, Tim Morgan, argues that there is a need for a new kind of economics he calls "exponential economics" to identify "key drivers of society and the economy." He says, "The first of these key drivers is that the economy is an energy equation. Society as we know it today is a product of the use of extraneous energy to leverage the limited capabilities of human labor. The leveraging effect of abundant extraneous energy alone permits the earth to support a population of almost seven billion people" (2010, 2). This is not an explicit reference to Georgescu-Roegen, but it reflects the same kind of thinking. Morgan identifies energy return on energy invested as a potentially important measure of the biophysical constraints on the economy (2010, 33).

These biophysical limits have an effect on distributional questions as well, which is the second assumption where steady state advocates differ from advocates of conventional economics. We can see in the growing policy debate around climate change response that distribution of consumption matters. The researcher Shoibal Chakravarty and his colleagues (2009) place climate change response as an issue of distribution and therefore one that cannot be solved by growth. They argue that the requirements of carbon emission reductions should not be allocated on the basis of nation-states but rather based on the distribution of one billion high emitters, individuals who are responsible through their personal lifestyles for the largest emissions and are located in nations around the world.

More significantly, the 2011 United Nations Human Development Report made explicit the links between sustainability and equity in distribution. An innovation in the Human Development Index (HDI) for 2011 was the inclusion of an inequality-adjusted HDI, for the first time recognizing in this metric that distribution of income matters for well-being. This contradicted the utilitarian assumptions of welfare analysis in neoclassical economics and reflects a growing acceptance of this part of the steady state economy paradigm challenge to the dominant paradigm.

The HDI itself is part of a larger effort to develop alternative metrics of economic well-being from those that have dominated the standard economic theory. The assumption of the neoclassical model is that well-being is largely a function of consumption and that money income is a reasonable metric for economic progress. Therefore, real gross domestic product per capita is a reasonable measure of economic progress. Inherent in the steady state economy paradigm is a challenge to this assumption, but here too there is an increasingly broader acceptance of the challenge to money income as a comprehensive measure of well-being, both among economists and policy makers. A good example is the report commissioned by the government of France on alternative metrics of progress. The authors say, "What we measure affects what we do; and if our measurements are flawed, decisions may be distorted. . . . [W]e often draw inferences about what are good policies by looking at what policies have promoted economic growth; but if our metrics of performance are flawed, so too may be the inferences we draw" (Stiglitz, Sen, and Fitoussi 2009, 8).

Although there has not been a complete paradigm shift toward acceptance of the idea of the steady state economy, the idea both in whole and in part continues to challenge mainstream thinking. The concept stakes out an intellectual space between the optimists, neoliberal (neoclassical) advocates for continued growth, and pessimists like Georgescu-Roegen. The most recent manifestation of the steady state concept is the sustainable degrowth movement, which provokes a number of questions about the steady state concept at its core.

Growth, Degrowth, and Resolved Problems

The steady state economy idea challenges the growth paradigm of the standard economic model. As long as natural resources are abundant, seemingly unlimited growth offers more for everyone. Growth allows societies to make everyone materially better off without having to address difficult issues of income or wealth distribution. As humanity fills the planet, however, biophysical limits appear to the advocates of the steady state economy to constrain future growth. Therefore, the steady state economy is the alternative paradigm that may be sustainable.

Several fundamental questions remain with the idea. At what levels of economic activity and population size should the steady state occur? For optimists, the answer is some future level beyond which we need not worry in the present. For others, particularly those in the European degrowth movement, the rich nations of the world are already beyond a level that could be sustainable as a steady state (see, e.g., Martinez-Alier et al. 2002; Kallis 2011.) The degrowth movement reflects a Georgescu-Roegen–like belief that society has already overshot the biophysical limits of the Earth and is trending toward collapse. These opposed perspectives give widely different answers to a stark question: Should there be more humans at lower levels of consumption for a longer period of time or fewer humans at higher levels of consumption for a shorter period of time?

Even if there were agreement either globally or at a smaller geographic scale that the steady state economy was desirable, there are many technical questions to be answered. These are similar to the questions that neoclassical growth theory addresses within the growth paradigm.

- What level of income and wealth inequality is necessary or tolerable in the steady state? How do policies about distribution affect production and consumption behaviors?
- How do different age structures in a population affect the functioning of the economy?
- What social welfare rules will be possible in the attempt to reach and maintain the steady state?
- What are the capital investment needs of the steady state and what policies will assure that they are met? This applies for all capital types—manufactured, human, natural, and social/cultural.
- What metrics of human well-being will facilitate achieving and maintaining the steady state economy?
- Are people willing to accept constraints on behavior necessary to achieve and maintain the steady state economy?
- Can one part of the steady state economy grow, necessitating that some other part decreases?
- Is the steady state sustainable in some meaningful way, or was Georgescu-Roegen correct in believing that the steady state is not any more possible than growth?

The assumption of the need for a steady state economy is that the current generation of humans has as an ethical or a moral obligation to future humans and perhaps to nonhuman species. Inherent in almost any definition of sustainability is the idea that there is an intergenerational imperative that we leave the future no worse off in terms of its ability to meet its needs. If the steady state economy is a necessary constraint on unsustainable growth in order to allow the future to meets its needs, the steady state economy becomes an article of trust for the present generation. We must trust that if the steady state is accomplished at some level that would be sustainable for the indefinite future, future generations will share in the commitment to pass that state on to those who follow them in their future. It is essentially a reciprocal intergenerational bargain. How might we be assured that those who follow us would accept that bargain?

Mark W. ANDERSON
The University of Maine

See also Community; Education, Higher; Energy Efficiency; Global Trade; Natural Capital; Population; Progress; Values

FURTHER READING

Barnett, Harold J., & Morse, Chandler. (1963). *Scarcity and growth: The economics of natural resource availability.* Baltimore: Johns Hopkins University Press.

Boulding, Kenneth. (1966). The economics of the coming spaceship Earth. In Herman Daly (Ed.), *Economics, ecology, ethics: Essays toward a steady-state economy.* San Francisco: W. H. Freeman.

Boulding, Kenneth. (1973). The shadow of the stationary state. *Daedalus, 102*(4), 89–101.

Chakravarty, Shoibal, et al. (2009). Sharing global CO$_2$ emission reduction among one billion high emitters. *Proceedings of the National Academy of Sciences, 106*(29), 11884–11888.

Cole, H. S. D.; Freeman, Christopher; Jahoda, Mari; & Pavitt, K. L. R. (1973). *Thinking about the future: A critique of the limits to growth.* London: Chatto & Windus.

Daly, Herman E. (1968). On economics as a life science. *Journal of Political Economy, 76,* 392–406.

Daly, Herman E. (1980). Introduction to *Essays toward a steady-state economy.* In Herman Daly (Ed.), *Economics, ecology, ethics: Essays toward a steady-state economy.* San Francisco: W. H. Freeman. Retrieved August 14, 2012, from http://josiah.berkeley.edu/2008Spring/ER291/Readings/3.19-4.01/ValuingTheEarth_Daly_Intro.pdf

Daly, Herman E. (1995). On Nicholas Georgescu-Roegen's contributions to economics: An obituary essay. *Ecological Economics, 13,* 149–154.

Daly, Herman E., & Cobb, John B., Jr. (1989). *For the common good: Redirecting the economy toward community, the environment, and a sustainable future.* Boston: Beacon Press.

Ehrlich, Paul. (1968). *The population bomb.* New York: Ballantine Books.

Georgescu-Roegen, Nicholas. (1971). *The entropy law and the economic process.* Cambridge, MA: Harvard University Press.

Georgescu-Roegen, Nicholas. (1975). Energy and economic myths. *Southern Economic Journal, 41,* 347–381.

Kallis, Georgos. (2011). In defence of degrowth. *Ecological Economics, 70,* 873–880.

Kuhn, Thomas. (1970). *The structure of scientific revolutions.* Chicago: University of Chicago Press.

Layard, Richard. (2005). *Happiness: Lessons from a new science.* New York: Penguin.

Martinez-Alier, Joan, et al. (2002). Sustainable degrowth: Mapping the context, criticisms, and future prospects of an emergent paradigm. *Ecological Economics, 69,* 1741–1747.

Meadows, Donella H.; Meadows, Dennis L.; Randers, Jorgen; & Behrens, William W., III. (1972). *The limits to growth.* New York: Universe Books.

Mill, John Stuart. (1848). Of the stationary state. *Principles of political economy—Book IV.*

Morgan, Tim. (2010). End-Game: The denouement of exponentials. *Strategy Insights, Issue Six.* London: Tullett Prebon.

Osborn, Fairfield. (1948). *Our plundered planet.* Boston: Little, Brown.

Ropke, Inge. (2004). The early modern history of ecological economics. *Ecological Economics, 50,* 293–314.

Samuelson, Paul A. (1943). Dynamics, statics, and the stationary state. *The Review of Economics and Statistics, 25*(1), 56–68.

Stiglitz, Joseph E.; Sen, Amartya; & Fitoussi, Jean-Paul. (2009). Report by the Commission on the measurement of economic performance and social progress. Retrieved November 28, 2011, from www.stiglitz-sen-fitoussi.fr

Vogt, William. (1948). *Road to survival.* New York: Sloane Associates.

World Commission on Environment and Development (WCED). (1987). *Our common future.* New York: Oxford University Press.

Education, Higher

Sustainability challenges the current paradigms and structures, as well as predominant practices, in higher education. Universities and colleges must go beyond the integration of key ideas in existing curricula in a quest for interdisciplinarity, "real world" research, and the opening of institutional boundaries so that the notion of sustainable communities is extended beyond academic walls. A connected view of sustainability across institutions is required to transform the educational experience of students. If the higher education sector is to be transformative, it needs to transform itself.

A history of higher education reveals that universities and colleges have been at the forefront of creating as well as deconstructing paradigms. They have led social change through scientific breakthroughs but also through the education of intellectuals, leaders, and future makers. In the United Kingdom, the professor Lord Nicholas Stern of Brentford, an opinion leader in climate change and lead author of the eponymous *Stern Review on the Economics of Climate Change,* connects these important roles to addressing sustainability challenges of our day. Higher education, he argues, can change the world through training and expanding young minds; researching answers to challenges and informing public policy; showing its own understanding and commitment through careful campus management; and being a responsible employer and active member of the business and local communities (Stern 2010). In an era of globalization, universities and colleges also have an impact through their global procurement and offshore partnerships as well as through the education of national and international students. Their potential influence on economic development and poverty alleviation as well as on health and community building should not be overlooked.

This catalyst potential needs grounding, however, in a context where universities and colleges are currently seen as contributing to the sustainability crisis and reproducing the paradigms that underpin our exploitative relationships with people and the environment.

The literature argues that sustainability challenges the current paradigms, structures, and predominant practices across social sectors including higher education (e.g., Sterling 1996; Calder and Clugston 2003; Lozano 2007). It is therefore not surprising to discover that universities and colleges that have committed to sustainability are struggling to meaningfully contribute to it (e.g., Lozano et al. 2010; Su and Chang 2010; Huisingh and Mebratu 2000).

In practice, it is relatively simple to initiate projects that address key sustainability issues, but these tend to engage a minority of those involved, failing to reach the core of staff, students, and others with a direct interest or, indeed, to influence the culture of the institutions. Equally the commissioning of a new sustainable building or development of specialist courses in the area provides some opportunity to shape minds and practices; attempts to mainstream this agenda across higher education, however, have so far failed to have an impact.

Sustainability is more a journey than a checklist, as worldviews pervading thought and practice need to be questioned. It engages universities and colleges in a quest for interdisciplinary, participatory pedagogies, "real world" research, and the opening of institutional boundaries so that the notion of sustainable communities is extended beyond university and college walls. The difficulty is that these need to occur in a connected way. The systemic complexity of this agenda challenges university silos and corridors of power, as well as the criteria and processes of decision making. Furthermore, sustainability is underpinned by democratic and participatory processes of change; cross-departmental (and faculty) teaching and research; and a redefinition of the teacher-student, the leader-employee, and the academia-community relationships. In other words, the transformation of a university toward sustainable development requires a realignment of all its activities with a critically reflective paradigm, which also supports the construction of more sustainable futures.

Milestones in Higher Education

A review of the sustainability movements and milestones in higher education is needed to understand the current expectations of and challenges to higher education. The journey began in the early 1970s with the Stockholm Conference on the Human Environment (1972) being the first to formally identify the role of higher education in progressing sustainable development at the international level. This was followed by the Belgrade Charter (1975), the Tbilisi Declaration (1977), and the United Nations Conference on Environment and Development (1992), all acknowledging the importance of education and higher education in furthering this agenda. More significant, however, was the signing of international declarations by university leaders, higher education associations, and government ministers committing to a step toward changes for sustainability. These documents call for universities and colleges to operate ethically and to be more accountable to those with a direct interest. They argue for better environmental and carbon management on campuses; the training of employees; the reorientation of the curriculum toward education for sustainable development; and a greater contribution to social agendas through research and public engagement. (See table 1 on pages 88–89.)

Although these international declarations provide visible commitment to encourage progress, they are not sufficient to change institutional and disciplinary practices in higher education (Bekessy, Samson, and Clarkson 2007). The review below indicates that it is government support combined with the reach of international partnerships (such as the International Association of Universities, the Global Higher Education for Sustainability Partnerships, the Pacific Network of Island Universities, the Copernicus Alliance, and Global University Network for Innovation) that is playing a critical role in promoting the innovation needed to reorient higher education toward sustainability.

Steps Forward

The higher education sector first committed to innovating for sustainability in the early 1990s. The key questions now become, What progress has there been, and how is it evidenced? In order to address these questions, it is important to look at international and regional progress in the areas of leadership and strategy; modeling practice; education and learning; and partnerships and outreach for sustainability in higher education.

Modeling Practice across Campuses

The majority of the universities engaged with sustainability are preoccupied with the greening of the campus. The evidence for this can be found within research papers published in journals of higher education, but also across institutional webpages that document extensive sustainability efforts to minimize waste and energy consumption; develop low carbon buildings; protect biodiversity and natural space; source sustainable goods and services; and model sustainability to influence behaviors of staff, students, and local communities.

The Greening the Campus movement can be traced back to North America, where higher education has taken great strides in demonstrating sustainability in practice within the management and administration of university sites (Wright and Elliott 2011). US and Canadian university networks have played a key role catalyzing efforts across the globe. Leaps forward in this area can be partly attributed to the US 2008 Higher Education Sustainability Act (HESA), which legislated for the University Sustainability Grants Program. In 2010 the program was approved for a budget of $50 million to support the implementation of major sustainability initiatives on campuses (see Campaign for Environmental Literacy 2008). The United States is the only country in the world that offers this type of incentive and support. More recently the Salix loan grant (in the United Kingdom) has supported institutional initiatives mostly associated with the refurbishment or development of faculty, administrative, and student housing buildings.

Examples of good practice in campus management for sustainability have been documented not only in Europe and the United States, but also in Africa, Asia, and particularly Latin America. The International Sustainable Campus Network (ISCN) Excellence Awards capture and celebrate the diversity of responses to challenges in this field. Interesting examples often not celebrated through high profile awards include the University of Hong Kong's systematic efforts to reduce environmental impact and conserve natural environments; the University Autónoma of the Madrid eco-campus, which creates innovative and effective opportunities for engaging staff and students in sustainability activities; and Mabada University in Lebanon, which recycles its water and generates its own electricity (Salame 2010). Equally, the Universidad Autónoma del Estado de Morelos (UAEM)

TABLE 1. Key International Declarations on Higher Education

Year	Declaration / Charter	Partners(s) Involved	Scope	Key Words
1990	Talloires Declaration	University Leaders for a Sustainable Future	Global	Unprecedented scale and speed of pollution and degradation; Major roles: education, research, policy, information exchange; Reverse the trends
1991	Halifax Declaration	Consortium of Canadian Institutions; International Association of Universities (IAU); United Nations University (UNU)	Global	Responsibility to shape their present and future development; Ethical obligation; Overcome root causes
1993	Kyoto Declaration on Sustainable Development	IAU	Global	Better communication of the what and why of SD*; Teaching and research capacity; Operations to reflect the best SD practice
1993	Swansea Declaration	Association of Australian Government Universities	Global	Educational, research, and public service roles; Major attitudinal and policy changes
1994	COPERNICUS University Charter for Sustainable Development	Association of European Universities	Regional (Europe)	Institutional commitment; Environmental ethics and attitudes; Education of university employees; Programs in environmental education; Interdisciplinarity; Dissemination of knowledge; Networking; Partnerships; Continuing education programs; Technology transfer
2001	Lüneburg Declaration	Global Higher Education for Sustainability Partnership	Global	Indispensable role; Catalyst for SD* building a learning society; Generate new knowledge to train leaders and teachers of tomorrow; Disseminate SD knowledge; State of the art knowledge; Continually review and update curricula; Serve teachers; Lifelong learners
2002	Unbuntu Declaration	UNU, United Nations Educational, Scientific and Cultural Organization (UNESCO), IAU, Third World Academy of Science, African Academy of Sciences and the Science Council of Asia, COPERNICUS-CAMPUS, Global Higher Education for Sustainability Partnership and University Leaders for Sustainable Future	Global	Called for the creation of a global learning environment for education in sustainable development; To produce an action-oriented tool kit for universities designed to move from commitment to action; To indicate strategies for taking sustainable development; To suggest strategies for reform, particularly in such areas as teaching, research, operations, and outreach; To make an inventory of best practice and case studies

TABLE 1. *Continued*

2005	Graz Declaration on Committing Universities to Sustainable Development, Austria	COPERNICUS CAMPUS, Karl-Franzens University Graz, Technical University Graz, Oikos International, UNESCO	Global	Called on universities to give status to SD* in their strategies and activities; Called for universities to use SD as a framework for the enhancement of the social dimension of European higher education
2005	Bergen	European education ministers, European Commission and other consultative members	Regional (Europe)	Made for the first time since 1999 a strong reference that the Bologna Process for establishing a European Higher Education Area by 2010 and promoting the European system of higher education worldwide should be based on the principle of sustainable development.
2006	American College and University Presidents' Climate Commitment	Association for the Advancement of Sustainability in Higher Education (AASHE)	National (US)	Called for an Emissions inventory; Within two years, universities are to set a date for becoming "climate neutral"; Integrating sustainability into the curriculum and make it part of the educational experience; Make action plan, inventory, and progress reports publicly available
2008	Declaration of the Regional Conference on Higher Education in Latin America and the Caribbean– CRES 2008	UNESCO	Regional (Caribbean and Latin American)	Emphasis on SD* for social progress; Cultural identities; Social cohesion; Poverty; Climate Change; Energy Crisis; Culture of Peace; Need contributes to democratic relations and tolerance; Solidarity and cooperation; Critical and rigorous intellectual ability
2008	Sapporo Sustainability Declaration	G8 University Network	Global	Universities should work closely with policy makers; Universities' leadership role is becoming increasingly critical; Educating; Disseminating information; Training leaders; Interdisciplinary perspective
2009	World Conference on Higher Education	UNESCO	Global	Advance understanding of multifaceted issues and our ability to respond; Increase interdisciplinary focus; promote critical thinking; Active citizenship; Peace, well-being, human rights; Contribute to education of committed ethical citizens
2009	Turin Declaration on Education and Research for Sustainable and Responsible Development, Italy	G8 University Network	Global	Called for new models of social and economic development consistent with sustainability principles; Ethical approaches to sustainable development; New approaches to energy policy; Focus on sustainable ecosystems

Source: author.

Note: "SD" = "sustainable development."

in Mexico provides an exemplary case study of how to progress campus change for sustainability through internal and external partnerships.

Programs such as the ISO 14001, a global standard for Environmental Management Systems (EMS), or Eco Campus have played a role in catalyzing efforts in this area. These activities, mostly driven by estates' directors (i.e., the directors of operations rather than the academic side of campuses) and their teams, rarely make an impact on students' formal learning opportunities. The Mirvac School of Sustainable Development at Bond University, Australia, provides an outstanding example of how sustainable buildings not only can contribute to minimizing ecological footprints, but also become a source of inspiration for curriculum work. Examples of campus activities extending their influence on core university provisions are rare.

The recent swell of interest in carbon may well reverse this trend in northern universities. In the United Kingdom, for example, the government's Carbon Reduction Commitment Energy Efficiency Scheme (CRC), introduced in April 2010, is a mandatory carbon emissions reporting and pricing program aimed at non-energy-intensive sectors in the nation's economy, including higher education. Higher education institutions affected by the legislation (i.e., those that use more than 6,000 megawatts of electricity per year) are required to measure and report their carbon emissions annually, using specific measurement rules. Beginning in 2012, they will be required to purchase allowances (at £12/tonne, or roughly US$18, in the first year) to cover their emissions from the previous year. Parallel to this, the Higher Education Funding Council for England published its Carbon Strategy in 2010, committing the university sector to the achievement of the British government's carbon reduction targets (set out in the Climate Change Act 2008). The Strategy also expects universities to promote carbon reduction through teaching, research, and public communications. The increasing interest in curriculum activities from professional associations such as the Association for the Advancement of Sustainability in Higher Education (in the United States), the Environmental Association for Universities and Colleges (in the United Kingdom), the Australasian Campuses Towards Sustainability (Australia), and the International Sustainable Campus Network (which brings together

practitioners from higher education with an interest in sustainability) signals a movement toward greater alignment between what is preached in classrooms and practiced on campuses.

Research for Sustainability in Higher Education

It is widely acknowledged that sustainability requires forms of research activity that challenge boundaries at several interfaces, not the least between academic disciplines and research paradigms, across professional roles, and in relation to professional values (e.g., the Marie Curie International Incoming Fellowships [IIF], which award grants to top researchers). It only has been since the beginning of the new millennium, however, that movements toward these more complex forms of research activity are evident in sustainability research arenas.

Interdisciplinary Research

Research councils and funding agencies, such as the European Union, are increasingly recognizing the need to uncover new conceptual and practical spaces for research. In recent years, they have directed resources and attention to interdisciplinarity and recognized it as a new source of insight to advance human understandings of the sustainability challenge (Tilbury 2011b). These funding sources are encouraging academics to go beyond their discipline boundaries and seek partnerships with colleagues who have similar interests but differing methodologies and/or perspectives. The result is emergent research landscapes with the potential for alternative academic frameworks and new sustainability pathways in the areas such as sustainable consumption; wildlife and water conservation; reducing poverty; community development; transition towns; sustainable business development; ecological resilience; sustainable food; and change management for sustainability. This expertise focuses on understanding how to plan, manage, and lead change for sustainability across an organization. It draws on the fields of education, psychology, sociology, and business management.

Research with Impact

There has also been a push toward research that has an impact in a social as well as in an academic sense. The

Research Excellence Frameworks (HEFCE), Research Quality Framework (DEEWPR), Performance Based Research (TEC), and similar systems used for assessing the quality of research in higher education institutions are still key for academics seeking promotion, funding, and/or external recognition for their research. Criteria that acknowledge the impact of the research on thinking, policy, and communities of practice are slowly making their way into these high profile assessment systems. This is beginning to influence the type of sustainability research that institutions and researchers are turning their attention to with an emphasis on more practical and concrete projects, which can create changes as well as make academic contributions.

In the context of higher education itself, and in this context of research impact, there has been a notable investment in research, which can change strategies for sustainability in universities and colleges. In Australia, for example, the Australian Teaching and Learning Council has invested in research-informed resource development (ALTC 2011). Similarly, in Africa, Mainstreaming Environment and Sustainability in African Universities (MESA) has received funding to support "situated inquiry" that is seeking to influence institutional thinking and practice. (*Situated inquiry* refers to the theory that knowledge depends on context; it contrasts with theories that stress the importance of individual learning.) In Asia, Japan's Education for Sustainable Development Research Center and China's Tongi Institute of Environment and Sustainable Development are progressing following similar lines of inquiry with government and United Nations Environment Programme (UNEP) funding.

From Informing to Transforming

Although there is still significant investment in exploratory research, particularly in the areas of science and technology for sustainability, there has also been increasing attention attached to transforming research practice itself (El Zoghbi 2011). This new wave of research is seeking to go beyond problem solving or technological developments, and instead questions the role of research in reproducing exploitative relationships with people and the environment. Underpinning this movement is an explicit challenge to dominant research paradigms and the professional practice of the researcher.

This trend is characterized by the phrase "research as social change" (Schratz and Walker 1995) and promotes forms of research that are conscious and explicit about the power, politics, and participatory relations underpinning research practice. They challenge the dominant role of the researcher as an expert and encourage participatory inquiry techniques so that research is undertaken "with people" rather than "on people." The

TABLE 2. Questioning Research Practice

Key Questions Driving Changes in Research Practice
Q. How can different disciplines combine to present new insights in the sustainability challenge?
Q. Who commissions the research?
Q. Whose interests does the research serve?
Q. What is the relationship between the researcher and the researched?
Q. Is the research "on" or "with" people?
Q. Who can access the research and how?
Q. How can the research transform and not just inform practice?
Q. How is complexity embraced within the research?
Q. How do researchers engage with, and recognize, systems within the research?
Q. Is there congruence between the "what" and the "how" of research?

Source: author.

movement is driven by a series of "critical" questions. (See table 2 above.)

Sustainability beyond the University Walls

Initial reports of sustainability in higher education would suggest that the issues and solutions for progressing sustainability lie with universities and the higher education sector itself. Through experience and over time, however, the sector has learned that it must reach beyond the university walls to address sustainability within the communities of practice that they serve. Since roughly the beginning of the millennium there has been a stepping up of activity relating to partnerships and outreach for sustainability.

The University of Western Sydney is an example where the sustainability efforts have been constructed through an approach situated within their locality and with a focus on supporting the communities closely linked to the university. The partnership is particularly active in issues of watershed management. The journey of transforming the institution toward sustainability has been shared particularly with community and government stakeholders (i.e., those people with a vested interest in the outcome of an enterprise). In Saudi Arabia, the King Abdullah University of Science and Technology runs a community-wide recycling and compost program where problems and solutions to the waste issue are co-constructed with local stakeholders (Salame 2011). In the Philippines, teacher education partnerships have redefined "town and gown" relationships (Galang 2010). At the University of Gloucestershire in the United Kingdom, an edible garden brought together local residents, students, and staff as well as local government support and enforcement agencies in learning skills in permaculture design, food awareness, and community building. (*Permaculture*, a portmanteau of *permanent* and *agriculture*, refers to the practice of incorporating various aspects of nature into agriculture, architecture, design, and other fields.)

The United Nations University (UNU)–accredited Regional Centres of Expertise (RCE), which focus on partnership learning and action for sustainability, are also worthy of attention. Since 2005 the UNU has acknowledged sixty-three RCEs in Africa, Australia, the Asia-Pacific region, Europe, the Middle East, South America, the Caribbean, North America, and Central America. RCEs seek to expand the span of local partnership work as well as connect people and activities across wider regions in order to link urban and rural development issues, to understand dynamics that cut across local boundaries, and to connect local and national activities.

In the United States, the Partnership for Education for Sustainable Development, established in 2003, brought together schools, science and research, faith organizations, nongovernmental organizations (NGOs), government agencies, and youth advocacy groups to support the implementation of sustainability initiatives.

Partnership platforms that bring together universities committed to this agenda continue to be important. For example, the Copernicus Alliance; the Pacific Network of Island Universities; the Japanese Higher Education for Sustainable Development Network; the Australasian Campuses Towards Sustainability network; the Association for the Advancement of Sustainability in Higher Education (US); the Mexican Consortium University for Sustainable Development (COMPLEXUS); and the Mainstreaming Environment and Sustainability in African Universities (MESA) Partnership have all experienced significant increases in their membership numbers. Their annual meetings confirm that universities are increasingly recognizing the need to work together to share common issues, but also to learn from best practice

and combine scarce resources to address the sustainability imperative.

Parallel to this key trend is a greater accountability of higher education to the communities that it serves, particularly in Western nations currently in economic decline. As national debt increases, governments are forced to rethink their investment strategies. They are asking questions regarding the value and impact of university activity on economic as well as social development. Universities are being held to account and, through various funding mechanisms, are being encouraged to establish stronger links with their local-regional communities to support the recovery. The result is a reorientation of university activity to provide this greater accountability in terms of outreach. It has led to an array of studies such as that undertaken by the New Economics Foundation, which found that the social impact of universities in the United Kingdom is worth over £1.31 billion or about US$2.1 billion. It opens with the tagline "benefits are felt by everyone, not just those who go to university." The study undertaken by the New Economics Foundation (Shaheen 2011) documents how universities in the United Kingdom add value to society in the form of health, well-being, citizenship, and political engagement.

Heila Lotz-Sisitka, an expert on environmental education and sustainability at Rhodes University in South Africa, reports a parallel trend in Africa, where universities are seeing sustainability as an opportunity to redefine university-community relationships (2011). She presents evidence that institutions are making tangible contributions to local communities through addressing issues of peace, security, conflict resolution, and HIV/AIDS. She cites Uganda Martyrs University and its improving livelihoods initiative, which has resulted in improved income, food security, water conservation, and sustainable livelihoods as well as better relationships between the university and the surrounding communities.

Education and Learning for Sustainability

Education has always been seen as key to improving quality of life, not just of individuals but also collectively for humankind (Galang 2010). The higher education declarations on sustainability (see table 1 on pages 88–89) explicitly acknowledge this and confirm the importance of learning, communication, and capacity building for sustainable development.

The US environmental studies professor David Orr reminds us, perhaps paradoxically, that the global issues that face us cannot be attributed to a lack of higher education. "Why is it that those who contribute to exploiting poor communities and the Earth's ecosystems are those who have BAs, MBAs, MSCs, and PhDs, and not the 'ignorant' poor from the [global] South?" (2004).

The paradigms deeply embedded in our higher education knowledge systems and relationships are contributing to unsustainable development. The United Nations Decade in Education for Sustainable Development International Implementation Scheme echoes this perspective and calls for reorientation of education toward more sustainable forms of living (UNESCO 2005). It acknowledges that it is not simply a matter of integrating new content into our education programs or building sustainability literacy across all subject areas, but it requires the unpacking of social, economic, cultural, and environmental assumptions, which serve the status quo and which are reproduced by our education systems (UNESCO 2002). As Angelina Galang, executive director of the Environmental Studies Institute at Miriam College in the Philippines, reminds us, centuries of teaching resource extraction need to be questioned and learning efforts redesigned so that professionals understand the responsibility and implications of sustainability for their area of influence (2010).

There is evidence to suggest that higher education does not understand the true nature of the challenge. The focus has been on developing new specialist courses on sustainable development (e.g., University of Philippines; The Energy and Resources Institute of India [TERI]; Dalhousie University), which are improving the sustainability literacy and capabilities of those interested in pursuing careers in this area. The teachers, architects, accountants, doctors, and business managers, however, are still being schooled into social assumptions and practices that serve to exploit people and the planet. Curriculum and pedagogy, which are at the core of higher education experiences, need to be transformed if universities and colleges are to make a meaningful contribution to sustainable development (UNECE 2010b).

The Asia Pacific region has played an important role in directing attention to pedagogy and learning for sustainability across education, including higher education, and shows a stronger overall trajectory in this respect (Ryan et al. 2010). The UN Decade in Education for Sustainable Development originated in this region with the proposal

from the Japanese government and NGOs at the World Summit for Sustainable Development (Nomura and Abe 2009). The Asia Pacific Regional Bureau of Education has provided much strategic guidance and practical tools in ESD (see for example UNESCO 2005; Elias 2006; Tilbury and Janousek 2007; Elias and Sachathep 2009).

Arguably the most ambitious initiatives in these areas have been driven by the Australian Research Institute in Education for Sustainability (ARIES) through its business education and teacher education projects. The ARIES work has challenged dominant assumptions within existing programs; developed inter- and intra-university partnerships to support systemic change; built staff confidence and expertise in sustainability; addressed the professional capacities and responsibilities of the students; and embraced the dual challenge of pedagogical and curriculum development for sustainability. This has been evidenced through independent evaluations commissioned by the Australian Federal Government, which funds this work.

A Higher Education Funding Council for England (HEFCE)–funded project, Leading Curriculum Change for Sustainability, seeks to embed education for sustainability into university quality assurance and enhancement systems and is another example of an ambitious curriculum change in higher education being encouraged by a government agency (HEFCE 2011). In a similar vein, Swedish, British, Australian, Canadian, Japanese, and Dutch aid agencies have played an important role in funding curriculum development for sustainability in Africa, Asia, and the Pacific Islands (e.g., MedIES 2010; AusAid 2012). Case studies of higher education change triggered or supported by such funding are documented across various journals such as the *Journal of Education for Sustainable Development;* the *Australian Journal of Environmental Education*; and the *South African Journal of Environmental Education and Environmental Education Research.*

There is also evidence from Latin America and parts of Southeast Asia that university education programs are being challenged to reorient themselves toward sustainability by school and community education initiatives whose influences are slowly making their way into higher education curricula (Galang 2010).

When studied closely, the initiatives identified above reveal learning transitions toward education for sustainable development. These shifts are summarized in table 3 on page 94.

Leadership and Strategy for Sustainability

The strategic implications of sustainability are that of innovation, not integration, of this agenda into mainstream institutional structures and practices. In other

TABLE 3. Learning Transitions toward Education for Sustainable Development (ESD)

Shifting From:	Moving Toward:
Bolt-on additions to existing curricula	Innovation within existing curricula
Passing on knowledge and raising awareness of issues	Questioning and getting to the root of issues
Teaching about attitudes and values	Encouraging clarification of existing values
Seeing people as the problem	Seeing people as change agents
Sending messages about sustainable development	Creating opportunities for reflection, negotiation, and participation
Raising awareness and trying to change behavior	Challenging the mental models that influence decisions and actions
More focus on the individual and personal change	More focus on professional and social change
Negative "problem-solving" approaches	Constructive creation of alternative futures
Isolated changes/actions	Learning to change

Source: Tilbury and Cooke (2005).

words, translating signatures on international declarations into institutional responses requires adjustments to academic priorities, organizational structures, financial systems, and audit systems. A recent project commissioned by the Australian Teaching and Learning Council recognizes that these changes do not just happen; they must be led (Scott et al. 2011). The Turnaround Leadership for Sustainability in Higher Education Project seeks to define the capabilities that make an educationally effective higher education leader for sustainability and produce resources to develop and enhance these leadership capabilities. This international project involves researchers from Australia, the United Kingdom, and the United States, and seeks to make a step-change contribution to an area that has been deprived of attention and forms an important piece of the transformation puzzle.

A review of journal articles accompanied by a web search reveals that there are several leadership for sustainability initiatives across the globe, which essentially target senior managers from the corporate sector (see for example the Cambridge Programme for Sustainability Leadership). Universities do operate as businesses at one level, but at another level academic change for sustainability requires a different model of leadership. Existing programs are thus of limited value for senior management teams working with higher education concerns. The lack of leadership development opportunities for higher education managers may explain why progress toward sustainability in higher education has been piecemeal (Lozano 2007; Tilbury 2011b).

Emerging practice may well change this scenario. For example, the Sustainable Development Education Academy at York University, established in 2009, is supporting Canadian teams engaged in teacher education to plan and implement academic and program change for sustainability. At another level, the Salzburg Global Academy founded the Sustainable Futures Academy (SFA) in 2010, recognizing the criticality of leadership in the transition toward more sustainable universities and colleges. The SFA has the reorientation of academic offerings toward sustainability firmly in its sights, and seeks to progress it through partnerships between the global North (i.e., the industrialized and developed nations of the world, mainly found in the north) and the global South that can embed sustainability into the core business of universities and colleges (Scott et al. 2011).

Integrating Sustainability into Higher Education

Sustainability is a multifaceted agenda for organizations, but when harnessed effectively, its integrative potential is substantial. Yet to achieve this level of engagement in academic institutions involves profound leadership challenges. Leading change for sustainability in universities requires more than knowledge of or commitment to the principles of sustainability. It requires a facility for bringing about change that deals with complexity, uncertainty, and multiple stakeholders, as well as ambiguous terminology. It is complex, confusing, time consuming, and difficult to implement, which explains why, to date, only a handful of university leaders have taken on the challenge.

Evidence suggests that despite this inertia, there are movements toward more sustainable planning and practice in higher education. Government incentives, socio-economic expectations, partnership platforms, student leadership, and experimental practice are all contributing to changes, although these may not be deep or systemic. University leaders now need to help join these dots of activity in ways that align mainstream practices to sustainability innovation in their institutions. Senior management teams, at this moment, hold the key to transforming higher education so that it can play its part in transforming social practices and contribute to more sustainable futures.

Daniella TILBURY
University of Gloucestershire

See also Aging; Collective Learning; Community; Design and Architecture; Local Solutions to Global Problems

This article was adapted by the editors from Daniella Tilbury's article "Higher Education in the World 4: Higher Education's Commitment to Sustainability: From Understanding to Action," published in 2011 by the Global University Network for Innovation (GUNI). Used with kind permission of Palgrave Macmillan. We are grateful to Prof. Tilbury for her help on the article.

FURTHER READING

Abdul-Wahab, Sabah A.; Abdulraheem, Mahmood Y.; & Hutchinson, Melanie. (2003). The need for inclusion of environmental education in undergraduate engineering curricula. *International Journal of Sustainability in Higher Education, 4*(2), 126–137.

American College and University Presidents' Climate Commitment. (2011). *American college and university presidents' climate commitment.* Retrieved May 18, 2011, from http://www.presidentsclimatecommitment.org/about/commitment

Association of Australian Government Universities. (1993). Swansea Declaration. Retrieved May 3, 2011, from http://www.iisd.org/educate/declarat/swansea.htm

AusAid. (2012). About Australia's aid program. Retrieved August 20, 2012, from http://www.ausaid.gov.au/makediff/Pages/default.aspx

Australian Learning and Teaching Council (ALTC). (2011). Sustainability resources for learning & teaching in higher education. Retrieved June 6, 2012, from http://sustainability.edu.au/resources

Baltic University Programme. (2011). Baltic University Programme: A regional university network. Retrieved June 6, 2011, from http://www.balticuniv.uu.se/

Barab, Sasha Alexander, & Luehmann, April Lynn. (2003). Building sustainable science curriculum: Acknowledging and accommodating local adaptation. *Science Education, 87*(4), 454–467.

Bawden, Richard. (2004). Sustainability as emergence: The need for engaged discourse. In Peter Blaze Corcoran & Arjen E. J. Wals (Eds.), *Higher education and the challenge of sustainability: Problematics, promise, and practice* (pp. 21–32). Dordrecht, The Netherlands: Kluwer Academic Publishers.

Bekessy, S. A.; Samson, K.; & Clarkson, R. E. (2007). The failure of non-binding declarations to achieve university sustainability: A need for accountability. *International Journal of Sustainability in Higher Education, 8*(3), 301–316.

Boks, Casper, & Diehl, Jan Carel. (2006). Integration of sustainability in regular courses: Experiences in industrial design engineering. *Journal of Cleaner Production, 14*(9–11), 932–939.

Calder, Wynn, & Clugston, Richard M. (2003). International efforts to promote higher education for sustainable development. *Planning for Higher Education, 31*, 30–44.

Campaign for Environmental Literacy. (2008). The University Sustainability Program. Retrieved August 23, 2012, from http://www.fundee.org/campaigns/usp/

COPERNICUS. (1994). *The University charter for sustainable development.* Retrieved May 3, 2011, from http://www.iisd.org/educate/declarat/coper.htm

Cortese, Anthony D. (2003). The critical role of higher education in creating a sustainable future. *Planning for Higher Education, 31*(3), 15–22.

Cotton, Debby R. E., & Winter, Jennie. (2010). It's not just bits of paper and light bulbs: A review of sustainability pedagogies and their potential for use in higher education. In Paula Jones, David Selby & Stephen Sterling (Eds.), *Sustainability education: Perspectives and practice across higher education* (pp. 39–54). London: Earthscan.

Elias, Derek. (2006). UNESCO's approach to implementing the decade of education for sustainable development (DESD) in Asia and the Pacific. *Australian Journal of Environmental Education, 22*(1), 83–86.

Elias, Derek, & Sachathep, Karampreet. (Eds.). (2009). *ESD currents: Changing perspectives from the Asia-Pacific.* Bangkok, Thailand: UNESCO Bangkok.

Elton, Lewis. (2003). Dissemination of innovations in higher education: A change theory approach. *Tertiary Education and Management, 9*, 199–214.

G8 University Network. (2008). G8 University Summit: Sapporo Sustainability Declaration (SSD). Retrieved May 4, 2011, from http://g8u-summit.jp/english/ssd/index.html

Galang, Angelina P. (2010). Environmental education for sustainability in higher education institutions in the Philippines. *International Journal of Sustainability in Higher Education, 11*(2), 138–150.

Global Higher Education for Sustainability Partnership. (2001). The Lüneburg declaration on higher education for sustainable development. Retrieved May 3, 2011, from http://www.lueneburg-declaration.de/downloads/declaration.htm

Global Reporting Initiative (GRI). (2002). Sustainability reporting guidelines. Retrieved June 11, 2012, from www.unep.fr/scp/gri/pdf/gri_2002_guidelines.pdf

El Zoghbi, Mona. (2011, May 19–20). The interdisciplinary researcher: Paradigms, practices and possibilities for sustainability. *PRISM conference report.* University of Gloucestershire, Cheltenham.

Ferreira, Jo-Anne; Ryan, Lisa; & Tilbury, Daniella. (2007a). Mainstreaming education for sustainability in initial teacher education in Australia: A review of existing professional development models. *Journal of Education for Teaching, 33*(2), 225–339.

Ferreira, Jo-Anne; Ryan, Lisa; & Tilbury, Daniella. (2007b). Planning for success: Factors influencing change in teacher education. *Australian Journal of Environmental Education, 23*, 45–55.

Ferreira, Jo-Anne; Ryan, Lisa; Davis, Julie; Cavanagh, Marian; & Thomas, Janelle. (Eds.). (2009). *Mainstreaming sustainability into pre-service teacher education in Australia.* Canberra: ARIES and Australian Government Department of the Environment, Water, Heritage and the Arts.

Ferreira, Jo-Anne, & Tilbury, Daniella. (2011). Higher education and sustainability in Australia: Transforming experiences. In *Higher education in the world 4, higher education's commitment to sustainability: From understanding to action.* Barcelona, Spain: GUNI.

Harvard College. (2009). Green campus loan fund. Retrieved May 20, 2011, from http://green.harvard.edu/loan-fund

Higher Education Funding Council for England (HEFCE). (2011). Research excellence framework. Retrieved June 13, 2011, from http://www.hefce.ac.uk/research/ref/

Huisingh, Don, & Mebratu, Desta. (2000). Educating the educators as a strategy for enhancing education on cleaner production. *Journal of Cleaner Production, 8*, 439–442.

International Association of Universities. (1991). The Halifax Declaration. Retrieved May 3, 2011, from http://www.iisd.org/educate/declarat/halifax.htm

International Association of Universities. (1993). Kyoto declaration on sustainable development. Retrieved May 4, 2011, from http://archive.www.iau-aiu.net/sd/sd_dkyoto.html

Lotz-Sisitka, Heila. (2011). The "event" of modern sustainable development and universities in Africa. In *Higher education in the world 4, higher education's commitment to sustainability: From understanding to action.* Barcelona, Spain: GUNI.

Lozano, Rodrigo. (2006). Incorporation and institutionalization of SD into universities: Breaking through barriers to change. *Journal of Cleaner Production, 14*(9–11), 787–796.

Lozano, Rodrigo. (2006). A tool for a graphical assessment of sustainability in universities (GASU). *Journal of Cleaner Production, 14,* 963–972.

Lozano, Rodrigo. (2007). Collaboration as a pathway for sustainable development. *Sustainable Development, 16*(6), 370–381.

Lozano, Rodrigo; Lukman, Rebeka; Lozano, Francisco J.; Huisingh, Don; & Zilahy, Gyula. (2010). *Jumping sustainability meme: SD transfer from society to universities.* (Paper presented at the *Environmental management for sustainable universities,* Delft, The Netherlands). Retrieved June 11, 2012, from http://repository.tudelft.nl/view/conferencepapers/uuid%3A66a6d957-f9e1-4913-bcf0-fbc4ebf15a1d/

Mah, Jeremy; Hunting, S.; & Tilbury, Daniella. (2006). *Education about and for sustainability in Australian business schools: Business schools project stage 2.* Canberra: Australian Government Department of the Environment, Water, Heritage and the Arts, and Australian Research Institute in Education for Sustainability.

Martin, Andrew, & Steele, Frances. (2010). *Sustainability in key professions: Accounting.* A report prepared by the Australian Research Institute in Education for Sustainability for the Australian Government Department of the Environment, Water, Heritage and the Arts.

Mediterranean Education Initiative for Environment & Sustainability (MEdIES). (2010). The MEdIES network for ESD Baltic University Programme. Retrieved August 20, 2012, from http://www.medies.net/staticpages.asp?aID=496

Ministry of the Environment, Japan. (2008). *Vision for university-led environment leadership initiatives for Asian sustainability.* Ministry of the Environment. Retrieved June 11, 2012, from http://www.env.go.jp/policy/edu/asia/en/education/

Mochizuki, Yoko, & Fadeeva, Zinaida. (2008). Regional centers of expertise on education for sustainable development (RCEs): An overview. *International Journal of Sustainability in Higher Education, 9*(4), 371–379.

Moore, Janet. (2005). Barriers and pathways to creating sustainability education programs: Policy rhetoric and reality. *Environmental Education and Research, 11*(5), 537–555.

Nobes, David C. (2002). Building on the foundations: Environmental science at the University of Canterbury, Christchurch, New Zealand. *International Journal of Sustainability in Higher Education, 3*(4), 371–379.

Nomura, Ko, & Abe, Osamu. (2009). The education for sustainable development movement in Japan: A political perspective. *Environmental Education Research, 15*(4), 483–496.

Nomura, Ko, & Abe, Osamu. (2011). Sustainability and higher education in Asia and the Pacific. In *Higher education in the world 4, higher education's commitment to sustainability: From understanding to action.* Barcelona, Spain: GUNI.

Orr, David W. (2004). *Earth in mind—On education, environment and the human prospect (10th anniversary ed.).* Washington, DC: Island Press.

Park, Tae Yoon. (2008). ESD of Korean universities. Presented at *International symposium "Sustainability in higher education: Learning from experiences in Asia and the world."* Rikkyo University, Japan.

Ryan, Alexandra; Tilbury, Daniella; Corcoran, Peter Blaze; Abe, Osamu; & Nomura, Ko. (2010). Sustainability in higher education in the Asia-Pacific: Developments, challenges, and prospects. *International Journal of Sustainability in Higher Education, 11*(3), 106–119.

Salame, Ramzi. (2011). Higher education commitment to sustainability in the Arab states. Presented at the *Fifth GUNI international Barcelona conference on higher education,* 23–26 November 2010. Barcelona, Spain.

Sanusi, Zainal Abidin, & Khelgat-Doost, Hamoon. (2008). Regional centre of expertise as a transformational platform for sustainability: A case study of Universiti Sains Malaysia, Penang. *International Journal of Sustainability in Higher Education, 9*(4), 487–497.

Schratz, Michael, & Walker, Rob. (1995). *Research as social change. New opportunities for qualitative research.* London: Routledge.

Scott, Geoff; Tilbury, Daniella; Sharp, Leith; & Deane, Elizabeth. (2011). Turnaround leadership for sustainability in higher education, Australian Learning and Teaching Council and the Sustainable Futures Leadership Academy, Sydney: Australia.

Shaheen, Faiza. (2011). *Degrees of value: How universities benefit society.* London: New Economics Foundation.

Sharp, Leith. (2002). Green Campuses: The road from little victories to systemic transformation. *International Journal of Sustainability in Higher Education, 3*(2), 128–145.

Sterling, Stephen. (1996). Education in change. In John Huckle & Stephen Sterling (Eds.), *Education for sustainability* (pp. 18–39). London: Earthscan.

Sterling, Stephen. (2004). An analysis of the development of sustainability education internationally: Evolution, interpretation and transformative potential. In John Blewitt & Cedric Cullingford (Eds.), *The sustainability curriculum: The challenge for higher education* (pp. 43–63). London: Earthscan.

Stern, Nicholas. (2010). Stern review on the economics of climate change. Retrieved June 1, 2012, from http://siteresources.worldbank.org/INTINDONESIA/Resources/226271-1170911056314/3428109-1174614780539/SternReviewEng.pdf

Su, H. Jenny, & Chang Tzu-chau. (2010). Sustainability of higher education institutions in Taiwan. *International Journal of Sustainability in Higher Education, 11*(2), 163–172.

Tertiary Education Commission, New Zealand. (2009). Performance based research fund. Retrieved June 11, 2012, from http://www.tec.govt.nz/Funding/Fund-finder/Performance-Based-Research-Fund-PBRF-/

The Energy and Resources Institute (TERI) University. (2011). About TERI University. Retrieved May 23, 2011, from http://www.teriuniversity.ac.in/index.php?option=com_content&view=article&id=56

Thomas, Ian. (2004). Tertiary or terminal: A snapshot of sustainability education in Australia's universities. *Proceedings of effective sustainability education conference 18–20 February, 2004,* University of New South Wales, Sydney.

Thomas, Janelle, & Benn, Suzanne. (2009). *Education about and for sustainability in Australian business schools stage 3.* A Report prepared by the Australian Research Institute in Education for Sustainability for the Australian Government Department of the Environment, Water, Heritage and the Arts.

Tilbury, Daniella. (2010). Change for a better world: Assessing the contribution of the DESD [Decade of Education for Sustainable Development]. In *Tomorrow Today.* Paris: UNESCO.

Tilbury, Daniella. (2011a). Are we learning to change? Mapping global progress in education for sustainable development in the lead up to Rio plus 20. *Global Environmental Research Education for Sustainable Development: Promises and Challenges, 14*(2), 101–107.

Tilbury, Daniella. (2011b). *Education for sustainable development: An expert review of processes and learning.* Paris: UNESCO.

Tilbury, Daniella, & Cooke, Kristina. (2005). *A national review of environmental education and its contribution to sustainability in*

Australia: Frameworks for sustainability. Canberra: Australian Government Department of the Environment, Water, Heritage and the Arts and the Australian Research Institute in Education for Sustainability.

Tilbury, Daniella; Crawley, Cathy; & Berry, Fiona. (2005). *Education about and for sustainability in Australian business schools: Stage 1*. Canberra: Australian Government Department of the Environment, Water, Heritage and the Arts and the Australian Research Institute in Education for Sustainability.

Tilbury, Daniella, & Janousek, Sonja. (2007). *Asia-Pacific guidelines for the development of national ESD [ecologically sustainable development] indicators*. Bangkok: UNESCO Asia and Pacific Regional Bureau for Education.

Tilbury, Daniella; Janousek, Sonja; Elias, Derek; & Bacha, Joel. (2007). *Monitoring and assessing progress during the UNDESD [United Nations Decade of Education for Sustainable Development] in Asia Pacific region: A quick guide to developing indicators*. Bangkok: UNESCO Asia and Pacific regional bureau for education IUCN.

Tilbury, Daniella; Keogh, Amanda; Leighton, Amy; & Kent, Jenny. (2005). *A national review of environmental education and its contribution to sustainability in Australia: Further and higher education*. Canberra: Australian Government Department of the Environment, Water, Heritage and the Arts and the Australian Research Institute in Education for Sustainability (ARIES).

Tilbury, Daniella, & Wortman, David. (2008). Education for sustainability in further and higher education: Reflections along the journey. *Journal for Planning in Higher Education, Society for College and University Planning US, 36*(4), 5–16.

United Nations (UN). (1992). *The Rio Declaration on Environment and Development*. Geneva: Centre for our Common Future.

United Nations (UN). (2002a). Agenda 21. Retrieved May 3, 2011, from http://www.un.org/esa/dsd/agenda21/

United Nations (UN). (2002b). Press conference on "Ubuntu Declaration" on education. Retrieved May 3, 2011, from http://www.un.org/events/wssd/pressconf/020901conf1.htm

United Nations Economic Commission for Europe (UNECE). (2010a). *UNECE annotated agenda for the Fifth meeting*, ECE/CEP/AC/.13/2010.1. Geneva: UN Economic and Social Council.

United Nations Economic Commission for Europe (UNECE). (2010b). *UNECE ESD competencies for educators: First draft for consultation*. Unpublished. Geneva: UN Economic and Social Council.

United Nations Educational, Scientific and Cultural Organization (UNESCO). (2002). *Education for sustainability, from Rio to Johannesburg: Lessons learnt from a decade of commitment*. Paris: UNESCO.

United Nations Educational, Scientific and Cultural Organization (UNESCO). (2005). *United Nations Decade of Education for Sustainable Development (2005–2014): International Implementation Scheme*. Paris: UNESCO.

United Nations Educational, Scientific and Cultural Organization (UNESCO). (2008). Declaration of the regional conference on higher education in Latin America and the Caribbean—CRES 2008. Retrieved May 3, 2011, from http://www.iesalc.unesco.org.ve/docs/wrt/declarationcres_ingles.pdf

United Nations Educational, Scientific and Cultural Organization (UNESCO). (2009). UNESCO World Conference on Education for Sustainable Development: Bonn Declaration. Retrieved May 4, 2011, from http://www.esd-world-conference-2009.org/fileadmin/download/ESD2009_BonnDeclaration080409.pdf

University Leaders for a Sustainable Future. (1990). Talloires Declaration. Retrieved May 3, 2011, from http://www.ulsf.org/programs_talloires.html

Verbitskaya, Ludmila A.; Nosova, Natilia B.; & Rodina, Ludmila L. (2002). Sustainable development in higher education in Russia: The case of St. Petersburg State University. *International Journal of Sustainability in Higher Education, 3*(3), 279–287.

Wright, Tarah, & Elliott, Heather. (2011). Canada and USA regional report. In *Higher education in the world 4, higher education's commitment to sustainability: From understanding to action*. Barcelona, Spain: GUNI.

Energy Efficiency

Energy efficiency is an often-misunderstood concept. Squeezing more work from energy via smarter technologies is often confused with a derogatory usage of the term "energy conservation." Energy efficiency means doing more (and often better) with less—the opposite of simply doing less or doing without. Energy inefficiency includes not only converting energy inefficiently into services, but also performing a task, however efficiently, that doesn't need to be performed—such as cooling a building with mechanical means when groundwater or ambient conditions could more cheaply do the same thing. Much of the confusion in terminology stems from mixing three different things—technological improvements in energy efficiency (such as thermal insulation), behavioral changes (such as resetting thermostats), and the price or policy tools used to induce or reward those changes.

Increasing energy end-use efficiency—technologically providing more desired service per unit of delivered energy consumed—is generally the largest, least expensive, most benign, most quickly deployable, least visible, least understood, and most neglected way to provide energy services. In the United States, it was largely responsible for halving primary energy use per dollar of real GDP during 1975–2010—making efficiency (together with smaller shifts in economic mix and behavior) as big as all sources of US energy supply combined—yet it often is dismissed as being unimportant.

Physical scientists find that despite energy efficiency's leading role in providing new energy services today, it has barely begun to tap its profitable potential.

In contrast, many engineers tend to be limited by adherence to past practice, and most economists by their assumption that any profitable savings must already have occurred. The potential of energy efficiency is also increasing faster through innovative designs, technologies, policies, and marketing methods than it is being used up through gradual implementation. The uncaptured "efficiency resource" lately is becoming bigger and cheaper even faster than oil reserves have, through stunning advances in exploration and production. The expansion of the "efficiency resource" is also accelerating, as designers realize that whole-system design integration can often make very large (one- or two-order-of-magnitude) energy savings cost *less* than small or no savings, and as energy-saving technologies often evolve discontinuously (such as LED lamps) rather than incrementally. Moreover, similarly rapid evolution and enormous potential apply also to marketing and delivering energy saving technologies and designs; research and development can accelerate both.

Terminology of Energy Efficiency

"Efficiency" means different things to the two professions most engaged in achieving it. To engineers, "efficiency" means a physical output/input ratio. To economists, "efficiency" means a monetary output/input ratio—and also, confusingly, "efficiency" may refer to the economic optimality of a market transaction or process. This article uses only physical output/input ratios (the engineering sense of "efficiency"), but the common use of monetary ratios confuses policymakers accustomed to economic jargon.

Mixing three different things—*technological* improvements in energy efficiency (such as thermal insulation), *behavioral* changes (such as resetting thermostats), and the *price* or *policy tools* used to induce or reward those changes—causes endless confusion.

Wringing more work from energy via smarter technologies is often, and sometimes deliberately, confused with a derogatory usage of the ambiguous term "energy conservation." Energy *efficiency* means doing more (and often better) with less—the opposite of simply doing less or worse or without. This confusion unfortunately makes the honorable and traditional term "energy conservation" no longer useful in certain societies, notably the United States, and underlies much of these societies' decades-long neglect or suppression of energy efficiency.

Deliberately reducing the amount or quality of *energy services*, however, remains a legitimate, though completely separate, option for those who prefer it or are forced by emergency to accept it. The 2000–2001 California electricity crisis—California is the most populous of the United States, and, as of 2012, the world's ninth largest economy, but inept regulation caused operators to shut down working power plants and create electricity shortages—ended abruptly when customers, exhorted to curtail their use of electricity, cut their peak load per dollar of weather-adjusted real gross domestic product (GDP) by 14 percent in the first half of 2001. Most of that reduction, undoing the previous five to ten years' demand growth, was temporary and behavioral, but later became permanent and technological.

Even without crises, some people do not consider an ever-growing volume of energy services to be a worthy end in itself, but seek to live more simply—with elegant frugality rather than involuntary penury—and to meet nonmaterial needs by nonmaterial means. (Trying to do otherwise is ultimately futile.) Such choices can save even more energy than technical improvements alone, although they are often considered beyond the scope of energy efficiency.

Several other terminological distinctions are also important. Technical improvements in energy efficiency may be applied in several ways:

- only to new buildings and equipment;
- installed in existing ones ("retrofitted");
- added during minor or routine maintenance ("slipstreamed");
- or conveniently added when making major renovations or expansions for other reasons ("piggybacked").

Efficiency saves energy whenever an energy service is being delivered, whereas *load management* (sometimes called "demand response" to emphasize reliance on customer choice) only changes the time when that energy is used—either by shifting the timing of the service delivery or by, for example, storing heat or "coolth" (pleasantly low temperatures) so energy consumption and service delivery can occur at different times. In the context chiefly of electricity, *demand-side management* comprises both these options, plus others that may even *in*crease the use of electricity. Most efficiency options yield comparable or greater savings in peak loads; both kinds of savings are valuable, and both kinds of value should be counted.

Energy statistics are traditionally organized by the economic sector of apparent consumption, not by the physical end-uses provided or services sought. End-uses were first seriously analyzed in 1976, rarely appear in official statistics nearly four decades later, and can be hard to estimate accurately. But end-use analysis can be valuable because matching energy supplies in quality and scale, as well as in quantity, to end-use needs can save much energy and money. Supplying energy of superfluous quality, not just quantity, for the task is wasteful and expensive.

Many subtleties of defining and measuring energy efficiency merit but seldom get rigorous treatment, such as:

- distribution losses downstream of end-use devices (an efficient furnace feeding leaky ducts or poorly distributing the heated air yields costlier delivered comfort);
- undesired or useless services, such as leaving equipment on all the time (as many factories and offices do) even when it serves no useful purpose;
- misused services, such as space-conditioning (heating, cooling, and ventilation) rooms that are open to the outdoors;
- conflicting services, such as heating and cooling the same space simultaneously (wasteful even if both services are provided efficiently);
- parasitic loads, as when the inefficiencies of a central cooling system reappear as additional fed-back cooling loads that make the system less efficient than the sum of its parts;
- misplaced efficiency, such as doing with energy-using equipment, however efficiently, a task that doesn't need the equipment—such as cooling with a mechanical chiller when groundwater or ambient conditions can more cheaply do the same thing.

This is a partial list. There are other, very technical, definitions of energy use and measurement that won't be mentioned here. The aim here is not to get mired in word games, but to offer a clear overview of what kinds of energy efficiency are available, what they can do, and how best to consider and adopt them.

Five Kinds of Efficiencies

The technical efficiency of using energy is the product of efficiencies successively applied along the chain of energy conversions: the conversion efficiency of primary into secondary energy, times the distribution efficiency of delivering that secondary energy from the point of conversion to the point of end-use, times the end-use efficiency of converting the delivered secondary energy into such desired energy services as hot showers and cold beer. Some analysts add another term at the upstream end—the extractive efficiency of converting fuel in the ground, wind or sun in the atmosphere, etc. into the primary energy fed into the initial conversion device—and another term at the downstream end—the "hedonic efficiency" of converting delivered energy services into human welfare and satisfaction. (Delivering junk mail with high technical efficiency, for instance, is futile if the recipients don't want it in the first place.)

Counting all five efficiencies permits comparing ultimate means—primary energy tapped—with ultimate ends—happiness or economic welfare created. Focusing only on intermediate means and ends loses sight of what human purposes an energy system is there to serve. Most societies pay attention to only three kinds of energy efficiency: extraction (because of its cost, not because the extracted fuels are assigned any intrinsic or depletion value), conversion, and perhaps distribution. End-use and hedonic efficiency are left to customers, are least exploited, and hence hold the biggest potential gains.

They also offer the greatest potential leverage. Since successive efficiencies along the conversion chain all multiply, they are often assumed to be equally important. Yet downstream savings—those nearest the customer—are the most important.

Analyses of energy use should, but seldom do, start with the desired services or changes in well-being, then work back upstream to primary supplies. This maximizes the extra value of downstream efficiency gains (because compounding losses are reversed to create compounding savings) and the capital-cost savings from smaller, simpler, cheaper upstream equipment. Similarly, most energy policy analysts ask how much energy could be supplied before asking how much is optimally needed and at what quality and scale it could be optimally provided. This backwards direction (upstream to downstream) and supply orientation lie at the root of many if not most energy policy problems.

Re-examining How We Use Energy

Some major opportunities to save energy involve redefining the service being provided. This is often a cultural variable. A Japanese person, asked why the house isn't heated in winter, might reply, "Why should I? Is the house cold?" In Japanese culture, the traditional goal is to keep the *person* comfortable, not to heat or cool empty space. Thus a modern Japanese room air conditioner may contain a sensor array and swiveling louvers that detect and blow air toward people's locations in the room, rather than wastefully cooling the entire space. Western office workers, too, can save energy (and can often see better, feel less tired, and improve aesthetics) by properly adjusting Venetian blinds, bouncing glare-free daylight up onto the ceiling, and turning off the lights. As the Danish professor of engineering, Jørgen Nørgård, has noted, energy-efficient lamps save the most energy when they are turned off; yet many Westerners automatically turn on every light when entering a room.

This example also illustrates that energy efficiency may be hard to distinguish from energy supply that comes from natural energy flows. All houses are already approximately 98 percent solar-heated, because if there were no sun (which provides 99.8 percent of the Earth's natural heat), the temperature of the Earth's surface would average approximately −272.6°C rather than +15°C. Thus, strictly speaking, engineered heating systems provide only the last 1–2 percent of the total heating required.

Mobility vs. Access

Service redefinition becomes complex in personal transport. Its efficiency is not just about vehicular fuel economy, people per car, or public transport alternatives. Rather, the underlying service should often be defined as access, not mobility. Typically the best way to gain access to a place is to be there already, so one needn't go somewhere else. This is the realm of spatial planning—no novelty in the United States, where it's officially shunned yet practiced (zoning laws often mandate *dispersion* of location and function, real-estate practices segregate housing by income, and other market distortions maximize unneeded and often unwanted travel). Obviously sprawl would decrease if not mandated and subsidized. Another way to gain access is virtually via telecommunications. Sometimes that's a realistic alternative to physically moving people. And if such movement is really necessary, it merits real competition, at honest prices, between all modes: personal or collective, motorized or human-powered, conventional or innovative. Creative policy tools can enhance that choice in ways that enhance property value, time saved, quality of life, and public amenity and security.

Historic Summaries of Potential

People have been saving energy for centuries, even millennia; this is the essence of engineering. Most savings were initially in conversion and end-use: pre-industrial households often used more primary energy than modern ones do, because fuelwood-to-charcoal conversion, inefficient open fires, and crude stoves burned much fuel to deliver sparse cooking and warmth. Lighting, materials processing, and transport end-uses were also very inefficient. Billions of human beings still suffer such primitive conditions today. Fast-growing economies like China's have the greatest *need* and the greatest *opportunity* to leapfrog to efficiency—because building correctly the first time is easier than fixing it later. But even the most

energy-efficient societies still have enormous and expanding room for further efficiency gains.

Many published engineering analyses show a smaller saving potential because of major conservatisms, often deliberate (because the real figures seem too good to be true), or because they assume only partial adoption over a short period rather than examining the ultimate potential for complete practical adoption. Many non-technological economic theorists argue that if cost-effective opportunities existed, they'd already have been captured in the marketplace, even in planned economies with no marketplace or mixed economies with a distorted one. This mental model—"don't bother to bend over and pick up that banknote lying on the ground, because if it were real, someone would have picked it up already"—often dominates governments' policy. It seems ever less defensible as more is learned about the reality of pervasive market failures (practical obstacles to a profitable action) and the astonishing size and cheapness of the energy savings empirically achieved by diverse enterprises.

Technological Progress, and Copying Nature

This engineering/economics divergence about the potential to save energy also reflects an implied assumption that technological evolution is smooth and incremental, as mathematical modelers prefer. In fact, while much progress is as incremental as technology diffusion, discontinuous technological leaps propel innovation and speed its adoption.

The late Canadian engineer, Ernie Robertson, noted that when turning limestone into a structural material, one is not confined to the conventional possibilities of cutting it into blocks or turning it into Portland cement. One can instead grind it up and feed it to chickens, whose ambient-temperature technology turns it into eggshell stronger than Portland cement. Were we as smart as chickens, we would have mastered this life-friendly technology. Extraordinary new opportunities to harness 3.8 billion years of biological design experience, as described by the US biologist Janine Benyus in *Biomimicry*, can often make energy-intensive industrial processes unnecessary. So, in principle, can the emerging techniques of molecular-scale self-assembly, as pioneered by the US nanotechnology researcher, Eric Drexler.

More conventional innovations can also bypass energy-intensive industrial processes. Making things that last longer, using materials more frugally, and designing and deploying those things to be repaired, reused, remanufactured, and recycled can save much or most of the energy traditionally needed to produce and assemble their materials (and can increase welfare while reducing GDP, which perversely swells when short-lived goods are quickly discarded and replaced). By combining many such options, it is now realistic to contemplate a long-run advanced industrial society that provides unprecedented levels of material prosperity with far less energy, cost, and impact than today's best practice.

Why is Energy Efficiency So Invisible?

In light of all these possibilities, why does energy efficiency, in most countries and at most times, command so little attention and such lackadaisical pursuit? Several explanations come to mind. Saved energy is invisible. Energy-saving technologies may look and outwardly act just like inefficient ones, so they're invisible too. They're also highly dispersed—unlike central supply technologies, such as large dams, that are among the most impressive and durable human creations. Many users believe energy efficiency is binary—you either have it or lack it—and that engineers already achieved it in the 1970s, so there's no more room for improvement. Major energy efficiency opportunities are disdained or disbelieved by policymakers indoctrinated in a theoretical economic paradigm that claims big untapped opportunities simply cannot exist.

Benefits of Energy Efficiency

Energy efficiency avoids the direct economic costs and the direct environmental, security, and other costs of the energy supply and delivery that it displaces. Yet most literature neglects several key side-benefits (economists call them "joint products") of saving energy. Below are just a few of these benefits.

Indirect Benefits of Improved Energy Efficiency

Improved energy efficiency, especially end-use efficiency, often delivers better services. Efficient houses are more comfortable; efficient lighting systems can look better and help you see better; efficient motors can be quieter, more reliable, and more controllable, improving industrial output and quality; efficient refrigerators can keep food fresher for longer; efficient supermarkets can improve food safety and merchandising. Such side-benefits can be one or even two orders of magnitude more valuable than the energy directly saved. For example, careful measurements show that in efficient buildings—where workers can see what they're doing, hear themselves think, breathe cleaner air, and feel more thermally comfortable—labor productivity typically rises substantially. Practitioners can market these attributes without ever mentioning lower energy bills.

Diminishing vs. Expanding Returns to Investments

Among the most basic, most often skipped over, yet most simply resolved economic/engineering disagreements is whether investing in end-use efficiency yields expanding or diminishing returns. Economic theory says diminishing—the more efficiency we buy, the more steeply the marginal cost of the next increment of savings rises, until it becomes too expensive. But engineering practice often says expanding—big savings can cost *less* than small or no savings—if the engineering is done unconventionally but properly.

Designing Whole Systems

Consider, for example, how much thermal insulation should surround a house in a cold climate. Conventional design specifies just the amount of insulation that will repay its marginal cost out of the present value of the saved marginal energy. But this is methodologically wrong, because the comparison omits the *capital cost of the heating system*—furnace, ducts, fans, pipes, pumps, wires, controls, and fuel source.

Optimizing a house as a system rather than a component (like insulation) by itself, and optimizing for lifecycle cost (capital plus operating cost, and preferably maintenance cost too), can make a superefficient house cheaper to build, not just to run, by eliminating costly heating and cooling systems. (Since the author built such a house in 1982–1984—now ripening its forty-fifth passive-solar banana crop high in the Rocky Mountains with no furnace—more than 30,000 buildings with no heating systems have been constructed in Europe; in recent years, these building have been built at a cost that is no more than the cost of building conventional buildings.) Optimizing whole systems for multiple benefits, not just components for single benefits, often boosts end-use efficiency by roughly an order of magnitude at negative marginal cost. These enormous savings were not previously much noticed or captured because of deficient engineering teaching and practice. Whole-system design integration isn't rocket science, but rediscovers the forgotten tradition of Victorian system engineering, before designers got specialized and forgot how components fit together.

Taking the Right Steps in the Right Order

Breakthrough results in energy efficiency need not just the right technologies, but also their application in the right sequence. For example, most practitioners designing lighting retrofits start with more efficient lighting fixtures ("luminaires")—improving optics, lamps, and ballasts (the devices used to start and regulate a gas-discharge lamp). But for optimal energy and capital savings, that should be step six, not step one. First come improving the quality of the visual task, optimizing the geometry and cavity reflectance of the space, optimizing lighting quality and quantity, and harvesting daylight. Then, after the luminaire improvements, come better controls, maintenance, management, and training.

Likewise, to deliver thermal comfort in a hot climate, most engineers retrofit a more efficient and perhaps variable-speed chiller, variable-speed supply fans, etc. But these should all be step five. The previous four steps are to expand the comfort range (by exploiting such variables as radiant temperature, turbulent air movement, and ventilative chairs); reduce unwanted heat gains within or into the space; exploit passive cooling (ventilative, radiative, ground-coupling); and if needed, harness nonrefrigerative alternative cooling. These preliminary steps can generally eliminate refrigerative cooling. If it's nonetheless still wanted, it can be made superefficient, then supplemented by better controls and coolth storage. Yet most designers pursue these seven steps in reverse order, worst buys first, so they save less energy, pay higher capital costs, yet achieve worse comfort and greater complexity.

Whole-system design is not what engineering schools appear to be teaching, nor what most customers currently expect, request, reward, or receive. When consumers don't specify the use of energy-efficient materials in building projects or renovations, the typical vendor will use the bare minimum materials to "meet code" (the worst you can build without risking jail). These less expensive, short-sighted decisions save money for the vendor, because paying energy bills once the project is done is the customer's responsibility.

Market Failures—And Their Business Opportunities

Any skilled practitioner of energy efficiency encounters a range of market failures daily. A 1997 compendium, Climate: Making Sense and Making Money, organizes sixty to eighty such market failures into eight categories—and illustrates the business opportunity each can be turned into. Some arise in public policy, some at the level of the firm, some in individuals' heads.

Most are glaringly perverse. For example, in all but fourteen of the United States, and in almost every other country, regulated distribution utilities are rewarded for selling more electricity and penalized for cutting customers' bills, so they're unenthusiastic about energy efficiency that hurts their shareholders. Nearly all architects and engineers, too, are paid for what they spend, not for what they save; "performance-based design fees" have been shown to yield superior design, but are rarely used. When markets and bidding systems are established to augment or replace traditional regulation of energy supply industries, negawatts (saved watts) are rarely allowed to compete against megawatts.

Indeed, dominant industries discourage competing investments by spreading disinformation. For example, from widely accepted claims that only nuclear power is big and fast enough to do much about climate change, one would hardly guess that its low- and no-carbon decentralized competitors already exceed its global output and capacity, and are adding enormously more megawatts and terawatt-hours per year every year—an order of magnitude more if electrical savings are also included (Lovins 2005b). Nor would one understand that nuclear expansion actually reduces and retards climate protection because it saves far less carbon, per dollar and per year, than investing instead in energy efficiency, renewable supplies, and combined-heat-and-power (also known as cogeneration—producing both electricity and useful heat simultaneously).

In short, scores of market failures—well understood but widely ignored—cause available and profitable energy efficiency to get only a small fraction of the investment it merits. Thus most of the capital invested in the energy system is being misallocated.

The most effective remedy would be to put systematic "barrier-busting"—turning obstacles into opportunities, stumbling-blocks into stepping-stones—atop the policy agenda, so market mechanisms could work properly, as economic theory correctly prescribes.

New Ways to Accelerate Energy Efficiency

Aggressively scrapping inefficient devices—paying bounties to destroy them instead of reselling them—could both solve many problems (e.g., oil, air, and climate in the case of inefficient vehicles) and boost global development by exporting only efficient, not inefficient, devices.

Winning the Oil Endgame (Lovins et al., 2004) offers a similarly novel policy menu for saving oil. Revenue and size-neutral "feebates" for widening the price spread between more and less efficient light vehicles in each size class—thus bridging the discount-rate spread between car-buyers and society—are far more effective than fuel taxes or efficiency standards, and can yield both consumer and producer surpluses. Tripled-efficiency heavy trucks and planes can be elicited, respectively, by "demand pull" from big customers (once they're informed of what's possible, as began to occur in 2005) and by innovative financing for insolvent airlines (on condition of scrapping inefficient parked planes).

A key player is now the military, which needs superefficient platforms for agile deployment and to cut the huge cost and risk of fuel logistics. Speeding ultralight, ultrastrong materials fabrication processes to market could transform civilian vehicle industries as profoundly as military research and development did to create the Internet, GPS, jet engines, and microchips. Only this time, that transformation could lead countries like the United States off oil, making oil no longer worth fighting over. The 2011 "grand synthesis"

Reinventing Fire, mentioned below, discusses how to eliminate US oil *and* coal use—and for that matter nuclear power—by 2050, at a cost $5 trillion cheaper than "business-as-usual"; the strategy does not rely on new inventions or the passage of national laws, but rather on businesses pursuing profit in the marketplace.

Altogether, the conventional agenda for promoting energy efficiency—price manipulations through subsidies and taxes, plus regulation or deregulation—ignores nearly all the most effective, attractive, and quickly spreadable methods.

By pursuing the entire efficiency potential systematically and comprehensively, concludes Jørgen Nørgård, "it is possible in the course of half a century to offer everybody on Earth a joyful and materially decent life with a per capita energy consumption of only a small fraction of today's consumption in the industrialized countries" (2000, 2).

Outlook for Improving Energy Efficiency

These quickly growing opportunities suggest that price may well become less important to the uptake of energy efficiency. Price remains important and should be correct, but is only one of many ways to get attention and influence choice; ability to respond to price can be far more important.

End-use efficiency may increasingly be marketed and bought mainly for its qualitatively improved services, just as distributed and renewable supply-side resources may be marketed and bought mainly for their distributed benefits. Outcomes would then become decreasingly predictable from economic experience or using economic tools. Meanwhile, disruptive technologies and integrative design methods are clearly inducing dramatic shifts *of,* not just along, demand curves, and are even making them less relevant by driving customer choice through non-price variables. If, as now seems unquestionable, light vehicles can achieve three- to five-fold fuel savings as a byproduct of breakthrough design integration, yet remain uncompromised and competitively priced, then the energy-price driven "tradeoff" paradigm becomes irrelevant. People will prefer such vehicles because they're *better*, not because they're clean and efficient, much as most people now buy digital media rather than vinyl phonograph records: they're a generally superior product that redefines market expectations.

This implies a world where energy price and regulation become far less influential than today, displaced by imaginative, holistic, integrative engineering and marketing.

In the world of consumer electronics—ever better, faster, smaller, cheaper—that world is upon us. In the wider world of energy efficiency, the master key to so many of the world's most vexing problems, it is coming rapidly over the horizon. We need only understand it and do it.

Amory B. LOVINS
Rocky Mountain Institute

This article was adapted by the editors, with kind permission from Rocky Mountain Institute, from Amory B. Lovins's 2005 technical article "Energy End-Use Efficiency." The original article was commissioned by Dr. Steven Chu (later US Secretary of Energy) for the InterAcademy Council (IAC), Amsterdam, as part of its 2005–2006 study "Transitions to Sustainable Energy Systems." Copyright © 2005 IAC. The original article is available on Rocky Mountain Institute's website: http://www.rmi.org/Knowledge-Center/Library/E05-16_EnergyEndUseEfficiency. A 2011 book treating these issues more fully, updating the references, and giving URLs for many of the older references below is A. B. Lovins & Rocky Mountain Institute, *Reinventing Fire: Bold Business Solutions for the New Energy Era* (White River Junction, VT: Chelsea Green; see www.reinventingfire.com).

The following author's note appears in the original article: "The author is grateful to many colleagues, especially Drs. David B. Brooks, Jørgen S. Nørgård, and Joel N. Swisher PE for their insightful comments, and to The William and Flora Hewlett Foundation for supporting the preparation of an *Encyclopedia of Energy* article (Lovins 2004) from which this paper was adapted and updated with IAC's consent."

See also Buildings and Infrastructure; Design and Architecture; Economics, Steady State; Geoengineering; Natural Capital; Nuclear Power; Progress; Waste—Engineering Aspects; Waste—Social Aspects

FURTHER READING

American Institute of Physics (AIP). (1975). *Efficient use of energy* (AIP Conference Proceedings #25.) New York: AIP.

Benyus, Janine M. (1997). *Biomimicry: Innovation inspired by nature.* New York: William Morrow.

Bodlund, Birgit; Mills, Evan; Karlsson, Tomas; & Johansson, Thomas B. (1989). The challenge of choices. In Thomas B. Johansson, Birgit Bodlund & Robert H. Williams (Eds.), *Electricity: Efficient end-use and new generation technologies, and their planning implications.* Lund, Sweden: Lund University Press.

Brohard, Grant J., et al. (1998). Advanced Customer Technology Test for Maximum Energy Efficiency (ACT2) Project: The final report. *Proceedings of the Summer Study on Energy-Efficient Buildings.* Washington, DC: American Council for an Energy-Efficient Economy.

Daly, Herman E. (1996). *Beyond growth: The economics of sustainable development.* Boston: Beacon Press.

Drexler, K. Eric. (1992). *Nanosystems: Molecular machinery, manufacturing, and computation.* New York: John Wiley & Sons.

Earth Track. (2011). Access subsidy publications. Retrieved August 22, 2012, from http://earthtrack.net/publications

E SOURCE. (2002). *Technology atlas series* (6 vols.), & *Electronic Encyclopedia* CD-ROM. Boulder, CO: E SOURCE.

Fiberforge, Inc. (2012). Homepage. Retrieved August 22, 2012, from www.fiberforge.com

Fickett, Arnold P.; Gellings, Clark W.; & Lovins, Amory B. (1990, September). Efficient use of electricity. *Scientific American, 263*(3), 64–74.

Hawken, Paul G.; Lovins, Amory B.; & Lovins, L. Hunter. (1999). *Natural capitalism: Creating the next industrial revolution.* New York: Little Brown.

International Project for Sustainable Energy Paths (IPSEP). (1989–1999). *Energy policy in the greenhouse* (Report to Dutch Ministry of Environment, International Project for Sustainable Energy Paths). El Cerrito, CA: IPSEP.

Krause, Florentin; Baer, Paul; & DeCanio, Stephen. (2001). Cutting carbon emissions at a profit: Opportunities for the US. El Cerrito, CA: IPSEP. Retrieved August 22, 2012, from http://epw.senate.gov/107th/krause.pdf

Lovins, Amory B. (1992). *Energy-efficient buildings: Institutional barriers and opportunities* (Strategic Issues Paper II). Boulder, CO: E SOURCE.

Lovins, Amory B. (1994). Apples, oranges, and horned toads. *Electricity Journal, 7*(4), 29–49.

Lovins, Amory B. (1995, June). The super-efficient passive building frontier (Rocky Mountain Institute Publication #E95-28). *ASHRAE Journal, 37*(6), 79–81.

Lovins, Amory B. (2003). Twenty hydrogen myths. Retrieved August 22, 2012, from http://www.rmi.org/Knowledge-Center/Library/E03-05_TwentyHydrogenMyths

Lovins, Amory B. (2004). Energy efficiency, taxonomic overview. *Encyclopedia of Energy, 2*, 382–401.

Lovins, Amory B. (2005a, September). More profit with less carbon. *Scientific American, 293*, 74–82.

Lovins, Amory B. (2005b, September 11). Nuclear economics and climate-protection potential. Snowmass, CO: Rocky Mountain Institute.

Lovins, Amory B., & Cramer, D. R. (2003). Hypercars, hydrogen, and the automotive transition. *International Journal of Vehicle Design, 35*(1/2), 50–85. Retrieved August 22, 2012, from http://www.rmi.org/Knowledge-Center/Library/T04-01_HypercarsHydrogenAutomotiveTransition

Lovins, Amory B., et al. (2002). *Small is profitable: The hidden economic benefits of making electrical resources the right size.* Snowmass, CO: Rocky Mountain Institute.

Lovins, Amory B., & Gadgil, Ashok. (1991). *The negawatt revolution: Electric efficiency and Asian development* (RMI Publication #E91-23). Snowmass, CO: Rocky Mountain Institute.

Lovins, Amory B.; Datta, E. Kyle; Bustnes, Odd-Even; Koomey, Jonathan G.; & Glasgow, Nathan J. (2004). *Winning the oil endgame.* Snowmass, CO: Rocky Mountain Institute.

Lovins, Amory B., & Lovins, L. Hunter. (1991). Least-cost climatic stabilization. *Annual Review of Energy and the Environment, 16,* 433–531.

Lovins, Amory B., & Lovins, L. Hunter. (1996). Negawatts: Twelve transitions, eight improvements, and one distraction. *Energy Policy, 24*(4), 331–344. Retrieved August 22, 2012, from http://www.rmi.org/Knowledge-Center/Library/U96-11_NegawattsTwelve Transitions

Lovins, Amory B., & Lovins, L. Hunter. (1997). *Climate: Making sense and making money.* Snowmass, CO: Rocky Mountain Institute.

Lovins, Amory B., & Lovins, L. Hunter. (2001, July/August). Fool's gold in Alaska. *Foreign Affairs, 80*(4), 72–85.

Lovins, Amory B., & Lovins, L. Hunter; Krause, Florentin; & Bach, Wilfrid. (1982). *Least-cost energy: Solving the CO_2 problem.* Andover, MA: Brick House. (Reprinted 1989 by Rocky Mountain Institute, Snowmass, CO).

Lovins, Amory B., & Williams, Brett D. (1999, April 8). A strategy for the hydrogen transition (*Proceedings of the 10th Annual Hydrogen Meeting*). Washington, DC: National Hydrogen Association.

Nadel, Steven. (1990). *Lessons learned* (Report #90-08). Albany, NY, & Washington, DC: New York State Energy R&D Authority, N.Y. State Energy Office, Niagara Mohawk Power Corp., & American Council for an Energy-Efficient Economy.

Nørgård, Jørgen S. (2000). Energy efficiency and the switch to renewable energy sources. Natural Resource System Challenge II: Climate change. Human systems and policy. In Antoaneta Yotova (Ed.), *UNESCO encyclopedia of life support systems.* Oxford, UK: EOLSS Publisher Co. Retrieved August 22, 2012, from http://www.eolss.net/Sample-Chapters/C12/E1-04-06-04.pdf

Reddy, Amulya K. N.; Williams, Robert H.; & Johansson, Thomas B. (1997). *Energy after Rio: Prospects and challenges.* New York: United Nations Development Program.

Repetto, Robert, & Austin, Duncan. (1997). *The costs of climate protection: A guide to the perplexed.* Washington, DC: World Resources Institute. Retrieved August 22, 2012, from http://www.wri.org/publication/costs-of-climate-protection

Romm, Joseph J.; Rosenfeld, Art H.; & Herrmann, Susan. (1999). The internet economy and global warming: A scenario of the impact of e-commerce on energy and the environment. Washington, DC: Center for Energy and Climate Solutions.

Romm, Joseph J., & Browning, William D. (1994). Greening the building and the bottom line: Increasing productivity through energy-efficient design. Snowmass, CO: Rocky Mountain Institute. Retrieved August 22, 2012, from http://www.enterpriseelectricboise.com/documents/GreenBuildingsTheBottomLine.pdf

Swisher, Joel N. (2002). *The new business climate: A guide to lower carbon emissions and better business performance.* Snowmass, CO: Rocky Mountain Institute.

Swisher, Joel N.; Jannuzzi, Gilberto de Martino; & Redlinger, Robert Y. (1997). *Tools and methods for integrated resource planning: Improving energy efficiency and protecting the environment.* Roskilde, Denmark: United Nations Environment Programme (UNEP) Collaborating Centre on Energy and Environment. Retrieved August 22, 2012, from http://www.uneprisoe.org/IRPManual/IRPmanual.pdf

von Weizsäcker, Ernst U.; Lovins, Amory B.; & Lovins, L. Hunter. (1995/97). *Factor four: Doubling wealth, halving resource use.* London: Earthscan.

Wilson, Alex, et al. (1998). *Green development: Integrating ecology and real estate.* New York & Snowmass, CO: John Wiley & Sons, & Rocky Mountain Institute.

F

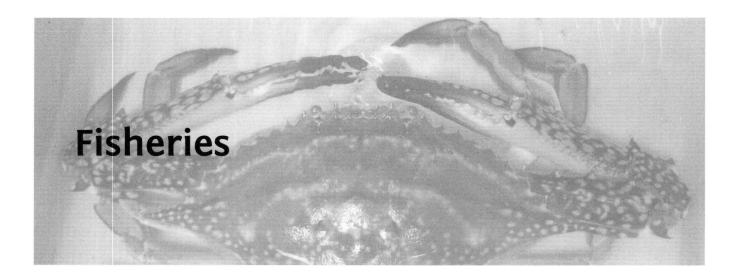

Fisheries

The history of fisheries provides an example of unsustainable human exploitation of a wild living resource. Serial depletions became global as fisheries expanded out from the coasts, fished at greater depths, and targeted new fish species from the 1960s onward. Ratchet-like processes make restoration difficult, while demand for nutritious seafood has outstripped supply in the oceans. Future prospects include more ecological and ethical fishing, favoring small-scale coastal fisheries. The future may see more fishing low in the food web, such as krill, and more farming of herbivorous fish to address pressing issues of seafood security.

The archaeological discovery of fish spears cleverly fashioned of bone in Africa, Europe, and Asia reveals that wild fish have been caught by humans for food for at least 100,000 years. Indeed, fisheries have provided significant economic, social, and cultural bases to human societies in both classical and medieval times.

History

A fermented fish sauce known as *garum* was a fishery product marketed extensively throughout the huge Roman Empire, forming, for example, a major economic activity in Pompeii, a Roman coastal town frozen in time by a volcanic eruption of Vesuvius in 60 CE (Sahrhage and Lundbeck 1992). *Garum*, a key ingredient in most Roman cooking, was made from plankton-feeding fish species such as sardines, anchovies, and small tuna caught in seine nets, processed on land, and exported in specially designed amphorae labeled by origin and quality (Corcoran 1963). There was also a significant Roman trade in piscivorous Nile perch from Egypt.

One of the first symptoms of overfishing, a reduction in fish size and age, was noted by the Roman satirist Juvenal in the first century."[O]ur sea has been totally ransacked to the point of exhaustion, since gluttony rages, the fish markets raking the nearest waters with nonstop nets—and we don't let the Tyrrhenian fish grow to size" (Juvenal 2004, *Satire* 5:92–96).

Herring, which are small schooling fish that feed on zooplankton, were caught in the North Sea from Roman times, but the fishery first appears of note in Saxon England, where villages were named after the fishery (e.g., Herringfleet, near Norwich) and fresh herring were delivered on contract to inland abbeys such as Barking in 670. In medieval times, English parliaments (such as that of King Edward III in 1357) proclaimed regulations (and taxes) for the herring fishery and its markets. Moreover, the Hanseatic League of peacefully trading city-states (such as Bergen, Amsterdam, and Lubeck) was largely built on profits from the herring trade; in 1600, more than 300,000 people made their living from herring in Holland alone (Sahrhage and Lundbeck 1992). Analysis of extensive Dutch and other records shows that herring were caught sustainably from the North Sea from earlier than 1100 up to the 1850s; sustainability in the Dutch records was indicated by calculating the daily catch rate of herring for a standard herring vessel, known as *catch per unit effort* (Poulsen 2008). The total annual North Sea catches in this period seem to have been between 100,000 and 200,000 tonnes—a big contrast to catches that expanded to more than 1.2 million tonnes in the twentieth century, when North Sea herring were almost wiped out by fishing, and the fishery had to be closed for fifteen years after the 1960s (Roberts 2008).

One note of warning from the Middle Ages is the Scanian herring population, which supported a large seasonal fishery in the channel between Sweden and Denmark (salted herring were exported in barrels as far as Rome). The fish disappeared in the sixteenth century, never to return (Roberts 2008). There has been no convincing analysis of the reason for this fishery collapse, but it is likely the result of overfishing and water temperature fluctuations, factors later implicated in a collapse of the Californian sardine fishery in the 1950s. (The sardine cannery highlighted in John Steinbeck's 1945 novel *Cannery Row* has not operated since.) Foreshadowed by these warning signs, the history of fisheries since 1950 paints a horror story of unsustainability. Fish populations are self-renewing resources in natural ecosystems; moreover, since at least the 1940s, fishery scientists have had access to sufficient quantitative ecological science to manage them effectively, so this should not have been the case. What has gone wrong?

Fishing Methods

Humans have invented many types of fishing gear in addition to spears, such as hooks, traps, and nets. Nets, with their characteristic nonslip knot, seem to date back thirty thousand years and were originally designed to catch small mammals flushed from copses on land (after large mammals like mammoths had been depleted). Trawls, which are bag nets dragged through the water, are very effective fishing devices and make fishers a lot of money, but they devastate sessile bottom-living creatures such as sea lilies, corals, and sponges, which perform an important service in marine ecosystems by providing cover to juvenile fish. Damage caused by trawls has long been recognized: In May 1376, the parliament of King Edward III of England set up a commission to investigate complaints by fishers that "so close net is fixed that even the smallest fish cannot escape therefrom . . . the net touches the ground under the water so evenly and heavily that spawn of fish and the flowers of the sea and other things wherewith the greater fish might live and be nourished are destroyed" and that a glut of trawl-caught fish had caused prices to drop so much that fish could be sold only for pig food (translated from Norman French by Given-Wilson et al. 2005). Four juries ("inquisitions") empaneled by the commission reported in 1377, and trawling was banned inshore (HMSO 1937).

Over the ensuing centuries, there were many more failed attempts to ban trawling, including a major UK Royal Commission led by the pioneering evolutionary biologist Thomas Huxley in the 1880s, yet today trawls are banned only in a few areas. In December 2006, the United Nations General Assembly failed to adopt a measure put forward by six countries that would have banned bottom trawling. Some trawlers today have freezer factories onboard: one giant trawler, the 180-meter-long *Atlantic Dawn*, built in Ireland with government subsidies, has been banned from European Union waters because it could catch the entire quota of some species in one day. Together with many other European trawlers, it often operates under joint ventures with West African government officials, where overfishing is rife and small-scale local fishers are badly affected by this exploitation of the resources of developing countries.

The Perils of Overfishing

The effects of improvements in the technology devised to catch wild fish have been serious. Symptoms of overfishing, such as reduction of fish size, failure of spawning or enough larvae or juvenile fish (termed "recruits"), and catches of fish before they are old and large enough to reproduce, all contribute to the loss of whole populations that breed together to form the next generation (termed "stocks" in fisheries jargon, which refers to catches as "harvest").

Three ratchet-like processes have prejudiced the chances of recovery from the depleted state of the world's ocean fishery resources (Pitcher 2001). First, Odum's ratchet, named after the pioneering US ecologist Eugene P. Odum's concerns with human-caused extinctions, describes how fishing itself acts as a selective force on ecosystems by removing long-lived, slow-growing fish in favor of those with life histories endowed with higher turnover. This process operates both within and among species irrespective of high fecundity evolved to buffer habitat volatility. When species become locally extinct, the past becomes hard to restore, just as a ratchet is hard to reverse.

Second, Ludwig's ratchet, named after the Canadian mathematical economist Donald Ludwig, describes the generation of overcapacity in fishing power through pressure from loans that can be repaid only by sustained catches that, on account of depletion, can be generated only by ratchet-like further investment in fishing technology. It is hard to go back to using yesterday's fishing gear.

Third, Pauly's ratchet, named after the eminent fisheries scientist Daniel Pauly, and otherwise known as the *shifting baseline syndrome,* refers to the psychological tendency for scientists and others to relate changes in the system to what things were like at the time of their own professional debut, regarding earlier accounts of great abundance as anecdotal and methodologically naïve. Interviews with fishers have demonstrated the ratchet in action (e.g., Lozano-Montes, Pitcher, and Haggan 2008). The combined effect of these three ratchets over time has been not only to bring about the collapse of many major commercial fisheries, but also to shift the structure of ecosystems toward lower trophic levels, to favor simpler organisms and energy pathways, and to compromise biodiversity in ways that might be hard to reverse. Many of these events have undoubtedly caught fisheries science, managers, and the public by surprise (Hilborn, Parrish, and Litle 2006).

Globally, fisheries have been overfished to such a degree that many believe that by midcentury we will face a global disaster scenario of local extinctions (Dulvy, Pinnegar, and Reynolds 2009), simplified food webs (Worm et al. 2006), and unstable and unpredictable ecosystem shifts (Daskalov et al. 2007; Pauly, Watson, and Alder 2005). There have been some reports that fisheries are improving (Worm et al. 2009), but, worldwide, only a few fisheries in four or five rich, developed nations, such as the United States and Australia, covering about 10 percent of the annual world catch, seem to be in a healthy state (Branch et al. 2011). These are the only fisheries for which sufficiently detailed quantitative information is available for management using quotas, and here it is possible that overfishing has been reversed. In contrast, in the South China Sea, analysis of catch per unit effort from the daily catch records of Hong Kong fishing vessels allowed to fish in Chinese waters reveals that many fish species showed a 90 percent reduction of biomass between 1973 and 1988 (Cheung and Pitcher 2008). This seems to characterize the situation in most of the world and its fish catches, including poorly managed European Union waters.

Massive depletions like this in potential seafood that can be gathered from the oceans come at a time of unprecedented need for food security as the human population burgeons. These changes occur in oceans challenged by climate changes of warming and acidification, with life support cycles threatened by a portfolio of toxic wastes and chemical pollution. Some pollution issues have been addressed internationally (e.g., PCBs), while others, such as flame retardants, sunscreen, heavy metals, and microplastic residues, continue unfettered (Thomson et al. 2009).

Estimates based on modeling suggest, on average, that global fishing intensity has expanded its geographical scope and increased tenfold, and up to twenty-five-fold in Asia, since the 1950s (Anticamara et al. 2008). Since the 1970s, fisheries have been targeting species in deeper water (for example, moving from 300 meters to 1,000 meters by 2000) (Morato et al. 2008). Deep-sea fish species are particularly vulnerable to depletion by fishing because they are long lived, late maturing, and slow growing, with sporadic recruitment of juvenile cohorts. These life history characteristics are adapted to the boom-and-bust regime of food supplies, spawning, and larval success in the deep-sea environment but have proved inimical to heavy fishing. In the international waters of the open ocean, seamounts—oases of long-lived fish adapted to similar sporadic feeding and spawning opportunities—were devastated by the trawling of large distant-water Soviet fleets in the 1970s and 1980s. By 2012, only a few of the world's half-million seamounts were fished sustainably by small-scale local fishing fleets (Pitcher et al. 2010).

This process of moving on to fish new areas, depths, and species is known as *serial depletion* (Swartz et al. 2010). In the early years, new areas, depths, and species typically came onstream for the fishing industry in an almost uncontrolled free-for-all. The problem with serial depletion is that total catches and economic benefits from the fishery are maintained, masking the true effects of overfishing. Many people argue that serial depletion in fisheries means that the world catch has reached its limit in terms of the capacity of oceans to produce fish of the type that we eat, so that catches are forecast to decline markedly—a trend that can already be seen in the world catch data.

Calculating the Catch

Despite all our technologies, the high value of seafood, and the global nature of the industry, total fishery landings are declining. The inherent limitations of marine resources are based on global primary production, using trophic level theory. Trophic level is defined as the organism's position relative to autotrophs (plants) in the food web and is calculated as the numeral 1 added to the weighted sum of the trophic level of all food inputs to a species. Plants (which make their own food from sunlight, a metabolic process catalyzed by chlorophyll) thus are defined as level 1, then exclusive plant eaters (like most zooplankton and a few fish like tilapia) are level 2, zooplankton-eating fish like herring are level 3, while seals and killer whales have trophic levels over 4. Most fish eaten by humans are about trophic level 3.5.

Ecological theory suggests that the average efficiency with which energy is transferred across trophic levels is about 10 percent, varying between about 8 and 14 percent. This is how the maximum production of level 3.3 fish can be estimated from the global production of phytoplankton at trophic level 1; the result is about 130 million tonnes per year, which is about the present level of catch (Chassot et al. 2010). Altering the calculation to look at production of krill at trophic level 2.2 gives about 850 million tonnes. Krill, however, form key forage organisms in many marine ecosystems (especially the Antarctic, where penguins, whales, and seals rely on krill for food), so that catches of krill would need to be limited to levels at which these other organisms are not compromised. Modeling suggests that an annual catch of about 260–360 million tonnes of krill might be sustainable without prejudice to other ecosystem inhabitants (Pitcher 2008), and would be a significant increase in sustainable world seafood production. It represents a policy of deliberately "fishing down the food web" to enhance seafood security.

World fisheries annually extract a reported 80 million tons of fish from the marine environment, which make up the primary source of protein for about 3 billion people and support the livelihoods of about 200 million people (Hilborn et al. 2003). Annual fishery catch data are assembled from reporting governments by the Food and Agriculture Organization of the United Nations at their Rome headquarters (Garcia and Grainger 2005). This data on reported fish landings do not show the total extraction of fish from the ocean, which are the figures needed by fishery ecologists (Pitcher et al. 2002). The reported catches are incomplete because, first, many fish are discarded into the sea because they will not command a good price (*high grading*), the skipper's fishing license does not cover them, or they are valueless small and juvenile fish caught in the tiny mesh of a prawn trawler, amounting to more than 30 million tonnes a year—as much as 35 percent of the total catch in some countries like the United States and India. Second, illegally caught fish are estimated to amount to more than 26 million tons a year worldwide (Agnew et al. 2009).

Next, other categories of unreported catches are made by millions of small-scale fishers in the developing countries, and by recreational anglers, whose catch can exceed that of commercial fisheries for some species in some areas such as the south Atlantic states of the United States. To overcome these problems, modeling based on ecological fish distributions, fishing records, and international access

agreements can be employed to estimate the true catches in each region of the globe (Watson et al. 2004). The upshot is that the true global fish catch is likely in the region of 130 to 150 million tonnes per year, hovering around the maximum possible given primary production levels.

Between 1960 and 2010, the proportion of primary production that ends up not in living marine organisms but sequestered by fish that end up dead in fisheries has risen from less than 10 percent to 40 percent in some areas, such as the North Sea. At this level of exploitation, we can expect to see major changes to the composition and volatility of marine ecosystems due to Odum's ratchet, as species with less resilience to fishing are reduced and others are targeted by fisheries (Pauly et al. 1998). Already, major increases in simpler organisms like jellyfish have been noted in ecosystems as far apart as the Bering Sea, the Mediterranean Sea, and the South China Sea (Purcell, Uye, and Lo 2007), while fishing down the food web has been detected in many ecosystems worldwide, despite controversy about its estimation from fish catches (Branch et al. 2011).

Sustainability

For sustainability, one conceptual issue impinges on policy formulation for fisheries. Some people have argued that sustainability should not be the goal of fisheries management. In a depleted ocean, sustainability can only preserve the present misery: restoration to former abundance and benefits should be a more legitimate goal (Pitcher and Pauly 1998). Historical reconstruction of past ecosystems and their fishery catches has often revealed what today would be thought astounding levels of abundance. In the Gulf of Maine, for example, analysis of daily catch records of sail-powered cod-fishing vessels showed that cod were one hundred times as abundant in the 1850s (Rosenberg et al. 2005).

Fish make up a healthy diet for humans because of the features of marine food webs, so the sustainability of seafood is an important matter. Unlike mammals, which store saturated fats, the metabolic energy reserves of many fish comprise unsaturated omega-3 oils. The energy reserves are used to fuel spawning migrations (as much as 1,000 kilometers upriver in sockeye salmon) and feeding migrations (4,000 kilometers across the Pacific for some tuna species, and between Norway and Iceland for a major population of Atlantic herring). These oils in fish come largely from eating food like copepods and krill, and, as it happens, they form healthy components of the human diet. Moreover, fish protein itself contains double-sulfur-bond amino acids like lysine and methionine, which are also important for the human diet. Some people think that fish made a vital contribution to early human evolution (Cunnane and Stewart 2010). In the twenty-first century, some health issues with fish as food derive from pollutants, such fat-soluble toxins and carcinogens (dioxins), which are particularly a problem with North Sea sand eels turned into agricultural feeds in Europe. Toxic levels of heavy metals (e.g., silver, copper, lead, mercury), some of which derive partly from natural sources, accumulate in predators at the apex of marine food webs (e.g., swordfish, marlin, and some large sharks).

The rapid decomposition of dead fish out of water (i.e., ready to cook and eat by humans) is an important issue with many consequences for human society, trade, and culture. Preservation of fish hence has been an imperative from ancient times. The origins of drying, salting, and smoking are lost in antiquity but were found in use by indigenous peoples in the Americas at first European contact. Canning (using steam) dates back to the early industrial age of Napoleonic France. The use of ice to preserve the catch dates back at least to Roman times but became widespread as fisheries expanded in the mid-nineteenth century. Ice was cut in blocks from frozen lakes and shipped in straw; in the 1860s one lake in Norway supplied 44,000 tonnes of ice to fishing ports on the east coast of England. Ice-making machines, invented in Australia in 1857, eventually supplanted this trade. The invention of railways in the mid-1800s led to great expansion of fisheries because for the first time fresh fish could be delivered before they spoiled to meet the demand from inland cities (Roberts 2008). Even before then, fast "cutter" sailing ships made daily deliveries of fresh herring and cod to Billingsgate fish market in London from a huge fleet fishing continuously on the North Sea. In Yarmouth in the 1870s, Hewitt's Short Blue Fleet of no fewer than two hundred sail-powered trawlers had a floating hospital and chapels for the fishers.

Since the 1990s, trade in fish has become increasingly global as the commoditization of standard fish products has increased (Lam and Pitcher 2012). Seafood companies operate on a global scale, and ownership of fisheries has become increasingly corporatized. For example, scampi (small marine crayfish called *Nephrops*) caught off the west of Scotland are cost-effectively shipped to China for processing, and the trimmed, cooked, and packaged frozen product is re-exported to Europe.

The high demand for fish while the human population is still increasing comes at a time when many foresee serious food shortages from terrestrial sources—made more worrisome by the depletions, pollution, and climate change affecting the oceans. Estimates by the United Nations and others suggest that the demand for fish will outstrip supply before 2020 (Pitcher 2008). Forecasts of demand for thirty to fifty years hence greatly exceed what likely can be caught, and aquaculture of carnivorous fish species like salmon and turbot will be hard pressed to fill the gap, because these species rely largely on fish caught to provide their food.

Coral reefs support many fisheries, which are mainly using hooks and lines with some cast and seine nets, and in some areas, prawn trawling in sandy areas between patch reefs (e.g., on the Great Barrier Reef in Australia). Most reefs are prosecuted by small-scale fishers from poor coastal fishing communities—perhaps more than 20 million people worldwide make their living from coral reef fisheries. All of this is threatened by reef overfishing, often with destructive dynamiting, and by the forecast acidification of the oceans from higher carbon dioxide levels. Present trends lead coral reef experts to foresee the loss of all coral reefs by the middle of the twenty-first century (Carpenter et al. 2008; Hughes et al. 2010).

Small-scale fisheries have a number of attractive features that are important in sustainability. They may be roughly defined as those operated by owner drivers and family members using fishing vessels less than 12 meters long from small coastal communities. Large-scale fisheries, often termed industrial fisheries, tend to be corporately owned, operate over large distances, employ about half a million people worldwide, land about 60 million tonnes annually, consume about 40 million tonnes of oil as fuel (Tyedmers, Watson, and Pauly 2005), discard more than 30 million tonnes back into the sea, and process about 35 million tonnes of fish into fishmeal for use in agriculture and fish farming (Pauly 2006). Small-scale fisheries, in contrast, employ more than 12 million people, land about 40 million tonnes annually, consume about 5 million tonnes of oil, have few discards, and process almost none of the catch into fishmeal. Large-scale enterprises have the advantage of fewer points of contact for management and governments but foster overfishing through overcapacity that is hard to control, are driven by fiscal need to maintain short-term profits regardless of the state of fish populations, and often create a powerful political lobby for continuing catches that governments find hard to resist and often subsidize. Globally, these subsidies to large-scale fisheries are estimated at $30 billion annually. Small-scale fisheries are more easily managed for sustainability because smaller, lower-tech fishing vessels allow more refuges for fish while local communities may develop a sustainability ethic and invest in their own future by not overfishing (Lam and Pauly 2010). Some subsidies go into small-scale fisheries—for example, traditional fisheries operated by aboriginal or indigenous people. A global estimate is $5 billion to $7 billion per year.

Overall, subsidies encourage overfishing by reducing the fish population level at which profit may be made (Sumaila et al. 2011). And, in 2011, it was discovered that fishery subsidies from the European Union have been diverted to operate illegal fisheries (Greenpeace EU Unit 2011). Nevertheless, some people argue that certain subsidies, such as those used to encourage less-harmful gear—for example, turtle excluders in tropical prawn trawl nets—or to set up and police marine protected areas, may be environmentally beneficial.

Solutions

Fishery scientists work out how much fish can be caught sustainably using mathematical models of fish populations (Walters and Martell 2004). Classically, fishery science looks at the population dynamics (demography) of single fish species using a modern version of equations devised during the Second World War. Smart computer analyses look for optima in complex models that may have hundreds of parameters covering growth, mortality, reproduction, and movements of the fish. These analyses define where the fishery for each species is in relation to reference points for management, such as the maximum sustainable yield (MSY), or Blim, the biomass below which the fish population might collapse because it would be no longer be ecologically sustainable (Pitcher 1998). Then the model is used to set a fishing quota that allows the fish population to move toward the relevant target (such as MSY) by managing the amount of fishing to be allowed in the subsequent year. The process is known as *stock assessment*. Simulations using feasible ranges of inputs for key parameters are used to work out the risks of exceeding management reference points, a process known as *Bayesian analysis.*

A trend has arisen toward considering all organisms in an ecosystem, called *ecosystem-based management*, because it has been realized that the single-species process does not allow for ecosystem interactions such as predation, food, and competition, or for the preservation of charismatic organisms such as seabirds or marine mammals that are generally not caught but have conservation value or contribute to ecosystem stability over time. Ecosystem models for fisheries, however, are still in their infancy, and although they can be employed to make comparisons among alternative fishery management policies, no consensus has been reached on how this should be done (Rice 2011). This could be critical for sustainability,

because preliminary studies suggest that MSY levels determined by ecosystem-based analyses are generally lower (Walters et al. 2005). Ecosystem-based management is explicitly mentioned in fishery policies worldwide, but surveys show that almost no countries have implemented it in a substantive fashion (Pitcher et al. 2008).

Using information from these analyses, fishery management aims to regulate the fish species, sizes, places, quantities caught, and gear used so that a fishery may be sustainable or that it will recover to a specified degree on the way to a long-term sustainable goal. Several studies have shown, however, that globally the quality and performance of fishery management in addressing declines and overfishing is poor. For example, two-thirds of the countries taking 96 percent of the world catch failed to comply with the forty-four key issues in the UN Code of Conduct for Responsible Fishing, and no countries received a "good" score.

Since the 1990s, the allocation of formal legal property rights to fisheries has been advocated by many as a solution to overfishing. The theory is that caring for property that is owned, like livestock on a farm, will be more likely to ensure sustainable fisheries (e.g., Branch 2009). This is termed *individual transferable quotas* (ITQs). But others argue that property invites fiscal speculation, and it is evident that the initial allocation of what was formerly a publicly owned resource creates long-term unfairness and other social problems that make the fisheries harder to govern (Bromley 2009). In some cases, quota owners have stopped fishing, borrow capital against their assets, and encourage other individuals to compete to lease their quota. This can result in almost poverty-level income for those actually engaged in the fishing, such as occurred with the British Columbia halibut fishery (Pinkerton and Edwards 2009). Where ITQs have been implemented for a considerable time (such as in Iceland, New Zealand, and parts of the United States and Canada), outcome analysis shows a mixed track record for fish populations managed in this fashion (Chu 2009). Current thinking suggests that fishing may better be regarded not as a property right but as a privilege accorded by society (mediated by government licenses). The fishery may still benefit from some long-term interest in having access to a sustainable resource. Effective fishery management in the face of these social and ecological issues requires several techniques; many people consider that there is no silver bullet (Hilborn, Parrish, and Little

2006), and management systems with an element of historical restoration, ecosystem thinking, and community support are most likely to succeed (Pitcher and Lam 2010).

Is fish farming a solution? Maybe. Most farming of captive fish targets profitable "table fish" like salmon, trout, bass, turbot, or halibut. These fish, however, are obligate piscivores, and their diet has to include double sulfur-bond amino acids like methionine and lysine, constituents most easily obtained from fish. Ecologically irresponsible fisheries have developed, designed to provide fishmeal to make food pellets to feed to other fish, and there has been a general failure to make plant or yeast-based substitutes. It is said that each tonne of farmed salmon takes small pelagic fish from twenty-five square kilometers of ocean, and there is increasing pressure to make these small fish available for direct human consumption instead of diverting them to make fish farm food (Goldburg and Naylor 2005). This type of fish farming has no future in a world short of fish protein, except in producing small amounts of luxury products. Some traditional fish farming uses omnivorous, detritivorous, or herbivorous fish, such as carp, mullet, milkfish, and tilapia, and in these cases the future might see a considerable expansion (Tacon et al. 2009).

Outlook

In the future, global capture fisheries will likely be required to become more ecologically and ethically responsible. Sustainable seafood labels (such as the Marine Stewardship Council) will likely proliferate despite concerns about their validity and effectiveness in mediating improvements in fishery management (Jacquet et al. 2009). Fisheries may be asked to pay to remediate harm done to publicly owned resources such as coastal marine ecosystems (Lam 2012). They will almost certainly be required to operate with fewer government subsidies. Fisheries will also have to adapt to climate change as the ecological ranges of target fish shift across political boundaries (Cheung et al. 2009; MacNeil et al. 2010), with economic implications that could be serious (Sumaila et al. 2011), while ocean acidification will affect the shells of mollusks, impacting shellfish fisheries. Many people consider that only large and networked marine protected areas can ensure the future of marine resources and elevate seafood security (Halpern, Lester, and Kellner 2008). Although there may be some areas where things can improve, many people now fear that a fisheries catastrophe is unlikely to be averted.

Tony J. PITCHER
University of British Columbia

See also Food Security; Global Trade; Local Solutions to Global Problems; Natural Capital; Shipping; Water

FURTHER READING

Agnew, David J., et al. (2009). Estimating the worldwide extent of illegal fishing. *PLoS ONE, 4*(2), 1–8.
Anticamara, Jonathan Alburo; Watson, Reg; Gelchu, Ahmed; & Pauly, Daniel. (2011). Global fishing effort (1950–2010): Trends, gaps, and implications. *Fisheries Research, 107*(1–3), 131–136.
Branch, Trevor A. (2009). How do individual transferable quotas affect marine ecosystems? *Fish and Fisheries, 10*(1), 39–57.
Branch, Trevor A.; Jensen, Olaf P.; Ricard, Daniel; Ye, Yimin; & Hilborn, Ray. (2011). Contrasting global trends in marine fishery status obtained from catches and from stock assessments. *Conservation Biology, 25*(4), 777–786.
Bromley, Daniel W. (2009). Abdicating responsibility: The deceits of fisheries policy. *Fisheries, 34*(6), 280–290.
Carpenter, Kent E., et al. (2008) One third of reef-building corals face elevated extinction risk from climate change and local impacts. *Science, 321*(5888), 560–563.
Chassot, Emmanuel, et al. (2010). Global marine primary production constrains fisheries catches. *Ecological Letters, 13*(4), 495–505.
Cheung, William W. L., & Pitcher, Tony J. (2008). Evaluating the status of exploited taxa in the northern South China Sea using intrinsic vulnerability and spatially explicit catch-per-unit-effort data. *Fisheries Research, 92*(1), 28–40.
Cheung, William W. L., et al. (2009). Projecting global marine biodiversity impacts under climate change scenarios. *Fish and Fisheries, 10*(3), 235–251.
Chu, Cindy. (2009). Thirty years later: The global growth of ITQs and their influence on stock status in marine fisheries. *Fish and Fisheries, 10*(2), 1–14.
Corcoran, Thomas H. (1963). Roman fish sauces. *The Classical Journal, 58*(5), 204–210.
Cunnane, Stephen C., & Stewart, Kathlyn N. (Eds.). (2010). *Human brain evolution: The influence of freshwater and marine food resources.* Hoboken, NJ: Wiley-Blackwell.
Daskalov, Georgi M.; Grishin, Alexander N.; Rodionov, Sergei; & Mihneva, Vesselina. (2007). Trophic cascades triggered by overfishing reveal possible mechanisms of ecosystem regime shifts. *Proceedings of the National Academy of Science of the USA, 104*(25), 10518–10523.
Dulvy, Nicholas K.; Pinnegar, John K.; & Reynolds, John D. (2009). Holocene extinctions in the sea. In Samuel T. Turvey (Ed.), *Holocene extinctions* (pp. 129–150). Oxford, UK: Oxford University Press.
Garcia, Serge M., & Grainger, Richard J. R. (2005). Gloom and doom? The future of marine capture fisheries. *Philosophical Transactions of the Royal Society B: Biological Sciences, 360*(1453), 21–46.
Given-Wilson, Chris; Brand, Paul; Curry, Anne; Ormrod, W. Mark; & Phillips, J. R. Seymore. (Eds.). (2005). *The Parliament rolls of Medieval England, 1275–1504.* London: Woodbridge.
Goldburg, Rebecca, & Naylor, Rosamond. (2005). Future seascapes, fishing, and fish farming. *Frontiers in Ecology and the Environment, 3*(1), 21–28.
Greenpeace EU Unit. (2011, October 2). Wide open to abuse: The Common Fisheries Policy. Retrieved June 21, 2012, from http://www.greenpeace.org/eu-unit/en/Publications/2011/Common-Fisheries-Policy-wide-open-to-abuse/
Halpern, Benjamin S.; Lester, Sarah E.; & Kellner, Julie B. (2008). Spillover from marine reserves and the replenishment of fished stocks. *Environmental Conservation, 36*(4), 268–276.
Her Majesty's Stationery Office (HMSO) Public Record Office. (1937). *Calendar of inquisitions miscellaneous (Chancery): Volume 3 (Edward III: 1348–1377).* London: HMSO.
Hilborn, Ray, et al. (2003). State of the world's fisheries. *Annual Review of Environment and Resources, 28*, 359–399.
Hilborn, Ray; Parrish, Julia K.; & Litle, Kate. (2006). Fishing rights or fishing wrongs? *Reviews in Fish Biology and Fisheries, 15*(3), 191–199.

Hughes, Terry P.; Graham, Nicholas J. A.; Jackson, Jeremy B. C.; Mumby, Peter J.; & Steneck, Robert S. (2010). Rising to the challenge of sustaining coral reef resilience. *Trends in Ecology and Evolution, 25*(11), 633–642.

Jacquet, Jennifer, et al. (2009). Conserving wild fish in a sea of market-based efforts. *Oryx, 44*(1), 45–56.

Juvenal. (2004). *Juvenal and Persius* (Susanna Morton Braund, Trans.). Cambridge, MA: Loeb Classical Library, Harvard University Press.

Lam, Mimi E. (2012). Of fish and fishermen: Shifting societal baselines to reduce environmental harms in fisheries. *Ecology and Society, 15*(3). (in press)

Lam, Mimi E., & Pauly, Daniel. (2010). Who is right to fish? Evolving a social contract for ethical fisheries. *Ecology and Society, 15*(3), 1–16.

Lam, Mimi E., & Pitcher, Tony J. (2012). Fish commoditization: Sustainability strategies to protect living fish. *Bulletin of Science, Technology and Society* (in press).

Lozano-Montes, Hector; Pitcher, Tony J.; & Haggan, Nigel. (2008). Shifting environmental and cognitive baselines in the upper Gulf of California (Mexico): Local fisher's knowledge reveals a slow-motion disaster. *Frontiers in Ecology and the Environment, 6*(2), 75–80.

MacNeil, M. Aaron, et al. (2010). Transitional states in marine fisheries: Adapting to predicted global change. *Philosophical Transactions of the Royal Society of London, B: Biological Sciences, 365*, 3753–3763.

Morato, Telmo; Watson, Reg; Pitcher, Tony J.; & Pauly, Daniel. (2006). Fishing down the deep. *Fish and Fisheries, 7*(1), 23–33.

Pauly, Daniel. (2006). Major trends in small-scale fisheries with emphasis on developing countries. *Maritime Studies (MAST), 4*(2), 6–23.

Pauly, Daniel; Christensen, Villy; Dalsgaaard, Johanne; Froese, Rainer; & Torres, Francisco, Jr. (1998). Fishing down marine food webs. *Science, 279*(5352), 860–863.

Pauly, Daniel, & Maclean, Jay. (2003). *In a perfect ocean: The state of fisheries and ecosystems in the Atlantic Ocean.* Washington, DC: Island Press.

Pauly, Daniel; Watson, Reg; & Alder, Jackie. (2005). Global trends in world fisheries: Impacts on marine ecosystems and food security. *Philosophical Transactions of the Royal Society B: Biological Sciences, 360*(1453), 5–12.

Pinkerton, Evelyn, & Edwards, Danielle N. (2009). The elephant in the room: The hidden costs of leasing individual transferable fishing quotas. *Marine Policy, 33*, 707–713.

Pitcher, Tony J. (1998). A cover story: Fisheries may drive stocks to extinction. *Reviews in Fish Biology and Fisheries, 8*(3), 367–370.

Pitcher, Tony J. (2001). Fisheries managed to rebuild ecosystems: Reconstructing the past to salvage the future. *Ecological Applications, 11*(2), 601–617.

Pitcher, Tony J. (2008). The sea ahead: Challenges to marine biology from seafood sustainability (Keynote paper, 41st European Marine Biology Symposium, September 4, 2006). *Hydrobiologia, 606*, 161–185.

Pitcher, Tony J., & Lam, Mimi. (2010). Fishful thinking: Rhetoric, reality and the sea before us. *Ecology and Society, 15*(2), 12, 27.

Pitcher, Tony J., & Pauly, Daniel. (1998). Rebuilding ecosystems, not sustainability, as the proper goal of fishery management. In Tony J. Pitcher, Paul J. B. Hart & Daniel Pauly (Eds.), *Reinventing fisheries management* (pp. 311–329). London: Chapman and Hall.

Pitcher, Tony J.; Clark, Malcolm R.; Morato, Telmo; & Watson, Reg. (2010). Seamount fisheries: Do they have a future? *Oceanography, 23*(1), 134–144.

Pitcher, Tony J.; Kalikoski, Daniela; Short, Katherine; Varkey, Divya; & Pramod, Ganapathiraju. (2008). An evaluation of progress in implementing ecosystem-based management of fisheries in 33 countries. *Marine Policy, 33*(2), 223–232.

Pitcher, Tony J.; Watson, Reg; Forrest, Robyn; Valtýsson, Hreiðar Þór; & Guénette, Sylvie. (2002). Estimating illegal and unreported catches from marine ecosystems: A basis for change. *Fish and Fisheries, 3*(4), 317–339.

Poulsen, Bo. (2008). *Dutch herring: An environmental history, c. 1600–1860.* Holland, The Netherlands: Askant Press.

Purcell, Jennifer E.; Uye, Shinichi; & Lo, Wen-Tseng. (2007). Anthropogenic causes of jellyfish blooms and their direct consequences for humans: A review. *Marine Ecology Progress Series, 350*, 153–174.

Rice, Jake. (2011). Managing fisheries well: Delivering the promises of an ecosystem approach. *Fish and Fisheries, 12*(2), 209–231.

Roberts, Callum. (2008). *The unnatural history of the sea.* Washington, DC: Island Press.

Rosenberg, Andrew A., et al. (2005). The history of ocean resources: Modeling cod biomass using historical records. *Frontiers in Ecology, 3*(2), 84–90.

Sahrhage, Dietrich, & Lundbeck, Johannes. (1992). *A history of fisheries.* Berlin: Springer.

Sumaila, U. Rashid, et al. (2010). A bottom-up re-estimation of global fisheries subsidies. *Journal of Bioeconomics, 12*(3), 201–225.

Sumaila, U. Rashid; Cheung, William W. L.; Lam, Vicky W. Y.; Pauly, Daniel; & Herrick, Samuel. (2011). Climate change impacts on the biophysics and economics of world fisheries. *Nature Climate Change, 1*, 449–456.

Swartz, Wilf; Sala, Enric; Tracey, Sean; Watson, Reg; & Pauly, Daniel. (2010). The spatial expansion and ecological footprint of fisheries (1950 to present). *PLoS ONE, 5*(12), 1–6.

Tacon, Albert; Metian, Marc; Turchini, Giovanni; & De Silva, Sena. (2009). Responsible aquaculture and trophic level implications to global fish supply. *Reviews in Fisheries Science, 18*(1), 94–105.

Thomson, Richard C.; Moore, Charles J.; vom Saal, Frederick S.; & Swan, Shanna H. (2009). Plastics, the environment and human health: Current consensus and future trends. *Philosophical Transactions of the Royal Society B, 364*(1526), 2153–2166.

Tyedmers, Peter H.; Watson, Reg; & Pauly, Daniel. (2005). Fuelling global fishing fleets. *Ambio, 34*(8), 635–638.

Walters, Carl J., & Martell, Steven J. (2004). *Fisheries ecology and management.* Princeton, NJ: Princeton University Press.

Walters, Carl J.; Christensen, Villy; Martell, Steven J.; & Kitchell, James F. (2005). Possible ecosystem impacts of applying MSY policies from single-species assessment. *ICES Journal of Marine Science, 62*(3), 558–568.

Watson, Reg; Kitchingman, Adrian; Gelchu, Ahmed; & Pauly, Daniel. (2004). Mapping global fisheries: Sharpening our focus. *Fish and Fisheries, 5*, 168–177.

Worm, Boris, et al. (2006). Impacts of biodiversity loss on ocean ecosystem services. *Science, 314*(5800), 787–790.

Worm, Boris, et al. (2009). Rebuilding global fisheries. *Science, 325*(5940), 578–585.

Food Security

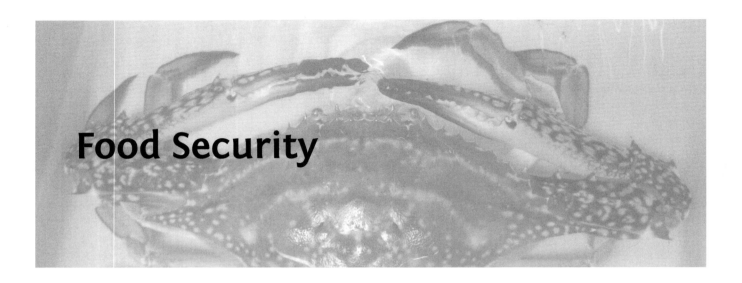

The term food security *refers to a population's or geographic region's access to food resources that meet its nutritional needs and cultural preferences. Expanding the world's food security depends on the conservation of water and arable land, as well as continuing innovations in agricultural practice. As the world's population climbs past 7 billion people to an unknown number later this century, immediate steps need to be taken to ensure that everyone on the planet has access to adequate food and nutrition.*

Prior to 1950, growth of the food supply came almost entirely from expanding cropland area. Then as frontiers disappeared and population growth accelerated after World War II, the focus quickly shifted to raising land productivity. In the most spectacular achievement in world agricultural history, farmers doubled the grain harvest between 1950 and 1973. Stated otherwise, growth in the grain harvest during this twenty-three-year span matched that of the preceding eleven thousand years (USDA 2010c).

This was the golden age of world agriculture. Since then, growth in world food output has been gradually losing momentum as the backlog of unused agricultural technology dwindles, soil erodes, the area of cultivable land shrinks, and irrigation water becomes scarce.

Gains in land productivity since 1950 have come primarily from three sources—the development of higher-yielding varieties, the growing use of fertilizer, and the spread of irrigation. The initial breakthrough in breeding higher-yielding varieties came when Japanese scientists succeeded in dwarfing both wheat and rice plants in the late nineteenth century. This decreased the share of photosynthate (a chemical product of photosynthesis) going into straw and increased that going into grain, making it possible to double yields.

The early breakthrough with corn (maize), the world's leading grain crop—over 750 million tonnes were produced in 2011 (IGC 2012)—came with hybridization in the United States. As a result of the dramatic advances associated with hybrid corn and the recent, much more modest gains associated with genetic modification, corn yields are still edging upward.

In 1974, Chinese scientists developed commercially viable hybrid rice strains. While they have raised yields somewhat, the gains have been small compared with the earlier gains from dwarfing the rice plant.

As farmers attempted to remove nutrient constraints on crop yields, fertilizer use climbed from nearly 13 million tonnes in 1950 to nearly 150 million tonnes in 2009. In some countries, such as the United States, several in western Europe, and Japan, fertilizer use has now leveled off or even declined substantially in recent decades (Heffer and Prud'homme 2010). In China and India, both of which use more fertilizer than the United States does, usage may also decline as farmers use fertilizer more efficiently.

After several decades of rapid rise, however, it is now becoming more difficult to raise land productivity. From 1950 to 1990, world grainland productivity increased by 2.2 percent per year, but from 1990 until 2010 it went up only 1.2 percent annually (USDA 2010c).

There are distinct signs of yields leveling off in the higher-yield countries that are using all available technologies. With wheat, it is hard to get more than 7.25 tonnes per hectare. This is illustrated by the plateauing of wheat yields in France (Europe's largest wheat producer), Germany, the United Kingdom, and Egypt (Africa's leading wheat grower) (FAO 2010b).

Japan, which led the world into the era of rising grain yields over a century ago, saw its rice yield plateau in the first decade of the twenty-first century, as it approached

4.5 tonnes per hectare. Yields in China, in 2011, also leveled off as they reached the Japanese level.

Among the big three grains, corn is the only one where the yield is continuing a steady rise in high-yield countries. In the United States, which accounts for 40 percent of the world corn harvest, yields now exceed an astonishing 9 tonnes per hectare. Iowa, with its super-high corn yields, produces more grain than Canada does (USDA 2010a).

Despite dramatic past leaps in grain yields, it is becoming more difficult to expand world food output for many reasons. Further gains in yields from plant breeding, even including genetic modification, do not come easily. Expanding the irrigated area is difficult. Returns on the use of additional fertilizer are diminishing in many countries.

In spite of the difficulties, some developing countries have dramatically boosted farm output. In India, after the monsoon failure of 1965 that required the import of one-fifth of the US wheat crop to avoid famine, a highly successful new agricultural strategy was adopted. It included replacing grain ceiling prices that catered to urban consumers with grain support prices to encourage farmers to invest in raising land productivity. The construction of fertilizer plants was moved from the public sector into the private sector, which could build them much faster. The high-yielding Mexican dwarf wheats, already tested in India, were introduced by the shipload for seed. These policy initiatives enabled India to double its wheat harvest in seven years (Brown 2001). No major country before or since has managed to double the harvest of a staple food so quickly.

Getting India's food distributed to the people who need it, however, is another matter: according to the *Wall Street Journal*, nearly 30 percent of the country's fresh produce perishes due to a lack of refrigeration, while thousands of tons of grain spoil in warehouses that are ill-equipped to handle surpluses (Mukherji and Pattanayak 2011). This is a classic example of the intricacies of food insecurity.

A similarly dramatic advance came in Malawi, a small country in Africa's Great Rift Valley with low grain yields, after the drought of 2005 left many hungry and some starving. In response, the government issued coupons good for 90 kilograms of fertilizer to each farmer at well below the market price, along with free packets of improved seed corn, their staple food. Costing some $70 million per year and funded partly by outside donors, this fertilizer and seed subsidy program helped Malawi's farmers nearly double their corn harvest within two years, leading to an excess of grain (World Bank 2008). Fortunately this grain could be exported profitably to nearby Zimbabwe, which was experiencing acute grain shortages.

Some years earlier, Ethiopia, taking similar steps, also achieved a dramatic jump in production. But because there was no way to export the surplus, prices crashed—a major setback to the country's farmers. This experience underlines a major challenge to Africa's agricultural development, namely the lack of public infrastructure, such as roads to get fertilizer to farmers and their products to market.

In Africa's more arid countries, such as Chad, Mali, and Mauritania, there is not enough rainfall to raise yields dramatically. Modest yield gains are possible with improved agricultural practices, but in many of these low-rainfall countries there has not been a Green Revolution for the same reasons there has not been one in Australia—namely, low soil moisture and the associated limit on fertilizer use. (The term *Green Revolution* refers to a program started in the 1960s to develop more productive food crops for use by farmers in the developing world.)

One encouraging practice to raise cropland productivity in semiarid Africa is the simultaneous planting of grain and nitrogen-fixing leguminous trees. At first the trees grow slowly, permitting the grain crop to mature and be harvested; then the saplings grow quickly, dropping leaves that provide nitrogen and organic matter, both sorely needed in African soils. The wood can then be cut and used for fuel. This simple, locally adapted technology, developed by scientists at the World Agroforestry Centre in Nairobi, has enabled farmers to double their grain yields within a matter of years as soil fertility builds (Sanchez 2001).

The shrinking backlog of unused agricultural technology and the resulting loss of momentum in raising yields worldwide signal a need for fresh thinking on how to raise cropland productivity. One way is to breed crops that are more tolerant of drought and cold. Corn breeders in the United States have developed corn strains that are more drought tolerant, enabling corn production to move westward into Kansas, Nebraska, and South Dakota. For example, Kansas, the leading US wheat-producing state, now produces more corn than wheat (USDA 2010a). Similarly, corn production is moving northward into North Dakota and Minnesota.

Another way to raise land productivity, where soil moisture permits, is to expand the land area that produces more than one crop per year. Indeed, the tripling of the world grain harvest from 1950 to 2000 was due in part to widespread increases in multiple cropping in Asia (Worldwatch 2001). Some of the more common combinations are wheat and corn in northern China, wheat and rice in northern India, and the double or triple cropping of rice in southern China and southern India.

The spread of corn-wheat double cropping on the North China Plain helped boost China's grain production to rival that of the United States. In northern India, the grain harvest in the 1960s was confined largely to wheat, but with the advent of the earlier-maturing high-yielding wheats and rices, wheat could be harvested in time to plant rice. This combination is now widely used throughout the Punjab, Haryana, and parts of Uttar Pradesh.

Another often overlooked influence on productivity is land tenure. A survey by the Rural Development Institute revealed that farmers in China with documented land rights were twice as likely to make long-term investments in their land, such as adding greenhouses, orchards, or fishponds (Zhu and Prosterman 2006).

In summary, while grain production is falling in some countries, either because of unfolding water shortages or spreading soil erosion, the overwhelming majority of nations still have a substantial unrealized production potential. The challenge is for each country to fashion agricultural and economic policies to realize that potential. Countries like India in the late 1960s or Malawi in the early twenty-first century give a sense of how to exploit these possibilities for expanding food supplies.

Water Shortages

With water shortages constraining food production growth, the world needs a campaign to raise water productivity similar to the one that nearly tripled land productivity over the last half century. Data on the efficiency of surface-water projects—that is, dams that deliver water to farmers through a network of canals—show that crops never use all the irrigation water simply because some evaporates, some percolates downward, and some runs off. Water-policy analysts Sandra Postel and Amy Vickers found that "surface water irrigation efficiency ranges between 25 and 40 percent in India, Mexico, Pakistan, the Philippines, and Thailand; between 40 and 45 percent in Malaysia and Morocco; and between 50 and 60 percent in Israel, Japan, and Taiwan" (Postel and Vickers 2004, 51–52).

China's irrigation plan is to raise efficiency from 43 percent in 2000 to 55 percent in 2020 (Chen 2009). Key measures include raising the price of water, providing incentives for adopting more irrigation-efficient technologies, and developing the local institutions to manage this process.

Raising irrigation efficiency typically means shifting from the less-efficient flood or furrow systems to overhead sprinklers or to drip irrigation, the gold standard of irrigation efficiency. Switching from flood or furrow to low-pressure sprinkler systems reduces water use by an estimated 30 percent, while switching to drip irrigation typically cuts water use in half (FAO 2002).

Drip irrigation also raises yields because it provides a steady supply of water with minimal losses to evaporation. In addition, it reduces the energy needed to pump water. Since drip systems are both labor intensive and water efficient, they are well suited to countries with a surplus of labor and a shortage of water. A few small countries—Cyprus, Israel, and Jordan—rely heavily on drip irrigation. This more-efficient technology is used on 1–3 percent of irrigated land in India and China, and on roughly 4 percent in the United States (Postel and Vickers 2004, 53).

In recent years, small-scale drip irrigation systems—literally an elevated bucket with flexible plastic tubing to distribute the water—have been developed to irrigate small vegetable gardens; somewhat larger systems using drums can irrigate larger areas. In both cases, the containers are elevated slightly so that gravity distributes the water. Large-scale drip systems using plastic lines that can be moved easily are also becoming popular. These simple systems can pay for themselves in one year. By simultaneously reducing water costs and raising yields, they can dramatically raise incomes of smallholders.

Sandra Postel of the Global Water Policy Project estimates that drip technology has the potential to profitably irrigate 10 million hectares of India's cropland, nearly one-tenth of the total. She sees a similar potential for China, which is now also expanding its drip irrigated area to save scarce water (Postel et al. 2001).

Institutional shifts—specifically, moving the responsibility for managing irrigation systems from government agencies to local water users associations—can also facilitate the more efficient use of water. Farmers in many countries are organizing locally so they can assume this responsibility, and since they have an economic stake in good water management they tend to do a better job than a distant government agency. Mexico is a leader in developing water users associations. As of 2008, farmers associations managed more than 99 percent of the irrigated area held in public irrigation districts (CONAGUA 2008). One advantage of this shift is that the cost of maintaining the irrigation system is assumed locally, reducing the drain on the treasury.

Low water productivity is often the result of low water prices. In many countries, subsidies lead to irrationally low water prices, creating the impression that water is abundant when in fact it is scarce. As water becomes scarce, it needs to be priced accordingly.

A new mind-set is needed, a new way of thinking about water use. For example, shifting to more water-efficient crops wherever possible boosts water productivity. Rice growing is being phased out around Beijing because rice is such a thirsty crop. Similarly, Egypt restricts rice production in favor of wheat. Any measures that raise crop yields on irrigated land also raise irrigation water productivity.

Bringing water use down to the sustainable yield of aquifers and rivers worldwide involves a wide range of measures not only in agriculture but throughout the economy. The more obvious steps, in addition to adopting more water-efficient irrigation practices, include using more water-efficient industrial processes. Recycling urban water supplies is another obvious step in countries facing acute water shortages. And because coal-fired power plants use so much water for cooling, shifting to wind farms eliminates a major drain on water supplies.

More Efficient Animal Protein

Another way to raise both land and water productivity is to produce animal protein more efficiently. With some 35 percent of the world grain harvest (690 million tonnes) used to produce animal protein (USDA 2010c), even a modest reduction in meat consumption or gain in efficiency can save a large quantity of grain.

World consumption of animal protein is on the rise everywhere. Meat consumption increased from 40 million tonnes in 1950 to 246 million tonnes in 2009 (FAO 2010c), more than doubling annual consumption per person to nearly 90 pounds. The rise in the consumption of milk and eggs is equally dramatic. Wherever incomes rise, so does meat consumption, reflecting a taste that apparently evolved over 4 million years of hunting and gathering.

As the oceanic fish catch and rangeland beef production have both leveled off, the world has shifted to grain-based production of animal protein to expand output. The efficiency with which various animals convert grain into protein varies widely: raising cattle is less efficient than raising pork, which is less efficient than raising chickens or farmed fish such as carp, tilapia, and catfish.

Global beef production, most of which comes from rangelands, grew less than 1 percent a year from 1990 to 2007, and has plateaued since. Pork production grew by 2 percent annually, and poultry by 4 percent. World pork production, half of it now in China, overtook beef production in 1979 and has continued to widen the lead since then. Poultry production eclipsed beef in 1995, moving into second place behind pork (FAO 2010c).

Fast-growing, grain-efficient fish farm output may also soon overtake beef production. In fact, aquaculture has been the fastest-growing source of animal protein since 1990, expanding from under 12 million tonnes in 1990 to 47 million tonnes in 2008, or an 8 percent increase a year (FAO 2010a).

Public attention has focused on aquacultural operations that are environmentally inefficient or disruptive, such as the farming of salmon, a carnivorous species that is typically fed fishmeal. But these operations account for less than one-tenth of world fish farm output. Worldwide, aquaculture is dominated by herbivorous species—mainly carp in China and India, but also catfish in the United States and tilapia in several countries—and shellfish. This is where the great growth potential for efficient animal protein production lies.

China accounts for 62 percent of global fish farm output (Li 2001, 26). Its output is dominated by finfish (mostly carp), which are grown in inland freshwater ponds, lakes, reservoirs, and rice paddies, and by shellfish (oysters and mussels), which are produced mostly in coastal regions. A multispecies system, using four types of carp that feed at different levels of the food chain, commonly boosts pond productivity over that of monocultures by at least half. China's fish farm output of 29 million tonnes is nearly triple the US beef output of 11 million tonnes (FAO 2010a).

Soybean meal is universally used in mixing feed for livestock, poultry, and fish. In 2010 the world's farmers produced 230 million tonnes of soybeans. Of this, an estimated 27 million tonnes were consumed directly as tofu or other meat substitutes. Some 200 million tonnes were crushed, yielding roughly 36 million tonnes of soybean oil and 154 million tonnes of highly valued high-protein meal (USDA 2010b).

Combining soybean meal with grain in a one-to-four ratio dramatically boosts the efficiency with which grain is converted into animal protein, sometimes nearly doubling it. Virtually the entire world, including the three largest meat producers—China, the United States, and Brazil—now relies heavily on soybean meal as a protein supplement in feed rations (USDA 2010c).

The heavy use of soybean meal to boost feed efficiency helps explain why the production of meat, milk, eggs, and farmed fish has climbed even though the 35 percent share of the world grain harvest used for feed has decreased slightly since 1990. It also explains why world soybean production has multiplied fifteenfold since 1950 (USDA 2010c).

Mounting pressures on land and water resources have led to the evolution of some promising new animal protein production systems that are based on roughage rather than grain, such as milk production in India. Since 1970, in what is known as the White Revolution, India's milk production has increased fivefold, jumping from 19 million to 100 million tonnes in 2009. In 1997 India overtook the United States to become the world's leading producer of milk and other dairy products (FAO 2010c).

What is so remarkable is that India has built the world's largest dairy industry based not on grain but almost entirely on crop residues—wheat straw, rice straw, and corn stalks—and grass gathered from the roadside. The value of India's annual milk output now exceeds that of its rice harvest (Government of India 2009, 11).

A second new protein-production model, one that also relies on ruminants and roughage, has evolved in four provinces in eastern China—Hebei, Shangdong, Henan, and Anhui—where double-cropping of winter wheat and corn is common. These provinces, dubbed the Beef Belt by Chinese officials, use crop residues to produce much of China's beef. This use of crop residues to produce milk in India and beef in China lets farmers reap a second harvest from the original grain crop, thus boosting both land and water productivity.

What Can Be Done?

While people in developing countries are focusing on moving up the food chain, in many industrial countries there is a growing interest in fresh, locally produced foods. In the United States, this interest is driven both by concerns about the climatic effects of transporting food from distant places and by the desire for fresh food that supermarkets with long supply chains can no longer deliver. This is reflected in the growth of both home gardens and local farmers' markets.

With the fast-growing local foods movement, diets are becoming more locally shaped and more seasonal. In the United States, this trend toward localization can be seen in the recent rise in farm numbers. Between the agricultural census of 2002 and that of 2007, the number of farms increased by nearly 80,000 to roughly 2.2 million (USDA 2010a). Many of the new farms, mostly smaller ones—and a growing share of them operated by women—cater to local markets. Some produce fresh fruits and vegetables exclusively for farmers' markets. Others, such as goat farms that produce milk, cheese, and meat, produce specialized products. With many specializing in organic food, the number

of organic farms in the United States jumped from 12,000 in 2002 to 18,200 in 2007 (Martin 2009).

Many market outlets are opening up for local US produce. Farmers' markets, where local farmers bring their produce for sale, increased from 1,755 in 1994 to over 6,100 in 2010, more than tripling over sixteen years (USDA 2012). These markets facilitate personal ties between producers and consumers that do not exist in the impersonal confines of a supermarket.

Many US schools and universities are now making a point of buying local food because it is fresher, tastier, and more nutritious, and it fits into new campus greening programs. Supermarkets are increasingly contracting seasonally with local farmers when produce is available. For example, in late 2010 Walmart announced a plan to buy more produce from local farmers for its stores. Upscale restaurants emphasize locally grown food on their menus. Some year-round food markets are evolving that supply only locally produced foods, including not only fresh produce but also meat, milk, cheese, eggs, and other farm products.

Home gardening was given a big boost in the spring of 2009 in the United States when First Lady Michelle Obama worked with children from a local school to dig up a piece of the White House lawn to start a vegetable garden. There was a precedent for this: Eleanor Roosevelt planted a White House victory garden during World War II; her initiative encouraged millions of victory gardens, which eventually grew 40 percent of the nation's fresh produce.

Although it was much easier to expand home gardening during World War II, when the United States was much more rural, there is still a huge gardening potential—given that the grass lawns surrounding US residences collectively cover some 7.3 million hectares (Milesi et al. 2005). Converting even a small share of this to fresh vegetables and fruit trees could make a meaningful contribution.

Many cities and small towns in the United States and Great Britain are creating community gardens that can be used by those who would otherwise not have access to land for gardening. Providing space for community gardens is now seen by many local governments as an essential service, like providing playgrounds or parks.

Urban gardens are gaining popularity throughout the world. A program organized by the UN Food and Agriculture Organization (FAO) to help cities in developing countries establish urban garden programs is being well received. In five cities in the Democratic Republic of the Congo, for example, it has helped twenty thousand gardeners improve their vegetable growing operations. Market gardens in Kinshasa, the country's capital, produce an estimated 73,000 tonnes of vegetables per year, meeting 65 percent of the city's needs (FAO 2010b, 5–7, 13).

In the city of El Alto near La Paz, Bolivia, FAO supports a highly successful micro-garden program for low-income families. Using small, low-cost greenhouses covering about 40 square meters each, some 1,500 households grow fresh vegetables the year round. Some of the produce is consumed at home; some is sold at local markets.

School gardens are another welcome development. Children learn how food is produced, a skill often lacking in urban settings, and they may get their first taste of fresh salad greens or vine-ripened tomatoes. School gardens also provide fresh produce for school lunches. California, a leader in this area, has six thousand school gardens (MacVean 2009).

Food from more-distant locations boosts carbon emissions while losing flavor and nutrition. A survey of food consumed in Iowa showed conventional produce traveled on average 2,400 kilometers, not including food imported from other countries. In contrast, locally grown produce traveled on average 90 kilometers—a huge difference in fuel use. And a study in Ontario, Canada, found that fifty-eight imported foods traveled an average of 4,500 kilometers (Xuereb 2005). In an oil-scarce world, consumers are worried about food security in a long-distance food economy.

The high prices of natural gas, which is used to make nitrogen fertilizer, and of phosphate, as reserves are depleted, suggest a much greater future emphasis on nutrient recycling—an area where small farmers producing for local markets have a distinct advantage over massive livestock and poultry feeding operations.

With food, as with energy, achieving security now depends on looking at the demand side of the equation as well as the supply side. We cannot rely solely on expanding production to reverse the deteriorating food situation of recent years. This is why a basic Plan B goal is to accelerate the shift to smaller families and halt the growth in world population at 8 billion by 2040; it passed the 7 billion mark in 2012. ("Plan B" refers to the Earth Policy Institute's contention that business-as-usual—Plan A—will lead to catastrophic climate change, overpopulation, etc.) A citizen of the United States living high on the food chain with a diet heavy in grain-intensive livestock products, including red meat, consumes twice as much grain as the average Italian and nearly four times as much as the average Indian. Adopting a Mediterranean diet can cut the grain footprint of people in the United States roughly in half, reducing carbon emissions accordingly.

Across the world, ensuring future food security was once the exclusive responsibility of the ministry of agriculture, but this is changing. One minister of agriculture alone, no matter how competent, can no longer be expected to secure food supplies. Indeed, efforts by ministers of health and family planning to lower human fertility may have a greater effect on future food security than efforts in the ministry of agriculture to raise land fertility.

Similarly, if ministries of energy cannot quickly cut carbon emissions, the world will face crop-shrinking heat waves that can massively and unpredictably reduce harvests. Saving the mountain glaciers, whose ice melt irrigates much of the cropland in China and India during the dry season, is the responsibility of the ministry of energy, not solely the ministry of agriculture.

If the ministries of forestry and agriculture cannot work together to restore tree cover and reduce floods and soil erosion, grain harvests will shrink not only in smaller countries like Haiti and Mongolia, as they are doing, but also in larger countries, such as Russia and Argentina—both wheat exporters.

And where water shortages restrict food output, it will be up to ministries of water resources to do everything possible to raise national water productivity. With water, as with energy, the principal potential now is in increasing efficiency, not expanding supply.

In a world where cropland is scarce and becoming more so, decisions made in ministries of transportation on whether to develop land-consuming, auto-centered transport systems or more-diversified systems that are much less land intensive will directly affect world food security.

In the end, it is up to ministries of finance to reallocate resources in a way that recognizes the new threats to security posed by agriculture's deteriorating natural support systems, continuing population growth, human-driven climate change, and spreading water shortages. Since many ministries of government are involved, it is the head of state who must redefine security.

At the international level, we need to address the threat posed by growing climate volatility and the associated rise in food price volatility. The tripling of wheat, rice, corn, and soybean prices between 2007 and 2008 put enormous stresses on governments and low-income consumers; the droughts in the United States, including the summer of 2012, and continued unusually hot summers in other places, are doing the same. This price volatility also affects producers, since price uncertainty discourages investment by farmers.

In this unstable situation, a new mechanism to stabilize world grain prices is needed—in effect, a World Food Bank (WFB). This body would establish a support price and a ceiling price for wheat, rice, and corn. The WFB would buy grain when prices fell to the support level and return it to the market when prices reached the ceiling level, thus moderating price fluctuations in a way that would benefit both consumers and producers. The principal role of the WFB governing board, representing major exporting as well as importing countries, would be to establish the price levels for acquiring and releasing grain.

And finally, we all have a role to play as individuals. Whether we decide to bike, bus, or drive to work will affect carbon emissions, climate change, and food security. The size of the car we drive to the supermarket and its effect on climate may indirectly affect the size of the bill at the supermarket checkout counter. At the family level, we need to hold the line at two children. And if we are living high on the food chain, we can eat less grain-intensive livestock products, improving our health while helping to stabilize climate. Food security is something in which we all have a stake—and a responsibility.

Lester R. BROWN
Earth Policy Institute

This article was adapted by the editors from chapter 12 ("Feeding 8 Eight Billion") of Lester Brown's book *World on the Edge: How to Prevent Environmental and Economic Collapse.* Used with kind permission of the Earth Policy Institute. © 2011 Earth Policy Institute. The book is available at http://www.earth-policy.org/images/uploads/book_files/wotebook.pdf

See also Agricultural Innovation; Fisheries; Local Solutions to Global Problems; Migration; Population; Water

FURTHER READING

Brown, Lester R. (2001). *Eco-economy: Building an economy for the Earth.* New York: W. W. Norton.

Chen Lei. (2009, September 27). Speech at the 3rd academician forum of Chinese academy of engineering on hydraulic & architecture engineering. Wuhan, China. Retrieved June 12, 2012, from http://www.mwr.gov.cn/english/speechesandarticles/chenlei/200909/t20090927_59303.html

China to improve irrigation efficiency. (2009, October 25). *Xinhua.* Retrieved July 19, 2012, from http://au.china-embassy.org/eng/xw/t622531.htm

Comisión Nacional del Agua (CONAGUA). (2008, February). *National water program 2007–2012.* Coyoacán, Mexico: CONAGUA.

Food and Agriculture Organization of the United Nations (FAO). (2002). *Crops and drops.* Rome: FAO.

Food and Agriculture Organization of the United Nations (FAO). (2010a). FishStat Plus: Universal software for fishery statistical time series [Electronic database]. Retrieved August 10, 2012, from www.fao.org/fishery/statistics/software/fishstat

Food and Agriculture Organization of the United Nations (FAO). (2010b). *Growing greener cities.* Rome: FAO.

Food and Agriculture Organization of the United Nations (FAO). (2010c). ProdSTAT [Electronic database]. Retrieved August 10, 2012, from http://faostat.fao.org

Government of India, Ministry of Agriculture, Department of Animal Husbandry, Dairying & Fisheries. (2009). *Annual report 2008–2009.* New Delhi: Government of India.

Heffer, Patrick, & Prud'homme, Michel. (2010). *Fertilizer outlook 2010–2014.* Paris: IFA.

International Grain Council (IGC). (2012, July 2). Grain market report. Retrieved July 12, 2012, from http://www.igc.int/en/downloads/gmrsummary/gmrsumme.pdf

Li, S. F. (2001). Aquaculture research and its relation to development in China. In L. X. Zhang, J. Liu, S. F. Li, N. S. Yang & P. R. Gardiner (Eds.), *Agricultural development and the opportunities for aquatic resources research in China* (pp. 17–28). Penang, Malaysia: World Fish Center.

MacVean, Mary. (2009, March 27). Maria Shriver says edible garden will be planted in capitol park flower bed. *Los Angeles Times.* Retrieved July 19, 2012, from http://articles.latimes.com/2009/mar/27/local/me-garden27

Martin, Andrew. (2009, February 8). Farm living (subsidized by a job elsewhere). *New York Times,* p. BU6. Retrieved July 19, 2012, from http://www.nytimes.com/2009/02/08/business/08feed.html

Milesi, Cristina, et al. (2005, July 19). Mapping and modeling the biogeochemical cycling of turf grasses in the United States. *Environmental Management, 36*(3), 426–438.

Mukherji, Biman, & Pattanayak, Banikinkar. (2011, June 8). New Delhi starts drive to root out hunger. *Wall Street Journal.* Retrieved July 12, 2012, from http://online.wsj.com/article/SB10001424052702304259304576372813010336844.html

Postel, Sandra; Polak, Paul; Gonzales, Fernando; & Keller, Jack. (2001, March). Drip irrigation for small farmers: A new initiative to alleviate hunger and poverty. *International Water Resources Association, 26*(1), 3–13.

Postel, Sandra, & Vickers, Amy. (2004). Boosting water productivity. In Worldwatch Institute, *State of the world 2004: Special focus; The consumer society* (pp. 46–65). New York: W. W. Norton.

Sanchez, Pedro. (2001). *The climate change–soil fertility–food security nexus.* Bonn, Germany: International Food Policy Research Institute.

United States Department of Agriculture (USDA). (2010a, January). *Crop production 2009 summary.* Washington, DC: USDA National Agricultural Statistics Service.

United States Department of Agriculture (USDA). (2010b, August). *Oilseeds: World markets and trade.* Washington, DC: USDA Foreign Agriculture Service.

United States Department of Agriculture (USDA). (2010c). Production, supply and distribution. Retrieved August 12, 2010, from www.fas.usda.gov/psdonline

United States Department of Agriculture (USDA). (2012). Farmers market growth: 1994–2012. Retrieved August 13, 2012, from http://www.ams.usda.gov/AMSv1.0/ams.fetchTemplateData.do?template=TemplateS&navID=WholesaleandFarmersMarkets&leftNav=WholesaleandFarmersMarkets&page=WFMFarmersMarketGrowth&description=Farmers%20Market%20Growth&acct=frmrdirmkt

World Bank. (2008). Malawi, fertilizer subsidies and the World Bank. Retrieved July 12, 2012, from http://web.worldbank.org/WBSITE/EXTERNAL/COUNTRIES/AFRICAEXT/MALAWIEXTN/0,,contentMDK:21575335~pagePK:141137~piPK:141127~theSitePK:355870,00.html

Worldwatch Institute. (2001). 1950 data from USDA. *Signposts 2001* [CD-ROM]. Washington, DC: Worldwatch Institute.

Xuereb, Marc. (2005, November). *Food miles: Environmental implications of food imports to Waterloo region.* Waterloo, Canada: Region of Waterloo Public Health.

Zhu Keliang, & Prosterman, Roy. (2006, July–August). From land rights to economic boom. *China Business Review.* Retrieved July 19, 2012, from https://www.chinabusinessreview.com/public/0607/zhu.html

Geoengineering

The term geoengineering *has been applied to speculative proposals for the intentional manipulation of the global environment aimed at controlling environmental processes at the largest possible scale. Currently, most geoengineering proposals are focused on providing "technological fixes" for global warming. Advances in the main enabling technologies of geoengineering, combined with future worries about environmental threats, will continue to fuel speculation in this field.*

Can humanity survive on Earth into the indefinite future without taking control of the climate system and biosphere through geoengineering? What is geoengineering and how is it related to planetary engineering and climate control? What are the most recent ideas and proposals to cool the Earth and eliminate carbon dioxide from the atmosphere? Is geoengineering a viable emergency response to an unprecedented problem? Has it been proposed or even practiced in the past? What role does history play in providing perspective on these issues and their governance?

The editors of the venerable *Oxford English Dictionary* recently proposed to define the noun *geoengineering* as "the modification of the global environment or the climate in order to counter or ameliorate climate change." An engineering practice defined by its scale (*geo*) need not be constrained, however, by the good that might result from it, such as the counteraction or amelioration of climate change. The *Urban Dictionary* definition drops the statement of purpose and simply defines geoengineering as "the intentional large-scale manipulation of the global environment; planetary tinkering; a subset of terraforming or planetary engineering." Of course, any manipulation techniques deployed on such a grandiose scale, like any engineering practice, could

be used for both good and ill—or they may result in huge unintended consequences—a planetary "oops!"

Space and Planetary Engineering

As the name *geoengineering* implies, the Earth is the focus of the field, but there are various engineering proposals underway regarding extraterrestrial resources. In his 1995 book *Terraforming: Engineering Planetary Environments*, the British physicist Martyn J. Fogg reviewed the history and some of the technical aspects of "orchestrated planetary change." He defined *planetary engineering* as the application of technology for the purpose of influencing the global properties of a planet and *terraforming* as the process of enhancing the capacity of a planetary environment to support life. The ultimate in terraforming would be to create an uncontained planetary biosphere emulating all the functions of the biosphere of the Earth—one that would be fully habitable for human beings. Many have speculated about doing this, for example, on Mars, yet in reality we have yet to learn how to make a small-scale sustainable ecosystem, as revealed by the failed experience of Biosphere 2 (the project to construct an enclosed ecosystem in the Arizona desert).

Fogg described how ecological-engineering techniques might be used someday to implant life on other planets and how geoengineering might be used to ameliorate (or perhaps exacerbate) the currently "corrosive process" of global change on the Earth. He presented order-of-magnitude calculations and the results of some simple computer modeling to assess the plausibility of various planetary-engineering scenarios. This is typical practice for most geoengineers. Fogg deemed it rash to proclaim impossible any program that does not obviously violate the laws of physics. Yet he, like many others in this field, focused only on possibilities, not on unintended consequences, and left unaddressed questions of whether the programs are desirable, or even ethical. According to Fogg, geoengineering is not simply, or even primarily, a technical problem, because people, their politics, and their infrastructures get in the way. That is, geoengineering involves the implications and dangers of attempting to tamper with an immensely complex biosphere on an inhabited planet.

Earth's moon is often mentioned as a base for further exploration, observation, or possible resource extraction, perhaps in mining the lunar surface or perhaps the asteroid belt. Small amounts of water, recently identified, could possibly provide fuel and oxygen for a lunar colony. A 2012 proposal suggested capturing an asteroid, towing it to the L1 point (a theoretical point in space where the gravitational attraction of the Sun and Earth approximately balance) and pulverizing some of it to create a dust cloud to cool the Earth. Such fantastic ideas are really academic exercises in gravitational computation. "Astroengineering," or modifying the properties of the Sun or a star, by intervening in its opacity, nuclear reactions, mass loss, chemical mixing, or other properties, is admittedly hyper speculative now, but who can say in the future?

Geoengineering Proposals

Recent geoengineering (or more accurately climate engineering) proposals come in two main flavors: solar radiation management (SRM; sometimes called "sunlight reduction methods") and carbon capture and sequestration or storage (CCS; sometimes called carbon dioxide removal [CDR]).

SRM proposals involve a variety of wild ideas to be deployed from the Earth's surface to outer space: genetically alter crops to increase the reflectivity of their leaves, paint roofs white, enhance the albedo (light reflected by a surface) of marine clouds, inject sulfates or reflective nanoparticles high into the atmosphere, or launch a space shield to shade the planet. Each of these ideas is based on making the Earth brighter to reflect more solar radiation, with the goal of offsetting infrared heating from greenhouse gases. But each of these ideas is also based on very simple physics with those doing the proposing having little to no understanding of the environmental or social consequences of these interventions. Some leading climate modelers have warned that the effects of SRM would be largely unpredictable and may have major adverse effects on weather systems and ecosystems across the globe, while the effects on the climate system would be difficult or impossible to verify in the short term. Prominent ethicists and political theorists opposing such

heavy-handed climate intervention warn that SRM, while seemingly cheap to implement, could be exceedingly costly in the long run if it serves as a disincentive to mitigation and adaptation, or leads to social or political turmoil.

Scientists already claim to know, based on the 1991 volcanic eruption of Mount Pinatubo in the Philippines, that stratospheric aerosols can cool the planet, but they can also cause drought in some regions as well as deplete stratospheric ozone. We also know that shading the planet without reducing carbon dioxide in the atmosphere will not stop ocean acidification. SRM may have many other physical and ecological side effects, and climate modelers are currently trying to investigate them to the best of their ability, while policy makers are warning that these techniques are not ready (and may never be ready) for field-testing or deployment.

SRM finds its greatest support among conservative libertarian groups, scientists with intellectual property interests, and military planners; most environmentalists oppose it. Its proposed techniques have been criticized for being impractical (white roofs), naive (cloud brightening), and overly expensive (space shades). Stratospheric SRM could turn the blue sky milky white, weaken starlight as well as sunlight, and interfere with direct beam solar-power generators. SRM raises more questions than answers: Could such programs buy time for more reasonable ideas like reducing carbon dioxide emissions? Are they sustainable in the long term? Or could SRM destabilize an already vulnerable climate system?

The aforementioned method of carbon capture and sequestration or storage (CCS) aims to reduce the carbon dioxide in the atmosphere from anthropogenic sources. To be effective, it would involve the capture, transportation, and indefinite safe storage of 27.2 billion tonnes of carbon dioxide annually, an amount equal to the world's emissions (IPCC 2007). Since carbon dioxide is a stable, fully oxidized molecule at very low concentration in the atmosphere of 0.04 percent (394 parts per million) (NOAA 2012, Mauna Loa Observatory smoothed average), capture and storage techniques would be quite inefficient and might involve caustic chemicals such as sodium hydroxide. CCS would also be quite costly, since it would require a huge expansion of our energy infrastructure and an astronomical amount of energy—by some estimates 30 percent more (Sathre 2011) than the current world energy use—to liquefy carbon dioxide (CO_2), pipe it, pump it, store it in drilled wells or in the sea floor in perpetuity, and monitor it at remote storage sites. No one knows if our human institutions are capable of safe, long-term storage of such a large amount of carbon dioxide.

Currently CCS finds limited on-site application where the CO_2 concentration is very high, the infrastructure is already in place, and the captured gas can be repurposed, such as at factory smokestacks, and in oil and gas fields. Reforestation (enhancing existing forest lands) and afforestation (creating new forests) are getting considerable attention from policy makers but are limited in scale by the amount of arable land and the need to grow food instead of trees. More speculative ideas include building millions of proprietary, technochemical "artificial trees" (or inverse tailpipes) to capture CO_2 from the air, or adding an iron solution to the ocean in the hope of stimulating algal blooms that will accelerate carbon drawdown.

Long and Checkered History

Visionary programs for weather and climate control have a long history, but with very few exceptions they have never worked. Mythological stories warn of the folly of trying to control nature. In the Greek tradition, the youthful Phaethon lost control of his father's sun chariot, and his recklessness caused extensive damage to the Earth before Zeus shot him out of the sky. Will someone or some group trying to "fix" the climate with SRM repeat Phaethon's blunder?

In the 1840s James Espy, the United States' first national meteorologist, collected and mapped weather observations and developed a theory of storms powered by convection, but he went off the deep end when he proposed lighting giant fires to generate artificial rains and to clear the air of miasmas (harmful fumes). Rain making by concussion had its day in the mid- to late nineteenth century as various writers (none very scientific) speculated that cannonading the clouds or setting off loud explosions should shatter the ethereal equilibrium, perhaps causing downpours or, in the right circumstances, shattering hail-producing clouds.

In the 1920s, with concerns about aviation safety rising, the independent inventor L. Francis Warren and Cornell chemistry professor Wilder D. Bancroft developed a program to dose the clouds with electrified sand delivered by airplane. Rain making and fog clearing were both on the agenda, but trials, supported by the US Army Air Corps, were less than promising. Two decades later

during World War II, the British burned thousands of liters of petrol in specially designed burners surrounding military airfields to evaporate fog and light the way for returning aviators. This successful program, called FIDO (Fog Investigation and Dispersal Operation), was deemed too expensive and impractical to continue after the war.

These early weather modification plans (some of surprisingly large scale) were couched in the context of the pressing issues and available technologies of their eras: Espy wanted to purify the air and make rain for the East Coast; Warren and Bancroft hoped to make rain and clear airports of fog in the 1920s. During World War II, with national survival at stake, the British FIDO project succeeded, briefly but at great expense, in clearing fog from military airports. FIDO "worked" to dissipate fog by using giant burners to heat the airfields. It was in operation within several months of Winston Churchill's order to use Petroleum Warfare Department resources. It was a crash program for national defense and used 3,000 gallons (over 11,000 liters) of petrol to land one airplane, but after the war, planes used avionics to make instrument landings.

Recent History

Prospects for larger-scale, even planetary, intervention in the climate system arrived after 1945 with the dawn of nuclear power, digital computing, and access to space. In 1945 the Russian inventor and engineer Vladimir Zworykin suggested that digital computers could provide a "perfect forecast" that would allow deployment of a rapid intervention force to intervene in beginning weather systems as they developed. In 1955 the noted mathematician John von Neumann warned, however, that intervention in atmospheric and climatic matters would merge each nation's affairs with those of every other, even more thoroughly than the threat of a nuclear war or any other war would have done. In 1962 his colleague, the meteorologist Harry Wexler, classified all such programs as hypothetical until the consequences of tampering with large-scale atmospheric events were assessed and the risk of irremediable harm to our planet or undesirable side effects were counterbalanced against the possible short-term benefits. As of 2012 we are nowhere near being able to conduct such comparisons, although the climate modeling community is trying. Table 1 (below) indicates proposed (P) and actual (A) geoengineering in the recent era.

Highlighting just a few of these entries, during the early Cold War, the General Electric Corporation (GE) developed methods for seeding clouds with dry ice and silver iodide, sparking a race of sorts for commercial applications and military control of the clouds. Although field tests were inconclusive at best, the Nobel laureate chemist Irving Langmuir hyped the possibilities, arguing that hurricanes could be redirected and that the climate might ultimately be controlled on a continental or oceanic scale with these techniques. Also in the 1950s the Soviets declared war on permafrost and sought to engineer an ice-free Arctic Ocean. By 1962 Harry Wexler, head of research in the US Weather Bureau, worried that some types of rocket fuel, when burned, might release chlorine that could damage stratospheric ozone and warned that a hostile power could even build a "bromine bomb" that could devastate the ozone layer. In fact, a type of military geoengineering was actually practiced by both the United States and the Soviet Union half a century ago, and it had nothing to do with staving off climate change. Soon after the discovery in 1958 of the so-called Van Allen radiation belts that are held in place by the Earth's magnetic field, the US military launched Operation Argus, a top-secret project to detonate atomic bombs in space, with the goal of generating an artificial radiation belt, disrupting radio communications in the ionosphere, and destroying incoming missiles. This was followed, in 1962, by the Starfish Prime detonation of a hydrogen bomb in space that damaged the natural radiation belts. In the 1990s a committee of the National Academy of Sciences suggested using naval guns to shoot sulfates into the high atmosphere, since it was cheaper than reducing carbon emissions. Opening up the most recent era in geoengineering history, in 2006 the Dutch atmospheric chemist and Nobel laureate Paul Crutzen published an editorial wondering if injecting sulfates into the stratosphere using cannons or airplanes might be a sound policy for combating global warming. Some took him seriously, but others found it reminiscent of Jonathan Swift's "modest proposal" to end hunger in Ireland. Whatever the case, when members of the general public are asked to choose between mitigating their carbon emissions and shooting sulfates into the stratosphere, they overwhelmingly choose the first option.

The Future

Geoengineering has been proposed, and in some cases practiced, many times in the past. The checkered history

TABLE 1. Geoengineering: Proposed (P) and Actual (A)

Year	Plan
1945	(P) Vladimir Zworykin proposes perfect prediction/control with digital computer.
1945	(P) Julian Huxley proposes nuclear weapons to dissolve polar ice cap.
1947	(A) GE-US Air Force Project Cirrus attempts diversion of Atlantic hurricane.
1950s	(P) Soviets "declare war" on permafrost and seek an ice-free Arctic Ocean.
1954	(P) Harrison Brown envisions CO_2 generators and scrubbers to regulate climate.
1955	(P) Irving Langmuir proposes Pacific Basin cloud seeding.
1955	(P) John von Neumann warns of global climate control and nuclear war.
1958	(A) Project Argus, three atomic bombs, detonated in magnetosphere.
1962	(P) Harry Wexler warns that a 100 kiloton (KT) bromine bomb could destroy ozone layer.
1962	(A) Project Stormfury critiqued by Fidel Castro and government of Mexico.
1962	(A) Starfish Prime, H-bomb detonated in magnetosphere; similar Soviet tests.
1965	(P) Gordon MacDonald warns that geoengineering could wreck the planet.
1967	(A) Monsoonal cloud seeding over Vietnam leads to UN ENMOD* treaty (1978).
1992	(P) US National Academy analyzes shooting sulfates into stratosphere.
2006	(P) Paul Crutzen's "modest proposal"

Source: Fleming (2010, 189–268).

Note: The UN ENMOD treaty refers to the Convention on the Prohibition of Military or Any Other Hostile Use of Environmental Modification Techniques (ENMOD).

of this field provides valuable perspectives on what might otherwise seem to be completely unprecedented challenges. It also reveals that environmental issues are as much sociocultural as they are technical. Effective responses, as pointed out by the American Meteorological Society's 2009 policy statement on geoengineering, thus must include robust mitigation and adaptation, involve respect for the complexities of nature, and be both historically and socially informed. Most geoengineering proposals involve rather vague "back of the envelope calculations [and] simple computer models" (Fleming 2010, 223). This is not good enough.

The noted aeronautical engineer Theodore von Karman once observed that "scientists study the world as it is, engineers create the world that has never been." This quote has an ominous ring, however, when it comes to issues involving geoengineering, since some "worlds" perhaps should never be. Still, geoengineering involves human affairs, so in our march from knowledge to action—from understanding to prediction and control—we will need to consider both the technical and the human elements, the engineering and the philosophical dimensions. Policy makers, mostly in the United States and United Kingdom, have attempted to set preliminary guidelines for experimentation in this field, but they are currently discussing a vague and as yet nonexistent entity. Moreover, the conversation has been dominated by technocratic voices from the West, who believe technical experts should control decision making and governance. Deliberations about fixing the planet—if that is desirable—need to be fully international, interdisciplinary, and intergenerational in scope.

Here is a historical rule of thumb that needs to be considered by proposers of geoengineering programs: any projection of the state of the climate, engineering, or society into the future (say eighty years from now, or 2100) must also consider the changes in these variables over at least the past eighty years (that is, since the early twentieth century). Science, technology, and social values are changing faster than the climate system, so any student of climate dynamics must also be a student of "science dynamics"—or what we usually call the history of science. This single requirement will help technical researchers understand the contingent nature of extrapolating geoengineering ideas into the future.

James Rodger FLEMING
Colby College

See also Anthropocene Epoch; Climate Change and Big History; Food Security; Natural Capital; Progress; Values; Waste—Engineering Aspects; Waste—Social Aspects; Water

FURTHER READING

American Meteorological Society. (2009). Policy statement on geoengineering the climate system. Retrieved May 25, 2012, from http://www.ametsoc.org/policy/2009geoengineeringclimate_amsstatement.html

Crutzen, Paul J. (2006). Albedo enhancement by stratospheric sulfur injections: A contribution to resolve a policy dilemma? An editorial essay. *Climatic Change, 77*, 211–220.

Fleming, James Rodger. (2010). *Fixing the sky: The checkered history of weather and climate control.* New York: Columbia University Press.

Fleming, James Rodger. (2011). Iowa enters the space age: James Van Allen, Earth's radiation belts, and experiments to disrupt them. *Annals of Iowa, 70*, 301–324.

Fogg, Martyn J. (1995). *Terraforming: Engineering planetary environments.* Warrendale, PA: Society of Automotive Engineers.

Intergovernmental Panel on Climate Change (IPCC). (2007). IPCC fourth assessment report: Climate change 2007. Retrieved August 6, 2012, from http://www.ipcc.ch/publications_and_data/publications_and_data_reports.shtml

National Oceanic & Atmospheric Administration (NOAA). (2012). Trends in atmospheric carbon dioxide: July 2012. Retrieved August 10, 2012, from http://www.esrl.noaa.gov/gmd/ccgg/trends/

Royal Society of London. (2009). *Geoengineering the climate: Science, governance, and uncertainty* (Royal Society policy document 10/09). London: Royal Society of London.

Sathre, Roger. (2011). The role of life cycle assessment in identifying and reducing environmental impacts of CCS (LBNL-4548E). Berkeley, CA: Lawrence Berkeley National Laboratory. Retrieved July 20, 2012, from http://escholarship.org/uc/item/2bv98328

United States Government Accountability Office (US GAO). (2011). Climate engineering: Technical status, future directions, and potential responses (GAO-11-71). Retrieved May 25, 2012, from http://www.gao.gov/products/GAO-11-71

von Neumann, John. (1955, June). Can we survive technology? *Fortune*, 106–108.

Global Trade

International trade is an important driver of economic growth, but there are concerns about its environmental costs. While open markets underpin growth, conditioning market access to achieve environmental goals can be an important tool for achieving sustainable development goals. The rules of the World Trade Organization, among the many environmental initiatives that could affect trade, will play a key role in balancing between the need for open markets and using trade measures to ensure that growth is sustainable.

In 2011, total world exports amounted to almost $US18 trillion dollars, representing over a quarter of global GDP and an increase of almost 500 percent since 1991 (author's calculations). This exponential increase in trade has been at the forefront of globalization, which has created economic growth, raised standards of living, and exposed people to new goods, services, ideas, and lifestyles. At the same time, global trade has presented a range of challenges, especially through its impact on the environment. How countries reap the benefits from trade while managing it in ways that are environmentally sustainable is a key goal of sustainable development. The World Trade Organization (WTO) is the primary multilateral agency responsible for regulating world trade. Based in Geneva, Switzerland, and comprising 155 members, the WTO plays an important role in balancing the development and growth opportunities from trade while allowing members the scope needed to regulate access to their markets in order to achieve environmental goals.

International Trade and Sustainable Development

The linkages between international trade and the environment are key elements of the broader question about how international trade contributes to sustainable development. The rising global environmental consciousness can be traced back at least as far as the 1972 United Nations (UN) Conference on the Human Environment, which agreed to a set of principles that made protection of the environment central to human development and recognized the need for international cooperation to address transboundary and global environmental challenges. Recognition of the need for economic growth to address development issues while also protecting the environment was the beginning of the economic and environmental strands of what is referred to as sustainable development. Yet the implication of international trade on the environment was little explored at this time and was not mentioned in the report on the UN Conference on the Human Environment.

It was not until the 1987 Report of the World Commission on Environment and Development—*Our Common Future*, the so-called Brundtland Report—that the goal of sustainable development was more fully articulated, and the impact of international trade became an important part of the conversation. In the Brundtland Report, the role of trade in promoting development was recognized and focused on the environmental impacts of over-exploitation and export of nonrenewable natural resources. The Brundtland Report also reflected developing-country demands for greater access for their exports of manufactured goods to developed countries' markets to facilitate a shift away from their reliance on exports of natural resources and to support development opportunities.

The 1992 UN Conference on Environment and Development produced the Rio Declaration on Environment and Development, and built on the Brundtland Report's articulation of the relationship between trade, development, and environmental protection. Significantly, the Rio Declaration observed, "environmental protection shall constitute an integral part of the development process and cannot be considered in isolation from it" (Rio Declaration on Environment and Development 1992, 2). Read in conjunction with Principle 12 of the Rio Declaration was a view that economic growth encouraged by international trade would give states the capacity to address environmental problems.

The Rio Declaration also addressed concerns about the use of trade restrictions to achieve environmental goals. For instance, Principle 12 states that such trade measures should not constitute a means of arbitrary or unjustifiable discrimination or a disguised restriction on international trade. Principle 12 also encourages states to avoid taking unilateral action to address environmental challenges outside the jurisdiction of the importing country and to address transboundary or global environmental problems based on international consensus. The focus at Rio on the links between trade and environment highlighted how this relationship had become central to the debate over what sustainable development meant in practice (Esty 1994, 183).

While the impact of international trade on sustainable development became a focus following the 1987 Brundtland Report, since the early 1970s international efforts to address transboundary and global environmental harms had led to the conclusion of multilateral environmental agreements (MEAs) that used trade measures to achieve their goals. The earliest MEA was the 1973 Convention on International Trade in Endangered Species, which protects wildlife by regulating trade. The 1987 Montreal Protocol on Substances that Deplete the Ozone Layer restricts trade in substances that deplete the ozone, especially chlorofluorocarbons (CFCs). And the 1989 Basel Convention restricts imports of hazardous wastes.

While the implications of international trade were becoming central to efforts to protect the environment, the international trading regime was slow to address the issue. In fact, prior to 1995 and the establishment of the WTO, there was little discussion of the issue under the General Agreement on Tariffs and Trade (GATT)—the key multilateral agreement regulating international trade at that time. Any discussion in the GATT on the linkages dismissed trade as a means of

achieving environmental goals (GATT Secretariat 1992, 23). This reflected the economic view that countries would be best off by liberalizing trade and using the gains from trade to address any environmental harms. In 1991, however, the Organisation for Economic Co-operation and Development (OECD) began to analyze trade and environmental issues, and this work helped lay the groundwork for consideration of trade and environmental issues in the so-called Uruguay Round trade negotiations, which led to the creation of the WTO and the establishment in the WTO of a Committee on Trade and Environment.

Further negotiations from 1996 to 2000 led to the launch of the WTO Doha Development Agenda in 2001—the latest round of multilateral trade negotiations—which included a mandate for the WTO to consider a range of trade and environmental issues, including the relationship between WTO rules and trade obligations in MEAs as well as negotiations to reduce trade barriers to environmental goods and services. Reforming trade measures to address environmental issues was also taken up in other parts of the WTO Doha Round, such as eliminating subsidies that cause the unsustainable exploitation of fish stocks.

The Rio+20 Conference in June 2012 made green growth central to achieving sustainable development. Green growth policies emphasize the environmental and economic dimensions of sustainable development and focus on the need for economic growth that is consistent with the sustainable use of natural resources. For instance, taking the environmental costs of production into account should lead to a more efficient use of resources that will lead to increased output and prosperity.

The green growth focus has also been picked up by the world's major economies as part of their growth strategy. For instance, the G20—a group of the world's 20 largest economies—has recognized the need for green growth as a means of increasing economic growth, rebalancing economies, and restoring financial stability. To achieve green growth goals, trade policies, such as reducing trade barriers to green goods and services as well as phasing out fuel subsidies, remain a focus as well.

Economic Impact on Sustainable Development

Despite international attention, there remains debate in the economic literature over what effects trade liberalization will have on the environment and sustainable development. United States economists Gene Grossman and Alan B. Krueger have developed a useful economic framework for thinking about the impact of trade on the environment in terms of the "scale effect," the "composition effect," and the "technique effect" (Grossman and Krueger 1991, 3).

The Scale Effect

The scale effect refers to the impact on the environment from the increase in size of the economy caused by trade liberalization. Trade liberalization reduces the price of imports as tariffs and other trade barriers are removed, leading to increased competition between imported and domestic goods and services. In order to compete, domestic firms are forced to innovate and improve their productivity—to use fewer inputs to produce a given level of output—which leads to more-efficient use of resources within an economy and drives economic growth. The concern here is that as trade liberalization increases the scale of an economy, this could cause environmental harms such as pollution, land degradation, and increased consumption of exhaustible natural resources, such as water. An alternative view—reflected in the Environmental Kuznets Curve (EKC) and discussed below—is that a country would be better off by liberalizing trade and using the surplus wealth from the subsequent economic growth to address the environmental harms caused by an expanding economy.

The Composition Effect

The composition effect describes changes in the composition of the economy as a result of trade liberalization, such as increased specialization in sectors with a comparative advantage. Where changes in economic composition lead to the production of less-polluting goods, then we can expect better environmental health to follow. The concern here is that such improvements in environmental health could arise from the relocation of polluting industry to developing countries. This is the pollution haven hypothesis and is addressed below.

The Technique Effect

The technique effect describes the use of more environmentally friendly production processes. One way that trade liberalization can influence the choice of production processes is by providing access to imports of cleaner technologies.

The net impact of the scale, composition, and technique effects on environmental health is difficult to determine in the abstract, and depends on an economy's natural resource endowment and comparative advantage. For instance, the scale effect could harm the environment where it leads to an increased depletion of nonrenewable resources. Environmental health, however, could improve as a result of the technique effect, which leads to more efficient and technologically advanced manufacturing; and the composition effect could shift production toward cleaner production or services. Assessing the interaction of these effects on the environment is further complicated by their dynamic interaction, which means the impact will change over time (Managi, Hibiki, and Tsurumi 2009, 347).

The Environmental Kuznets Curve

The relationship between economic growth and environmental health has been described as following an inverted U-shaped curve illustrating how, as a country begins growing and focuses on lifting its population out of poverty, environmental health can suffer as industry and manufacturing expand, low-cost energy sources such as coal and biomass are utilized, and resources such as water and forests are exploited. As economic growth leads to increased national wealth, however, an expanding middle class demands tougher environmental regulation and improvements in environmental health.

The claim underlying the EKC is that economic growth is consistent with, and indeed a precondition for, environmental health. The message of the Rio Declaration was that trade is a means of driving growth and improving the capacity of states to address environmental harms. There are limits to this view, however (Hallegatte et al. 2011, 20). For instance, it may be more economical to prevent pollution now than to clean it up later. And some environmental harm, such as loss of biodiversity and species extinction, can be irreversible. Moreover, the EKC may itself describe a form of market failure where people do not properly account for the benefits of access to clean water and air. There is also evidence that the relationship between economic growth and environmental health described by the EKC applies to localized visible pollution but not to less-visible global issues such as ozone depletion and climate change. For instance, Grossman and Krueger have estimated that emissions of sulfur dioxide increase until per capita income reaches US$5,000–$6,000 and declines thereafter (Grossman and Krueger 1994, 353). Increased economic growth, however, has not seemed to translate into reduced greenhouse gas emissions or reduced losses of biodiversity.

The Pollution Haven Hypothesis

There are concerns that improvements in environmental health caused by changes in the composition of an economy in developed countries has been the result of polluting industries relocating to less-regulated countries—the so-called pollution haven hypothesis. Trade liberalization could support this outcome by making it easier for businesses to shift production to lower-regulating countries and then export back to higher-regulating countries. That would make it increasingly difficult for developing countries to follow a similar path and shed their polluting industries, as there are fewer developing countries to where polluting industries can relocate. For some developing countries, however, the change in trade patterns caused by different levels in environmental regulations is a source of comparative advantage, and attracting polluting industry supports economic development.

There is conflicting evidence as to whether trade leads to pollution havens (Brunnermeier and Levinson 2004). One reason is the lack of industry-level data across countries and the limited utility of anecdotal evidence on why companies relocate. Some studies suggest that decisions on where to locate depend on different levels of stringency in environmental regulations, while others suggest that the cost differentials caused by different environmental regulations are too small to matter (Cole 2004).

There is some evidence of a positive correlation between trade openness, a decline in manufacturing in developed countries, and corresponding increase in manufacturing in developing countries (Levinson and Taylor 2008, 249). Yet Arik Levinson from Georgetown University shows that imports into the United States have in fact become greener rather than dirtier, suggesting that environmental regulation has not contributed to pollution havens in developing countries (Levinson 2007, 22). This conclusion is supported by a study by Judith M. Dean and Mary E. Lovely from the US International Trade Commission and Syracuse University, who show that the pollution embodied in China's exports has fallen over time (Dean and Lovely 2008, 12).

Instead, the decline in manufacturing in developed countries has been driven more by significant improvements in technology and productivity than the shifting of manufacturing to developing countries and an increase in imports of polluting products (Levinson 2007, 23). For instance, approximately half the decline in air pollution from manufacturing in the United States has come from improvements in the way that goods are produced (Levinson 2007, 22). Other reasons for the lack of pollution havens are that industries may find it more profitable to manufacture close to their main market, and there are often other significant barriers to investing in developing countries with low environmental regulation, such as rule of law issues and barriers to trade and investment (Levinson 2007, 22). Moreover, an absence of formal environmental regulation in one country may not indicate that there are no environmental costs. Sheoli Pargal and David Wheeler from the World Bank have demonstrated how communities in developing countries can mobilize to force companies to clean up their manufacturing operations (Pargal and Wheeler 1996).

For global environmental problems, such as destruction of the ozone layer or climate change, there is the additional concern that the relocation of industry in response to tougher regulations would lead to no net reduction in global harm. For instance, the global nature of greenhouse gas emissions means that if actions by one country to reduce their greenhouse gas emissions leads to the relocation of carbon-intensive industry to countries with less-strict climate change laws, there will be no net reduction in global greenhouse gas emissions—a phenomenon referred to as carbon leakage.

A further issue is whether responsibility for the carbon embedded in international trade should be assumed by the consuming/importing country or the producing/exporting country (the latter is currently the case). The distinction will affect how we assign responsibility for the impact of trade on climate change. Over the period 1990–2008, for example, the embedded greenhouse gas emissions in developed-country imports from developing countries was larger than the total reductions in greenhouse gas emissions mandated under the Kyoto Protocol—an international agreement that requires an overall reduction in developed countries' greenhouse gas emissions by 5 percent below their 1990 level (Peters et al. 2011).

A Regulatory Race to the Bottom?

Another issue is the potential for a regulatory freeze caused by firms shifting production to jurisdictions with lower-cost environmental and labor regulations, which would lead countries to compete for business by not raising environmental standards—in turn opening the possibility of a regulatory "race to the bottom" as countries seek to maintain or attract new industry by lowering their environmental protections. As with the pollution haven hypothesis, such concerns arise from the possibility of firms shifting production as a result of open markets, but in this case firms use the threat of relocation to dampen or drive down environmental and social regulation in developed countries.

There is limited empirical support for the claim that international trade drives a race to the bottom of environmental regulations (Drezner 2001; Jaffe et al. 1995). For instance, the Commission for Environmental Cooperation—an international organization through which the United States, Canada, and Mexico cooperate on environmental matters—issued a report on the environmental impact of the North American Free Trade Agreement (NAFTA), a trade agreement between those three countries, and concluded that there was no evidence of a weakening of environmental regulations and instead, there is evidence of strengthening environmental regulations as Canada and Mexico in particular have raised their laws to the higher US standard. Some of the reason for this is similar to why there is limited evidence of pollution havens: the incentive for firms to relocate overseas to avoid environmental regulations is limited by their costs when compared to the larger determinants of competitive position, such as labor, material costs, capital costs, and exchange rate swings (Grossman and Krueger 1991, 24).

Another reason that a race to the bottom might not be happening is that competitors in higher-polluting industries tend to be in developed countries, which have strong environmental regulations. This limits the competitive effect of environmental regulations, as there is often little difference in environmental regulatory costs across developed countries. Moreover, firms from developed countries, such as the United States, Japan, and the European Union (EU), tend to build state-of-the art-facilities overseas irrespective of environmental regulations. And in some markets, consumers are willing to pay more for green goods, creating an economic incentive to invest in cleaner production processes.

There are also political economy reasons that help explain the lack of evidence of a race to the bottom. The reasoning is that in countries that value environmental health, consumer groups and environmental organizations are likely to mobilize and lobby in support of stronger environmental laws. These political forces make it increasingly difficult for governments to respond only to demands for reduced environmental regulation.

Despite a lack of evidence of pollution havens or a race to the bottom, fears over the economic harm to industry of pricing carbon to address climate change has been a key reason why the US Congress has failed to pass legislation that would reduce US greenhouse gas emissions. Such fears are also behind Canada's refusal to comply with its commitments under the Kyoto Protocol, and why Japan has stepped back from the greenhouse gas reduction targets it had set for itself.

Environmental Regulation as a Driver of Innovation

Environmental laws have benefited companies by being a spur for innovation. This was first proposed by US professor Michael Porter, who argued that environmental regulation creates competitive pressures for firms to innovate (Porter 1991, 68). His proposition has been challenged on the grounds that if there are profitable opportunities, firms can be assumed to exploit them anyway. Or, in other words, why would firms need to wait for environmental regulation (Palmer, Oates, and Portney 1995, 121)? One reason could be that these opportunities are not exploited because of market failures. For instance, increasing energy efficiency reduces energy consumption and energy costs, but efficiency is not pursued when electricity costs are paid by renters, delinking any incentive for owners to increase the energy efficiency of their buildings.

Some empirical evidence supports the Porter hypothesis. Some companies did innovate their production processes and organizational structure in response to the US Clean Air Act Amendments in 1990, which created a cap-and-trade system to regulate emissions of sulfur dioxide (Burtraw 2000). Others have observed, however, that "with literally hundreds of thousands of firms subject to environmental regulation in the United States alone, it would be hard *not* to find instances where regulation seemingly has worked to a polluting firm's advantage." This suggests that even though environmental regulation can end up costing less than expected or lead to innovative breakthroughs, it does not mean that all environmental regulation will benefit businesses (Palmer, Oates, and Portney 1995).

The WTO and Sustainable Development

Evidence pertaining to the impact of international trade on environmental health is mixed. A balance between working out how to liberalize trade to drive growth and recognizing the need for trade restrictions to respond to environmental concerns is being defined under the rules of the WTO. This arises from the WTO's central role in the liberalization of trade barriers and the role of WTO rules in disciplining the extent to which a country can restrict access to its markets in pursuit of environmental goals.

The WTO comprises a series of agreements, the main one being the GATT, which regulates trade in goods. Under the GATT, WTO members have agreed to bind their tariff rates, to not impose quantitative limits on imports, and to avoid discrimination—to treat imports of goods from other WTO members no less favorably than like domestic goods (the national treatment [NT] commitment) and to not discriminate against imports from one WTO member to the another (the most favored nation [MFN] commitment). Another WTO agreement—the General Agreement on Trade in Services (GATS)—regulates trade in services, and like the GATT includes market access, national treatment, and MFN commitments.

The WTO also includes agreements that regulate so-called behind-the-border measures—rules that are applied domestically but which also have an impact on trade. For instance, US domestic regulation that addresses how a dolphin-safe label can be used on canned tuna products can affect imports of tuna and is subject to the WTO Technical Barriers to Trade (TBT) Agreement. The TBT Agreement includes NT and MFN commitments and seeks to harmonize such regulations by requiring WTO members to base them on international standards where they exist and would be effective and appropriate for achieving the country's goals.

Another WTO agreement relevant to sustainable development is the WTO Sanitary and Phytosanitary (SPS) Agreement. For instance, under the SPS Agreement, quarantine measures to prevent the spread of a particular pathogen must be based on a risk assessment and be the least trade-restrictive option. The SPS Agreement also encourages members to base their SPS measures on international standards where they exist. Other relevant WTO agreements are the WTO Agreement on Trade in Intellectual Property Rights (TRIPS), which mandates a minimum level of protection for intellectual property, such as patents, trademarks, and copyrights; and the WTO Agreement on Subsidies and Countervailing Duties.

An important part of the WTO is its dispute settlement system, which is like an international court comprising a panel and opportunity to appeal a decision to the WTO Appellate Body, which adjudicates whether a country is complying with its commitments. In the event that the WTO finds that a member is not acting in accordance with its commitment, that country is required to bring its laws or regulations into conformity with its WTO commitments. Failure to do so can lead to the complaining WTO member restricting imports from that country.

International Trade Law and Sustainable Development

The WTO rules determine the balance between trade liberalization as a driver of growth and the use of trade restrictions to achieve environmental sustainability. For instance, countries may wish to restrict the access of imports to their markets as a reflection of consumer desire to not accept products whose production creates environmental harms, be they overfishing, loss of biodiversity, and the impact on endangered species, or emissions of greenhouse gases. For example, concern in the United States about the impact on endangered sea turtles of shrimp fishing led that country to ban imports of shrimp caught without nets that reduced the turtle by-catch.

Trade restrictions aimed at the policies of exporting countries could also be part of a country's effort to use access to its market to encourage changes in how other countries produce particular goods. For instance, the EU's recent imposition of a charge on aircraft carbon dioxide emissions is partly intended to encourage other countries to also regulate aircraft carbon dioxide emissions. At the same time, developing countries are concerned that the use of trade measures to achieve environmental goals can be protectionist and reduce export opportunities that affect growth and development.

Restricting Trade to Achieve Environmental Goals

The preamble to the WTO recognizes that trade should be conducted consistent with sustainable development.

How the WTO Appellate Body interprets the WTO rules determines how countries navigate between the benefits of free trade and the use of trade measures to achieve other environmental or human health goals. In this regard, the WTO US Shrimp-Turtle case is particularly relevant, in that the United States banned the import of shrimp from countries that did not use turtle-excluder devices on their nets. The United States sought to justify the measure under the WTO exceptions provision in GATT Article XX, which allows for the adoption of measures that are otherwise inconsistent with WTO commitments, such as the NT and MFN commitments. GATT Article XX (which provision is largely replicated under the GATS) enumerates a list of policy goals, such as the conservation of exhaustible natural resources and protection of human, animal, or plant life or health that can be understood as recognition by WTO members that achieving these policy goals trumps free trade.

In the Shrimp-Turtle case, the WTO Appellate Body articulated how GATT Article XX strikes a balance between trade and environmental protection—between the right of a WTO member to adopt trade measures to achieve environmental goals and the rights of WTO members under other WTO provisions (WTO 1998). This balance is inherent in the concept of sustainable development and the emphasis on trade as a driver of environmentally and socially sustainable economic growth.

The WTO Appellate Body explained that GATT Article XX does allow WTO members to condition access to their markets in order to conserve exhaustible natural resources, such as sea turtles. GATT Article XX, however, also requires that such measures not be applied in ways that constitute arbitrary and unjustifiable discrimination, and a disguised restriction on international trade. This means that measures that condition market access based on the policies of exporting countries must be applied equally to domestic production, which goes some way toward addressing concerns that these measures are really about protecting domestic industry.

In addition, the importing country cannot require other countries to adopt the same environmental policies. For instance, the Appellate Body found that the United States could not insist that all exporting countries use nets with turtle-excluder devices. Instead, the United States should focus on whether the exporting country achieves the goal of reducing the impact of shrimp fishing on endangered turtles. The United States, therefore, needed to be open to countries demonstrating the effectiveness of other means for achieving this goal.

The WTO Appellate Body also observed that, where possible, a negotiated solution to addressing transboundary and global environmental harm is ideal; countries, however, do not have a duty to negotiate or to conclude an agreement, as this would give other countries a veto over an importing country's environmental policy. But where the importing country has negotiated a solution to the harm with some countries, then failure to seek to negotiate with other countries can constitute arbitrary and unjustifiable discrimination that breaches GATT Article XX.

Subsidizing Sustainable Development

The WTO subsidies rules have important implications for sustainable development. The WTO agreements of relevance are the Agreement on Agriculture and the Agreement on Subsidies and Countervailing Duties.

The use of subsidies has been a focus in the trade arena because of developed countries' use of subsidies in agriculture production, which has distorted trade in agricultural goods. It has impacted those developing countries that rely on agriculture as well as access to developed-country markets as an important driver of economic growth. The WTO Agreement on Agriculture includes some disciplines on agriculture subsidies, and the subject has been a key discussion point in WTO Doha Round negotiations.

Subsidies for renewable energy have been challenged as being inconsistent with the WTO subsidies agreement, which defines what a subsidy is and which subsidies are prohibited under the WTO rules because of their impact on international trade. The Nobel prize–winning economist Joseph Stiglitz has argued in the climate change context that a failure to price carbon is a subsidy that the WTO should condemn (Stiglitz 2006). Under WTO rules, however, a failure to regulate is not the same thing as a subsidy. Instead, subsidies by countries such as Canada to promote renewable energy have been challenged by the EU and Japan before the WTO dispute settlement body, and the United States has challenged the WTO consistency of Chinese subsidies for wind energy manufacturers.

Intellectual Property Rules and Innovation

A country's access to technology can have important implications for its ability to address a range of complex challenges, from climate change to public health crises. The TRIPS agreement has been controversial because it mandates a common floor for intellectual property protection. The incentive this provides companies for innovation and investment in research and development

(R&D) may not outweigh the losses to some countries from reduced access to particular technologies or generic medicines. As the US professor Keith Maskus, a specialist in international trade analysis, has observed, ". . . it is impossible to guarantee as a matter of logic or fact that stronger IPRs [intellectual property rights] will generate economic gains for all countries" (Maskus 2000, 39).

In the public health context, the potential for TRIPS to prevent developing countries from accessing cheap generic drugs to address health crises led to agreement by the WTO membership to the 2001 Declaration on the TRIPS Agreement and Public Health. The Declaration highlights the need to balance higher intellectual property protection with its impact on the price of medicines, and confirmed the right of WTO members to issue compulsory licenses to respond to public health crises. In 2003, the WTO waived application of TRIPS Article 31(f) to allow for the export of medicines under compulsory license to countries that did not have the manufacturing capabilities to produce that product.

The impact of TRIPS on sustainable development is an issue in the context of climate change as well. Developing countries claim that the need to adhere to the WTO TRIPS agreement reduces their access to the technologies required to address climate change. The response from developed countries has been that intellectual property protection underpins the innovation and R&D needed to respond to climate change.

Free Trade Agreements and Sustainable Development

Bilateral and regional free trade agreements (FTAs) are an increasingly significant source of rules regulating international trade. Many FTAs now go beyond the WTO and include specific commitments on environment and labor issues. For instance, the 2011 South Korea-EU FTA includes a chapter on trade and sustainable development that requires both countries to enforce all MEAs and international labor agreements to which they are a party, and not to lower their environmental or labor standards to encourage trade and investment, thereby

addressing concerns about international trade leading to a regulatory race to the bottom. The 2011 South Korea-US FTA contains similar environmental and labor provisions but goes further by requiring the parties to adopt a range of MEAs and labor agreements.

Many FTAs also establish committees to monitor the impact of trade on the environment and coordinate areas of future cooperation. For instance, under the Chile-US FTA, the parties have agreed to cooperate in areas such as aquaculture, environmental education, and natural resources management.

Looking Forward

While international trade can drive economic growth and development, it can also exacerbate environmental ills, such as pollution and the depletion of natural resources. Some of these environmental harms are mitigated, however, where international trade shifts economies away from polluting industry to cleaner goods and a more services-orientated economy. Moreover, trade can increase access to environmental goods that can be used to improve and clean production processes.

Sustainable development is about finding ways for economies to grow in an environmentally and socially sustainable manner. The challenge lies in finding ways to encourage open markets and efficient economies while also giving countries the opportunity to condition access to their economies in order to achieve sustainable development goals. The WTO, as the organization responsible for regulating international trade, with a complex set of trade rules and jurisprudence, plays a key role in terms of how this balance gets struck. Decisions of the WTO dispute settlement body have gone a long way toward tracing out an appropriate line between ensuring that the tariff reductions negotiated at the WTO are not undone by the imposition of environmental regulations or trade restrictions, while giving countries enough scope to respond to the legitimate demands of their constituents to mitigate environmental or human health risks.

Free trade agreements are a growing area of trade rules that go further than WTO rules to craft new obligations that more explicitly address some of the concerns about the relationship between trade and sustainable development. For instance, the commitment in some FTAs not to lower trade and labor standards in order to attract trade and investment limits the potential for trade to lead to pollution havens or a regulatory race to the bottom.

The need for countries to reduce their greenhouse gas emissions is a new and growing challenge for sustainable development, and is raising complex issues for international trade. The concerns about the costs to industry from pricing carbon in advance of other countries has led countries to extend the carbon price to imports, thereby restricting international trade. The EU decision to include EU and non-EU airlines under its cap-and-trade system is the latest example of this and has led to a strong diplomatic reaction from the United States, China, and India, to mention a few. How countries navigate between climate change action and the international trade implications will become increasingly significant as they adopt more-ambitious climate change laws.

The EU decision to seek ways to reduce carbon dioxide emissions from aviation also points to a growing focus on the impact of transport—whether by land, sea, or air—on the environment. The environmental harms from transportation in terms of pollution and the introduction of invasive species have been an issue of concern under NAFTA. Climate change concerns, however, have changed the dimension and scope of the issue to include a focus on greenhouse gas emissions from the entire transportation sector. How countries regulate this sector will be important for climate change and could have profound impacts on trade and trade routes.

Finally, restricting the export of raw materials and other precious earths on environmental grounds is another growing trade and environmental issue that will involve the WTO. For instance, the WTO has already dismissed a claim by China that restrictions on its exports of raw materials was for environmental reasons, and further WTO litigation on Chinese exports of so-called rare earths has commenced. At the same time, as the United States considers whether to export natural gas, some members of Congress have been calling for these resources to be kept within the United States.

The range of concerns and challenges that arise from the complex inter-relationship between international trade and sustainable development has made this issue a key focus for policy makers at both the domestic and international levels. Encouraging open markets to drive economic growth and development in ways that are socially and environmentally sustainable will also be one of the primary challenges going forward.

Joshua MELTZER
Brookings Institution; Georgetown University Law School; John Hopkins School of Advanced International Studies

See also Economics, Steady State; Natural Capital; Progress; Shipping

FURTHER READINGS

Basel Convention on the Control of Transboundary Movements of Hazardous Wastes and Their Disposal. Opened for signature 22 March 1989, 28 I.L.M. 649 (entered into force 5 May 1992).

Brunnermeier, Smita B., & Levinson, Arik. (2004, March). Examining the evidence on environmental regulations and industry location. *Journal of Environment & Development, 13*(1), 6–41.

Burtraw, Dallas. (2000). Innovation under the tradable sulfur dioxide emission permits program in the US electricity sector (Discussion paper no. 00-38). Washington, DC: OECD Workshop on Innovation and the Environment.

Cole, Matthew A. (2004). Trade, the pollution haven hypothesis and the Environmental Kuznets Curve: Examining the linkages. *Ecological Economics, 48*(1), 71–78.

Commission for Environmental Cooperation of North America (CEC). (2002). *Free trade and the environment: The picture becomes clearer.* Montreal, Canada: CEC.

Convention on International Trade in Endangered Species of Wild Fauna and Flora. Opened for signature 3 March 1973, 993 U.N.T.S. 243, 12 I.L.M. 1085 (entered into force 1 July 1974).

Copeland, Brian Richard, & Taylor, M. Scott. (2003). *Trade and the environment: Theory and evidence.* Princeton, NJ: Princeton University Press.

Dean, Judith M., & Lovely, Mary E. (2008, March). Trade, growth, production fragmentation, and China's environment (Working paper no. 13860). Cambridge, MA: National Bureau of Economic Research.

Drezner, Daniel W. (2001, Spring). Globalization and policy convergence. *International Studies Review, 3*(1), 53–78.

Esty, Daniel C. (1994). *Greening the GATT: Trade, environment, and the future.* Washington, DC: The Peterson Institute for International Economics.

General Agreement on Tariffs and Trade (GATT) Secretariat. (1992). *International Trade 90-91: Vol. 1.* Geneva: GATT.

Grossman, Gene M., & Krueger, Alan B. (1991). Environmental impact of a North American Free Trade Agreement (Working paper no. 3914). Cambridge, MA: National Bureau of Economic Research.

Grossman, Gene M., & Krueger, Alan B. (1994). Economic growth and the environment. *Quarterly Journal of Economics, 110*(2), 353–377.

Hallegatte, Stéphane; Heal, Geoffrey; Fay, Marianne; & Treguer, David. (2011, November). From growth to green growth: A framework (Policy research working paper no. 5872). Washington, DC: World Bank.

Jaffe, Adam B.; Peterson, Steven R.; Portney, Paul R.; & Stavins, Robert N. (1995, March). Environmental regulations and the competitiveness of US manufacturing: What does the evidence tell us? *Journal of Economic Literature, 33*, 132–163.

Montreal Protocol on Substances that Deplete the Ozone Layer. Opened for signature 16 September 1987, 26 I.L.M. 1541 9 (entered into force 1 January 1989).

Nordstrom, Hakan, & Vaughan, Scott. (1999). *Trade and environment.* Geneva: The World Trade Organization.

Levinson, Arik. (2007). Technology, international trade, and pollution from US manufacturing (Discussion paper no. 07-40). Cambridge, MA: National Bureau of Economic Research.

Levinson, Arik, & Taylor, M. Scott. (2008). Unmasking the pollution haven effect. *International Economic Review, 49*(1), 223–254.

Managi, Shunsuke; Hibiki, Akira; & Tsurumi, Tetsuya. (2009). Does trade openness improve environmental quality? *Journal of Environmental Economics and Management, 58*(3), 346–363.

Maskus, Keith E. (2000). *Intellectual property rights in the global economy.* Washington, DC: The Peterson Institute for International Economics.

Pargal, Sheoli, & Wheeler, David. (1996). Informal regulation of industrial pollution in developing countries: Evidence from Indonesia. *Journal of Political Economy, 104*(6), 1314–1327.

Palmer, Karen; Oates, Wallace E.; & Portney, Paul R. (1995). Tightening environmental standards: The benefit-cost or the no-cost paradigm? *Journal of Economic Perspectives, 9*(4), 119–132.

Peters, Glen P.; Minx, Jan C.; Weber, Christopher L.; & Edenhofer, Ottmar. (2011, May). Growth in emissions transfers via international trade from 1990 to 2008. *Proceedings of the National Academy of Sciences, 108*(21), 8902–8908.

Porter, Michael E. (1991, April). America's green strategy. *Scientific American, 264*(4), 168.

Rio Declaration on Environment and Development. (1992). Principle 4. Retrieved April 25, 2012, from http://www.unesco.org/education/information/nfsunesco/pdf/RIO_E.PDF

Stiglitz, Joseph E. (2006). *Making globalization work.* New York: W. W. Norton & Company.

The World Trade Organization (WTO). (1998, October 12). WTO Appellate Body report, United States import prohibition of certain shrimp and shrimp products (WT/DS58/AB/R). Geneva: WTO.

The World Trade Organization (WTO). (2008). *World Trade report 2008: Trade in a globalizing world.* Geneva: WTO.

Tamiotti, Ludivine, et al. (2009). *Trade and climate change.* Geneva: The World Trade Organization (WTO) & United Nations Environment Programme (UNEP).

United States Central Intelligence Agency (US CIA). (2012). The world factbook: World. Retrieved August 30, 2012, from https://www.cia.gov/library/publications/the-world-factbook/geos/xx.html

Local Solutions to Global Problems

A sustainable future requires human activities to change on a global scale, but global agreements have not been very effective. At the local level, however, there are many examples of successful efforts to solve problems within social-ecological systems. Studying these examples has led to an understanding of the principles of self-governance. Scaling up these insights by using social media tools can help address the challenges involved in global change.

Human societies have been affecting the environment for thousands of years. Initially their impacts were local, but these were still enough to leave traces in the geological record. During the twentieth century, the scale of human impacts became increasingly global; for example, the disruption of important biochemical cycles of phosphorus and carbon led to eutrophication (a process that causes the depletion of oxygen in water) of waterways around the world, as well as global climate change. Many people have come to fear that the scale of human impacts on the environment may exceed planetary capacity to sustain human societies (Rockström et al. 2009).

Countries commonly address the increasingly global challenges by defining policies that operate on a global scale. Some of these policies have been successful, such as the phasing out of several groups of halogenated hydrocarbons that were shown to deplete the ozone layer. The Montreal Protocol from 1987, for instance, led to a measurable reduction of halogenated hydrocarbons in the atmosphere, to the point where the ozone layer is expected to be fully recovered by 2050.

Despite such successes in global governance, many global sustainability challenges are difficult to address at that scale. For example, climate change has been a topic of international policy negotiations since the early 1990s. At that time, scientific studies showed that immediate stabilization and future reduction of worldwide greenhouse gas emissions (e.g., carbon dioxide [CO_2]) were needed in order to avoid an average global temperature increase of 2°C. Yet in spite of various global treaties, emissions of fossil-fuel-related CO_2 have increased by more than 40 percent. According to statistics provided by the US Energy Information Administration (EIA 2012), the global emissions from fossil fuels in 1990 were 21.6 trillion metric tons of CO_2, which increased to 30.3 trillion metric tons of CO_2 by 2009.

Addressing global-scale problems from the top down has not been effective. This might be because of the nature of the problem. In 1968, the US ecologist Garrett Hardin looked at the problem from a new angle in his essay published in *Science*, titled, "The Tragedy of the Commons," which concluded that overuse of common resources was inevitable because users would never self-organize. Hardin used the model of a pasture open to all, in which each herder received an individual benefit from adding sheep to graze on the common land and suffered costs from overgrazing only later (a cost shared with other herders). The only way to avoid overharvesting the commons, besides private property rights, would be an intervention such as taxing the use of common resources.

Climate change policy can be viewed as a commons problem. Each individual, firm, or nation must absorb the costs of changing lifestyle and production techniques as part of reducing emissions from the use of fossil fuels. The benefit will be a reduction in the level of climate change for future generations. But how do we overcome the tragedy of the climate commons?

According to insights from Hardin, the options are to either define carbon emission rights or impose a carbon tax. These are indeed the types of solutions discussed at international negotiations; however, so far, they have not produced much change in the trend of rising greenhouse gas emissions.

Governing the Commons

If Hardin is right, why are so many common resources not overharvested? In the mid-1980s, a group of scholars from disciplines such as anthropology, sociology, political science, and biology started to compare case studies and discovered that the empirical evidence was not consistent with conventional theory as was advocated by Hardin. They became concerned about the theory's dominance and the consequences of privatization and nationalization policies, which were increasingly being adopted for natural resource management.

In order to understand the diversity of outcomes from individual case studies, there was a need for synthesis of these individual case studies. This happened through meetings of the National Research Council (NRC) starting in 1983. The NRC studied a large number of cases that showed both successes and failures in the self-organization of resource users. The resources included local fisheries, irrigation systems, pastures, and forests. Hundreds of case studies were analyzed and coded systematically with the aim of detecting patterns in the data to determine what the specific rules were that lead to successful governance of common resources.

Elinor Ostrom (1933–2012) was a leading scholar in the community studying these cases, and performed an influential meta-analysis of them, which was published in 1990. Ostrom, a political scientist, and her colleagues, had studied for decades the conditions that lead communities to solve collective action problems. In 2009, she was awarded a Nobel Prize in Economic Sciences for her contributions to the understanding of how people self-organize when they share common resources.

Ostrom had been unable to find a specific rule using statistical analysis; by considering many case studies, however, she discovered qualitative patterns that she called "design principles." Successful governance of common-pool resources, Ostrom determined, follows the same basic design principles:

1. *Well-defined boundaries.* Boundaries define who is allowed to harvest from a resource, as well as the limits of the resource system itself. Physical boundaries may be clearly marked by fences, rivers, specific tree species, or other markers. Social boundaries, such as permits, gender, kinship, or ethnicity, can be used to define who is allowed to have access.
2. *Proportional equivalence between benefits and costs.* The rules that participants use in practice should avoid unequal distribution of resources and revenues in order to avoid conflict.

3. *Collective-choice arrangements.* Having local resource users involved in creating and modifying rules leads to better acceptance of the rules by all. It also prevents elites from generating policies that benefit themselves disproportionally.
4. *Monitoring.* A cost-effective and transparent monitoring plan needs to be organized to ensure that the rules are followed and infractions enforced. Reliable monitoring can raise confidence among resource users.
5. *Graduated sanctions.* Mistakes can happen, and therefore there should be some tolerance of mistakes unless they become persistent violations of the rules, in which case more severe sanctions might be needed to guarantee compliance.
6. *Conflict-resolution mechanisms.* There should be low-cost ways to resolve conflicts among participants. Sometimes rules might be interpreted differently among participants, and easy ways to clarify such misunderstandings may reduce the number of conflicts that arise, and help maintain trust among participants.
7. *Minimum recognition of rights.* The rights of local users to craft their own rules should be recognized by higher levels of governance. If this is not the case, participants can be dissatisfied and challenge the authorities.
8. *Nested enterprises.* When resources are part of a larger system, different nested layers should be organized to match the activities of the local users and the biophysical conditions. Fitting the social and ecological scales to the problem at hand is crucial to a sustainable future.

These design principles have been tested in many publications since Ostrom, and they are well supported empirically. They show that a common feature of successful self-governance cases is that the rules people use in practice are understood and have been accepted by the participants. This is possible in small communities where the same common resource is shared over many years.

One of the questions that came out of the meta-analysis was whether the results can be generalized. Analysis of successful cases of self-governance is biased, since failing communities disappear and are therefore underrepresented in the data. Are the success cases historical artifacts? To study the principles of self-governance in greater depth, Ostrom and her colleagues used controlled experiments to test specific hypotheses. In the process, they made new discoveries.

Experiments

Controlled experiments are being used more frequently in the quest to derive an alternative theory of the governance of the commons. Since the late 1980s, laboratory and field experiments have been performed that confirm the basic insights gained from the field studies (Ostrom, Gardner, and Walker 1994). This is important for the development of theory because observations in field studies might be disregarded by some scholars as anecdotal. Replicating field observations in controlled experiments with diverse populations around the world provides specific insights into what enhances the likelihood of successful self-governance of common-pool resources.

In a typical experiment, researchers create a situation where a number of human participants make decisions in a controlled situation in which the researcher controls aspects such as what decisions can be made, what information is available, and whether participants can communicate and how. The people voluntarily consent to take part in such an experiment. They receive instructions on the actions that can be taken and the consequences of those actions that result in monetary rewards. Decisions are made in private during a number of rounds. In each round, every participant receives an endowment that is used to invest in harvesting from a collective resource, or a risk-free return. The more participants who invest in the collective resource, the lower the reward per unit of investment. The best outcome for the group occurs when each participant harvests a moderate amount from the collective resource. Participants can gain more individually if they increase their share of the harvesting while other participants stay at the same level. If each participant uses this reasoning, however, overharvesting of the common resource can be expected.

Ostrom and colleagues performed a series of experiments, which showed that participants (in this case, undergraduate students of a US university) would overharvest the resource if they could not communicate or have any institutional arrangements to govern their common resources (Ostrom, Gardner, and Walker 1994). On average, participants harvest the level of earnings similar to the predicted outcome of selfish rational participants; if "cheap talk" or costly sanctioning is allowed, however, participants are able to derive much higher earnings as a group and avoid overharvesting.

In cheap talk, participants are allowed to communicate, face-to-face or in chat-rooms on the Internet, but they cannot enforce their agreements. In the conventional theory, cheap talk has been viewed as irrelevant; therefore, the findings on its effectiveness made by Ostrom and colleagues were considered remarkable.

In costly sanctioning, users pay a fee to reduce the earnings of someone else. The use of costly sanctioning was observed by Ostrom in field studies, but was not consistent with the theory of norm-free, completely rational, selfish behavior of the actors. Ostrom and her colleagues replicated the situation in the laboratory and they showed that participants did choose to use costly sanctioning, and that this led to a reduction of the harvesting rate. As a consequence, while the gross earnings are higher, the net earnings do not rise due to the cost of sanctioning.

Therefore, the net benefits of costly sanctioning are not necessarily positive.

These findings have been replicated by many other studies, including experiments in the field involving traditional resource users with more complex resources, and experiments with public goods. For example, experiments were performed with forest resource users in rural Colombia wherein the researchers framed the experiment in terms of investing hours in collecting fuel wood from the common resource instead of talking about abstract resources and monetary payments. The participants received a payoff table that helped them decide how much time to spend for fuel wood extraction and how much time for alternative activities. These field experiments produced the same conclusions as were found for experiments using abstract instructions that were performed with undergraduate students in the United States.

In public goods experiments, every participant also receives an endowment in each round, but the question becomes how much to invest in a public fund and how much to keep. All the investments in the public fund are increased by the experimenter, and the resulting public good is equally shared among the participants. For example, in a group of five participants, the experimenter might double the investments in the public fund. All participants will see a doubling of their endowment by investing the whole endowment in the public fund. If, however, a participant keeps the endowment and receives a share of the public good, this participant is free-riding on the investments of others. The expected outcome of selfish rational participants is that nobody will invest in the public good.

Public good experiments show that participants invest initially about half of their endowment in the public good (Fehr and Gächter 2000). When communication and costly sanctioning are not possible, most groups will decline their investments in the subsequent rounds. But when communication or costly sanctioning is possible, we see an increase of investments into the public good up to 100 percent of the endowment.

In sum, controlled experiments show that participants overcome the tragedy of the commons if they can communicate with each other and sanction free-riders. In line with the field studies, groups are able to self-govern their common resources under the right conditions. What are the underlying mechanisms that cause this? More in-depth analysis shows that a critical factor is that most participants are conditional cooperators.

Conditional Cooperation

Controlled experiments show that participants in experiments do not behave as selfish rational actors. There is increasing evidence that people value the earnings of others. But there is variation in people's preferences for the earnings of others. Some individuals make decisions as if they are selfish and rational. Those participants never invest in the public good. Other participants are altruistic and invest a high amount, independent of what others are doing. Most participants will cooperate if others do the same, leading to the term "conditional cooperators"; in other words, those who cooperate in collective action situations if they expect others will do so as well (Fischbacher, Gächter, and Fehr 2001). In heterogeneous groups, conditional cooperators will reduce their level of contributions to the public good if they see that there are others who do not invest the same level as they do.

Field experiments show that the percentage of conditional cooperators in a community, as identified from participation in experiments, is a good predictor of the success of governance of common resources. Devesh Rustagi and Stefanie Engel of the Swiss Federal Institute of Technology together with economist Michael Kosfeld (2010) showed this in a study of a forestry program in Ethiopia. Individuals who were identified as conditional cooperators also invested more time in the actual monitoring of the rule-in-use of the villages and their common forests.

The observation that most participants are conditional cooperators explains why communication is so important. Communication enables participants to signal their intentions and trustworthiness. Not only do participants cooperate if they expect that others will, but they also value and receive emotional benefits if others receive good earnings too, and the earnings are fairly distributed among the participants.

Other studies show that when information is provided about the historical behavior of current participants in an experiment, the level of cooperation increases (e.g., Chaudhuri and Paichayontvijit 2006). If participants can choose with whom to participate, they will avoid free-riders (Ahn, Isaac, and Salmon 2008). Information on the characteristics of others in the group will thus affect the decisions of individuals. If a participant finds out that others in a group are not willing to cooperate, he or she will reduce their level of cooperation or leave the group if possible.

Critique and Challenges

The work of Ostrom focuses on small communities. There is a convincing amount of evidence that small communities are able to overcome the tragedy of the commons in the right context. They have the ability to develop and maintain trust relationships and monitor the behavior of the population. Larger groups make it more difficult for individuals to evaluate the trustworthiness of other participants while making it easier for anyone to free-ride on the actions of others. The information that a person can derive regarding the reputation of others can have an important influence on decision making.

Ostrom's advice for larger problems, such as global climate change, is to use a polycentric approach—meaning, use global- and national-level policies for certain aspects of the solution, and nurture and stimulate local initiatives to address other aspects of the solution. For a problem like climate change, local initiatives could focus on indicators appealing to the local level, such as carpooling to reduce air pollution, bicycling to improve health, and using solar energy to reduce the energy bill.

Empirical studies have shown the abilities of communities to self-govern, and their ability to develop and maintain trust relationships and monitor the behavior of the population. This does not mean that the local level is the only way to address collective action problems. The strengths of local bottom-up approaches can be employed to address the challenges of global-scale change.

Despite the ability of communities to self-organize there are profitable opportunities to reduce emissions that are not implemented. For example, research shows that the US national carbon emissions can be reduced by more than 7 percent without new regulation, technology, or infrastructure simply by taking advantage of existing opportunities (Dietz et al. 2009).

If there is proverbial low-hanging fruit, such as profitable ways to reduce carbon emissions, why don't individuals take advantage of it? To understand this, we have to look into the factors that influence individual decision making, since focusing on individuals themselves and providing factual information alone may not be effective. Research in social psychology shows the importance of social influence on individual motivation. Blending insights from social psychology on social influence with insights on collective action and the commons may lead to concrete ideas on how to develop a bottom-up approach for global change.

As noted previously, in larger groups participants find it more difficult to evaluate each other's trustworthiness, and easier to free-ride on others' actions. One's reputation can have an important influence on other people's decisions. New information technologies reduce the costs of communicating with a larger number of people in different locations. What are the implications of this for collective action situations?

Since there has been limited focus on the potential impacts of information technology on the governance of shared resources, different areas of research need to be explored to identify those potential impacts. New technologies can monitor activities and deliver accurate information on the consequences of one's decisions as well as the decisions of others. Such real-time feedback may have an important effect on the decisions that people make.

Social Influence and Social Norms

Feedback provides information about someone or some group's performance so that people may understand the effect of their actions and adjust them to some desired level. In energy-use studies, for example, providing feedback could mean displaying current energy use to users, which enables them to make more-informed decisions about reducing energy use.

Feedback is more effective when it is specific, frequent, and related to goals that people set. For instance, one can install smart meters and monitor energy use in real time, and determine which appliances use the most energy. Such monitoring enables motivated users to reach their energy-saving goals.

But this might not be sufficient for broad-scale change; additional motivation may be required. Studies in social psychology have shown that providing feedback on how one's actions relate to the actions of others also influences behavior. An illustrative example of this is a study on energy use by Robert Cialdini, one of the key scholars of social influence. He and his colleagues studied the effect of providing social feedback on energy bills in a few hundred households in California (Schultz et al. 2007). When residents' energy bills showed that their households had a higher energy use than similar households in the neighborhood, the residents reduced their energy use in the weeks and months after receiving this social feedback. Residents who received feedback that their energy use was lower than similar neighboring households increased their energy use. So there was no net effect from providing factual information.

In the other half of the households followed in the study, information was added to the energy bill. Those

with less energy use than average got a smiley face (☺) on their bills, and those with higher energy use than average got a frowny face (☹). With this treatment, the energy-efficient households continued to be efficient, and households that used more energy than average reduced their energy use. The net effect in this treatment was a positive effect of social influence.

The study was implemented by OPOWER, a customer engagement platform in the United States for the utility industry, which works with utility companies to send customers information on how they are doing compared to the neighborhood (Schultz et al. 2007). Another study analyzed about 600,000 households, of which half received the targeted feedback on their energy bills. The energy savings found of about 2 percent was modest but statistically significant (Allcott 2011).

Many similar experiments have been done related to recycling of towels in hotels, voter turnout, drinking behavior of college students, littering, donations to charity, and the like. All these studies show that providing information on what others do has an effect on the actions of individuals. In most cases there is an increase of contributions to the public good. But more understanding of the right social feedback in the right context is needed in order to develop concrete applications for enhancing collective action in diverse situations.

In the context of collective action and the commons literature, it appears that information about contributions of others stimulates conditional cooperators to cooperate. For instance, households that use more energy than their neighbors may be motivated by social pressure to comply with the social norm within their neighborhood. Households that get energy bills with information about others and see that they use less energy than others may feel discouraged in their contributions to the public good. Getting an additional smiley face may motivate the conditional cooperator to remain cooperative even though others don't meet the norm yet.

Studies from social psychology show that even small details in the feedback on social information can have an important impact on the effects. It is too simple to say that showing others' contributions to the public good will reinforce cooperation in every case. The results, however, provide hope for possible tools to stimulate cooperation in collective action situations like energy use, water use, and recycling.

Using Social Media to Catalyze Collective Action

As of 2011, about 5 billion of the world's 7 billion people had a mobile phone (Gartner 2011). In some regions in the world, there are fewer people with proper sanitation than a mobile phone. Almost 1 billion people have an account on Facebook (Facebook 2012), and people are increasingly texting, tweeting, poking, finding their destinations based on GPS directions from their iPhones, taking pictures with their smartphones and sharing them with friends, and video chatting with people on the other side of the world. The world is becoming one big village exchanging an enormous amount of information.

As of 2010, the majority of the people in the world live in urban environments (UN 2012). The abilities of self-organization as found in small-scale rural environments do not directly apply to those urban environments where many unrelated people interact with each other. Although mobile devices and other computational devices are increasingly owned and used all over the world, not everybody has access to the same quality of services or equipment, or has the same level of expertise to use new technologies. The insights discussed in this section are mainly based on research in western societies and may not apply directly to other societies. This will be an area of research in the coming years.

Will it be possible to use the escalating amount of information that people produce and access to develop tools to catalyze collective action? While this is an open question to be addressed by scientific studies, there are a number of trends that suggest a positive answer.

The challenges involved in scaling up the findings on self-governance will be to capture the ability of people to develop and maintain trust relationships, know the reputations of others, and have the ability to contribute to the community. This may not be possible within an urbanized world where people often do not know their neighbors. By using social media, however, people can connect with their friends in a small community not limited by physical constraints. Even though people themselves experience a small community, social networks work on a global level.

Activities are increasingly monitored in real time. On a smartphone, people can check on traffic jams en route to their destinations. Smart meters enable people to monitor household energy use. Remote sensing provides information on the energy efficiency of homes. Smart water meters monitor the use of water. Supermarkets scan purchases and have accurate information on the stock and flows of consumer goods in people's households. Car insurance companies provide devices to monitor a person's driving style and provide discounts for safe driving.

All these activities allow researchers to provide rough estimates on carbon footprints, water footprints, and other sustainability indicators. Such numbers include a large degree of uncertainty, but it should be possible to provide an indication of degrees of impact. A particular activity, such as purchasing an organic local lunch, provides information for a number of sustainability indicators. Given that one of the challenges of collective action is monitoring, making use of crowd-sourcing techniques makes monitoring of self-reported activities a community activity.

If there is technology that combines this information, assuming that individuals provide consent, people could keep track of the impact of their activities compared to the common known statistics. Compare this with apps for smartphones, where people can keep track of the calories they burn and consume based on information they collect. An app like "The Eatery," for example, uses feedback from other users to rate the healthiness of meals and enables individuals to track their eating habits over time.

This information might be shared with others in a social network. Because an individual finds water footprints important, for example, he or she might use social media to share with others any information gathered. Doing so may affect individuals' reputations, enabling them to derive feedback and help from friends, and empowering them to reach their own goals.

Such a technology may seem utopian; to achieve it, many technical, cultural, ethical, and legal issues must be addressed. If such a technology were available, however, we could perform more systematic analyses on the incentives that motivate people to change their behavior for the common good. We must also work out functional questions, such as how to avoid an information overload, how to keep people involved, and what indicators are most useful.

Why might this technology be effective? As discussed above, most people are conditional cooperators and will contribute to the public good if others do the same. It has also been shown that people are influenced by information on what others like them are doing. Providing people with accurate, real-time feedback on various indicators of sustainability may stimulate behavioral change. While such behavioral change might affect only a small portion of the population, it may also provide opportunities for households to innovate and create sustainable lifestyles that will propagate to the broader population. In the past, this was achieved most effectively in small communities, since activities could be monitored by others. In an increasingly urbanized world, information technology may enable us to scale up the strength of the community governance to higher levels.

Developing tools to catalyze collective action introduces a number of ethical concerns. Some people may argue that this is social engineering, where people are manipulated to reach the goals of those who control the software. Other people may be concerned about potential privacy violation through software. These are valid concerns, but already part of the debate in the common daily use of social media. The proposed tool would make use of existing trends in social media use, tools, and infrastructure. It is part of public debate to explore the changing social norms on privacy and use of information technology.

Conclusion

Rapid information technology development makes it possible to derive accurate, real-time information on the consequences of our decisions and the decisions of others. Increasingly, people participate in various online social networks that make it possible to share and compare information, and connect people with similar interests. This provides opportunities to apply the strengths of community self-governance to work on a global scale.

The opportunities to provide real-time feedback on resource use have been successfully implemented in various projects on energy use. Energy is a logical starting place owing to the availability of smart meters. Similar tools might be applied to water use, vaccinations, carbon footprints of people's groceries, recycling, and many more areas.

Connecting insights gained from collective action with social influence research shows that there are interesting opportunities for testing whether the power of small-group cooperation can be scaled up using modern information technology. This approach, however, presents several challenges. Although individuals share a lot of their private activities with the public through social media networks, the idea of having their behaviors tracked might be perceived as a frightening infringement on their privacy. Conversely, we face global challenges in an increasingly urbanized world that we share with strangers. Top-down nation- and state-based approaches seem to be ineffective in addressing global challenges such as climate change. Lessons from small-scale self-governance situations are inspirational, but cannot immediately scale up to an increasingly global-scope world.

Opportunities are emerging from low-cost monitoring devices that provide personalized feedback to others. Various initiatives are underway to implement such tools in practice, especially as related to energy use. Such applications are promising and need to be studied in detail to enhance our understanding of how to scale up the power of self-governance to address the challenges associated with global change.

Marco A. JANSSEN
Arizona State University

The author and editors are saddened by the loss of Elinor Ostrom during production of this volume.

See also Cities and the Biosphere; Collective Learning; Community; Economics, Steady State; Education, Higher; Progress; Property Rights; Values

FURTHER READING

Ahn, T. K.; Isaac, R. Mark; & Salmon, Timothy C. (2008). Endogenous group formation. *Journal of Public Economic Theory, 10*(2), 171–194.
Allcott, Hunt. (2011). Social norms and energy conservation. *Journal of Public Economics, 95*(9–10), 1082–1095.
Chaudhuri, Ananish, & Paichayontvijit, Tirnud. (2006). Conditional cooperation and voluntary contributions to a public good. *Economics Bulletin, 3*(8), 1–14.
Dietz, Thomas; Gardner, Gerald T.; Gilligan, Jonathan; Stern, Paul C.; & Vandenbergh, Michael P. (2009). Household actions can provide a behavioral wedge to rapidly reduce U.S. carbon emissions. *Proceedings of the National Academy of Sciences USA, 106*, 18452–18456.
Energy Information Administration (EIA). (2012). International energy statistics. Retrieved May 3, 2012, from http://www.eia.gov/cfapps/ipdbproject/iedindex3.cfm?tid=90&pid=44&aid=8&cid=regions&syid=1990&eyid=2009&unit=MMTCD
Facebook. (2012). Newsroom: Key facts. Retrieved May 4, 2012, from http://newsroom.fb.com/content/default.aspx?NewsAreaId=22
Fehr, Ernst, & Gächter, Simon. (2000). Cooperation and punishment in public good experiments. *American Economic Review, 90*(4), 980–994.
Fischbacher, Urs; Gächter, Simon; & Fehr, Ernst. (2001). Are people conditionally cooperative? Evidence from a public goods experiment. *Economics Letters, 71*(3), 397–404.
Gartner. (2011). Gartner says worldwide mobile connections will reach 5.6 billion in 2011 as mobile data services revenue totals $314.7 billion. Retrieved May 3, 2012, from http://www.gartner.com/it/page.jsp?id=1759714
Hardin, Garrett. (1968). The tragedy of the commons. *Science, 162*, 1243–1248.
Janssen, Marco A. (2012). Elinor Ostrom (1933–2012), *Nature* 487: 172.
Ostrom, Elinor. (1990). *Governing the commons: The evolution of institutions for collective action.* New York: Cambridge University Press.
Ostrom, Elinor; Gardner, Roy; & Walker, James. (1994). *Rules, games, and common-pool resources.* Ann Arbor: University of Michigan Press.
Rockström, Johan, et al. (2009). Planetary boundaries: Exploring the safe operating space for humanity. *Ecology and Society, 14*(2), 32. Retrieved January 24, 2012, from http://www.ecologyandsociety.org/vol14/iss2/art32/
Rustagi, Devesh; Engel, Stefanie; & Kosfeld, Michael. (2010). Conditional cooperation and costly monitoring explain success in forest commons management. *Science, 330*, 961–965.
Schultz, P. Wesley; Nolan, Jessica M.; Cialdini, Robert B.; Goldstein, Noah J.; & Griskevicius, Vladas. (2007). The constructive, destructive, and reconstructive power of social norms. *Psychological Science, 18*(5), 429–434.
United Nations (UN). (2012). World urbanization prospects, the 2011 revision. Retrieved May 3, 2012, from http://esa.un.org/unpd/wup/CD-ROM/Urban-Rural-Population.htm

M

Migration

Humankind will face unprecedented and systemic environmental disruption in the twenty-first century, making it necessary to explore the complex interrelationship between environmental factors and mobility and to consider the multitude of factors that cause migration. In most developed countries, shortages of labor will intensify pressure on policy makers to bring in more migrants to meet growing labor and demographic gaps. Social and economic transformations will give migrants the means and reasons to move. The growth of communications technologies has collapsed the social distance between people and is laying the groundwork for a twenty-first century characterized by more openness to migration.

Projections of climate and environmental change in the twenty-first century include scenarios of extreme weather, deforestation, declining fish stocks, pollution of water supplies, and degradation of agricultural land. These scenarios are based on uncertain emissions estimates and uncertain projections of the physical effects of climate change from a range of models. The 2006 Stern Review on the Economics of Climate Change, commissioned by the British government, noted that without a reduction in carbon emissions the livelihoods of people could be affected by changes in food production, access to water, health, and use of land and the environment (Stern 2006). Climate change would have extremely severe consequences for developing countries because of various geographical factors (such as the availability of fresh water) and the relative lack of economic and political resources needed to respond to severe environmental stress. The Intergovernmental Panel on Climate Change (IPCC), which is the principal international body for assessing climate change, has noted that shoreline erosion, coastal flooding, and agricultural disruption can promote human migration as an adaptive response. The debate about the implications of climate change for migration revolves around the magnitude and permanence of displacement by environmental factors.

As the French migration scholar Etienne Piguet (2011) reminds us, climate has always played a role in human migration and environmental change, prompting and facilitating the colonization of the planet by our ancestors. More recently, excessive periods of rain were linked to the Irish potato famine in the mid-nineteenth century, and the droughts of the 1930s in the United States are permanently captured in the literature arising from the Dust Bowl experiences. The relationship between migration and climate change remains undertheorized, and there has been little systematic research on the topic. This is urgently needed.

In the twenty-first century, climate change could make many parts of the world less habitable, threatening the security and livelihoods of millions of people. Constant and extreme drought could become more frequent and severe in certain regions. Extreme weather would intensify storms and floods, with more rain falling in South Asia and less falling in interior sub-Saharan Africa by 2050. Agricultural yields in sub-Saharan Africa and Central and South Asia could, as a consequence, fall dramatically. As a result of melting glaciers in South Asia, China, and the Andes, flooding would increase during the wet season, and water supplies would diminish during the dry season, potentially affecting more than a billion people. Sea-level rise could lead to the significant loss of coastal lowlands by 2050 (these statistics were helpfully summarized in Brown 2007). Such dramatic changes will inevitably be associated with great increases in migratory pressures, with those pressures rising as climate change and environmental stresses become more pronounced. As the Oxford University scholars

Ian Goldin and Geoffrey Cameron, and researcher Meera Balarajan stress (2011), climate and environmental change will compound the effect of other underlying structural changes, which together will lead to much higher levels of migration in the future.

Impact of Environmental and Climate Change on Migration

The climate change migration researcher Shuaizhang Feng and his colleagues (2010) attempted to analyze the linkages between climate change, crop yields, and Mexico–US cross-border migration. They found a significant effect of climate-driven changes in crop yields on the rate of emigration to the United States, with a 10 percent reduction in yields leading to a 2 percent increase in migration. They then projected that by 2080 climate change will induce an additional 1.4 to 6.7 million Mexicans to migrate to the United States. Their analysis highlights the difficulties associated with linking assumptions regarding the future evolution of climate change with changes in crops and crop yields and subsequently deriving the implications for migration in an ill-defined future. The study by Feng and colleagues fails to take into account either the mitigation and adaptation strategies that Mexico could apply—including the use of new improved varieties of seeds—or the changing demographic and economic structure of Mexico and the United States. By 2080, these technological, social, and economic developments will lead to changes that will overwhelm the *ceteris paribus* (i.e., indicating that something would be the case if everything else under consideration remains the same) calculations on which the study is based. As a first step in developing climate and crop models, the study by Feng and colleagues makes important strides, but it does not provide insight into the nature or scale of future climate-induced migration from Mexico to the United States, and its results are not more generally applicable.

There can be no doubt, as the food security researcher David Lobell and his coauthors (2011) have shown, that new approaches are needed to understand climate impacts on crop yields as the results are likely to be non-linear. For African maize, for each one-degree increase above 30°C, the final crop yield decreases by 1 percent under optimal rain-fed conditions and by 1.7 percent under drought conditions. The implication is that virtually all African maize would be harmed under drought conditions and that the number of peak temperature days has a very strong impact on outcomes. Climate change associated with high temperature peaks, as well as irregular rains and other drought conditions, could be potentially disastrous for the millions of people who depend on these crops. Although the impact on crops and climate is becoming clearer, drawing firm conclusions regarding the migration impact is not yet possible.

As with the other factors that influence the supply of migrants in the future, it is impossible to arrive at a reliable estimate of the number of people who will migrate in response to environmental changes. In the words of William B. Wood, the official US Department of State geographer, "there is usually no simple relationship between environmental causes and societal effects" (Castles 2002, 4). While there is widespread agreement that humankind will face unprecedented and systemic environmental disruption in the twenty-first century, how people respond to these challenges will be heavily influenced by local conditions and the political response of states (Castles 2002).

The term "environmental refugees" was first coined by the US environmental author Lester Brown in the 1970s and has been used with increasing frequency in recent years, even though it has no agreed upon definition in international law and is not part of the United Nations framework for refugees. The United Nations High Commissioner for Refugees (UNHCR) avoids the term, which risks undermining its well-established refugee regimes, preferring instead to refer to "environmentally displaced persons," a term that does not carry the misleading reference to cross-border movements. The International Organization for Migration (IOM) refers to "environmental migrants" as "persons or groups of persons who, for reasons of sudden or progressive changes in the environment that adversely affect their lives or living conditions, are obliged to have to leave their habitual homes, or choose to do so, either temporarily or permanently, and who move either within their territory or abroad." This debate may evolve as individuals who are clearly forced to flee their country (such as may be the case for Maldivians) at some future date perhaps win the right to relocate as "environmental refugees" (Boana, Zitter, and Morris 2008).

The dramatic forecasts of as many as two hundred million "environmental refugees" by 2050 have been widely cited in official reports, but they have not held up to wider scrutiny (Brown 2007; Black 2001). Goldin, Cameron, and Balarajan believe it is unlikely that climate change alone will lead to a ten-fold increase in the number of refugees and displaced persons, and double the total number of migrants, as implied by these "guesstimates." Nevertheless, few analysts would expect drastic environmental changes to have no significant effect on mobility. Environmental stress in the twenty-first century will have unpredictable impacts on international migration but will certainly intensify migration pressure in developing countries, where changes are expected to be most dramatic and the adaptive capacity is the weakest.

Environmental change will shape migration patterns based on how such damage affects people's livelihoods and on the capacity of local communities and households to adapt. A United Nations University report found that "the principal pathway through which environmental change affects migration is through livelihoods . . . The more direct the link between environmental quality and livelihoods, the stronger the role of environmental push factors in migration choices" (Warner et al. 2008, 6).

In the case of sudden environmental catastrophes, people typically migrate to nearby areas and often return to their homes. Dramatic floods in central and southern Mozambique in March 2000 displaced about one million people from their homes, but within a few months, most had been able to return (Black 2001, 6). The 2004 Asian tsunami caused the deaths of approximately 200,000 people and displaced approximately 500,000 more. Most of this movement occurred within the local region, and very few people actually crossed borders to seek refuge (Brown 2007, 16). A year later, in 2005, Hurricane Katrina caused the largest movement of people in the history of the United States. Over a period of two weeks, as many as 1.5 million people fled the US Gulf Coast (three times more than moved during the Dust Bowl migration of the 1930s). With up to one-third of New Orleans' residents yet to return, those scattered by the disaster have remained in the United States, and the impact on international migration has been negligible (Knight 2009). In part, this is indicative of the size of the United States and the potential for domestic migrants to escape the disaster.

International migration is contemplated when the socioeconomic basis of people's livelihoods is severely and permanently threatened and domestic alternatives are exhausted. Families may send a member overseas to diversify their sources of income (e.g., if farming is less productive or if traditional sources of employment are less lucrative). Historical examples suggest, however, that people prefer to move only short distances (and often do not cross borders) in response to slow-onset environmental change. In the case of encroaching desertification in the Sahel, for example, the response of many residents appears to be temporary internal movement and/or the diversification of income-generating opportunities (Black

2001, 4). A survey of 204 families in the arid Nandom region of northern Ghana that was suffering from desertification indicated that, while migration within Ghana was a common response to environmental stress, none of the families had members who had left Ghana. This reflects, in part, that employment and other opportunities exist elsewhere in Ghana, and more than 700,000 north–south migrants were counted in Ghana's 2000 census (Knight 2009).

Insofar as people's basis for earning a living is compromised, pressure for international migration may mount, but this will depend on the extent to which there may be other near-by alternatives and on government (and other adaptive) measures to support the increasingly precarious existence of people under threat from environmental change. Scenarios that include large swatches of land being affected by climate change would limit local adaptive strategies and provoke more varied and radical responses. As many experts have noted, in Sudan, and elsewhere in the Sahel, environmental stress may also lead to tensions and conflict over land and resource use, and political refugees may traverse borders (Homer-Dixon 1991).

Studies by the Dutch government and the US Geological Survey warned in 2009 that sea levels could rise by 55 centimeters to 1.5 meters during the twenty-first century (McKie 2009). The implications of a dramatic rise in sea level would be particularly serious for the inhabitants of the Maldives, where 80 percent of the country is less than 1 meter above sea level and 47 percent of houses are within 100 meters of the coast. Storm surges in 2007 inundated fifty-five of its islands, and rising sea levels are projected to make these surges more regular and severe.

In 2008, Maldives' then President Mohamed Nasheed publicly discussed investing funds from tourism to buy land for relocation in nearby India, Sri Lanka, or Australia. In the meantime, inhabitants of the lower-lying islands are likely to continue moving to Male, the most populated island and the country's capital, which has a seawall and uses desalination plants. Population pressures, however, are already being felt on the islands and especially in Male, which is one of the most densely populated islands in the world. As sea levels rise in the

Indian Ocean and the islands in the Maldives become less habitable, the population will become more concentrated in Male, and the number of people attempting to emigrate could increase.

Climate change also poses a major threat to Bangladesh, where many of the country's people live in densely populated coastal areas. Rising sea levels will exacerbate coastal flooding, and tropical cyclones and storm surges would be more severe. Fluctuating rainfall patterns and melting glaciers in the Himalayas would lead to higher flows during the monsoon season. A lead author of the IPCC report, Atiq Rahman, speculates that thirty-five million people could be displaced from the coastal regions of Bangladesh by 2050 (Vidal 2008). It is still unclear precisely how these climate threats would influence outmigration from Bangladesh, and overseas development assistance has already begun to focus on building infrastructure and systems that will aid internal migration, and diminish the human impact of floods and storms (Ministry of Environment and Forests 2008). The way in which environmental change impacts people's livelihoods and generates migration pressure will be heavily determined by states' social policies and their capacity to respond to immediate crises. As UN Environmental Affairs Officer Oli Brown notes:

> It is clear that many natural disasters are, at least in part, "man-made." A natural hazard (such as an approaching storm) only becomes a "natural disaster" if a community is particularly vulnerable to its impacts. A tropical typhoon, for example, becomes a disaster if there is no early-warning system, the houses are poorly built, and people are unaware of what to do in the event of a storm. (2007, 11)

This observation is also reflected in contemporary thinking about how famines occur, influenced by the 1998 Nobel economics laureate Amartya Sen's widely cited work comparing the 1943 Bengal famine with Ethiopia's 1968–1973 famine (Sen 1981). The proximate cause of declining food production may be (partially) environmental, but the systemic cause of food shortages, scarcity, and starvation actually depends on a country's socioeconomic structure and political response.

We can also examine the very different impacts of comparable extreme weather events on Bangladesh and the United States. The 1991 tropical cyclone Gorky killed 138,000 people and left as many as ten million others homeless in Bangladesh. The following year, a relatively stronger storm (Hurricane Andrew) hit Florida and Louisiana, killing only sixty-five people and leading to very little permanent displacement (Brown 2007, 11–12). The human impact of future extreme weather patterns will be shaped by the quality of housing, early warning systems, states' capacities, and disaster resilience, among

other factors. Furthermore, the poorest people are often the most affected by such disasters because so many live in marginal and vulnerable areas. The contrasting impact of the devastation caused by the 2010 earthquake in Haiti that killed more than 200,000 people with a death toll of approximately five hundred people associated with the much stronger Chilean earthquake a few months later highlights the need to focus on both the nature of extreme events as well as local vulnerabilities.

Conceptualizing the Environmental Change/Migration Relationship

The University of Oxford researcher Gunvor Jonsson in a paper on the environmental factors that affect migration, notes that "claims that climate change will shape the future of global migration are continuously being made in academia as well as popular and policy circles (2010, 2)." Drawing on thirteen case studies of environmentally induced migration in Africa, with particular reference to the Sahel, she "questions the empirical basis for such claims . . . (and) highlights some of the conceptual and methodological flaws that recur in many of these studies." Jonsson identifies that the terminology is often confused, with concepts such as environment and climate, change and variability being conflated. Second, she highlights the extent to which extreme climate variability and unstable environments have long been the norm for many Sahelian people; in this context, mobility can be a successful coping mechanism, potentially reducing environmental stress. Third, Jonsson criticizes the use of static push–pull frameworks that suggest that migrants are being "pushed out" of marginal and degraded environments, while neglecting the intertwined environmental, political, economic, and cultural factors. Fourth, she points to flaws in the sampling and questionnaires used, particularly in some of the later studies. In conclusion, her paper calls for more open research that explores the complex interrelationship between environmental factors and mobility instead of starting from the assumption of a simplistic causal relationship.

Jonsson's study is based on a critical review of these same thirteen empirical studies of the relationship between environmental change and migration in Africa. Jonsson highlights that climate is only one aspect of the environment and that humans have for many thousands of years exercised an influence over their environment and ecosystem, and that it in turn has influenced their actions and opportunities. As Hein de Haas, codirector of the International Migration Institute (1998, 2001) has shown, the migration of people into areas has an impact on the environment, and changing environmental conditions in turn contribute to the nature of society and to the propensity and type of migration. It should also be noted that outmigration may also relieve pressure on land and natural resources, and the potential subsequent recovery in turn may influence future migration patterns (Olsson, Eklundh, and Ardo 2005).

Jonsson points to the difficulty of distinguishing between climate change and its natural variability. In Africa, and not least in the Sahel, rainfall has been highly variable for as long as records have been kept. There is considerable disagreement among scientists whether the current conditions are caused by global warming or a protracted natural cycle. While the IPCC predicts increased water stress and reduced agricultural production as a result of climate change, this will serve to compound already high levels of variability and environmental stress. Jonsson argues that the key question is not whether changing environment and migration are related, but to what extent this is the case. In seeking to conceptualize the relationship, Jonsson and also Piguet (2009) try to provide clarity about the weight of environmental change in the relationship.

In providing insights into the relationship of environmental change to migration, Jonsson draws on recent conceptual contributions to the literature on migration, and notably to those, such as de Haas (2008), who show that social capital and networks, as well as the internal dynamics of societies, shape patterns of migration. Jonsson seeks to go beyond the Norwegian political scientist Astri Surhke's (1994) distinction between the "maximalists," who argue that environmental change will lead to large-scale migration, and the "minimalists," who see it as one of many contextual variables that contribute to migration. The maximalists are represented in the literature by the British environmentalist Norman Myers (1993, 1997, 2005), who claimed that there were 25 million "environmental refugees" in the 1990s and that this would rise to 200 million by 2050. The "minimalist" position was taken by the University of Sussex professor Richard Black (2001), who questioned whether "environmental refugees" was a helpful notion and discounted what he considered to be unfounded and unhelpful projections. The journalist and environmental consultant Fred Pearce (2011) highlights the range of views on this issue.

Jonsson argues that the nexus between migration and the environment needs to be understood in terms of the broader complex and dynamic interaction of numerous factors that result in a decision to migrate. She highlights that in response to environmental change people draw on a range of responses, including resilience, adaptation, and survival strategies. For many African societies, this is not new. Yet, as Jonsson notes, the bias in much of the literature on environmental change is that people historically have lived under stable climatic

conditions, whereas in much of Africa risk and instability have been a way of life, not least in the Sahel where drought is a recurrent phenomenon. As part of the coping mechanism, there have been high levels of migration in and out of the region for as long as records have existed.

From her review of the relationship between environmental change and migration Jonsson finds that:

> environmental stressors such as drought do not necessarily lead to migration. This is usually because migration—particularly long-distance and international migration—requires resources and during drought, resources are scarce . . . Moreover, migration requires social networks outside that the migrant can draw upon for support, and if a community has no previous history or tradition of migration, such facilitating networks will not be present to help people migrate during drought. (2010, 11)

Jonsson finds that to the extent there is migration it tends to occur within the borders of the migrants' countries of residence. In part, this is because migrants want to return home when conditions improve, and this is easier if they have only moved a short distance, such as to local towns.

When international migration occurs, it tends to be associated with other contextual factors. A number of studies went so far as to indicate that environmental change, on its own, could not explain migration. In some regions, patterns of migration existed before, and independent of, environmental change, while in others environmental change had no discernible impact. Where environmental change is associated with chronic deficits of food, the link to migration is clearer. As Sen (1981) and others have convincingly shown, famines and food deficits are not simply the result of the environmental change but have complex social and political determinants. In seeking to identify the relationship between environmental change and migration, a number of the studies examined by Jonsson point to the extent to which migration is an integral factor in the lives of many communities. Migration can be understood in terms of the long-standing patterns of building resilience and diversifying incomes in high-risk environments. In these contexts, in certain communities environmental change may lead to a reduction in migration, because it disrupts traditional social patterns, increases the pace of urbanization, reduces incomes below the thresholds needed to pay for transport and migration, and reduces the potential for obtaining work in neighboring countries. As Jonsson notes, citing the work of the University of Oslo anthropologist Jon Pedersen (1995), the relationship between drought and population growth and movement is complex, and there are not simple causal relationships. The difficulty of coming to firm conclusions is illustrated by the evidence collected by the Belgian geographer Sabine Henry, Catholic University of Louvain professor Bruno Schoumaker, and French expert on migration Cris Beauchemin (2004) as well as by the Dutch human geographer Kees van der Geest (2009), who found that migration actually decreased during the severe drought years. The US public health professor Sally Findley (1994, in Jonsson 2010, 28) found that during drought in the Sahel, short-range migration almost doubled, but migration to France almost halved. Jonsson, in examining these studies, notes that migration requires resources and that therefore the poorest people do not migrate long distances. By the time famine sets in, it is often too late to migrate.

In projecting the likely interaction of environmental change and migration, it is important to distinguish between, first, environmental change associated with human settlement and the resulting land degradation, water depletion, and pollution; second, environmental change associated with the long-term "natural" cycle of climate variability, which gives rise to recurring droughts or other environmental stress; and, third, the more recent overlay with anthropogenic climate change. Societies may be able to adapt to the longer-term cycles of droughts or floods and the gradual degradation of resources, but may be unable to develop sustainable strategies to compensate for the higher levels of instability and long-term shifts associated with climate change. Whereas temporary migration of certain members of the community may have provided a viable response to environmental change in the past, when these impacts are compounded by climate change, temporary migration patterns, which for generations have allowed communities to survive environments with high stress, may result in the permanent migration of individuals or even whole families.

It is as important to understand the reasons why people do not migrate in response to environmental stress as why they do. As Jonsson asks, "Why have not many more people left the poor South?" (2010, 24). The University of Durham anthropologist Kate Hampshire (2002, in Jonsson 2010, 25), in her examination of the seasonal migration of the Fulani from northern Burkina Faso,

highlights the complexity of the reasons why individuals migrate, with economics, politics, gender, culture, and history all contributing to decision making. As Stephen Castles has highlighted, migration cannot be seen as something distinct from broader social relationships and change processes.

In summarizing the results of thirteen case studies, Jonsson concludes that "long-distance international or intercontinental migration is a very unusual outcome of environmental change. Migration occurring in the context of poverty and hunger is usually short-distance, while international migration, for example to Europe, requires many resources and networks that these people simply do not have" (2010, 27).

Piguet, on the basis of his review of the consequences of extreme weather and natural disasters on migration patterns, noted that "the victims have little mobility, and the majority of the displaced return as soon as possible to reconstruct their homes in the disaster zone" (2011). He draws the conclusion that, on the global level, the potential for hurricanes and cyclones to provoke long-term and long-distance migration remains limited. He similarly argues that the relationship between drought and migration is limited, highlighting the finding that during the 1994 drought in Bangladesh only 0.4 percent of households resorted to emigration.

While drought or extreme weather may not lead to mass migration, Piguet (2011) reminds us that rising ocean levels may be expected to lead to permanent displacement. At present, over 150 million people live at an altitude of one meter or less. Approximately 75 percent of these individuals live in the major river deltas and estuaries of South Asia (near the Ganges–Brahmaputra and Indus Rivers, with a combined population of over 140 million) and East Asia (near the Mekong, Pearl, and Yangzi [Chang] rivers, with a combined population of over 130 million). While the overwhelming majority of these people may be expected to move within their countries, for the less populated islands of Maldives (population 394,999) and Tuvala (population 10,472), sea level rise would give them no alternative but to resettle in another country.

Climate change scenarios depict an unpredictable future that is still, to a certain extent, contingent on what governments do today to reduce carbon emissions and mitigate the worst of its effects. The environmental effects of climate change will also be accompanied and compounded by population growth and urbanization over the coming half-century. While climate change will influence the lives of millions, if not billions, of people, it will impact migration in the same way as other factors. As people's livelihoods are compromised and they face social and economic distress and possible famine, they will seek greater security and better opportunities. While many will move locally, others will draw on social and family networks to move internationally. Rather than think of "environmental migrants" as a separate class, we should consider the changing environmental landscape to be another factor that adds to the pressure to migrate from developing countries to their wealthier neighbors or even farther afield.

The Future of Migration

To understand future migration, we need to go beyond climate to examine the factors that will determine both the future supply of and demand for migrants, with particular reference to the anticipated impact of environmental change and labor markets. Reducing international migration to a mere "push" and "pull" phenomenon neglects the role of local and national context, networks, and social capital in determining who moves and where they go.

Many factors will make people inclined and equipped to migrate in the future, and structural changes will generate pressure on governments, especially in advanced economies, to accept more migrants. The direction of flows will be predominantly from developing to developed countries, although movement between developing countries and between the richest countries will continue to be significant.

On the supply side—persistent and large, although for the most part declining—intercountry inequality will mean that large wage gaps will continue to offer incentives for individuals to move. As economic growth in low-income countries provides more people with the resources and capabilities to migrate, they will do so in larger numbers. The high levels of fertility found in developing countries in the first years of the twenty-first century will lead to large cohorts of young, working-age adults who are more inclined to seek their fortunes abroad. In addition, increasing environmental stress due to climate change and resource degradation will provide an added impetus for migration. As more people's livelihoods are threatened, they will look for opportunities to move. The growing supply of potential migrants will include both low-skilled and high-skilled migrants.

In most of the developed countries, shortages of labor will intensify pressure on policy makers to bring in more migrants to meet growing labor and demographic gaps. Persistently low fertility rates in developed countries means that sustaining current levels of economic growth and public services will require large influxes of migrants just to stabilize the size of workforces. Already, many developed countries rely on undocumented workers to fill low-skilled jobs. High-skilled labor will also be in greater demand in the future, as footloose companies continue to pressure governments to relieve mobility restrictions. Developed countries will also have to compete with emerging destination countries, such as China, for increasingly scarce labor. The sharp decline in fertility in many developing countries, coupled with rapid economic growth, means that by the middle of the twenty-first century, we may face a situation where there are too few migrants moving to developed countries to meet the demand for workers.

Globalization

Since 1990 or thereabouts, there has been a tidal wave of globalization, which has had political, economic, social, and technological dimensions (Goldin and Reinert 2012). Two particular features will accelerate migration in the future: the progressive reduction of barriers to global economic flows and growing "transnationalism," by which people's interactions and identities become less circumscribed by national boundaries.

Globalization is not only influencing how policy makers think about migration, it is also leading more and more people to move. The University of Warwick political scientist Jan Aart Scholte (2000) characterizes globalization as the "deterritorialization" of exchanges and relationships. The growth of communications technologies has collapsed the social distance between people separated by thousands of miles. In early 2009, an estimated 1.5 billion people were regular users of the Internet, and the United Nations (UN) estimates that more than 60 percent of people worldwide have a mobile phone subscription (up from less than 20 percent in 2002). Air transport costs also fell rapidly between the 1960s and 1990s, enabling people to travel, do business, or move their families more easily (Bordo, Taylor, and Williamson 2005). Whereas in the mid-nineteenth century, a family fleeing Russia for the United States would have left home without being certain that they would ever speak to or see their relatives and friends again, today those social ties would remain intact. It is now cheaper than ever for people to keep in touch across vast distances, and for even those on modest salaries to afford periodic airline tickets to visit home. The result is a significant reduction in the social and psychological costs and risks of migrating.

Greater connectivity not only makes it easier to keep in touch with friends and family after leaving, it also enhances sprawling transnational social networks that link people around the world. Globalization and migration are intertwined processes that point to a cosmopolitan future, where people, goods, ideas, and finance are able to flow more freely across national borders. As trade has been increasingly liberalized, some economists have turned to labor mobility as the next frontier where more openness can produce global economic benefits (World Bank 2005; Pritchett 2006). And as more people's everyday lives and relationships transcend borders, the way in which we conceive of national homogeneity and citizenship is being transformed. The process of globalization advances in fits and starts. It is creating the institutions, relationships, and ideas that are laying the groundwork for a twenty-first century characterized by more openness to migration. Within this enabling environment, growing supply and demand for migrants will produce higher cross-border flows of people.

Skilled Labor Movement

Debates over the global movement of skilled labor already tend toward the industry position. As a 2005 report on skilled migration noted, "much of what appears to be governments changing the way they compete for the world's skilled workers is really the selective removal of their own barriers in the international labor market" (Kapur and McHale 2005, 38). Competition for skilled migrants is not only national, it is also becoming local in areas that have been economically devastated by the movement of manufacturing industries overseas and subsequent population decline. A grassroots effort for economic revitalization in Cleveland, Ohio, has focused on attracting migrants. "I think that's the future of Cleveland," one local activist said. "If we don't get some good, talented, capable people here, we're in trouble" (Smith 2009). Philadelphia also started a similar campaign and brought in more than 100,000 new migrants between 2000 and 2006 (Smith 2009). Their campaign to boost the regional economy by attracting skilled international migrants featured new coalitions between civic leaders, migrant groups, chambers of commerce, and city halls.

In the foreseeable future, the management of migration at a national level should involve progressively lowering barriers to skilled migration. Research on innovation, entrepreneurship, and endogenous growth highlights the potential benefits of increasing a country's volume and diversity of human capital. Restrictive immigration policies have been shown to have a direct impact on the rates of innovation in the United States (and presumably other countries as well) (Kerr and Lincoln 2008). Developed countries that maintain obstacles to skilled migration will lose out to emerging economies that become more open to mobility. Armed with a growing volume of evidence, multinational corporations are exerting considerable pressure on governments to permit mobility for their workers and recruits. Even local communities are finding that as manufacturing industries are shipped overseas, they are also competing for talent to revitalize their economies. While nationalist backlashes and the recessionary impulse toward scaling back on globalization may reverse the trend toward more skilled migration, such an effect is likely to be temporary. In the medium term, it will be overwhelmed by the economic demand for more migration.

The future, as the French social activist and philosopher Simone Weil (1909–1943) is thought to have said, is made of the same stuff as the present. Most people will move for the same reasons in the future as they do today: to pursue welfare, prosperity, peace, security, fulfillment, and opportunity for both themselves and their families. The social and economic transformations at hand, however, presage a twenty-first century that will give more people the means and reasons to move. How many people make the journey to another country will depend on the pace of development in emerging economies, immigration policies in destination countries, and the design of effective mechanisms to manage and integrate foreigners into their new homes. Migration controls will remain relevant in the coming decades, but they will be limited in their ability to radically curtail migration (Castles 2002).

Developed countries will face difficult choices between a future of economic prosperity, security, and health in old age and one of greater cultural uniformity generated by long-settled populations. If we agree that prosperity and social welfare are primary goals of government policy, then governments and electorates may well prefer to accept more social, linguistic, and cultural diversity that higher rates of migration will produce in the interests of a more dynamic and secure future. The global governance of migration is still relatively underdeveloped and immature in the context of the increasingly transnational character of international migration and relative to trade and financial flows.

Ian GOLDIN and Geoffrey CAMERON
Oxford Martin School, University of Oxford

Note: This article was adapted from Ian Goldin's article "Migration and Global Environmental Change." The original review article was commissioned as part of the UK Government's Foresight Project, "Migration and Global Environmental Change." As such, the views expressed do not represent the policy of any government or organization. This article has been adapted with kind permission from Foresight. The original publication is available at http://www.bis.gov.uk/assets/foresight/docs/migration/drivers/11-1172-dr3-future-global-migration-impact-environmental-change. "Migration and Global Environmental Change" was, in turn, partially based on the 2011 book *Exceptional People: How Migration Shaped Our World and Will Define Our Future*, by Ian Goldin, Geoffrey Cameron, and Meera Balarajan. Adapted with kind permission from Princeton University Press, which owns the copyright to that book.

See also Aging; Climate Change and Big History; Community; Food Security; Mobility; Population; Water

FURTHER READING

Black, Richard. (2001). Environmental refugees: Myth or reality. *UNHCR New Issues in Refugee Research Working Paper No. 34*. Geneva: UNHCR.

Boana, Camillo; Zitter, Roger; & Morris, Tim. (2008). Environmentally displaced people. *Forced Migration Policy Briefing 1*. Oxford, UK: Refugee Studies Centre, 7–8.

Bordo, Michael D.; Taylor, Alan M.; & Williamson, Jeffery G. (2005). *Globalization in historical perspective*. Chicago: University of Chicago Press.

Brown, Oli. (2007). Climate change and forced migration: Observations, projections and implications. *Human Development Report Office Occasional Paper 2007/17*, 9–10.

Castles, Stephen. (2002). Environmental change and forced migration: Making sense of the debate. *UNHCR New Issues in Refugee Research, Working Paper No. 70*. Geneva: UNHCR.

Feng, Shuaizhang; Krueger, Alan B.; & Oppenheimer, Michael. (2010). Linkages among climate change, crop yields and Mexico–US cross-border migration. *PNAS Proceedings of the National Academy of Sciences of the Unites States of America, 107*, 14257–14262.

Goldin, Ian; Cameron, Geoffrey; & Balarajan, Meera. (2011). *Exceptional people: How migration shaped our world and will define our future*. Princeton, NJ: Princeton University Press.

Goldin, Ian, & Reinert, Kenneth. (2012). *Globalization for development: Meeting new challenges*. Oxford, UK: Oxford University Press.

de Haas, Hein. (1998). Socio-economic transformations and oasis agriculture in southern Morocco. In L. de Haan and P. Blaikie (Eds.), *Looking at maps in the dark: Directions for geographical research in land management and sustainable development in rural and urban environments of the Third World* (pp. 65–78). Utrecht/Amsterdam: KNAG/FRW UvA.

de Haas, Hein. (2001). *Migration and agricultural transformations in the oases of Morocco and Tunisia*. Utrecht: Netherlands: KNAG.

de Haas, Hein. (2008). Migration and development: A theoretical perspective (Working paper series). Oxford, UK: International Migration Institute, University of Oxford.

Henry, Sabine; Schoumaker, Bruno; & Beauchemin, Cris. (2004). The impact of rainfall on the first outmigration: A multi-level event-history analysis in Burkina Faso. *Population and Environment, 25*, 397–422.

Homer-Dixon, Thomas F. (1991). On the threshold: Environmental changes as causes of acute conflict. *International Security, 16*, 76–116.

Jonsson, Gunvor. (2010). The environmental factor in migration dynamics—A review of African case studies. *International Migration Institute Working Paper 21*. Oxford, UK: IMI.

Kapur, Devesh, & McHale, John. (2005). *Give us your best and brightest: The global hunt for talent and its impact on the developing world*. Washington, DC: Center for Global Development.

Kerr, William R., & Lincoln, William F. (2008). *The supply side of innovation: H-1B Visa reforms and US ethnic invention* (Working Paper 09-005). Boston: Harvard Business School.

Knight, Sam. (2009, June19). The human tsunami. *Financial Times*.

Lobell, David; Banziger, Marianne; Magorokosho, Cosmos; & Vivek, Bindiganavile. (2011). Nonlinear heat effects on African maize. *Nature Climate Change, 1*, 42–44.

McKie, Robin. (2009, March 8). Scientists to issue stark warning over dramatic new sea level figures. *The Observer*.

Milanovic, Branko. (2003). The two faces of globalization: Against globalization as we know it. *World Development, 31*, 667–683.

Ministry of Environment and Forests. (2008). *Bangladesh Climate Change Strategy and Action Plan 2008*. Dhaka, Bangladesh: Ministry of Environment and Forests, Government of the People's Republic of Bangladesh.

Myers, Norman. (1993). Environmental refugees in a globally warmed world. *BioScience, 43*, 752–761.

Myers, Norman. (1997). Environmental refugees. *Population and Environment, 19*, 167–182.

Myers, Norman. (2005). Environmental refugees: An emergent security issue. *13th Economic Forum*. Prague.

Olsson, L., Eklundh, L., & Ardo, J. (2005). A recent greening of the Sahel—Trends, patterns and potential causes. *Journal of Arid Environments, 63*, 556–566.

Pearce, Fred. (2011, April 30). Search for climate refugees. *New Scientist*.

Pedersen, Jon. (1995). Drought, migration and population growth in the Sahel: The case of the Malian Gourma: 1900–1991. *Population Studies, 49*, 111–126.

Piguet, Etienne. (2009). Environment and migration: A methodological challenge. *Environmental Change and Migration: Assessing the Evidence and Developing Norms for Response*. University of Oxford, Refugee Studies Centre and the International Migration Institute.

Piguet, Etienne. (2011). Storms in a tea cup? *Global—The International Briefing*, First Quarter, 18–19.

Pritchett, Lant. (2006). *Let their people come: Breaking the gridlock on global labor mobility*. Washington, DC: Center for Global Development.

Scholte, Jan Aarte. (2000). *Globalization: A critical introduction*. Basingstoke, UK: Palgrave MacMillan.

Sen, Amartya. (1981). *Poverty and famines: An essay on entitlement and deprivation*. Oxford, UK: Oxford University Press.

Smith, Robert L. (2009, May 20). Waves of immigrants now calling Philadelphia home; New welcoming center idea behind the lure. *The Plain Dealer (Cleveland)*.

Stern, Nicholas. (Ed.). (2006). *The economics of climate change: The Stern Review*. Cambridge, UK: Cambridge University Press.

Suhrke, Astri. (1994). Environmental degradation and population flows. *Journal of International Affairs, 47*, 473–496.

van der Geest, Kees. (2009). Migration and natural resources scarcity in Ghana. Case study report for the Environmental Change and Forced Migration Scenarios Project. Retrieved May 30, 2012, from http://www.each-for.eu

Vidal, John. (2008, September 8). UK gives £50m to Bangladesh climate change fund. *The Guardian*.

Warner, Koko; Afifi, Tamer; Dun, Olivia; Stal, Marc; & Schmidl, Sophia. (2008). Human security, climate change, and environmentally induced migration. *United Nations University Institute for Environment and Human Security, Report*. United Nations University.

World Bank. (2005). *Global economic prospects: Economic implications of remittances and migration*. Washington, DC: World Bank.

Mobility

Urban mobility helps build dynamic and efficient urban areas. Social and economic factors and technological processes help create extensive, effective, and sustainable urban mobility patterns. In order to reach a greater level of mobility, cities need to provide transportation alternatives—both motorized and nonmotorized modes of transportation—transportation integration, and Transit-Oriented Development (TOD). Urban planning plays a major role in developing sustainable urban mobility. Different perspectives and approaches build possible scenarios unveiling the future of sustainability for mobility.

Although *mobility* can be broadly defined, one aspect of mobility, in the context of cities, is the urban dynamic that individual and public transportation support. Specifically, mobility relates to the circulation of people and goods within an urban area. Urban mobility is characterized by various forms of transportation in the context of regional cultural traditions and socioeconomic developments throughout the world.

There are many fine examples of cities where urban mobility has been improved through the implementation of advanced transportation systems that have simultaneously reduced inhabitants' automobile dependence. In the United States, the New York City subway system and the Chicago "L" train system are examples, as is the Curitiba Bus Rapid Transit (BRT) system in Brazil. By prioritizing public transportation, the cities of Brisbane, Adelaide, Perth, Melbourne, and Sydney, in Australia, and Auckland, in New Zealand, have also significantly improved their mobility patterns.

The sustainability of urban mobility depends on the relationship between a city's physical structure, its available natural resources, and its transportation. People use fewer natural and material resources and occupy less urban land the more they have access to an environmentally friendly and efficient urban transport system. Stated simply, implementing sustainable transportation systems inexorably fosters better cities.

Infrastructure and Networks

The availability of a variety of transportation alternatives and their related infrastructures obviously contributes to increased urban mobility and might include, for example, automobiles / road networks, buses / bus routes, bicycles / bikeways, walking / sidewalks and public spaces, and subways / railroad networks.

Transportation facilities such as stations, terminals, stops, and integration hubs are all components of a public transportation system, and their presence, quality, and number ameliorate urban mobility. Amenities such as benches, trash bins, signs, flower beds, drinking fountains, sidewalks, and public spaces in transportation facilities encourage their use, thereby contributing to increased urban mobility.

Integration

Integration is the key to sustainable mobility. The simple availability of different transportation modes cannot guarantee the sustainability of an urban mobility system. To be sustainable, transportation modes and their related infrastructures must be interconnected; the more the transportation modes of that system are integrated, the more a city's urban mobility system becomes efficient and sustainable. For instance, bus routes should be integrated with subway systems, subway systems with bikeways, bikeways with sidewalks and public spaces, and so on, with all of these structures operating as part of an integrated and smooth-running multimodal transportation network.

The transportation planner and scholar Michael J. Bruton (1975) suggests that integration should be planned to function simultaneously on two levels: the physical and the operational.

On the physical level, transportation facilities are interconnected, allowing for a continuous flow of users, for instance, by placing a bus stop and a subway entrance as close together as possible to reduce the distance passengers must walk to get from one to the other. Integrating additional transportation modes results in a more advanced system with higher urban mobility.

On the operational level, coordinated operations are implemented, such as scheduling, ticketing, fare collection, embarking and disembarking, and information systems that allow passengers a clear and smooth transition between modes.

Finally, the integration of nonmotorized transportation modes, such as bicycles and walking, with collective modes, such as mass transit, strengthens urban sustainability and environmental friendliness. Modern and dynamic cities should pursue this kind of transportation integration.

Urban Traffic Congestion

In large cities and important urban hubs, creating a balance between individual and collective transportation modes reduces urban congestion and car dependency by encouraging people to use mass transit. Traffic congestion is a major problem in large cities worldwide that wastes time, resources, and energy, directly affecting not only their economies but the health of those cities' inhabitants and environments as well. Mass transit, together with careful urban planning, offers the best alternatives for large cities in their attempt to reduce daily traffic problems and conserve resources.

Transit-Oriented Development (TOD)

One of the goals of effective urban planning is to achieve the aforementioned equilibrium between individual and collective transportation while prioritizing mass transit. Transit-oriented development (TOD) is one possible approach. A TOD is a planned and coordinated effort to promote mixed-use development in the area surrounding a transit stop, and includes, but is not limited to housing, parks, businesses, government offices, and civic facilities. TOD mass transit may take a variety of forms: subway, light rail, and bus rapid transit (BRT), among others. As noted by the urban- and transportation-planning scholar

and researcher Evandro C. Santos (2011), some important cities have been structured as TODs—among them: Stockholm, Copenhagen, Zurich, Tokyo, Melbourne, Guatemala City, and Singapore. Other notable examples are Portland, Oregon; Denver, Colorado; and the San Francisco Bay Area, California, in the United States, and Vancouver, Toronto, and Calgary in Canada.

Because of their commitment to collective transportation, these cities are considered more efficient and sustainable than others of comparable size (in terms of population, occupied area, and economic development). Their effectiveness can be measured by their levels of reduced traffic congestion and preservation of natural resources like fuel, urban land, and urban infrastructure (principally the road network and underground systems—drainage, water supply, and sewage collection).

Sustainable Transportation

In order to think about urban mobility within the context of a sustainable and environmentally friendly city, urban planners must address the issue of sustainable transportation and more efficient and less harmful modes of transporting passengers and freight. Sustainable transportation is achieved primarily by using cleaner technology for personal vehicles (as one essential aspect, among others, of an integrated change that focuses primarily on mass transit and nonmotorized transportation options). Special mention should be made of the infrastructure that supports such technology (e.g., electric vehicle–charging stations and hydrogen-fueling stations). Singapore, for example, has developed a hydrogen-based transportation infrastructure, and Vancouver is investing in electric car–charging stations. Regular and electric bicycle rental systems are becoming increasingly popular worldwide as an efficient alternative for reducing traffic congestion and, particularly in cities that attract high numbers of tourists, improving the visitor's experience.

Load capacity and resource consumption both factor into sustainability measures. Through continuous research, improvements in engine technology—such as hybrid, electric, hydrogen cell, and solar powered engines, collectively known as zero- and low-emission vehicles—will reduce resource consumption, increase load capacity, and be critical to future transportation improvements.

Continuously rising gasoline prices have stimulated research related to more efficient vehicles, thus contributing new possibilities for more sustainable urban transportation. Sustainable transportation will be possible, however, only when more efficient, higher-capacity transportation modes have been successfully developed. Whether a balance can be found between the costs of providing transportation and the savings in time, energy, and resources will dictate the extent to which sustainable transportation will become available and will determine the nature of modern, more efficient cities.

Nonmotorized Transportation

Nonmotorized transportation—walking and bicycling—complements the major modes of motorized urban transportation. Two vital factors allow nonmotorized and motorized transportation to be linked: the availability of resources and of infrastructure for nonmotorized transportation such as sidewalks, bikeways, and high quality public spaces. Integrating these motorized and nonmotorized modes is mutually beneficial. Cities can achieve efficient transportation alternatives by joining nonmotorized transportation modes with mass transit. To do this, urban planning must promote a less car-dependent future along with environmentally friendly design.

Walkability

Walkability is a term that describes how easy it is for pedestrians to move around a location and is essentially a walking index that measures how open and closed public spaces allow pedestrians a safe and comfortable walking experience. Initially developed by the Canadian politician and environmental activist Chris Bradshaw (1993), walkability has become one of the criteria used to quantify an urban area's quality of life. It helps gauge the state of pathways, sidewalks, and public spaces, encouraging urban authorities to improve conditions, and furnishes them the guidelines to do so. The more "walkable" a location proves to be, the healthier and more environmentally friendly it is.

The scholar and researcher Evandro C. Santos (2006b) adapted the walkability index to assess two basic, complementary aspects: safety and comfort. In order to achieve a favorable rating, walkable areas need to score high in two categories: physical characteristics and design. According to the American Association of State Highway and Transportation Officials (AASHTO 2004), a number of factors need to be evaluated.

1. Width (A minimum of 1.5 meters of barrier-free path is suggested, but depending on the pedestrian flow, the width may be higher. A practical approach might be to provide enough width for two wheelchairs to pass each other without touching or for two pedestrians carrying umbrellas to pass each other without touching umbrellas.)
2. Pavement conditions (A nonslip, well maintained, and even pavement is required.)
3. Grading (No more than a 2 percent transversal grading, and no more than a 15 percent longitudinal grading is permitted; otherwise, a handrail is recommended.)
4. Street lighting (Contributes to safer walking at night)
5. Crossings and curb ramps (Clearly marked, they provide smooth and safe connections between edges and for mobility-impaired pedestrians such as wheelchair users and the elderly. Features such as tactile pavement [a strip of tiles with different texture and color from the rest of the pavement] and sound signals can be placed in the barrier-free path, close to curb ramps, and at street intersections, thus allowing vision-impaired people to cross safely.)
6. Trees (Guarantee shade while purifying the air and enhancing the beauty of the landscape)
7. Street furniture (Trash bins, benches, drinking fountains, signs, and other fixtures provide convenience and comfort for pedestrians.)
8. Absence of obstacles (The absence of barriers on the paths ensures safe walking, especially for the elderly and vision-impaired pedestrians.)

Bikeways

Bicycles are a form of nonmotorized transportation and, as urban vehicles, should be separated from busy motorized traffic (as is already done in such cities as Copenhagen and Amsterdam). Bicycles and pedestrians may also be subject to different rules (prescribed by local custom and law) than those that apply to motorized transportation modes. In addition, because bicycles are more vulnerable than automobiles, trucks, and buses, they should be protected to some extent from general traffic by designated bike lanes or bikeways.

According to the American Association of State Highway and Transportation Officials (1999), bike lanes are defined as clearly marked, in-ground strips that identify the dedicated path for bicycles amid general traffic and ideally should be three meters wide in order to provide safe circulation. Such bike lanes and bikeways may be positioned either adjacent to a street or on a completely different track and should be integrated with the regular, nonmotorized transportation network. Depending on the amount of bicycle flow, cities could reserve the right to designate an increased minimum width.

Urban Planning

Urban planning is the tool that allows cities to grow and develop socially, economically, and environmentally. Through zoning and controlled land use, urban planning determines the direction and characteristics of such growth and development.

The major issue in urban planning that affects millions of people worldwide (especially in large cities and particularly pronounced in North America) is the phenomenon of suburbanization. The outward expansion of a city's boundaries into the less expensive land on its outskirts compromises city development by creating distant suburbs and, consequently, urban sprawl. This growth forces residents to undertake long commutes in order to accomplish their daily tasks. Urban sprawl has enormous negative impacts on infrastructure costs, the environment, and social development. Urban sprawl is often regarded either as having resulted from bad urban planning—because decisions that concern cities directly affect their outskirts—or, worse, as having resulted from a complete lack of urban planning.

In terms of mobility and sustainability, urban planning should be concerned with a city's attempt to achieve a balanced environment, and this equilibrium between private and collective modes of transportation and the movement of goods and their distribution must be maintained. In order to be sustainable in terms of mobility, cities need to be compact, walkable, integrated, and livable.

Approaches to urban planning, such as the New Urbanism described by the consultant and real estate developer Peter Katz (1994), advocate livable, sustainable communities and promote the creation and restoration of diverse, walkable, compact, vibrant, mixed-use communities. Such communities have the same components as conventional developments, but are constructed in a more integrated fashion in order to form self-contained communities. Such communities are spread all over the world, balancing essential topics such as general sustainability, land use, transportation, buildings, energy, materials management, water, green infrastructure, economic development, and community engagement. Walkable and bicycle-friendly communities are examples of such development.

Zoning and ordinances should prioritize mass transit and public transportation. They should also govern and manage street parking and parking lots. Allowing higher-density building along transit corridors (as is the case with TOD) supports sustainability, and as Katz (1994) notes, TOD has been shown, for example, to reduce infrastructure costs while promoting vibrant neighborhoods and fighting urban sprawl.

Regional Considerations

Although urban mobility is a universal concern, each city will have its own particular way to deal with mobility components. Each city will have to arrange and manage those components to serve its distinctive needs in accordance with its own conditions, preferences, and possibilities, which, in turn, are based on individual cultural, technological, economic, and historical factors. For example, while in the Americas the United States has developed a powerful automobile industry with a related urban infrastructure that makes automobiles both affordable and popular, cities like Amsterdam, Barcelona, Berlin, Paris, Tokyo, Beijing, Cape Town, Perth (Australia), and Auckland (New Zealand) have significantly improved their mobility patterns by investing in collective and nonmotorized transportation (illustrated by the number of bikeways and bike routes that have been constructed in many of those cities). Despite the great preference for cars in the United States and Canada, some US and Canadian cities have reported great progress in providing and encouraging the use of collective and nonmotorized transportation such as in Boulder (Colorado), Chicago (Illinois), Davis and San Francisco (California), and Ottawa (Canada).

Because of limited fossil fuel resources and rising gasoline prices, there is a worldwide trend toward the research and development of technologies that rely on renewable and clean energy sources to propel transportation. Such technological developments will create new possibilities for urban mobility.

Future Mobility Patterns

A mobility pattern can be understood as the way in which urban and regional dynamics occur, meaning the way transportation modes, facilities, available infrastructure, and legislation are locally organized in order to successfully achieve mobility, allowing people and goods to move within urban and regional areas efficiently and safely.

It is possible that the world's long-term mobility patterns will change over time within urban, intercity, national, and international areas and that they will affect the transportation industry and people's lifestyles because of their direct impact on car-dependent communities. Areas that focus on developing alternative modes of transportation, such as designing urban spaces for less car dependency, will be less impacted socially, economically, and environmentally. In order to make a projection of the future within a time frame, it is most usual to think of the short, medium, and long terms. These periods vary drastically from activity to activity. More perishable (subject to decay), less complex, or more susceptible (subject to some influence) activities tend to adopt shorter time frames compared with more complex activities, where it generally takes longer to perceive an outcome. In the area of financial operations, for instance, long-term borrowing and investing is usually considered to take place over a period of more than three years; the medium term for the same activity is usually defined as between one and three years; and the short-term occurs during a period of less than one year. In urban planning the immediate term is comprised of those actions and changes that are to be implemented within a one-year time frame; the short term describes actions and changes implemented over a period of one to five years; the medium term denotes a five-to-ten-year period; and long-term changes are implemented after ten years. A mobility pattern is a very complex and multi-related system that involves different domains such as the economy, social interactions, technological development, and the quality of the environment, among others; therefore the future (of a mobility pattern) can be defined as a time frame long enough to allow for a complete cycle of changes (which directly impact such areas) to occur, thereby configuring new paradigms and new standards for urban development that affect an entire population's quality of life. It has been estimated that this entire cycle of changes takes place over a period of twenty-five to fifty years. Future mobility patterns will directly affect urban design, transportation components, infrastructure systems, national economies, and the natural environment. Defining the future of mobility and making predictions about future mobility pattern trends (and their sustainability) is necessary because of the speed with which profound social, economic, and environmental changes are occurring worldwide.

Three different, interactive, and chronological scenarios based on the availability of fossil fuels have been considered here in order to framework future developments in mobility patterns and the consequences they will have on people's daily lives. It should be noted, however that there are other ways of predicting future developments (such as technological improvements, planning efforts, economic and social achievements, behavioral changes, and changes to and/or the introduction of relevant legislation and policy) in urban mobility.

A World with Cheap Fossil Fuels

In a hypothetical future with cheap fossil fuels, urban sprawl would detrimentally affect our urban land areas. Although there have been periods in the past where fossil fuels were cheap, it is neither predicted nor expected to happen in the near or distant futures, in spite of the existence of huge remaining petroleum reserves around the world. Cheap fuel during the last half of the twentieth century dictated urban design and city layouts worldwide—especially in the automobile-dependent United States. In terms of urban land use and occupation and the maintenance of the same urban planning trends that generated urban sprawl, it appears that cheap fossil fuels might have the same effect as cheap electric or hydrogen vehicles: they would contribute to an increased mobility pattern while concomitantly increasing traffic congestion, This is the paradox of "individual" mobility. Urban sprawl is a worldwide phenomenon affecting developed countries (especially the United States). The reach for cheap land and affordable housing and the twentieth century's low gasoline prices—especially from the 1950s onward—strongly contributed to the creation of suburbs in the United States, where more than half of the US population lives today (US Census Bureau 2010).

As the US scholar and researcher on urban change J. John Palen (2012) has pointed out, the US suburban era in fact began in the nineteenth century. It started with electric streetcars that operated between 1890 and 1920 and from (approximately) 1920 to 1950 the automobile became the dominant mode of transportation. With the ascendance of the automobile, mass suburbanization occurred (between 1950 and 1990)—a process perpetuated by the "metro sprawl" that took place between 1990 and 2010. Technological developments in private and public transportation and improvement of the mobility paradigm were fundamental conditions underlying these phenomena.

Mass-produced and affordable housing, low-priced land, government incentives, middle-class mobility, technological developments—especially in transportation and telecommunications—economic growth, and cheap fuels contributed to the US focus on the car. The thousands of mass-produced houses that were built in Levittown, New Jersey, in 1954 helped to create the common, widespread image of suburbia (Glaeser 2011). Two important factors contributed to this suburban sprawl during the 1950s and 1960s: federal government subsidies that made home ownership cheaper than renting and the availability of high-quality school systems. These strongly influenced the design of US cities.

According to the director of the National Center for Environmental Health and the Agency for Toxic Substances and Disease Registry at the US Centers for

Disease Control and Prevention, Howard Frumkin (2009), urban sprawl is a long-standing urban expansion process that encroaches upon rural areas and has the following characteristics: low-density land use, heavy reliance on automobiles for transportation, segregation of land uses, and a loss of opportunities for some groups, especially those in inner cities. The direct effects of this reliance on the automobile are principally pollution, congestion and degradation, and injuries and fatalities suffered by pedestrians and bicyclists. The urban sprawl phenomenon contributes considerably to the planet's carbon footprint.

Urban sprawl also has a significant impact on public health standards. The consequences of the lack of physical activity that results from excessive driving can directly lead to obesity, mental health problems (such as depression and anxiety caused by long commutes and disconnection from the landscape), and other severe illnesses that can be attributed to a sedentary lifestyle. This is a global public health issue that particularly affects highly motorized and developed countries.

The suburban lifestyle reflects preferences many people in the United States share, but the major shift in lifestyle that suburbanization presents also has profound health implications. Some of these health effects are environmental and are conditioned by issues such as land use, transportation, urban and regional design, and planning. Urban sprawl can negatively affect water quality and quantity and produces a heat island effect (air temperatures in densely built urban areas are higher than the temperatures of the surrounding rural country): both are a result of deforestation; impervious surfaces; water runoff; and agricultural land contaminated by fertilizers, herbicides, and insecticides. Oil, grease, and toxic chemicals from roadways and parking lots also have detrimental environmental effects.

As a suburban nation, the United States (and similar developed countries) should actively search for sustainable mobility patterns that can reduce and reverse these public health issues.

Suburbs, however, are not necessarily unpleasant. Many people are attracted by the privacy, quiet and calm environments, safety, and other amenities they have to offer, in spite of the sometimes frustratingly long commutes required for those who live there but work elsewhere. According to data from the American Community Survey (2002), if we count 250 workdays per year, we can calculate the average total number of days spent commuting to work in the top ten US cities: New York: 6.7 days; Chicago: 5.7 days; Philadelphia: 5.3 days; Los Angeles: 4.9 days; Dallas and Houston: 4.4 days; Detroit and Phoenix: 4.3 days; San Antonio: 4.1 days; and San Diego: 3.9 days.

Some distinctly suburban features are part of the US national culture (Palen 2012) including ranch-style houses, neat lawns, good schools, cleanliness, safe neighborhoods, a small-town atmosphere, and overscheduled parents and children. Although these elements are caricatures, they collectively make up what might be referred to as the myth of suburbia.

In order to consider density as a parameter for establishing future mobility patterns, it is important to analyze when and where new developments are being planned. In the opinion of the urban planners and scholars Claudio Acioly and Forbes Davidson (1996), the issue of the density of new developments is seen as critical for a wide range of environments. The affordability of low-density areas that have expensive services, high maintenance, and expensive transportation is an issue for debate in places with geographically and economically divided populations like Brazil, New Zealand, and states such as California in the United States. Low-density suburbs have triggered extensive and expensive land use, thereby creating, predictably, urban sprawl. An alternative that might reverse the situation that was created by the past availability of affordable fuels would be to try to limit the number of new settlements. This, in turn, would increase the demand for existing land and buildings, and result in higher densities, which could easily result in the displacement of low-income groups.

A World with Expensive Fossil Fuels

There are no reliable data about how long the world reserves of petroleum are expected to last. Amid this uncertainty, politics and speculation play major roles, provoking price surges. Fuel prices have skyrocketed since the beginning of the twenty-first century, and there is no hope of cheap fuel prices in the near or distant future. Since 1988, the price of the Intercontinental Exchange—formerly the International Petroleum Exchange—Brent crude oil barrel prices jumped from nearly US$15 to US$120 per barrel, an increase of 800 percent that peaked at US$145 per barrel in July 2008 (Oilnergy 2012).

Urban design and mobility patterns reflect these increasing fuel prices, which are adjusted somewhat to fit household budgets according to new and challenging economic realities. Since the 2008 financial crisis, housing prices are determined by a market more concerned than ever before by commuting times and costs. The automobile industry is also focused on offering fuel efficient vehicles like hybrid (electric—gasoline), flex fuel (ethanol—gasoline), and fully electric vehicles (that correspond to user preferences) in order to help make commutes affordable.

Many new neighborhoods are attempting to offer carpooling as an alternative in tough economic times. Cities are endeavoring to offer more public transit and implement nonmotorized transportation alternatives by the improvement and/or implementation of decent sidewalks, bikeways, and bike lanes that are fully integrated with public and mass transit.

As fuel prices rise, new approaches to urban design and mobility patterns will be needed to respond to new requirements. Researchers, developers, manufacturers, and companies worldwide are exploring alternative fuels and advanced technologies like ethanol, soy oil by-products, biodiesel, hydrogen cells, batteries, more efficient vehicular engines, lighter and tougher chassis, and other parts and components. In addition, efforts are increasingly geared toward producing efficient hydrogen-propelled and hybrid buses, hybrid and fully electric cars, and solar powered vehicles, as well as many other developments and inventions that will be popular with consumers.

Population density, location, mixed land use, transportation alternatives, and transportation mode integration are key words for urban development in a world that is facing exorbitant future fuel costs. Inevitably people will choose lower-cost options for transportation—such as walking, bicycling, and public transportation—as fuel prices increase. In providing adequate infrastructure that allows and encourages people to utilize such options, special attention should be given to the public sector. Increased support for public infrastructure in the form of sidewalks, safe crossings, bikeways and bike-lane networks, as well as supportive amenities like street furniture (benches, trees, trash bins, signs, bus stops, and adequate pavement), and first-rate public places designed to allow people to assemble helps increase the number of healthy transportation options.

A World with Scarce or Very Expensive Fossil Fuels

In order to explore the scenario of a world with scarce and/or very expensive fossil fuels, it is necessary to understand that changing mobility patterns will drastically affect people's current lifestyle choices. The scarcity and/or higher prices of fossil fuels would generate different mobility patterns. It is also necessary to consider that transitioning from one scenario to another could take several years or even decades.

This third scenario is the one that hypothesizes the most dramatic change, and if it came to be, would be a great test of humanity's capacity to create new mobility patterns and design new city layouts. Attempts to replace fossil fuels as the major vehicle propellant are currently focusing on a multitude of diverse renewable electricity sources such as hydroelectric, geothermal and nuclear plants, as well as solar and wind-powered systems. Although a great proportion of generated electricity comes from burned fossil fuels, renewable sources come with a lower price tag and fewer negative impacts.

In this scenario, significant changes in social behavior can be expected as a result of educational campaigns and governmental programs focused on collective, public, and nonmotorized forms of transportation. Positive results in terms of quality of life can be expected from electricity-based and collective transportation options. Some of these results may include an amelioration of environmental conditions and a reduction of traffic congestion because of expected very low or even zero emissions.

In spite of the existence of efficient and environmentally friendly public transit systems, bikeways, and people-friendly public places in many urban areas, there is still a heavy reliance on cars and thus on fossil fuels. Data from the International Energy Agency (IEA 2010) listed the 2009 world energy supply by power source: oil: 37.2 percent; coal: 19.7 percent; gas: 24.2 percent (and of that figure fossil fuel represents 81 percent); renewable (hydro, solar, wind, geothermal power, and biofuels): 6.5 percent; nuclear: 11.3 percent; and others (including combustible [renewable and waste] and heat) 1.1 percent. As the data illustrate, oil was the most popular energy fuel, and oil and coal combined represented almost 57 percent of the world's 2009 energy supply, demonstrating its tremendous dependency on fossil fuels—a great part of which was allocated for transportation activities. The importance of renewable energy is just starting to emerge in this process. The same IEA report listed data about how 2008's global electricity generation was distributed: coal: 41 percent; gas: 21.3 percent; hydro: 15.9 percent;

nuclear: 13.5 percent; oil: 5.5 percent; and others: 2.8 percent. These figures indicate to what extent, even in the domain of electricity generation, the world is greatly dependent on fossil fuels. Optimistically, IEA (2010) predicts that the outlook for the total global energy production, listed by fuel, will be as follows in 2030: oil: 29.5 percent; gas: 20.4 percent; renewable energies: 18.6 percent; coal: 18.2 percent; nuclear: 9.9 percent; and hydro: 3.4 percent. This signifies two important things: a decrease of oil (−7.7 percent) and an increase of renewable energy (+12.1 percent) in the matrix by that date.

Changing mobility parameters and patterns will not be an easy task in the long run, even for those communities and cities that are already adopting alternative transportation methods. Adopting alternative transportation methods may very likely require profound departures from current standards and procedures and therefore enormous public- and/or private-sector investments. Urban sprawl is not inevitable, and smart growth—a variety of efforts to shape growth so sprawl is limited—may offer solutions that can be implemented by advocating and encouraging development that offers transportation alternatives, preserves open space, revitalizes older communities, and limits wasteful and expensive suburban sprawl. Smart growth in a higher-density design can result in advantages including an increase in good mobility patterns, that is, mobility patterns that are sustainable and integrated, and improved nonmotorized transportation.

A sustainable mobility pattern is one that achieves the best balance possible between efficiency and efficacy. Any city that attempts to create a new sustainable mobility pattern should create mechanisms that reverse the historical trend of car dependency while they strongly invest in integrated and (maximally) multimodal transportation that includes both public transit and nonmotorized modes in order to connect its most important sites.

Evandro C. SANTOS
Jackson State University

See also Buildings and Infrastructure; Cities and the Biosphere; Community; Design; Energy Efficiency; Local Solutions to Global Problems; Migration

FURTHER READING

Acioly, Claudio, Jr., & Davidson, Forbes. (1996). Density in urban development. *Building Issues, 3*(8), 3–25.

American Association of State Highway and Transportation Officials (AASHTO). (1999). *Guide for the development of bicycle facilities* (3rd ed.). Washington, DC: AASHTO.

American Association of State Highway and Transportation Officials (AASHTO). (2004). *Guide for the planning, design, and operation of pedestrian facilities.* Washington, DC: AASHTO.

American Community Survey. (2002). America's ten largest cities: Average total days spent commuting to work. In J. John Palen (Ed.), *The urban world* (9th ed.) (p. 260). Boulder, CO: McGraw-Hill.

American Public Transportation Association. (2011). Transit oriented development: Reports and publications. Retrieved July 12, 2011, from http://fta.dot.gov/about/library.html

Bradshaw, Chris. (1993). A rating system for neighborhood walkability: Towards an agenda for local "heroes" (14th International Pedestrian Conference. Boulder, CO). Retrieved February 12, 2011, from http://www.cooperativeindividualism.org/bradshaw-chris_walkable-communities.html

Bruton, Michael J. (1975). *Introduction to transportation planning.* London: Hutchinson & Co. Ltd.

City of Melbourne. (1985). Streets for people: A pedestrian strategy for the Central Activities District of Melbourne. In Quentin Stevens (Ed.), *The lucid city: Exploring the potential of public spaces* (2007). New York: Routledge.

Frumkin, Howard. (2009). Urban sprawl and public health. In H. Patricia Hynes & Russ Lopez (Eds.), *Urban health: Readings in the social, built, and physical environments of US cities* (pp. 141–168). Boston, MA: Jones and Bartlett.

Glaeser, Edward. (2011). *Triumph of the city.* New York: Penguin Group.

Goodwill, Julie, & Hendricks, Sara J. (2002). Building transit oriented development in established communities. *Journal of Public Transportation* (Center for Urban Transportation Research at the University of South Florida). Retrieved August 11, 2011, from http://www.nctr.usf.edu/jpt/journal.htm

International Energy Agency (IEA). (2010). Key world energy statistics. Retrieved March 7, 2012, from http://www.iea.org/textbase/nppdf/free/2010/key_stats_2010.pdf

Katz, Peter. (1994). *The new urbanism: Toward an architecture of community.* New York: McGraw-Hill.

Oilnergy.com. (2012). ICE Brent crude oil closing price [begin July 1988]. Retrieved March 6, 2012, from http://www.oilnergy.com/1obrent.htm

Palen, J. John. (2012). *The urban world* (9th ed.). Boulder, CO: McGraw-Hill.

Santos, Evandro C. (2006a). *Survey on the Urban Bikeability Index: A diagnosis and lecture of urban conditions for the development of biker-outes and bikelanes in Montevideo, Uruguay* (Seminario de la Bicicleta Urbana: Ciudad en Dos Ruedas, 1st). Montevideo, Uruguay: United Nations Educational, Scientific and Cultural Organization (UNESCO) and Goethe Institut of Montevideo.

Santos, Evandro C. (2006b). Diagnosis of Walkability's Index of main Brazilian southern cities (Curitiba, Porto Alegre, Blumenau, Londrina, Maringa, Foz do Iguacu, Cascavel). Multimedia CD-ROM Vols. 1–7. Curitiba, Brazil: Brazilian Association of Portland Cement—South region (ABCP-Sul).

Santos, Evandro C. (2011). *Curitiba, Brazil: Pioneering in developing bus rapid transit and urban planning solutions.* Saarbrücken, Germany: LAP Lambert Academic Publishing.

Stevens, Quentin. (2007). *The lucid city: Exploring the potential of public places.* New York: Routledge

United States (US) Census Bureau. (2010). Population division, population estimates program. Retrieved March 7, 2012, from http://2010.census.gov/2010census/

United States Department of Transportation, Federal Transit Administration. (n.d.). Technology. Retrieved August 15, 2011, from http://fta.dot.gov/about/12351_technology.html

Wright, Charlie L. (1992). *Fast wheels, slow traffic: Urban transport choices.* Philadelphia, PA: Temple University Press.

Natural Capital

Sustainable development includes the premise that intergenerational well-being increases over time only if a comprehensive measure of wealth per capita increases—based on not only manufactured capital, knowledge, and human capital (education and health), but also natural capital (e.g., healthy ecosystems). As data from some of the world's poorest countries shows, a country's wealth may decline even if gross domestic product increases and the United Nations Human Development Index (a composite measure of GDP per head, life expectancy at birth, and education) records an improvement. Since no current development indicators can reveal whether development is sustainable, national and international organizations should routinely estimate the comprehensive wealth of nations as part of evaluating environmental sustainability.

Are humanity's dealings with nature sustainable? Can we expect world economic growth to continue in the foreseeable future? Should we be confident that knowledge and skills would increase in ways that would lessen our reliance on nature in relation to humanity's growing numbers and rising economic activity?

Discussions of these questions are now several decades old. If they remain alive and continue to be shrill, it is because two opposing empirical perspectives shape them. On the one hand, if we look at specific examples of what economists call *natural capital* (aquifers, ocean fisheries, tropical forests, estuaries, the atmosphere as a carbon sink—ecosystems, generally), convincing evidence suggests that, given the rates at which we currently exploit them, they are likely to change character dramatically for the worse, with little advance notice. Indeed, many ecosystems have already collapsed, with short notice (Hassan, Scholes, and Ash 2005; MEA 2003). On the other hand, if we study historical trends in the prices of marketed resources (e.g., minerals and ores), improvements in life expectancy, or growth in recorded incomes in regions that are currently rich and in those that are on the way to becoming rich, resource scarcities would not appear to have occurred. Let's consider the troubled nations of sub-Saharan Africa and suggest that resource scarcities are acute there today. Those who focus on natural capital (ecologists, generally) will say that people in the world's poorest regions are so poor because they face acute resource scarcities relative to their numbers, while those who focus on traditional capital (economists, usually) will say that people in poor countries experience serious resource scarcities because they are poor. When experts disagree over such a fundamental matter as causation, the rest of us have little to work with.

Those conflicting intuitions are related to an intellectual tension between the concerns people share about carbon emissions and acid rains that sweep across regions, nations, and continents; and about declines in the availability of firewood, fresh water, coastal resources, and forest products in as small a locality as a village in a poor country. That is why "environmental problems" present themselves in different ways to different people. Some people associate environmental problems with population growth, while others associate them with wrong sorts of economic growth. Some people associate environmental problems with urban pollution in emerging economies, while others view them through the lens of poverty.

Each of those visions is correct; not just one environmental problem exists. A large collection of them does, and they manifest at different spatial scales and operate at different speeds (Dasgupta 1993, 2004; Ehrlich and Ehrlich 1981, 1990; Sachs 2008). In this reckoning, environmental pollutants are the reverse of natural resources. Roughly speaking, "resources" are "good" (many being sinks into which pollutants are discharged), whereas "pollutants" (the degrader of resources) are "bad." Pollution is the other side of conservation. That is why we can study pollution and conservation in a unified way (Dasgupta 1982).

Despite the conflicting intuitions, most economists appear to be convinced that scientific and technological advances, the accumulation of reproducible capital (machinery, equipment, buildings, roads), growth in human capital (health, education, skills), and improvements in an economy's institutions (which are also capital assets) can overcome diminutions in natural capital. Otherwise, explaining why twentieth-century economics has been so detached from the environmental sciences is hard. Judging by the profession's writings, economists see nature, when they see it at all, as a backdrop from which we can draw resources and services in isolation. Macroeconomic forecasts routinely exclude natural capital. Accounting for nature, if it comes into the calculation at all, is usually an afterthought to the real business of "doing economics." Economists have been so successful in this enterprise that if someone exclaims, "Economic growth!" few people need to ask, "Growth in what?" Most people know that the economists mean growth in gross domestic product (GDP).

The rogue word in GDP is "gross." Since GDP is the total value of the final goods and services an economy produces, it does not deduct the depreciation of capital that accompanies production—in particular, it doesn't deduct the depreciation of natural capital. The quantitative models that appear in leading economic journals and textbooks consider nature to be a fixed, indestructible factor of production. The problem with this assumption is that it is wrong: nature consists of degradable resources. Agricultural land, forests, watersheds, fisheries, freshwater sources, river estuaries, and the atmosphere are self-regenerative capital assets, but they suffer from depletion or deterioration when they are overused (excluding oil and natural gas, which are at the limiting end of self-regenerative resources). To assume away the physical depreciation of capital assets is to draw a wrong picture of the future production and consumption possibilities open to a society.

Here is an illustration of what goes wrong in economic accounts when we ignore depreciation. The US economics and sustainable development professor Robert Repetto and his colleagues (1989), as well as the US environmental economist Jeffery Vincent and his colleagues (1997), estimated the decline in forest cover in Indonesia and Malaysia, respectively. They found that including depreciation means the national accounts look quite different: net domestic saving rates are some 20–30 percent lower than recorded saving rates. In their work on the depreciation of natural resources in Costa Rica, Raul Solorzano

of that country's Ministry of Environment and Energy and his colleagues (1991) found that the depreciation of three resources (forests, soil, and fisheries) amounted to about 10 percent of GDP and more than 33 percent of domestic saving.

Including Natural Capital in Economics

We can reconstruct economics to include natural capital in a seamless way. As it stands, property rights to natural capital are frequently unprotected or ill specified, which typically leads to their overexploitation and so to waste and inequity. The example of overexploitation in the context of a "small" problem discussed below, namely, the economic failure that can accompany deforestation in a small region, illustrates this idea. Every economy faces innumerable such small problems, and the performance of the macroeconomy depends on how it tackles each small problem. If good policies are in place to reduce the economic losses small problems generate, the macroeconomy can be expected to function well, but not otherwise. When economic statistics include natural capital, however, the recent economic history of nations looks very different from what we see when we use conventional economic indicators, such as GDP per head, or the United Nations (UN) Human Development Index (HDI), to judge economic performance. The HDI is a composite measure of GDP per head, life expectancy at birth, and education.

Lack of Property Rights to Natural Capital

Why do market prices not reflect nature's scarcity value? If natural capital really was becoming scarcer, wouldn't its prices have risen, signalling that all is not well?

Prices might reveal social scarcities if markets themselves functioned well. For many types of natural capital, though, most especially ecological resources, markets not only don't function well, but often don't even exist. In some cases, they don't exist because relevant economic interactions happen over large distances, making the costs of negotiation too high (e.g., the effects of upland deforestation on downstream farming and fishing activities). In other cases, they don't exist because large temporal distances separate the interactions (e.g., the effect of carbon emission on climate in the distant future, in a world where forward markets don't exist because future generations are not present today to negotiate with us). Then there are cases, such as the atmosphere, aquifers, or the open seas, where the migratory nature of the resource keeps markets from existing. These cases are "open access resources," and they experience the tragedy of the commons—a dilemma that happens when several individuals, acting alone and by their own self-interest, ultimately deplete a shared limited resource.

Each of the above examples points to a failure to have secure *property rights* to natural capital. We can state the problem this way: ill-specified or unprotected property rights prevent markets from forming or make them function incorrectly when they do form.

"Property rights" in this context means not only private property rights but also communal property rights (e.g., rights over common property resources, such as woodlands, in South Asia and sub-Saharan Africa) and state property rights. At an extreme end are "global property rights," a concept that is implicit in current discussions on climate change. The concept isn't new, however. The idea that humanity had collective responsibility over the state of the world's oceans was explicit in the 1970s, when politicians claimed that the oceans were a "common heritage of mankind."

Failure to establish secure property rights to natural capital typically means that the services natural capital offers are underpriced in the market, which is another way of saying that the use of nature's services is implicitly subsidized. At the global level, what is the annual subsidy? One calculation suggested that it is 10 percent of annual global income (Myers and Kent 2000), though the possibility exists that the margin of error in that estimate is very large. An article the South African environmental economics professor Rashid Hassan and his colleagues wrote (2005) contains quantitative information that could help generate more-reliable estimates of nature's subsidies; international organizations such as the World Bank have the resources to undertake that work, but they appear reluctant to do so.

Nature's Subsidies

Since nature is underpriced, it is overexploited. So an economy could enjoy growth in real GDP and improvements in HDI for a long spell even while its overall productive base shrinks. As proposals for estimating the social scarcity prices of natural resources remain contentious, economic accountants ignore them and governments remain wary of doing anything about them. Consequently, the use of nature is indirectly subsidized.

An easy way for governments to earn revenue in countries that are rich in forests is to issue timber concessions to private firms. Imagine that a government awards concessions in the upland forests of a watershed. Since forests stabilize both soil and water flow, deforestation causes soil erosion and increases fluctuations in water supply downstream. If the law recognized the rights of those who suffer damage from deforestation, it would require

the upstream timber firm to compensate downstream farmers. Compensation is unlikely, however, when (a) the cause of damage is many miles away, (b) the state has awarded the concession, and (c) the victims are scattered groups of farmers. (For example, the social ecologist Marcus Colchester [1995] has recounted that political representatives of forest-dwellers in Sarawak, Malaysia, have routinely given logging licenses to members of the state legislature.) Compounding the problems is the fact that damages are not uniform across farms: location matters. Those who deforestation harms may not know the underlying cause of their deteriorating circumstances. Because the timber firm isn't required to compensate farmers, its operating cost is less than the social cost of deforestation—the firm's logging costs and the damage suffered by all who are adversely affected. So the export contains an implicit subsidy, paid for by people downstream. This scenario does not include forest inhabitants, who now live under even more straitened circumstances or, worse, find themselves evicted without compensation. The subsidy is hidden from public scrutiny, but it amounts to a transfer of wealth from the exporting to the importing country. Some of the poorest people in a poor country subsidize the incomes of the average importer in what could well be a rich country.

Quantifying Economic Failure

The spatial character of nature's hidden subsidies is self-evident, but getting a quantitative feel involves hard work. The literature is sparse as a result. As in many other scientific fields, scientists have made some of the best advances in studies of localized problems. Basing their estimate on a formal hydrological model, the environmental economics professors Subhrendu Pattanayak and Randall Kramer (2001) reported that the drought mitigation benefits that farmers enjoy from upstream forests in a group of Indonesian watersheds are 1–10 percent of average agricultural incomes. In another paper, Pattanayak and the US economist David Butry (2005) studied the extent to which upstream forests stabilize soil and water flow in Flores, Indonesia. They found that downstream benefits were 2–3 percent of average agricultural incomes.

In a study in Costa Rica on pollination services, the US ecological economics professor Taylor Ricketts and his colleagues (2004) discovered that forest-based pollinators increased the annual yield in nearby coffee plantations by as much as 20 percent. Subsequently, analysis of the results of some two dozen studies, involving sixteen crops on five continents, discovered that the density of pollinators and the rate at which they visit a site declines rapidly at exponential rates with the site's distance from the pollinators' habitat (Ricketts et al. 2008). At 0.6 kilometers from the pollinators' habitat, for example, the visitation rate drops to 50 percent of its maximum.

Eliminating Nature's Subsidies

How should societies eliminate nature's subsidies? In the case of the upstream firm and downstream farmers, the state could tax the firm for felling trees. The firm in this case would be the "polluter," and the farmers the "pollutees." Today we call pollution taxes "green taxes." They invoke the *polluter-pays principle* (PPP). The efficient rate of taxation would be the damage the farmers suffer. What the state does with the tax revenue is a distributional matter, as discussed later.

A "market-friendly" way to eliminate the subsidies is available. The Swedish economist Erik Lindahl (1958 [1919]) suggested that the state (or the community) could introduce private property rights to natural capital, the thought being that markets would emerge to price nature's services appropriately. That proposal, however, doesn't make clear who should gain the property rights. In the example of the upstream firm and downstream farmers, the sense of natural justice might suggest that the farmers should gain the rights. Under a system of "pollutees' rights," the farmers would receive compensations from the timber firm for the damage it inflicts on them. Such a property-rights regime also invokes PPP.

Conversely, the timber firm might gain the rights instead. In that case, the farmers would have to compensate the firm for not felling trees. The latter system of property rights invokes the *pollutee-pays principle* (a reverse PPP of sorts), which, in the current example, would seem repellent. Proponents have argued, however, that in terms of efficiency, it's a matter of indifference which system of private property rights prevails.

Market-based systems have attracted much attention among ecologists and development experts under the label *payment for ecosystem services*, or PES. (See Daily and Ellison 2002, and Pagiola, Landell-Mills, and Bishop 2002 for sympathetic reviews of a market-based PES.) The ethics underlying PES seem attractive. If decision makers in Brazil believe that decimating the Amazon forests is the true path to economic progress, shouldn't the rest of the world pay Brazil not to raze the forests? If the lake on a farm is a sanctuary for migratory birds, shouldn't bird lovers pay the farmer not to drain it for conversion into farmland? Never mind that the market for ecosystem services could be hard to institute. A system involving PES would require owners of ecological capital and beneficiaries of ecological services to negotiate. The former group would then have an incentive to conserve their assets.

Hundreds of PES programs operate around the globe. China, Costa Rica, and Mexico, for example, have initiated large-scale programs in which landowners receive payment for increasing biodiversity conservation, expanding carbon sequestration, and improving hydrological services. Although PES may be good for conservation, however, one can imagine situations where the system would be bad for poverty reduction and distributive justice. Many of the rural poor in undeveloped countries enjoy nature's services from assets they don't own. Even though they may be willing to participate in a system of property rights in which *they* are required to pay for ecological services (as they do in a careful study of a silvopastoral project in Nicaragua reported by Pagiola, Rios, and Arcenas 2008), the weaker among the farmers might end up paying a disproportionate amount. Some may even become worse off than they were earlier. Perhaps in those situations the state should pay the resource owner instead, using funds obtained from general taxation. Who should pay depends on the context (Bulte et al. 2008).

A PES system in which the state plays an active role is attractive for wildlife conservation and habitat preservation. In poor countries, property rights to grasslands, tropical forests, coastal wetlands, mangroves, and coral reefs are often ambiguous. The state may lay claim to the assets ("public" property being the customary euphemism), but if the terrain is difficult to monitor, inhabitants will continue to reside there and live off its products. Inhabitants are therefore key stakeholders. Without inhabitants' engagement, the ecosystems cannot be protected. Meanwhile, flocks of tourists visit the sites regularly. An obvious action for the state is to tax tourists and use the revenue to pay local inhabitants to protect their site from poaching and free riding. Local inhabitants would then have an incentive to develop rules and regulations to protect the site.

Measuring Sustainable Development

Whenever economists have probed the matter, they have found that all economies subsidize large numbers of economic transactions with nature. Some of those transactions are large (e.g., construction of dams that alter ecosystems), but mostly they are small. How do those subsidies affect overall economic performance? More fundamentally, how should we measure economic performance?

A famous 1987 report by an international commission (widely known as the Brundtland Commission Report) defined *sustainable development* as "development that meets the needs of the present without compromising the ability of future generations to meet their own needs" (World Commission for Environment and Development 1987). In this reckoning, sustainable development requires that, relative to their populations, each generation should bequeath to its successor at least as large a *productive base* as it had itself inherited. Notice that the requirement derives from the relatively weak notion of justice among the generations. Sustainable development demands that, relative to population numbers, future generations have no less of the means to meet their needs than we do ourselves; it demands nothing more. But how is a generation to judge whether it is leaving behind an adequate productive base for its successor?

Shadow Prices as Social Scarcities

As noted earlier, neither GDP nor HDI is of help, because neither is a measure of a country's productive base. So, what does measure the productive base? A society's productive base is the stock of all its capital assets, including its institutions. To estimate the change in an economy's productive base over a certain period, we need to know how to combine the changes that take place in its capital stocks.

Intuitively, we clearly must do more than just keep a score of capital assets (so many additional pieces of machinery and equipment; so many more miles of roads; so many fewer square miles of forest cover; and so forth). An economy's productive base declines if the economy does not compensate the decumulation of assets by the accumulation of other assets. Contrarily, the productive base expands if the economy more than compensates the decumulation of assets by the accumulation of other assets. The ability of one asset to compensate for the decline in some other asset depends on technological knowledge (e.g., double glazing can substitute for central heating up to a point, but only up to a point) and on the quantities of assets the economy happens to have in stock (e.g., the protection that trees provide against soil erosion depends on the existing grass cover). The values to impute to assets are their *shadow prices*. Formally, an asset's shadow price is the net increase in societal well-being that would result if an additional unit of that asset became available, other things being equal. Since shadow prices reflect the social scarcities of capital assets, only in exceptional circumstances would they equal market prices.

An operational sense of the concept of *sustainable development* is trying to be made here. In the concept of social well-being, not only the well-being of those who are alive today but also of those who will be here in the future must be included. Some ethical theories go beyond a purely anthropocentric view of nature, by insisting that certain aspects of nature have intrinsic value. The concept of social well-being invoked here would include intrinsic values, if the situation demands them. An ethical theory on its own isn't enough to determine shadow prices, however, because the theory has nothing upon which to act. Theories need descriptions of states of affairs, too. To add a unit of a capital asset to an economy is to perturb that economy. To estimate the contribution of that additional unit to societal well-being, a description of the state of affairs both before and after making the addition is needed, now and in the future. In short, estimating shadow prices involves both evaluation and description.

Not surprisingly, estimating shadow prices is a formidable problem. Ethical values are probably impossible to commensurate when they encounter other values. That doesn't mean ethical values don't impose bounds on shadow prices; they do. The language of shadow prices, therefore, is essential if we wish to avoid making somber pronouncements about sustainable development that amount to saying nothing. Most methods currently deployed to estimate the shadow prices of ecosystem services are crude, but deploying them is a lot better than doing nothing to value them.

The Wealth of Nations

The value of an economy's entire stock of capital assets measured in terms of their shadow prices is its *wealth*. Sometimes we call it *comprehensive wealth*, to remind ourselves that the measure should include *all* capital assets (building and machinery, roads and rail tracks; health and skills; natural capital; and knowledge and institutions), not just reproducible capital (buildings and machinery, roads and rail tracks). Comprehensive wealth (henceforth, wealth) is a number, expressed, say, in international dollars.

Evidence shows that an economy's wealth measures its overall productive base (see e.g., Dasgupta 2004; Dasgupta and Mäler 2000; Hamilton and Clemens 1999). So, if we wish to determine whether a country's economic development has been sustainable over a specific period of time, we have to estimate the changes in its wealth relative to growth in population that took place over that period. The theoretical result raised here gives meaning to the title of perhaps the most famous economics book ever written, *An Inquiry into the Nature and Causes of the Wealth of Nations*. It is important to note that the author, Adam Smith, did not write about either the GDP or the HDI of nations; he wrote about the wealth of nations. We have come full circle now, by identifying sustainable development with the accumulation of (comprehensive) wealth.

An Empirical Exercise

The economists Kirk Hamilton and Michael Clemens (1999) estimated in an important paper the change in the wealth of 120 nations during the period 1970–2000. They defined an economy's wealth as the value of its reproducible capital assets and three classes of natural capital assets: commercial forests, oil and minerals, and the quality of the atmosphere in terms of its carbon dioxide content. The economists presented the shadow prices of oil and minerals as their market prices minus extraction costs. The shadow price of global carbon emission into the atmosphere was the damage caused by bringing about climate change. That damage, they estimated, was US$20 per ton, which, is in all probability, a serious underestimate. Forests were valued in terms of their market price minus logging costs. Contributions of forests to ecosystem functions were ignored.

The list of natural resources Hamilton and Clemens considered was incomplete. It didn't include water resources, fisheries, air and water pollutants, soil, and ecosystems. The authors also ignored improvements in human health and skills, and they didn't consider increases in knowledge, nor improvements or deteriorations in the countries' institutions. Moreover, their estimates of shadow prices were extremely approximate. Nevertheless, one has to start somewhere, and theirs was a first pass at what is an enormously messy enterprise.

Table 1, below, shows an assessment of the character of economic development in select poor countries or regions during 1970–2000. Economists have discovered ingenious ways to estimate the accumulation of knowledge and changes in the effectiveness of an economy's institutions; international organizations such as the World Bank

regularly publish these estimates. The first column of figures in the table presents estimates of the average annual percentage rate of change in wealth in each region during 1970–2000. These estimates are a refinement of estimates the economist Kenneth Arrow and his colleagues (2004) published, which in turn were an improvement on those of Hamilton and Clemens—adding the average annual public expenditure on health and education, the average annual rate of growth in knowledge, and changes in the effectiveness of their institutions to the Hamilton-Clemens estimates for each region.

Except for sub-Saharan Africa, wealth increased in every country in the sample. In judging whether an economy has experienced sustainable development during a period, however, we must discover whether wealth increased *relative to population growth*. The simplest way to determine whether this increase happened is to ask whether wealth *per head* has increased. To estimate movements in wealth per head, the figures have been collated for the average annual population growth rate in each region during 1970–2000. They appear in the second column of figures in the table. The third column presents the difference between the figures in the first and second columns, which gives estimates of the change in wealth per head in each region.

Before summarizing the findings, it will be useful to get a feel for what the table is telling us. Consider Pakistan. During 1970–2000, wealth increased at an average annual rate of 1.3 percent, while Pakistan's population grew at a 2.7 percent rate. The third column shows that Pakistan's per capita wealth *declined* in consequence, at an annual rate of 1.4 percent, implying that in 2000, the average Pakistani was poorer than in 1970. If we were to judge Pakistan's economic performance in terms of growth in GDP per capita, we would obtain a different picture. The fourth column of the table shows that Pakistan grew at 2.2 percent a year. In the fifth column, we find that the HDI for Pakistan improved during the

TABLE 1. The Progress of Poor Nations

Country/Region	% Annual Growth Rate 1970–2000				
	Wealth	Population per Head	Wealth per Head	GDP per Head	Δ HDI*
Sub-Saharan Africa	−0.1	2.7	−2.8	−0.1	+
Bangladesh	1.4	2.2	−0.8	1.9	+
India	1.6	2.0	−0.4	3.0	+
Nepal	1.8	2.2	−0.4	1.9	+
Pakistan	1.3	2.7	−1.4	2.2	+
China	5.9	1.4	4.5	7.8	+

Source: Adapted from Arrow et al. (2004).

Note: "Δ HDI" = change in Human Development Index (HDI) between 1970 and 2000. The HDI is a composite statistic that shows relative levels of quality of living in different nations.

This table shows an assessment of the character of economic development in a selection of poor countries or regions during the period 1970–2000. Please refer to the text above the table for an explanation of the columns.

period. Pakistan achieved this growth in GDP and improvement in HDI by depleting the country's natural capital assets. Movements in GDP per capita and HDI tell us nothing about sustainable development.

The striking message of the table is that during 1970–2000, economic development in all countries on the list (other than China) was negative. To be sure, sub-Saharan Africa offers no surprise. Wealth, not just wealth per head, declined at an annual rate of 0.1 percent while population grew at 2.7 percent. Even without performing any calculation, we would have known that the productive base in sub-Saharan Africa declined relative to its population. The table confirms that it did, at 2.8 percent each year. The fourth column of numbers in the table shows that GDP per capita in sub-Saharan Africa declined at 0.1 percent annually. The region's HDI, though, showed an improvement—confirming once again that studying movements in HDI enables us to say nothing about sustainable development.

The table shows that Pakistan is the worst performer in the Indian subcontinent, although the remaining countries in South Asia didn't perform well either. Admittedly, each country became wealthier, but population growth was sufficiently high to more than neutralize the growth in wealth. Relative to their populations, the productive base in each economy declined. South Asia did not sustain economic development.

China was the single exception in the sample. The country invested so much in reproducible capital assets that its wealth grew at an annual rate of 5.9 percent. Population grew at a relatively low rate—1.4 percent per year, which is why China's wealth per capita expanded at an annual rate of 4.5 percent. Per capita GDP also grew, at an annual rate of 7.8 percent, and HDI improved. In China, GDP per capita, HDI, and wealth per head moved parallel to one another.

These figures are all very rough, but they show how accounting for natural capital can make a substantial difference in how the development process is viewed. We should remember that the figures for several shadow prices used to create table 1 on page 171 are conservative. For example, a price of US$20 per ton of carbon in the atmosphere is almost certainly a good deal below its true global social cost. The methods used to value improvements in health and education also are almost certainly defective, but in the opposite direction: they were underestimated. One of the most important problems economists face today is finding more-effective ways to quantify the progress and regress of nations. As long as economists rely on GDP, HDI, and the many other ad hoc measures of human well-being, they will continue to paint a misleading picture of economic performance.

The figures in the third column of the table are not to be taken literally, because of their imperfections.

Nevertheless, with all the above caveats (and more!) in mind, the overarching moral that emerges is salutary: development policies that ignore our reliance on natural capital are seriously harmful—they don't pass the mildest test for equity among contemporaries, nor among people separated by time and uncertain contingencies.

Sir Partha DASGUPTA
University of Cambridge and University of Manchester

This article, originally titled "Nature's Role in Sustaining Economic Development," was prepared for the Special Issue of the Philosophical Transactions of the Royal Society on the occasion of the Society's 350th anniversary in 2010. Used by kind permission of the Royal Society. The original article is available online at http://rstb.royalsocietypublishing.org/content/365/1537/5.full

See also Economics, Steady-State; Global Trade; Local Solutions to Global Problems; Population; Progress

FURTHER READING

Arrow, Kenneth J. (2004). Are we consuming too much? *Journal of Economic Perspectives, 18*(1), 147–172.

Bulte, Erwin H.; Lipper, Leslie; Stringer, Randy; & Zilberman, David. (2008). Payments for ecosystem services and poverty reduction: Concepts, issues, and empirical perspectives. *Environment and Development Economics, 13*(3), 245–254.

Colchester, Marcus. (1995). Sustaining the forests: The community-based approach in South and South-East Asia. *Development and Change, 25*(1), 69–100.

Daily, Gretchen, & Ellison, Katherine. (2002). *The new economy of nature: The quest to make conservation profitable.* Washington, DC: Island Press.

Dasgupta, Partha. (1982). *The control of resources.* Cambridge, MA: Harvard University Press.

Dasgupta, Partha. (1993). *An inquiry into well-being and destitution.* Oxford, UK: Clarendon Press.

Dasgupta, Partha. (2004) . *Human well-being and the natural environment* (2nd ed.). Oxford, UK: Oxford University Press.

Dasgupta, Partha, & Mäler, Karl-Göran. (2000). Net national product, wealth, and social well-being. *Environment and Development Economics, 5*(1), 69–93.

Ehrlich, Paul R., & Ehrlich, Anne H. (1981). *Extinction: The causes and consequences of the disappearance of species.* New York: Random House.

Ehrlich, Paul R., & Ehrlich, Anne H. (1990). *The population explosion.* New York: Simon and Schuster.

Hamilton, Kirk, & Clemens, Michael. (1999). Genuine savings rates in developing countries. *World Bank Economic Review, 13*(2), 333–356.

Hassan, Rashid; Scholes, Robert; & Ash, Neville. (Eds.). (2005). *Ecosystems and human well-being: Current state and trends: Vol 1* (Millennium Ecosystem Assessments series). Washington, DC: Island Press.

Lindahl, Erik R. (1958). Just taxation: A positive solution. In Richard Abel Musgrave & Alan T. Peacock (Eds.), *Classics in the theory of public finance.* London: Macmillan. Translated from the original article in Swedish, published in 1919.

Millennium Ecosystem Assessment (MEA). (2003). *Ecosystems and human well-being.* Washington, DC: Island Press.

Myers, Norman, & Kent, Jennifer. (2000). *Perverse subsidies: How tax dollars undercut our environment and our economies.* Washington, DC: Island Press.

Pagiola, Stefano; Landell-Mills, Natasha; & Bishop, Joshua. (2002). Making market-based mechanisms work for forests and people. In

Stefano Pagiola, Joshua Bishop & Natasha Landell-Mills (Eds.), *Selling forest environmental services: Market-based mechanisms for conservation and development*. London: Earthscan.

Pagiola, Stefano; Rios, Ana R.; & Arcenas, Agustin. (2008). Can the poor participate in payments for environmental services? Lessons from the silvopastoral project in Nicaragua. *Environment and Development Economics*, *13*(3), 299–326.

Pattanayak, Subhrendu K., & Butry, David T. (2005). Spatial complementarity of forests and farms: Accounting for ecosystem services. *American Journal of Agricultural Economics*, *87*(4), 995–1008.

Pattanayak, Subhrendu K., & Kramer, Randall A. (2001). Worth of watersheds: A producer surplus approach for valuing drought mitigation in Eastern Indonesia. *Environment and Development Economics*, *6*(1), 123–146.

Repetto, Robert; Magrath, William; Wells, Michael; Beer, Christine; & Rossini, Fabrizio. (1989). *Wasting assets: Natural resources and the National Income Accounts*. Washington, DC: World Resources Institute.

Ricketts, Taylor H.; Daily, Gretchen C.; Ehrlich, Paul R.; & Michener, Charles D. (2004). Economic value of tropical forests in coffee production. *Proceedings of the National Academy of Sciences*, *101*(34), 12579–12582.

Ricketts, Taylor H., et al. (2008). Landscape effects on crop pollination services: Are there general patterns? *Ecology Letters*, *11*(5), 499–515.

Sachs, Jeffrey D. (2008). *Common wealth: Economics for a crowded planet*. New York: Penguin Press.

Sachs, Jeffrey D.; Gallup, John Luke; & Mellinger, Andrew. (1998). Geography and economic development. In Boris Pleskovic & Joseph E. Stiglitz (Eds.), *Annual World Bank Conference on Development Economics*. Washington, DC: World Bank.

Smith, Adam. (1977). *An inquiry into the nature and causes of the wealth of nations*. Chicago: University of Chicago Press. (First published in 1776.)

Solorzano, Raul, et al. (1991). *Accounts overdue: Natural resource depreciation in Costa Rica*. Washington, DC: World Resources Institute.

Tomich, Thomas P.; van Noordwijk, Meine; & Thomas, David E. (2004). Environmental services and land use change: Bridging the gap between policy and research in Southeast Asia. *Agriculture Ecosystems & Environment*, *104*(1), 229–244.

Tomich, Thomas P., et al. (2005). *Forest and agroecosystem tradeoffs in the humid tropics*. Nairobi, Kenya: Alternatives to Slash-and-Burn Programme.

Vincent, Jeffery R.; Ali, Rozali Mohamed; & Associates. (1997). *Environment and development in a resource-rich economy: Malaysia under the new economic policy*. Cambridge, MA: Harvard Institute for International Development.

World Commission on Environment and Development. (1987). *Our common future*. New York: Oxford University Press.

Nuclear Power

Debate about the use of nuclear technology (and its destructive and constructive capabilities) continues to rage more than sixty-five years after the United States used nuclear bombs in World War II. Energy is a basic need of human civilization, and scientists have long viewed nuclear power as a sustainable option—creating little immediate pollution and using only small amounts of fuel to make massive amounts of power. Nuclear energy, however, is once again under public scrutiny. Many observers fear that nuclear power may become too expensive for some nations—particularly the developing nations it could benefit most.

When the first nuclear weapons exploded over Japan in 1945, observers all over the world knew that human life had changed in an instant. In the years since, nuclear technology has struggled to define itself as a public good when the public has seemed more inclined to view it as an evil. Its proponents argue that the electricity that nuclear reactors generate has the capacity to power the world more cleanly than any other resource. Opponents are less sure.

As the debate rages, nuclear power has become an increasingly important part of international dynamics: it can liberate nations from the need to trade in fossil fuels, allowing them to acquire inexpensive power that might advance society in important ways. At the same time, however, nations in Africa elect to receive nuclear waste from France and elsewhere, which could ultimately have negative health implications for an entire region.

As an energy source or as a weapon, atomic technology has remained one of the most important transborder issues since the mid-1900s.

Its Beginning as a Bomb

By the late 1930s, World War II threatened the global order. Leaders of every nation were searching for any edge that would help them defeat enemy forces. In Germany, leaders believed that nuclear technology might be a decisive force in the war effort. In reaction, scientists in the United States enlisted the German-born US physicist Albert Einstein to write a letter about their research to President Franklin D. Roosevelt to stress the technology's potential—particularly if the enemy developed it. Roosevelt authorized government funding for atomic research in October 1939 (Boyer 1994, 36–37).

Eventually science and the military would unite in a way never before seen. Scientists first needed to demonstrate the viability of an atomic reaction, however. In 1940, the US physicists Enrico Fermi and Leo Szilard received government support to construct a reactor at Columbia University, while other reactor experiments took place at the University of Chicago. By December 1942, Fermi achieved what scientists considered the first self-sustained nuclear reaction. With the war raging in Europe, it was time to test the reaction out of doors, a process that would greatly increase the scope and scale of the experiment.

Under the leadership of General Leslie Groves in February 1943, the US military acquired over 200,000 hectares of land near Hanford, Washington (in the arid and sparsely populated eastern half of the state), one of three primary US locations selected for Project Trinity. Hanford used water power to separate plutonium and produce the grade necessary for weapons use while Oak Ridge in Tennessee coordinated the production of uranium. Each production facility then fueled the heart of

174

the undertaking, located in Los Alamos, New Mexico, under the direction of the US physicist J. Robert Oppenheimer (Hughes 1989, 143–145).

Oppenheimer supervised the team of nuclear theoreticians who would devise the formulas necessary to produce atomic reactions within a weapon. Scientists from various fields participated in this complex theoretical mission. After theories were debated and materials delivered, the project became one of assembling and testing the technology in the form of a bomb. This work had to take place within the vast Los Alamos compound under complete secrecy (Hughes 1989, 143–145).

By 1944, World War II had wrought terrible destruction on the world. Although the European theater of war would soon close with Germany's surrender, the US atomic project forged ahead. Japan refused to surrender the Pacific theater, propelling the United States and Japan forward in a terrifying game of brinksmanship that would culminate in the Japanese cities Hiroshima and Nagasaki becoming live test laboratories of atomic explosions. The US bomber *Enola Gay* released a uranium bomb on Hiroshima on 6 August 1945, and the aircraft *Bock's Car* released a plutonium bomb on Nagasaki three days later. Death toll estimates vary between 150,000 and 300,000, most of whom were Japanese civilians. The atomic age, and life with the bomb, had begun.

Atomic Futures

Experiments and tests with nuclear and hydrogen bombs continued for nearly twenty years after World War II. Many of the scientists who worked on the original experiments, however, envisioned nonmilitary applications for the technology. Oppenheimer eventually felt that the bomb changed the public's attitude toward scientific exploration. "We have made a thing," he said in a 1946 speech, "a most terrible weapon, that has altered abruptly and profoundly the nature of the world . . . a thing that by all the standards of the world we grew up in is an evil thing" (Boyer 1994, 95–96).

Many scientists involved believed that atomic technology required controls unlike those of any previous innovation. As a result, shortly after the bombings, a movement began to establish a global board of scientists who, with no political affiliation, would administer the technology. Wresting control of this new tool for global influence from the US military, however, proved impossible. The US Atomic Energy Commission (AEC), formed in 1946, placed the US military and governmental authority in control of the weapons technology and other potential uses for the technology. With the "nuclear trump card," the United States catapulted to the top of global leadership.

In the 1950s, scientists applied nuclear reaction to peaceful purposes, notably power generation. The nuclear reaction required is a fairly simple process: similar to power generators that use fossil fuel, nuclear plants use thermal energy to turn turbines that generate electricity. The thermal energy comes from nuclear fission, which occurs when a neutron that a uranium nucleus emits then strikes another uranium nucleus, which then emits more neutrons and emits more heat as it breaks apart. If the new neutrons strike other nuclei, self-sustaining chain reactions take place. These chain reactions are the source of the nuclear energy, which then heats water to power the turbines.

Soon thereafter, the AEC seized this sensible application and began plans for "domesticating the atom." It was quite a leap, though, to make the US public comfortable with the most destructive technology ever known. The AEC and other organizations sponsored a barrage of popular articles concerning a future in which atomic bombs were used to create roads and radiation was employed to cure cancer (Boyer 1994).

The atomic future the media presented included images of atomic-powered agriculture and automobiles. Optimistic projections envisioned vast amounts of energy being harnessed, without reliance on limited natural resources like coal or oil. For many US citizens, this new technology meant control of everyday life; for the administration of US president Dwight Eisenhower, the technology meant expansion of US economic and commercial capabilities.

As the Cold War took shape around nuclear weapons, the Eisenhower administration looked for ways to define a domestic role for nuclear power, even as Soviet missiles threatened everyone in the United States. Project Plowshares grew out of the administration's effort to turn the destructive weapon into a domestic power producer. The list of possible applications was awesome: laser-cut highways would pass through mountains; nuclear-powered greenhouses built by federal funds in the Midwest would enhance crop production; and irradiated soils would simplify weed and pest management. Although domestic nuclear power production, with the help of massive federal subsidies, would prove to be the long-term product of government effort, the atom could never fully escape its dangerous military capabilities, which were most apparent when nuclear power plants experienced accidents.

Accidents Fuel Public Doubt

Nuclear power became increasingly popular in the 1970s, despite several nuclear power plant accidents and mounting criticism about the technology's safety. In 1979, the

United States experienced its first nuclear accident in a residential area outside Harrisburg, Pennsylvania. The accident at Three Mile Island (TMI) nuclear power plant fundamentally altered the landscape of US power generation. Although TMI involved only a relatively minor release of radioactive gas, panic ripped through the state, and Harrisburg was partially evacuated (Hampton 2001, 23–25).

While the international community took notice of the TMI accident, there was not a widespread perception that the accident gravely threatened the world. The world's other superpower had even greater difficulty with its atomic industry, which was plagued by accidents throughout this era. None, however, compared to the Chernobyl meltdown that occurred in Ukraine in 1986. During a routine test, the plant's fuel elements ruptured and caused an explosive force of steam that burst the cover plate off the reactor, releasing fission products into the atmosphere. A second blast released burning fuel from the core and created a massive explosion that burned for nine days. Experts estimate that the accident released thirty to forty times more radioactivity than the atomic bombs dropped on Hiroshima and Nagasaki. Hundreds of people died in the months after the accident, and hundreds of thousands of Ukrainians and Russians had to abandon entire cities (Black 2006, 197–198).

The implications of nuclear weapons and nuclear power had already become a great source of interest to environmental organizations before Chernobyl. After Chernobyl, however, international environmental organizations such as Greenpeace dubbed nuclear power a transborder environmental disaster waiting to happen. Yet, interestingly, even within the environmental movement, nuclear power maintained significant support due to its reputation as a clean source of energy. Whereas almost every other method for producing large amounts of electricity emits smoke or other pollutants, nuclear power creates only water vapor. This view consistently overlooked the hazardous waste produced. When the public worried about nuclear power, it was primarily because of the misunderstanding that it could behave like a nuclear detonation (Josephson 2000, 184).

International Expansion Checked by Events

Although these accidents decreased the US domestic appetite for nuclear power generation, the international community refused to judge the technology so quickly. Since the early 1990s, nuclear power has become one of the world's fastest-growing sources of electricity. In the first decade of the twenty-first century, nations that depended on nuclear power for at least one-quarter of their electricity included Belgium, Bulgaria, Hungary, Japan, Lithuania, Slovakia, South Korea, Sweden, Switzerland, Slovenia, and Ukraine (IAEA 2010).

The international trend, however, abruptly paused in 2011 with the dramatic events at the Fukushima Daiichi reactor in Japan. On 11 March 2011, an earthquake led to a tsunami whose tides overwhelmed coastal areas of Japan, including the nuclear reactors at the Fukushima facility. Of its six reactors, three are known to have experienced full meltdowns. The immediate emergency brought great confusion and, ultimately, wholesale evacuation of a twenty-kilometer area. The Fukushima disaster focused attention on the need to position reactors properly; for many observers, however, the event presented additional evidence that this technology was not suitable for domestic use. Could nations ever feel confident that they had considered every possible variable that a nuclear reactor could suffer?

In response to the Fukushima disaster, Germany instituted plans to close all of its reactors by 2022, and Japan took all fifty-four of its reactors out of service. In each case, the nation's decision carries dramatic economic implications. Germany and Japan have committed to pay to import more of their energy supplies, while other nations (including Russia for natural gas, and France and the Czech Republic for nuclear-generated electricity) will benefit by becoming lucrative energy suppliers. Only a year prior, the prospect of nuclear power offered more energy autonomy for many energy-intensive nations, including the United States, China, India, Brazil, Japan, Germany, and France. Developing this infrastructure appeared to assure nations of a strong scenario for energy security before 2010. Today, however, the risk of the next possible accident constrains the industry.

The wild card that could restore nuclear power's promise, according to some, is technological innovation. While engineers very likely may improve their siting of reactors and better prepare for the next tsunami, nuclear energy seems to be stained in the mind of international consumers by its potential—albeit slight—for cataclysm. Perhaps the technology will rise again as collective memory of the 2011 event in Japan begins to fade and the reality of sustainable energy development re-emerges. Given the increased issues of safety and security, however, the cost of new reactors may prove prohibitive for most nations.

Nuclear Weapons and the Balance of International Peace

According to the Bulletin of the Atomic Scientists, nine countries possess nuclear weapons capability—the United States, China, France, Russia, Britain, India, Pakistan, Israel, and North Korea—and thirty nations have some 440 commercial nuclear power reactors. Currently, nations are building fewer nuclear power plants than were under construction during the 1970s and 1980s, but the newer plants are much more efficient and capable of producing significantly more power. Additionally, nuclear power is a source for needs other than public electricity. In addition to commercial nuclear power plants, more than 280 research reactors are operating in fifty-six countries, with more on the way. These reactors have many uses, including research and training and the production of medical and industrial isotopes. Reactors are also used for marine propulsion, particularly in submarines. Over 150 ships of many varieties, including submarines, are propelled by more than 200 nuclear reactors.

Nuclear power has also become a volatile tool of international politics. Nations such as North Korea and Iran have used their pursuit of purportedly peaceful nuclear technology to raise the ire of many Western nations in hopes of forcing them into negotiations. Particularly in the case of Iran, many nations are suspicious of its claims

of "peaceful" uses. Fearing their own security, Israel and other nations have demanded that Iran be prohibited from developing new nuclear technology of any sort. These fears seem to have made it more attractive for rogue nations to increase the threat level.

Outlook

Regardless of the use to which it is put, nuclear energy continues to be plagued by its most nagging side effect: even if the reactor works perfectly for its service lifetime, the nuclear process generates dangerous waste. In fact, reactor wastes from spent fuel rods are believed to remain toxic to humans for thousands of years. At present, each nuclear nation makes its own arrangements for the waste. US nuclear utilities now store radioactive waste at more than seventy locations while they await authorization of an effort to construct and open a nuclear waste repository inside Nevada's Yucca Mountain. This decades-long controversy was most recently defunded in 2010 on the federal level, leaving the United States with no specific strategy for its waste storage.

Internationally, the situation is not much clearer. Opponents in Germany have obstructed nuclear waste convoys, and shipments of plutonium-bearing waste to Japan have met similar dispute. Nuclear power appears desirable for many developed societies until the time comes to contend with the waste. Some observers have voiced concern that less-developed nations will offer themselves as waste dumps for more-developed nations. The income from such an arrangement may be too much to turn down for many nations.

Rising energy prices of all sorts, however, bring the nuclear industry robust interest in the twenty-first century. In particular, new attention is focused on reprocessing used nuclear materials. In this way, the very idea of "nuclear waste" is redefined. Proponents argue that there is no such thing as waste if the spent rods can be reprocessed to fuel other types of plants. These efforts are particularly advanced in France, the global leader in nuclear power (IAEA 2010).

The most sustainable energy future likely includes nuclear power. Despite the Fukushima event, China has twenty-five nuclear power reactors under development and the United States recently approved the construction of its first two reactors since TMI. The industry, however, must invest in developing technologies that ameliorate the shortcomings that have nagged the utility since it began commercial production. Facilitating this international effort, the International Framework for Nuclear Energy Cooperation, originally established in 2006, comprises twenty-five partner countries, twenty-eight observer and candidate partner countries, and three international organization observers. Controversy in the United States erupted in 2012 when President Barack Obama nominated a geologist to oversee the Nuclear Regulatory Commission. Normally, this post would be held by a representative of the utility industry; by nominating Allison Macfarlane, Obama emphasized the issue of waste and its long-term geological implications.

In the energy industry, many continue to believe that nuclear power remains the best hope to power the future. In addition, in nations with scarce supplies of energy resources, nuclear power—even with its related concerns—remains the most affordable alternative and possibly the most sustainable energy for the future.

Brian BLACK
Pennsylvania State University

See also Energy Efficiency; Geoengineering; Natural Capital; Progress; Waste—Engineering Aspects

FURTHER READING

Adelstein, Jake. (2012). *Reconstructing 3/11*. New York: Abiko Free Press.

Black, Brian. (2006). *Nature and environment in twentieth-century American life*. New York: Greenwood.

Boyer, Paul. (1994). *By the bomb's early light*. Chapel Hill: University of North Carolina Press.

Brennan, Timothy J., et al. (1996). *A shock to the system: Restructuring America's electricity industry*. Washington, DC: Resources for the Future.

Brower, Michael. (1992). *Cool energy: Renewable solutions to environmental problems* (Rev. ed.). Cambridge, MA: MIT Press.

Cantelon, Philip, & Williams, Robert C. (1982). *Crisis contained: The Department of Energy at Three Mile Island*. Carbondale: Southern Illinois University Press.

Cooke, Stephanie. (2009). *In mortal hands: A cautionary history of the nuclear age*. New York: Bloomsbury.

Darst, Robert G. (2001). *Smokestack diplomacy: Cooperation and conflict in East-West environmental politics*. Cambridge, MA: MIT Press.

The Economist. (2012, March 12). Nuclear energy: The dream that failed. Retrieved June 12, 2012, from http://www.economist.com/node/21549098

Erikson, Kai. (1994). *A new species of trouble: The human experience of modern disasters*. New York: W. W. Norton.

Garwin, Richard L., & Charpak, Georges. (2001). *Megawatts and megatons: A turning point in the nuclear age*. New York: Knopf.

Hampton, William. (2001). *Meltdown: A race against nuclear disaster at Three Mile Island: A reporter's story*. Cambridge, MA: Candlewick Press.

Hughes, Thomas P. (1983). *Networks of power: Electrification in Western society, 1880–1930*. Baltimore, MD: Johns Hopkins University Press.

Hughes, Thomas P. (1989). *American genesis*. New York: Penguin Books.

International Atomic Energy Agency (IAEA). (2010). *International status and prospects of nuclear power: 2010 edition*. Retrieved July 23, 2012, from www.iaea.org/Publications/Booklets/NuclearPower/np10.pdf

Josephson, Paul R. (2000). *Red atom: Russia's nuclear power program from Stalin to today*. New York: W. H. Freeman.

Mahaffey, James. (2009). *Atomic awakening: A new look at the history and future of nuclear power*. New York: Pegasus.

May, Elaine Tyler. (1988). *Homeward bound*. New York: Basic Books.

May, Ernest R. (1993). *American Cold War strategy*. Boston: Bedford Books.

McNeill, J. R. (2000). *Something new under the sun: An environmental history of the twentieth-century world*. New York: Norton.

Melosi, Martin V. (1985). *Coping with abundance: Energy and environment in industrial America*. New York: Alfred A. Knopf.

Moorhouse, John C. (Ed.). (1986). *Electric power: Deregulation and the public interest*. San Francisco: Pacific Research Institute for Public Policy.

Nye, David E. (1990). *Electrifying America: Social meanings of a new technology*. Cambridge, MA: MIT Press.

Poole, Robert W., Jr. (Ed.). (1985). *Unnatural monopolies: The case for deregulating public utilities*. Lexington, MA: Lexington Books.

Smil, Vaclav. (1988). *Energy in China's modernization: Advances and limitations*. Armonk, NY: M. E. Sharpe.

Smil, Vaclav. (1994). *Energy in world history*. Boulder, CO: Westview Press.

Tucker, William. (2008). *Terrestrial energy: How nuclear energy will lead the green revolution and end America's energy odyssey*. New York: Bartleby.

Weiner, Douglas R. (1988). *Models of nature: Ecology, conservation, and cultural revolution in Soviet Russia*. Bloomington: Indiana University Press.

Population

The increase of their own numbers has always interested humans. With billions of people in today's environmentally challenged world and hundreds of thousands added each day, population growth is among the most significant issues facing humanity today. All environmental problems—climate change; water, energy, and food security; and the overextraction of the world's natural resources—connect to human numbers. Uncertainties cloud the future of population, including global migration, the spread of diseases such as HIV/AIDS, and the way in which family planning is funded (or not). When women have the power to make their own decisions on childbearing, population growth slows.

Many doubt that we need to worry about population growth. Humanity has been growing steadily for centuries. If population growth is a bomb, as some have suggested, it seems to be a dud. Indeed, so dramatic have been the changes in childbearing in recent years, with the spread of effective modern contraception—supplemented in many countries by safe and legal abortion services—that the worry has shifted to countries like Japan and several in Europe (such as Italy) where population has begun to ebb, or to nations that will need to draw many more immigrants to avoid imminent demographic decline.

It's almost amusing to see this new phase of "population crisis" based not on growth but on decline. The likelihood of future decreases in population drives far more writing, broadcasting, and blogging than does population growth, despite the fact that growth remains the overwhelming global dynamic and probably will for decades to come. On any given day, after all, more than twice as many people worldwide begin their lives

(373,000) as reach life's end (159,000) (UN DESA 2007). That's cold comfort all the same in countries from Spain to South Korea, where women are having little more than one child on average. Politicians and demographers worry about the future of such countries' retirement programs, the vibrancy of their economies, and their capacity to project military power or defend their territories.

Author Ben Wattenberg, senior fellow at the American Enterprise Institute in Washington DC, is right that, when given the choice, women typically decide to have fewer kids. In every country in which a variety of contraception options is readily accessible and backed up by safe abortion for the inevitable cases of contraceptive failure, women average roughly two children or less—barely replacing themselves and their partners, and signaling a future of gradual population decline if there is no net immigration.

But Wattenberg is shortsighted when he implies that more people equal greater prosperity. What happens in societies in which people younger than thirty vastly outnumber those older, and the number of workers always outpaces the numbers of jobs? Why do we face an explosion of dangerous infectious diseases that no one had heard of thirty years ago?

Our numbers take on special urgency as we face the reality that through human-induced climate change we are turning our long-hospitable home into a harsh and alien place, a "different planet" in the words of leading climatologist James Hansen of NASA (Revkin 2007). It is the global transformation our descendants are least likely to forgive, whatever rates of economic growth they may manage to record in the insubstantial calculus of monetary currency. And of all the threats the world faces, other than nuclear war, climate change poses the greatest risks to humanity, perhaps even posing the danger that some future generation will fail to renew our species through parenthood. Human annihilation probably isn't at the forefront of the minds of most women contemplating whether or not to have a child, but their own prospects, and those of their hypothetical children, factor heavily in the decision. Those opportunities and risks are clearly tied to the condition of the world in which they live and the number of other people trying to navigate it.

Bearing Wanted Children

Women aren't seeking more children, but more for their children, and we can be thankful for that. Avoiding unintended pregnancy and childbearing is an essential strategy for achieving the dreams that women hold for their children. Women who aspire to be mothers want to bear wanted children and nurture them to adulthood, with the best possible future in mind. This leads to two questions: What effects do more people have on the world? And what effect does more reproductive autonomy for women have on the number of children they have?

These questions are as old as humanity, and to fully address them we need to start at the very beginning. How can we begin to guess how population will affect our future without grappling with how it shaped our past? How strong is the link between women's control over their reproduction and low fertility? What connection might women's standing in society have to the development of culture and civilization in the past? And how might better access to contraception and greater equality between women and men influence the future of population?

Exploring the dynamic triangle of women's lives, human numbers, and nature may shed light on history and the likely future of women's opportunities, rights, and status. Just as importantly, it could help answer increasingly urgent questions about humanity's place in our fast-changing home. For even if there has been no single, global demographic detonation, that's no inoculation against the risks associated with a large and still-growing global population.

Limits to Growth

"Limits to growth" hasn't been a very popular idea since a book with that title brought the scorn of economists and cornucopian thinkers in the 1970s (Meadows et al. 1972). The idea that such constraints are out there, however, is coming back. There's not enough water for those alive today in the Horn of Africa, not enough atmosphere for those alive on Earth to use fossil fuels the way that people in the United States or Australia or Canada do. In Afghanistan and more than a dozen countries in sub-Saharan Africa, ill health, hunger, and violence make

youth as risky a phase of life today as it was in Charles Dickens's London. Parents need to have more than three children per woman to replace themselves in such populations, since infants have only a two-thirds probability of making it to age thirty.

While it's too simplistic to blame rapid population growth for the high death rates in these countries, overcrowding is likely one of several interacting factors. Parents in Rwanda and Malawi, for example, divide their subsistence farms between so many sons that each tiny plot can barely support a family. Many in the younger generations look for alternative livelihoods, but these aren't easy to find in either country. Malawi suffers from recurrent famine, and more than one in three newborns fails to make it to mid-reproductive age. Also some see the 1994 genocidal war of Rwanda as an example of what can happen when population densities reach intolerable levels in countries that lack decent government and decent economic options for their citizens (Diamond 2005, 311–328).

Even when birthrates hit the critical replacement value, whatever it is in a specific population, it takes time for human numbers to stabilize. Population change has its own momentum. If most parents are members of a "youth bulge" in the population—maybe they're baby boomers—then even if they average 2.1 children per couple the sum of all people will keep growing. Only a small group of older people is leaving the population, while a big, bawling, baby-boom "echo" is being born, comparable in number to their parents. Until deaths equal births, with the generations of reproducers about equal in size to those dying, the beat of growth goes on.

Below-Replacement Fertility Levels

Some writers fear that below-replacement fertility—any level too low to replace parents in a population—amounts to a sentence of demographic self-extinction. Actually, below-replacement fertility has been nearly as common in human experience as above-replacement fertility. For our species, obviously, family sizes too small to keep population from shrinking have never been fatal and, except for some small groups, it rarely has lasted long enough to threaten survival. Most countries today with fertility rates below replacement are still growing demographically, generally due to still-young populations or net immigration or both; although, among the dozen countries with the smallest families, population stability or decline is indeed the rule. Moreover, it's inaccurate to say that birthrates in low-fertility countries are in any kind of free fall. Most countries that have reached 1.1 births per woman have experienced leveling and even slight rises in fertility, suggesting that 1.1 births may be something of a fertility floor.

To be sustainable, then, a population will need some, but not too many, three-child families. Human numbers are staggeringly sensitive to small differences in fertility. Two or three thousand years with 1.8 children per woman, and vines start to snake up vacant skyscrapers and break the windows. The same few millennia with 2.4 children per woman, and people are stacked up on each other's heads. Such sensitivity to small differences in fertility is one reason demographic trends and data merit attention. However you feel about population as an issue, whether the Earth holds 5 billion or 15 billion people in 2100 will have a lot do with how rapidly and dangerously the global climate warms, the survival of anything we can call wild, and much more besides.

Wild Cards: Migration, HIV/AIDS, and Family Planning

There are three demographic forces that are neither well understood nor well integrated into demographers' analyses and their projections of future population: migration, the containment of HIV/AIDS, and the future of family planning.

Migration

Migration, in particular, is not well understood by demographers. An intellectual chasm separates scholars of historic human migration, most of whom see the process as linked to variations in local and regional population growth, and those who study contemporary international and *internal* (domestic) migration. Some experts in international migration argue that population growth or high density does not play a significant role in spurring people to move from one place to another. Migration is, in this view, chiefly a function of globalization, ease of travel, and the uneven pace of development. People, like capital, flow from areas of low to high opportunity regardless of what's happening to population (Zlotnik 2004). (Zlotnik actually reports a slight correlation between fertility rates in migrant-sending countries and the volume of emigration from these countries, but she judges it insignificant.)

No one doubts, however, that migrants contribute to the population growth of the countries to which they move, and they often help fill gaps in the receiving countries' age structures as well. Japan and the European nations that face the prospect of declining ratios of workers to retirees could at least slow this decline by accepting many more immigrants than they do today.

In an increasingly interconnected world, with older and wealthier populations close to younger and poorer ones, large numbers of people will likely be on the move for years to come. Eventually, however, fading job prospects or problems related to ever denser populations—rising costs of housing and transportation, for example—could dampen immigration into some countries; so, of course, could improving job prospects in the countries from which large streams of people emigrate. Few people migrate to satisfy a lifelong aspiration or a yen for travel. What woman, giving birth, hopes her child will grow up and move to another country? Yet humans have always migrated and no doubt always will. Best would be a world where development levels are roughly equal, where few people are desperate to leave their countries of birth, and where migration to most countries is safe, legal, and in rough equilibrium with emigration out of them. That world is possible, but not yet in sight.

HIV/AIDS

The second demographic wild card is the global HIV/AIDS pandemic, the future of which depends on how billions of people have sex over the next several decades and on whether governments get serious about preventing transmission. Already AIDS deaths exceed those of the Black Death of fourteenth-century Europe (when world population was a fraction of today's size). In southern Africa, Swaziland and Lesotho may now be losing population, no doubt the first countries on the continent to do so other than through war. Even more dramatic than population decline is an unprecedented hollowing out of age structure projected for the next few decades in these and other countries devastated by HIV. The ranks of the middle-aged appear likely to be thinned out, as though by a dark intelligence aiming at the most productive members of society. In most of the continent the sheer power of high birthrates is greater than that of deaths from AIDS, but other countries may join Swaziland and Lesotho in time.

Population activists strive to assure that falling birthrates, outcomes of intentional reproduction rather than inability to bear wanted children, are the overwhelming factor in slowing or reversing population growth. Population decline stemming mostly from premature death or involuntary infertility would be no sane person's triumph.

Reproductive health is a concept that elegantly brings all this together: intentional pregnancy, health care for mother and child, and prevention of the sexually transmitted infections that can contribute to AIDS deaths or infertility. Perhaps understandably, governments and international agencies spend almost all new funding for reproductive health on HIV/AIDS prevention and treatment. Few doubt that HIV/AIDS deserves more money and attention than it receives even now. But a comparable attention to broader reproductive health would combat HIV/AIDS as well as other sexually transmitted infections. It would also improve access to family planning services, which are not only needed for HIV prevention but also lead to positive demographic change.

Funding Family Planning

Finally, there's a third wild card: the future of support from the world's governments for funding family planning. Demographers assume that birthrates will keep drifting downward, as they've been trending for decades, but there are no guarantees. In some countries in Africa there's scarcely a flicker of the fertility revolution sweeping the rest of the world. Women in Niger, for example, have 7.6 children on average, down from 8 in the 1970s, but actually fewer than the 8.2 children women reported as ideal in a 1998 survey. Their male partners dreamt at that time of having 10.8 children each, and those with more than one wife considered 15.3 children ideal (CARE International/Niger and Demographic and Health Surveys 1999, 114).

These are extremes in the fertility spectrum, with family-size ideals trending downward in most of the world's remaining high-fertility countries. There's good reason to believe that many women in high-fertility countries would welcome smaller families but don't have ready access to birth control or health services. For many developing countries, especially those in sub-Saharan Africa with large rural populations and financially strapped governments, it's no easy matter to build clinics and dispensaries, keep them consistently stocked with a full range of contraceptives, and staff them all with capable health care providers. The world population projections produced by the United Nations, and relied upon by journalists and analysts, are based on the assumption that governments are making the right investments and will assure that the needed health care personnel and contraceptives are available. That's rosy and wrong: the gaps remain huge and hard to bridge, especially in rural areas, where 57 percent of the population of the developing world still lives.

Demographic possibilities for the next few centuries range from human extinction (global nuclear war, collision with a comet, a species-wide pandemic, etc.) to the theoretical "constant-fertility" population of trillions if average family size stays where it is today. But the standard UN projections, capably produced by expert demographers, are useful for thinking about the future in a world without major surprises: somewhere around 9 billion people by midcentury, and another billion more or less by 2100.

Zen and the Art of Population Maintenance

It's not hard to see why population size is not a pressing day-to-day concern among the staffs of reproductive health clinics. It can be difficult to keep a focus on slowing population growth, if you had one to begin with, while working with people, especially people all over the world. Faces are so unique, personalities so distinct, babies so appealing, and human beings so essentially interesting that any visceral feeling that there are just *too many people* often fades as the work proceeds. And with population size itself so sensitive and controversial, a common strategy for traveling through this minefield is to simply ignore the issue altogether.

This scarcely means that the rest of us need to ignore human numbers. Population is too vital a human issue to be swept under rugs for long. Some writers refer to populations in many developing countries as "out of control," while those of most industrialized countries have been "successfully limited," or words to this effect. The reality is that *all* populations are out of control. None are limited. Not even in communist China can the government actually micromanage the reproductive decisions, let alone the reproductive *outcomes*, of millions of women and men. (China's one-child policy, introduced in 1979, became a national law in 2001; its application is stricter in urban areas, and more flexible in rural areas and among ethnic minorities.) Migration streams, too, have mostly mocked governmental efforts at control. What governments can do is establish the policies, set up the programs, and create the conditions under which population trends are likely to bend in good directions.

The best way to "control" population is to give up control, in fact to give control *away* to those who can best decide for themselves when to bear a child. Enlightenment will arrive only after one has given up the search, and positive population outcomes only after the forcing stops. It's worth considering where this Zen-like approach to population came from, where it has detoured, and where it is headed (Pirsig 1984).

A Brief History of Population Thinking

From at least the Axial Age (roughly 800 BCE to 200 BCE, a time when revolutions in thinking were happening simultaneously in China, India, and the Western world) until the late eighteenth century, most organized efforts to influence the size of populations aimed at boosting it. Women have been extolled, pressured, or coerced into having children early and often, whether or not they would have timed their own childbearing that way if left to their own devices (contraceptive or otherwise). But let's consider for a moment the strategies that have gained the greater attention since the English reverend and economist T. Robert Malthus (1766–1834) wrote, the kind designed to slow demographic growth by reducing family size and birthrates.

Malthus didn't have a distinct plan for addressing the forces behind his "principle of population." The first true promoter of actually *acting* on population issues appears to have been Francis Place (1771–1854), a self-educated son of the English working class. Married at age nineteen to a woman two years his junior, Place fathered fifteen children and lived in poverty. In late middle age he became the world's first birth control theorist and propagandist. In an 1822 book on Malthus's population principle, Place proposed substituting contraception for late marriage to moderate birthrates.

By joining Malthus in identifying population growth as a driver of poverty, Place proposed a function for population policy and for family planning that would both help and haunt the two concepts ever after. On the one hand, the alleviation of poverty has been one of the great endeavors of humanity since the French Revolution. If bringing population growth to an end could demonstrably help that cause, the future of the effort might be secure. If the goal was to eliminate not poverty but the poor themselves, on the other hand, only a handful of well-off misanthropes were likely to sign up for the cause.

Place did stress one value that underlies mainstream population policies up to the present: control of births not by government or other outsiders, but by women and couples themselves, "so that none," in Place's words, "need to have more [children] than they wish to have" (Speert 2004, 443). Yet some later theorists doubted that women could be trusted to actually *want* the small families needed to slow or end population growth. The US ecologist Garrett Hardin, who originated the concept of the *tragedy of the commons*, argued in 1980 that, "it is an empirical fact that in every country in the world the number of children wanted by the average family is greater than the number needed to produce population equilibrium in that nation" (1980, 118). Less than two decades later, the human reproduction scientist Malcolm Potts demonstrated that this was anything but an empirical fact; even as early as the 1960s, countries that provided relatively unconstrained access to family planning and safe abortion services saw fertility rates heading toward or even reaching replacement levels of just two children per woman (Potts 1997).

In stressing the childbearing intentions of couples themselves, however, Place established a standard for judging population-related policies and programs: their conformance with individual rights and choices. The word "voluntary" hardly does the concept justice. Do policies help women and their partners have children when and only when that is their intention, or do they hinder this reproductive autonomy? Had the early pioneers of birth control focused more on this distinction, which shines more brightly in our day than in theirs, they might have avoided some damaging detours and dangerous liaisons that have marred the struggle for universal access to family planning ever since.

Population Strategies

The United Nations, the United States Agency for International Development (USAID), and many of the world's governments have traditionally operated on an assumption that contrasted with the view of many population writers: that women able to decide at any given time whether to become pregnant would end up on average having two children. Even as early as the late 1960s, when Paul Ehrlich (author of *The Population Bomb*) and others were writing pessimistically about population growth, evidence was accumulating that this assumption was valid.

In 1969, one year after the world's governments declared the ability to freely plan one's family a human right, the United Nations launched a Fund for Population Activities to consolidate monies from donor governments and distribute them to family-planning programs in poor countries. For a decade or more, there wasn't much data to prove this was a canny strategy. Organizing, promoting, and providing family planning services is detail work, and the US government paid for reams of technical reports to work out the minutiae.

Despite the half loaf of imperfect programs, however, the neo-Malthusian model of "population control" actually began to work. Population was not really controlled, of course. It never is. But gradually, and then at accelerating speeds in several countries, use of contraceptives went up, average family size went down, and population growth rates slowed. The mostly Roman Catholic island nation of Malta followed Japan's track to replacement fertility in the 1960s. Thailand, Taiwan, Singapore, Hong Kong, South Korea, Tunisia, Sri Lanka, and Colombia experienced comparable fertility falls in the 1970s and 1980s. From the late 1980s to 2005, Iran's fertility plummeted from nearly six children per woman to two, after the country's Shia Muslim government ordered contraceptive counseling and provision for all newlyweds. And if Mexico once was characterized by large families, it is no longer: average fertility hovered in 2007 around 2.2 children per woman, leading some Mexican leaders to worry about population aging and even future decline. Stories of family-size decline are similar in Morocco, Indonesia, and many other countries still considered part of the developing world (UN DESA 2007, 73).

By the 1980s it was obvious that women and many of their partners wanted later pregnancies and fewer of them. Where governments introduced family planning programs, contraceptive use rose almost immediately, followed not long after by falling fertility and population growth rates. The correlation among the three—government commitment to family planning programs, contraceptive prevalence, and completed family size—is more consistent than the commonly cited one between girls' average years of completed education and how many children they end up having.

The difference that family planning programs have made to childbearing patterns—and the difference these have made to the world—are truly revolutionary. As revolutions go, however, this one has been pretty shy. No loyal constituency touts the fact that most acts of human sexual intercourse today are protected against the risk of conception. A handful of demographers and public health advocates point out that this means healthier mothers and children, fewer abortions, and more opportunities for women. Next to no one notices that the world's current total fertility rate (2.6 children per woman) is just one-quarter of a child above its replacement fertility rate (2.34, and much too high for comfort, since it is elevated from the theoretical norm of 2.05 to 2.1 by significant numbers of deaths among young people).

Policy makers and bureaucrats would have a hard time legislating as huge a change in childbearing patterns as has occurred voluntarily. China is a special case, with an ancient cultural preference for the collective over the individual good and a communist government acutely aware of the pressure the country's 1.34 billion people exert on its natural resources. Even China's low fertility, however, arguably owes more to a growing preference for small families—true among Chinese populations in Taiwan and in other countries as well—than the government's unevenly enforced one-child policy.

It's not even clear that falling birthrates are the result, as is often claimed, of "changing ideas about the family." Sure, some ideas have changed, but did women and their partners around the world suddenly decide in the last three decades that large families weren't such a great idea after all? Not likely. The history of women's efforts to prevent pregnancy suggests that few have ever actually wanted frequent childbearing and large families, unless to conform to cultural norms. When researchers Bamikale Feyisetan and John Casterline studied the growing use of contraceptives in Latin America, Asia, and Africa from the 1970s through the 1990s, they found that downshifts in desired family size were much less influential than satisfaction of long pent-up demand for small families. The demand to time reproduction was already there—who knows for how long?—when contraception became an option (Feyisetan and Casterline 2000).

The Return of Nature

The classical Greeks had an ambiguous relation to sex. Why, Greek men wondered, couldn't they just arrange with a priest to receive a son at the local temple and be done with the messy business of relating to women? This male discomfort with reproduction has helped shape population dynamics for a very long time; it's reflected in most of the world's great religions and in the modern culture of global commerce. That culture manages to shunt sexual and reproductive realities into the shadows, even while it uses adolescent sexual imagery to market products and equates population stability with the end of prosperity.

The skills human females developed to keep their offspring alive, from assisted birth to communicative group parenting, facilitated ancient bursts of population growth that eventually gave *Homo sapiens* earthly dominion. That growth helped give rise to art, technology, and new social organizations, but it also tended to push groups up against natural and social constraints. Women more than men understood the risks of childbearing during hard times—and the risks of frequent childbearing at all times.

Now the tide has indeed turned. Most women around the world use contraception, and women globally give birth to an average of just 2.6 children. Human population grows more slowly than it did in the 1970s, but nonetheless it surpassed 7 billion in 2012 in a rapidly warming world.

It's a good time to ask, what next? Will fertility move lower still? Will human population eventually peak and then subside, but with fast-changing national and ethnic balances because family size varies so much around the world? Or will governments and the public continue to lose interest in population and family planning, leaving fertility to settle about where it is and population to keep growing until rising death rates set in?

Possibilities we can imagine and work toward, as the British climate and energy specialist Michael Grubb has written, are "futures to guide us, not forecasts to fool us" (2004, 469).

Growth and Grandchildren

All historical eras are shaped by the material and environmental realities of their time. Our own reflects the adjustments society and nature have made to accommodate the unprecedented 7 billion human beings now alive.

And this is just where we are *today*, while the beat of growth goes on. Little if any of this would have transpired had human numbers peaked long ago. Such a peak might have occurred by now, even with the gains in life expectancy of the past century, if the status and

reproductive intentions of women had found consistent support rather than silence and censure.

Beginning little more than a century ago, social acceptance of contraception began to grow and to spread around the world. That led to dramatic declines in birthrates that gathered force as human population throttled past a few billion. Who knows how much closer we would be to a meltdown of Greenland's ice or the collapse of critical ocean fisheries had this collective wisdom—a public good derived from individuals acting in their private interest—not dampened the rise of population? Given the increasingly plausible threat of one or more interacting environmental catastrophes, the slowing of population growth is a triumph of human wisdom and good fortune. This realization is only slowly dawning, however, on the community of journalists and other opinion leaders.

The dominant concerns in many countries about population aging and decline are hardly baseless. These developments may well challenge societies. Populations may have more old people than young for a while, because yesterday's baby boomers are heading toward old age even as young women are having fewer children. Over time, however, extreme age disparities should subside as these large generations pass on, the more so when average fertility returns to close to two children per woman. Assuming it will.

What might eventually unfold is something far more appealing than continually aging societies: birth cohorts of consistently equal size across generations. The most demographically stable age structure for a population would be for each year's "class" of babies to be the same size as the one the year before, and ten, twenty-five, or even fifty years before. No single age group, young or old, would naturally claim any more of society's attention than any other, at least based on their numbers. That's a population structure worth striving for.

For now, population aging is the inevitable outcome of two of the most positive developments of modern times: longer life spans and the realized intentions of women to have fewer children, later in their lives. Modern views on human rights and equality hardly would have allowed most women to continue giving birth to many more children than they wanted. And populations hardly could have continued growing in the twenty-first century at the same torrid pace as in the middle decades of the twentieth. Some populations had to be the first to experience the leveling off of growth and then decline, and in most cases this has occurred with no significant increases in death rates. That's rare, maybe even unprecedented, in human history.

Humanity still grows by 78 million people annually—the rough equivalent of a new Texas, California, and Florida (or somewhat less than a new Turkey, Iran, or Germany) each year. Unless death rates rise catastrophically or birthrates plummet far more than anyone expects, the end of world population growth is still decades away.

What dominates our experience in the first decades of the third millennium are the technologies and institutions we have invented, disseminated, tinkered with, and improved over thousands of years to make human life on such scales possible. We've done well. Not only are more people alive than ever, but most of us live longer than our ancestors did. Quite a few of us spend our entire lives in comfort and with tools and toys that those ancestors never could have imagined.

Perils of Adaptation

Despite the sense of dread and certainty coming from doomsayers on population and the environment, there don't seem to be any bright ideas for accommodating a lot more people. The gap between those with high and low incomes seems to grow wider by the year, driven at least in part by three megatrends closely related to population growth: rising housing costs, rising energy costs, and falling paychecks for unspecialized low-wage labor.

The adaptations we make to adjust to the growth of population tend to become problems themselves. As housing costs rise, owners and renters alike find themselves searching farther from downtowns for a place to live. Morning rush hour increasingly begins in the dark hours before dawn, but there are only so many of those hours available. People get by with less sleep, but they can't get by without any (Weiss 2002). They pay for their longer commutes not only in lost time, but in greater use of gasoline—just as the cost per liter is climbing. That, too, is driven up by population and economic growth not only in fully developed nations such as the United States but halfway around the world, where most of the 2.54 billion people living in China and India would like—and increasingly can afford—to drive automobiles.

In economics as in nature, scale matters. Growth in working-age populations tends to push down wages for work that requires few specialized skills, as evidenced by factories and call centers of Asia, and lawns and offices of Los Angeles. Experts disagree about how strong this population-wage relationship is and how much of an economic problem results.

People feel the impacts of population growth all over the world. Even in western Europe, whose population grows by only 0.2 percent each year, centuries of much faster growth have left population density more than five times higher on average than in the United States. Truly wild land is all but nonexistent. If you can find a forest, the chances are good it's a rectangular field of trees machine-planted in orderly ranks.

The Future of Population

The upshot of this is that there's far less to fear from the possibility of population decline than from ongoing growth. Here we venture out on the limb of prediction, as it seems to be a stout branch. Very low fertility rates will bounce back to two-child-plus replacement values once populations actually decline significantly. That process is only just beginning, and only in a handful of countries. Thanks to immigration, the population momentum of past growth, and young age structures, the populations of most countries with subreplacement fertility are still growing. Others are just beginning to see their populations level off, and a few have seen some demographic erosion.

When population really does decline, however, the laws of supply and demand will mean that land and housing will become more affordable, while employers will more highly value scarce young workers. Contrast Italy, where 90 percent of those aged twenty to twenty-four live with their parents (is it any wonder that Italian women have an average of 1.3 children?), to societies in which young people of modest means have their choice of inexpensive fixer-uppers for homes (Martinelli 2003, 12). Unemployment will be lower, labor participation among adults of all ages and both sexes higher. Labor will be compensated more fairly. Savings rates will rise as older workers rely less on pay-as-you-go social security systems, which will evolve toward needs-based supplemental income programs as their revenue base fails to keep pace with entitlement payments. Legacies divided into fewer parts than ever before will convey even middle-class wealth down the generations.

Perhaps humanity will have succeeded in saving and healing much of nature and the environment. Perhaps women will feel they have not only economic security but also the support of their partners and communities. If so, very many women will want—and have—two or maybe three children over their lifetimes. Other women will settle for one, or none at all. Some will adopt rather than give birth. Some will take advantage of the improving technology of fertility enhancement. In a world of level and declining populations, intentional reproduction will mean never having to say you're sorry about your choices.

This looks like a world worth working toward, even if demography were unrelated to destiny. The vision won't address every population issue—or solve every environmental problem. Lower birth rates alone can't stop climate change. We'll still have to learn how to moderate our consumption of materials and energy, and to jump-start new technologies that conserve them. The pressures to emigrate to find decent jobs won't go away any time soon, although they may be easing in some countries—Mexico is the best example—where large proportions of young people are beginning to shrink at last. And we'll still have to coexist with widely varying views on abortion, which will always be an issue because there will always be a need for the procedure. Not everyone, of course, sees the logic of stressing both pregnancy prevention and safe options for terminating unwanted pregnancies as early as possible.

All of us will need to rise above our genes and their urge for self-replication. Is it critical that a "nation," however defined, survives for centuries or that one's daughter carry on one's genetic lineage? Some elemental urge within us says yes. But that desire implies an *us* that at some point confronts a human *them*. Families, tribes, ethnic groups, and nations have accomplished great things, but frankly, not lately. Maybe we should simply appreciate the cultural and historical value of these groups, rather than putting all our resources into securing their long-term institutional future at the expense of humanity's as a whole.

The clearest principle to guide us in the future is that those who bear children should be the ones, more than anyone else, to decide when to do so. The rest will work itself out. We will not self-destruct through too much reproduction, nor will we fade sadly away through too little. With a bit of luck, an understanding of our place in nature, and a grateful nod to the long line of successful mothers who preceded us, humanity's moment on this rich but finite planet instead may stretch out for longer than we can now imagine. Humanity really could be as countless as the stars—just not *all at once*, but over millennia to come. Wanting not more people, but more *for* all people, we might find ourselves at home again, with more nature than we thought possible, in an Eden we can keep.

Robert ENGELMAN
Worldwatch Institute

This article was adapted by the editors from Robert Engelman's book *More: Population, Nature, and What Women Want*. Copyright © 2008 Robert Engelman. Reproduced with kind permission of Island Press, Washington, DC. The editors are grateful to Dr. Engelman for his help with the article adaptation.

See also Aging; Collective Learning; Community; Economics, Steady State; Migration; Progress; Values

FURTHER READING

Cammack, Diana. (2001). *Malawi at the threshold: Resources, conflict and ingenuity in a newly democratic state.* Cambridge, MA: Committee on International Security Studies, American Academy of Arts and Sciences.

CARE International / Niger and Demographic and Health Surveys. (1999). *Enquête démographique et de santé: Niger 1998* [Demographics and health survey: Niger 1998]. Niamey, Niger: CARE International.

Diamond, Jared. (2005). *Collapse: How societies choose to fail or succeed.* New York: Viking.

Feyisetan, Bamikale, & Casterline, John B. (2000). Fertility preferences and contraceptive change in developing countries. *International Family Planning Perspectives, 26*(3), 100–109.

Gasana, James. (2002, October/November). Remember Rwanda? *World Watch, 15*(5), 24–33.

Grubb, Michael. (2004, April 1). Power to the people. *Nature, 428*(1), 469–470.

Hardin, Garrett. (1980). Second thoughts on "The Tragedy of the Commons." In Herman Daly (Ed.), *Economics, ecology, ethics: Essays toward a steady-state economy* (p. 118). New York: W. H. Freeman.

Homer-Dixon, Thomas. (2006, September). Review of *States, security, and civil strife in the developing world* by Colin H. Kahl. *Population and Development Review, 32*(3), 585–587.

Martinelli, Nicole. (2003, March 31). Why do they do it in the road? *Newsweek*, p. 12.

Meadows, Donella H.; Meadows, Dennis L.; Randers, Jørgen; & Behrens, William W., III. (1972). *The limits to growth: A report for the Club of Rome's Project on the Predicament of Mankind.* New York: Universe Books.

O'Connor, Anahad. (2004, June 29). Wakefulness finds a powerful ally. *New York Times*, p. D1.

Percival, Val, & Homer-Dixon, Thomas. (1996). Environmental scarcity and violent conflict: The case of Rwanda. *The Journal of Environment & Development, 5*(3), 270–291.

Pirsig, Robert. (1984). *Zen and the art of motorcycle maintenance: An inquiry into values.* New York: Bantam.

Potts, Malcolm. (1997, March). Sex and the birth rate. *Population and Development Review, 23*(1), 1–39.

Revkin, Andrew C. (2007, January 1). A new middle stance emerges in debate over climate. *New York Times*, p. A16.

Speert, Harold. (2004). *Obstetrics and gynecology: A history and iconography.* New York: Parthenon Publishing.

United Nations Department of Economic and Social Affairs (UN DESA), Population Division. (2007). *World population prospects: The 2006 revision*, highlights (Working Paper No. ESA/P/WP.202). Retrieved June 19, 2012, from http://www.un.org/esa/population/publications/wpp2006/WPP2006_Highlights_rev.pdf

van Ginneken, Jeroen K., & Wiegers, Margreet. (2005). Various causes of the 1994 genocide in Rwanda with emphasis on the role of population pressure (Presentation during the session on demography of political conflict and violence, annual meeting of the Population Association of America). Philadelphia, PA.

Weiss, Eric M. (2002, June 10). The coffee is hot, and so is pre-dawn business. *Washington Post*, p. A1.

Zlotnik, Hania. (2004). Population growth and international migration. In Douglas S. Massey & J. Edward Taylor (Eds.), *International migration: Prospects and policies* (pp. 13–34). Oxford, UK: Oxford University Press.

Progress

Progress (Latin: progressus) originally meant moving across country to a chosen destination. Progress toward individual betterment was a derivative meaning that entered the English language with John Bunyan's Pilgrim's Progress (1678). The idea that society as a whole might progress took shape during the Industrial Revolution. Technological "progress," especially that which has allowed humans to exploit resources and spread themselves more extensively and pollute more prodigiously, prompts the question: change is everywhere, but is it really for the better?

New awareness of ecology and the radical impact of recent human activity on other forms of life has raised new questions about human progress. The study of energy flows sustaining human activity offers a promising way to construct quantitative estimates of our quite extraordinary success in enlarging our ecological niche at the expense of other species. Moreover, human webs of communication, permitting more extensive and efficacious cooperation across time, seem responsible for the collective learning and the accumulation of skills that produced this amazing result. The extraordinary multiplication of human numbers has drawn attention to demography as a fundamental variable as well. More generally, recognition that we are inescapably part of much larger evolutionary processes—cosmological, terrestrial, biological, and human—invites a recasting of our ideas about progress to take account of processes of which humans were previously unaware, yet which influenced or even controlled what they were able to do.

Ever since 1492, when Renaissance-age Europeans first made contact with peoples in the Americas, advances of geographical and mathematical knowledge have accumulated rapidly. Scientific progress became obvious by 1687, when Isaac Newton (1642–1727) published mathematically formulated laws of motion, making eclipses as well as more ordinary movements of sun, moon, planets—and even cannonballs—predictable. Writers like the French scientist Bernard de Fontenelle (1657–1757) concluded that progress of knowledge was real and might be expected to continue indefinitely into the future, but unchanging laws of nature meant that human society as a whole would remain much as before.

As long as most people lived just about the same way their parents and grandparents had done, any other opinion would have seemed absurd. But beginning about 1750 a cluster of changes began in Great Britain, western Europe, and the northern American colonies that historians later called the Industrial Revolution. The central feature of that revolution was expanding the output of useful goods by using inanimate forms of power—first falling water, then coal and steam, and then electricity—to drive large, often complicated machines. As a flood of useful things began to come from such machines, human lives in these places began to change unmistakably, and sometimes for the better, as cheaper manufactured goods became available.

Engines of Change

But at first the biggest improvement for most people was not industrial at all. Rather, food supplies increased enormously in Europe due to the rapid spread of potato cultivation after 1763, when all the principal governments of the continent set out to imitate the Prussians who, fifteen years before, had pioneered official efforts to persuade peasants to plant their fallow fields with potatoes. Potatoes meant more work, since they had to be hoed in summer to remove weeds. But as long as enough hands could be found for that task, potatoes multiplied the amount of food European fields could produce without diminishing the grain harvest in the slightest. This, together with use of turnips and other fodder crops as a parallel alternative to fallowing, radically diminished age-old risks of famine and provoked two centuries of population growth for humans and for their domesticated animals. That in turn assured a supply of people, horses, and cattle for intensified cultivation in the European countryside, and soon provoked a surge of migrants looking for wage work in burgeoning industrial towns.

Economic expansion thus became self-sustaining, and as new styles of farming and new forms of industry spread, the daily experience of almost everyone in western Europe began to change in obvious ways. These novelties soon began to affect the entire world as well. Not all changes were for the better. Living conditions in crowded industrial cities were often horrible, and alternating patterns of boom and bust meant insecurity for all and inflicted severe suffering on unemployed wage earners. But new possibilities and cheaper goods were just as real. Think, for example, of what it meant for ordinary persons—especially those with small babies to swaddle and keep more or less clean—when, as the utopian socialist Robert Owen tells us in his autobiography (*The Life of Robert Owen Written by Himself*), in 1858 the cost of cotton cloth in England had shrunk to one-seventieth of what it had been sixty years before when he started work as a teenager. During that same life span, steam railways, introduced in 1825, drastically cheapened and sped up overland transport for goods and people, and after 1837 electric telegraphs allowed instant communication, at first only for a few, later for nearly anyone with an urgent message to send.

As significant novelties multiplied, it became obvious that human lives and the whole structure of society were changing as never before. Ever since, a cascade of new technologies, new products, and new experiences has continued and even accelerated, spreading from an initial focus in Great Britain and adjacent parts of Europe quite literally around the Earth.

As always, new possibilities brought new risks and damaged or destroyed old ways of life. Most of the time, most people welcomed enlarged possibilities and liked to have access to cheaper machine-made goods. Yet costs were real, too. Everywhere artisans found they could not compete with machine-made products, and old-fashioned agrarian empires found that they had to allow European goods, merchants, missionaries, and soldiers to intrude on their territories more or less at will. The flood of new products soon affected even the most remote hunters and foragers whose ways of life were upset by encounters with such items as iron tools and, not least, handguns.

But looked at from the center of disturbance, the rapid growth of wealth, population, and political power that Britain, France, Germany, and the United States all experienced between 1800 and 1914 seemed a thoroughly good thing to almost everyone. Accordingly, the idea that human society was destined to progress in desirable directions soon took hold among these peoples. An early champion of that idea was a French nobleman, the Marquis de Condorcet (1743–1794), who wrote *Sketch for a Historical Picture of the Progress of the Human Mind* in the year of his death. His confidence in human progress toward perfection remains surprising, considering the fact that he was in prison and about to have his head cut off by the French revolutionary government when he wrote his sketch.

In the next century, as desirable novelties multiplied, the idea of progress took firm hold among Europeans. In Germany, the philosopher Georg Wilhelm Friedrich Hegel (1770–1831) made progress a universal principle of reality, moving from thesis to antithesis and then to synthesis, which immediately became a new thesis to keep the process going. The German philosopher and economist Karl Marx (1818–1883) claimed to have stood Hegel on his head by proving that class struggle toward equality and freedom under communism was the path of the future. Before that, in France another nobleman, Count Henri de Saint-Simon (1760–1825), founded a different socialist movement aimed at hastening progress toward a similarly free and equal future. One of his younger associates, Auguste Comte (1798–1857), founded what became the academic discipline of sociology with parallel aims. Meanwhile in England the philosopher and economist John Stuart Mill (1806–1873) and the historian Henry Thomas Buckle (1821–1862) explored a more open-ended liberal version of progress in their articles and books.

In 1851, the reality of material progress was spectacularly demonstrated when Prince Albert, Queen Victoria's husband, organized a very successful Great Exhibition in the Crystal Palace, London. Beneath a specially constructed iron-and-glass structure, exhibitors from far and wide displayed a vast array of new machines and products for public admiration and instruction. Thereafter, similar world's fairs became quadrennial events, achieving a new peak of success in 1893, when Chicago hosted the World's Columbian Exposition. That fair celebrated four hundred years of progress since Columbus's discovery of the Americas, and met with altogether unusual success. A still new transcontinental railroad network made it possible for more than 21 million persons to attend the fair; and at night, when incandescent electric bulbs lit up plaster-covered temporary buildings, the dazzling whiteness seemed like a preview of heaven to many of the fair's visitors. Progress never seemed so certain and so obvious, before or since.

The success of the Columbian Exposition depended partly, too, on the fact that the idea of progress had enlarged its scope and persuasiveness after 1867, when the English naturalist Charles Darwin (1809–1882) published *The Origin of Species*. Darwin argued that plants and animals had evolved through geological time thanks to a process of natural selection; in another book, *The Descent of Man* (1871), he specifically discussed human evolution from apelike ancestors. This challenged the biblical story of creation head-on and provoked intense, prolonged, and (as of yet) unresolved, controversy. Accordingly, one of the innovative features of the Columbian Exposition was a World Parliament of Religions, where spokesmen for each of the world's principal faiths had a chance to come before the public, looking for shared principles and, in some instances, even exploring the plausibility of religious progress through time.

There had always been doubters who discounted the desirability of all the tumultuous changes that beset nineteenth-century societies; and in the course of the twentieth century, doubts about human progress multiplied. The long stalemate of trench warfare in World War I (1914–1918) made the military side of technological progress, of which their nineteenth-century predecessors had been so proud, seem anything but desirable to millions of European and American soldiers. The postwar boom, followed by the Great Depression (1929–1938) and World War II (1939–1945), broadened and deepened that skepticism. Renewed economic growth after 1950 was counterbalanced by fears of sudden atomic annihilation and by uneasy awareness that rapid population growth in Africa and Asia was widening the gap between the rich and poor peoples of the Earth.

By the beginning of the twenty-first century, though nearly all the world's politicians still promised to accomplish all sorts of good things if elected to office, most writers and commentators on public affairs were taking a much gloomier view of the future. Emphatic rejection of the nineteenth-century faith in progress became general. That was partly because continuing improvements in human comfort and diet as experienced by people in the world's wealthiest countries, like air-conditioning in summer and fresh fruit and vegetables in supermarkets all year round, swiftly came to be taken for granted, while innumerable medical breakthroughs, like antibiotics and heart surgery, also being taken for granted, had the immediate effect of prolonging life and thereby multiplying the pains and debilities of old age, as well as adding to the world population.

Destructive capabilities of biological, chemical, and nuclear weapons also multiplied; while gaps between rich and poor, rivalries among ethnic and religious groups, and the decay of local communities seemed only to increase. All too obviously, change was everywhere, but was it really for the better? Did happiness increase with longer life and more things to own and look after? Or did accumulating material goods merely get in the way of leading a good life?

These are valid reproaches against rosy nineteenth-century predictions of moral and political progress. But material progress remains undeniable. One unfortunate aspect of life that deserves attention is the issue of violence, particularly since violence and progress often are thought of as going hand in hand. This is not necessarily the case, as the Harvard University psychologist Steven Pinker writes (in remarkable detail) in his 2011 book *The Better Angels of Our Nature: Why Violence Has Declined*. Pinker notes that even the Nazis' depredations didn't come close to those of the Mongol Golden Horde's in terms of sheer percentages of populations killed, and that human violence has in fact been on the decline since prehistory. Under the Aztecs, approximately 5 percent of the population met a violent end; people living in the twenty-first century, on the other hand, are far less likely to die a violent death (or, for that matter, to encounter any form of violence) than people living in any previous century. Surely this is a sign of some progress.

In theory, this decline in violence bodes well for the environment, too, as the more resources a society diverts to warfare (or to preventing the threat of warfare, or to the prevention of more localized conflicts such as gang violence), the less resources it will be able to put toward protecting its environment. The authors of *Our Common Future* noted in chapter 11 ("Peace, Security, Development, and the Environment") of their 1987 book that "even where war is prevented, and where conflict is contained, a state of 'peace' might well entail the diversion into armament production of vast resources that could, at least in part, be used to promote sustainable forms of development" (UN Documents Cooperation Circles n.d.). A government is less likely to put funding into solar technology or mass transportation, for instance, if it (or its populace) is worried about fending off enemies near and far. Obviously warfare is not an ideal state of affairs for anyone or anything.

No one can doubt that increasing knowledge and skills have enlarged human command of energy flows at a very rapid rate since 1750, and have done so more slowly throughout history. The resulting increase in human capabilities, both for good and for ill, is clearly cumulative, and constitutes a kind of progress that deserves to be recognized as such. Where such relatively new innovations as the Internet will take us as a species remains to be seen, of course. While some decry new technologies such as instant messaging as another step in the breakdown of communication (and indeed, civilization as we know it), others point to technology's role in events such as the Arab Spring as a harbinger of a more just—and *progressive*—future for humanity.

William H. McNEILL
University of Chicago, Emeritus

See also Anthropocene Epoch; Cities and the Biosphere; Climate Change and Big History; Collective Learning; Community; Economics, Steady State; Population; Values

FURTHER READING

Bunyan, John. (2009). *Pilgrim's progress*. Oxford, UK: Oxford University Press. (Originally published in 1678)

Darwin, Charles. (2003). *The origin of species*. New York: Signet. (Originally published in 1867)

Darwin, Charles. (2007). *The descent of man*. Sioux Falls, SD: NuVision Publications. (Originally published in 1871)

Condorcet, Marquis de. (1796). *Sketch for a historical picture of the progress of the human mind. Philadelphia*: Lang and Uftick.

Marx, Karl, & Engels, Frederich. (1988). *Das Kommunistische Manifest* [The communist manifesto]. New York: W. W. Norton & Company. (Originally published in 1848)

Muir, Diana. (2002). *Reflections in Bullough's Pond: Economy and ecosystem in New England*. Lebanon, NH: University Press of New England.

Nisbet, Robert A. (1994). *History of the idea of progress* (2nd ed.). Piscataway, NJ: Transaction Publishers.

Owen, Robert. (1920). *The life of Robert Owen written by himself*. Charleston, SC: Nabu Press. (Originally published in 1857–1858)

Pinker, Steven. (2011). *The better angels of our nature: Why violence has declined*. New York: Viking Adult.

United Nations (UN) Documents Cooperation Circles. (n.d.). Our common future, chapter 11: Peace, security, development, and the environment. Retrieved July 13, 2012, from http://habitat.igc.org/open-gates/ocf-11.htm

World Commission on Environment and Development (WCED). (1987). *Our common future*. New York: Oxford University Press.

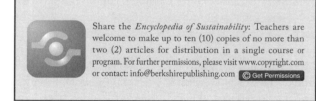

Property Rights

Private property as a legal institution varies greatly among legal systems and has taken different forms over time. There are conflicting views on how private property relates to environmental ills, but the dominant moral justification for property rights today—that a well-constructed system of private property can generate net social benefits to make nearly everyone better off—could play an important role in the emerging law of sustainability.

Private property is a social and economic institution that establishes rules for the control and use of things—both the tangible (land, cars, computers) and the intangible (patents, copyrights). Land and the objects growing on it or attached to it sometimes are termed *real property*, or *realty*. All other property sometimes is termed *personal property* or *personalty*. Property can be owned by individuals, families, or groups, and can also be owned by communities or by public bodies of any size. In some situations property is said to be owned by citizens collectively, and in these cases the state manages it as trustee for the people. The varieties are many.

Private property is a vital institution worldwide and commonly is viewed as being beneficial overall. The benefit most often mentioned is that the prospect of acquiring property offers an incentive for individuals to work hard. It encourages people to create and invest in ways that promote economic growth, benefiting the community as well as the owner (Pipes 1999). Yet, as noted below, private property has another face. In practice, property rights can be and have been morally problematic and a tool of exploitation, and the institution requires

careful crafting to be morally legitimate (Cohen 1927; Freyfogle 2007b; Singer 2000a; van der Walt 2009). Property is an institution that can help reduce ecological degradation and promote sustainability, as many have argued, but it is also an institution that can encourage and sanction activities that are ecologically degrading. In short, private property plays varied, conflicting roles in the quest for ecological health and sustainable development.

Many commentators feel that sustainability requires a reconsideration of property rights in nature, beginning with its basic elements (Burden 2011; Duncan 2002; Freyfogle 2003; Grinlinton and Taylor 2011; McElfish 1994). As a real-life, legal institution, private ownership is more complex than is commonly understood. It is also more flexible than may be appreciated, in that lawmaking communities have many options when defining what can be owned and what it means to own. A well-designed system of property rights can encourage activities consistent with environmental and social goals, while a poorly designed or out-of-date system can foster economic and political inequality at the same time it facilitates land uses that are degrading and unsustainable. Opinions vary widely as to how much today's property systems need to change to promote sustainability, mostly due to differing views on sustainability and on the justice of allowing property owners to act unsustainably if they choose. The need to reduce poverty and economic injustice (which—in the view of many—calls for reform of current property arrangements) is also relevant to the discussion of property rights.

This essay considers property as a functioning, complex legal institution that varies greatly among legal systems and that has taken different forms over time. Property in this sense—as a real-world institution—is distinct from property understood as a cultural or economic ideal, as a largely unchanging abstraction that exists independently of a political and cultural context. In this abstract view of property, humans typically have some right to property that can be developed logically into a particular regime of ownership. Scholars who study real-world property arrangements and who see property not as an intellectual creation, but as the evolving product of contested social, political, and economic choices, generally do not share this perspective. Nonetheless, ideal views of property often appear not just in popular rhetoric, but also in scholarly theorizing, particularly in that of free-market advocates.

This essay does not cover long-standing claims that the ownership of property can have a corrupting influence on the owner, a view embraced by Plato and various religious traditions that has bearing on sustainability issues. The essay also says little about clashes over property between local residents and regional, national, and global forces. Such clashes can arise over the identity of owners—that is, who owns particular land parcels and the associated resources (often water)—or can relate to who sets the rules of ownership—that is, which lawmaking community (local or tribal, national, international) prescribes the rules on what can be owned, who can own, and what it means to own. These kinds of disputes commonly arise with the growth and activities of imperialistic regimes, both political and economic. They also come up regularly in the context of clashes over indigenous property rights, particularly when indigenous communal ownership arrangements conflict with the market-based property ownership systems typical of developed nations (Hickford 2012; Walker 2008). Today disputes about the acquisition of land and resources in developing countries by outside interests (wealthy individuals, global corporations) are particularly prominent, with critics condemning the rising trend as a massive land grab that wipes away existing property arrangements, displaces the poor, and heightens exploitation (Pearce 2012).

Finally, this essay does not cover intellectual property rights directly, although much of what is said about property as a dynamic, socially constructed, morally complex institution also pertains to intellectual property. Its focus is property rights in the natural world, particularly land and natural resources.

Origins and Mechanisms

Private property is a social institution that is created by, and exists within, a lawmaking community (Freyfogle 2007b; Singer and Beerman 1993). Property ownership does not arise when a person seizes a tract of land and proclaims to the world that "this is mine." It arises instead when a group of people agree to recognize that a person has special rights to control a piece of land. Such a social agreement might come voluntarily through a fair governance process, or less voluntarily (or even under duress) in a community in which power rests in the hands of the few. In any event, property is defined by relationships among people: it exists only when a community recognizes the property rights and stands ready to protect them. In this sense, property is a product of law—whether formal or informal, written or oral—and does not exist in the absence of at least an elementary norm-enforcing system.

According to anthropologists, nearly every known human society (even societies where significant resources are used communally) has recognized property rights in one form or another (Maine 1861; Richards 2002; Sack 1986). Individuals and families typically have special control rights over clothing, utensils for food production and preparation, and shelters, although these rights can differ widely. With respect to rights to use land and natural resources, the more common approach has been to recognize distinct *use rights* in nature, that is, rights that entitle the property owner to use a specific part of nature in a specific way (e.g., to hunt, forage, graze livestock, grow crops, divert water, or extract minerals). In a use-right system, multiple owners can have rights to engage in different activities on a single tract of land. Individuals or families might hold some use rights, while a larger group, such as all members of a tribe or residents of a village, might exercise others.

Such a use-right system can be distinguished from a system in which an owner has more complete rights to undertake most or all permissible uses of a specific tract and can halt uses of the tract by others—either all uses by outsiders or those uses that actually interfere with the owner's activities. This more territorial approach toward land governance has a lengthy history; it reflects, for instance, territorial claims that tribal groups have long made to the exclusive control of tribal lands in relation to other tribal groups. What is newer is the application of territorial thinking to the delineation of private rights within a lawmaking community. Only in recent centuries have societies found it useful to allocate rights in land so that an owner gains the right to use a tract for all, or nearly all, purposes. Even in such a territorial-based system, however, it is common for particular parts of nature—water, wildlife, and navigable watercourses above all—to remain communally owned and for communal rights to limit entitlements vested in individual landowners. Further, exclusive rights during the main production season (e.g., crop growing) may yield to specific use rights by others during the off-season (e.g., gleaning fields or pasturing livestock after harvest).

To appreciate the moral complexity of property it is essential to understand how the arrangement works in practice. In a landscape with no property rights, individuals could use parts of nature as they liked but would lack a communally enforced right to halt interferences by others. What a person gains under a system of private property is the essential right, while using the thing owned, to halt all or most interferences. Indeed, property law as a subject of study is best approached by learning what remedies an owner has to protect against interruptions or competing uses. These protections, or remedies, come from the community. Without community-supported protections the world is simply one in which might makes right.

Put most simply, private property works in this manner: formal or informal law within a community empowers an owner to draw upon communal law-enforcement mechanisms to constrain the liberties of other community members (Freyfogle 2010). With such constraints, an owner can use property without material interference by others. The owner gains the right to control and use a particular thing (which might, as noted previously, be a specific use right). All others, in turn, are prohibited from using the thing without the owner's consent and are subject to communal sanction if they violate the owner's rights. Property owners thus do not want local government to leave them alone—on the contrary, they want government close at hand. They want government, when summoned, to halt invasions of their rights and to punish violators.

Law that prescribes the elements of ownership can stem from multiple levels of government, meaning that an owner's rights to a parcel of land could be set by laws and regulations coming from multiple lawmaking sources in combination. In some jurisdictions, private owners themselves can set up owner-run governing structures (e.g., homeowners' associations) that impose additional limits on land uses. Such owner-driven arrangements can blur the line between private contract and public governance.

Moral Complexity

Discussions of private property often stress how such systems can greatly benefit individual owners, but what is easily missed is that ownership of property, particularly of land and scarce resources, can give an owner considerable power over the lives and activities of other people (Bollier 2003; Cohen 1927; Gray 2002; van der Walt 2009). To control land and scarce resources is to wield control over people who require access to them in order to live: for instance, those who control water in an arid region inevitably have power over all others who need the water (Worster 1986). Such power is particularly acute when ownership is limited to elites and when competition for resources is not mediated by a fair, competitive market. Private property, in short, readily can become (as it has been and still is in many settings) an institution of domination that empowers owners to exploit workers and to demand various forms of homage from them. Since private property only operates when communal power supports it and when owners have the state's law-enforcement tools available to them, the arrangement entails the use of public power to constrain private liberties and therefore is subject to the full range of moral claims that can be made against misuses of public power.

For centuries, serious writers on property have sought to ground private ownership in ways that make such assertions of power—such restrictions on the liberties of nonowners—morally legitimate (Philbrick 1938; Schlatter 1951). Various writers have asserted that property is based on natural law or is divinely ordained. This culture-bound line of moral argument enjoys little support today among scholars of property, though it remains alive in popular culture (Becker 1977). The more common understanding among these scholars now is that property is a social creation that takes a variety of forms in terms of what can be owned, what it means to own, and how the rights of one owner fit with the rights of others. To say that a person owns a tract of land says almost nothing unless one probes the specific elements of the property regime that includes the tract.

A more persuasive justification for property than the natural law or natural-rights approach incorporates the centuries-old claim that individuals own their labor and thus ought to own all value created by that labor. This labor theory is most often associated with seventeenth-century English philosopher John Locke, although it existed before his day (Becker 1977; Christman 1994). Locke used the labor theory to help construct a narrative about property's origins that seemed to protect property against claims by the English king. Locke's reasoning helped undergird liberal political theory, but it did not successfully provide a defensible foundation for private ownership, particularly private rights in land. Locke explained why a person who mixed labor with land might own the value created, but did not explain why the laborer should own the land itself, and also failed to explain why one person could mix labor with land while others had no access to land. Its limitations aside, Locke's theory had unexpected consequences in that a literal reading of it challenged the dominant land-use pattern of his day, in which one person owned land, a tenant labored on it, and the owner claimed much of the produce as rent (Scott 1977). If ownership was grounded in labor, why did the tenant not own all that he produced? Indeed, why did slaves not own what they produced? From the eighteenth century onward (later in the United States) this labor theory was put to use philosophically to challenge the legitimacy of existing property arrangements, providing a starting point for socialist and communist critiques.

The dominant moral justification for property rights today is much different, and is based on the premise that a well-constructed system of private property generates net social benefits that are distributed in such a way that nearly everyone becomes better off, even if some people benefit far more than others (Becker 1977; Freyfogle 2003). This is a utilitarian—or, more generally, consequentialist—argument in that it justifies property based on its overall effects. As a justification it has considerable power and it can undergird many forms of property, but consequentialism succeeds in legitimizing property (that is, in legitimizing coercive governmental acts to protect property) only if and when a particular property-rights system does, in fact, promote widespread welfare so that nearly all people, nonowners included, end up better off because of it. Furthermore, each element of ownership needs to be evaluated separately to ensure that it is tailored to achieve good results for the community; it is not enough to say that a system of ownership brings good results overall. As discussed below, this important moral limit on property could play an important role in the emerging law of sustainability.

Basic questions of morality also attach to property rights when their original acquisition took place under circumstances that today are deemed wrongful (Singer 2011). Should current owners be required to relinquish property—even when they have purchased the property fairly—if the title rests upon earlier exploitation or outright theft (Sax 1999)? Is a property system morally well-grounded if it seems to generate overall benefits over large populations (nations, the international community) but does not benefit local people who need access to the property to survive and thrive?

Evolution and Legal Flexibility

Citizens, particularly those in nations with long histories of private ownership, routinely assume that private property has a relatively fixed form and that the rules of ownership are essentially timeless. The historical record is much to the contrary: laws of property ownership can and have taken many forms, and even within a single jurisdiction the meaning and rules of ownership typically evolve over time (Banner 2011). As noted previously, jurisdictions vary based on whether they mostly embrace a system of discrete-use rights in nature or whether instead they tend to divide landscapes into territorial pieces. Property regimes, however, differ on many other points as well.

One of the first questions to ask in any jurisdiction is what rights come with a parcel of land. Does ownership include a right to use surface or subsurface water? A right to exploit subsurface minerals, storage capacities, and geothermal resources? A right to control or harvest wildlife? Answers can differ widely. In many jurisdictions, particular natural resources are not included in the bundle of rights a landowner acquires. Instead, they are made available for use as discrete resources, and prospective users are required in the manner set by law to gain a separate use right for the resource.

A second question has to do with an owner's ability to exclude others. For property to function well, an owner needs a right of use free from interference—but what about intrusions by outsiders that do not interrupt what an owner is doing? Often land ownership is defined so that the public (the local public, usually) can use private land surfaces for various purposes (hunting, livestock grazing, travel, recreational use, etc.) so long as they do not disrupt the primary owner's activities. In recent years Great Britain, following the lead of Scandinavian countries, has expanded public rights to engage in recreational uses of rural lands provided that landowner activities are not disrupted (Shoard 1999). Through the early nineteenth century (and in some settings much later) the United States expressly allowed extensive public uses of unenclosed rural lands, but since then it increasingly has curtailed these once valuable public land-use rights (Freyfogle 2007b). Owners now typically can halt invasions by outsiders (though sometimes only with effort), whether or not these outsiders cause actual land-use conflicts.

A fundamental issue in any property-rights system has to do with the intensity of uses allowed and with the vague but widely embraced principle that private owners should not cause harm. Generally speaking (though with exceptions), owners of a thing must use it in ways that avoid harming other owners or surrounding communities. How, though, should the term *harm* be defined? What activities should the law deem harmful? Jurisdictions vary widely and definitions can evolve on this point. Agrarian communities typically have protected agrarian activities and viewed disruptive industrial activities with suspicion (Horwitz 1977). With the coming of industrialism, lawmakers tended to redefine harm to allow more intensive land and resource uses, thereby encouraging factories, cities, and industrial transport systems, even when such intensive activities disturbed older agrarian land uses (Freyfogle 2003; Novak 1996). The definition of harm, that is, changed with the advent of industrialization so that only the most disruptive industrial activities were deemed harmful. This redefinition, it should be noted, did not expand property rights but only reconfigured them; owners gained enhanced rights to use property intensively but partially relinquished their ability to halt interferences by neighbors.

A do-no-harm rule in some form (with, as noted, various and evolving definitions of harm) is commonly used in a property-rights system to help reconcile conflicts over land and resource uses. Such conflicts are quite common, both among nearby landowners and between and among landowners and owners of discrete resource-use rights. For instance, mining activities by an owner of subsurface mineral rights can easily clash with the land uses of the surface owner. Pollution, noise, and blockages of wind, light, and water by one property owner can harm other owners and surrounding communities. Much of the law dealing with private property relates directly to the lawmaking task of reconciling conflicting land or resource uses, either by prescribing clear property-use rights in advance (*ex ante*) or by providing more vague standards for assessments of an activity's legitimacy after the fact (*ex post*).

Rules designed to reduce conflicts can and do vary widely and change over time. For instance, a rule could require property owners to use what they own in ways that alter nature only slightly. Alternatively, a conflict-resolution rule could favor property users who are first chronologically, or could assess competing activities based on reasonableness or social benefits, favoring the more reasonable or beneficial. Some conflict-resolution rules operate by dividing use rights on a fair-share basis (for instance, giving landowners above an aquifer fair-share rights to withdraw water from it). Other rules insist that owners accommodate the needs of neighbors by adjusting their own activities so as to reduce conflicts. Many such rules can be seen (and perhaps are expressly intended) to reduce the external harms that a particular land use creates; that is, to "internalize" harms so that landowners causing them take the harms into account in their economic calculations. Such internalization of land-use harms—compelling the one who causes harm to pay for it—helps the market work efficiently. It can also reduce inefficient forms of degradation.

Conflicts also arise between individual property owners and the larger public. Here, too, it is common for legal systems to embrace a do-no-harm principle, sometimes phrased generally, and sometimes expressed in detailed regulations. Under this principle, property uses are illegitimate when they cause substantial harm to public rights, public property, or the common good. In this setting, also, harm is a term that typically evolves in meaning over time.

A hotly contested issue in some industrialized nations has centered on the legal right of landowners to develop lands intensively. Does or should landownership inherently include a right to develop? Put otherwise: can lawmakers properly restrict private development when a restriction greatly reduces land values? A sound response should consider how the contested land-use limit affects the common good. It would consider in particular not only the harmfulness of the development, but whether a restriction on development would hamper the ability of the property-rights system to benefit the community as a whole. A property system that allows pollution or degradation can hurt the public interest in a way that saps the institution's moral legitimacy.

Ecological Degradation

The literature on environmental problems has long featured conflicting commentary on how private property relates to environmental ills. Is private property part of the solution, part of the problem, or both?

A long-standing claim by market proponents is that the creation and strict enforcement of property rights can reduce misuses of nature, not only resource exhaustion but also pollution and ecological disruption (Anderson and Leal 2001). At the center of this argument is the dilemma known as the tragedy of the commons, which applies to resources that are open to all users without limit. With no limits on use, competing users tend to overuse the resources and exhaust them, consuming more than their annual yields and decreasing their productive capacities. In the view of many, this principle largely explains our environmental ills: too much of nature is open to free public use, and if all parts of nature were privately owned, our environmental plight would greatly improve. The proposed solution is to divide the commons into private shares, giving each owner the ability and incentive to avoid overuse.

A common criticism of this reasoning is that private owners in fact do not always, or even routinely, take good care of what they own in terms of long-term ecological health. The reasons for misuse are readily explained by economic theory. Some misuses are linked to externalities that are not, and perhaps cannot be, internalized. Others are due to the discounting of future declines and to competitive market pressures. Indeed, the most economically productive use of a particular resource sometimes involves immediate exploitation, with profits invested elsewhere. Critics of privatization as a solution to resource overuse also note that land-use patterns (particularly in rural areas) are guided by custom and inertia, with owners often unaware of or unconcerned about long-term decline. Further (and as noted below), good land use can require actions taken at large spatial scales, leaving individual owners unable to use land well given their small parcel sizes. Yet another critical response is that private property, and the rhetoric of private ownership, is often deployed as a shield to ward off requirements that owners use their lands responsibly—in other words, that private property has become a tool to resist legal measures and policies expressly designed to promote sustainability.

Related to the tragedy of the commons is a less familiar story of ecological decline, a story that has to do not with a commons that is undivided, but instead with a natural commons that is excessively divided. Scholars who write about the tragedy of the commons typically propose that lawmakers impose limits on how each user acts at the level of the commons. The proposed limits sometimes take the form of laws that prescribe use rights in the commons (e.g., the right to graze fifty cows during a specific season), but more often they involve dividing the commons into territorial shares and setting conflict-avoidance rules on how owners can use their shares. In any event, the key step is to set limits at the scale of the commons and to prescribe limits on use at that level. According to some observers, however, a key cause of ecological degradation today is that our commons have been overly fragmented; they have been divided into small pieces (individual property shares, small political jurisdictions) with no lawmaking group possessing enough legal power to ensure that collective individual use of the commons does not cause degradation. Put otherwise, too much power has been vested in (or assumed by) individual owners and local political jurisdictions with not enough authority retained at larger scales to prescribe overall policy and to set necessary, large-scale limits. This problem is seen readily in the case of global climate change, which requires action at the planetary level for resolution. At present inadequate power resides at that high level to set policy and limits, and thus activities contributing to climate change continue. The problem also is seen easily in the case of river basins, fisheries, aquifers, and large-scale wildlife habitats. The underlying issue in all of these instances is that rights to control nature have been excessively divided and delegated, producing what is sometimes termed the tragedy of the anticommons or the tragedy of fragmentation (Freyfogle 2003; Heller 1998). In this narrative, vesting managerial power at the level of the individual owner can weaken the ability of the larger community to undertake conservation efforts (Odum 1982).

It is important to recall that a property system loses moral legitimacy to the extent it allows owners to engage in degradation that harms the community. As discussed above, the legitimacy of a property system today rests on its capacity to foster the common good, and a system becomes less legitimate—and less helpful to the lawmaking community—to the extent individual owners can engage in harmful activity. That said, a property-rights system needs a strong element of stability and predictability if it is to induce economically productive investments. Transitions to new, more ecologically sound ownership rules therefore need to consider legitimate expectations and to accommodate them (for instance, by phasing out existing harmful land uses over time).

Public Property

Any discussion of private property needs to take note of publicly owned property and how private rights interface with public rights. In many jurisdictions the law vests overall ownership of water and wildlife in the public or the state, with private owners gaining only tailored use rights in them (Freyfogle 2003). Navigable waters and the land beneath them (including coastal waters) are typically viewed as public assets. In many jurisdictions subsurface resources are publicly owned, as are the rights to use airspace. Beyond that, the public often is viewed as having legitimate claims to the use of personal property that makes up a cultural heritage (e.g., artwork) and to historic sites and structures that similarly incorporate a community's history and self-awareness (Hyde 2010).

A recognition of such public rights is essential because their existence could properly tailor or qualify any private

rights that might impinge on them (Bollier 2003; Gooden and Tehan 2010; Rodgers et al. 2011). The public's ownership of flowing water thus could vest the public with power to insist that private water uses remain consistent with a river's ecological health. The public's ownership of wild animals, even when found on private land, can similarly give the public a legitimate voice in land uses that diminish the land's value as wildlife habitat. Private rights to use specific parts of nature (water, rivers, beaches, wildlife) often are said to be subject to public trust responsibilities and broader governmental powers to regulate in the public interest.

Public property and private property as categories are, in fact, far from distinct. Indeed, it may make more sense to view them not as separate categories but rather as poles on a continuum of property arrangements, varying from arrangements in which the public has essentially total control to ones in which the ongoing public role is slight (Freyfogle 2007a). Private rights, as stated previously, are intertwined with public power, given that law (formal or informal) prescribes the elements of ownership, and legal power (again, formal or informal) provides the necessary enforcement. What a private owner can do is often and necessarily limited by public lawmaking processes, and as such the public plays a major role in how private lands are used. On the other hand, many publicly owned lands are used by private parties who have specific use rights—rights that are themselves a form of private property (e.g., rights to graze animals, to cut timber, to hunt or fish or to extract minerals on public lands). In sum, public and private are intertwined complexly to widely varying degrees on essentially all lands.

Property and Sustainability

Given that much of nature around the world is subject to systems of private property, it is inevitable that the push for sustainability will include calls for changes in private rights. It is clear that a great deal of degradation occurs on private lands, and that other degradation on private lands, public lands, and in public waters is linked to discrete-use rights. These private activities must change in some way—change that could be prompted by education and cultural shifts, social pressure, economic incentives, and market forces. But property as an institution is fundamentally a creation of law, and owners look to the law for guidance on what they can and cannot do. Similarly, the institution's moral legitimacy—particularly in the case of private rights in nature (that is, in physical things not created by human labor)—is rooted today in its promotion of the common good. For these reasons, the law needs to change so that it curtails land and resource uses that undercut sustainability and so that it promotes collective action to address ecological challenges affecting large spatial scales (Beatley 1994; Bosselmann 2008; Bromley 1991; Burden 2011; Duncan 2002; Grinlinton and Taylor 2011).

As an overall principle, property law should limit uses of nature by property owners to activities consistent with overall environmental goals. It needs to allow only activities that sustain ecological integrity or health at appropriate spatial scales. Under this principle, a person who seeks to engage in a particular activity would, as a matter of law, need to site the activity in a place that is ecologically well suited for it. As part of the push for sustainability, the long-standing legal principle of do-no-harm should be interpreted and applied so that harm includes ecological degradation and other consequences inconsistent with sustainable living. Using this interpretation, this principle would limit significant pollution and would also curtail land-cover changes, mining activities, and other intensive land uses that noticeably degrade ecological function, at least at larger spatial scales. A particular challenge here will come from the need to define harm as including ills that arise from land uses that are acceptable in isolation but that become harmful when too many landowners engage in them— what might be termed carrying-capacity harms. In the case of carrying-capacity harms, the guiding legal principle might properly be a version of fair share or correlative rights, requiring that all landowners cut back proportionately.

Due to the many reasons for promoting good land and resource uses at large spatial scales (for instance, use of the planet's atmospheric commons and uses of transboundary watercourses), more planning and rule making is needed at higher levels (even new levels) of government. The aim here would be to overcome the many tragedies of fragmentation caused by the excessive delegation of governance power to small jurisdictions and individual property owners. Large-scale conservation planning will require the relocation of many current human activities: for instance, relocation to create migratory corridors for wildlife or to reconnect rivers to their floodplains. Such relocation necessarily will require the compensated expropriation of land and resources, including an end to particular land uses that are legitimate in the abstract but nonetheless inconsistent with community-level conservation efforts. Property systems typically have allowed expropriation (upon payment of compensation) when needed to foster the common good (Reynolds 2010). Sustainability will likely require an increased use of this collective tool.

A critical issue in some countries (the United States, conspicuously) is the need to ban development and other intensive uses of many privately owned lands (Freyfogle 2007b). Realistically and in fairness to taxpayers, such bans on development need to take place without requiring taxpayers to compensate the owner of every land parcel where development is unwanted. Some nations have made this transition successfully, without undercutting the ability of private property to function well as a productive social institution. The transition needs to be made in all jurisdictions, in ways that promote fairness and do not exacerbate economic or political inequality.

Sustainability also seems to call for greater attention to and respect for public interests in water, wildlife, rivers and oceans, the atmosphere, and other parts of nature that are either publicly owned or subject to public trust responsibilities. Many ideas about property ownership that now prevail arose during an era when ecological interconnections were little known. Water, flowing air, and wildlife do not recognize property boundaries. The severance of links among land parcels interferes with the promotion of healthy ecological processes, particularly processes that produce what have begun to be referred to as ecological services (benefits that come from the functioning of healthy ecosystems, such as clean air and freshwater). New ownership norms, protecting public property and public-trust interests, could greatly aid in promoting ecological health.

Finally, it is useful to take note of the rising call for greater recognition of individual rights to a healthy environment or, more narrowly, rights of access to clean water, clean air, adequate sanitation, and other minimum resources needed to sustain a decent life. Laws and proposed laws that embody such individual rights tend to stand apart from systems of private property. But when and as individual environmental rights are recognized, such claims will call into question current distributions of property rights. They will also call into question legal definitions of how owners can use what they own. Plainly, if citizens have rights to use an ecologically healthy river, then landowners along the river must cut back when their land uses interfere with these rights. The rising call to recognize human environmental rights, including rights of access to resources, thus is adding pressure to calls for changes in property law, and is further stimulating efforts to bring the elements of ownership into line with ecological goals.

Eric FREYFOGLE
University of Illinois

See also Community; Education, Higher; Local Solutions to Global Problems; Natural Capital; Values; Water

FURTHER READING

Alexander, Gregory S. (1997). *Commodity & propriety: Competing visions of property in American legal thought 1776–1970.* Chicago: University of Chicago Press.

Alexander, Gregory S. (2006). *The global debate over constitutional property: Lessons for American takings jurisprudence.* Chicago: University of Chicago Press.

Alexander, Gregory S. (2009). The social-obligation norm in American property law. *Cornell Law Review, 94*(4), 745–819.

Anderson, Terry L., & Leal, Donald R. (2001). *Free market environmentalism* (Rev. ed.). New York: Palgrave Macmillan.

Arnold, Craig Anthony. (2002). The reconstitution of property: Property as a web of interests. *Harvard Environmental Law Review, 26,* 282–364.

Banner, Stuart. (2011). *American property: A history of how, why, and what we own.* Cambridge, MA: Harvard University Press.

Beatley, Timothy. (1994). *Ethical land use: Principles of policy and planning.* Baltimore: Johns Hopkins University Press.

Becker, Lawrence C. (1977). *Property rights: Philosophical foundations.* London: Routledge & Kegan Paul.

Bollier, David. (2003). *Silent theft: The private plunder of our common wealth.* New York: Routledge.

Bosselmann, Klaus. (2008). *The principle of sustainability: Transforming law and governance.* Aldershot, UK: Ashgate.

Bromley, Daniel W. (1991). *Environment and economy: Property rights and public policy.* Oxford, UK: Blackwell.

Burden, Peter D. (2011). *Earth jurisprudence: Private property and earth community* (Doctoral dissertation). Adelaide, Australia: Adelaide Law School, University of Adelaide.

Burden, Peter D. (Ed.). (2011). *Exploring wild law: The philosophy of Earth jurisprudence.* Kent Town, Australia: Wakefield Press.

Caldwell, Lynton Keith, & Shrader-Frechette, Kristin. (1993). *Policy for land: Law and ethics.* Lanham, MD: Rowman & Littlefield.

Christman, John. (1994). *The myth of property: Toward an egalitarian theory of ownership.* New York: Oxford University Press.

Cohen, Morris. (1927). Property and sovereignty. *Cornell Law Quarterly, 13,* 8–30.

Cole, Daniel H. (2002). *Pollution & property: Comparing ownership institutions for environmental protection.* Cambridge, UK: Cambridge University Press.

Dagan, Hannoch. (2011). *Property: Values and institutions.* New York: Oxford University Press.

Duncan, Myrl L. (2002). Reconceiving the bundle of sticks: Land as a community-based resource. *Environmental Law, 32,* 773–807.

Freyfogle, Eric T. (2003). *The land we share: Private property and the common good.* Washington, DC: Island Press.

Freyfogle, Eric T. (2006). *Why conservation is failing and how it can regain ground.* New Haven, CT: Yale University Press.

Freyfogle, Eric T. (2007a). *Agrarianism and the good society: Land, culture, conflict, and hope.* Lexington: University Press of Kentucky.

Freyfogle, Eric T. (2007b). *On private property: Finding common ground on the ownership of land.* Boston: Beacon Press.

Freyfogle, Eric T. (2010). Property and liberty. *Harvard Environmental Law Review, 34,* 75–118.

Gooden, Lee, & Tehan, Maureen. (Eds.). (2010). *Comparative perspectives on communal lands and individual ownership: Sustainable futures.* Abington, UK: Routledge.

Gray, Kevin. (2002). Land law and human rights. In Louise Tee (Ed.), *Land law: Issues, debates, policy.* Cullompton, UK: Willan Publishing.

Grinlinton, David, & Taylor, Prue. (Eds.). (2011). *Property rights and sustainability: The evolution of property rights to meet ecological challenges.* Leiden, The Netherlands: Martinus Nijhoff Publishers.

Heller, Michael A. (1998). The tragedy of the anticommons: Property in the transition from Marx to markets. *Harvard Law Review, 111*(3), 621–688.

Hickford, Mark. (2012). *Lords of the land: Indigenous property rights and the jurisprudence of empire.* New York: Oxford University Press.

Horwitz, Morton J. (1977). *The transformation of American law 1780–1860.* Cambridge, MA: Harvard University Press.

Hyde, Lewis. (2010). *Common as air: Revolution, art, and ownership.* New York: Farrar, Straus and Giroux.

Jacobs, Harvey M. (Ed.). (2004). *Private property in the 21st century: The future of an American ideal.* Cheltenham, UK: Edward Elgar.

McElfish, James M., Jr. (1994). Property rights, property roots: Rediscovering the legal protection of the environment. *Environmental Law Reporter, 24,* 10231–10249.

MacPherson, C. B. (Ed.). (1978). *Property: Mainstream and critical positions.* Toronto: University of Toronto Press.

Maine, Henry. (2001). *Ancient law.* New Brunswick, NJ: Transaction Publishers. (Originally published in 1861)

Mostert, Hanre. (2002). *The constitutional protection and regulation of property and its influence on the reform of private law and landownership in South Africa and Germany: A comparative analysis.* Berlin: Springer.

Munzer, Stephen R. (1990). *A theory of property.* Cambridge, UK: Cambridge University Press.

Novak, William J. (1996). *The people's welfare: Law & regulation in nineteenth-century America.* Chapel Hill: University of North Carolina Press.

Odum, William E. (1982). Environmental degradation and the tyranny of small decisions. *BioScience, 32,* 728–729.

Oksanen, Markku. (1998). *Nature as property: Environmental ethics and the institution of ownership* (Doctoral dissertation). Turku, Finland: University of Turku.

Ostrom, Elinor. (1990). *Governing the commons: The evolution of institutions for collective action.* Cambridge, UK: Cambridge University Press.

Pearce, Fred. (2012). *The land grabbers: The new fight over who owns the Earth.* Boston: Beacon Press.

Philbrick, Francis S. (1938). Changing conceptions of property in law. *University of Pennsylvania Law Review, 86,* 691–732.

Pipes, Richard. (1999). *Property and freedom.* New York: Alfred Knopf.

Reynolds, Susan. (2010). *Before eminent domain: Toward a history of expropriation of land for the common good.* Chapel Hill: University of North Carolina Press.

Richards, John F. (Ed.). (2002). *Land, property, and the environment.* Oakland, CA: ICS Press.

Rodgers, Christopher P.; Straughton, Eleanor A.; Winchester, Angus J. L.; & Pieraccini, Margherita. (Eds.). (2011). *Contested common land: Environmental governance past and present.* London: Earthscan.

Rose, Carol M. (1994). *Property and persuasion: Essays on the history, theory, and rhetoric of ownership.* Boulder, CO: Westview Press.

Ryan, Alan J. (1987). *Property.* Minneapolis: University of Minnesota Press.

Sack, Robert David. (1986). *Human territoriality: Its theory and history.* Cambridge, UK: Cambridge University Press.

Sax, Joseph. (1999). *Playing darts with Rembrandt: Public and private rights in cultural treasures.* Ann Arbor: University of Michigan Press.

Schlatter, Richard. (1951). *Private property: The history of an idea.* London: George Allen & Unwin.

Scott, William B. (1977). *In pursuit of happiness: American conceptions of property from the seventeenth century to the twentieth century.* Bloomington: Indiana University Press.

Shoard, Marion. (1999). *A right to roam.* Oxford, UK: Oxford University Press.

Singer, Joseph William. (2000a). *Entitlement: The paradoxes of property.* New Haven, CT: Yale University Press.

Singer, Joseph William. (2000b). *The edges of the field: Lessons on the obligations of ownership.* Boston: Beacon Press.

Singer, Joseph William. (2011). Original acquisition of property: From conquest & possession to democracy & equal opportunity. *Indiana Law Journal, 86,* 763–778.

Singer, Joseph William, & Beerman Jack M. (1993). The social origins of property. *Canadian Journal of Law & Jurisprudence, 6,* 217–248.

Sreenivasan, Gopal. (1995). *The limits of Lockean rights in property.* New York: Oxford University Press.

van der Walt, André J. (1999). *Constitutional property clauses: A comparative analysis.* Cape Town, South Africa: Juta and Company.

van der Walt, André J. (2009). *Property in the margins.* Oxford, UK: Hart Publishing.

Waldron, Jeremy. (1988). *The right to private property.* New York: Oxford University Press.

Walker, Cherryl. (2008). *Land-marked: Land claims and land restitution in South Africa.* Johannesburg, South Africa: Jacana Media.

Worster, Donald. (1986). *Rivers of empire: Water, aridity, and the growth of the American West.* New York: Oxford University Press.

S

Shipping

The shipping industry must cope with several environmental issues; some sources put the industry's contribution to carbon dioxide emissions at almost 5 percent of the world's total. Although the public often considers transportation by ship to be environmentally friendly, shipping faces several sustainability issues, above all greenhouse gas emissions from burning fuel. Figures suggest that the situation is going to worsen. In the future, alternative fuel and energy sources, strict legal regulations, and economic incentives will play key roles in preventing pollution the shipping industry causes.

The public has long treated shipping as one of the more environmentally friendly modes of transportation; road transportation and aviation seem to lag far behind shipping. The enormity of freight carriers in the early twenty-first century facilitates a positive picture of the industry; carriers' massive sizes mean that they can ship large amounts of goods at one time.

The shipping industry must cope with environmental issues as well, however. Ships produce several types of greenhouse gas emissions. The contamination of the sea and navigable rivers due to the sewage that ships dispose of (both legally and illegally) is immense. A side effect of shipping is the increased amount of garbage in the seas. Although the shipping industry directly may not cause all of the garbage, the virtual endlessness of the oceans makes the criminal prosecution for garbage illegally disposed of at sea close to impossible. The disposal of the ships themselves is costly and becomes more complicated the more sophisticated ship designs become. Temptation is high to conduct shipbreaking (the breaking up of ships for scrap recycling) in countries with minimum regulations, a practice that endangers the environment and the people conducting the work. (The countries where shipbreaking is most common include India, Bangladesh, China, Turkey, and Pakistan.) The shipping industry needs to tackle these issues—to name just a few.

Awareness is growing, though, and the International Maritime Organization (IMO), a United Nations agency responsible for the security and safety of shipping and the prevention of environmental damage, has begun to collaborate with several governmental bodies of various states. Firms themselves have initiated industry coalitions and pools, and some of these have taken first steps.

Will these efforts be enough? How will the shipping industry and the sustainability issues it faces evolve in the upcoming years and decades of the twenty-first century? To assess where it is going, it is important to know the industry's current status. Figures of the present and forecasts of their development provide a starting point. It is possible to make predictions and venture speculations based on contemporary analyses. No guarantee exists for the actual future developments, however, as unexpected events may shift the industry's development into radically new directions.

Shipping and Its Impact in Figures

Almost all freight carriers in the early twenty-first century use bunker fuel as their source of power. Bunker fuel, or fuel oil, is a residual mass from petroleum distillation, a waste or by-product, which makes its use sound environmental practice to the layperson. Bunker fuel is full of pollutants, however, and causes a high amount of carbon dioxides, nitrogen oxides, and sulphur oxides, all of which cause heavy damage to human health and the environment (Sarvana 2009). Scientists believe sulphur oxides cause acid rain, and nitrogen oxides cause smog (Biello 2009).

A modern container ship with the power of around 100,000 horsepower consumes between 12.5 and 14.5 tonnes of bunker fuel per hour (AECOM 2010, 15). Many people tend to leverage this statistic, however, by considering that such a ship can transport up to 12,000 containers, which makes the fuel consumption seem relatively environmentally friendly when looked at per ton and per kilometer.

Other statistics put shipping's impact in a clearer context: depending on the source, shipping is said to be responsible for between 600 and 800 million tonnes of carbon dioxides yearly, which is equivalent to almost 5 percent of the world's total carbon dioxide emissions. This amount is more than the total of what all countries on the African continent combined produce in a year (Vidal 2007). The amount of nitrous oxide emissions a single ship fueled with bunker oil causes in one year is even higher than the amount twenty-two thousand cars cause (Biello 2009).

The problem of ship fuels and maritime emissions is likely to grow worse. By 2020, scientists expect the estimated carbon dioxide emissions to increase by almost 75 percent (Vidal 2007). The US Environmental Protection Agency (EPA), a federal agency of the US government designed to protect human health and the environment, estimates that the nitrous oxide emissions the shipping industry causes will double by 2030, then amounting to 1.9 million tonnes a year if the industry makes no further effort (EPA 2009). Similar calculations exist for particulate matter, which scientists estimate will triple by 2030, reaching a total of 154,000 tonnes (EPA 2009). These figures are only estimates, and estimates beyond ten years are never exact; they also do not account for varying scenarios, such as "business as usual" or scenarios including dramatic technology improvements.

The easiest way to reduce fuel consumption is to slow down. If the world fleet reduced its average speed by 10 percent, the reduction of carbon dioxide emissions would amount to 19 percent (IBS n.d.). This deceleration would also make sense from an economic point of view: fuel costs amount to 41 percent of the operating costs of a tanker ship (Biello 2009). Slowing down would lead to longer lead time, however, and customers often are not prepared to wait.

Are Emissions the Key Issue?

Emission reduction is the dominating topic and is likely to remain so. Most forecasts or analyses of the shipping industry's future predict emission reduction to expand its position of prevalence (e.g., Pruzan-Jorgensen, Peder, and Furrag 2010). This focus of analyses might then become a self-fulfilling prophecy.

The industry should not neglect ballast water or ship-breaking, however; it might solve many other sustainability issues apart from emissions along the way. For instance, most ship designers who aim to create an environmentally friendly vehicle do not consider only emission reduction, but also consider the ship's entire environmental footprint, thus also accounting for the ship's disposal at the end of its lifetime. Ideas for handling ballast water and the contamination of the sea also are on their way, included in discussions about minimizing emissions.

Several regulations already are in place to handle garbage and sewage on board (IMO 2011). Although still difficult, it is easier to track garbage and sewage as the source of sea pollution than the emission of greenhouse gases. For instance, a *garbage management plan*, which is obligatory for large vessels, ensures the whereabouts of every item brought onboard. The illegal disposal of garbage at sea would reduce the expected weight of garbage at the point of destination.

The industry needs fiercer regulations governing emissions, however; regulations are nowhere near as sophisticated as the regulations governing sewage and garbage. The regulations for garbage and sewage already apply to 99 percent of the world's merchant tonnage (IMO 2011), while supranational regulations for emissions still are scarce and, in most cases, resemble more declarations of intent than actual laws that entail punishment in case of noncompliance. Because emissions have such a radical effect on the environment and the topic is so ubiquitous, especially in the media, their omnipresence is likely to prevail. There is not only a great need for closer concerns, but also a great gap in current regulations.

Short- and Medium-Term Perspectives

The short- or medium-term perspectives refer to initiatives or concepts that will come into being or will develop between 2020 and 2025. In the last decades of the twentieth century, the damage and the long-term effects environmental pollution causes had been established. In the first decade of the twenty-first century, pollution reduction was the main theme. In the future, the industry will go a step further: in the short and medium term, the main theme will be the industry's transition from pollution reduction to pollution prevention. In the particular case of shipping, the dominant topics of interest will be the prevention of different types of emissions the industry causes. Reducing the impact of the current sources of power or finding new sources of energy for ships can achieve prevention of emissions. Both options accompany a reinforced regulation of the shipping sector.

The "command and control" instruments that policy makers discovered in the 1980s (Hart 2010) either will be fortified in the areas where they already affect the shipping industry or will at least be transferred to it.

Scientists from all over the world work on substituting fuel or bunker oil, and their approaches differ. Some rely on new sources of energy, such as solar and wind energy. Others retrieve solutions scientists already had examined in the past but found inefficient or without practical application. There is an assortment of alternatives to fuel oil. A variety of these alternatives stem from renewable energy sources, which are energies derived from natural resources such as sunlight, wind, and tides, which replenish naturally. Experts simply deem others environmentally friendlier than the currently used bunker oil. Some examples, finally, are just auxiliaries that help in an environmentally friendly way to reduce the fuel consumed. Among the more environmentally friendly modes of propulsion are hydrogen fuel cells, natural gas, and Flettner rotors. The "true" environmentally friendly ones use wind, wave, and solar power. Finally, the use of compressed air to avoid friction loss counts as an auxiliary method.

A first alternative for fuel oil would be fuel cells, which convert the energy of a fuel into electric energy. The fuel in this case would be hydrogen. This is not an entirely new idea, but its application so far has been restricted mostly to submarines. The great advantage of using hydrogen as an energy source is its independence of the ambient air and the fact that the fuel combustion is near to silent, both of which suit submarines. The process of energy generation does not cause direct emissions. The necessary preceding step of attaining hydrogen, however, does produce emissions. So far, hydrogen fuel cells are available only for excursion boats because the currently available types of fuel cells do not render the energy necessary for speeding a freight carrier. Plans are under way to expand this technology. The European Union is heavily subsidizing the research (FCH JU 2012), and some countries already have set clear goals. For instance, by 2040, South Korea wants to cover 22 percent of its energy consumption by using hydrogen fuel cells (Green Car Congress 2005). The first ship to use fuel cell technology is the *Viking Lady* (pictured at the top of this article) which uses a 320-kilowatt molten carbonate fuel cell that operates on liquefied natural gas (Biello 2009). Since 2009, the *Viking Lady* has run for over 18,000 hours on this hybrid system; the next step to reducing the need for fuel is increasing the fuel cell's capacity for energy storage (Schuler 2012).

Another type of alternative fuel is natural gas. Scientists believe that using natural gas instead of bunker oil could cut carbon dioxide emissions by up to 20 percent (Kahn Ribeiro and Kobayashi 2007). Natural gas is used mostly for inland ferries, such as in Norway, but some supply ships have used natural gas as well (Biello 2009). A great advantage is that it might work as an interim solution, too. Ships with diesel motors can be reequipped with motors that run on natural gas so that entirely new constructions are not necessary. Pioneers in this technology run into several problems. First, access is hard to find because only a few, if any, ports have filling stations (Biello 2009). Second, although natural gas itself may be cheaper than diesel, the technology's level of costs compared to traditional fuel's costs is an obstacle (Kahn Ribeiro and Kobayashi 2007). Experts believe it will take another ten to twenty years for this technology to be available commercially (Biello 2009).

Rotor ships, or Flettner ships, are not exactly an innovative idea because they have been around since the 1920s. In the search for alternative fuel powers, however, scientists revert to ideas of the past and see whether they are transferrable to the future. Flettner ships have large cylinders on deck, which include rotor sails. The rotors cause a perpendicularly moving airstream that meets with the horizontally moving natural airstream around the ship. This creates a physical effect called the Magnus effect, which can create propulsion. The disadvantage is that the rotors need energy to start spinning. Scientists nonetheless believe it is worth investigating. The Finnish company Wärtsilä already is designing plans for cruise ships to use both natural gas and Flettner rotors as sources of power (Reinikainen 2009).

Finally, in terms of more environmentally friendly possibilities, electric boats are an option. Similar to electric automobiles, a battery produces the energy for the ship. Critics argue that this is only a shift of the problem because although this system minimizes the emissions on the ship itself, the generation of energy that supplies the battery still remains an issue. Commercial electric ships are still a long way off; the available batteries are strong enough to last only one day and even that only for private small motorboats. Enlarging the currently used batteries to make them suitable for freight carriers for longer periods would make them disproportionally heavier and thus inappropriate for ships.

A very clean source of power is solar energy. Solar power already is an established source for private households, so the transfer to using it in shipping seems only logical. The first Atlantic crossing with a boat having solar propulsion took place in 2006. The ships using solar energy have solar panels installed on their decks, and simple daylight is enough to keep the batteries running. As with the hydrogen fuel cells, however, the solar panels available are just about strong enough to keep a small passenger boat going but nowhere near suitable for placement on freight carriers. Also, putting solar panels on the decks of a freight carrier means losing space for containers the carrier could transport. This trade-off so far does not favor the solar energy option.

When people think of green energy, the second concept that springs to mind, after solar energy, is wind energy. A transfer to shipping is conceivable. Large foil kites attached to the ship's deck capture wind energy. Contrary to earlier examples, freight carriers already use this technology, and plans for oil tankers exist. Although this scenario sounds like the rediscovery of sailing ships, the ships currently using kites are hybrid vehicles using two types of propulsion. Scientists estimate that this type of propulsion will cut fuel costs by 20 percent (BBC News 2008); however, the return to using sails means the return to a dependence on the weather. The payments shipping companies would need to make for delayed arrivals could offset the savings in fuel costs. Also, as with the solar panels, the installations necessary to secure the kites to the ship would take up space that otherwise could hold more cargo.

Another energy source stems from the idea of using what is around the ships, namely, water that causes waves. Wind passing over the surface of the sea creates waves, and both the wind power transferred to the sea and the motion of the waves can power a ship engine. Several so-called wave farms, large installations of machines in the sea, already exist that capture the wave power and supply the energy grid of the nearest land. Additionally, ships using wave power can use the ocean current. So far, ships using wave power are by far slower than freight carriers with diesel engines are, and they use wave power engines only as supplementary power.

The time of commercially used hovercraft boats came—and has already passed again. The production of the cushion filled with high-pressure air was too expensive, and the operation of the ships was not economically efficient. Hovercraft ships serve mainly in disaster relief and military or survey operations. The idea to use high-pressure air has lingered, nevertheless. The Dutch company DK Group has invented a system that pumps compressed air beneath a ship's hull, thus reducing the resistance between the water surface and the ship, which in turn reduces the fuel needed to move the ship—similar to a hovercraft boat. The caveat is that, as with the rotors of the Flettner ship, energy is needed to pump the air under the ship. The company has conducted tests and ordered the first commercial ship; however, this innovation is still far away from conquering the market.

Shipping companies need to act, and they need to act fast. Working proactively might save them precious resources because it goes hand in hand with anticipating future legislation and regulations. One example of this affects shipping companies that call at European ports: there are plans to include the industry into the European Trading System (ETS) in the medium term. The ETS is a framework of the European Union (EU) that was installed in 2005 and is part of the EU's efforts to reduce carbon dioxide by 20 percent by 2020 (compared to 2005) (European Commission n.d.). Companies receive allowances for their yearly carbon dioxide emissions, and if their emissions exceed their assigned limit, they have to purchase further allowances. Producing emissions that exceed their allowance incurs great costs for companies. Reducing emissions therefore entails an economic incentive. Several industries have been included in the strategy, with the latest addition being the aviation industry. It is the logical next step to include the shipping industry into the EU's ETS. The EU has opened the debate on the topic to discuss openly with different parties and stakeholders how to include the industry in the system. Several obstacles—not unlike those the inclusion of the aviation industry entailed—need resolution first. Domestic sea transportation, or those routes that start and end within the waters belonging to EU countries, is relatively easy to consider. The transportation that starts or ends in non-EU countries' waters and that reaches international waters in between ports is the delicate issue. Similar to complaints from the aviation industry, ship owners fear a competitive disadvantage.

It is tempting to adopt the aviation system for the shipping industry, after acknowledging the differences.

First, the aviation industry had already been under scrutiny for its emissions, and reliable emission data had been available before the introduction of the ETS (Kågeson 2007). Figures for fuel consumption and the accompanying emissions from shipping vary depending on the source. Unlike airplanes, which often are produced in series, a process that facilitates the generation of emission data per series and not per individual airplane, ships often are built individually with large differences between two types of ships.

Second, assigning the allowances for the emissions might create a problem. The owner of the ship, an external charterer, or an operator the owner hires might affect the operation of the ship. As the operator changes, so do the legal responsibilities. Ships also change flags sometimes; that is, the countries where they are registered and, accordingly, the legal regulations they are subject to change.

Finally, the European Trading System is—as the name implies—a European concept and not spread among other, non-EU nations. Although the EU countries taken together might represent one of the largest economies of the world, only three European ports exist among the twenty busiest ports in the world (World Shipping Council 2010). The majority of the world's containers pass through ports that do not belong to the ETS or abide by it. Other countries such as New Zealand have installed trading strategies or have projects under development, as does the Republic of Korea (Australian

Government n.d.), but none of them individually operates the tonnage and welcomes the mass of ships necessary to induce a sustainable change.

Other countries struggle to introduce efficient and lasting trading strategies at all, let alone specific ones for the shipping sector.

Although not very likely in the near future, the United States and China might be inclined to implement federal trading programs as well. In the United States, regional initiatives prevail with the Regional Greenhouse Gas Initiative as a pioneering example; it comprises nine East Coast states and takes on only the power sector so far. The Californian Emissions Trading Scheme started operating in 2012, and although the shipping industry is not included yet, it could really make a difference because of the immense economic power and thus industries that California represents (California Environmental Protection Agency 2011).

As of 2012, therefore, the shipping industry is not included in any trading system, nationally or internationally. First blueprints exist to include it, however, and within the next one or two decades, the shipping industry must deal with the trading of emissions allowances.

The Long-Term Perspective

Utopian-like pictures depict a far distant future where shipping has zero impact on the environment, without any carbon dioxide, nitrogen oxide, sulphur oxide, or noise emissions; where ballast water either is no longer necessary because scientists have found alternative ways to stabilize a ship, or where it does not harm entire ecosystems anymore; and where designers construct ships that are 100 percent recyclable. This vision supposes accomplishing all of this, of course, without raising prices for customers or consumers and with supply chains that are still flexible and secure.

This all sounds too good to be true, of course. Nonetheless, this scenario ought to be the ultimate goal toward which scientists, shipping companies, consumers, and other stakeholders should be working.

When it comes to the far future, there are two ways of approaching the subject: applying scenario techniques or following the path of technology.

Many scientists create scenarios whose existence depends on certain environmental conditions. Irrespective of the topic, most scenarios researchers develop are extreme ones, and the most likely outcome is a mixture of several scenarios. These scenarios often describe the general environment, atmosphere, or macroeconomic (study of economics in terms of whole systems) state.

The environmental conditions that experts believe to matter for the shipping industry's future are

the development of trade and economic growth, the awareness of and commitment to sustainability issues, the locus of power and global leadership, and the discovery of solutions for scarce resources (Wärtsilä 2010). The Finnish company Wärtsilä worked together with researchers to produce such scenarios and found three likely to emerge. The Rough Seas scenario depicts a scene where economic growth is limited, wealth is divided unequally, resources are so scarce that they have become a source of power, and every country looks out for itself. For sustainability, this scenario means that solutions are not international, but local. The limited economic growth and the regionalization efforts have led the shipping industry into an economic downturn, thus also reducing the environmental pollution it causes simply because of less traffic on the seas. Government control is fierce and mandates citizens to use resources only scarcely. This situation leads to resource savings but does not tackle the world's problems, such as environmental pollution enforced by the population growth at the root of these problems.

The Yellow River scenario shows China dominating the world's economy. Production has shifted to Africa, where living standards are rising, while consumption takes place in China, Europe, and the United States. The Western response to China's rise in power is heavy investment in research and development—from which the environment also benefits through new technologies that help to save resources and minimize pollution. Global agreements still do not exist, but both China and the Western countries rely on technology to solve the world's problems.

Finally, in the Open Seas scenario, global coordination is everything. Governments cooperate on global trade issues as well as environmental and sustainability issues. Unlike the first two scenarios, this scenario does not see climate change as a threat to humankind, but as an opportunity for business. Ships used as desalination plants (which remove salts and minerals), therefore, or as a recycling facility anchoring outside of the megacities, are a common sight. Sustainable cruise trips are en vogue.

Another trend or future researchers foresee involves similar conditions that largely will influence the future, such as the price of oil, the awareness of sustainability issues, and the desire to change within the society (PWC/IFK 2009). Experts participating in a survey about the future of transportation and logistics in 2009 do not believe in a major energy turnaround by 2030, but they expect a major growth in the renewable energy sector by then (PWC/IFK 2009). The omnipresent notion will be that those who reap the benefits will pay the costs of emissions. This idea requires exact and accurate data as grounds for financial calculations. Experts are convinced that the tracking, documentation, and disclosure of caused emissions will be compulsory for all types of logistics companies by 2030, and technology will need to facilitate this work (PWC/IFK 2009).

The flow of trade between countries suggests other conclusions. Although the trade flow between North America and Europe might be the largest in absolute numbers, in terms of growth, it lags far behind the trade volumes of intra-Asian trade and China-to-Africa trade (PWC/IFK 2010). The growth of the trade between North America and Europe used to be as large as the growth of the newly emerged flows of trade between Africa and Asia. One hypothesis might be that the more developed countries become, the less trade occurs between them. If this assumption holds true, then the more developed Asia and Africa become over the next decades, the less trade they will conduct with each other. Regionalization would be a consequence. Regionalization ultimately would mean less traffic at sea, which in turn implies less pollution at sea. This line of thinking might be considered very bold because most experts expect the volume of worldwide trade to grow, but their predictions reach only until the 2030s, while these hypotheses could be tested against reality within a century.

A more microeconomic or fine-grained perspective is taken when scientists follow the path of technology and venture guesses on future radical innovations or on incremental developments of already existing technology.

For shipping technology, this means creating even larger ships, creating ships that use other types of propulsion, or creating ships that inherit both characteristics.

As described in the previous section on medium-term developments, scientists pursue different paths for finding alternatives to fossil fuel. The culmination of these efforts, however, is the combination of several of them. Almost all major shipping companies have started plans on their "ship of the future." By 2030, Maersk, the Japanese shipping company Nippon Yusen Kaisha (NYK), and several other shipping companies want to be operating commercial freight carriers that have the minimum impact on the environment. A zero impact would be the optimum, but to acquire that state by 2030 is wishful thinking.

The A. P. Moller Maersk Group (or Maersk), currently the biggest shipping company in the world, already operates the largest container ships in the world, which can transport up to 12,000 standard containers at a time. By 2030, the company plans to have so-called Triple-E vessels at sea (Dasgupta 2011). Triple-E stands for exploiting economies of scale, increasing energy efficiency, and being environmentally improved. This type of ship can transport 18,000 standard containers at a time and purportedly can produce 50 percent less carbon dioxide emissions than the industry average on a Europe–Asia route (Dasgupta 2011). Ships of these dimensions,

however, require ports and authorities to follow in their developments of ports of the future; only a few, if any, ports are equipped to host such enormous vehicles. A port that could host ships of these proportions would have a competitive advantage because few will be equipped or rebuilt to do so. (It should be noted that the underlying issue of consumption—do we really need all of these things?—is not addressed by the ability to ship more and more materials across the oceans, however efficiently they are shipped.)

One of Maersk's competitors, NYK, is not missing the trend. NYK's Eco ship combines several "green" propulsion systems by using solar panels, retractable sails, and engines fueled by liquid natural gas (NYK n.d.). Similar designs that feature solar, wind, wave power energy, or a combination among them are only a playground for designers in the early twenty-first century, but drafts include finalization dates of between 2020 and 2030 (Marine Insight 2011).

Where to Go from Here

The figures do not suggest a bright future for the environment. The growth of the shipping industry and a significant increase in the volume of transported goods are likely. As the number of ships and the frequency at which they sail increases, however, so do the emissions they cause. Medium-term solutions include stricter legal regulations and a fiercer control of the companies' compliance. More long-term solutions include technology that does not seek to reduce the environmental impact of diesel, but seeks substitutes of bunker oil. These alternative fuels can separately, or even combined, contribute to alleviating the shipping industry's impact on the environment.

Anna GROBECKER and Julia WOLF
*EBS Universität für Wirtschaft und Recht
(EBS Business School, Germany)*

See also Economics, Steady State; Energy Efficiency; Fisheries; Global Trade; Progress; Water

FURTHER READING

AECOM. (2010). Freight best practice—Operational efficiency research. Retrieved on September 4, 2012, from http://www.freightbestpractice.org.uk/categories/3589_216_adroddiadau-ymchwil--research-reports-.aspx

Australian Government Department of Climate Change and Energy Efficiency. (n.d.). Emission trading schemes by country. Retrieved March 22, 2012, from http://www.climatechange.gov.au/government/international/global-action-facts-and-fiction/ets-by-country.aspx

British Broadcasting Company (BBC) News. (2008). Kite to pull ship across Atlantic. Retrieved March 22, 2012, from http://news.bbc.co.uk/2/hi/7201887.stm

Biello, David. (2009, November 30). World's first fuel cell ship docks in Copenhagen. *Scientific American.* Retrieved March 26, 2012, from http://www.scientificamerican.com/article.cfm?id=worlds-first-fuel-cell-ship

California Environmental Protection Agency. (2011). Cap and trade. Retrieved March 22, 2012, from http://www.arb.ca.gov/regact/2010/capandtrade10/capandtrade10.htm

Dasgupta, Soumyajit. (2011). Maersk's Triple-E vessels: The world's largest container ships might change the face of the shipping industry. *Marine Insight.* Retrieved March 22, 2012, from http://www.marineinsight.com/sports-luxury/futuristic-shipping/maersk%E2%80%99s-triple-e-vessels-the-worlds-largest-container-ships-might-change-the-face-of-shipping-industry/

European Commission. (n.d.). Emission Trading System (EU ETS). Retrieved March 22, 2012, from http://ec.europa.eu/clima/policies/ets/index_en.htm

Fuel Cells and Hydrogen Joint Undertaking (FCH JU). (2012). About FCH JU. Retrieved March 22, 2012, from http://www.fch-ju.eu/page/who-we-are

Green Car Congress. (2005). South Korea sets off down the hydrogen road. Retrieved March 22, 2012, from http://www.greencarcongress.com/2005/08/south_korea_set.html

Hart, Stuart. (2010). *Capitalism at the crossroads: Next generation business strategies for a post-crisis world* (3rd ed.). Upper Saddle River, NJ: Wharton School Publishing.

IBS Marine Consulting Group. (n.d.). Slower steaming could cut ship emissions by 15%. Retrieved March 22, 2012, from http://www.ibsmarine.com/index.php/20120307383/News-and-Events/IBS-News/Slower-steaming-could-cut-ship-emissions-by-15

International Maritime Organization (IMO). (2011). Pollution prevention. Retrieved April 8, 2012, from http://www.imo.org/OurWork/Environment/PollutionPrevention/Pages/Default.aspx

Kågeson, Per. (2007). Linking CO_2 emissions from international shipping to the EU ETS. *Natureassociates.se.* Retrieved March 22, 2012, from http://www.natureassociates.se/?page_id=134

Kahn Ribeiro, Suzana, & Kobayashi, Shigeki. (2007). Transport and its infrastructure. In *Climate change 2007: Mitigation.* Contribution of Working Group III to the Fourth Assessment Report of the Intergovernmental Panel on Climate Change. Cambridge, UK: Cambridge University Press.

Marine Insight. (2011). 10 Future ships that would change the face of the shipping industry. Retrieved March 22, 2012, from http://www.marineinsight.com/sports-luxury/futuristic-shipping/10-future-ships-that-would-change-the-face-of-the-shipping-industry/

Nippon Yusen Kaisha (NYK). (n.d.). NYK Super Eco Ship 2030. Retrieved March 22, 2012, from http://www.nyk.com/english/csr/envi/ecoship/

Reinikainen, Kari. (2009). Wind and LNG power Wartsila's cruise ferry design. *Cruise Business Review.* Retrieved March 26, 2012, from http://www.cruisebusiness.com/index.php?option=com_content&view=article&id=495:wind-and-lng-power-wartsilas-cruise-ferry-design&catid=48:top-headlines-category&Itemid=116

Sarvana, Adam. (2009). No safe harbor: The shipping industry's pollution problem part I: Low-hanging fruit. *Public Education Center DCBureau.org.* Retrieved March 22, 2012, from http://www.dcbureau.org/20090831730/natural-resources-news-service/no-safe-harbor-the-shipping-industrys-pollution-problem-part-i-low-hanging-fruit.html

United States Environmental Protection Agency (EPA). (2009). Regulatory announcement: Proposal of emission control area designation for geographic control of emissions from ships. Retrieved March 22, 2012, from http://www.epa.gov/nonroad/marine/ci/420f09015.htm

Vidal, John. (2007). CO_2 output from ships twice as much as airlines. *The Guardian.* Retrieved March 22, 2012, from http://www.guardian.co.uk/environment/2007/mar/03/travelsenvironmentalimpact.transportintheuk

PriceWaterhouseCoopers / Institute for Future Studies and Knowledge Management (PWC/IFK). (2009). *Transportation and logistics 2030: Vol. 1. How will supply chains evolve in an energy-constrained, low-carbon world?* London: PriceWaterhouseCoopers.

PriceWaterhouseCoopers / Institute for Future Studies and Knowledge Management (PWC/IFK). (2010). *Transportation and logistics 2030: Vol. 3. Emerging markets—New hubs, new spokes, new industry leaders?* London: PriceWaterhouseCoopers.

Pruzan-Jorgensen, Peder Michael, & Farrag, Angie. (2010). Sustainability trends in the container shipping industry. BSR. Retrieved April 8, 2012, from http://www.bsr.org/reports/BSR_Sustainability_Trends%20_Container_Shipping_Industry_September_2010.pdf

Schuler, Mike. (2012, March 14). *Viking Lady* going full hybrid as FellowSHIP Fuel Cell Project enters phase III. Retrieved September 4, 2012, from http://gcaptain.com/viking-lady-full-hybrid-fellowship/

Wärtsilä. (2010). Shipping scenarios 2030. Retrieved March 26, 2012, from http://www.shippingscenarios.wartsila.com/

World Shipping Council. (2010). Top 50 world container ports. Retrieved on March 22, 2012, from http://www.worldshipping.org/about-the-industry/global-trade/top-50-world-container-ports

Values

Conceptualizations of human values play a central role in the theory and practice of sustainability. How humans value the natural environment is central to how resources are distributed. A values typology, an arrangement of values by type, shows how humans express worth. Theories of sustainability must account for values differences, their measurement, and a system to weigh expressions of value over space and time.

However one defines sustainability, the concept, at its core, is about balancing human values in a world of limits. The Brundtland Commission, tasked with uniting countries in pursuing sustainable development, issued the Brundtland Report, commonly known as *Our Common Future*, in October 1987. The report stated that sustainability reflects an understanding that trade-offs are required for people within the present time and between people of the present and people of the future. Human well-being depends on, in part, natural, human, technological, and cultural resources. When these resources are limited, decisions must be made about their allocation across various uses. Values obviously matter in these allocations because different allocations serve different means, ends, and people. In the broadest sense, social processes and the outcomes these processes produce are sustainable if they continue to support what people consider important, which is determined by their values. "[M]ost debates over social policies, decisions, and actions are fundamentally disagreements over the relevance and priority of particular values" (Leiserowitz, Kates, and Parris 2006, 440).

Values matter in defining what is sustainable. They are the foundation upon which human behaviors are built. This case is made by the sociological researcher and president of the Social and Environmental Research Institute Paul Stern and colleagues when they say, "[N]orm-based actions flow from three factors: acceptance of particular personal values, beliefs that things important to those values are under threat, and beliefs that actions initiated by the individual can help alleviate the threat and restore the values" (Stern et al. 1999, 83).

If people are to use values to define and measure what it means to achieve sustainability, they must think about the different ways values can be characterized and, because not all humans hold the same values, the different ways of weighing values in social decision making.

The Nature of Human Values

Diverse frameworks of types are used to compare and contrast values. Discussions of values typically are anthropocentric, meaning they are based on how humans express what they consider worthwhile or valuable. For example, the social psychologist and cross-cultural researcher Shalom Schwartz suggests a formal definition: "A value is a (1) belief (2) pertaining to desirable end states or modes of conduct, that (3) transcends specific situations, (4) guides selection or evaluation of behavior, people, and events, and (5) is ordered by importance relative to other values to form a system of value priorities" (Schwartz 1994, 20). Such definitions, by design, do not explain the content of values.

In one way of thinking about content, values are desirable outcomes, outcomes that might be components of sustainability or might be equally important with sustainability. These outcomes are states of being or developments that humans find to be worthwhile inherently. Peace, freedom, progress, growth, or environmental quality are all concepts that express what some people see as human values. The US research scientist Anthony Leiserowitz and colleagues identify multiple attempts to characterize such values as outcomes that are both implicit and explicit in the sustainability literature (Leiserowitz, Kates, and Parris 2006).

An alternative way to think about values is in terms of motivation. Schwartz outlines what he terms "motivational" values (1994, 24). His model has four higher-order value types with a total of ten motivational types of values clustered under the higher-order values: (1) openness to change, (2) self-direction, (3) stimulation, (4) hedonism, (5) self-enhancement, (6) achievement, (7) power, (8) conservation, (9) security, (10) tradition, (11) conformity, (12) self-transcendence, (13) universalism, and (14) benevolence. Schwartz finds these value types to be consistently related in both theoretical and empirical ways. In Schwartz's model, some combinations of these motivational values might be more consistent with sustainability than other combinations.

Several authors think of values in terms of their orientation, for whom or to what end the object of the value is supporting some particular behavior (Schultz et al. 2005, 458–459). There are five broad categories of orientation or object of value: (1) self, (2) other individuals (individual altruism), (3) other groups of humans (collective altruism), (4) all living things (individually or as a system), and (5) all aspects of the natural world, living or not (even larger systems thinking).

Finally, in the sustainability realm, there is a combined approach to the structure of what is valuable. In this sense, specific sustainability values relate to both orientation and motivation. A typology of values in this sense is presented below. (See figure 1 on page 215.)

Sustainability Context for Values

Although many discussions cover the meanings of *sustainability* as a noun or *sustainable* as an adjective, most of them entail some element of underlying values. As a three-part concept, sustainable development addresses the interactions between economy, community, and the environment and speaks to cooperation and competition both within generations and between generations (UNDP 2011, 1). There is a growing interest in sustainability science, an emerging discipline "that seeks to understand the fundamental character of interaction between nature and society" (Kates et al. 2001). Central to the conduct of sustainability science is the importance of stakeholder engagement (i.e., the involvement of all of those who have an interest in the outcome of a policy dealing with sustainability), which makes explicit the ways in which values affect our understanding of what is sustainable (van Kerkhof and Lebel 2006). This new understanding of the central role of values in sustainability challenges traditional approaches of science. "Many decisions are also affected by values, attitudes, and belief systems that are completely unrelated to or in direct conflict with rationales based on scientific information" (Hart and Calhoun 2010, 260).

Inherent in most views of sustainability is the tension between how we allocate resources across people in the present (intragenerational equity) and across people of the present and future (intergenerational equity). Although people clearly need trade-offs here about what specific bequests they owe to the future, in a general sense, sustainability is a legacy construct, a framework for asking what condition the present should leave the state of the world for the future (Norton 2005). In economic terms, sustainability is thus considered a problem of capital investment and depreciation. "Strong" sustainability assures we provide the future an undiminished stock of natural capital essential to human well-being. This approach values environmental quality as measured by the aspects of natural systems that provide ecosystem services to humans. The alternative, often favored by neoclassical economists (who favor determining prices, outputs, and income distributions in markets through supply and demand), is "weak" sustainability. In this view, economists view capital types—natural, artificial, and human—as largely interchangeable. Our obligation to the future in this view is to leave the future an aggregate stock of capital capable of serving human needs and wants (Solow 2000). Aggregate capital stock is the sum of human capabilities, physical and technological resources, and natural processes humans have available to them for the production of goods and services they find desirable.

The debate over weak versus strong sustainability often has focused on whether we can know what future generations will want or need. Advocates of strong sustainability presume to know something about what the future will value and, hence, presume that natural capital should be undiminished (Norton 2005, chap. 8). Advocates of weak sustainability are uncertain about future values and therefore conclude that our obligation to the future is to provide undiminished opportunities derived from all capital types. One type of capital can be substituted for another across a broad range of production opportunities.

This debate, then, revolves around the nature of values, how people think about what is valuable about the natural environment, and how they might measure those values. Whether natural capital is irreplaceable or not partly depends on how we think about environmental values.

Typology of Environmental Values

In its simplest version, measuring environmental values is seen as essentially a trade-off between anthropocentric (considering humans the most significant entity in the universe) and biocentric (considering all forms of life as having intrinsic value) views of nature. The New Ecological Paradigm (Dunlap 2008) creates a one-dimensional scale of environmental worldviews (which reflects underlying values) contrasting a pro-ecological ideal with a dominant social ideal. The German researchers Michael Wiseman and Franz X. Bogner create an alternative scale with two dimensions: (1) preservation concern and apathy and (2) utilization

concern and apathy (Wiseman and Bogner 2003). The US philosopher Bryan Norton explores this view of environmental values when he compares the approaches of economics with that of environmental ethics (2005, 160–161). Each field claims that its respective views on how to value nature (economism versus intrinsic value theory) can be comprehensive and monistic. That is to say, each theory claims to capture all the relevant value types (comprehensive) using a single conceptual framework (monistic). Norton assesses these claims and asserts, "If we reject this sharp dichotomy between instrumental and intrinsic values and the associated classification of natural objects as instruments or as moral beings, a pluralistic and integrative position emerges as a possibility: there are many ways in which humans value nature" (Norton 2005, 187). What is valued about the natural world is complex, and environmental values clearly are not always dichotomous. In other words, a person might value an aspect of the natural environment due to multiple motivations at the same time—values are not necessarily mutually exclusive.

To get at this complexity of environmental values types, figure 1 (on page 215) is a typology of values. This typology includes values that both motivate and reflect different orientations. To begin with, a fundamental distinction exists between anthropocentric and biocentric value (Dietz, Fitzgerald, and Shwom 2005, 341).

Biocentric Values

Biocentric value is sometimes called intrinsic value, the worth of an aspect of the natural world without reference to humans—the value of nature in and of itself. Some have challenged whether such a concept is an oxymoron in the sense that value inherently is a human construct that is meaningless when invoked without reference to humans (Norton 2005). That logical problem notwithstanding, many people believe that nature is valuable whether or not it provides humans with goods or services. For them, this sense is clearly different from *existence value*, a human-centered concept discussed below.

At least three potential orientations of biocentric or intrinsic value exist, all of which imply some sense of the extension of rights beyond humans (Stone 1974):

1. The value of the individual member of a species.
2. The value of the species as a whole.
3. The value of ecosystems, including nonbiotic elements of ecosystem function.

Many interpret the US ecologist and environmentalist Aldo Leopold's (1949) concept of the land ethic as an

Figure 1. Typology of Values

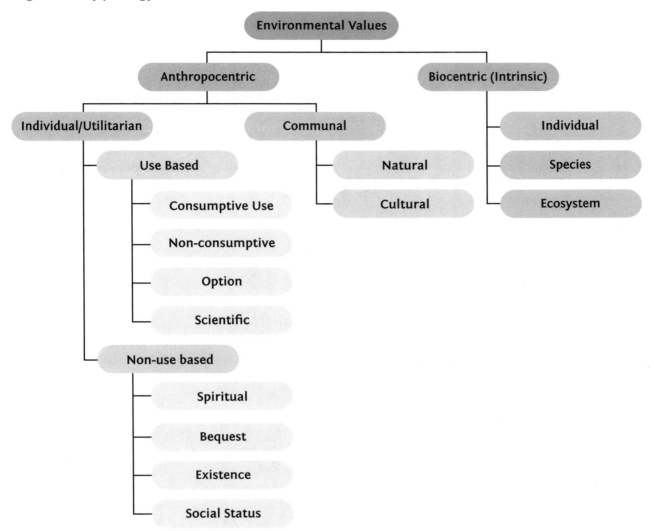

The values labeled in this figure are broken down into a hierarchy of subcategories, but the weight of a category's value is subjective. Human values types are organized in a hierarchy to reflect relationships with each other, recognizing that humans may express several values simultaneously.

expression of this type of value. Leopold argued for expansion of the human community to include "the land," what we might call nature today. In this view we should use the same ethical standards to define our relationship to aspects of the natural world that we use when we consider other humans. A tree is not merely an instrument for creating human well-being; it is an entity that has value in and of itself, without reference to its usefulness to humans.

Whether or not it is appropriate to talk about intrinsic value, intrinsic value clearly is not measurable in any meaningful sense because measurement would imply some human orientation. This type of value is

also called *biospheric altruism* (Dietz, Fitzgerald, and Shwom 2005).

Individual Anthropocentric Values

In contrast to intrinsic value, nature can also be worthwhile in reference to what its meaning is to humans; so we speak of anthropocentric or human-centered value. Nature provides for humans in multiple ways. Sometimes the worth of these is called *utilitarian value* because the environment contributes to human well-being (or utility, for economists). Four of these values are use-based in that they derive from direct use, while four are values that generate utility without direct use.

Consumptive use value is the worth from nature generated by "consuming" the aspect of nature. So, the worth humans gain from killing a turtle to make turtle soup from the meat or a bowl from the turtle shell is termed consumptive use value. This value is often measured in economics in terms of market values, or willingness to pay. These market values are usually excludable (one that readily can be prevented from consumption) and "rival" (one person's consumption means another cannot consume the same thing), resulting in a good that economists call a private good. The non-excludable and non-rival nature of non-consumptive use values typically are part of the explanation for public goods market failure. Scenic vistas are of this type; it is generally hard to exclude people from enjoying them, and one person's viewing of them does not diminish their scenic character. Hence they are termed *public goods*, ones that no private firm will provide and therefore need to be provided by the government.

Of course, the turtle could also be useful to people in non-consumptive ways. For example, people benefit from watching turtles in the wild or maintaining turtles as pets. In such uses, the turtle would generate *non-consumptive use values*. These values are often non-rival. For example, one person's enjoyment in watching a turtle normally does not diminish another person's ability to also get value from watching the same turtle, although the viewing platform might get crowded. The non-excludable and non-rival nature of non-consumptive use values are part of the typical explanation for public goods market failure.

Even if a person does not eat or watch turtles now, at least two other uses of turtles might make him or her value them. First, someone who thinks that eating or watching turtles in the future would be worthwhile might value the option of preserving the turtle for that future use. Scientists who invoke the precautionary

principle in advocating the preservation of certain natural resources often are appealing to *option value*. (The precautionary principle posits that if we are uncertain of something, such as the ramifications of a new technology, it is best to err on the side of caution because it is often too late after the technology has been introduced.) Tropical forests may be important because they may hold a plant or animal species from which pharmaceuticals will be derived in the future. This example is related to the last use-based value, *scientific value*, which might be considered as a specific example of option value. An aspect of nature may be worth protecting because through its study, we learn important lessons about nature, potentially applicable beyond this specific instance.

Four instances of nonuse of parts of nature are valued because they produce some indirect utility. Human history contains many examples of elements of the natural world that are central parts of belief systems (Hornborg 2001). Society might say that these have spiritual value and that the believers would be diminished if those elements of nature were lost. So, if turtles were part of some culturally significant belief system, they might have *spiritual value*.

Another nonuse value is *bequest value*. People may not eat, view, or study turtles, and they may not value doing any of these activities in the future. Yet they may feel an obligation to preserve turtles so that humans in the future may have those opportunities. This perspective is altruistic, where the focus is not oneself or nature; rather, it is a sense of obligation to future humans. Bequest value is also called *altruistic option value*.

Even if people do not eat turtles, or watch, study, or worship them, do not think they will wish to do so in the future, and do not care if future generations have these opportunities, they still might get value just knowing that turtles exist. People often confuse *existence value* with intrinsic value, but the concept is very different. The focus of intrinsic value is the aspect of nature, without reference to humans. Existence value is human centered. The presence of turtles is valuable simply because it makes people feel good knowing that they exist.

Finally, utilitarian value can be derived from a person's desire to be well regarded by other people. So, when a person acts to preserve the natural world and lets other people know about the act, this might be a source of social status (Gordon 1977). Here, the person gains *status value* from telling people he or she works to preserve turtles.

Communal Anthropocentric Values

Norton argues that one of the shortcomings of neoclassical economic thinking is the assumption that all values are individualistic. In this model, total value is the sum of the values of all the individuals. He proposes that some values transcend individuals and accrue to the community, but not as the sum of individual valuations. "Communal goods are understood as goods that emerge on a community level, a scale larger than that on which the goods of individuals are observed or calculated, and they are not commensurable with, or reducible to, individual goods or aggregations of individual goods" (2005, 240). Hence, these are known as *communal values*, the ways in which elements in the natural world are important to the community beyond their value to individuals. Sources of this value could be a landscape feature, the Bavarian Alps or the Mississippi River delta, that helps to define a sense of place. Or it could be a cultural artifact, like the Sydney Opera House, that gives a sense of human engagement with place. It might even be legend; think of Paul Bunyan, the mythic giant woodcutter claimed by several forest-based communities from Maine to Michigan. Each of these gives a sense of place that defines community and thus is a collective value.

Outlook

Whatever definition of sustainability is adopted, it is about what matters to people, now and in the future. The difficulty is that choices are necessary. "Measurement of environmental values, especially as they are understood and projected across time, is a central problem for any theory of sustainability" (Norton 2005, 155). Human, natural, technological, and cultural resources are scarce, and allocating those resources to serve the values of one person limits their availability to serve the values of another. Because what people value varies both from person to person and over time, the obvious problem is how to use values to make choices both within and between generations.

Making these choices is even more difficult than it first appears. How do we weigh the values of different people? In other words, whose values count and by how much? How do we measure and compare different types of values? What if the turtle is at the same time the central icon representing transcendent authority for a spiritual community, in the way that salmon were sacred to Native American groups in the Pacific Northwest, the source of tissue thought to be effective in the future for treating a prevalent disease, a focus of nature-based tourism economy in a developing nation, and a common meat source for soup production and threatened by overharvesting. It would have potential spiritual value, option value, non-consumptive use value, and consumptive use value. Although some economists assert that all relevant values can be measured in dollar terms, no commensurable metric is available for these different values, nor is there an obvious way to compare them systematically if such a metric existed.

Indeed, the criticism of neoclassical welfare theory is that it presumes to make such comparisons, but the method is unsatisfying on ethical terms, creating what some call an accounting problem (Norton and Toman 2003, 233). Welfare economics, the study of human well-being from the distribution and consumption of goods and services, assumes that the present value of net benefits is the appropriate measure of value and that human welfare is improved as long as those whose net benefits are increased could (but do not necessarily) compensate those whose net benefits decrease and remain better off. The assumption that relevant values can be measured in the same terms and that the distribution of net benefits does not matter makes this approach unacceptable in a sustainability context. To be clear about the latter point—the standard theory of welfare economics implies that a bigger pie is always better than a smaller pie, a concept underlying growth theory. Most sustainability definitions, however, include the concept of preserving the future while also enhancing the economic status of the have-nots. This latter addition implies that some redistribution should be made, and thus over time sustainable development should lead to a shrinking of the income gap.

The challenge for sustainability science then is to develop a theory that accommodates multiple values that are not readily commensurable within a system of fair weightings across space and time.

Mark W. ANDERSON & Mario TEISL
University of Maine

See also Collective Learning; Community; Education, Higher; Economics, Steady State; Natural Capital; Nuclear Power; Progress

FURTHER READING

Dietz, Thomas; Fitzgerald, Amy; & Shwom, Rachael. (2005). Environmental values. *Annual Review of Environment and Resources, 30*, 335–372.

Dunlap, Riley E. (2008). The new environmental paradigm scale: From marginality to worldwide use. *Journal of Environmental Education, 40*(1), 3–18.

Gordon, Theodore J. (1977). Lifestyle of the future: Conspicuous conservation. *Vital Speeches of the Day, 43*(18), 557–563.

Hart, David D., & Calhoun, Aram J. K. (2010). Rethinking the role of ecological research in the sustainable management of freshwater systems. *Freshwater Biology, 55*(Suppl. 1), 258–269.

Hornborg, Alf. (2001). *The power of the machine.* Walnut Creek, CA: Alta Mira Press.

Kates, Robert W., et al. (2001). Sustainability Science. *Science, 292*, 641–642.

Leopold, Aldo. (1949). *A Sand County almanac.* New York: Oxford University Press.

Leiserowitz, Anthony A.; Kates, Robert W.; & Parris, Thomas M. (2006). Sustainability values, attitudes, and behaviors: A review of multinational and global trends. *Annual Review of Environment and Resources, 31*, 413–444.

Norton, Bryan. (2005). *Sustainability: A philosophy of adaptive ecosystem management.* Chicago: University of Chicago Press.

Norton, Bryan, & Toman, Michael A. (2003). Sustainability: Ecological and economic perspectives. In Bryan G. Norton (Ed.), *Searching for sustainability: Interdisciplinary essays in the philosophy of conservation biology.* Cambridge, UK: Cambridge University Press.

Schultz, P. Wesley, et al. (2005). Values and their relationship to environmental concern and environmental behavior. *Journal of Cross-Cultural Psychology, 36*(4), 457–475.

Schwartz, Shalom H. (1994). Are there universal aspects in the structure and content of human values? *Journal of Social Issues, 50*(4), 19–45.

Solow, Robert M. (2000). Sustainability: An economist's perspective. In. R. N. Stavins (Ed.), *Economics of the environment.* New York: W. W. Norton.

Stern, Paul C.; Dietz, Thomas; Abel, Troy; Guagnano, Gregory A.; & Kalof, Linda. (1999). A value-belief-norm theory of support for social movements: The case of environmentalism. *Human Ecology Review, 6*(2), 81–97.

Stone, Christopher D. (1974). *Should trees have standing? Toward legal rights for natural objects.* San Francisco: William Kaufman.

United Nations Development Programme (UNDP). (2011). *Sustainability and equity: A better future for all.* New York: UNDP.

Van Kerkhof, Lorrae, & Lebel, Louis. (2006). Linking knowledge and action for sustainable development. *Annual Review of Environment & Resources, 31*, 445–477.

Wiseman, Michael, & Bogner, Franz X. (2003). A higher-order model of ecological values and its relationship to personality. *Personality & Individual Differences, 34*(5), 783–794.

Berkshire's authors and editors welcome questions, comments, and corrections. Send your emails about the *Berkshire Encyclopedia of Sustainability* in general or this volume in particular to: sustainability.updates@berkshirepublishing.com

Waste—Engineering Aspects

Waste minimization and pollution prevention have been the initial steps in moving away from the unsustainable industrial, municipal, agricultural, mining, and other processes in recent decades that have led to massive amounts of wastes to be collected and stored in landfills, incinerated, or otherwise handled in ways that have threatened the environment and public health. Green chemistry, green engineering, and other systematic approaches allow processes to be seen from a life cycle perspective and eliminate unsustainable aspects of processes. Waste management is increasingly adopting sustainable approaches, which are preferable to the ever increasing need to handle and treat wastes.

The amount and type of waste generated are indirectly proportional to the sustainability of a process. Environmental awareness of waste grew in the second half of the twentieth century. With this awareness came the public demand for environmental safeguards and remedies to environmental problems, along with an expectation of a greater role for government. In the United States, a number of laws were on the books prior to the 1960s, such as early versions of federal legislation to address limited types of water and air pollution and some solid waste issues, such as the need to eliminate open dumping.

The nineteenth century showed rapid industrial and urban growth across Europe and the United States, and with it came new kinds and greater amounts of wastes. An 1897 report to Great Britain's Royal Commission on River Pollution describes extensive pollution of the Tawe River in Wales from "alkali works, copper works, sulfuric acid liquid, sulfate of iron from tin-plate works, and by slag, cinders and small coal" (Markham 1994). Two years later in the United States, key legislation to protect waterways and riparian ecosystems was written in the form of the Rivers and Harbors Act of 1899 (the law that set the stage for wetland protection around the world).

The need for such laws was not exclusive to Great Britain and the United States. Indeed, nearly every nation now has its own set of regulations to address unique waste needs. For example, sparsely populated countries with wide open spaces sometimes do not insist on strict landfilling rules often required by more densely populated countries.

Environmental awareness and commensurate regulation grew throughout the twentieth century. The tumultuous decade of the 1960s was a particularly important time when environmental issues came to be seen as one of a number of social causes, including the civil rights and anti-war movements. Major public demonstrations on the need to protect "spaceship earth" encouraged elected officials to address environmental problems, exemplified by air pollution "inversions" that capped polluted air in urban valleys (leading to acute diseases and increased mortality from inhalation hazards), the "death" of Lake Erie from industrial waste, the shrinking of the Aral Sea from wanton irrigation practices, and rivers catching on fire in industrialized regions.

One of the key features of the new environmental laws was the requirement to conduct environmental assessments for large public projects, like roadways and dams. For example, several nations in North America and Europe require environmental impact statements (EISs). These usually require that after notification of the intent to undertake a large project, the environmental agencies will identify what needs to be included in the EIS, if one is required. This includes a description of the project and alternatives. The EIS also describes the environmental impacts, especially those expected to be significant, and the measures needed to mitigate these impacts. The public and other interested parties review the EIS. The environmental agencies need sufficient information to determine both the direct and indirect effects of a project. An example of a direct effect would be releases of contaminants into the air or water. An indirect effect would be to provide access to a roadway or other amenities that lead to urban sprawl.

Numerous environmental laws have been enacted around the world to address environmental problems. Those that specifically address waste generally consider hazardous and nonhazardous wastes. For example, two principal US laws governing solid wastes are the Resource Conservation and Recovery Act (RCRA) and Superfund (Comprehensive Environmental Response, Compensation, and Liability Act, or CERCLA). The RCRA law covers active waste sites for both hazardous and solid wastes, whereas Superfund and its amendments generally address abandoned hazardous waste sites. Other countries also address active and abandoned waste sites, but in various ways.

Municipal Solid Waste

When engineers and managers discuss solid waste, they generally mean municipal solid waste (MSW), which includes all wastes generated within a municipality, but may also include industrial waste and agricultural material that find their way into the waste stream that a municipality must handle. Addressing MSW means that engineers need to know how these wastes are generated in order to devise plans for collection, transport, and disposal. In most cases, MSW varies, but almost always consists mainly of food waste and garbage from residential areas. (See table 1 below.) Depending on the location,

it may also include street sweepings, commercial and institutional nonhazardous wastes, as well as localized construction and demolition waste (Pariathamby 2011).

Defining Wastes

The term *waste* has many connotations. In general, a waste is something that is to be discarded because it is deemed to have no value. It may even be harmful. All of these aspects of wastes depend on perception, however. The old adage that one person's trash is another person's treasure is quite accurate. Minimizing or eliminating wastes from a process can be achieved by assigning value to what would have been discarded and sent to a landfill, emitted to the atmosphere, or discharged into a water body.

A working definition of waste, then, is that it is any process's by-product that must be discarded. Such wastes are distinguished in two ways. First, where are they likely to be found after they are discarded? A water pollutant is a waste that finds its way to water. Likewise land and air pollutants are likely to be found in the soil and atmosphere, respectively, after they are released. Second, wastes are distinguished according to their harm. Usually, this distinction is between nonhazardous and hazardous wastes.

Some wastes are common to many countries or pollutants from the wastes can be transported long distances in the atmosphere. Therefore, such wastes represent an international problem, such as nuclear waste, for example. Indeed, the amount of nuclear waste from electrical power generation is expected to increase substantially this century. The International Atomic Energy Agency (IAEA)

TABLE 1. Mean Composition of Municipal Solid Waste in the US and the UK

	United States	United Kingdom
Paper and cardboard	31%	23%
Food	13%	18%
Garden / yard waste	13%	14%
Plastics	12%	10%
Metals	8%	4%
Textiles	8%	3%
Wood	7%	4%
Glass	5%	7%
Other*	3%	17%

Sources: McLeod and Cherrett (2011); UK Defra (2009); and US EPA (2008).

Note: The "other" category for the United Kingdom includes furniture (1.3%) and electrical waste (2.2%), which are included in the wood, metals, and other waste categories in the United States.

developed a system to categorize these wastes into three classes according to levels of radioactivity (Marra and Palmer 2011). Exempt wastes have sufficiently low concentrations of radionuclides (atoms with unstable nuclei) to be excluded from regulation. Low- and intermediate-level wastes contain enough radioactive material to require actions to ensure the protection of workers and the public for short or extended periods of time. High-level wastes have sufficiently high levels of radioactive materials that require containment and segregation for long periods of time, depending on the half-lives of the radionuclides (perhaps millions of years). Risk is a function of exposure, so even exempt and very low-level waste must be disposed of properly. For example, a small quantity of radioactive materials in one electronic product may not present much risk, but if millions of these products find their way to landfills, the risks could be substantial.

Active Hazardous Waste Facilities

The growing number of identified hazardous wastes in the 1970s and 1980s caused nations to revamp older solid waste laws. Notably, waste began to be appreciated as the by-product of unsustainable and unsystematic thinking. This was a step toward life cycle analysis for industrial and municipal operations. Particularly hazardous wastes had to be monitored from "cradle-to-grave" (Vallero 2011b). This means that manifests must be prepared to keep track of the waste, including its generation, transportation, treatment, storage, and disposal. The new laws often added provisions for hazardous wastes while strengthening requirements against open dumping and other traditional solid waste management.

Protecting groundwater became the prominent interest of hazardous waste laws, which were expanded in the 1980s to address leaks, including those from underground storage tanks that contain petroleum and other hazardous substances. For example, certain chemicals became associated with gasoline and other fuel tanks, which are now referred to as BTEX, for benzene,

toluene, ethylbenzene, and xylenes. When BTEX is detected in soil or groundwater, there is often a leaking underground storage tank or there has been a spill of petroleum-based fuel.

In the developed world, large facilities can treat and dispose of many types of hazardous wastes. These facilities are able to take advantage of economies of scale by incorporating many treatment processes that might not be economical for individual generators. For example, in the Czech Republic from 1993 to 1998, very large companies enjoyed economies of scale in controlling pollution at their facilities compared to smaller firms. This relationship is neither linear nor is it universal, because moderately large firms in the Czech Republic performed less efficiently on average than small firms at controlling air pollutant emissions (Earnhart and Lizal 2011).

Comprehensive facilities are able to exploit the combined opportunities made possible by having many different types of waste present at a single site. These include using waste acids and alkalies to neutralize each other; waste oxidants to treat cyanides; organic contaminants in water, salts, and acids to precipitate organic compounds from wastewater; onsite incinerators to dispose of organic vapors generated by other onsite processes; ash, calcium, and magnesium oxides to aid in stabilization processes; and combustible solids and liquids to produce blended liquid fuels.

Abandoned Hazardous Waste Sites

Throughout the world, hazardous waste has been disposed of improperly, requiring cleanup operations. Thousands of these sites have been identified and approximately two thousand sites require immediate action. Environmental regulations lay out explicit steps for cleaning up contamination (Vallero 2011b).

Cleaning up abandoned disposal sites involves isolating and containing contaminated material, removing and treating contaminated sediments, and direct treatment of the hazardous wastes involved in the original places they are found (in situ). In the United States, for example, CERCLA (commonly known as Superfund) was enacted in 1980 to create a tax on the chemical and petroleum industries and to provide extensive federal authority for responding directly to releases or threatened releases of hazardous substances that may endanger public health or the environment. The law established prohibitions and requirements concerning closed and abandoned hazardous waste sites; established provisions for the liability of persons responsible for releases of hazardous waste at these sites; and established a trust fund to provide for cleanup when no responsible party could be identified.

There are two basic approaches for reducing the risks presented at hazardous waste sites:

1. Short-term removals, where actions may be taken to address releases or threatened releases requiring prompt response. This is intended to eliminate or reduce exposures to possible contaminants.
2. Long-term remedial response actions to reduce or eliminate the hazards and risks associated with releases or threats of releases of hazardous substances that are serious but not immediately life threatening. These actions are usually part of a contingency plan, which sets guidelines and procedures required when responding to releases and threatened releases of hazardous substances.

The decision on which of these approaches to take is based on the immediacy and potential contact with the hazard. If this threat is high, it is likely that barriers would be installed, alternative sources of drinking water made available, and other measures taken to prevent exposures. These may be followed by longer term cleanup efforts, known as remediation.

Sustainable Approaches

Waste generation is a necessary reality associated with public health, environmental quality, and economic development. Until recently, societies have assumed an almost inexhaustible supply of resources. Such inertia has been, and will continue to be, difficult to overcome. The transition from open dumps to engineered facilities, such as landfills, can be seen as the first major step toward sustainability. This was a difficult but largely successful step in much of the developed world; open dumps remain in the developing world, however, in part because of the lack of infrastructure for collection and the scarcity of funds to provide the engineered system.

The second step in the transition was to develop ways to treat and prevent exposures to hazardous substances

found in wastes. These efforts continue throughout the world. The appreciation for the risks from these hazards has provided the emphasis for waste reduction and pollution prevention. These steps depend on life cycle perspectives, that is, on considering the processes that have led or could lead to the generation of wastes. The logical next step is to find alternatives that lead to less waste while providing the same benefits to society.

The first steps have been completely achieved mainly because, like other environmental problems, waste management has traditionally been a reaction to problems as they arise individually on a case-by-case basis. Indeed, the waste was an accepted feature or afterthought that had to be addressed if we wanted a particular good. The new and future paradigm is to view processes proactively and systematically with an eye toward preventing the generation of wastes rather than building ever increasing capacity to address waste as inevitable by-products. In this way, the volume of wastes is reduced; waste streams not only are rendered less toxic and reusable, but processes are ultimately changed to eliminate the wastes completely (Vallero 2011a). Waste managers thus now have a number of approaches available to them, beyond waste collection, storage, and treatment.

Indeed, everyone is a "waste manager," since everything we do has the potential to generate wastes. Waste production varies according to what we choose to eat, the form of transportation we decide to employ, the materials we use to do our jobs, the items we purchase, what we decide to throw in the trash can versus the recycling container, what we repurpose, and even what we advertise online. Thus, we should view each of our decisions using a personal life cycle assessment.

Recycling

One major societal shift has been the increasing acceptance of recycling in recent decades. In the United States, for example, each person generated slightly more waste in 2010 than in 1980. The good news is that during the same time frame, each person's recycling rate increased even more rapidly. Recycling in 1980 amounted to less than 10 percent of the average municipal waste, but increased to 34 percent in 2010. This means that recycling more than tripled, which substantially reduced the volume of waste delivered to landfills. Landfills had to handle nearly 90 percent of the waste generated by the average household in 1980. Largely because of recycling, landfills now have to handle only about half of the household waste generated. This has reduced the acreage that would have gone to waste sites and has provided sorely needed cost savings to cash-strapped municipalities.

Land Preservation

In addition to recycling solid wastes, engineers, scientists, planners, and designers in governments, industries, agriculture, and other areas are increasingly employing waste minimization, pollution prevention, and other systematic approaches. Green chemistry and engineering apply scientific principles to consider every element of the process or product's life cycle. This mutually benefits the client, the public, and the environment. Waste products can decrease in volume and mass as green designs replace traditional methods of manufacturing, use, and disposal.

Wastes must be managed (and, ideally, avoided) by means of applying the laws of science in addition to the societal shifts of recycling and reusing. Generally, land is the environmental receptacle of wastes. The US ecologist and environmentalist Aldo Leopold, in his famous essays, posthumously published as *A Sand County Almanac*, argued for a holistic approach toward land: "A thing is right when it tends to preserve the integrity, stability, and beauty of the biotic community. It is wrong when it tends otherwise" (Leopold 1949, 262).

Land is threatened in a number of ways. Topsoil can be lost. Soil and water can be contaminated by chemical pollutants, such as from the leachate (a solution that contains contaminants through the leaching of soil) from landfills, hazardous waste storage and treatment facilities, and even from atmospheric pollutants, for example, sulfur and nitrogen compounds that lead to acid rain.

Land can be altered physically in a manner that renders the land less useful or makes its future usage sustainable. Construction, agriculture, transportation, and other human activities lead to the release of chemical contaminants, but also result in landscape damage, such as soil erosion, habitat destruction, and loss of resources, such as wetlands and coastal ecosystems. Biological threats include invasive plant species that can greatly reduce biodiversity, as well as invasive animal species that will upset ecological balances, such as predator-prey relationships. Microbes are also threats to land, such as when medical wastes are improperly disposed, increasing potential exposures to pathogens.

Sustainable waste management thus must consider more than landfills, incinerators, infrastructure, and other "built forms." It requires a view of the totality of matter and energy, with an eye toward ways to reduce "leakage" from the system. The US architect and sustainability pioneer William McDonough and the German chemist Michael Braungart captured quite well the need to shift the waste paradigm:

> For the engineer that has always taken—indeed has been trained his or her entire life to take—a traditional, linear, cradle to grave approach, focusing on "one-size fits-all" tools and systems, and who expects to use materials and chemicals and energy as he or she has always done, the shift to new models and more diverse input can be unsettling. (McDonough and Braungart 2002, 165)

Land Use Planning

Thoughtful land use planning can enhance health, safety, and general welfare (Vallero and Vallero 2011). The plan recognizes the connection between people and land. A good plan not only protects things at the surface, but considers ways to preserve and protect groundwater and to conserve sensitive habitats, geologic features, soil, and topography. Plans must include measures beyond zoning, such as siting open space areas and roadways to prevent air pollution, minimize congestion, and reduce reliance on fossil fuels, so that several modes are encouraged, including walking, bicycling, and public transit use.

Thoughtful land management can help to reduce wastes that contribute to climate change. For example, zoning that encourages cleanup and new land uses of previously contaminated zones, known as brownfields, can reduce the amount of waste from vehicles (e.g., exhaust, spillage, and tires) because such sites are often centrally located in old industrial zones (US EPA 2009). Proper land use planning reduces wastes directly and indirectly. When development occurs in outlying areas, it is often followed by a demand for services and infrastructure, such as roads, sewers, and electricity. This entails moving earth, cutting down trees, and other major environmental changes. The direct effects of infrastructure expansion also include disposal of the removed materials, which often find their way to landfills or are burned onsite. Indirect waste generation can result from poorly sited structures, such as those allowed near coasts and hazard zones (e.g., subsidence areas above underground mines). This may require demolition in future years, with the need to dispose of material. Proper land use planning is thus an important means of waste reduction.

Waste Management Hierarchy

Managing wastes typically starts with finding effective means of collecting, storing, and treating wastes. Waste managers may well know that such a reactive approach is not ideal, but the existing problems often dictate such immediacy. Increasing recycling and waste reduction, however, are being employed, beginning at the top of the hierarchy in figure 1 on page 225 and proceeding downward, if necessary (ideally, if the waste is eliminated,

Figure 1. Hierarchy of Waste Management Choices

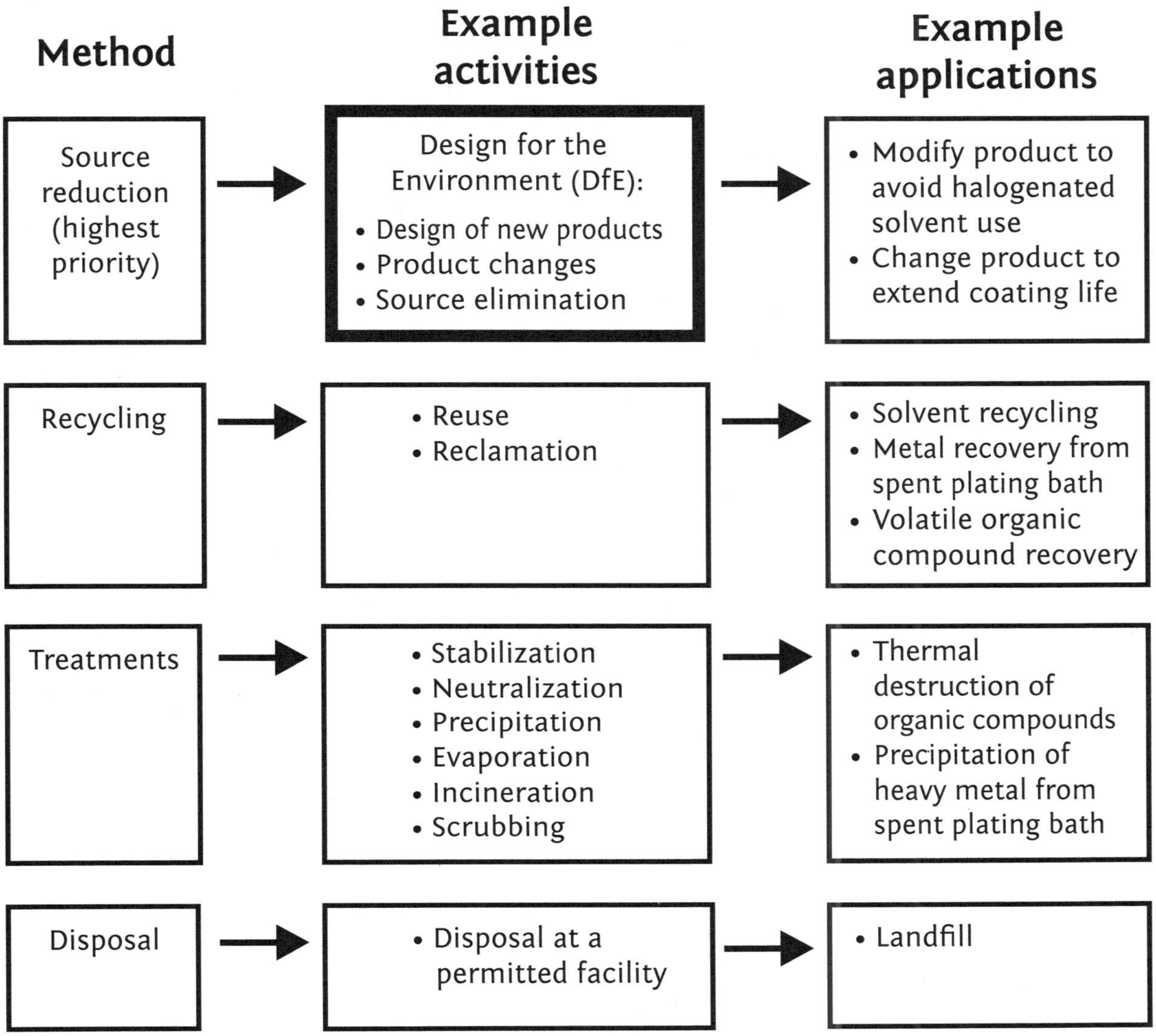

Method	Example activities	Example applications
Source reduction (highest priority)	Design for the Environment (DfE): • Design of new products • Product changes • Source elimination	• Modify product to avoid halogenated solvent use • Change product to extend coating life
Recycling	• Reuse • Reclamation	• Solvent recycling • Metal recovery from spent plating bath • Volatile organic compound recovery
Treatments	• Stabilization • Neutralization • Precipitation • Evaporation • Incineration • Scrubbing	• Thermal destruction of organic compounds • Precipitation of heavy metal from spent plating bath
Disposal	• Disposal at a permitted facility	• Landfill

Source: Adapted from Vallero (2009).

Waste management starts with collecting, storing, and treating wastes. In this hierarchy of waste management, recycling and waste reduction processes are employed beginning at the top and progressing downward as necessary until the waste is eliminated or disposed of properly. Waste minimization is an umbrella term used for strategies and technologies that use source reduction and recycling. In the United States the term "pollution prevention" is often used instead of source reduction as listed in the top left of the figure.

there is no further need to follow the sequence). In the United States, the term *pollution prevention* is often preferred to *source reduction* (on the top left of the figure), and waste minimization is used as an umbrella term for strategies and technologies that use source reduction and recycling.

Life Cycles and Comparative Risk

Life cycles are the fundamental means of evaluating the sustainability of process, which is contrary to

"single-purpose" thinking. Such a thing has been the rule, not the exception. Examples of single-purpose designs are dramatically illustrated in advertisement. In the late 1970s, a company had just introduced a new disposable razor. The magazine ad showed the well-shaved man flipping the plastic and metal razor into the air, whereupon it incrementally disappeared! The singularity of use was the selling point. The razor was used and then discarded. Recent examples exist at all scales. So-called McMansions displace homes whose only flaw was that they were too small. Small items are packaged in boxes ten sizes too large (one size fits all?). Nanosilver is added to bandages (indeed, it may be antimicrobial, but does it have other potential impacts?).

Among the most frustrating sectors engaged in single-purpose thinking is the electronics industry. This sector employs some of the most creative and innovative members of society. To date, however, computers, tablets, and cell phones contain materials that are toxic and/or difficult to recycle. Indeed, many recyclers do not yet accept e-wastes for these reasons. E-waste is an international problem. Many countries are drafting legislation to address this problem via reuse, recycling, and waste reduction. The European Union (EU) required that member countries implement the EU directive on waste electrical and electronic equipment. For example, the United Kingdom produces about 1 million tonnes of e-waste each year, and about 10 percent of this waste is being shipped illegally to countries in Asia, Africa, and Eastern Europe. Similarly, the United States has about 7 million tonnes of e-waste, of which an estimated 20 percent will be exported to Asia. E-waste production is also rapidly increasing in China, India, and Brazil (Cui and Roven 2011).

An environmental problem is usually more complex than the existence of a particular substance. Indeed, the same quantity of a particular substance in one place and time may be quite beneficial, but harmful in another setting. For example, a car's fuel tank is designed to hold 40 liters of gasoline, but the same amount spilled from an underground storage tank could contaminate an aquifer used for drinking water. The spill could result in unacceptable concentrations of benzene, toluene, ethylbenzene, and xylenes, which are all classified as toxic to humans.

Waste is an expression of inefficiency. The efficiency of a system is stated as:

$$Efficiency = \frac{E_{in} - E_{out}}{E_{in}} \times 100$$

Where, E_{in} = Energy entering a control volume, and E_{out} = Energy exiting a control volume.

According to the second law of thermodynamics, if no energy enters or leaves the system, the potential energy of the state will always be less than that of the initial state. The tendency toward disorder, or entropy, requires that external energy is needed to maintain any energy balance in a control volume, such as a heat engine, a waterfall, or an ethanol processing facility. Entropy is ever present. Losses must always occur in conversions from one type of energy (e.g., mechanical

energy of farm equipment ultimately to chemical energy of the fuel). The equation above is actually a series of efficiency equations for the entire process, with losses at every step. Reliable information in the life cycle inventory (LCI) thus is needed to estimate sustainability, that is, to conduct a life cycle analysis (LCA). The LCA considers relevant energy and material inputs and environmental releases. From this LCI, the amount of waste and other potential environmental impacts are evaluated. Thus, the LCA process is a systematic, four-component process (US EPA 2006):

1. *Goal Definition and Scoping*—Define and describe the product, process, or activity. Establish the context in which the assessment is to be made, and identify the boundaries and environmental effects to be reviewed for the assessment.
2. *Inventory Analysis*—Identify and quantify energy, water, materials usage, and environmental releases (e.g., air emissions, solid waste disposal, wastewater discharges).
3. *Impact Assessment*—Assess the potential human and ecological effects of energy, water, materials usage, and the environmental releases identified in the inventory analysis.
4. *Interpretation*—Evaluate the results of the inventory analysis and impact assessment to select the preferred product, process, or service with a clear understanding of the uncertainty and the assumptions used to generate the results.

Note that these steps track closely with the life cycle stages dictated by the laws of physics, especially the laws of thermodynamics. For example, the first law of thermodynamics states that mass and energy must be conserved. That is, all mass and energy in a system must be considered when anything is manufactured, not just what finds its way into a product. Indeed, any mass that is not in the product is potential waste. For example, the part of ore that is removed during refining, the catalysts and reagents, the energy needed for chemical reactions, and the packaging needed to ship the products will be wastes unless they are reused, used in another process (e.g., excess heat from one process used to increase reactions in another), or eliminated (i.e., a step that is removed from production).

Figure 2. Decision Logic for Design for Environment (DfE) Approaches

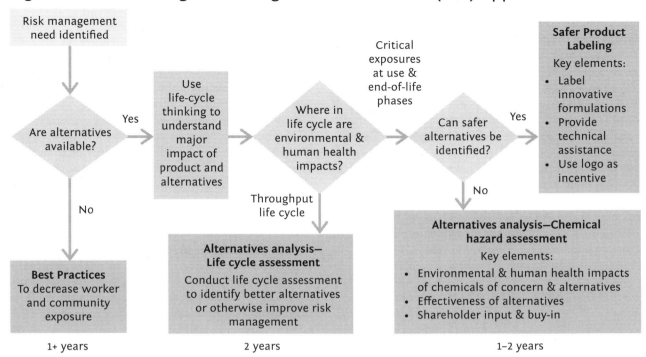

Source: Adapted from Sommer (2010).

The design for the environment (DfE) process shows that a product can be made safer at various points in the life cycle depending on the decisions made in the process. This drive toward the availability of safer products can greatly reduce toxicity, exposure, and risks that may be present during extraction, manufacture, use, and disposal.

The second law of thermodynamics also comes into play—that is, entropy, because every step involves losses. For example, energy production requires the conversion of energy in several steps. If a fossil fuel is burned, this converts chemical energy to heat, which is used to boil water to turn a turbine. The heat is thus converted to mechanical energy, which generates electrical energy, which must be transmitted at high voltage. At various points in the grid, transformers regulate the voltage, so that the electricity can be used. Each of these steps involves losses. If a step can be made more efficient or eliminated, the fuel demand will be reduced commensurately. Less coal is needed, so less extraction is needed, and thus, less mining waste results. Less bottom ash (solid waste) and fly ash (air pollution) from coal combustion are produced. All of these savings can result from smart land use that simply prevents costly and destructive development.

Also, the life cycle can help to highlight possible routes and pathways of exposure to constituents during extraction, manufacture, use, and disposal. This can drive the availability of safer products, that is, design for the environment (DfE). The DfE process shown in figure 2 (above) indicates that a product can be made safer at various points in the life cycle, and that these

improvements can greatly reduce toxicity, exposures, and risks. (See figure 2 above.)

Single-minded solutions are all too common. For instance, phosphorus (P) is an essential nutrient for plants. When large enough quantities reach a lake, however, phosphates will contribute to eutrophication (a process where water bodies receive too many nutrients, which causes excessive plant growth) and even fish kills due to low dissolved oxygen. Reformulating a detergent to be "phosphate free," however, may be insufficient if this does not translate directly into an ecologically acceptable product, where producing the substitute includes steps that are harmful. The substitute substance may indeed help the detergent to clean clothing like the phosphate did, but may be toxic to certain species or may build up in sediment.

Each substitute has unique inherent properties. For example, could the substitute ingredient be extracted and stored by plant life so as to damage sensitive habitats, release toxic materials during manufacturing, and generate persistent chemical by-products that remain hazardous in storage, treatment, and disposal? Unfortunately, unsuitable substitutions are not all that rare. Dichlorodiphenyltrichloroethane (DDT) was replaced with even more toxic pesticides, for instance, aldrin and dieldrin. Substituting incineration for landfills has led to the release of certain pollutants, for example, dioxins and heavy metals, in far more toxic forms than would be found in the landfill leachate.

Even substitutions that are generally accepted may not be appropriate for specific scenarios. For example, it is important to keep organic solvents out of waste streams, so substituting water soluble compounds for petroleum distillates in coating and painting, for example, has been preferable from an environmental perspective. Certain toxic substances, however, such as certain heavy metal compounds, are highly soluble in water (i.e., hydrophilic). The life cycle perspective considers the potential that water may be in some ways worse than organic solvents, for example, as a transport medium for metal pigments in the paint, increasing the rate of hydrophilic compounds entering ecosystems and leading to human exposures.

Future Waste Reduction Measures

Worldwide, there have been major advances in waste management. Communities, companies, and individuals have increasingly embraced ways to prevent the generation of wastes. For example, Sioux Falls, South Dakota, has established standards for recycling by licensing haulers, enhanced educational programs, and tracked business recycling rates; the city has built a facility to handle construction and demolition materials, integrated sustainable processes (e.g., co-digestion of fats, oil, and grease in existing anaerobic treatment systems), and decreased methane emissions from landfills. These measures are expected to increase waste generation by 7 percent, reduce landfill space by 15 percent, and speed up landfill gas collection by five years (Sioux Falls 2012). London, Canada, has instituted similar measures with much success. From 2008 to 2011, organic wastes were reduced by 11 percent, and recycling increased by 17 percent. With these and other enhancements, 41 percent of wastes generated are not finding their way to landfills. In India, the Ashoka Pulp and Paper Company was under pressure from the public to improve environmental performance and to conserve water, especially in summer months. As part of a United Nations (1997) program, the company implemented numerous waste minimization options that not only reduced wastes but saved nearly twice as much money as was invested. Similarly successful UN programs have been implemented in Africa, Asia, and Latin America.

Life cycle–based waste management depends on finding alternatives to substances that are toxic, energy inefficient, and difficult to treat. This can be done using an alternatives assessment, which is a formal technique to characterize the hazards of substances based on a full range of human health and environmental information (US EPA 2012b). Chemical choices made based on these assessments improve potential for unintended consequences beforehand (a priori). This approach, however, could advance beyond hazard to address benefits and utility, that is, to look at a process that currently calls for helium and find points in the life cycle where the need for helium can be reduced or eliminated.

Selecting an alternative substance or process is easiest if substitutes are commercially available. For example, when pulp and paper companies wanted to reduce the generation of toxic dioxins from their bleaching process, they found that other industries were whitening without using chlorine compounds. This eliminated the chlorination step, which meant that dioxin production was also eliminated from the process.

Such substitutions are not always obvious. They may be used in industries unfamiliar to one's sector. For example, there may be a sustainable process of using microfibers in the textile industry to reduce the need for toxic dyes. These are making use of optical properties rather than chemicals. Such an approach could be adapted to plastics, electronics, and other industries. There may be few clearinghouses shared by textile, plastic, and electronics companies, however. Alternative approaches in the future thus will require some solid detective work.

Conversely, it is possible that the alternative approach has some underlying and yet-to-be-manifested deficiencies and hazards. Again, a complete life cycle assessment could help, including various "what if" scenarios. For example, a chemical ingredient may be safe if used as intended. Once the product finds its way into the marketplace, however, it may find many unintended and incidental uses. A complete life cycle takes into consideration such uses, making use of reliable data to predict possible hazards. These include consideration of a substance's carcinogenicity, reproductive and developmental toxicity, neurotoxicity, sensitization and irritation, hormonal activity, and potential to cause ecological damage.

Waste reduction and elimination must not be justified solely using cost-benefit economics, such as those based on the return on monetary investment that can be expected over the life of a product. Often, the waste manager is presented with a list of options, but they all begin with the waste arriving at the facility. Obviously, the manager's span of control dictates the number and diversity of options. Even if limited in options, however, sustainable waste management is a continuous quest for upstream improvements. Products that end up in the waste stream must also be evaluated using methods beyond a comparison of the initial investment as a fraction of the total cost of manufacture, use, and disposal.

While treating wastes has been a necessary component of waste management, eliminating wastes before they are generated is a more preferable goal.

Daniel Alan VALLERO
Duke University

See also Buildings and Infrastructure; Design and Architecture; Economics, Steady State; Energy Efficiency; Geoengineering; Local Solutions to Global Problems; Shipping; Waste—Social Aspects

FURTHER READING

Council on Environmental Quality. (2010). National Environmental Policy Act. Retrieved July 15, 2010, from http://ceq.hss.doe.gov/

Cui, Jirang, & Roven, Hans R. (2011). Electronic waste. In Trevor M. Letcher & Daniel Alan Vallero (Eds.), *Waste: A handbook for management* (pp. 281–296). Burlington, MA: Elsevier Academic Press.

Earnhart, Dietrich, & Lizal, Lubomir. (2011). The evolution of economies of scale regarding pollution control: Cross-sectional evidence from a transition economy. *Journal of Management Policy and Practice, 21*(2), 62–83.

Leopold, Aldo. (1949). *A Sand County almanac.* New York: Oxford University Press.

Markham, Adam. (1994). *A brief history of pollution.* New York: St. Martin's Press.

Marra, John, & Palmer, Ronald. (2011). Radioactive waste management. In Trevor M. Letcher & Daniel Alan Vallero (Eds.), *Waste: A handbook for management* (pp. 101–108). Burlington, MA: Elsevier Academic Press.

McDonough, William, & Braungart, Michael. (2002). *Cradle to cradle: Remaking the way we make things.* New York: North Point Press.

McLeod, Fraser, & Cherrett, Tom. (2011). Waste collection. In Trevor M. Letcher & Daniel Alan Vallero (Eds.), *Waste: A handbook for management* (pp. 61–76). Burlington, MA: Elsevier Academic Press.

Pariathamby, Agamuthu. (2011). Municipal waste management. In Trevor M. Letcher & Daniel Alan Vallero (Eds.), *Waste: A handbook for management* (pp. 109–126). Burlington, MA: Elsevier Academic Press.

Sioux Falls. (2012). Waste minimization. City of Sioux Falls, SD. Retrieved August 1, 2012, from http://www.siouxfalls.org/public-works/environmental-recycling-hazardous/green/smp/waste-minimization.aspx

Sommer, Libby. (2010). US EPA design for the environment program: Exposure-based chemical prioritization workshop. Research Triangle Park, NC: US EPA.

United Kingdom Department of Environment, Food and Rural Affairs (UK Defra). (2009). Commercial and industrial waste in England: Statement of aims and actions 2009. Retrieved May 3, 2012, from http://archive.defra.gov.uk/environment/waste/topics/documents/commercial-industrial-waste-aims-actions-091013.pdf

United Nations (UN). (1997). Earth Summit+5: Special session of the General Assembly to review and appraise the implementation of Agenda 21: Success stories from India. Retrieved August 1, 2012, http://www.un.org/esa/earthsummit/unido3.htm

United Nations Environment Programme (UNEP). (2002). Chemicals: North American regional report, regionally based assessment of persistent toxic substances, global environment facility. Nairobi, Kenya: UNEP.

United States Environmental Protection Agency (US EPA). (2006). Life cycle assessment: Principles and practice (Report No. EPA/600/R-06/060). Retrieved May 3, 2012, from http://www.epa.gov/nrmrl/std/lca/pdfs/chapter1_frontmatter_lca101.pdf

United States Environmental Protection Agency (US EPA). (2008). Municipal solid waste generation, recycling, and disposal in the United States: Facts and figures for 2008. Retrieved April 6, 2012, from http://www.epa.gov/osw/nonhaz/municipal/pubs/msw2008rpt.pdf

United States Environmental Protection Agency (US EPA). (2009). Opportunities to reduce greenhouse gas emissions through materials and land management practices (Report No. EPA530-R-09-017). Retrieved July 31, 2012, from http://www.epa.gov/oswer/docs/ghg_land_and_materials_management.pdf

United States Environmental Protection Agency (US EPA). (2012a). Risk management sustainable technology: Life cycle perspective. Retrieved July 31, 2012, from http://www.epa.gov/nrmrl/std/lifecycle.html

United States Environmental Protection Agency (US EPA). (2012b). Alternatives assessments. Retrieved March 15, 2012, from http://www.epa.gov/dfe/alternative_assessments.html

Vallero, Daniel Alan. (2009). Hazardous waste. In *McGraw-Hill Encyclopedia of Science & Technology.* New York: McGraw-Hill.

Vallero, Daniel Alan. (2011a). Green engineering and sustainable design aspects of waste management. In Trevor M. Letcher & Daniel Alan Vallero (Eds.), *Waste: A handbook for management* (pp. 11–22). Burlington, MA: Elsevier Academic Press.

Vallero, Daniel Alan. (2011b). Hazardous wastes. In Trevor M. Letcher & Daniel Alan Vallero (Eds.), *Waste: A handbook for management* (pp. 393–424). Burlington, MA: Elsevier Academic Press.

Vallero, Daniel Alan, & Letcher, Trevor M. (2012). *Unraveling environmental disasters.* Burlington, MA: Elsevier Academic Press.

Vallero, Daniel J., & Vallero, Daniel Alan. (2011). Land pollution. In Trevor M. Letcher & Daniel Alan Vallero (Eds.), *Waste: A handbook for management* (pp. 445–468). Burlington, MA: Elsevier Academic Press.

Waste—Social Aspects

Waste has increased since the nineteenth century, and some cities (a focal point of waste generation) are trying to take control by encouraging more recycling and reuse, while reclamation efforts are beginning to deal with the landfill waste from generations past. The industrial sector is also beginning to control waste, as major retailers such as Walmart begin initiatives to reduce unnecessary packaging, saving them money in the long term. While waste reduction efforts require the partnership of many, it will also be a benefit for many heading into the future.

The past, present, and future of waste are ensnared with society and the resulting consumption whether people live in small or large communities. As people continue to move to cities, consumption will continue to increase, and as a result, continued advancement in the way we use, reuse, and dispose of waste will be necessary. When people lived in small communities or farms, most waste was reused. As cities emerged and became centers of living and commerce, the management of waste often failed to keep pace. In New York City in the late nineteenth century, human and animal waste (from horse traffic) that mixed with food waste and other trash caused preventable diseases and contaminated the city's water supply. In the early twentieth century, backyard incinerators in Los Angeles, California, fouled the air forty years before the explosion of the car culture and resulting smog (Humes 2012). In the early twenty-first century, curbside recycling can be found in many communities around the globe, but landfilling is still the standard for most. In developing countries with large populations concentrated in cities, proper waste disposal remains a civic and public health issue. A look into the future, however, shows many options for mitigating the harmful social and environmental effects of waste and entombing it in landfills.

Many residents of cities and localities work to provide options for waste reduction and reclamation, which have important implications for the present and future. Aside from requiring residents to recycle common items, communities work to reclaim, repair, and reuse many goods that are commonly placed in the landfill or recycling streams. All across the United States, for example, "reuse" organizations actively solicit unwanted but usable material such as lumber, house fixtures, bricks, tools, and all other manner of materials to sell to do-it-yourselfers, artists, tinkerers, and people hoping to meet their needs while saving money. There are other reuse and recycling organizations that accept used electronic items, recycle the broken, and repair and resell the usable material in an effort to keep this material out of the landfill. Another way to bring reuse and reclamation out of the sole purview of waste managers and into the social realm is the development of so-called repair cafés. In Amsterdam, the Netherlands, the Repair Café Foundation sponsors monthly gatherings of volunteers to repair broken appliances, mend clothing, and fix just about anything else that people bring in. Some are motivated by the cost to have their item repaired, which is free, and others come out of a desire to interrupt the cycle of planned obsolescence of many consumer goods. According to the Repair Café Foundation, similar groups in Africa and Australia continue this work (McGrane 2012). In Thailand, the Princess Mother of Thailand, Srinagarindra, created a program in 1992 that collects aluminum can tabs to create prosthetic limbs for children, impoverished adults, and even animals. All over the country enthusiastic troops of schoolchildren, citizens, and office and factory workers collect massive numbers of can tabs for this program.

Waste and Industrial Production

Industrial production associated with a predominantly consumer society is another major source of waste across the globe. In the European Union, manufacturing creates more waste than any other sector of the economy. The United States has a similar problem (OECD 2012). Any item produced must go through the "materials economy," a complex system of extracting natural resources, producing the item from the resources, distributing those items to wholesalers or retailers, consuming (purchasing) those items, and finally disposing of the entire item or remnants of the item (Leonard 2007). The materials economy is important to understand because of not only the externalities of industrial production but also because during each phase of the materials economy, waste is produced and must be handled and processed. Another byproduct of the production of goods is the packaging used to secure and sell items, most of which goes to landfills. Industrial production and the energy used in that production also create a variety of hazardous and toxic wastes that must be intensively managed. As the production of consumer goods increases, so do the resources needed and the resulting waste created. In the 1960s, the disposal of products and their associated packaging displaced all other categories of household waste, such as inorganics and food and yard waste. In 2000, households in the United States produced more than 50 percent more waste associated with products and packaging over 1960 levels (Humes 2012).

In addition to many national, regional, and local recycling efforts across the world to mitigate the effects of household waste through community recycling, composting, and reuse, the chief players in the industrial economy also work to reduce the amount of waste produced by the industrial production of items. The major producers and retailers of goods undertake reduction activities not only for an environmental benefit, but also for an economic benefit. As the global economy becomes more competitive, producers and retailers seek to find an edge in the present, constantly looking forward to the future for a competitive advantage.

One example of this is the recent effort by the retailer Walmart. According to Walmart's sustainability initiatives, the retailer seeks to reduce packaging by 5 percent globally by 2013 and seeks to find alternatives to environmentally harmful packing such as polyvinyl chloride (PVC). While it may be an obvious marketing ploy, reducing on-shelf and shipping packaging by 5 percent across the retailer's supply chain diverts a significant amount of material from the materials stream, especially considering the gross amount of material Walmart sells globally. On the other side of this initiative are the economic benefits Walmart reaps. A 5 percent reduction in packaging results in 5 percent more space in its heavy delivery trucks. This allows more material to be transported in fewer trucks, which saves fuel and prevents air pollution. This reduction in packaging also allows Walmart to fit more items on its shelves, thus increasing the number of goods a store can sell in a space, which benefits the retailer's profits. It also reduces the need for larger stores or more stores, which reduces the externalities associated with construction and operation of large commercial spaces.

This reduction from such a major player in the materials economy forces producers down the materials economy chain from Walmart (the producers of goods purchased by Walmart) to reduce the packaging of its goods to comply with Walmart's packaging standards. This creates a ripple effect though the supply chain because those producers then begin to reduce their packaging in all of their goods sold to retailers, and the entire distribution sector of the materials economy will benefit from the packaging reduction imposed by Walmart (SPC n.d.; Walmart Corporate 2012).

Affecting the supply chain is the most effective way to influence the amount of waste produced because the type and amounts of material used determine the way in which material is used and then discarded. The supply chain approach is the hallmark of the "zero waste" movement. The problem with this approach is that is requires the producers of goods to change their processes, and in most cases it is voluntary. Many producers of goods use the materials and processes they do in a least-cost scenario to maximize profit. Radically restructuring their processes can be expensive and time consuming. Usually these producers will change their behavior only in response to outside influences such as a major purchaser requiring it (such as the Walmart example) or through regulatory activity.

Waste, Disposal, Reclamation, and Zero Waste

No matter what initiatives and programs are created to reduce household and industrial waste, when people organize into societies and live in cities and towns, they will create waste. There are many recent efforts by municipal and regional governments, however, to handle what waste is produced in a way that costs the least and has the least impact and produces value-added benefit to the communities that create the waste. In most cases, these efforts rely on a combination of waste management and social- and behavior-change scenarios. One city employing these scenarios in the United States is Portland, Oregon. In 2012, the city of Portland eliminated weekly trash pickup, reducing it to once every two weeks—a first for any major US city. In addition to reducing trash pickup to every two weeks, it increased green waste (yard debris and food waste) pickup to once a week. The recycling goes to a materials recovery facility, and the green waste goes to a local composting facility, which transforms it into usable soil. This change in service placed a priority on recycling of material because a large majority of household trash is either recyclable or compostable. It also required residents to improve household recycling to keep trash down to a level that will fit into a once-every-two-weeks schedule. This small change reaped big benefits. In the first quarter of 2012, the city of Portland collected approximately 44 percent less trash, or 9,000 tonnes, than in the first quarter of 2011. Aside from the environmental benefits of diverting that much material from the landfill, it resulted in twenty-five fewer heavy garbage trucks traveling the streets of Portland. This system attracted administrators from across the United States who seek to improve diversion rates to comply with state laws and save money on collection, which accounts for more than 35 percent of public- and private-sector expenses (Millman 2012).

On the very edge of the future, some companies work to extract and recycle material buried in landfills long ago. Before recycling efforts, everything went into a landfill, including commodity items such as metals, paper, and plastic. Because nothing placed in a landfill actually fully decomposes, much of this material is available to be extracted, sold, and recycled, while the rest can be converted to clean-burning natural gas to create power. Enhanced Landfill Mining (ELFM), a public-private partnership from the United Kingdom and Belgium, seeks to create the world's first complete landfill reclamation project. The lead company, Group Machiels, which owns a number of landfills in Belgium, is using one of its landfills to research and promote the idea of ELFM. The Houthalen-Hechteren Landfill in Belgium contains almost 15 million tonnes of material. Through a complex process of extraction, testing, and sorting of the landfill material, Group Machiels hopes to recycle approximately 45 percent of the material and turn the rest of it into energy. At the same time Group Machiels hopes to make a profit from reclaiming the material. When the project is complete, the company will restore the site to its natural state or use it for further development. The company believes that the project will be the future of landfill reclamation and influence the design of future landfills. ELFM has attracted attention from Chile, Bulgaria, Hungary, and Romania, which are all hoping to apply some of ELFM's techniques to landfills in their countries (Group Machiels 2011; Schiller 2011).

The Organisation for Economic Co-operation and Development (OECD) and the United Nations Division for Sustainable Development (DSD) forecast that the global production of waste could increase four- to fivefold by 2025. Although exact numbers are difficult to obtain, these organizations project approximately 2.7 billion tonnes of trash per year will go into landfills around the world by 2025 (OECD 2000; DSD 2009).

The "zero waste" movement seeks to counter this projected increase in trash creation through affecting the supply chain that supplies all consumer goods in the global economy and actively managing the goods that are already in the consumer cycle. Primarily, the zero waste philosophy works to deemphasize the manner in which the waste stream is currently managed, which deals with discards by means of recycling, incineration, and landfilling.

Zero waste encourages the creation of durable goods with longer life cycles and with materials that can be easily repurposed when the good's primary use is completed or the good can be completely reused altogether. The idea is to prevent further energy and materials inputs, which is evident in the recycling and waste infrastructure. A primary example of this is returnable glass bottles (Palmer 2005). In the recycling modality, the glass bottle is crushed and melted to form new glass. This is a labor- and energy-intensive process. In the zero waste modality, the glass bottle is sanitized and reused again for its original intent. Similarly, in the recycling modality, when a building is demolished, the material is recycled into other material—the wood may be ground to create compost or wood chips, the glass from windows crushed to make new glass, and the metals (pipes, wire) smelted to create new metal products. Again, this is an energy-intensive process, which involves heavy equipment, trucks, and chippers and smelters. Zero waste encourages the physical deconstruction of the building and the reuse of each component in another construction project, thus maintaining the embodied energy in the material.

The chief target of the zero waste philosophy, however, is the design philosophy of planned obsolescence, wherein producers of goods create items that must be replaced or are perceived to need replacing before their time. An example of this is most consumer electronics; manufacturers convince consumers that the newest media player, computer, or television is better than the one currently owned, when in fact the current items are perfectly usable. Other manufacturers intentionally build in obsolescence by using low quality materials that simply cannot hold up to long-term, consistent use. Interrupting the cycle of planned obsolescence is the subject of the book *Cradle to Cradle* by the US architect William McDonough and the German chemist Michael Braungart. Moving to zero waste is possible only through the cooperation of all producers of goods and requires international standards among these producers all the way up and down the supply chain. Most of these changes will require a major paradigm shift economically and in industrial design.

Indeed, the only way to a true zero waste society is by a complete re-engineering of the supply chain. Because of the complexity of the shift, it remains one of the major challenges of the zero waste movement. Most successful zero waste systems are achieved on a small scale, where the supply inputs can be tightly controlled, such as large events or defined communities such as college and university campuses.

Outlook

Many of the governmental programs and community efforts concerning waste reduction and recycling look to the future to mitigate the harmful effects of waste, keep usable material out of the landfills, and provide for the common good. Likewise, private industry works to reduce the amount of waste created in the production of goods and wasteful packaging in an effort to maintain competitive in the market and produce greater profit. The future of waste reduction and mitigation worldwide will not be the responsibility of one community, nation, or economic sector. It will be a partnership among all players for their own individual reasons, but the result will benefit all global citizens.

Michael D. SIMS
Independent scholar, Eugene, Oregon

See also Cities and the Biosphere; Community; Design and Architecture; Local Solutions to Global Problems; Natural Capital; Waste—Engineering Aspects

FURTHER READING

Group Machiels. (2011). Enhanced landfill mining. Retrieved July 10, 2012, from http://www.machiels.com/company-detail.aspx?ID=885c55e0-f3b6-4fe6-aa25-1fa7bfc312dd (in Dutch)

Humes, David. (2012). *Garbology: Our dirty love affair with trash.* New York: Penguin Group.

Leonard, Annie. (2007). The story of stuff project. Washington, DC: Free Range Studios. Retrieved July 10, 2012, from www.storyofstuff.com

McDonough, William, & Braungart, Michael. (2002). *Cradle to cradle: Remaking the way we make things.* New York: North Point Press.

McGrane, Sally. (2012, May 8). An effort to bury a throwaway culture one repair at a time. *The New York Times.* Retrieved July 4, 2012, from http://www.nytimes.com/2012/05/09/world/europe/amsterdam-tries-to-change-culture-with-repair-cafes.html?pagewanted=all

Millman, Joel. (2012). Portland puts new twist on trash pickup. *Wall Street Journal.* Retrieved July 7, 2012, from http://online.wsj.com/article/SB10001424052702304458604577490532687633866.html

Organisation for Economic Co-operation and Development (OECD). (2000). Strategic Waste Prevention: OECD reference manual. Retrieved on July 9, 2012, from http://www.oecd.org/officialdocuments/displaydocumentpdf/?cote=env/epoc/ppc(2000)5/final&doclanguage=en

Palmer, Paul. (2005). *Getting to zero waste.* San Francisco: Purple Sky Press.

Rathje, William, & Murphy, Cullen. (2001). *Rubbish! The archaeology of garbage.* Phoenix: University of Arizona Press.

Rogers, Heather. (2006). *Gone tomorrow: The hidden life of garbage.* New York: The New Press.

Royte, Elizabeth. (2006). *Garbage land: On the secret trail of trash.* New York: Black Bay Books.

Schiller, Ben. (2011, September 7). Trash to cash: Mining landfills for energy and profit. Retrieved September 25, 2012, from http://www.fastcompany.com/1778461/trash-cash-mining-landfills-energy-and-profit

Strasser, Susan. (2000). *Waste and want: A social history of trash.* New York: Holt Press.

Sustainable Packaging Coalition (SPC). (n.d.). Homepage. Retrieved July 10, 2012, from http://www.sustainablepackaging.org/

United Nations, Division for Sustainable Development (DSD). (2009). Agenda 21, Section II: Environmentally sound management of solid wastes & sewage-related issues. Retrieved July 9, 2012, from http://www.un.org/esa/dsd/agenda21/res_agenda21_21.shtml

Walmart Corporate. (2012). Sustainability. Retrieved July 8, 2012, from http://www.walmartstores.com/Sustainability/

Water

Although water covers the majority of the planet's surface, less than 2.5 percent is freshwater, most of which is frozen in glaciers or ice caps occurs as groundwater, which can be difficult to access. Water scarcity has been a growing concern as populations rise and resources dwindle; available freshwater is vulnerable to overuse and contamination. Because many bodies of water cross boundaries, sustainable management of freshwater resources will be impossible without national and international transboundary water management systems. The Millennium Development Goals set targets for addressing such issues, but as of 2012 some of those targets are not on track to be met by 2015.

Across geological time, our planet has been a dynamic environment of perpetual change. The present represents a momentary end point of a continuum by which earth materials have been constantly cycled and the organisms that are dependent on energy provided by the sun and various earth materials have evolved. This will continue far into the geological future. If we take stock of this present moment in time, however, we discover that humans, and our activities, are imposing a disturbance to this continuum in relation to water, with consequences for the planet and for ourselves.

An exponential rate of population growth, of about 1 percent per annum globally, has seen the world's population increase from 1 billion in 1800, through 6 billion at the turn of the twenty-first century, to 7 billion in 2012. According to many current projections, the world's population will reach 9 billion by 2050, with a slight slowing down due to decreased birthrates. The initial escalation in the world's population coincided with the Industrial Revolution. Since then living conditions have steadily improved, which, together with medical advances, have

increased life expectancy. The rapid growth rate has increased demands for food and water, the availability of which are not necessarily distributed evenly over space or time. It is important to remember, at this point, that freshwater resources are limited (freshwater makes up less than 2.5 percent of the total water on the Earth). Of this small proportion that is potentially useful to humans, most is locked up as ice in glaciers and ice caps or occurs as groundwater, which can be difficult to access. It is truly a precious resource.

A Key Element

Inextricable links between water and food are evident when we consider that approximately 65–70 percent of global water use is associated with food production. Much of that water is used for irrigated agriculture; it has been suggested that the increased food production arising out of the very rapid population growth during the latter part of the twentieth century could be supported only by increasing irrigation—the so-called Green Revolution (WWAP 2012). The Food and Agriculture Organization (FAO) expects that water consumption via irrigation uses will, by 2050, increase by 11 percent with most of that occurring within regions already experiencing water scarcity (FAO 2011). Unfortunately, there is a limit to the amount of land available for food production, especially irrigated food production. This means, first, that expansion for irrigation will be at a cost to other land uses such as native forests. Second, there will come a point at which, simply, no further expansion can take place. There is also a finite limit to the amount of water available for consumption, even though water is largely a renewable resource. As a consequence of all these factors, it is estimated that water shortages will be experienced by nearly a quarter of all developing countries within twenty years (FAO 2011), while the expansion of irrigated agriculture will slow down.

It is important to note, at this point, that water is *the* key element that sustains life: it is essential for a range of biological processes such as photosynthesis and respiration, the transport of solutes (for example, nutrients, glucose in blood; waste products in perspiration, exhaled air, and urine; nutrients in plants). Its availability therefore is central to human survival and to life on Earth. In addition, access to clean freshwater is also vital for good health and well-being. Within this context, and in order to understand the implications of increasing demands for water, we need to ask, what are the basic requirements to sustain human life? The World Health Organization recommends that each person requires 40 liters of water per day for drinking and sanitation, a guideline value embedded within the United Nations (UN) General Comment on Water, section 2, paragraph 12 (UN 2003). This translates to approximately 15 cubic meters per person per year (m³/person/year). When additional water required for agriculture and industry is factored in, the minimum requirements equal 1,200 m³/person/year. Not being able to meet this minimum requirement can have dire consequences. Even in developed countries, prolonged severe drought can impose critical water shortages. A drought in eastern Australia from 1999 to 2007 reduced some major water storage dams to less than 5 percent capacity. This generated drought contingency plans that included no water allocated to irrigators for food and fodder production; drilling for groundwater to provide reliable drinking water supplies to small rural townships; minimization or cessation of environmental flows; and the disconnection of wetlands from river systems to ensure as much water as possible would reach downstream communities. In developing countries, long-term, and even seasonal drought have life-threatening consequences. Water shortages for drinking purposes and limited food production are the causes of famine, where

large numbers of people have to stop work, leave school or other educational and training institutions, and migrate away from their homes and communities to less hostile environments. Water shortage famines, inducing such social dislocation, as well as high mortality and illness are particularly frequent in arid and semi-arid regions such as parts of Africa, the Middle East, and Central Asia. As surface water sources dry up, they become particularly vulnerable to contamination from human and animal excreta, so that water-starved people become increasingly at risk of gastrointestinal illnesses. The human scale of water and food shortages imposed by drought can be enormous; for example, in 2011 more than 10 million people were adversely affected by drought in the Horn of Africa (African Ministerial Conference on the Environment 2011).

Populations in the developed countries of the world meet minimum water requirements; even under non-drought conditions, however, many developing countries do not, in which case they are considered to be experiencing some degree of scarcity. A classification system for identifying water scarcity (the Falkenmark Stress Indicator, or FSI) can be used to classify whether a country has sufficient water to meet its needs and to maintain ecosystem health (more than 1,700 m³/person/year); is experiencing water stress (between 1,000 and 1,700 m³/person/year); or is characterized by water scarcity (less than 1,000 m³/person/year). Where a country is experiencing water availability, less than 500 m³/person/year, the consequences will include salinization of land by irrigation and a progressive loss of productive agricultural land. This condition is referred to as a "water barrier." Table 1 (below) shows these categories, the number of countries included, and their total populations estimated for 1995 and predicted for 2025 (Jury and Vaux 2007). These data, although arbitrary, still provide some measure by which we can understand the scale of water issues globally and the degree by which water scarcity may shift in the near future.

As human populations grow, there are attendant risks not simply to the volume of water available per person, but

TABLE 1. The Global Extent of Water Stress and Scarcity

Category	Annual Water Resources (m³/person/year)	Number of Countries		Population (millions)	
		1995	2025	1995	2025
Below water barrier	<500	12	17	65	218
Water scarce	<1,000	18	29	166	802
Water stressed	1,000–1,700	11	19	294	2,027
Water stressed or scarce	<1,700	29	47	460	2,829

Sources: Jury and Vaux (2007).

to the *quality* of water. Water quality is impacted by the addition of contaminants that include sediments from eroding catchments; nutrients and agrichemicals from intensive pastoral and agricultural land uses; heavy metals and other elements derived naturally from parent rock and soils or from human activities such as mining and industry; pathogens; and complex compounds sourced from sewage treatment plants, industry, and intensive land uses. Contamination by any of these pollutants can affect human health and well-being through, for example, the effects of parasites, diarrheal and other waterborne diseases, metal and other toxicities, and reduced access to potable water. Large scale water-related crises directly linked to poor water quality include contamination of groundwater by naturally occurring arsenic in Bangladesh (affecting nearly 70 million people) (IAEA n.d.) and fluoride in China and India (affecting 2.7 million and 6 million respectively) (Fluoride Action Network 2004). Contamination of water is also widespread in urban areas, particularly those that have developed rapidly with limited planning, including mega-cities, which can be characterized by poor sanitation and increased pollution of surface and groundwaters (e.g., Mexico City, Mumbai, Shanghai, and Dhaka). Sanitation is one of the most significant issues surrounding water quality in the world. There are direct links between sanitation and poverty, quality of drinking water, human health, and condition of aquatic environments. The importance of sanitation for human health and well-being was acknowledged in the United Nations Millennium Declaration of 2000, which set the target of "halving by 2015, the proportion of the population without sustainable access to safe drinking water and basic sanitation" (UN 2000). Improvements in access to safe drinking water have occurred since that declaration was made, although it varies a great deal from country to country, and even between different communities. Most progress has occurred in rural regions, with little change in urban areas. On a regional scale, Oceania has barely improved at all. (See table 2 below.) Nevertheless, the UN's latest reporting suggests that "if current trends continue, the world will meet or exceed the MDG [Millennium Development Goals] drinking water target

TABLE 2. Progress Toward Meeting 2015 Millennium Goals for Water and Sanitation

Goal	Africa		Asia				Oceania	Latin America and Caribbean	Caucasus and Central Asia
	Northern	Sub-Saharan	East	Southeast	South	West			
Reduce proportion of the population without improved drinking water by half	H	L	M	M	M	H	L	H	M
Reduce proportion of population without sanitation by half	M	VL	L	L	VL	M	L	M	H

Source: UN (2012b).

Note: The letters within the boxes for each category identify the relative level of compliance. VL = Very low; L = Low; M = Moderate; H = High. The gray shading refers to progress in each category:

☐ Target already met or expected to be met by 2015
▨ Progress insufficient to reach the 2015 target if current trends continue
▮ No progress, or deterioration

by 2015. By that time an estimated 86 percent of the population in developing regions will have gained access to improved sources of water" (UN 2010). By contrast, the Millennium Development goal for sanitation will not be met. On a global scale, 2.5 billion people are still without access to improved sanitation—including 1.2 billion who have no facilities at all and are forced to defecate in the open (UN 2012a). This latter number is significant: open defecation is an affront to human dignity; has enormous implications for women in some developing countries, where they can use only designated areas at night with associated risks of assault; and is a principal cause of oral-fecal transmission of disease. Reporting by the UN suggests that the greatest single obstacle to improving sanitation is the political will to "mobilise resources to tackle the issue" (UN 2010).

Challenges

Access to freshwater is not enough, in itself, for survival; the water must be of a quality that is appropriate for its use. Furthermore, short-term goals provide an impetus for improvements into the future, but the scale of issues and the capacity to implement improved conditions represent significant challenges.

The changes that are currently occurring in the human population, as well as those changes being imposed by human activities, have stimulated discussion about the risks and uncertainties that lie ahead, and the possible strategies that need to be implemented to provide for future generations. The imperative for such an approach is captured by the following:

> Critical challenges lie ahead in coping with progressive water shortages and water pollution. By the middle of this century, at worst 7 billion people in sixty countries will be water-scarce, at best 2 billion people in forty-eight countries. (WWAP 2012)

Past practices in a rapidly changing world have been largely exploitive. Although water was identified as a largely renewable resource, it was not understood that it was a *finite* resource, particularly within the context of increasing demands. Now, the same volume has to be shared by an increasingly large population, which has been, and in many cases continues to be, willing to pollute, overuse, and waste. Not only does it have to be shared, however, but the *use* of water has to be managed at levels that can be sustained over the long term. Furthermore, the resource has to be *developed* while the environment is simultaneously protected.

Adding further complexity to this picture is that an increasingly valuable resource can be the focus of political tension because water crosses political borders. When this occurs, the water within the lakes and rivers is referred to as *transboundary water*. Currently in the world there are approximately 263 transboundary lake and river basins covering almost half the Earth's total land surface, as well as approximately 300 transboundary aquifer systems. The political scale of this is evident in the fact that 146 nations share a river with at least one other bordering country. At one extreme, the Danube River in Europe flows through eighteen nations. Other important rivers where transboundary issues arise include the Congo, Nile, Rhine, Jordan, Ganges, and Mekong rivers. Examples of transboundary lakes include four of the Great Lakes in North America, which straddle the border between Canada and the United States, and Lake Tanganyika in Africa, which is bounded by Tanzania, Zambia, Burundi, and the Democratic Republic of the Congo.

Problems associated with sharing water resources across boundaries can be minimized through multilateral and bilateral agreements to protect and conserve the resource and through institutional frameworks such as river basin commissions. In the absence of such instruments, however, conflict can arise out of over abstraction, diversion, and different management plans and practices. In some cases serious transboundary conflict can arise. Examples of this include, but are not limited to, conflicts surrounding the Jordan River (Israel, Jordan, Syria, Lebanon, and Palestine); the Ganges (India and Bangladesh); the Blue Nile (Egypt, the Sudan, and Ethiopia); the Tigris-Euphrates (Iraq, Turkey, and Syria); and the Aral Sea (Kazakhstan, Uzbekistan, Turkmenistan, Tajikistan, and Kyrgyzstan). International conflicts can also arise out of shared groundwater resources (for example between the United States and Mexico). In some cases, there can be actual or potential conflicts within countries across provincial or state boundaries, such as occurs in India (the Narmada River) and Australia (the Murray-Darling system). Research at the University of Oregon in the United States, however, has shown that cooperation and collaboration are more often involved in transboundary water management than conflict: in a total of more than 1,500 conflicts occurring since the middle of the twentieth century, only 37 have involved violence, of which 30 occurred between Israel and its neighbors (Jury and Vaux 2007). The management and protection of transboundary water is highly complex because of hydrological, social, economic, and geopolitical factors. Treaties that include institutional mechanisms for cooperation, however, are important tools for averting or minimizing conflict and optimizing mutual benefits across the participant nations. At the Sixth World Water Forum held at Marseilles, France, in 2012, the Ministerial Declaration acknowledged this key role of international conventions and agreements, and stated the intention to "further promote and encourage coordinated, equitable, reasonable and optimal water utilization in transboundary basins, with a view to deepening mutual trust among riparian countries and achieve sound cooperation" (IFC Secretariat 2012).

Sustainability

Unsustainable water use occurs when the resource and its dependent ecosystems diminish over time as a result of inappropriate or inadequate management. According to Peter Gleick, the US scientist who raised awareness of the impending "water crisis" in the mid-1990s, there are two possible routes toward unsustainable water use. First, it can develop in response to variations in the stocks and flows of water that impact on its availability over time and space (for example, this can occur when management does not respond appropriately to reduced resources during prolonged drought). Second, it can develop as water demands change in response to population growth, improvements in technology, increasing standards of living and life expectancies, and evolving social values. In the case of population growth, this will reduce the volume of water available per person, impose the need to manipulate which sector gets water and when, and, as sources increasingly fail to meet demand, "mining" of unrenewable resources (such as most groundwater) will occur. Ultimately this reduces the overall benefits to the population and more broadly to the environment.

What Is Not Sustainable?

It is easy to recognize what is *not* sustainable. Many examples of unsustainable water use and development exist. For example, the over abstraction of groundwater can cause land subsidence whereby large areas are lowered by several meters, such as occurs across Tokyo, Japan. Over abstraction of groundwater along coastal areas can induce seawater intrusion of aquifers so that what were once freshwater systems become progressively more saline as pumping continues over time. In systems where groundwater and streams are connected, any lowering of the water table by over abstraction will reduce stream flow, sometimes changing a stream from being perennial to one that flows only during wetter periods or seasons. Within an urban setting, rapid and unregulated expansion of a city may exceed the existing infrastructure water supply capacity, creating water shortages. This is particularly evident in megacities around the world such as Mexico and most cities in India and China. It is also a major issue for smaller towns and cities, however, where

urban migration is associated with extremely rapid population growth and the development of informal settlements that are not connected to the water and sewerage infrastructure, such as Honiara, in the Solomon Islands, and Tarawa, Kiribati, in Oceania. Finally, overallocation of water resources for consumptive uses with no provisions for the environment will have far-reaching ecological consequences. Unsustainable practices will have medium- to long-term impacts, including complex outcomes. In India, for example, a very heavy reliance on groundwater as a reliable source of freshwater has generated a dependence on its supply for the large-scale production of food staples including rice, sugar cane, and wheat. Continued unsustainable over abstraction has the potential to reduce production that has not only socioeconomic implications at a regional scale, but also disastrous consequences for global food prices. In this case, unsustainable practices at a regional scale have global consequences. A familiar example of unsustainable water use, arising out of unrestrained resource exploitation, has occurred in Central Asia, where the rapid development of irrigated cotton reliant on surface freshwater sourced from the Aral Sea has generated the collapse of multiple systems. Agriculture has failed because of salinization and waterlogging of land, the volume of the Aral Sea has been reduced by approximately three-quarters, water dependent ecosystems such as those within wetland, lake, and riparian settings have collapsed, and a host of social, economic, and health problems have emerged for the inhabitants of the region. Former seaside towns can be tens of kilometers from the present shoreline, and images of large boats abandoned on a dry lakebed have become iconic. These are cautionary tales clearly demonstrating past and current mistakes. The challenge for the future is to determine what *is* sustainable.

What Is Sustainable?

The Brundtland Commission (1987) defined sustainability as "development that meets the needs of the present without compromising the ability of future generations to meet their own needs." A later definition by the United Nations Educational, Scientific and Cultural Organization (UNESCO) in 1999 expanded a little further: "[S]ustainable water resource systems are those designed and managed to fully contribute to the objectives of society, now and in the future, while maintaining their ecological, environmental, and hydrological integrity." A number of questions arise from these definitions. Whose needs, and at what spatial scale(s)? What time frames are involved, particularly when reference is made to "future generations"? Frequently, fifty years or approximately two generations provide the basis for planning. In a rapidly changing world, however, personal survival may be reliant on a series of short-term solutions that, because of their urgency, are dislocated from longer-term goals. In any case, how can we know what the needs of future generations will be? In addition, how do we know what the *demands* of future generations will be? We can assume that future generations will expect the same benefits from water resources that we currently experience, so maintaining quality is also an imperative. But returning to the issue of a growing population, will it be possible to meet future needs if demands exceed supply?

Attempts to define sustainability, such as those mentioned here, have stimulated debate that is still ongoing. As part of that process, more questions have arisen. researcher Daniel Loucks, a US expert on the development and application of economics, ecology, and systems analysis methods to the solution of environmental and regional water resources problems, asked, "[J]ust how can water resources management be sustainable when we cannot look into the future with any degree of certainty?" (Loucks 2012). That uncertainty is linked to change, which is an inevitable companion to time. In terms of water resources, changes will occur to natural systems (for example, shifting positions of rivers as they meander through floodplains); to engineered infrastructure due to corrosion, settlement, and loss of structural integrity; to water demands and use in response to societal needs; and finally, to the volumes of water being delivered to, and draining, catchments in response to climate variability and climate change. Sustainability, then, becomes not only a particular approach to use and management of the resource, but also to planning and development that ensures, in part at least, that the system is capable of adapting to those changes or is resilient to change. It also needs to be an approach that can respond to future stresses that are as yet unknown or little understood. Where the direction of change can be predicted, such as rate of population growth, developing sustainable approaches should be straightforward. This is not necessarily the case, however. Theoretically, there will be a threshold for intensive food production and water resources development beyond which sustainable practices are impossible. If such a threshold exists, in reality, is it approached progressively in a predictable manner, and for which appropriate planning can be developed? Is the transition from sustainable to unsustainable a recognizable phase of change or does it occur as an abrupt tipping point?

Water Futures

We are moving progressively forward in time with a rapidly expanding population and a finite resource that is essential to our existence. That resource has to be available to everyone, it needs to be of a high quality, and it must be shared across all users, including the environment. And this has to be done within a setting of climate change and other uncertainties. Increasingly, the future has been viewed pessimistically, and this is understandable given the rate of population growth, the specter of climate change, and the geopolitical instability that has characterized the world in the last decade. This pessimism is reflected in statements made initially by Peter Gleick in 1998 (571):

A wide range of ecological and human crises result from inadequate access to, and the inappropriate management of, freshwater resources. These include destruction of aquatic ecosystems, and extinction of species, millions of deaths from water-related illnesses, and a growing risk of regional and international conflicts over scarce, shared water resources.

Ten years later this view had not progressed much further, when William Jury and Henry Vaux, scientists at the University of California, in the United States, said, "[W]ithout immediate action and global cooperation, a water supply and water pollution crisis of unimaginable dimensions will confront humanity, limiting food production, drinking water access, and the survival of innumerable species on the planet" (Jury and Vaux 2007, 3). Despite such pessimism, these writers all recognize an imperative for the future: water management and development needs to be predicated on national and international cooperation and the political will to meet goals set within realistic time frames.

These views were expressed at the same time that significant agendas were being developed on the international stage. At the Rio World Summit, in 1992, values and directions for sustainable water resources management were outlined in Chapter 18 of Agenda 21 (the 21 referring to the twenty-first century). At the United Nations Millennium Summit in 2000, heads of governments resolved to embed a new ethic of stewardship (care of resources for future generations) and conservation within resource management and development. In particular, the resolution was made to "stop the unsustainable exploitation of water resources, by developing water resources strategies at regional, national and local levels which promote both equitable access and adequate supplies" (UN 2000). A number of key international meetings in 2012, including the Rio+20 Summit and the Sixth World Water Forum in France, reaffirmed the critical importance of water to sustainable development.

Within the context of an acknowledged water crisis and the need to collectively manage the resource in a sustainable manner, governments and individuals recognize a number of salient issues surrounding the future of water. These include scarcity; water contamination and reduced quality, particularly with reference to sanitation; the effects of climate change; and transboundary water management.

Water Resource Management Strategies

The challenge of managing water within the context of increasing stress and scarcity is a major challenge that requires a hierarchical approach, from the building of foundational scientific data (and its analysis) at the base through to regulatory tools at the top. These tools include water laws that operate at local, state, national, and international scales. Over the past two decades, many countries have been reforming their water allocation laws, in order to improve water security and to provide for equity for all users, including the environment. As part of that process, some countries have significant hurdles to clear: for example, the United States has a highly fragmented approach across multiple jurisdictions that is a challenge to water allocation and environmental protection. In Chile, a deeply flawed approach to developing a free water market in the 1980s has required the promulgation of new codes to rectify social inequities and mitigate environmental degradation. Other countries, however, are taking coordinated national approaches for the unified management of water, with such highly diverse examples as South Africa with its National Water Act (1998); the Republic of China, which introduced a new water law system in 2002; and Australia with its National Water Initiative (introduced in 2004), which has included major water reforms in allocation and the introduction of water trading. Beyond national jurisdictions, overarching international laws and conventions not only protect environmental values, but also play a key role in the collaborative and increasingly unified approach to management and use of water. These institutional tools include the universally applicable Convention on the Law of the Non-navigational Uses of International Watercourses, which was signed and adopted by the UN General Assembly in 1997; the 1971 Ramsar Convention on Wetlands of International Importance, which is an intergovernmental treaty that provides a framework for the conservation and sustainable use of wetlands and their resources; and the 1992 United Nations Economic Commission for Europe (UNECE) Convention on the Protection and Use of Transboundary Watercourses and International Lakes, which has provided the basis of numerous bilateral and multilateral agreements relating to high-value river systems such as the Danube. A further international tool for water management is provided by institutions that have a mandate to enable cooperative water management across national boundaries. For example, the United Nations can help member nations establish appropriate legal or institutional mechanisms for sustainable water management, such as the Mekong River Commission in Southeast Asia or the development of water governance frameworks across the highly diverse Island Nations of the Pacific.

Using objectives, targets, and actions embodied within the various international agreements that have been put in place, the simplest approach for water resource management involves: (a) augmenting supply; (b) controlling demand; and (c) managing uncertainty.

Augmenting Supply

Augmenting supply is an exploitive approach typified by forecasting future water demands and comparing this with how much water can be supplied. If the supply cannot meet demand, the solution is in further development of the water supply system, such as the construction of additional dams and supply infrastructure, the diversion of water from one catchment to another via an engineered distribution system, or desalination of sea water. Although this approach was the dominant paradigm in the past and still continues, particularly in many developing countries, it is increasingly limited by environmental, economic, and social concerns.

Controlling Demand

A progression away from this approach can occur if the underlying concept is "flipped" so that rather than developing a bigger supply system, the demands are reduced. This is what Peter Gleick (1998) refers to as *backcasting*. In using this approach, potential needs are identified and planning focuses more on water efficiencies and technological solutions to lower water use. Water efficiencies include simple remedies such as lining open irrigation distribution channels to reduce seepage or converting channels to pipelines to reduce evaporative losses. Water efficiencies within urban environments also involve water conservation measures, such as water reuse and recycling programs, water restrictions, the use of water efficient appliances, and rainwater tanks to supplement the main supply. Technological solutions include plant breeding to select for water efficient crop species and engineered structures that store and release water with minimal losses. Economic approaches are also an example of backcasting, by which market pricing can reflect scarcity and hence the value of water per unit.

Managing Uncertainty

It has been argued that realigning supply and demand within a framework of sustainability has many benefits, but there is a risk that water will increasingly become associated with power. In this scenario, the interests of the poor will be increasingly marginalized in preference to the powerful agricultural and industry sectors. Already there is inequity in water access, water pricing, and water use, some of which can be addressed through formal processes of legislation and policy, but also through participatory decision making, which is embedded within the Millennium Development Goals. This is particularly evident when water resources in developed countries are compared with those that are poor and developing. Moreover, on a smaller spatial scale, inequity also occurs between domestic water use in wealthy suburbs connected to the water utility, compared to that of slums and illegal settlements at the fringes of rapidly developing cities. The vulnerability of the poor is also evident when progress toward targets set by the Millennium Goals for water access and sanitation are examined. (See table 2 on page 236.) The latest reporting indicates that (a) compliance and (b) progress differ significantly across regions. (See table 2.) The most vulnerable are the poorest—sub-Saharan Africa and Southeast Asia.

The Future

The way forward is no more uncertain than at any time in the past—we have never been able to see into the future. We are simply more fully aware of highly complex changes and risks that need to be integrated into planning and management. Governments have made their position clear, through such instruments as the Millennium Goals, that forward planning as a series of shorter time steps will progressively address shortfalls in water access and water quality. Importantly, in 2000 the Global Water Partnership stated, in the report *Towards Water Security: A Framework for Action* that "the water crisis is mainly a crisis of governance." By 2012, the Global Water Partnership had developed this further by stating,

> Some countries still have to put adequate policies, laws and plans for managing water into place and link them to broader national development priorities. Others already have clear policies and strategies, but do not have the political will, funds or capacity to take action to solve water problems. Weak governance, corruption and interest groups that resist change exacerbate the problems. These barriers exact a heavy toll on the poor and hold back progress towards the Millennium Development Goals. (GWP 2012)

What this means for the future is that institutional arrangements must be put in place by which water is effectively managed strategically and sustainably at local, regional, national, and international levels. Management systems will need to include institutions, laws, and policies that are administered adequately and transparently. These systems and their administration also need to operate in harmony with the capacities, abilities, and expectations of the stakeholders involved (i.e., those people who have a stake in an enterprise, in contrast to corporate shareholders), so that their social mores and collective knowledge are incorporated into planning processes. Miguel Solanes and Andrei Jouravlev, of the Economic Commission for Latin America and the Caribbean (ECLAC), suggest that "every society has natural conditions, power groups, power structures, and requirements that must be considered specifically" (Solanes and Jouravlev 2006, 67). This is particularly relevant to countries or regions where there are significant cultural and biophysical differences (for example, Oceania), which are not amenable to a single model for future water governance. It might be argued, for example, that slow progress in Oceania toward meeting the Millennium Goals for water and sanitation is partly because of the mismatch between constitutional law and customary laws. There can also be a wariness that faces integrated water resource management (IWRM) efforts, which either are controlled by external consultants or do not consider that local professionals and communities may not have the necessary skills and knowledge to continue developing management strategies beyond the implementation or planning stages. In this sense, progress in the future for sustainable water management depends not only on effective and transparent governance but also on education. This latter is an extremely powerful tool by which improved knowledge increases the ability of local professionals to undertake planning, management, and monitoring; empowers the disadvantaged; and increases both reliance and adaptability of populations to future uncertainty. The education of girls and women is central to improved hygiene (by understanding the significance of oral-fecal transmission of disease for example), improved water management, and decision making, as well as an improved capacity for water law.

The issue of water is enormous; its magnitude is the size of our projected human population. Once we have the knowledge of how the world is changing, and the uncertainties that come with those changes, it becomes imperative that individually as well as collectively we take responsibility for using and managing water not only for the present but also for the future. The fact that the future spreads so widely ahead of us does not mean that we cannot plan and act with an ethos that includes those unknown generations that advance before us. A number of options are possible to ensure that future management of water is sustainable, equitable, and realistic. These include, for example, strategies that recognize economic value of water through pricing mechanisms; acknowledge and embed gender and socioeconomic equity within water governance and water resources management; and ensure water use is maintained within the limits of ecological sustainability. Investment in education, water efficiency technology, research, and planning is, of course, integral to such future strategic planning.

These strategies are not wholly the responsibility of institutions or governments. Communities are capable of taking affirmative, positive action for a better future. In Sri Lanka, for example, the Wanaraniya Water Project involved women in the village taking full responsibility for the construction of a dam and pipeline to provide a reliable source of water. In this project, where the men were paid for their labor, the women satisfied their need for safe and secure water supplies, but also made significant progress strategically. Outcomes of the project included community benefits in health, livelihoods, and education, together with political and social empowerment of the women (Aladuwaka and Momsen 2010). Collaborative efforts between stakeholders can also be highly effective mechanisms by which sustainable and efficient water use occurs. In Japan, the Toyogawa Water Resource Development Project is a highly successful collaborative approach to water use across the agriculture, industry, and domestic sectors. In particular, it incorporates participatory irrigation management by which farmers are key decision makers for the allocation and use of water, in partnership with water utilities and government (Kono et al. 2012). The direct involvement of farmers in decision making has reversed their focus from augmenting supply to meet their water needs to strategically controlling demand.

It is now widely recognized that the move away from competitive, hierarchical approaches to water resources management toward more collaborative, participatory approaches is a significant step into the future of water sustainability.

Sara G. BEAVIS
The Australian National University

See also Agricultural Innovation; Buildings and Infrastructure; Climate Change and Big History; Fisheries; Food Security; Local Solutions to Global Problems; Migration

FURTHER READING

African Ministerial Conference on the Environment. (2011, September 13–14). *Drought in the Horn of Africa: Opportunities and responses.* (Meeting of the expert group). Bamako, Mali.

Aladuwaka, Seela, & Momsen, Janet. (2010). Sustainable development, water resources management and women's empowerment: The Wanaraniya Water Project in Sri Lanka. *Gender & Development*, *18*(1), 43–58.

Brundtland Report. (1987). *Our common future: A report to the United Nations General Assembly.* New York: United Nations World Commission on Environment and Development.

Fluoride Action Network. (2004, May). Skeletal fluorosis: Recent reports from India. Retrieved August 1, 2012, from http://www.fluoridealert.org/fluorosis-india.htm/

Food and Agriculture Organization (FAO) of the United Nations. (2011). *The state of the world's land and water resources for food and agriculture: Managing systems at risk.* Rome & London: Land & Water Division, FAO, & Earthscan.

Gleick, Peter H. (1998). Water in crisis: Paths to sustainable water use. *Ecological Applications, 8*(3), 571–579.

Global Water Partnership (GWP). (2000). *Towards water security: A framework for action.* Stockholm: GWP.

Global Water Partnership (GWP). (2012). *Strategy for 2009–2013.* Stockholm: GWP.

International Atomic Energy Agency (IAEA). (n.d.). Arsenic contamination of groundwater in Bangladesh. Retrieved August 1, 2012, from http://www-tc.iaea.org/tcweb/publications/factsheets/arsenic_contamination.pdf

International Forum Committee (IFC) Secretariat. (2012). Ministerial Declaration: Global Water Framework 6th World Water Forum, Marseilles, France. Retrieved August 1, 2012, from http://www.worldwaterforum6.org/fileadmin/user_upload/pdf/process_pol_elem/Ministerial_Declaration_Final_EN.pdf

Jury, William A., & Vaux, Henry J., Jr. (2007). The emerging global water crisis: Managing scarcity and conflict between water users. *Advances in Agronomy, 95*, 1–76.

Kono, Satoshi; Ounvichit, Tassanee; Ishii, Atsushi; & Satoh, Masayoshi. (2012). Participatory system for water management in the Toyogawa Irrigation Project, Japan. *Paddy and Water Environment, 10*(1), 75–81.

Loucks, Daniel P. (2012). Sustainable water resources management. *Water International, 25*(1), 3–10.

Solanes, Miguel, & Jouravlev, Andrei. (2006, June). Water governance for development and sustainability. Santiago, Chile: United Nations, CEPAL.

United Nations (UN). (2000). Resolution adopted by the General Assembly 55/2 United Nations Millennium Declaration. Retrieved August 1, 2012, from http://www.un.org/millennium/declaration/ares552e.htm/

United Nations (UN). (2003). Water for people, water for life (World water development report). New York: UN.

United Nations (UN). (2010). Millennium Development Goals report. Retrieved July 19, 2012, from http://www.un.org/millenniumgoals/pdf/MDG%20Report%202010%20En%20r15%20-low%20res%2020100615%20-.pdf

United Nations (UN). (2012a). Millennium Development Goals 2012 report. New York: UN.

United Nations (UN). (2012b). Millennium Development Goals: 2011 progress chart. Retrieved July 19, 2012, from http://www.un.org/millenniumgoals/pdf/%282011E%29_MDReport2011_ProgressChart.pdf

United Nations Educational, Scientific and Cultural Organization (UNESCO) Working Group MIV. (1999). *Sustainability criteria for water resource systems.* Cambridge, UK: Cambridge University Press.

World Water Assessment Programme (WWAP). (2012). *The United Nations World Water Development Report 4: Managing water under uncertainty and risk.* Paris: UNESCO.

Directory of Sustainability Programs

The following material is intended for people—students, teachers, professionals, and anyone else—interested in sustainability education. This is not to be considered a complete list; rather, it should be used as a tool to get started in researching the vast array of sustainability programs in the world. Berkshire Publishing Group invites readers to add comments and further recommendations at TheSustainabilityProject.com.

Addressing the challenge of sustainability will take approaches from every angle. To equip future generations with the awareness of the challenges and the tools we have at hand will require extensive educational materials, programs, and resources for students and teachers. The *Berkshire Encyclopedia of Sustainability* provides a window into this world and we hope the following collection of resources will open many more views on this expansive field.

Through the pages of this encyclopedia, authors have explored education from many angles, from business education in volume 2 (*The Business of Sustainability*) to environmental law education in volume 3 (*The Law and Politics of Sustainability*) to environmental education in India in volume 7 (*China, India, and East and Southeast Asia: Assessing Sustainability*). Julie Newman, director of the Yale Office of Sustainability, introduced readers to the challenge of education for sustainability in volume 1, *The Spirit of Sustainability*. She begins:

> Our educational system is designed to contribute to the well-being of society at the present and into the future through the creation and dissemination of knowledge and the education of its citizenry. The challenge at hand is to understand and determine how best to design our educational systems in a manner that both contributes to and, in essence, designs a sustainable future. One

broad-level approach is shaped by the United Nations Educational, Scientific, and Cultural Organization (UNESCO), which proposes that the goal of the United Nations Decade of Education for Sustainable Development (2005–2014) is to implement a process to ". . . make decisions that consider the long-term future of the economy, ecology and equity for all communities; to reorient education systems, policies and practices in order to empower everyone, young and old, [and] to make decisions and act in culturally appropriate and locally relevant ways to redress the problems that threaten our common future (De Rebello, 2003)."

Following the 1972 Earth Summit in Stockholm, Sweden, interdisciplinary environmental education became popular. Twenty five years ago, publication of the Brundtland report, commonly known as *Our Common Future*, further contributed to the development of broader interdisciplinary program with a focus on "sustainability." The fact that the UN declared the years 2005–2014 as a "Decade of Education for Sustainable Development" was extraordinary. The publication of "World Trends in Education for Sustainable Development" in 2011 was a major initiative and a milestone. There are international journals (e.g. the *International Journal of Sustainability in Higher Education*). There have been declarations such as The Talloires Declaration, which has over 400 institutional signatories vowing that higher education institutions will be leaders in sustainability. There are supporting agencies that provide resources and convene conferences for educators (e.g., ACTS Australasian Campuses Towards Sustainability, AASHE Association for the Advancement of Sustainability in Higher Education). Numerous conferences have been dedicated to sustainability in higher education; one of the most recent was the GUNI Report 2011 *Higher Education in the World 4,*

Higher Education's Commitment to Sustainability; From Understanding to Action. (The article in this volume titled "Education, Higher," is an adaptation of this report.)

Sustainability has a place in all disciplines of higher education from science to drama and theater. The introduction of sustainability courses and degree programs in higher education, however, has prompted many questions. For example, is there clarity between education *about* sustainability, and education *for* sustainability? (For instance, a university may provide education about sustainability, by teaching about ecology, natural resource use, etc., but its physical campus—and indeed, even its offshore business dealings—may be at odds with the sustainability issues that are taught about on the campus; the campus itself, therefore, may not be practicing what it preaches.) It is increasingly evident that education *about* sustainability needs to be different from traditional forms of education (Environmental Science Scientist 2009; Jones et al. 2010).

There are many critics of sustainability in higher education. Walter Leal Filho in 2000 summarized some criticism as including: sustainability is not a subject *per se*, it's too theoretical, it's too broad, it's too recent a field, and it's a fashion. In a recent communication with Berkshire Publishing Group he said "I am sad to say that many of the barriers still remain today." It is very important to address such criticism, especially with an emerging subject such as sustainability. Librarians need to know how to categorize sustainability materials in the best way possible so that students can find what they are looking for. Such barriers have been addressed in a positive way, however, and a good example is the paper by education professor Janet Moore (2005) in which she offers recommendations on how to create institutional change and sustainability education. ("Seven recommendations for creating sustainability education at the university level: A guide for change agents," *International Journal of Sustainability in Higher Education*, 6:4, pp. 326–339.)

Sustainable Management Education

In *The Business of Sustainability*, Nicola Acutt provides a look at sustainability management education in the twenty-first century:

> Sustainable management education is about more than changing lightbulbs or switching to recycled paper on campus. It is about rethinking what is taught and how it is taught, and reassessing the connections between what is learned in the classroom and the impact of managers' actions in the world. It is the combination of educational context, learning processes, and content designed to prepare business students to engage in the imperative—and interconnected—management issues of the twenty-first century. . . . It is ultimately about imparting the knowledge, teaching the skills, and

developing the competencies and courage of managers, entrepreneurs, and leaders to create a future that is ecologically sound, socially just, and economically viable for future generations.

Outlook on Law Education

In *The Law and Politics of Sustainability*, contributors grappled with the concept of sustainability law, which, while still a somewhat amorphous field, is gaining prominence in international law as sustainable development is invoked more and more. The 2012 United Nations Conference on Sustainable Development (known as "Rio+20") is one example of the increasing prominence of the field. It was one of the largest United Nations events in history and, it is to be hoped, will help to push the nascent field of sustainability law along. More established than sustainability law, which considers an inherent interconnection among environmental, economic, and social issues, is environmental law.

In volume 3, University of Cambridge law professor Catherine MacKenzie gives readers a sense of the emergence of environmental law education worldwide:

> Environmental law education has developed rapidly over the last forty years in response to the development of environmental law in the same period. The curriculum is now well defined, and some law schools have developed significant expertise in this area of law. The challenge now is to integrate environment and sustainability into all aspects of mainstream legal education so that environment and sustainability become a central aspect of legal decision making, instead of an optional subject designed primarily for specialists. Courses on environmental law are generally integrated into professional and advanced degrees, but integration of sustainability into all areas of law school operations is still at an early stage in many schools.
>
> Environmental law is one aspect of state, national (in the United States, federal), and international law and is usually studied in those contexts. A law school may, for example, offer courses on the environmental laws of its own state, national (federal) environmental law, and international environmental law. Within the European Union (EU), the environmental law of the EU is often offered.
>
> Schools with extensive environmental law curricula often subdivide environmental law further according to topic. Such schools may, for example, offer separate courses on state biodiversity law, national or federal biodiversity law, international biodiversity law, and (within the EU) EU biodiversity law. This degree of specialization is possible only in a small number of U.S. and other law schools that have highly developed environmental law programs.

In the United States, Vermont Law School (VLS) has the largest, and often top-ranked, environmental law program. Other highly ranked environmental law programs in the United States generally include Florida State University, Georgetown University, Lewis and Clark Law School, New York University, Pace University School of Law, University of California at Berkeley, University of Colorado at Boulder, University of Maryland, University of Oregon, and Stanford University.

Sustainability in Continuing Professional Development

Accredited educational programs are compulsory for many professions. For example, to become a planning officer in local government, it will almost certainly require a course of education that is recognized and "accredited" by that profession. After graduation, there is an expectation that practitioners will undertake continuing professional development (CPD). For some professions this is compulsory. CPD credits are obtained by way of attending conferences, research presentations, publishing and attending workshops. CPD is required for an individual to become certified and for an individual to retain their certified status. This is to ensure retention of competency and professional standards of practice.

Knowledge continues to advance in all professions. "Greening the workplace" is becoming a catch phrase. In many professions we are seeing more and more expectations of sustainability credentials and sustainability literacy. What opportunities are there for CPD in sustainability? More and more professional institutes are offering programs. For example, the Association of Energy Engineers has the Certified Sustainable Development Professional (CSDP) Program which, among other things, "raises the professional standards of those engaged in sustainable development." There is the International Society of Sustainability Professionals (ISSP) for those who are committed to making sustainability standard practice. In 1999 Professional Practice for Sustainable Development (PP4SD) was launched and works with professional institutes to create a common curriculum framework for sustainable development (Martin, 2009). Finally, some individuals have made it their business as consultants to offer educational and CPD opportunities in sustainability.

Sustainability Science: An Emerging Discipline

In the directory that follows, we highlight just some of the academic programs that are part of the new discipline of "sustainability science," which includes dozens of undergraduate doctoral degree programs in sustainability. Kansas State University Geography Professor Lisa Harrington explores the development of this discipline and the efforts to define it in her piece "Sustainability Science" in *Measurements, Indicators, and Research Methods*. Here she helps readers distinguish sustainability science from other disciplines:

> Sustainability science refers to the general pursuit of knowledge related to sustainable development, or strengthening societal transformation to more sustainable conditions. Like sustainable development concepts (or simply "sustainability"), sustainability science recognizes various spheres of interest, including environmental sustainability, economic development, human development, and cultural sustainability. Although science, broadly speaking, has traditionally avoided applications of value judgments, sustainability science developed with explicit recognition that sustainability involves choosing among what people may judge to be better or worse outcomes, and that the alternatives among which we choose are judged on the basis of human (and environmental) well-being. As noted by the Harvard professor of international science, public policy, and human development, William C. Clark, "Sustainability science is a field defined by the problems it addresses rather than by the disciplines it employs."

For more articles on education within the pages of the *Berkshire Encyclopedia of Sustainability*, please see:

- "Education"—Julie Newman (Volume 1)
- "Education, Business"—Nicola J. Acutt (Volume 2)
- "Education, Higher"—James Elder (Volume 2)
- "Education, Environmental Law"—Catherine MacKenzie (Volume 3)
- "Sustainability Science"—Lisa Harrington (Volume 6)
- "Education, Environmental (India)"—Vivek Bhandari (Volume 7)
- "Education, Environmental (China)"—Xia Ji (Volume 7)
- "Education, Environmental (Japan)"—Osamu Abe (Volume 7)
- "Female Education (India and China)"—Leemamol Mathew (Volume 7)
- "Education, Higher (Africa)"—Alex Awiti (Volume 9)
- "Education, Environmental"—Bob Stevenson (Volume 9)
- "Education, Higher"—Daniella Tilbury (Volume 10)

Key Organizations and Resources for Educators

We hope that the following list of organizations and resources will be helpful to educators and others. Please note that this list is NOT, by any means, to be considered a complete list; an organization's or program's appearance (or not) on this list does not imply any endorsement by the publisher or the editors of the *Berkshire Encyclopedia of Sustainability*. Berkshire Publishing Group invites readers to add further recommendations at TheSustainabilityProject.com.

For K-12 (Kindergarten–12th Grade) Teachers and Schools

- Arizona State University Global Institute of Sustainability: http://sustainability.asu.edu/education/k-12-education.php
- Children's Environmental Literacy Foundation: http://celfeducation.org/About.html
- The Cloud Institute for Sustainability Education: www.cloudinstitute.org/
- Green Schools National Network: www.greenschoolsnationalconference.org/
- Institute of Sustainable Education: www.ise-lv.eu/index.php?show=1
- *International Journal of Sustainability in Higher Education*: www.emeraldinsight.com/products/journals/journals.htm?id=ijshe
- The International Schools Association, Education for Sustainability—A Curriculum Framework K–12: www.isaschools.org/index.php?Itemid=62&id=24&option=com_content&task=view
- *Journal of Education for Sustainable Development*: http://jsd.sagepub.com/
- *Journal of Sustainability Education*: http://susted.com/
- *Journal of Teacher Education for Sustainability*: http://www.ise-lv.eu/publications.php?show=39&pub=3
- State of Washington Office of Superintendent of Public Instruction, Education for Environment and Sustainability: www.k12.wa.us/EnvironmentSustainability/default.aspx
- US Department of Education, Green Ribbon Schools: www2.ed.gov/programs/green-ribbon-schools/index.html
- US Partnership for Education for Sustainable Development: www.uspartnership.org/
- University of Wisconsin, La Crosse, Sustainability at UW–La Crosse: www.uwlax.edu/sustainability/html/educational-resources.htm

For Colleges and Universities

- American Association for the Advancement of Sustainability in Higher Education (AASHE): www.aashe.org
- Environmental Association for Universities and Colleges (EAUC): www.eauc.org.uk/2009_green_gown_awards
- Higher Education Associations Sustainability Consortium (HEASC): www.heasc.aashe.org

- Second Nature: www.secondnature.org
- Sustainability Education and Economic Development (SEED) Center, www.theseedcenter.org
- InTeGrate: www.serc.carleton.edu/integrate

For Businesses

- Beyond Grey Pinstripes: www.beyondgreypinstripes.org
- National Environmental Education Foundation: www.neefusa.org
- Rocky Mountain Institute: www.rmi.org
- SustainableBusiness.com: www.sustainablebusiness.com

General

- Earth Day: www.earthday.org
- Global Footprint Network: www.footprintnetwork.org
- International Institute of Sustainable Development (IISD): www.iisd.org
- Redefining Progress: www.ecologicalfootprint.org
- Stockholm Environmental Institute (SEI): www.sei-international.org
- Worldwatch Institute: www.worldwatch.org
- World Resources Institute: www.wri.org

Directory of Academic Sustainability Programs and Research Centers

There is a vast amount of research on sustainability. Some tertiary educational institutes have "sustainability research clusters," or sustainability research institutes, and even research departments, focused entirely on sustainability. Some countries have established institutes with a focus on research in sustainability, such as the Canada-based International Institute for Sustainable Development (IISD). Almost every discipline has launched sustainability research such as "agriculture and sustainability" or "design and sustainability."

Below is a partial list of selected academic insitutions that have sustainability degree programs or research institutes. This list does not include the myriad programs in environmental studies and only captures a slice of this burgeoning field of study. We are grateful to the American Association for the Advancement of Sustainability in Higher Education (AASHE), which has made material similar to this directory publicly available and keeps it maintained on their website: http://www.aashe.org/. As before, Berkshire Publishing Group invites readers to add further recommendations at TheSustainabilityProject.com. We particularly welcome suggestions for programs outside of the United States.

This is NOT to be considered a complete list, or to suggest that any one program is better than any other; it is but a starting point of some of the many programs in the world for the student interested in studying sustainability. Please visit TheSustainabilityProject. com if you would like to suggest a program that is not on this list.

ACADEMIC PROGRAMS WITH A GENERAL SUSTAINABILITY FOCUS

Acadia University
Environmental & Sustainability Studies
BA in Environmental and Sustainability Studies
Wolfville, Nova Scotia, Canada
http://environment.acadiau.ca/

Antioch University
Glen Helen Ecology Institute
Various programs

Antioch University-Los Angeles
MA in Urban Sustainability
Los Angeles, CA, USA
www.antiochla.edu/academics/
ma-urban-sustainability

Antioch University, New England
MA in Advocacy for Social Justice and Sustainability
Keene, NH, USA

Appalachian State University
Department of Sustainable Development
BS in Sustainable Development
BA in Sustainable Development
Minor in Sustainable Development
Boone, NC, USA
http://susdev.appstate.edu/

Arizona State University
School of Sustainability
Ph.D. in Sustainability
MS in Sustainability
MA in Sustainability
BS in Sustainability
BA in Sustainability
Minor in Sustainability
Tempe, AZ, USA
http://schoolofsustainability.asu.edu/

Art Institute of Portland, The
Sustainability Studies Minor
Portland, OR, USA
www.artinstitutes.edu/portland/degree-programs/
sustainability-minor.aspx

Auburn University
Office of Sustainability
Minor in Sustainability Studies
Auburn, AL, USA
www.auburn.edu/projects/sustainability/website/
student_resources/student_minor.php

Baldwin Wallace College
Sustainability Program
BA in Sustainability
Berea, OH, USA
www.bw.edu/academics/sustainability/

Blekinge Institute of Technology
Programme in Sustainable Product-Service System Innovation
Strategic Leadership Towards Sustainability (MSLS) and Sustainable Product-Service System Innovation (MSPI)
Karlskrona, Sweden
http://bth.se/mspi

Boston Architectural College
Master of Design Studies in Sustainable Design
Boston, MA
www.the-bac.edu/x3199.xml

California State Polytechnic Institute
John T. Lyle Center for Regenerative Studies
MS in Regenerative Studies
Minor in Regenerative Studies
Pomona, CA
www.csupomona.edu/~crs/graduate.html

Central Piedmont Community College
Sustainability Technologies
AAS in Sustainability Technologies
Charlotte, NC, USA
www.cpcc.edu/gs/degree_programs/
sustainability-technologies-a40370

Clarion University of Pennsylvania
Physics Department
Sustainability Science and Policy Minor
Clarion, PA, USA
www.clarion.edu/13412/

Columbia University
Department of Sustainable Development
Ph.D. in Sustainable Development
MS in Sustainability Management
*BA Major and Concentration in Sustainable
    Development*
New York, NY, USA
www.college.columbia.edu/bulletin/depts/sustdev.php

Dalhousie University
Environment, Sustainability and Society (ESS)
    program
BS in Environment, Sustainability, and Society
BA in Environment, Sustainability, and Society
Halifax, Nova Scotia, Canada
http://sustainability.dal.ca/index.php

Dominican University of California
Sustainable Communities Program
BA in Sustainable Communities
San Rafael, CA, USA
www.dominican.edu/academics/ahss/hum/
    undergraduate/sustainable/

Drew University
Environmental Studies
BA in Environmental Studies and Sustainability
Madison, NJ, USA
www.drew.edu/depts/depts.aspx?id=73168

Eastern Mennonite University
Applied Social Sciences
BS in Environmental Sustainability
Harrisonburg, VA, USA
www.emu.edu/applied-social-sciences/
    environmental-sustainability/

Emory University
Institute of the Liberal Arts
Sustainability Minor
Atlanta, GA, USA
www.ila.emory.edu/ila-undergraduate/sub-
    undergraduate-sus.shtml

Furman University
Department of Earth and Environmental Sciences
BS in Sustainability Sciences
Greenville, SC, USA
www2.furman.edu/academics/EES/Pages/
    home.aspx

George Mason University
College of Science
BA in Environmental and Sustainability Studies
Sustainability Studies Minor
Manassas, VA, USA
http://cos.gmu.edu/academics/undergraduate/
    minors/sustainability-studies

Goucher College
Arts in Cultural Sustainability
MA in Cultural Sustainability
Baltimore, MD, USA
www.goucher.edu/x33261.xml

Harvard University Extension School
Sustainability & Environmental Management
*MA in Sustainability and Environment
    Mangement*
Cambridge, MA, USA
www.extension.harvard.edu/programs/
    environmental-sustainability/overview/

Illinois Institute of Technology
Environmental Management and Sustainability
*MS in Environmental Management and
    Sustainability*
Chicago, IL, USA
www.stuart.iit.edu/graduateprograms/ms/
    environmentalmanagement/

Johns Hopkins University
Department of Earth and Planetary Sciences
*BA in Global Environmental Change and
    Sustainability*
*Global Environmental Change and Sustainability
    Minor*
Baltimore, MD, USA
http://eps.jhu.edu/gecs/

Leiden University/Delft Technical University/
    Erasmus University (the Netherlands)
Industrial Ecology Program
MS Industrial Ecology
Delft, the Netherlands
http://ie.leidendelft.nl/

Lipscomb University
Institute for Sustainable Practice
MS in Sustainability
BA in Sustainbility Practice
BS in Sustainable Practice

Nashville, TN, USA
http://sustainability.lipscomb.edu/page.
    asp?SID=193&Page=5291

Maharishi University of Management
Department of Sustainable Living
BS in Sustainable Living
Fairfield, IA, USA

Meredith College
Department of Biological Sciences Programs
BA in Environmental Sustainability
Minor in Environmental Sustainability
Raleigh, NC, USA
www.meredith.edu/biology/programs.htm#baenv

Messiah College
BA in Sustainability Studies
Grantham, PA, USA
www.messiah.edu/sustainability/academics.html

Michigan State University, East Lansing
Sustainability Specialization Minor
East Lansing, MI, USA
www.reg.msu.edu/AcademicPrograms/
    ProgramDetail.asp?Program=5333

Missouri Southern State University
Interdisciplinary Studies
Sustainability Minor
Joplin, MO, USA
www.mssu.edu/catalog04-06/
    InterdisciplinaryStudies.pdf

Mountain State University
BS in Environmental Sustainability
Beckley, WV, USA
www.mountainstate.edu/programs/environmental-
    sustainability/environmental-sustainability.aspx

Murdoch University
Perth, Western Australia
School of Engineering and Energy
BS in Sustainable Energy Management
www.eepe.murdoch.edu.au/areas/energy/
    undergrad/energybsc.html

National University of Ireland Galway;
MA in Rural Sustainability
    www.nuigalway.ie/geography/ma/rs/

Northern Arizona University
Arts in Sustainable Communities
MA in Sustainable Communities
Flagstaff, AZ, USA
http://home.nau.edu/sus/

Otago Polytechnic
Dunedin, New Zealand
www.otagopolytechnic.ac.nz/about/sustainable-
    practice.html

Pennsylvania State University
Online Degrees
BA in Energy and Sustainability Policy
State College, PA, USA

Philadelphia University
BS in Environmental Sustainability
Philidelphia, PA, USA
http://philau.edu/schools/liberalarts/ugradmajors/
    envirosustain/

Portland State University
Graduate School of Education
MS in Leadership for Sustainability Education
Portland, OR, USA
www.pdx.edu/elp/lse

Prescott College
Ph.D. in Sustainability Education
Prescott, AZ, USA
www.prescott.edu/academics/phd/index.html

Presidio Graduate School
MPA in Sustainable Management
San Francisco, CA, USA
www.presidioedu.org/programs/
    mpa-sustainable-management

Ramapo College
Environmental Studies
MA in Sustainability Studies
Mahwah, NJ, USA
www.ramapo.edu/masters-sustainability/

Rochester Institute of Technology
Department of Civil Engineering Technology,
    Environmental Management & Safety
Ph.D. in Sustainability
BS in Environmental Sustainability

Rochester, NY, USA
www.rit.edu/cast/cetems/bs-ms-in-environmental-
    sustainability-health-and-safety.php

San Diego State University
Environmental Studies and Sustainability
San Diego, CA, USA
http://environment.sdsu.edu/

San Francisco State University
Environmental Studies Program
BA in Environmental Sustainability and Social Justice
San Francisco, CA, USA
http://bss.sfsu.edu/envstudies/concentrations.html

Savannah College of Art and Design
MA in Design for Sustainability
Minor in Design for Sustainability
Savannah, GA, USA
www.scad.edu/design-for-sustainability/index.
    cfm#programButtons

Saybrook University
College of Psychology and Humanistic Studies
MA in Organizational Systems, Leadership of
    Sustainable Systems Specialization
San Francisco, CA, USA
www.saybrook.edu/phs/academicprograms/os/lss

Slippery Rock University
Department of Geography, Geology, & the
    Environment
MS in Sustainable Systems
Slippery Rock, PA, USA
http://academics.sru.edu/gge/MS3/ms3.html

St. Petersburg College
BS in Sustainability Management
St. Petersburg, FL, USA

Stony Brook University
Sustainability Studies
BA in Sustainability Studies
Stony Brook, NY, USA
www.stonybrook.edu/commcms/sustainability/

Temple University
Fox School of Business
Corporate Social Responsibility Minor
Philidelphia, PA, USA
www.fox.temple.edu/features/corporate_social_
    responsibility.html

The City College of New York
Sustainability in the Urban Environment Program
MS in Sustainability
New York, NY
www1.ccny.cuny.edu/prospective/sustainability/

United Nations University
Institute for Sustainability and Peace
Master of Science in Sustainability, Development,
    and Peace
Tokyo, Japan
http://isp.unu.edu/index.html

University College
BS in Sustainability
St. Louis, MO, USA
http://ucollege.wustl.edu/node/895

University of Alaska, Fairbanks
Natural Resources and Sustainability
Ph.D. in Natural Resources and Sustainability
Fairbanks, AK, USA
www.uaf.edu/nrs/

University of Dayton
Initiative on Sustainability, Energy and the
    Environment
Sustainability, Energy and the Environment (SEE)
    minor
Dayton, OH, USA
http://see.udayton.edu/

University of Florida
College of Design, Construction, and Planning
BS in Sustainability and the Built Environment
College of Liberal Arts and Sciences
Minor in Sustainability Studies
Gainsville, FL, USA
www.dcp.ufl.edu/sustainability

University of Massachusetts Dartmouth
Sustainability Studies
Online Sustainable Development Program
Sustainability Minor
North Dartmouth, MA, USA
www1.umassd.edu/sustainability/studies/
    academics_certificate_graduate.cfm

University of Minnesota Twin Cities
Sustainability Studies Minor
Sustainability Studies Minor

Saint Paul, MN, USA
http://sustainabilitystudies.umn.edu/
    index.htm

University of Missouri—Kansas City
Environmental Studies Program
Environmental Sustainability Minor
Kansas City, MO, USA
http://cas.umkc.edu/Environmental_
    Studies/

University of New Haven
Sustainability Studies
BS in Sustainability
New Haven, CT, USA
www.newhaven.edu/89939/

University of New Mexico
Sustainability Studies Program
Sustainability Studies Minor
Albuquerque, NM, USA
http://sust.unm.edu/

University of North Carolina Chapel Hill
Environment and Ecology Department
Sustainability Studies Minor
Chapel Hill, NC, USA
www.cee.unc.edu/sustainability_minor.cfm

University of Oklahoma
Department of Geography
BA in Environmental Sustainability
BS in Environmental Sustainability
Norman, OK, USA

University of Rochester
Chemical Engineering
MS in Alternative Energy
Rochester, NY, USA
www.che.rochester.edu/altenergy.htm

University of Saskatchewan
School of Environment and Sustainability
Ph.D. in Environment and Sustainability
Master of Environment and Sustainability
    (M.E.S.)
Master of Sustainable Environmental
    Management (M.SEM.)
Saskatoon, SK, Canada
www.usask.ca/sens/index.php

University of South Florida
School of Sustainability
MA in Global Sustainability
Tampa, FL, USA
http://sgs.usf.edu/ma_main.php

University of Southern Maine
Department of Environmental Science
Environmental Sustainability Minor
Portland, ME, USA
www.usm.maine.edu/esd/degree/index.htm

University of Texas, Arlington
Environmental and Sustainability Studies
Minor in Environmental and Sustainability Studies
Arlington, TX, USA
www.uta.edu/sustainability/academics/academic-
    programs.php

University of Tokyo
Graduate Program in Sustainability Science
Masters in Sustainability Science
Tokyo, Japan
www.sustainability.k.u-tokyo.ac.jp/

University of the Pacific
School of Engineering and Computer Science
Sustainability Minor
Stockton, CA, USA
http://web.pacific.edu/x26083.xml

Virginia Polytechnic Institute and State
    University
College of Natural Resources and the
    Environment
Executive Master of Natural Resources (XMNR)
Blacksburg, VA, USA
www.cnr.vt.edu/xmnr/

Western Kentucky University
Geography and Geology Department
Sustainability Minor
Bowling Green, KY, USA
www.wku.edu/geoweb/envcrse/sustain.htm

Western New England College
School of Arts and Sciences
BS in Sustainability
Springfield, MA, USA
www1.wnec.edu/artsandsciences/index.
    cfm?selection=doc.8258

Wilson College
Environmental Sustainability
BA in Environmental Sustainability
Chambersburg, PA, USA
www.wilson.edu/wilson/asp/content.asp?
  id=3229

University of Glasgow
*MSc Programme in Environmental Science,
  Technology and Society (E-STS)*
Glasgow, Scotland, UK
www.gla.ac.uk/postgraduate/taught/
  environmentalsciencetechnologysociety/

GRADUATE BUSINESS PROGRAMS IN SUSTAINABILITY

Antioch University, New England
Keene, NH, USA
MBA in Sustainability
www.antiochne.edu

Bainbridge Graduate Institute
Seattle, WA, USA
MBA in Sustainable Business
www.bgi.edu

Bodø Graduate School of Business
University of Norway
Bodø, Norway
MS in Sustainable Management
www.english.hhb.no

College of Business
Colorado State University
Fort Collins, CO, USA
MSBA in Global Social Sustainable Enterprise
www.biz.colostate.edu/gsse/pages/default.aspx

College of Graduate & Professional Studies
Franklin Pierce University
Rindge, NH, USA
MBA Energy Sustainability
www.franklinpierce.edu/academics/gradstudies/
  programs_of_study/mba_energy_sustainability.
  htm

The Earth Institute
Columbia University

New York, NY, USA
MS Sustainability Management
http://ce.columbia.edu/Sustainability-
  Management

Green Mountain College
Poultney, VT, USA
Green MBA
http://greenmba.greenmtn.edu/

Goddard College
Plainfield, VT, USA
MA in Sustainable Business and Communities
www.goddard.edu/
  masterarts_businesscommunities

Maharishi University of Management
Fairfield, IA, USA
Sustainable Business (MBA)
www.mum.edu/mba/

Maine Business School
University of Maine
Orono, ME, USA
MBA Track in Business & Sustainability
www.mbs.maine.edu/~mba_msa/bus_sust_
  track.htm

Marlboro College
Brattleboro, VT, USA
MBA in managing for sustainability
http://gradschool.marlboro.edu/academics/mba/

Marylhurst University
Online Degrees
Portland, OR, USA
MBA in Sustainabile Business
http://onlinedegrees.marylhurst.edu

Presidio Graduate School
San Francisco, CA, USA
MBA in Sustainable Management
www.presidioedu.org/programs/
  mba-sustainable-management

Royal Roads University
Victoria, BC, Canada
MA in Environment and Management
http://royalroads.ca/program/
  environment-and-management-ma

School of Business
Duquesne University
Pittsburgh, PA, USA
MBA Sustainability
http://mba.sustainability.duq.edu/

School of Business and Leadership
Dominican University of California
San Francisco, CA, USA
Green MBA
www.greenmba.com/

ACADEMIC CENTERS AND RESEARCH INITIATIVES ON SUSTAINABLE AGRICULTURE

Agricultural Sustainability Institute
University of California, Davis
Davis, CA, USA
http://asi.ucdavis.edu/

Center for Agroecology and Sustainable Food
    Systems
University of California, Santa Cruz
Santa Cruz, CA, USA
http://casfs.ucsc.edu/

Center for Organic and Sustainable
    Agriculture
Alfred State College
Alfred, NY, USA
www.alfredstate.edu/cosa/introduction

Center for Environmental Farming Systems
North Carolina State University
Raleigh, NC, USA
www.cefs.ncsu.edu/

Center on Agriculture, Food and Environment,
    New Entry Sustainable Farming Project
Tufts University
Medford, MA, USA
http://nutrition.tufts.edu/1177953852962/
    Nutrition-Page-nl2w_1178370556099.html

Center for Organic Agriculture
University of Florida
Gainsville, FL, USA
http://fycs.ifas.ufl.edu/organic/

Center for Sustaining Agriculture and Natural
    Resources
Washington State University
Puyallup, WA, USA
http://csanr.wsu.edu/

C.S. Mott Group for Sustainable Food Systems
Michigan State University
East Lansing, MI, USA
www.mottgroup.msu.edu/

Sustainable Agriculture Resource Consortium
California Polytechnic State University, San
    Luis Obispo
San Luis Obispo, CA, USA
http://sarc.calpoly.edu/

DESIGN SCHOOL ACADEMIC CENTERS AND RESEARCH INITIATIVES ON SUSTAINABILITY

Brooke Byers Institute for Sustainable Systems
Georgia Institute of Technology
Atlanta, GA, USA

Center for Sustainability
Pennsylvania State University
State College, PA, USA

Center for Sustainable Cities
University of Kentucky
Lexington, KY, USA

Center for Sustainable Communities
Ambler College, Temple University
Ambler, PA, USA

Center for Sustainable Building Research
University of Minnesota, USA
Minneapolis, MN, USA

Center for Sustainable Design
Mississippi State
Mississippi State, MS, USA

Center for Sustainable Systems
University of Michigan
Dearborn, MI, USA

Center for Urban and Community
  Design
University of Miami
Coral Gables, FL, USA

College of Environmental Design
University of California, Berkeley
Berkeley, CA, USA

Design Center for Global Needs
San Francisco State University
San Francisco, CA, USA

Ecological Design Center
University of Oregon
Eugene, OR, USA

ecoMOD Project
University of Virginia
Charlottesville, VA, USA

Engineering and Design Institute
Philidelphia University
Philidelphia, PA, USA

Environmental Institute
Cleveland State University
Cleveland, OH, USA

Green Design Institute
Carnagie Mellon University
Pittsburgh, PA, USA

Green Design Research Collaborative
Iowa State University
Ames, IA, USA

International Center for Sustainable New Cities
Illinois Institute of Technology
Chicago, IL, USA

Powell Center for Construction and
  Environment
University of Florida
Gainsville, FL, USA

Sustainable Systems Research Center
Rochester Institute of Technology
Rochester, NY, USA

BUSINESS SCHOOL ACADEMIC CENTERS AND RESEARCH INITIATIVES ON SUSTAINABILITY

Allwin Initiative for Corporate Citizenship
Dartmouth College
Hanover, VT, USA
http://mba.tuck.dartmouth.edu/initiative/

Batten Institute's Sustainable Business Inititive
University of Virginia
Charlottesville, VA
www.darden.virginia.edu/web/Batten-Institute/

Brooke Byers Institute for Sustainable Systems
Georgia Institute of Technology
Atlanta, GA, USA
http://sustainability.gatech.edu/

Building Sustainable Value Research Center
University of Western Ontario
London, ON, Canada
www.ivey.uwo.ca/centres/sustainability/

Center for the Advancement of Social
  Entrepreneurs
Duke University
Durham, NC, USA
www.caseatduke.org/

Center for Corporate Citizenship
Boston College
Boston, MA, USA
www.bcccc.net/

Center for Sustainable Enterprise
University of North Carolina, Chapel Hill
Chapel Hill, NC
www.kenan-flagler.unc.edu/cse/

Center for Sustainable Enterprise
Illinois Institute of Technology
Chicago, IL, USA
www.stuart.iit.edu/cse/

Center for Sustainable Global Enterprise
Cornell University
Ithaca, NY, USA
www2.johnson.cornell.edu/sge/index.cfm

Center for Social Innovation
Stanford University

Stanford, CA, USA
http://csi.gsb.stanford.edu

Center for Responsible Business
University of California, Berkeley
Berkeley, CA
http://responsiblebusiness.haas.berkeley.edu/

Centre for Corporate Social Responsibility
Queen's University
Kingston, ON, Canada
http://business.queensu.ca/centres/crl/index.php

Erb Institute for Global Sustainable Enterprise
University of Michigan
Ann Arbor, MI
http://erb.umich.edu/

Fowler Center for Sustainable Value
Case Western Reserve University
Cleveland, OH, USA

Institute for Sustainable Enterprise
Fairleigh Dickinson University
Madison, NJ, USA
http://view.fdu.edu/default.aspx?id=
    2354

Social Enterprise Program
Columbia University
New York, NY, USA
www4.gsb.columbia.edu/socialenterprise/

Socially, Environmentally and Ethically
    Responsible (SEER) Business Practice Program
Pepperdine University
Los Angelos, CA

Weatherhead Institute for Sustainable Enterprise
Case Western Reserve University
Cleveland, OH, USA
http://weatherhead.case.edu/initiatives/
    sustainable-enterprise/

SUSTAINABLE DEVELOPMENT ACADEMIC RESEARCH CENTERS

Atkinson Center for a Sustainable Future (ACSF)
Cornell University
www.sustainablefuture.cornell.edu/index.php

Center for Sustainable Development
Rose-Hulman Institute of Technology
Terre Haute, IN, USA
www.rose-hulman.edu/csd/

Center for Sustainable Development and
    International Peace
University of Denver
Denver, CO, USA
www.du.edu/korbel/sdip/

Center for Sustainable Suburban Development
University of California, Riverside
Riverside, CA, USA
http://cssd.ucr.edu/

The Earth Institute
Columbia University
New York, NY, USA
www.earthinstitute.columbia.edu/sections/view/9

Sustainability Institute of Clarion University
Clarion University
Clarion, PA, USA
www.clarion.edu/123581/

ECOLOGICAL AND ENVIRONMENTAL ECONOMICS ACADEMIC CENTERS AND RESEACH INITIATIVES

Australian Centre for Biosecurity and
    Environmental Economics
Australian National University
Canberra, Australia
www.acbee.anu.edu.au/

The Beijer Institute for Ecological Economics
Royal Swedish Academy of the Sciences
Stockholm, Sweden

Brooke Byers Institute for Sustainable Systems
Georgia Institute of Technology
Atlanta, GA, USA

Centre for Applied Business Research in Energy
    and the Environment
University of Alberta
Edmonton, AB, Canada
www.business.ualberta.ca/Centres/cabree.aspx

Centre for Ecological Economics and Ethics
Bodø Graduate School of Business

Bodø, Norway
www.english.hhb.no/index.php?ID=16700

Centre for Research on Energy and Environmental
  Economics and Policy
Universita Commerciale Luigi Bocconi, Milano
Milano, Italy
www.iefe.unibocconi.eu/

Centre for Strategic Economic Studies
Victoria University
Victoria, Australia
www.cfses.com/

Center for Economic and Social Studies of the
  Environment
Universite Libre De Bruxelles
Brussels, Belgium
http://dev.ulb.ac.be/ceese/CEESE/fr/accueil.
  php?menu=0

Center for Environmental and Resource Economic
  Policy
North Carolina State University
Raleigh, NC, USA

Center for Integrative Environmental Research
University of Maryland
College Park, MD, USA

Economics and Environment Network
Australian National University
Canberra, Australia

Environmental Finance Center
University of North Carolina at Chapel Hill
Chapel Hill, NC, USA

Global Development and Environment Institute
Tufts University
Medford, MA, USA

Gund Institute of Ecological Economics
University of Vermont
Montpelier, VT, USA
www.uvm.edu/giee/

Harvard Environmental Economics
  Program
Harvard University
Cambridge, MA, USA

Institute for the Economy and the
  Environment
University of St. Gallen
St. Gallen, Switzerland

Institute for Environmental Economics and
  World Trade
Leibniz Universitat, Hannover
Hannover, Germany
www.iuw.uni-hannover.de/start_institut.
  html?&L=1

New Zealand Centre for Ecological Economics
Massey University
Palmerston North, New Zealand

Portugese Ecological Economics and
  Environmental Management Centre
New University of Lisbon
Lisbon, Portugal

Research Center for Environmental Economics
Ruprecht-Karls Universitat
Heidelburg, Germany
www.eco.uni-heidelberg.de/index_e.html

Research in Economics, Business, and the
  Environment
University of Vigo
Vigo, Spain

SUSTAINABILITY AND ENVIRONMENTAL EDUCATION ACADEMIC CENTERS AND RESEARCH INITIATIVES

Center for Environmental and Sustainability
  Education
Florida Gulf Coast University
Fort Myers, FL, USA
www.fgcu.edu/cese/

Center for Global Environmental Education
Hamline University
St. Paul, MN, USA
www.hamline.edu/cgee/frogs/

Environmental Education Center
Morehead State University
Moorehead, KY, USA
http://eec.moreheadstate.edu/

Canadian Centre for Environmental Education
Royal Roads University
Victoria, BC, Canada
www.ccee.ca/

Center for Environmental Education
Murray State University
Murray, KY, USA
http://coekate.murraystate.edu/cee/

Center for Environmental Education
University of Louisville
Louisville, KY, USA
http://louisville.edu/education/research/centers/
environmental-ed

Center for Environment & Conservation
Education
University of Tennessee at Martin
Martin, TN, USA
www.utm.edu/departments/cece

Center for Environmental Education &
Sustainability
Western Kentucky University
Bowling Green, KY, USA
www.wku.edu/cees/

Center for Environmental Sustainability Education
University of Wisconsin-Milwaukee
Milwaukee, WI, USA
www4.uwm.edu/sce/dci.cfm?id=661

Center for Geography and Environmental
Education
University of Tennessee
Knoxville, TN, USA
http://eeintennessee.org/net/org/info.
aspx?s=45142.0.0.37935

Environmental Education and Training
Partnership
University of Wisconsin—Stevens Point
Stevens Point, WI, USA
www.eetap.org/

Global Environmental Management Education
Center
University of Wisconsin—Stevens Point
Stevens Point, WI, USA
www.uwsp.edu/cnr/gem/

Merry Lea Environmental Learning Center
Goshen College
Wolf Lake, IN, USA
www.goshen.edu/merrylea/about/index.php

Robert A. Macoskey Center for Sustainable
Systems Education and Research
Slippery Rock University
Slippery Rock, PA, USA
www.sru.edu/academics/colleges/ches/macoskey/
Pages/index.aspx

Steinbrenner Institute for Environmental
Education & Research
Carnegie Mellon University
Pittsburgh, PA, USA
www.cmu.edu/steinbrenner/
index.html

Sustainability Education Center
Ramapo College of New Jersey
Mahwah, NJ, USA
www.ramapo.edu/ramapogreen/sustainabilityctr/

Wallerstein Collaborative For Urban
Environmental Education
New York University
New York, NY, USA
http://steinhardt.nyu.edu/wallerstein/

SUSTAINABLE ENGINEERING ACADEMIC CENTERS

Brook Byers Institute for Sustainable Systems
Georgia Institute of Technology
Atlanta, GA, USA

Center for Sustainability in Engineering
California Polytechnic State
University
San Luis Obispo, CA, USA

Center for Sustainable Engineering
Carnegie Mellon University
Pittsburgh, PA, USA

Center for Environmental Resource Management
University of Texas at El Paso
El Paso, TX, USA

Center for Green Chemistry & Green Engineering
Yale University
New Haven, CT, USA

Center for Sustainable Energy Systems (press release)
Massachusetts Institute of Technology
Cambridge, MA, USA

Center for Sustainable Urban Engineering
University of Cincinnati
Cincinnati, OH, USA

Consortium on Green Design and Manufacturing
University of California, Berkeley
Berkeley, CA, USA

Engineering and Design Institute
Philadelphia University
Philadelphia, PA, USA

International Sustainable Engineering Initiative
Michigan Technological University
Houghton, MI, USA

Power Systems Engineering Research Center and National Center of Excellence (NCE) on SMART Innovations
Arizona State University
Tempe, AZ, USA

Sustainable Energy Science and Engineering Center
Florida State University
Tallahassee, FL, USA

University of Cambridge
Centre for Sustainable Development
MPhil in Engineering for Sustainable Development
Cambridge, UK

University of Cambridge
Programme for Sustainable Leadership
Cambridge, UK
http://www.cpsl.cam.ac.uk/

University of Strathclyde
David Livingstone Centre for Sustainability (DLCS)
Various postgraduate degrees
Glasgow, Scotland, UK

ENVIRONMENTAL LAW ACADEMIC CENTERS

Australian Centre for Environmental Law
Australian National University
Canberra, Australia
http://law.anu.edu.au/acel

California Center for Environmental Law & Policy
University of California, Berkeley
Berkeley, CA, USA
www.law.berkeley.edu/clee.htm

Canadian Institute of Resources Law
University of Calgary
Calgary, AB, Canada
http://cirl.ca/

Center for Water Law and Policy
Texas Tech University
Lubbock, TX, USA
www.law.ttu.edu/acp/centers/water/

Center for Environmental Law and Policy
Yale University
New Haven, CT, USA
http://envirocenter.research.yale.edu/

Center for Energy and Environmental Security
University of Colorado at Bolder
Boulder, CO, USA
http://cees.colorado.edu/

Center for Environment, Energy & Natural Resources Law
University of Houston
Houston, TX, USA
www.law.uh.edu/eenrcenter/

Center for Environmental Law and Land Use
Loyola University New Orleans
New Orleans, LA, USA
www.loyno.edu/environment-land-use/

Center for Oceans Law and Policy
University of Virginia
Charlottesville, VA, USA
www.virginia.edu/colp/

Centre for Environmental Law
Macquarie University
Sydney, Australia
www.law.mq.edu.au/MUCIEL/index.htm

Centre For Global Environmental and Natural
  Resource Law
University of British Columbia
Vancouver, BC, Canada
www.law.ubc.ca/enlaw/

Centre for Law and the Environment
University College London
London, United Kingdom
www.ucl.ac.uk/laws/environment/
Environmental Law Center
University of California, Los Angeles
Los Angeles, CA, USA
www.law.ucla.edu/centers-programs/
  environmental-law/Pages/default.aspx

Environmental Law Centre
University of Victoria
Victoria, BC, Canada
www.elc.uvic.ca/

Environmental and Natural Resources Law
Stanford University
Stanford, CA, USA
www.law.stanford.edu/program/centers/enrlp/

Frank J. Guarini Center on Environmental and
  Land Use Law
New York University
New York, NY, USA
www.law.nyu.edu/centers/elc/index.htm

Institute for Energy and the Environment
Vermont Law School
Burlington, VT, USA
www.vermontlaw.edu/Academics/Environmental_
  Law_Center.htm

Land Use Institute
Vermont Law School

Burlington, VT, USA
www.vermontlaw.edu/x3704.xml

Land Use Law Center
Pace University
White Plains, NY, USA
http://web.pace.edu/page.cfm?doc_id=23239

Marine & Environmental Law Institute
Dalhousie University
Halifax, NS, Canada
http://law.dal.ca/Institutes/Marine%20&%20
  Environmental%20Law%20Institute/

National Energy-Environment Law and Policy
  Institute
University of Tulsa
Tulsa, OK, USA
www.utulsa.edu

Natural Resource Law Center
University of Colorado at Bolder
Boulder, CO, USA
www.colorado.edu/law/centers/nrlc/

Natural Resources Law Institute
Lewis & Clark College
Portland, OR, USA
www.lclark.edu/law/programs/environmental_
  and_natural_resources_law/
  natural_resources_law_institute/

New Zealand Centre for Environmental Law
University of Auckland
Auckland, New Zealand
www.nzcel.auckland.ac.nz/uoa/law/about/assns/
  nzcel/nzcel.cfm

POLIS Project on Ecological Governance
University of Victoria
Victoria, BC, Canada
www.polisproject.org/

Tulane Institute on Water Resources Law & Policy
Tulane University
New Orleans, LA, USA
www.law.tulane.edu/enlaw/

Vermont Law School
Environmental Law Programs

*Online Master of Environmental Law
   and Policy*
Online LLM in Environmental Law

URBAN SUSTAINABILITY ACADEMIC CENTERS AND RESEARCH INITIATIVES

Brooke Byers Institute for Sustainable Systems
Georgia Institute of Technology
Atlanta, GA, USA

Center for Sustainable Cities
University of Southern California
Los Angeles, CA, USA

Center for Sustainable Communities
Temple University
Philadelphia, PA, USA

Center for Sustainable Urban Development
Columbia University
New York, NY, USA

Center for Sustainable Urban Engineering
University of Cincinnati
Cincinnati, OH, USA

Center for Sustainable Urban Infrastructure
University of Colorado Denver
Denver, CO, USA

Center for Sustainable Urban Neighborhoods
University of Louisville
Louisville, KY, USA

Center for Urban & Environmental Solutions
Florida Atlantic University
Boca Raton, FL, USA

Center for Urban & Regional Studies
University of North Carolina at Chapel Hill
Chapel Hill, NC, USA

Center for Urban Environmental Studies
Northeastern University
Boston, MA, USA

Hixon Center for Urban Ecology
Yale University
New Haven, CT, USA

Idaho Urban Research and Design Center
University of Idaho
Boise, ID, USA

Institute for Sustainable Cities
Hunter College, City University of
   New York
New York, NY, USA

International Center for Sustainable
   New Cities
Illinois Institute of Technology
Chicago, IL, USA

Partnership for the Transformation of Urban
   Communities
Tulane University
New Orleans, LA, USA

Urban Center for People and the
   Environment
University of California, Los Angeles
Los Angeles, CA, USA

Urban Sustainability Initiative
University of California, Berkeley
Berkeley, CA, USA

Urban Sustainability Initiative
University of Nevada, Las Vegas
Las Vegas, NV, USA

Urban Ecology Research Lab
University of Washington
Seattle, WA, USA

OTHER SUSTAINABILITY RESEARCH INSTITUTES

Adirondack Ecological Center
College of Environmental Science and Forestry,
   State University of New York
Newcomb, NY, USA
www.esf.edu/aec/research/currentresearch.htm

Center for Energy, Environment, and
   Sustainability
Wake Forest University
Winston Salem, NC, USA

Center for the Environment
Harvard University
Cambridge, MA, USA
http://environment.harvard.edu/

Centre for Sustainability Studies
Lund University
Lund, Sweden

China Project (China's atmospheric environment)
Harvard University
Cambridge, MA, USA
http://chinaproject.harvard.edu/

David E. Shi Center for Sustainability
Furman University
Greenville, SC, USA
www2.furman.edu/academics/sustainability/Pages/
    default.aspx

Helmholtz Centre for Environmental
    Research—UFZ
Leipzig, Germany
www.ufz.de/index.php?en=11382

Institute for Sustainable Resources
Queensland University of Technology
Brisbane, Australia
www.isr.qut.edu.au/

International Institute for Environment and
    Development (IIED)
London, UK
www.iied.org/

Institute for Resources Environment and
    Sustainability
University of British Columbia
Vancouver, BC, Canada
www.ires.ubc.ca/

Institute for Sustainable Solutions
Portland State University
Portland, OR, USA
www.pdx.edu/sustainability/

Institute for Systems Science, Innovation &
    Sustainability Research (ISIS)
University of Graz
Graz, Austria
www.uni-graz.at/en/innoxwww.htm?=

Rocky Mountain Institute
Snowmass, CO, USA
www.rmi.org

Stockholm Environmental Institute
Stockholm, Sweden
www.sei-international.org

Stockholm Resilience Center
University of Stockholm
Stockholm, Sweden

Sustainability Research Unit
Nelson Mandela Metropolitan University
Port Elizabeth, South Africa
www.nmmu.ac.za/default.asp?id=9045&bhcp=1

Sustainability Science Program
Harvard University
Cambridge, MA
www.hks.harvard.edu/centers/cid/programs/
    sustsci

Sustainability Solutions Initiative
University of Maine
Orono, ME, USA
www.umaine.edu/sustainabilitysolutions/

Master Bibliography: The Most Cited Works

The following list includes books, articles, and reports that have been cited the most by *Encyclopedia of Sustainability* authors. Following this is a list of all books, articles, reports, and websites that were cited at least three times by *Encyclopedia of Sustainability* authors. The last three works in this list were cited an equal number of times (hence the unusual number 21): *Collapse: How Societies Choose to Fail or Succeed; The River Runs Black: The Environmental Challenge to China's Future;* and *Something New Under the Sun: An Environmental History of the Twentieth-Century World.*

Top 21 Cited Works, in Order of Frequency Cited

1. **Brundtland Commission.** (1987). *Our common future: Report of the World Commission on Environment and Development.* Oxford, UK: Oxford University Press.
2. **Daly, Herman E., & Cobb, J. B.** (Eds.). (1989). *For the common good.* Boston: Beacon Press.
3. **Meadows, Donella H.; Meadows, Dennis L.; Randers, Jorgen; & Behrens, William W., III.** (1972). *The limits to growth.* New York: Universe Books.
4. **McDonough, William, & Braungart, Michael.** (2002) *Cradle to cradle: Remaking the way we make things.* New York: North Point Press.
5. **Hawken, Paul; Lovins, Amory; & Lovins, L. Hunter.** (1999). *Natural capitalism: Creating the next Industrial Revolution.* Boston: Little, Brown.
6. **Costanza, Robert, et al.** (1997). The value of the world's ecosystem services and natural capital. *Nature, 387,* 253–260.
7. **Hardin, Garrett.** (1968). The tragedy of the commons. *Science, 162*(3859), 1243–1248.
8. **Millennium Ecosystem Assessment (MA).** (2005). *Ecosystems and human well-being: Synthesis.* Washington, DC: Island Press.
9. **Stern, Nicholas.** (2007). *The economics of climate change: The Stern Review.* Cambridge, UK: Cambridge University Press.
10. **Benyus, Janine M.** (1997). *Biomimicry: Innovation inspired by nature.* New York: Morrow Publishing.
11. **Leopold, Aldo.** (1949). *A Sand County almanac and sketches here and there.* New York: Oxford University Press.
12. **Schumacher, E. F.** (1973). *Small is beautiful: A study of economics as if people mattered.* London: Sphere Books.
13. **Carson, Rachel.** (1962). *Silent spring.* Boston: Houghton Mifflin Company.
14. **Norton, Bryan G.** (2005). *Sustainability: A philosophy of adaptive ecosystem management.* Chicago: University of Chicago Press.
15. **Ostrom, Elinor.** (1990). *Governing the commons: The evolution of institutions for collective action.* Cambridge, UK: Cambridge University Press.

16. **Rees, William, & Wackernagel, Mathis.** (1996). Ecological footprints and appropriated carrying capacity: Measuring the natural capital requirements of the human economy. In Ann Marie Jansson, Carl Folke, Monica Hammer & Robert Costanza (Eds.), *Investing in natural capital: The ecological economics approach to sustainability* (pp. 362–390). Washington, DC: Island Press.

17. **Smith, Adam.** (1977). *An inquiry into the nature and causes of the wealth of nations.* Chicago: University of Chicago Press. (First published in 1776.)

18. **The Earth Charter Initiative.** (2000). The Earth Charter. Retrieved August 2, 2010, from http://www.earthcharterinaction.org/content/pages/Read-the-Charter.html

19. **Diamond, Jared M.** (2005). *Collapse: How societies choose to fail or succeed.* New York: Viking Press.

20. **Economy, Elizabeth C.** (2005). *The river runs black: The environmental challenge to China's future.* Ithaca, NY: Cornell University Press.

21. **McNeill, J. R.** (2000). *Something new under the sun: An environmental history of the twentieth-century world.* New York: W. W. Norton & Company.

Master Bibliography

The following list includes books and articles—as well as some websites—that have been cited the most by *Encyclopedia of Sustainability* authors. A more complete list of all works cited in the set may be found at TheSustainabilityProject.com.

Agyeman, Julian; Bullard, Robert D.; & Evans, Bob. (Eds.). (2003). *Just sustainabilities: Development in an unequal world*. Cambridge, MA: MIT Press.

Altieri, Miguel A. (1995). *Agroecology: The science of sustainable agriculture*. Boulder, CO: Westview Press.

Andersen, Mikael Skou, & Ekins, Paul. (Eds.). (2009). *Carbon energy taxation*. Oxford, UK: Oxford University Press.

Andrews-Speed, Philip. (2009). China's ongoing energy efficiency drive: Origins, progress and prospects. *Energy Policy*, *37*(4), 1331–1344.

Auty, Richard M. (1993). *Sustaining development in mineral economies: The resource curse thesis*. London: Routledge.

Auty, Richard M., & Mikesell, Raymond F. (1998). *Sustainable development in mineral economies*. Oxford, UK: Oxford University Press.

Baker-Fletcher, Karen. (1999). *Sisters of dust, sisters of spirit: Womanist wordings on God and creation*. Minneapolis, MN: Fortress Press.

Basel Action Network (BAN). (2004). Dante's digital junkyard. Retrieved March 28, 2012, from http://www.ban.org/ban_news/dantes_digital_040406.html

Bean, Michael J., & Rowland, Melanie J. (1997). *The evolution of national wildlife law* (3rd ed.). Westport, CT: Praeger.

Benyus, Janine M. (2002). *Biomimicry: Innovation inspired by nature*. New York: Harper Perennial.

Berkes, Fikret. (2008). *Sacred ecology* (2nd ed.). New York: Routledge.

Berry, Thomas. (1990). *The dream of the Earth*. San Francisco: Sierra Club Books.

Berry, Thomas. (2000). *The great work: Our way into the future*. New York: Bell Tower.

Birnie, Patricia; Boyle, Alan; & Redgwell, Catherine. (2010). *International law and the environment* (3rd ed.). Oxford, UK: Oxford University Press.

Brundtland Report. (1987). *Our common future: A report to the United Nations General Assembly*. New York: United Nations World Commission on Environment and Development.

Bruton, Michael J. (1975). *Introduction to transportation planning*. London: Hutchinson & Co. Ltd.

Buckley, Ralf C. (2003). *Case studies in ecotourism*. Wallingford, UK: CAB International.

Buckley, Ralf C. (2009). *Ecotourism: Principles and practices*. Wallingford, UK: CAB International.

Buckley, Ralf C. (2011). *Conservation tourism*. Wallingford, UK: CAB International.

Bullard, Robert. (2000). *Dumping in Dixie: Race, class, and environmental quality*. Boulder, CO: Westview Press.

Burke, Lauretta; Reytar, Kathleen; Spalding, Mark; & Perry, Alison. (2011). *Reefs at risk revisited.* Washington, DC: World Resources Institute.

Callicott, J. Baird. (1999). *Beyond the land ethic: More essays in environmental philosophy.* Albany: State University of New York Press.

Carbon Disclosure Project (CDP). (2010). Homepage. Retrieved September 21, 2010, from https://www.cdproject.net/

Carson, Rachel. (1962). *Silent spring.* Boston: Houghton Mifflin.

Cervero, Robert. (1998). *The transit metropolis: A global inquiry.* Washington, DC: Island Press.

Christian Aid. (2007). *Human tide: The real migration crisis.* London: Christian Aid.

Christian, David. (2004). *Maps of time: An introduction to big history.* Berkeley & Los Angeles: University of California Press.

Coggins, George Cameron; Wilkinson, Charles F.; Leshy, John D.; & Fischman, Robert L. (2007). *Federal public land and resources law* (6th ed.). New York: Foundation Press.

Collier, Paul, & Hoeffler, Anke. (2004). Greed and grievance in civil war. *Oxford Economic Papers, 56*(4), 563–595.

Costanza, Robert, et al. (1997). The value of the world's ecosystem services and natural capital. *Nature, 387*(6630), 253–260.

Courtney, Rob. (2006, July). Evolving hazardous waste policy for the digital era. *Stanford Environmental Law Journal, 25,* 199–227.

Crosby, Alfred W. (1972). *The Columbian exchange: Biological and cultural consequences of 1492.* Westport, CT: Greenwood Press.

Crosby, Alfred W. (1986). *Ecological imperialism: The biological expansion of Europe, 900–1900.* Cambridge, UK: Cambridge University Press.

Daly, Herman E. (1977). *Steady-state economics: The economics of bio-physical equilibrium and moral growth.* San Francisco: W. H. Freeman.

Daly, Herman E. (1996). *Beyond growth: The economics of sustainable development.* Boston: Beacon Press.

Daly, Herman E., & Cobb, John B., Jr. (1989). *For the common good: Redirecting the economy toward community, the environment, and a sustainable future.* Boston: Beacon Press.

Daly, Herman, & Farley, Joshua. (2004). *Ecological economics: Principles and applications.* Washington, DC: Island Press.

Daly, Herman E., & Townsend, Kenneth N. (Eds.). (1993). *Valuing the Earth: Economics, ecology, ethics.* Cambridge, MA: MIT Press.

Dana, Samuel T., & Fairfax, Sally K. (1980). *Forest and range policy: Its development in the United States* (2nd ed.). New York: McGraw-Hill.

Daneel, Martinus L. (2001). *African earthkeepers: Wholistic interfaith mission.* Maryknoll, NY: Orbis Books.

Dawson, Chad P., & Hendee, John C. (2009). *Wilderness management: Stewardship and protection of resources and values* (3rd ed.). Golden, CO: Fulcrum Books.

Dean, Warren. (1987). *Brazil and the struggle for rubber: A study in environmental history.* Cambridge, UK: Cambridge University Press.

Diamond, Jared. (1998). *Guns, germs and steel: The fate of human societies.* New York: W. W. Norton & Company.

Diamond, Jared. (2005). *Collapse: How some societies choose to fail or succeed.* New York: Viking Press.

Diaz, Robert J., & Rosenberg, Rutger. (2008). Spreading dead zones and consequences for marine ecosystems. *Science, 321*(5891), 926–929.

Drayton, Heather L. (2007, Fall). Economics of electronic waste disposal regulations. *Hofstra Law Review, 36*(1), 149–183.

Dudley, Nigel. (Ed.). (2008). *Guidelines for applying protected areas management categories.* Gland, Switzerland: International Union for Conservation of Nature.

Duffield, Mark. (2001). *Global governance and the new wars: The merging of development and security.* London: Zed Books.

Economy, Elizabeth C. (2005). *The river runs black: The environmental challenge to China's future.* Ithaca, NY: Cornell University Press.

Ehrlich, Paul Ralph. (1968). *The population bomb.* New York: Ballantine Books.

The Earth Charter Initiative. (2000). The Earth Charter. Retrieved August 2, 2010, from http://www.earthcharterinaction.org/content/pages/Read-the-Charter.html

Elkington, John. (1997). *Cannibals with forks: The triple bottom line of 21st century business.* Oxford, UK: Capstone Publishing Limited.

Environmental Performance Index (EPI). (2012). Environmental Performance Index. Retrieved February 1, 2012, from http://epi.yale.edu/

Ezroj, Aaron. (2010). How the European Union's WEEE & RoHS Directives can help the United States develop a successful national e-waste strategy. *Virginia Environmental Law Journal, 28*, 45–72.

Fairhead, James, & Leach, Melissa. (1996). *Misreading the African landscape: Society and ecology in a forest-savanna mosaic.* Cambridge, UK: Cambridge University Press.

Fehm, Sarah. (2011, Fall). From iPod to e-waste: Building a successful framework for extended producer responsibility in the United States. *Public Contract Law Journal, 41*(1), 173–192.

Foltz, Richard C.; Denny, Frederick M.; & Baharuddin, Azizan. (Eds.). (2003). *Islam and ecology.* Cambridge, MA: Harvard University Press.

Foreman, Dave. (2004). *Rewilding North America: A vision for conservation in the 21st century.* Washington, DC.: Island Press.

Fort, Timothy L., & Schipani, Cindy A. (2004). *The role of business in fostering peaceful societies.* Cambridge, UK: Cambridge University Press.

Forum on religion and ecology. (2009, February 9). Homepage. Retrieved April 27, 2009, from www.yale.edu/religionandecology

Fox, Matthew. (1983). *Original blessing: A primer in Creation Spirituality presented in four paths, twenty-six themes, and two questions.* Santa Fe, NM: Bear & Company.

Freyfogle, Eric T., & Goble, Dale D. (2009). *Wildlife law: A primer.* Washington, DC: Island Press.

Fridell, Gavin. (2007). *Fair trade coffee: The prospects and pitfalls of market-driven social justice.* Toronto: University of Toronto Press.

Friedman, Thomas. (2008). *Hot, flat, and crowded: Why we need a green revolution—and how it can renew America.* New York: Farrar, Straus and Giroux.

Gadgil, Madhav, & Guha, Ramachandra. (1992). *This fissured land: An ecological history of India.* Berkeley: University of California Press.

Gallagher, Kevin P. (2009, November). NAFTA and the environment: Lessons from Mexico and beyond.

Gebara, Ivone. (1999). *Longing for running water: Ecofeminism and liberation* (David Molineaux, Trans.). Minneapolis, MN: Fortress Press.

Glacken, Clarence J. (1967). *Traces on the Rhodian shore: Nature and culture in Western thought from ancient times to the end of the eighteenth century.* Berkeley: University of California Press.

Global Reporting Initiative (GRI). (n.d.). Homepage. Retrieved August 12, 2011, from http://www.globalreporting.org/

Gottlieb, Roger S. (2006). *A greener faith: Religious environmentalism and our planet's future.* Oxford, UK: Oxford University Press.

Grim, John. (Ed.). (2001). *Indigenous traditions and ecology: The interbeing of cosmology and community.* Cambridge, MA: Harvard Divinity School, Center for the Study of World Religions.

Gunderson, Lance H., & Holling, C. S. (Eds.). (2002). *Panarchy: Understanding transformations in human and natural systems.* Washington, DC: Island Press.

Hackett, Steven. (2011). *Environmental and natural resources economics: Theory, policy, and the sustainable society* (4th ed.). New York: M. E. Sharpe.

Hardin, Garett. (1968, December 13). The tragedy of the commons. *Science, 162*(3859), 1243–1248.

Hart, John. (2006). *Sacramental commons: Christian ecological ethics.* Lanham, MD: Rowman & Littlefield.

Harvey, Graham. (2005). *Animism: Respecting the living world.* New York: Columbia University Press.

Hawken, Paul. (2005). *The ecology of commerce: A declaration of sustainability.* New York: HarperCollins Business

Hawken, Paul; Lovins, Amory B.; & Lovins, L. Hunter. (1999). *Natural capitalism: Creating the next Industrial Revolution.* New York: Back Bay Books.

Hays, Samuel P. (1959). *Conservation and the gospel of efficiency: The Progressive Era conservation movement, 1890–1920.* Cambridge, MA: Harvard University Press.

Hirsch, Philip, & Warren, Carol. (Eds.). (1998). *The politics of environment in Southeast Asia: Resources and resistance.* London: Routledge.

Homer-Dixon, Thomas F. (1999). *Environment, scarcity, and violence.* Princeton, NJ: Princeton University Press.

Honey, Martha. (2008). *Ecotourism and sustainable development: Who owns paradise?* (2nd ed.). Washington, DC: Island Press.

Hull, Eric V. (2010). Poisoning the poor for profit: The injustice of exporting electronic waste to developing countries. *Duke Environmental Law and Policy Forum, 21*(1), 1–48.

Hunter, David; Salzman, James; & Zaelke, Durwood. (2007). *International environmental law and policy* (3rd ed.). New York: Foundation Press.

International Energy Agency (IEA). (2011). *World energy outlook 2011* (Chap. 14). Paris: IEA.

International Union for Conservation of Nature (IUCN). (2011). IUCN red list of threatened species. Retrieved February 1, 2012, from www.iucnredlist.org

Jackson, Jeremy B. C., et al. (2001). Historical overfishing and the recent collapse of coastal ecosystems. *Science, 293*(5530), 629–638.

Jacobs, Jane. (1961). *The death and life of great American cities.* New York: Random House.

Kates, Robert W., et al. (2001, April 27). Sustainability science. *Science, 292*(5517), 641–642.

Kaza, Stephanie, & Kraft, Kenneth. (Eds.). (2000). *Dharma rain: Sources of Buddhist environmentalism.* Boston: Shambhala.

Kaza, Stephanie. (Ed.). (2005). *Hooked: Buddhist writings on greed, desire, and the urge to consume.* Boston: Shambhala.

Kearns, Laurel & Keller, Catherine. (Eds.). (2007). *EcoSpirit: Religions and philosophies for the Earth.* New York: Fordham University Press.

Kelly, Kevin. (1994). *Out of control: The new biology of machines, social systems, and the economic world.* Reading, MA: Perseus Books.

Kormos, Cyril F. (Ed.). (2008). *A handbook on international wilderness law and policy.* Golden, CO: Fulcrum Books.

Kuhn, Thomas S. (1970). *The structure of scientific revolutions* (2nd ed.). Chicago: University of Chicago Press.

Laszlo, Chris. (2008). *Sustainable value: How the world's leading companies are doing well by doing good.* Stanford, CA: Stanford University Press.

Leonard, Annie. (2007). The story of stuff project. Washington, DC: Free Range Studios. Retrieved July 10, 2012, from www.storyofstuff.com

Leopold, Aldo. (1949). *A Sand County almanac and sketches here and there.* New York: Oxford University Press.

Lotze, Heike K., et al. (2006). Depletion, degradation, and recovery potential of estuaries and coastal seas. *Science, 312*(5781), 1806–1809.

MacArthur, Robert H., & Wilson, Edward O. (1967) *The theory of island biogeography.* Princeton, NJ: Princeton University Press.

McCrea, Hannah. (2011, Summer). Germany's take-back approach to waste management: Is there a legal basis for adoption in the United States? *Georgetown International Environmental Law Review, 23*(4), 513–529.

McCully, Patrick. (1996). *Silenced rivers: The ecology and politics of large dams.* London: Zed Books.

McDonough, William, & Braungart, Michael. (2002). *Cradle to cradle: Remaking the way we make things.* New York: North Point Press.

McNeill, J. R. (2000). *Something new under the sun: An environmental history of the twentieth-century world.* New York: W. W. Norton & Company.

Meadows, Donella H.; Meadows, Dennis L.; Randers, Jorgen; & Behrens, William W., III. (1972). *The limits to growth*. New York: Universe Books.

Meadows, Donella H.; Meadows, Dennis L.; & Randers, Jørgen. (2004). *The limits to growth: The 30-year update.* White River Junction, VT: Chelsea Green Publishing.

Millennium Ecosystem Assessment (MA). (2005). *Ecosystems and human well-being: Synthesis.* Washington, DC: Island Press.

Naess, Arne. (1973). The shallow and the deep, long-range ecology movement: A summary. *Inquiry, 16,* 95–100.

Nash, James A. (1991). *Loving nature: Ecological integrity and Christian responsibility.* Nashville, TN: Abingdon Press.

Nash, Roderick F. (2001). *Wilderness and the American mind* (4th ed.). New Haven, CT: Yale University Press.

Norton, Bryan G. (2005). *Sustainability: A philosophy of adaptive ecosystem management.* Chicago: University of Chicago Press.

Orr, David W. (1994). *Earth in mind: On education, environment and the human prospect.* Washington, DC: Island Press.

Ostrom, Elinor. (1990). *Governing the commons: The evolution of institutions for collective action.* Cambridge, UK: Cambridge University Press.

Pauly, Daniel, & Maclean, Jay L. (2003). *In a perfect ocean: The state of fisheries and ecosystems in the North Atlantic Ocean.* Washington, DC: Island Press.

Pauly, Daniel; Christensen, Villy; Dalsgaard, Johanne; Froese, Rainer; & Torres, Francisco, Jr. (1998). Fishing down marine food webs. *Science, 279*(5352), 860–863.

Pearce, David, & Atkinson, Giles D. (1993). Capital theory and the measurement of sustainable development: An indicator of weak sustainability. *Ecological Economics, 8*(2), 103–108.

Peerenboom, Randall. (2002). *China's Long March to the rule of law.* Cambridge, UK: Cambridge University Press.

Pigou, Arthur C. (1932). *The economics of welfare* (4th ed.). London: Macmillan and Company.

Pimentel, David, & Pimentel, Marcia H. (2008). *Food, energy and society* (3rd ed.). Boca Raton, FL: CRC Press (Taylor and Francis Group).

Pimentel, David.; Westra, Laura; & Noss, Reed F. (Eds). (2000). *Ecological integrity: Integrating environment, conservation, and health.* Washington, DC: Island Press.

Pratt, Laura A. W. (2011, Winter). Decreasing dirty dumping? A re-evaluation of toxic waste colonialism and the global management of transboundary hazardous waste. *Texas Environmental Law Journal, 35*(2), 147–178.

Pryde, Philip R. (1991). *Environmental management in the Soviet Union.* Cambridge, UK: Cambridge University Press.

Putnam, Robert D. (2000). *Bowling alone: The collapse and revival of American community.* New York: Simon & Schuster.

Quadri, Shaza. (2010). An analysis of the effects and reasons for hazardous waste importation in India and its implementation of the Basel Convention. *Florida Journal of International Law, 22*(3), 468–493.

Rangan, Haripraya. (2000). *Of myths and movements: Rewriting Chipko into Himalayan history.* London: Verso.

Rappaport, Roy A. (1968). *Pigs for the ancestors: Ritual in the ecology of a New Guinea people.* New Haven, CT: Yale University Press.

Rasmussen, Larry L. (1996). *Earth community Earth ethics.* Maryknoll, NY: Orbis Books.

Raymond, Robert. (1984). *Out of the fiery furnace: The impact of metals on the history of mankind.* Melbourne, Australia: Macmillan.

Rees, William E. (1992). Ecological footprints and appropriated carrying capacity: What urban economics leaves out. *Environment and Urbanization, 4*(2), 121–130.

Rees, William, & Wackernagel, Mathis. (1996). Ecological footprints and appropriated carrying capacity: Measuring the natural capital requirements of the human economy. In Ann Marie Jansson, Carl Folke, Monica Hammer, & Robert Costanza (Eds.), *Investing in natural capital: The ecological economics approach to sustainability* (pp. 362–390). Washington, DC: Island Press.

Roberts, Callum. (2007). *The unnatural history of the sea. The past and future of humanity and fishing.* London: Gaia Books.

Rockström, Johan, et al. (2009, September 24). A safe operating space for humanity. *Nature, 461*(7263), 472–475.

Rolston, Holmes, III. (1994). *Conserving natural value.* New York: Columbia University Press.

Ruether, Rosemary Radford. (1992). *Gaia & God: An ecofeminist theology of Earth healing.* San Francisco: Harper San Francisco.

Sala, Osvaldo E., et al. (2000). Global biodiversity scenarios for the year 2100. *Science, 287*(5459), 1770–1774.

Sands, Philippe. (2003). *Principles of international environmental law* (2nd ed.). Cambridge, UK: Cambridge University Press.

Sassen, Saskia. (2001). *The global city: New York, London, Tokyo* (2nd ed.). Princeton, NJ: Princeton University Press.

Scheffer, Marten. (2009). *Critical transitions in nature and society.* Princeton, NJ: Princeton University Press.

Schumacher, E. F. (1973). *Small is beautiful: A study of economics as if people mattered.* London: Sphere Books.

Scott, Douglas W. (2004). *The enduring wilderness: Protecting our national heritage through the Wilderness Act.* Golden, CO: Fulcrum Publishing.

Sen, Amartya K. (2001). *Development as freedom.* New York: Oxford University Press.

Sen, Amartya K. (1981). *Poverty and famines: An essay on entitlement and deprivation.* Oxford, UK: Clarendon Press.

Shapiro, Judith. (2001) *Mao's war against nature: Politics and the environment in revolutionary China.* Cambridge, UK: Cambridge University Press.

Shiva, Vandana. (1989). *Staying alive: Women, ecology and development.* London: Zed Books.

Shuman, Michael H. (2000). *Going local: Creating self-reliant communities in a global age.* New York: The Free Press.

Singer, Peter. (1975). *Animal liberation: A new ethics for our treatment of animals.* New York: Random House.

Smil, Vaclav. (1994). *Energy in world history.* Boulder, CO: Westview Press.

Smil, Vaclav. (2003). *Energy at the crossroads: Global perspectives and uncertainties.* Cambridge, MA: MIT Press.

Smith, Adam. (1977). *An inquiry into the nature and causes of the wealth of nations.* Chicago: University of Chicago Press. (Originally published in 1776.)

Solow, Robert M. (1993). Sustainability: An economist's perspective. In Robert Dorfman & Nancy Dorfman (Eds.), *Economics of the environment: Selected readings* (3rd ed., pp. 179–187). New York: Norton.

Soulé, Michael E., & Terborgh, John. (Eds.). (1999). *Continental conservation: Scientific foundations of regional reserve networks.* Washington, DC: Island Press.

Speth, James Gustave. (2008). *The bridge at the edge of the world: Capitalism, the environment, and crossing from crisis to sustainability.* New Haven, CT: Yale University Press.

Steffen, Will; Crutzen, Paul J.; & McNeill, J. R. (2007). The Anthropocene: Are humans now overwhelming the great forces of nature? *AMBIO, 36*(8), 614–621.

Steinbeis-Europa-Zentrum & Comite Richelieu. (2006). *Nanomaterial roadmap 2015: Roadmap report concerning the use of nanomaterials in the aeronautics sector.* Retrieved March 14, 2008, from http://www.nanoroad.net/download/roadmap_as.pdf

Stern, Nicholas. (2007). *The economics of climate change: The Stern Review.* Cambridge, UK: Cambridge University Press.

TerraChoice Environmental Marketing Inc. (2009). The seven sins of greenwashing. Retrieved June 1, 2009, from http://sinsofgreenwashing.org

Tester, Jefferson W.; Drake, Elisabeth M.; Driscoll, Michael J.; Golay, Michael W.; & Peters, William A. (2005). *Sustainable energy: Choosing among energy options.* Cambridge, MA: MIT Press.

Thomas, David S. G., & Middleton, Nicholas J. (1994). *Desertification: Exploding the myth.* Chichester, UK: John Wiley & Sons.

Tladi, Dire. (2000). The quest to ban hazardous waste import into Africa: First Bamako and now Basel. *Comparative and International Law Journal of South Africa, 33*(2), 210–222.

Tucker, Mary Evelyn, & Berthrong, John. (Eds.). (1998). *Confucianism and ecology: The interrelation of heaven, Earth, and humans.* Cambridge, MA: Harvard Center for the Study of World Religions.

Vitousek, Peter M., et al. (1997). Human alteration of the global nitrogen cycle: Sources and consequences. *Ecological Applications, 7*(3), 737–750.

Wackernagel, Mathis, & Rees William E. (1996). *Our ecological footprint: Reducing human impact on the Earth.* Gabriola Island, Canada: New Society Publishers.

Walker, Brian, & Salt, David. (2006). *Resilience thinking: Sustaining ecosystems and people in a changing world.* Washington, DC: Island Press.

Wang, Alex. (2007). The role of law in environmental protection in China: Recent developments. *Vermont Journal of Environmental Law, 8*, 195–233. Retrieved July 13, 2011, from http://www.vjel.org/journal/VJEL10057.html

Weaver, David B., & Lawton, Laura J. (2007). Twenty years on: The state of contemporary ecotourism research. *Tourism Management, 28*(5), 1168–1179. doi:10.1016/j.tourman.2007.03.004

White, Lynn, Jr. (1967, March 10). The historical roots of our ecologic crisis. *Science, 155*(3767), 1203–1207. Retrieved January 27, 2012, from http://www.sciencemag.org/content/155/3767/1203.citation

Widawsky, Lisa. (2008). In my backyard: How enabling hazardous waste trade to developing nations can improve the Basel **Convention's** ability to achieve environmental justice. *Environmental Law, 38*(2), 577–626.

Worm, Boris, et al. (2006). Impacts of biodiversity loss on ocean ecosystem services. *Science, 314*(5800), 787–790.

Worm, Boris, et al. (2009). Rebuilding global fisheries. *Science, 325*(5940), 578–585.

Wouters, Patricia, & Ziganshina, Dinara. (2011). Tackling the global water crisis: Unlocking international law as fundamental to the peaceful management of the world's shared transboundary waters—Introducing the H2O paradigm. In R. Quentin Grafton & Karen Hussey (Eds.), *Water resources planning and management* (pp. 175–229). Cambridge, UK: Cambridge University Press.

Wright, Charlie L. (1992). *Fast wheels, slow traffic: Urban transport choices.* Philadelphia: Temple University Press.

Contributors to Volumes 1–10 of the *Encyclopedia of Sustainability*

The following is a list of the more than 900 contributors who wrote for the ten volumes of the *Berkshire Encyclopedia of Sustainability*. Please refer to the series page that appears on page VI for the names of the volumes that appear after each article title.

A

Abadie, Luis María
Basque Centre for Climate Change (BC3)
Ecolabels (co-author: Ibon Galarraga) (Vol. 6)
Energy Efficiency (co-author: Ibon Galarraga) (Vol. 8)
Property Rights (Vol. 8)
European Union Greenhouse Gas Emission Trading Scheme (EU ETS) (co-author: Ibon Galarraga) (Vol. 9)

Abe, Osamu
Rikkyo University
Education, Environmental (Japan) (Vol. 7)

Abedin, Jakerul
Macquarie University
Transboundary Water Issues (Vol. 7)

Acutt, Nicola J.
Presidio Graduate School
Education, Business (Vol. 2)

Adam, Paul
University of New South Wales
Wetlands (Vol. 4)

Adcock, Christina
University of British Columbia
Northwest Passage (Vol. 8)

Aderibigbe, Ibigbolade S.
University of Georgia
Indigenous Traditions—Africa (Vol. 1)

Adler, Nancy J.
McGill University
Corporate Citizenship (Vol. 2)

Adnan, Md. Sarfaraz Gani
Chittagong University of Engineering and Technology (CUET)
Dhaka, Bangladesh (co-author: Carolyn Roberts) (Vol. 7)

Adriaens, Peter
University of Michigan
Investment, CleanTech (Vol. 2)

Ahmed, A. Karim
National Council for Science and the
   Environment
Precautionary Principle (Vols. 1, 3)

Alam, Shawkat
Macquarie University
*Convention for the Safe and Environmentally
   Sound Recycling of Ships* (Vol. 3)

Albright, Scott M.
University of Hawaii at Hilo
Jakarta, Indonesia (Vol. 7)
Warsaw, Poland (Vol. 9)

Alexander, Karen
University of New Hampshire
Shifting Baselines Syndrome (Vol. 5)

Allen, Craig R.
US Geological Survey, Nebraska
   Cooperative Fish & Wildlife Research
   Unit, University of Nebraska
Resilience (co-authors: Ahjond Garmestani
   and Shana M. Sundstrom) (Vol. 5)

Allison, Elizabeth
California Institute of Integral Studies
Biodiversity (Vol. 1)
Forests (Vol. 1)
Gross National Happiness (Vol. 6)
The Himalaya (Vol. 7)

Amaral, Renata Campetti
Baker & McKenzie, São Paulo
Environmental Law—South America
   (co-authors: Gustavo Boruchowicz,
   Alejandra Bugna, Alessandro De
   Franceschi da Cruz, Antonio Ortuzar Jr.,
   María Eugenia Reyes, María Victoria
   Romero, and Cristina Rueda) (Vol. 3)

Amati, Marco
Macquarie University
Greenbelts (Vol. 4)

Anderson, E. N.
University of California, Riverside
Indigenous Traditions—Asia (Vol. 1)

Anderson, Laura
University of Vermont
Recreation, Outdoor (co-author: Robert E.
   Manning) (Vol. 4)
Parks and Preserves—National (co-author:
   Robert E. Manning) (Vol. 4)

Anderson, Mark W.
University of Maine, Orono
National Environmental Policy Act (Vol. 3)
New Ecological Paradigm (NEP) Scale (Vol. 6)
Economics, Steady State (Vol. 10)
Values (co-author: Mario Teisl) (Vol. 10)

Anderson, T. Michael
Wake Forest University
Plant-Animal Interactions (Vol. 5)

Ando, Shotaro
National Institute of Livestock and
   Grassland Science, Japan
Sugarcane (Vol. 4)

Andreas, Robert
College of Micronesia
Pacific Island Environmental Philosophy
   (co-author: James D. Sellmann) (Vol. 8)

Andreen, William
University of Alabama School of Law
Clean Water Act (Vol. 3)

Andrejko, Dennis A.
University at Buffalo; State University of
   New York
International Green Construction Code (Vol. 3)

Antal, Áron
Corvinus University of Budapest
*International Organization for
   Standardization (ISO)* (co-authors: Gyula
   Vastag and Gergely Tyukodi) (Vol. 6)

Anwana, EnoAbasi D.
Regional Institute for Population Studies,
   University of Ghana
Migration (Africa) (co-authors: Samuel
   N. A. Codjoe and Delali B. K. Dovie)
   (Vol. 9)

Arora, Aanchal
TERI University, New Delhi
Automobiles and Personal Transportation
   (co-author: Kaushik Ranjan
   Bandyopadhyay) (Vol. 7)

Asher, Jana
StatAid
Human Development Index (HDI)
   (co-author: Juan Carlos Rosa) (Vol. 6)

Ashton, Weslynne S.
Illinois Institute of Technology
Industrial Ecology (co-author: Reid J. Lifset)
   (Vol. 4)

Anthony, Kenneth R. N.
Australian Institute of Marine Science
Ocean Acidification—Management
   (co-author: Elizabeth Mcleod) (Vol. 5)

Awiti, Alex O.
Aga Khan University, Nairobi, Kenya
Education, Higher (Africa) (Vol. 9)

Ayers, John C.
Vanderbilt University
Sands and Silica (Vol. 4)

Azaransky, Sarah
University of San Diego
Liberationist Thought (Vol. 1)
Politics (Vol. 1)

Azoulay, David
Center for International
   Environmental Law
Nanotechnology Legislation (Vol. 3)

B

Baffes, John
The World Bank
Coffee (Vol. 4)
Cotton (Vol. 4)
Tea (Vol. 4)

Bagaeen, Samer G.
University of Brighton
Dubai, United Arab Emirates (Vol. 9)

Bai, Xuemei
The Australian National University
Cities—Overview (Vol. 7)

Bailey, Joseph K.
University of Tennessee
Community Ecology (co-authors: Randy K.
   Bangert, Mark A. Genung, Jennifer A.
   Schweitzer, and Gina M. Wimp)
   (Vol. 5)

Bajracharya, Roshan M.
Kathmandu University
Agricultural Intensification (co-author: Bed
   Mani Dahal) (Vol. 5)

Balraj, Dianne
Queen's University, Canada
Chromium (co-author: J. Andrew Grant)
   (Vol. 4)
Manganese (co-author: J. Andrew Grant)
   (Vol. 4)
Mining—Nonmetals (co-author: J. Andrew
   Grant) (Vol. 4)
Potassium (co-author: J. Andrew Grant)
   (Vol. 4)
Sulfur (co-author: J. Andrew Grant)
   (Vol. 4)
Tin (co-author: J. Andrew Grant)
   (Vol. 4)
Titanium (co-author: J. Andrew Grant)
   (Vol. 4)

Bandyopadhyay, Kaushik Ranjan
TERI University, New Delhi
Automobiles and Personal Transportation
(co-author: Aanchal Arora) (Vol. 7)

Banerjee, Tirtho
Journalist, Lucknow, India
Ganges River (Vol. 7)

Bangert, Randy K.
Trinidad State Junior College
Community Ecology (co-authors: Joseph K.
Bailey, Mark A. Genung, Jennifer A.
Schweitzer, and Gina M. Wimp) (Vol. 5)

Barkemeyer, Ralf
University of Leeds
Corporate Accountability (Africa) (co-author:
Jo-Anna Russon) (Vol. 9)

Barker, Rene Allen
Texas State University
Aquifers (co-author: Glenn Longley) (Vol. 4)

Barnhill, David Landis
University of Wisconsin, Oshkosh
Ecology, Deep (Vol. 1)
Ecology, Social (Vol. 1)

Barthel, Pierre-Arnaud
University of Paris-East—Marne-la-Vallée,
CNRS-Latts
Cairo, Egypt (Vol. 9)

Bartolome, James W.
University of California, Berkeley
Succession (co-author: Lynn Huntsinger)
(Vol. 5)

Basile, George
Arizona State University
*Framework for Strategic Sustainable
Development (FSSD)* (co-authors:
Karl-Henrik Robèrt and Göran Broman)
(Vol. 6)

Bassett, Luke H.
Yale Divinity School
Ecovillages (Vol. 1)

Bassett, Thomas J.
University of Illinois at Urbana-Champaign
Bushmeat (Vol. 4)

Bastakoti, Ram Chandra
Asian Institute of Technology, Klong
Luang, Pathumthani, Thailand
Mekong-Lancang River (co-authors: Joyeeta
Gupta and Hao Li) (Vol. 7)

Bateson, Matthew
World Business Council for Sustainable
Development
Energy Efficiency (co-author: David Gagne)
(Vol. 2)

Baugh, Tom
Independent scholar, Hidden Springs,
North Carolina
Conservation Biology (Vol. 1)

Bauman, Whitney
Florida International University
Ecocentrism (co-author: Willis Jenkins)
Ecological Footprint (Vol. 1)
Sikhism (Vol. 1)
White's Thesis (Vol. 1)

Baumann, Henrikke
Chalmers University of Technology
Life Cycle Assessments (LCAs) (Vol. 2)

Beavis, Sara G.
The Australian National University
Hydrology (Vol. 5)
Sanitation (Vol. 8)
Water (Vol. 10)

Beck, Abby
University of Nevada, Las Vegas
Las Vegas, United States (co-author:
Krystyna Stave) (Vol. 8)

Becker, Marc
Truman State University
Social Movements (Latin America) (Vol. 8)

Beinart, William
University of Oxford
Africa, Southern (Vol. 9)

Bekefi, Tamara
Daedalus Strategic Advising
Risk Management (co-author: Marc J.
   Epstein) (Vol. 2)

Belzile, Jacqueline
University of British Columbia
Focus Groups (co-author: Gunilla Öberg)
   (Vol. 6)

Bendik-Keymer, Jeremy
LeMoyne College
Development—Concepts and Considerations
   (Vol. 1)

Bennett, Judith A.
University of Otago
Oceania (Vol. 8)

Benzoni, Francisco
U.S. Fourth Circuit Court of Appeals
Utilitarianism (Vol. 1)

Berkes, Fikret
University of Manitoba
Indigenous Traditions—The Arctic (Vol. 1)

Beyerlin, Ulrich
Max Planck Institute for Comparative
   Public Law and International Law
Environmental Law, Soft vs. Hard
   (co-author: Thilo Marauhn) (Vol. 3)

Bhandari, Vivek
Independent scholar, Jaipur, India
Education, Environmental (India)
   (co-author: Rahul Ghai) (Vol. 7)

Bharucha, Zareen Pervez P.
University of Essex
Agriculture—Developing World (Vol. 4)
Agriculture (South Asia) (Vol. 7)
Water Security (Vol. 7)

Bharvirkar, Ranjit
Itron Inc.
Utilities Regulation and Energy Efficiency
   (co-authors: Chris Greacen, Chuenchom
   Sangarasri Greacen, Fredrich Kahrl,
   Mahesh Patankar, Priya Sreedharan, and
   James H. Williams) (Vol. 7)

Bhushan Sharan, Awadhendra
Centre for the Study of Developing
   Societies, Delhi
Delhi, India (Vol. 7)

Bidwell, R. G. S.
Queen's University, Canada
Light Pollution and Biological Systems
   (co-authors: Robert Dick, Peter Goering,
   and David Welch) (Vol. 5)

Biggs, Reinette (Oonsie)
Stockholm Resilience Center, Stockholm
   University
Regime Shifts (co-authors: Juan C. Rocha
   and Garry D. Peterson) (Vol. 5)

Binder, Claudia
University of Munich
Material Flow Analysis (MFA) (Vol. 6)

Birch, Eugenie L.
University of Pennsylvania
Urbanization (Europe) (co-authors:
   Alexander M. Keating and Susan M.
   Wachter) (Vol. 9)

Black, Brian
Pennsylvania State University
Nuclear Power (Vol. 10)

Blanco-Canqui, Humberto
Kansas State University
Soil Conservation (Vol. 5)

Bleischwitz, Raimund
Wuppertal Institute for Climate,
Environment and Energy
Conflict Minerals (co-author: Lena Guesnet)
(Vols. 4, 9)

Blume, Richard
The Natural Step International
Natural Step Framework, The (TNSF)
(co-author: Anthony Thompson) (Vol. 2)

Bo Wenjing
Chinese Academy of Sciences
Urban Vegetation (co-author: Jiang
Gaoming) (Vol. 5)

Boas, Ingrid
University of Kent
Climate Change Migration (India) (Vol. 7)

Bocchino, Clara
North-West University, Potchefstroom,
South Africa
Rural Development (Vol. 9)

Bode, Michael
University of Melbourne
Biodiversity Hotspots (co-authors: Kerrie
A. Wilson, Takuya Iwamura, and Hugh
P. Possingham) (Vol. 5)

Boehringer, Ayse Martina
University of Giessen
Environmental Law—Europe (co-author:
Thilo Marauhn) (Vol. 3)

Boer, Benjamin
Sydney Law School
Soil Conservation Legislation (co-author:
Ian Hannam) (Vol. 3)

Bohannon, Richard
College of St. Benedict and St. John's
University
Architecture (Vol. 1)
Christianity—Evangelical and Pentecostal
(Vol. 1)

Boone, Randall B.
Colorado State University, Fort Collins
Biological Corridors (Vol. 9)

Borin, Norm
Orfalea College of Business, California
Polytechnic State University
Greenwashing (Vol. 2)
Marketing (Vol. 2)

Boruchowicz, Gustavo
Baker & McKenzie, Buenos Aires
Environmental Law—South America
(co-authors: Renata Campetti Amaral,
Alejandra Bugna, Alessandro De
Franceschi da Cruz, Antonio Ortuzar Jr.,
María Eugenia Reyes, María Victoria
Romero, and Cristina Rueda) (Vol. 3)

Boyd, Doreen S.
University of Nottingham
Remote Sensing (Vol. 6)

Brade, Isolde
Leibniz Institute for Regional Geography,
Leipzig
Moscow, Russia (co-author: Tatyana G.
Nefedova) (Vol. 9)

Bratspies, Rebecca M.
City University of New York School of Law
*Environmental Law—United States and
Canada* (co-author: John Martin Gillroy)
(Vol. 3)

Bratton, Susan Power
Baylor University
Stewardship (co-author: Austin Cook-
Lindsay) (Vol. 1)

Brinkman, Todd J.
University of Alaska Fairbanks
Hunting (Vol. 5)

Briones, Ruth P.
Greenergy Solutions Inc., Quezon City,
    The Philippines
Public-Private Partnerships (Vol. 7)

Broadbent, Jeffrey P.
University of Minnesota
Environmental Law—East Asia (co-authors:
    Yu-Ju Chien, Koichi Hasegawa, Jun Jin,
    Dowan Ku, and Taehyun Park) (Vol. 3)

Broman, Göran
Blekinge Institute of Technology
*Framework for Strategic Sustainable
    Development (FSSD)* (co-authors: Karl-
    Henrik Robèrt and George Basile) (Vol. 6)

Bromberg, Gidon
EcoPeace / Friends of the Earth Middle East
Jordan River Project (Vol. 1)
Transboundary Water Issues (co-author:
    Jessica C. Marx) (Vol. 9)

Bronstein, Judith L.
University of Arizona
Mutualism (co-author: Ginny M.
    Fitzpatrick) (Vol. 5)

Brooking, Tom
University of Otago
New Zealand (co-authors: Eric Pawson and
    Hamish G. Rennie) (Vol. 8)

Broughton, Edward I.
Columbia University
Bhopal Disaster (Vol. 3)

Brown, Donald A.
Pennsylvania State University
Climate Change (Vol. 1)
Ethics, Global (Vol. 1)

Brown, Lester R.
Earth Policy Institute
Food Security (Vol. 10)

Bruce, C. Andrea
University of the West Indies
Systems Thinking (co-authors: Anthony
    M. H. Clayton and Nicholas Radcliffe)
    (Vol. 6)

Buckley, Lauren B.
University of North Carolina at Chapel
    Hill
Ecological Forecasting (Vol. 5)

Buckley, Ralf
Griffith University, Australia
Parks and Preserves—Wilderness Areas
    (Vol. 4)
Tourism (Vol. 4)
Ecotourism (Vols. 7, 9)
Ecotourism (the Americas) (co-author:
    Fernanda de Vasconcellos Pegas) (Vol. 8)

Bugge, Hans Christian
University of Oslo
Brundtland Report (Vol. 3)

Bugna, Alejandra
Baker & McKenzie, Buenos Aires
Environmental Law—South America
    (co-authors: Renata Campetti Amaral,
    Gustavo Boruchowicz, Alessandro De
    Franceschi da Cruz, Antonio Ortuzar Jr.,
    María Eugenia Reyes, María Victoria
    Romero, and Cristina Rueda) (Vol. 3)

Burroughs, Richard
University of Rhode Island
Coastal Management (Vol. 5)

Bushaw-Newton, Karen L.
Northern Virginia Community College,
    Annandale
Dam Removal (Vol. 5)

C

Caddell, Richard
Swansea University
Convention for the Safety of Life at Sea (Vol. 3)
*Convention on Civil Liability for Oil
    Pollution* (Vol. 3)
Convention on Persistent Organic Pollutants
    (Vol. 3)

Cameron, Geoffrey
Oxford Martin School, University of Oxford
Migration (co-author: Ian Goldin) (Vol. 10)

Cameron, Peter D.
University of Dundee
Investment Law, Energy (co-author: Abba
    Kolo) (Vol. 3)

Campagna, Michele
University of Cagliari
Geographic Information Systems (GIS)
    (Vol. 6)

Cannon, Jonathan Z.
University of Virginia School of Law
Law (Vol. 1)

Carey, Mark
University of Oregon
Glaciers (Vol. 4)

Carpenter, Carol
Yale University
Ecology, Cultural (co-author: Michael Dove)
    (Vol. 1)

Cartier, Laurent E.
University of Basel
Gemstones (Vol. 4)

Carton, Adrian
University of Western Sydney
Food in History (Vol. 4)

Castley, J. Guy
Griffith University
Parks and Preserves (Vol. 9)

Castro, José Esteban
Newcastle University
Southern Cone (Vol. 8)

Cater, Carl Iain
Aberystwyth University
Travel and Tourism Industry (co-author:
    Tiffany Low) (Vol. 9)

Cavill, Sue
WEDC (Water, Engineering and
    Development Centre), Loughborough
    University
Public–Private Partnerships (co-author:
    M. Sohail) (Vol. 2)
Water Use and Rights (co-author: M. Sohail)
    (Vol. 2)

Cerf, Doug
California Polytechnic State University,
    San Luis Obispo
Accounting (co-authors: Arline Savage and
    Kate Lancaster) (Vol. 2)

Chandra, Satish
International Society for Tropical Root Crops
Root Crops (Vol. 4)

Chappells, Heather
Dalhousie University and Saint Mary's
    University
Heating and Cooling (Vol. 4)
Lighting, Indoor (Vol. 4)
Buildings and Infrastructure (Vol. 10)

Chapple, Christopher Key
Loyola Marymount University
Hinduism (Vol. 1)
Jainism (Vol. 1)
Sacrifice (Vol. 1)
Religions (Vol. 7)

Cheng, Gong
Minzu University of China
Traditional Chinese Medicine (TCM)
  (Vol. 7)

Chiabai, Aline
Basque Center for Climate Change (BC3)
Biodiversity Conservation (Vol. 9)

Chick, Anne
Kingston University
Design, Industrial (Vol. 2)
Packaging (Vol. 2)

Chien, Yu-Ju
University of Minnesota
Environmental Law—East Asia (co-authors:
  Jeffrey Broadbent, Koichi Hasegawa,
  Jun Jin, Dowan Ku, and Taehyun Park)
  (Vol. 3)

Childers, Dan
Arizona State University
Phoenix, United States (Vol. 8)

Chouvy, Pierre-Arnaud
French National Centre for Scientific
  Research
Drug Production and Trade (Vol. 4)

Christensen, Karen
Berkshire Publishing Group
Home Ecology (Vol. 5)
Community (Vol. 10)

Christensen, Norman L. Jr.
Duke University
Fire Management (Vol. 5)

Christian, David
Macquarie University; WCU Professor,
  Ewha Womans University, Seoul
Anthropocene Epoch (Vol. 10)
Climate Change and Big History (Vol. 10)
Collective Learning (Vol. 10)

Chryssavgis, John
Greek Orthodox Archdiocese of America
Christianity—Eastern Orthodox (Vol. 1)

Cioc, Mark
University of California, Santa Cruz
Rivers (Vol. 4)
Germany (Vol. 9)
Rhine River (Vol. 9)

Clarke, Matthew
Deakin University
Genuine Progress Indicator (GPI) (Vol. 6)

Clark, Meghan
Saint Anselm College
Community (Vol. 1)

Clarke, Alan
University of Pannonia
Ecotourism (Vol. 4)

Clayton, Anthony M. H.
University of the West Indies
Fisheries Indicators, Marine (co-author:
  Michael Haley) (Vol. 6)
Systems Thinking (co-authors: Nicholas
  Radcliffe and C. Andrea Bruce) (Vol. 6)

Cleary, David
The Nature Conservancy
Amazon River (Vol. 8)

Clingerman, Forrest
Ohio Northern University
Sacred Texts (Vol. 1)
Theocentrism (Vol. 1)
Values (Vol. 1)

Codjoe, Samuel N. A.
Regional Institute for Population Studies,
  University of Ghana
Migration (Africa) (co-authors: Delali B. K.
  Dovie and EnoAbasi D. Anwana)
  (Vol. 9)

Colbeck, Ian
University of Essex
Air Pollution Indicators and Monitoring
(co-author: Zaheer Ahmad Nasir)
(Vol. 6)

Comtois, Claude
Université de Montréal
Shipping and Freight Indicators (Vol. 6)

Conicelli, Bruno Pirilo
University of São Paulo
Groundwater Management (co-authors:
Ricardo Hirata and Juliana Baitz
Viviani-Lima) (Vol. 5)

Connett, Paul
American Environmental Health Studies
Project (AEHSP); St. Lawrence
University
Zero Waste (Vol. 2)

Connolly, Rebecca L.
University of Sydney
Genetically Modified Organisms Legislation
(Vol. 3)

Conradie, Ernst M.
University of the Western Cape
Christianity—Mainline Protestant (Vol. 1)

Conte, Christopher A.
Utah State University
Africa, East (Vol. 9)

Cook-Lindsay, Austin
Baylor University
Stewardship (co-author: Susan Power
Bratton) (Vol. 1)

Coombs, Casey L.
United Nations correspondent, *Diplomatic
Courier*
Thorium (Vol. 4)
Uranium (Vol. 4)

Costanza, Robert
University of Vermont
Ecological Economics (Vol. 2)

Costilow, Kyle C.
The Ohio State University
Forest Management (co-authors: Charles E.
Flower and Miquel A. Gonzalez-Meler)
(Vol. 5)

Craker, Lyle
University of Massachusetts, Amherst
Medicinal Plants (Vol. 4)

Crawford, Colin
Tulane University Law School
New Orleans, United States (Vol. 8)
Rio de Janeiro, Brazil (Vol. 8)

Crowson, Phillip Charles Francis
University of Dundee
Minerals Scarcity (Vol. 4)

Cui Can
Beijing Institute of Technology Law School
National Pollution Survey (China)
(co-author: Gong Xiangqian) (Vol. 7)

Cullet, Philippe
University of London
Water Use and Rights (India) (Vol. 7)

Cumming, Graeme S.
University of Cape Town
Complexity Theory (Vol. 5)

Cumo, Christopher M.
Independent scholar, Canton, Ohio
Agriculture (China and Southeast Asia) (Vol. 7)
Agriculture, Small-Scale (Vol. 9)
Diet and Nutrition (Vol. 9)

Currie, Duncan E. J.
Globe Law
Fishing and Whaling Legislation (co-author:
Kateryna M. Wowk) (Vol. 3)

Curtin, Deane
Gustavus Adolphus College
Nonviolence (Vol. 1)

Cybriwsky, Roman Adrian
Temple University
Tokyo, Japan (Vol. 7)

D

da Cruz, Alessandro F.
Baker & McKenzie, Porto Alegre, Brazil
Environmental Law—South America
(co-authors: Renata Campetti Amaral,
Gustavo Boruchowicz, Alejandra Bugna,
Antonio Ortuzar Jr., María Eugenia
Reyes, María Victoria Romero, and
Cristina Rueda) (Vol. 3)

Dahal, Bed Mani
Kathmandu University
Agricultural Intensification (co-author:
Roshan M. Bajracharya) (Vol. 5)

Dameron Hager, Irene
The Ohio State University
Great Lakes and Saint Lawrence River
(Vol. 8)

Dane, Andrew
Short Elliott Hendrickson Inc.
Energy Industries—Bioenergy (Vol. 2)
Green-Collar Jobs (co-author: Gary Paul
Green) (Vol. 2)
Stormwater Management (Vol. 5)

Dasgupta, Partha, Sir
University of Cambridge and University of
Manchester
Natural Capital (Vol. 10)

Dávila, Julio D.
University College London
Bogotá, Colombia (Vol. 8)

Davis, Diana K.
University of California at
Davis
Middle East (Vol. 9)

Davison, Aidan
University of Tasmania
Technology (Vol. 1)

Dawson, Chad P.
State University of New York
Wilderness Areas (co-author: John C.
Hendee) (Vol. 5)

De Gruchy, Steve (1961–2010)
University of KwaZulu-Natal
Development, Sustainable (Vol. 1)

Deakin, Elizabeth
University of California, Berkeley
Bicycle Industry (Vol. 2)
Public Transportation (Vol. 2)

Deane-Drummond, Celia
University of Chester
Wisdom Traditions (Vol. 1)

Dehejia, Makarand V.
Alliance for Sustainable Energy &
Industry, LLC
Salt (Vol. 4)

Denny, Frederick Mathewson
University of Colorado at Boulder
Islam (Vol. 1)

DePriest, Michael S.
University of Alabama
Algae (co-author: Juan M. Lopez-Bautista)
(Vol. 4)

Dernbach, John C.
Widener University Law School
Cap-and-Trade Legislation (Vol. 2)

Dey, Christopher
University of Sydney
Sydney, Australia (Vol. 8)

Dhanasarnsombat, Sansanee
ENHESA Inc.
Environmental Law—Southeast Asia
  (co-authors: James Kho, Koh Kheng-Lian,
  Lye Lin Heng, Chit Chit Myint, Dominic
  J. Nardi Jr., and Deny Sidharta) (Vol. 3)

Dick, Robert
Royal Astronomical Society of Canada
Dark Sky Initiatives (Vol. 3)
Light Pollution and Biological Systems
  (co-authors: R. G. S. Bidwell, Peter
  Goering, and David Welch) (Vol. 5)

Didham, Raphael K.
CSIRO Ecosystem Sciences
Habitat Fragmentation (co-authors: Timm
  F. Döbert and James P. Ruffell) (Vol. 5)

Dimarco, Romina D.
University of Tennessee
Keystone Species (co-author: Martin A.
  Nuñez) (Vol. 5)

Döbert, Timm F.
The University of Western Australia
Habitat Fragmentation (co-authors: Raphael
  K. Didham and James P. Ruffell) (Vol. 5)

Dodgen, Randall
Sonoma State University
Huang (Yellow) River (Vol. 7)

Doevenspeck, Martin
University of Bayreuth, Germany
Goma, Democratic Republic of the Congo (Vol. 9)

Dornbos, William E.
Yale University
Environmental Performance Index (EPI)
  (co-authors: John W. Emerson, Marc A.
  Levy, and Daniel C. Esty) (Vol. 6)

Dougherty, Michael L.
Illinois State University
Mining—Metals (Vol. 4)
Rural Development (the Americas) (Vol. 8)
Volume Introduction (Vol. 8)

Dove, Michael
Yale University
Ecology, Cultural (co-author: Carol
  Carpenter) (Vol. 1)

Dovey, Kathryn
Global Business Initiative on Human Rights
Human Rights (Vol. 2)

Dovie, Delali B. K.
Regional Institute for Population Studies,
  University of Ghana
Migration (Africa) (co-authors: Samuel N. A.
  Codjoe and EnoAbasi D. Anwana) (Vol. 9)

Drummond, José Augusto
Universidade de Brasília
Brazil (Vol. 8)

Duke, Duncan
Johnson Graduate School of Management,
  Cornell University
Base of the Pyramid (co-authors: Mark B.
  Milstein, Stuart Hart, and Erik Simanis)
  (Vol. 2)
Poverty (co-authors: Mark B. Milstein,
  Stuart Hart, and Erik Simanis) (Vol. 2)

Dummer, Trevor J. B.
Dalhousie University
Public Health (Vol. 7)

Dutfield, Graham
University of Leeds
Intellectual Property Rights (Vol. 6)

Dyball, Robert
The Australian National University
Human Ecology (Vol. 5)

E

Eagle, Josh
University of South Carolina
Ocean Zoning (Vol. 3)

Eardley-Pryor, Roger
University of California, Santa Barbara
Lake Victoria (Vol. 9)

Eaton, Heather
Saint Paul University
Feminist Thought (Vol. 1)

Edens, Bram
Statistics Netherlands
National Environmental Accounting (Vol. 6)

The Editors
Desalination (Vol. 4)
Appalachian Mountains (Vol. 8) (co-author: Timothy Silver)
Sahara (Vol. 9)
Sahel (Vol. 9)

Eggers, Dee
University of North Carolina at Asheville
Regulatory Compliance (Vol. 6)

Eiselen, Sieg
University of South Africa
E-Waste (Vols. 7, 8, 9)

Eisen, Joel Barry
University of Richmond School of Law
Utilities Regulation (Vol. 3)
Energy Industries—Renewables (China) (Vol. 7)

Eisenbise, Kathryn S.
Manchester College
Christianity—Anabaptist (Vol. 1)

Elder, James L.
The Campaign for Environmental Literacy
Education, Higher (Vol. 2)

Elkington, John
SustainAbility; Volans Ventures
Social Enterprise (Vol. 2)
Triple Bottom Line (Vol. 2)

Ellwood, Elizabeth R.
Boston University
Biodiversity (co-author: Richard B. Primack) (Vol. 5)

Emerson, John W.
Yale University
Environmental Performance Index (EPI) (co-authors: Marc A. Levy, William E. Dornbos, and Daniel C. Esty) (Vol. 6)

Engelman, Robert
Worldwatch Institute
Population Indicators (Vol. 6)
Population (Vol. 10)

Enstad, Craig
Boston University
Lake Chad (Vol. 9)

Epstein, Marc J.
Rice University
Performance Metrics (co-author: Priscilla S. Wisner) (Vol. 2)
Risk Management (co-author: Tamara Bekefi) (Vol. 2)

Erasga, Dennis Saturno
De La Salle University–Manila
Armed Conflict and the Environment (Vol. 3)
Indigenous Peoples (Vol. 7)

Ernstson, Henrik
Stockholm University & University of Cape Town
Social Network Analysis (SNA) (Vol. 6)

Esty, Daniel C.
Yale University; Connecticut Department
of Energy and Environmental Protection
(DEEP)
Environmental Performance Index (EPI)
(co-authors: John W. Emerson, Marc A.
Levy, and William E. Dornbos) (Vol. 6)

Evans, Sterling
University of Oklahoma
Central America (Vol. 8)
Mexico (co-author: Amanda Prigge) (Vol. 8)

Evely, Anna Clair
University of St. Andrews
Community and Stakeholder Input (Vol. 6)

Evenden, Matthew
University of British Columbia
Canada (co-author: Graeme Wynn)
(Vol. 8)

Evered, Kyle T.
Michigan State University
The Balkans (Vol. 9)
Volga River (Vol. 9)

F

Fagan, William F.
University of Maryland
Edge Effects (co-author: Leslie Ries)
(Vol. 5)

Fagg, Lawrence W.
Catholic University of America
Time (Vol. 1)

Farley, Joshua
University of Vermont
Natural Capital (Vol. 5)

Ferguson, Ken
University of Glasgow
Fencing (Vol. 5)

Feris, Loretta Annelise
University of Cape Town
World Constitutionalism (Vol. 3)

Fershee, Joshua P.
University of North Dakota School
of Law
Energy Subsidies (Vol. 3)

Figueroa, Robert Melchior
University of North Texas
Ecology, Political (Vol. 1)
Racism (Vol. 1)

Fiksel, Joseph
The Ohio State University
Integrated Product Development (IPD) (Vol. 2)
Supply Chain Management (Vol. 2)

Fitzpatrick, Ginny M.
University of Arizona
Mutualism (co-author: Judith L. Bronstein)
(Vol. 5)

Fleming, James Rodger
Colby College
Geoengineering (Vol. 10)

Fletcher, Thomas H.
Bishop's University
Love Canal (Vol. 3)

Flippen, J. Brooks
Oklahoma State University
Chesapeake Bay (Vol. 8)

Flower, Charles E.
University of Illinois, Chicago
Nitrogen (Vol. 4)
Forest Management (co-authors: Kyle C.
Costilow and Miquel A. Gonzalez-
Meler) (Vol. 5)
Global Climate Change (co-authors: Miquel
A. Gonzalez-Meler and Douglas J.
Lynch) (Vol. 5)

Fogel, Daniel S.
Wake Forest University; EcoLens
Financial Services Industry (Vol. 2)
European Union Greenhouse Gas Emission Trading Scheme (Vol. 3)
University Indicators (co-author: Emily Yandle Rottmann) (Vol. 6)

Font, Xavier
Leeds Metropolitan University
Travel and Tourism Industry (co-author: Andreas Walmsley) (Vol. 2)

Forbes, Kevin F.
The Catholic University of America
Energy Industries—Natural Gas (co-author: Adrian DiCianno Newall) (Vol. 2)
Energy Industries—Wind (co-author: Adrian DiCianno Newall) (Vol. 2)

Forbes, William
Stephen F. Austin State University
Korean Peninsula (Vol. 7)
London, United Kingdom (Vol. 9)

Fort, Timothy L.
The George Washington University School of Business
Peace Through Commerce: The Role of the Corporation (Vol. 2)

Foulk, Jonn A.
United States Department of Agriculture
Fiber Crops (Vol. 4)

Franzreb, Kay E.
University of Tennessee
Ecosystem Management (co-authors: Becky L. Jacobs, John D. Peine, and Maggie R. Stevens) (Vol. 3)

Fredericks, Sarah E.
University of North Texas
Agenda 21 (Vol. 1)

Energy (Vol. 1)
Millennium Development Goals (Vol. 1)
Challenges to Measuring Sustainability (Vol. 6)
Environmental Justice Indicators (Vol. 6)

Freestone, David
The George Washington University Law School
Kyoto Protocol (Vol. 3)
Law of the Sea (Vol. 3)

Fremuth, Michael Lysander
University of Cologne
European Union (EU) (co-author: Erik Pellander) (Vol. 9)

Frey, Sibylle
Giraffe Innovation Ltd.
Telecommunications Industry (Vol. 2)

Freyfogle, Eric T.
University of Illinois College of Law
Conservation (Vol. 1)
Natural Resources Law (Vol. 3)
Nuisance Law (Vol. 3)
Natural Resource Law (Vol. 4)
Property Rights (Vol. 10)

Friedlander, Jay
College of the Atlantic
Fast Food Industry (Vol. 2)

Fulkerson, Gregory M.
State University of New York, College at Oneonta
Development, Rural—Developed World (co-authors: Alexander R. Thomas and Polly J. Smith) (Vol. 2)
Development, Rural—Developing World (co-authors: Alexander R. Thomas and Polly J. Smith) (Vol. 2)
Ecological Modernization Theory (Vol. 3)

G

Gade, Daniel
University of Vermont
Andes Mountains (Vol. 8)

Gagne, David
Berkshire Publishing Group
Energy Efficiency (co-author: Matthew
  Bateson) (Vol. 2)
Energy Industries—Oil (Vol. 2)
Mining (co-author: Dirk van Zyl) (Vol. 2)

Galarraga, Ibon
Basque Centre for Climate Change (BC3)
Ecolabels (co-author: Luis María Abadie)
  (Vol. 6)
Energy Efficiency (co-author: Luis María
  Abadie) (Vol. 8)
*European Union Greenhouse Gas Emission
  Trading Scheme (EU ETS)* (co-author:
  Luis María Abadie) (Vol. 9)

Gale, Robert
University of New South Wales
Triple Bottom Line (Vol. 6)

Galloway, William
Environmental Innovators Program, Keio
  University
Smart Growth (Vol. 2)
Architecture (Vol. 8)

García Latorre, Jesús
Federal Ministry of Agriculture, Forestry,
  Environment & Water Management,
  Austria
Desertification (co-author: Juan García
  Latorre) (Vol. 5)

García Latorre, Juan
Association for Landscape Research in
  Arid Zones, Spain
Desertification (co-author: Jesús García
  Latorre) (Vol. 5)

García Molyneux, Cándido T.
Covington & Burling LLP
Restriction of Hazardous Substances Directive
  (Vol. 3)

Garmestani, Ahjond
US Environmental Protection Agency,
  National Risk Management Research
  Laboratory
Resilience (co-authors: Craig R. Allen and
  Shana M. Sundstrom) (Vol. 5)

Gaustad, Gabrielle
Rochester Institute of Technology
Recycling (Vol. 4)

Geall, Sam
chinadialogue
Five-Year Plans (co-author: Sony Pellissery)
  (Vol. 7)
Media Coverage of the Environment (Vol. 7)

Genung, Mark A.
University of Tennessee
Community Ecology (co-authors: Joseph K.
  Bailey, Randy K. Bangert, Jennifer A.
  Schweitzer, and Gina M. Wimp) (Vol. 5)

George, Daniel
Pennsylvania State University College of
  Medicine
Health, Public and Environmental
  (co-author: Peter Whitehouse) (Vol. 2)
Pharmaceutical Industry (co-authors: Chris
  Laszlo and Peter Whitehouse) (Vol. 2)

Gerber, Nicolas
University of Bonn
Biological Indicators—Genetic (co-author:
  Jan Henning Sommer) (Vol. 6)

Gerth, Karl
University of Oxford
Consumerism (Vol. 7)

Ghai, Rahul
Independent development practitioner,
    Western Rajasthan, India
Education, Environmental (India)
    (co-author: Vivek Bhandari) (Vol. 7)

Giles-Vernick, Tamara
Institut Pasteur
Africa, Central (Vol. 9)

Gillroy, John Martin
Lehigh University
Customary International Law (Vol. 3)
*Environmental Law—United States and
    Canada* (co-author: Rebecca M.
    Bratspies) (Vol. 3)

Gimblett, H. Randy
University of Arizona
Viewshed Protection (Vol. 5)
Computer Modeling (Vol. 6)

Gingerich, Elizabeth F. R.
Valparaiso University College of Business
    Administration
Global Reporting Initiative (GRI) (Vol. 2)

Glass, Jacqueline
Loughborough University
Building Standards, Green (Vol. 2)
Property and Construction Industry (Vol. 2)
Design Quality Indicator (DQI) (Vol. 6)

Glibert, Patricia M.
University of Maryland Center for
    Environmental Science
Eutrophication (Vol. 5)

Globus, Robin
University of Florida
New Age Spirituality (Vol. 1)

Goble, Dale D.
University of Idaho, Moscow
Lacey Act (Vol. 3)

Godfrey, Phoebe C.
University of Connecticut
*Activism—Nongovernmental Organizations
    (NGOs)* (Vol. 2)

Goering, Peter
Muskoka Heritage Foundation
Light Pollution and Biological Systems
    (co-authors: R. G. S. Bidwell, Robert
    Dick, and David Welch) (Vol. 5)

Goldin, Ian
Oxford Martin School, University of Oxford
Migration (co-author: Geoffrey Cameron)
    (Vol. 10)

Goldman, Lisa
Environmental Law Institute
Environmental Law—Africa, Saharan (Vol. 3)

Gong Xiangqian
Beijing Institute of Technology Law School
National Pollution Survey (China)
    (co-author: Cui Can) (Vol. 7)

González Márquez, José Juan
Metropolitan Autonomous University
*Environmental Law—Central America and
    the Caribbean* (Vol. 3)

Gonzalez-Meler, Miquel A.
University of Illinois at Chicago
Forest Management (co-authors: Kyle C.
    Costilow and Charles E. Flower) (Vol. 5)
Global Climate Change (co-authors: Charles
    E. Flower and Douglas J. Lynch) (Vol. 5)

Gonzales, Tirso
University of British Columbia Okanagan
Indigenous Traditions—South America
    (co-author: Maria E. Gonzalez) (Vol. 1)

Gonzalez, Maria E.
University of Michigan
Indigenous Traditions—South America
    (co-author: Tirso Gonzales) (Vol. 1)

Goodall, Melissa
Antioch University New England
Global Environment Outlook (GEO) Reports
(co-author: Maria Ivanova) (Vol. 6)

Gordon, Robert B.
Yale University
Copper (Vol. 4)

Gorman, Antonia
Humane Society of the United States
Creation (Vol. 1)
Eschatology (Vol. 1)

Gorringe, T. J.
University of Exeter
Culture (Vol. 1)

Gottlieb, Roger S.
Worcester Polytechnic Institute
Ecocide (Vol. 1)
Spirit and Spirituality (Vol. 1)

Grainger, Alan
University of Leeds
Desertification (Africa) (Vol. 9)

Gralton, Anna M.
University of Tasmania
Food, Value-Added (co-author: Frank
Vanclay) (Vol. 4)

Grant, J. Andrew
Queen's University, Canada
Chromium (co-author: Dianne Balraj)
(Vol. 4)
Manganese (co-author: Dianne Balraj)
(Vol. 4)
Mining—Nonmetals (co-author: Dianne
Balraj) (Vol. 4)
Potassium (co-author: Dianne Balraj) (Vol. 4)
Sulfur (co-author: Dianne Balraj) (Vol. 4)
Tin (co-author: Dianne Balraj) (Vol. 4)
Titanium (co-author: Dianne Balraj)
(Vol. 4)

Greacen, Chris
Palang Thai
Utilities Regulation and Energy Efficiency
(co-authors: Ranjit Bharvirkar, Chuenchom
Sangarasri Greacen, Fredrich Kahrl,
Mahesh Patankar, Priya Sreedharan, and
James H. Williams) (Vol. 7)

Greacen, Chuenchom Sangarasri
Palang Thai
Utilities Regulation and Energy Efficiency
(co-authors: Ranjit Bharvirkar, Chris
Greacen, Fredrich Kahrl, Mahesh
Patankar, Priya Sreedharan, and James
H. Williams) (Vol. 7)

Green, Gary Paul
University of Wisconsin, Madison
Extension
Green-Collar Jobs (co-author: Andrew
Dane) (Vol. 2)
Green Collar Jobs (co-author: Yifei Li) (Vol. 7)

Griffiths, Jesse
European Network on Debt and
Development (Eurodad)
World Bank (Vol. 9)

Grim, John A.
Yale University
Cosmology (Vol. 1)
Indigenous and Traditional Peoples (Vol. 1)

Grissino-Mayer, Henri D.
The University of Tennessee
Tree Rings as Environmental Indicators
(co-author: Grant L. Harley) (Vol. 6)

Grobecker, Anna
European Business School, Germany
Global Reporting Initiative (GRI)
(co-author: Julia Wolf) (Vol. 6)
Shipping and Freight (co-author: Julia Wolf)
(Vol. 9)
Shipping (co-author: Julia Wolf) (Vol. 10)

Grorud-Colvert, Kirsten
Oregon State University
Parks and Preserves—Marine (co-author:
    Sarah E. Lester) (Vol. 4)
Marine Protected Areas (MPAs) (co-author:
    Sarah E. Lester) (Vol. 5)

Grove, Deborah Puretz
Grove Associates LLC
Data Centers (co-author: David Rosenberg)
    (Vol. 2)

Grynspan, Rebeca
United Nations Development Programme
Millennium Development Goals (co-author:
    Luis F. Lopez-Calva) (Vol. 6)

Gu, Dejin
Sun Yat-sen University Law School
Activism, Judicial (co-author: Jingjing Liu)
    (Vol. 7)

Gudmarsdottir, Sigridur
Reykjavik Academy
Pilgrimage (Vol. 1)

Guesnet, Lena
Bonn International Center for Conversion
Conflict Minerals (co-author: Raimund
    Bleischwitz) (Vols. 4, 9)

Guo, Xiumei
Curtin University
One-Child Policy (co-author: Dora
    Marinova) (Vol. 7)
Aging (co-author: Dora Marinova) (Vol. 10)

Gupta, Aarti
Environmental Policy Group, Wageningen
    University
Transparency (Vol. 2)

Gupta, Joyeeta
UNESCO-IHE Institute for Water
    Education, Delft, the Netherlands

Mekong-Lancang River (co-authors: Ram
    Chandra Bastakoti and Hao Li) (Vol. 7)

Gusset, Markus
University of Oxford
Species Reintroduction (Vol. 5)

Gutknecht, Jessica L. M.
Helmholtz-Centre for Environmental
    Research—UFZ
Microbial Ecosystem Processes (Vol. 5)

Gutschick, Vincent P.
New Mexico State University
Extreme Episodic Events (Vol. 5)

Guyomard, Ann-Isabelle
University of Nantes
Water Act (France) (Vol. 3)

H

Haag, James
Suffolk University
Anthropic Principle (Vol. 1)

Haberl, Helmut
Alpen-Adria Universitaet Klagenfurt,
    Wien, Graz, Office Vienna
*Human Appropriation of Net Primary
    Production (HANPP)* (Vol. 6)

Hackett, Steven C.
Humboldt State University
Weak vs. Strong Sustainability Debate
    (Vols. 3, 6)

Haddad, Brent M.
University of California, Santa Cruz
Water (Overview) (Vol. 4)

Haley, Michael
EcoReefs Inc.
Fisheries Indicators, Marine (co-author:
    Anthony M. H. Clayton) (Vol. 6)

Halim, Sadeka
University of Dhaka
Gender Equality (co-author: Muhammad
   Zakir Hossin) (Vol. 7)

Hall, C. Michael
University of Canterbury
Advertising (Vol. 6)
Murray-Darling River Basin (Vol. 8)
Small Island States (Vol. 8)

Hall, Charles A. S.
State University of New York, Syracuse
Petroleum (Vol. 4)

Haluza-DeLay, Randolph
The King's University College (Alberta)
Globalization (Vol. 1)
Place (Vol. 1)

Handley, George
Brigham Young University
Mormonism (Vol. 1)

Haney, Alan
University of Wisconsin–Stevens Point
Ecological Restoration (Vol. 5)

Hannam, Ian
University of New England (Australia)
Soil Conservation Legislation (co-author:
   Benjamin Boer) (Vol. 3)

Harkness, Michael Dale
Cornell University
Energy Industries—Solar (Vol. 2)

Harley, Grant L.
The University of Tennessee
Tree Rings as Environmental Indicators
   (co-author: Henri D. Grissino-Mayer)
   (Vol. 6)

Harms, Robert
Yale University
Congo (Zaire) River (Vol. 9)

Harper, Krista M.
University of Massachusetts, Amherst
Danube River (Vol. 9)

Harrington, Eileen M.
University of San Francisco
Nonprofit Organizations, Environmental
   (Vol. 1)
Unitarianism and Unitarian Universalism
   (Vol. 1)

Harrington, Lisa M. Butler
Kansas State University
Sustainability Science (Vol. 6)

Harris, Adrian
Faith, Spirituality and Social Change
   Project
Paganism and Neopaganism (Vol. 1)

Hart, John
Boston University
Christianity—Roman Catholic (Vol. 1)
Cosmic Commons (Vol. 1)
Sacrament (Vol. 1)

Hart, Stuart
Johnson Graduate School of Management,
   Cornell University
Base of the Pyramid (co-authors: Mark
   B.Milstein, Erik Simanis, and Duncan
   Duke) (Vol. 2)
Poverty (co-authors: Mark B. Milstein,
   Erik Simanis, and Duncan Duke)
   (Vol. 2)

Hartman, Laura M.
Augustana College (Illinois)
Council of All Beings (Vol. 1)
Creation Spirituality (Vol. 1)
Property and Possessions (Vol. 1)

Harvey, Graham
The Open University
Nature Religions and Animism (Vol. 1)

Hasegawa, Koichi
University of Tohoku
Environmental Law—East Asia (co-authors:
Jeffrey Broadbent, Yu-Ju Chien, Jun Jin,
Dowan Ku, and Taehyun Park) (Vol. 3)

Hayes, Peter
Nautilus Institute at Global Studies,
RMIT University
Energy Security (East Asia) (co-authors:
Fredrich Kahrl, David F. von Hippel,
and James H. Williams) (Vol. 7)

Heiman, Michael K.
Dickinson College
Waste Management (Vol. 5)

Heller, Trudy
Executive Education for the Environment
*Information and Communication Technologies
(ICT)* (Vol. 2)

Hemmings, Alan D.
University of Canterbury
Environmental Law—Antarctica (Vol. 3)

Hendee, John C.
University of Idaho
Wilderness Areas (co-author: Chad P.
Dawson) (Vol. 5)

Henley, Jane
World Green Building Council
Building Rating Systems, Green (co-author:
Michelle Malanca) (Vol. 6)

Hermanus, Mavis
University of the Witwatersrand
Mining (Africa) (co-authors: Ingrid Watson
and Tracy-Lynn Humby) (Vol. 9)

Herring, Horace
The Open University
Energy Efficiency Measurement (Vol. 6)

Herron, Michael W.
University of North Carolina, Charlotte
Natural Resource Economics (co-author: Peter
M. Schwarz) (Vol. 4)

Heymann, Matthias
Aarhus University
Natural Gas (Vol. 4)

Higgins, Luke B.
Drew University
Process Thought (Vol. 1)

Hildén, Mikael
Finnish Environment Institute (SYKE)
Ecosystem Health Indicators (co-author:
David J. Rapport) (Vol. 6)

Hilger, Tim
National University of Singapore
Nanotechnology (co-author: Darryl S. L.
Jarvis) (Vol. 7)

Hill, Deborah
University of Kentucky
Tree Planting (Vol. 5)

Hill, R. Benjamin
Kenan-Flagler Business School, University
of North Carolina
Airline Industry (Vol. 2)

Himley, Matthew D.
Illinois State University
Mining (Andes) (Vol. 8)

Hipel, Keith W.
University of Waterloo (co-author: Sean B.
Walker)
Brownfield Redevelopment (Vol. 5)

Hirata, Ricardo
University of São Paulo
Groundwater Management (co-authors:
Bruno Pirilo Conicelli and Juliana Baitz
Viviani-Lima) (Vol. 5)

Hobgood-Oster, Laura
Southwestern University
Animals (Vol. 1)

Holm, Poul
University of Dublin Trinity College
Oceans and Seas (Vol. 4)

Holthaus, Gary
Island Institute; The Atheneum School
Subsistence (Vol. 1)

Horgan, John C.
Concordia University–Wisconsin
Shanghai, China (Vol. 7)

Horton, Lynn R.
Chapman University
Grassroots Environmental Movements (Vol. 3)

Hossin, Muhammad Zakir
ASA University Bangladesh (ASAUB)
Gender Equality (co-author: Sadeka Halim) (Vol. 7)

Howarth, Robert W.
Cornell University
Shale Gas Extraction (Vol. 5)

Hsieh, Hsin-Neng
New Jersey Institute of Technology
Cradle to Cradle (Vol. 2)

Hughes, Robert M.
Amnis Opes Institute & Oregon State University
Index of Biological Integrity (IBI) (Vol. 6)

Humby, Tracy-Lynn
University of the Witwatersrand
Mining (Africa) (co-author: Ingrid Watson, Mavis Hermanus) (Vol. 9)

Hund, Andrew J.
Independent scholar, Excursion Inlet, Alaska
Reforestation (Vol. 5)

Huntsinger, Lynn
University of California, Berkeley
Grasslands (co-author: Li Wenjun) (Vol. 4)
Ranching (co-author: Paul F. Starrs) (Vol. 4)
Succession (co-author: James W. Bartolome) (Vol. 5)

Hunziker, Roland
World Business Council for Sustainable Development (WBCSD)
Cement Industry (co-author: Caroline Twigg) (Vol. 2)

Hurley, Andrew
University of Missouri, St. Louis
Mississippi and Missouri Rivers (Vol. 8)

Hussey, Karen
The Australian National University
Water Security (Vol. 3)
Water Energy (Vol. 4)

I

Ilesanmi, Adetokunbo O.
Obafemi Awolowo University, Ile-Ife, Nigeria
Lagos, Nigeria (Vol. 9)

Irons, Gordon
McMaster University
Steel Industry (Vol. 2)

Irvine, Sandy
City of Sunderland College
Rio Earth Summit (UN Conference on Environment and Development) (Vol. 8)

Ivanova, Maria
University of Massachusetts, Boston
Global Environment Outlook (GEO) Reports (co-author: Melissa Goodall) (Vol. 6)

Ives, Christopher
Stonehill College
Buddhism (Vol. 1)

Iwamura, Takuya
The University of Queensland
Biodiversity Hotspots (co-authors: Michael
 Bode, Hugh P. Possingham, and Kerrie
 A. Wilson) (Vol. 5)

J

Jackson, Tim
University of Surrey
Consumer Behavior (Vol. 2)

Jackson, Wes
The Land Institute
Agricultural Innovation (Vol. 10)

Jacobs, Becky L.
University of Tennessee
Ecosystem Management (co-authors: Kay E.
 Franzreb, John D. Peine, and Maggie R.
 Stevens) (Vol. 3)

Jacoby, Jill B.
University of Wisconsin, Superior
Rain Gardens (Vol. 5)
Participatory Action Research
 (Vol. 6)

Jaeger, Jochen A. G.
Concordia University Montréal
Road Ecology (Vol. 5)

Jain, Abhimanyu G.
National Law School of India University
Cod Wars (United Kingdom v. Iceland)
 (Vol. 3)
International Court of Justice (Vol. 3)
Trail Smelter Arbitration (United States v.
 Canada) (Vol. 3)

Jain, Vaneesha
Luthra and Luthra Law Offices
*Montreal Protocol on Substances That Deplete
 the Ozone Layer* (Vol. 3)
Traditional Knowledge (India) (Vol. 7)

James, George A.
University of North Texas
Chipko Movement (Vol. 1)

Jameton, Andrew
University of Nebraska Medical Center
Health Care Industry (co-authors: Peter
 Whitehouse, Jeffrey Zabinski, and
 Charlotte A. Smith) (Vol. 2)

Jantzi, Terrence
Eastern Mennonite University
Peace (co-author: Aaron Kishbaugh) (Vol. 1)

Jarvis, Darryl S. L.
National University of Singapore
Nanotechnology (co-author: Tim Hilger)
 (Vol. 7)

Jenkins, Willis
Yale Divinity School
Anthropocentrism (Vol. 1)
Ecocentrism (co-author: Whitney Bauman)
 (Vol. 1)
Ethics, Environmental (Vol. 1)
Nature (Vol. 1)
Sustainability Theory (Vol. 1)
Volume Introduction (Vol. 1)

Jhunjhunwala, Ashok
Indian Institute of Technology (IIT)
 Madras
*Information and Communication Technologies
 (ICT)* (co-author: Janani Rangarajan)
 (Vol. 7)

Ji, Xia
University of Regina
Education, Environmental (China) (Vol. 7)

Jiang Gaoming
Chinese Academy of Sciences
Urban Vegetation (co-author: Bo Wenjing)
(Vol. 5)

Jiang, Hong
University of Hawaii at Manoa
Great Green Wall (China) (Vol. 7)

Jin, Jun
Tsinghua University
Environmental Law—East Asia (co-authors:
Jeffrey Broadbent, Yu-Ju Chien, Koichi
Hasegawa, Dowan Ku, and Taehyun
Park) (Vol. 3)

Johnston, Lucas F.
Wake Forest University
International Commissions and Summits
(Vol. 1)
*Indigenous and Traditional Resource
Management* (co-author: Todd LeVasseur)
(Vol. 4)

Jones, Kevin Edson
University of Alberta
Citizen Science (Vol. 6)

Jones, Richard
Royal Entomological Society, United
Kingdom
Honeybees (Vol. 4)
Insects—Beneficial (Vol. 4)
Insects—Pests (Vol. 4)

K

Kaak, Paul
Azusa Pacific University
Urban Agriculture (Vol. 5)

Kaempfer, William H.
University of Colorado, Boulder
*Convention on International Trade in
Endangered Species* (Vol. 3)

Kahrl, Fredrich
Energy and Environmental Economics, Inc.
Energy Security (East Asia) (co-authors:
Peter Hayes, David F. von Hippel, and
James H. Williams) (Vol. 7)
Utilities Regulation and Energy Efficiency
(co-authors: Ranjit Bharvirkar, Chris
Greacen, Chuenchom Sangarasri
Greacen, Mahesh Patankar, Priya
Sreedharan, and James H. Williams)
(Vol. 7)

Kalfagianni, Agni
VU University Amsterdam
*Multilateral Environmental Agreements
(MEAs)* (Vol. 8)

Karlaganis, Georg
United Nations Institute for Training and
Research (UNITAR)
Chemicals Legislation and Policy (co-author:
Franz Xaver Perrez) (Vol. 3)

Karlberg, Michael
Western Washington University
Bahá'í (Vol. 1)

Kearns, Laurel D.
Drew Theological School and University
Christianity—Society of Friends / Quakers
(Vol. 1)
Fundamentalism (Vol. 1)
*National Religious Partnership for the
Environment* (Vol. 1)
Wise Use Movement (Vol. 1)

Kearns, Robin A.
The University of Auckland
Auckland, New Zealand (Vol. 8)

Keating, Alexander M.
University of Pennsylvania
Urbanization (Europe) (co-authors:
Eugenie L. Birch and Susan M. Wachter)
(Vol. 9)

Keeling, Arn
Memorial University of Newfoundland
Mackenzie River (Vol. 8)

Khan, Ayesha
West Bengal National University of
    Juridical Sciences
Civil Disobedience, Environmental (Vol. 3)

Kho, James
Ateneo de Manila University School of
    Government
Environmental Law—Southeast Asia
    (co-authors: Sansanee Dhanasarnsombat,
    Koh Kheng-Lian, Lye Lin Heng, Chit
    Chit Myint, Dominic J. Nardi Jr., and
    Deny Sidharta) (Vol. 3)

Kirk-Duggan, Cheryl A.
Shaw University Divinity School
African Diasporan Religions (Vol. 1)

Kishbaugh, Aaron
Independent scholar, Singers Glen,
    Virginia
Peace (co-author: Terrence Jantzi) (Vol. 1)

Klein, Natalie
Macquarie University Law School
Eco-Terrorism (Vol. 3)

Knapp, Don
ICLEI–Local Governments for
    Sustainability USA
Municipalities (Vol. 2)

Knox, John H.
Wake Forest University
*North American Free Trade Agreement
    (NAFTA)* (Vol. 8)

Knudsen, Sanne H.
University of Utah
Exxon Valdez (Vol. 3)

Kogan, Marcos
Oregon State University
Pest Management, Integrated (IPM)
    (Vol. 4)

Koh Kheng-Lian
National University of Singapore
Environmental Law—Southeast Asia
    (co-authors: Sansanee Dhanasarnsombat,
    James Kho, Lye Lin Heng, Chit Chit
    Myint, Dominic J. Nardi Jr., and Deny
    Sidharta) (Vol. 3)

Koivurova, Timo
University of Lapland
Environmental Law—The Arctic (Vol. 3)

Kolb, Charles C.
National Endowment for the Humanities
Afghanistan (Vol. 9)

Kolo, Abba
University of Dundee
Investment Law, Energy (co-author: Peter
    D. Cameron) (Vol. 3)

Konijnendijk, Cecil C.
University of Copenhagen
Urban Forestry (co-authors: Kjell Nilsson
    and Phillip Rodbell) (Vol. 5)

Kontogianni, Areti
University of the Aegean
Externality Valuation (Vol. 6)

Kormos, Cyril F.
The WILD Foundation
Wilderness Act (Vol. 3)

Kosloff, Laura
EcoSecurities Consulting Ltd.
Climate Change Mitigation (co-author:
    Mark C. Trexler) (Vol. 3)

Kotzé, Louis
North-West University
Environmental Law—Africa, Sub-Saharan
(co-author: Werner Scholtz) (Vol. 3)

Kover, T. R.
Katholieke Universiteit Leuven
Hybridity (Vol. 1)
Order and Harmony (Vol. 1)

Krasnova, Irina
Moscow State Academy of Law
*Environmental Law—Russia and Central
Asia* (co-authors: Bakhtiyor R.
Mukhammadiev and Dinara Ziganshina)
(Vol. 3)

Kricsfalusy, Vladimir V.
University of Saskatchewan
Population Dynamics (Vol. 5)

Ku, Dowan
Environment and Society Research
Institute
Environmental Law—East Asia (co-authors:
Jeffrey Broadbent, Yu-Ju Chien, Koichi
Hasegawa, Jun Jin, and Taehyun Park)
(Vol. 3)

Kwak, Thomas J.
United States Geological Survey
Fisheries Indicators, Freshwater (Vol. 6)

L

Lal, Sanjay
Clayton State University
Gandhism (Vol. 7)

Lancaster, Kate
California Polytechnic State University,
San Luis Obispo
Accounting (co-authors: Doug Cerf and
Arline Savage) (Vol. 2)

Lang, Daniel J.
Leuphana University of Lüneburg
Transdisciplinary Research (co-author:
Arnim Wiek) (Vol. 6)

Larsen, Larissa
University of Michigan
Detroit, United States (Vol. 8)

Laszlo, Chris
Case Western Reserve University;
Sustainable Value Partners
Pharmaceutical Industry (co-authors: Daniel
George and Peter Whitehouse) (Vol. 2)
Sustainable Value Creation (Vol. 2)

Leaf, Murray J.
University of Texas, Dallas
Green Revolution (Vol. 4)
Rice (Vol. 4)

Lejeune, André
University of Liège
Energy Industries—Hydroelectric
(Vol. 2)

Lemanski, Charlotte
University College London
Cape Town, South Africa (Vol. 9)

Leonard, Liam
Institute of Technology, Sligo
Community Capital (Vol. 2)

Lester, Sarah E.
University of California, Santa Barbara
Parks and Preserves—Marine (co-author:
Kirsten Grorud-Colvert) (Vol. 4)
Marine Protected Areas (MPAs) (co-author:
Kirsten Grorud-Colvert) (Vol. 5)

Leung, David W. M.
University of Canterbury
Biotechnology Industry (Vol. 2)

LeVasseur, Todd
College of Charleston
Indigenous and Traditional Resource Management (co-author: Lucas Johnston) (Vol. 4)

Levy, Marc A.
Columbia University
Environmental Performance Index (EPI) (co-authors: John W. Emerson, William E. Dornbos, and Daniel C. Esty) (Vol. 6)

Lewis, James G.
Forest History Society, Durham, North Carolina
United States (Vol. 8)

Lewis, Joanna I.
Georgetown University
Climate Change Mitigation Initiatives (China) (Vol. 7)

Li, Hao
Chanjiang River Scientific Research Institute, Wuhan, China
Mekong-Lancang River (co-authors: Ram Chandra Bastakoti and Joyeeta Gupta) (Vol. 7)

Li, Pansy Hon-ying
The Hong Kong Polytechnic University
Guangzhou, China (co-author: Carlos Wing-Hung Lo) (Vol. 7)

Li Wenjun
Peking University
Grasslands (co-author: Lynn Huntsinger) (Vol. 4)

Li, Yifei
University of Wisconsin, Madison
Green Collar Jobs (co-author: Gary P. Green) (Vol. 7)

Lian Ming
Shanghai Bi Ke Clean Energy Technology Co., Ltd.

Energy Industries—Coal (co-authors: Zhao Ning, Song Quanbin, and Xu Guangwen) (Vol. 2)
Coal (co-authors: Song Quanbin, Xu Guangwen, and Zhao Ning) (Vol. 4)

Lide, James H.
History Associates Incorporated
Yangzi (Chang) River (Vol. 7)
Scandinavia (Vol. 9)

Lidicker, William Z. Jr.
University of California, Berkeley
Biological Corridors (Vol. 5)

Liese, Walter
University of Hamburg
Bamboo (Vol. 4)

Lifset, Reid J.
Yale University
Industrial Ecology (co-author: Weslynne S. Ashton) (Vol. 4)

Lillington, Ian R.
Swinburne University
Permaculture (Vol. 5)

Ling, Christopher
Royal Roads University
Urbanization (Vol. 8)

Liroff, Richard A.
Investor Environmental Health Network
Chemistry, Green (Vol. 2)

Liu, Jingjing
Vermont Law School
Environmental Law—China (co-author: Adam Moser) (Vol. 3)
Activism, Judicial (co-author: Dejin Gu) (Vol. 7)

Liu, KeShun
United States Department of Agriculture
Soybeans (Vol. 4)

Lo, Carlos Wing-Hung
The Hong Kong Polytechnic University
Guangzhou, China (co-author: Pansy
  Hon-ying Li) (Vol. 7)

Locke, Harvey
Strategic Advisor, Yellowstone to Yukon
  Conservation Initiative
*Yellowstone to Yukon Conservation Initiative
  (Y2Y)* (Vol. 8)

Lockyer, Joshua
Arkansas Tech University
Ecovillages (co-author: James R. Veteto)
  (Vol. 8)

Lofthouse, Vicky
Loughborough University
Design, Product and Industrial
  (Vol. 4)

Longley, Glenn
Texas State University
Aquifers (co-author: Rene Allen Barker)
  (Vol. 4)

Lopez-Bautista, Juan M.
University of Alabama
Algae (co-author: Michael S. DePriest)
  (Vol. 4)

Lopez-Calva, Luis F.
The World Bank
Millennium Development Goals (co-author:
  Rebeca Grynspan) (Vol. 6)

Lovell, Sarah Taylor
University of Illinois, Urbana-Champaign
Agroecology (Vol. 5)
Buffers (Vol. 5)

Lovins, Amory B.
Rocky Mountain Institute
Energy Efficiency (Vol. 10)

Lovins, L. Hunter
Natural Capitalism Solutions
Development, Sustainable (Vol. 2)
Natural Capitalism (Vol. 2)

Low, Tiffany
University of Bedfordshire
Travel and Tourism Industry (co-author:
  Carl Iain Cater) (Vol. 9)

Lu, Jiang
Shanxi University
Energy Security (Europe) (Vol. 9)

Lund-Durlacher, Dagmar
Department of Tourism and Hospitality
  Management, MODUL University
  Vienna
Hospitality Industry (Vol. 2)

Lunney, Daniel
Office of Environment and Heritage
  New South Wales, Australia
Charismatic Megafauna (Vol. 5)

Lye Lin Heng
National University of Singapore
Environmental Law—Southeast Asia
  (co-authors: Sansanee Dhanasarnsombat,
  James Kho, Koh Kheng-Lian, Chit Chit
  Myint, Dominic J. Nardi Jr., and Deny
  Sidharta) (Vol. 3)

Lynch, Douglas J.
University of Illinois at Chicago
Global Climate Change (co-authors: Charles
  E. Flower and Miquel A. Gonzalez-
  Meler) (Vol. 5)

Lyon, Kimberly
Multilateral Relations at the World
  Wildlife Fund
Ecosystem Services (co-authors: Emily
  McKenzie and Amy Rosenthal) (Vol. 5)

M

MacDonald, Kate
University of Melbourne
Corporate Accountability (co-author: Shelley Marshall) (Vol. 8)

MacDonald, Mary N.
Le Moyne College
Indigenous Traditions—Oceania (Vol. 1)

MacKenzie, Catherine P.
University of Cambridge
Education, Environmental Law (Vol. 3)
Reducing Emissions from Deforestation and Forest Degradation (REDD) (Vol. 6)
Rule of Law (Africa) (Vol. 9)

Magee, Darrin
Hobart and William Smith Colleges
South-North Water Diversion (Vol. 7)

Majer, Jonathan David
Curtin University
Indicator Species (Vol. 5)

Majzoub, Tarek
Beirut Arab University
Environmental Law—Arab Region (co-author: Fabienne Quilleré-Majzoub) (Vol. 3)
Urbanization (Western Asia and Northern Africa) (co-author: Fabienne Quilleré-Majzoub) (Vol. 9)

Malanca, Michelle
World Green Building Council
Building Rating Systems, Green (co-author: Jane Henley) (Vol. 6)

Malandrino, Ornella
Salerno University
Energy Labeling (Vol. 6)

Malcolm, Rosalind
University of Surrey
Rule of Law (European Union) (Vol. 9)

Mank, Bradford C.
University of Cincinnati College of Law
Massachusetts v. Environmental Protection Agency (Vol. 3)

Manning, Robert E.
University of Vermont
Tragedy of the Commons, The (Vol. 1)
Parks and Preserves—National (co-author: Laura Anderson) (Vol. 4)
Recreation, Outdoor (co-author: Laura Anderson) (Vol. 4)

Marauhn, Thilo
University of Giessen
Environmental Law—Europe (co-author: Ayse Martina Boehringer) (Vol. 3)
Environmental Law, Soft vs. Hard (co-author: Ulrich Beyerlin) (Vol. 3)

Marcotullio, Peter J.
Hunter College, City University of New York
New York City, United States (Vol. 8)

Marinova, Dora
Curtin University
One-Child Policy (co-author: Xiumei Guo) (Vol. 7)
Aging (co-author: Xiumei Guo) (Vol. 10)

Marshall, Shelley
Monash University
Corporate Accountability (co-author: Kate MacDonald) (Vol. 8)

Martin-Schramm, James B.
Luther College
Population (Vol. 1)

Marx, Jessica C.
EcoPeace / Friends of the Earth Middle
  East
Transboundary Water Issues (co-author:
  Gidon Bromberg) (Vol. 9)

Mateo, Nicolás
Agronomist, San José, Costa Rica
Agriculture, Tropical (the Americas)
  (co-author: Rodomiro Ortiz) (Vol. 8)

Mather, Diarmid
Curtin University
Mining (Australia) (co-author: Erkan Topal)
  (Vol. 8)

Mathew, Leemamol
Institute of Rural Management
Education, Female (co-author: Fengping
  Zhao) (Vol. 7)

Mathewes, Charles
University of Virginia
God (co-author: Chad Wayner) (Vol. 1)

Mathews, Freya
La Trobe University
Dualism (Vol. 1)

Mayer, Audrey L.
Michigan Technological University
Gross Domestic Product, Green (Vol. 6)

Mayer, Heike
University of Bern
Local Food Movements (Vol. 4)

McAnally, Elizabeth
California Institute of Integral Studies
Earth Day (Vol. 1)

McBroom, Matthew W.
Stephen F. Austin State University
Best Management Practices (BMPs)
  (co-author: Yanli Zhang) (Vol. 5)

McCarty, John P.
University of Nebraska, Omaha
Agriculture—Genetically Engineered Crops
  (co-author: L. LaReesa Wolfenbarger)
  (Vol. 4)

McCook, Stuart
University of Guelph
Cacao (Vol. 4)

McDaniel, Jay
Hendrix College
Beauty (Vol. 1)
Meditation and Prayer (Vol. 1)
Simplicity and Asceticism (Vol. 1)

McIntyre, Owen
University College Cork
Gabčíkovo–Nagymaros Dam Case (Hungary
  v. Slovakia) (Vol. 3)

McKenzie, Emily
Natural Capital Project at the World
  Wildlife Fund
Ecosystem Services (co-authors: Kimberly
  Lyon and Amy Rosenthal) (Vol. 5)

Mcleod, Elizabeth
The Nature Conservancy
Ocean Acidification—Management
  (co-author: Kenneth R. N. Anthony)
  (Vol. 5)

McNamara, Nora
Missionary Sisters of the Holy Rosary
Microfinance (Vol. 9)

McNeely, Jeffrey A.
International Union for Conservation of
  Nature (IUCN)
Endangered Species (Vol. 7)

McNeill, J. R.
Georgetown University
Mediterranean Sea (Vol. 9)

McNeill, William H.
University of Chicago
Progress (Vol. 10)

Melosi, Martin V.
University of Houston
Waste Management (Vol. 4)

Meltzer, Joshua
Brookings Institution; Georgetown
University Law School; John Hopkins
School of Advanced International
Studies
Global Trade (Vol. 10)

Menzies, Gillian F.
Heriot Watt University
Facilities Management (Vol. 2)

Mickey, Sam
California Institute of Integral Studies
Individualism (Vol. 1)

Migliavacca, Paolo
Bocconi University
Energy Industries—Hydrogen and Fuel Cells
(co-authors: Stefano Pogutz and
Angeloantonio Russo) (Vol. 2)

Miles, Kate
University of Sydney
Investment Law, Foreign (Vol. 3)

Miller, Jennie R. B.
Yale School of Forestry & Environmental
Studies
Food Webs (co-author: Oswald J. Schmitz)
(Vol. 5)

Milne, Janet E.
Vermont Law School
Green Taxes (Vol. 3)
Taxation Indicators, Green
(Vol. 6)

Milstein, Mark B.
Johnson Graduate School of Management,
Cornell University
Base of the Pyramid (co-authors: Stuart
Hart, Erik Simanis, and Duncan Duke)
(Vol. 2)
Poverty (co-authors: Stuart Hart, Erik
Simanis, and Duncan Duke) (Vol. 2)

Minteer, Ben
Arizona State University
Pragmatism (Vol. 1)

Mintz, Joel A.
Nova Southeastern University
Enforcement (Vol. 3)

Mitchell, Bruce
University of Waterloo, Ontario, Canada
*Water Resource Management, Integrated
(IWRM)* (Vol. 5)

Mitra, Arup
Institute for Economic Growth, Delhi
Labor (Vol. 7)

Miyamoto, Yotaro
Kansai University
Shinto (Vol. 1)

Moberg, Mark A.
University of South Alabama
Caribbean (Vol. 8)
Fair Trade (Vol. 8)

Mohr, Steve H.
Institute of Technology, Sydney
Lithium (co-author: Gavin M. Mudd)
(Vol. 4)

Moncel, Remi
World Resources Institute
Copenhagen Climate Change Conference 2009
(Vol. 3)

Mondal, Pinki
Columbia University
Parks and Preserves (co-author: Harini
    Nagendra) (Vol. 7)

Montelongo, Ivett
Gonzales & Asociados (Gonzales &
    Associates)
Mexico City (Vol. 8)

Montgomery, Heather A.
International Christian University
Microfinance (Vol. 7)

Morris, Peter J. T.
The Science Museum, London
Rubber (Vol. 4)

Morrone, Juan J.
National Autonomous University of
    Mexico (UNAM)
Biogeography (Vol. 5)

Morse, Stephen
University of Surrey
Development Indicators (Vol. 6)
Sustainable Livelihood Analysis (SLA)
    (Vol. 6)

Moscoso, Victor J.
Researcher, Daedalus Strategic Advising
Guatemala City (co-author: J. Rodolfo
    Neutze) (Vol. 8)

Moser, Adam
Vermont Law School
Environmental Law—China (co-author:
    Jingjing Liu) (Vol. 3)

Moynihan, Ruby
University of Dundee
Transboundary Water Law (co-author:
    Patricia Wouters) (Vol. 3)

Mudd, Gavin M.
Monash University
Gold (Vol. 4)
Iron Ore (Vol. 4)
Lead (Vol. 4)
Lithium (co-author: Steve H. Mohr)
    (Vol. 4)
Mineral Sands (Vol. 4)
Nickel (Vol. 4)
Platinum Group Metals (Vol. 4)
Silver (Vol. 4)

Muers, Rachel
University of Leeds
Future Generations (Vol. 1)

Mughal, Muhammad Aurang Zeb
Durham University
Pakistan (co-author: Anita M. Weiss)
    (Vol. 9)

Mukhammadiev, Bakhtiyor R.
United States Embassy, Tashkent
*Environmental Law—Russia and Central
    Asia* (co-authors: Irina Krasnova and
    Dinara Ziganshina) (Vol. 3)

Mukonyora, Isabel
Western Kentucky University
Green Belt Movement (Vol. 1)

Mulder, Herman
Independent ESG Advisor & Board
    Member
Equator Principles (Vol. 2)

Muradov, Nazim
Florida Solar Energy Center
Hydrogen Fuel (Vol. 4)

Mwaniki, Fiona
Farmer Voice Radio (FVR), Nairobi, Kenya
Education, Environmental (co-authors:
    Robert B. Stevenson and Aravella
    Zachariou) (Vol. 9)

Myint, Chit Chit
SEEgreen, Myanmar (Burma)
Environmental Law—Southeast Asia
   (co-authors: Sansanee Dhanasarnsombat,
   James Kho, Koh Kheng-Lian, Lye Lin
   Heng, Dominic J. Nardi Jr., and Deny
   Sidharta) (Vol. 3)

N

Nævdal, Eric
Ragnar Frisch Centre for Economic
   Research
Safe Minimum Standard (SMS) (Vol. 5)

Nadarajah, Yasothara
Royal Melbourne Institute of Technology
   (RMIT)
Kuala Lumpur, Malaysia (Vol. 7)

Nagendra, Harini
Ashoka Trust for Research in Ecology and
   the Environment
Parks and Preserves (co-author: Pinki
   Mondal) (Vol. 7)

Nagle, John Copeland
University of Notre Dame
Clean Air Act (Vol. 3)
Endangered Species Act (Vol. 3)

Nardi, Dominic J., Jr.
University of Michigan
Environmental Law—India and Pakistan
   (co-author: Armin Rosencranz)
   (Vol. 3)
Environmental Law—Southeast Asia
   (co-authors: Sansanee Dhanasarnsombat,
   James Kho, Koh Kheng-Lian, Lye Lin
   Heng, Chit Chit Myint, and Deny
   Sidharta) (Vol. 3)
*Association of Southeast Asian Nations
   (ASEAN)* (Vol. 7)

Nasir, Zaheer Ahmad
University of Essex
Air Pollution Indicators and Monitoring
   (co-author: Ian Colbeck) (Vol. 6)

Nasr, Nabil
Golisano Institute for Sustainability,
   Rochester Institute of Technology
Remanufacturing (Vol. 2)

Nefedova, Tatyana G.
Institute of Geography, Russian Academy
   of Sciences
Moscow, Russia (co-author: Isolde Brade)
   (Vol. 9)

Neidel, J. David
National University of Singapore
*Reforestation and Afforestation (Southeast
   Asia)* (Vol. 7)

Nelson, Fred
Maliasili Initiatives Ltd.
Poaching (Vol. 4)

Nelson, Melissa
San Francisco State University
Indigenous Traditions—North America (Vol. 1)

Nesamani, K. S.
Ford Foundation International Fellowship
   Program
Public Transportation (Vol. 7)

Neutze, J. Rodolfo
Councilman, Guatemala City
Guatemala City (co-author: Victor J.
   Moscoso) (Vol. 8)

Newall, Adrian DiCianno
Energy consultant
Energy Industries—Natural Gas (co-author:
   Kevin Forbes) (Vol. 2)
Energy Industries—Wind (co-author: Kevin
   Forbes) (Vol. 2)
Energy Conservation Incentives (Vol. 3)

Newman, Julie
Yale University
Education (Vol. 1)

Nijman, Jan
University of Amsterdam
Mumbai, India (Vol. 7)

Nilsson, Kjell
University of Copenhagen
Urban Forestry (co-authors: Cecil C.
   Konijnendijk and Phillip Rodbell) (Vol. 5)

Njuki, Caroline Muthoni
Intergovernmental Authority on
   Development (IGAD)
African Union (AU) (co-author: J.
   Manyitabot Takang) (Vol. 9)
Immigrants and Refugees (Vol. 9)

Nolon, Sean F.
Vermont Law School
Environmental Dispute Resolution (Vol. 3)

Norgaard, Richard
University of California, Berkeley
Economics (Vol. 1)

Norton, Bryan
Georgia Institute of Technology
Intergenerational Equity (Vol. 3)

Notarnicola, Bruno
University of Bari Aldo Moro, Taranto,
   Italy
Life Cycle Assessment (LCA) (co-authors:
   Ettore Settanni and Giuseppe Tassielli)
   (Vol. 6)
Life Cycle Costing (LCC) (co-authors: Ettore
   Settanni and Giuseppe Tassielli) (Vol. 6)

Nuñez, Martin A.
University of Tennessee
Keystone Species (co-author: Romina D.
   Dimarco) (Vol. 5)

O

Öberg, Gunilla
University of British Columbia
Focus Groups (co-author: Jacqueline Belzile)
   (Vol. 6)
Quantitative vs. Qualitative Studies (Vol. 6)

O'Brien, Kevin J.
Pacific Lutheran University
Ecology (Vol. 1)
Ethics, Communicative (Vol. 1)

O'Connor, Anthony M.
University College London
Tunis, Tunisia (Vol. 9)
Urbanization (Africa) (Vol. 9)

Oelschlaeger, Max
Northern Arizona University
Wilderness (Vol. 1)

Oestigaard, Terje
The Nordic Africa Institute, Uppsala,
   Sweden
Water (Vol. 1)
Nile River (Vol. 9)

Ogunseitan, Oladele A.
University of California, Irvine
Coltan (Vol. 4)
Electronics—Raw Materials (Vol. 4)

Oh, Irene
The George Washington University
Justice (Vol. 1)

Oldenski, Lindsay
Georgetown University
Outsourcing and Offshoring (Vol. 7)

Ormond, Thomas
Regional government of South Hesse,
   Germany
Waste Shipment Law (Vol. 3)

Ortiz, Rodomiro
Swedish University of Agricultural
    Sciences (SLU)
Agriculture, Tropical (the Americas)
    (co-author: Nicolás Mateo) (Vol. 8)

Ortuzar, Jr., Antonio
Baker & McKenzie, Santiago
Environmental Law—South America
    (co-authors: Renata Campetti Amaral,
    Gustavo Boruchowicz, Alejandra
    Bugna, Alessandro De Franceschi da
    Cruz, María Eugenia Reyes, María
    Victoria Romero, and Cristina Rueda)
    (Vol. 3)

Otiso, Kefa M.
Bowling Green State University
Nairobi, Kenya (Vol. 9)

P

Padovani, Florence
Paris 1 Sorbonne University
Three Gorges Dam (Vol. 7)

Pandey, Pramod Kumar
Iowa State University
Pollution, Nonpoint Source (co-author:
    Michelle Lynn Soupir) (Vol. 5)

Pardo Buendia, Mercedes
University Carlos III of Madrid
Principle-Based Regulation (co-author:
    Luciano Parejo) (Vol. 3)

Pardy, Bruce
Queen's University, Canada
Administrative Law (Vol. 5)

Parejo, Luciano
University Carlos III of Madrid
Principle-Based Regulation (co-author:
    Mercedes Pardo Buendia) (Vol. 3)

Paritsis, Juan
University of Colorado
Disturbance (co-authors: Alan J. Tepley and
    Thomas T. Veblen) (Vol. 5)
Outbreak Species (co-author: Thomas T.
    Veblen) (Vol. 5)

Park, Jacob
Green Mountain College
Investment, Socially Responsible (SRI)
    (Vol. 2)

Park, Taehyun
Kangwon University
Environmental Law—East Asia (co-authors:
    Jeffrey Broadbent, Yu-Ju Chien, Koichi
    Hasegawa, Jun Jin, and Dowan Ku)
    (Vol. 3)

Patankar, Mahesh
Customized Energy Solutions
Utilities Regulation and Energy Efficiency
    (co-authors: Ranjit Bharvirkar, Chris
    Greacen, Chuenchom Sangarasri
    Greacen, Fredrich Kahrl, Priya
    Sreedharan, and James H. Williams)
    (Vol. 7)

Patel, Amrita
National Dairy Development Board, India
White Revolution of India (Vol. 7)

Pattberg, Philipp
VU University Amsterdam
Public-Private Partnerships (Africa) (Vol. 9)

Pattison, Ian
University of Southampton
Catchment Management (Vol. 5)
Fish Hatcheries (Vol. 5)

Pawson, Eric
University of Canterbury
New Zealand (co-authors: Tom Brooking
    and Hamish G. Rennie) (Vol. 8)

Pearman, Peter B.
Swiss Federal Research Institute WSL
Biological Indicators—Species
    (co-author: Niklaus E. Zimmermann)
    (Vol. 6)

Pegas, Fernanda de Vasconcellos
Griffith University, Australia
Ecotourism (the Americas) (co-author: Ralf
    Buckley) (Vol. 8)

Peine, John D.
University of Tennessee
Ecosystem Management (co-authors: Kay E.
    Franzreb, Becky L. Jacobs, and Maggie
    R. Stevens) (Vol. 3)

Pellander, Erik
University of Cologne
*Convention on Long-Range Transboundary
    Air Pollution* (Vol. 3)
MOX Plant Case (Ireland v. United
    Kingdom) (Vol. 3)
*United Nations—Overview of Conventions
    and Agreements* (Vol. 3)
European Union (EU) (co-author: Michael
    Lysander Fremuth) (Vol. 9)

Pellissery, Sony
Institute of Rural Management, Anand
Energy Industries—Renewables (India)
    (co-author: Badrinarayanan
    Seetharaman) (Vol. 7)
Five-Year Plans (co-author: Sam Geall)
    (Vol. 7)
Rural Development (co-author: Li Sun)
    (Vol. 7)
Rural Livelihoods (Vol. 7)

Perrez, Franz Xaver
Ambassador, Federal Office for the
    Environment, Switzerland
Chemicals Legislation and Policy (co-author:
    Georg Karlaganis) (Vol. 3)

Peterson, Garry D.
Stockholm Resilience Center, Stockholm
    University
Regime Shifts (co-authors: Reinette [Oonsie]
    Biggs and Juan C. Rocha) (Vol. 5)

Phansey, Asheen A.
Dassault Systèmes SolidWorks Corp.;
    Babson College
Biomimicry (Vol. 2)
Materials Substitution (Vol. 4)

Pichura, Alexander
Pichura Consult—Architects
Architecture (Vol. 9)

Pimentel, David
Cornell University
Malnutrition (co-author: Patricia J.
    Satkiewicz) (Vol. 4)
Fertilizers (co-author: Patricia J. Satkiewicz)
    (Vol. 4)

Pitcher, Tony J.
University of British Columbia
Fisheries (Vol. 10)

Plachcinski, Douglas
American Institute of Certified Planners
Food Security (Vol. 4)
Rare Earth Elements (Vol. 4)

Pogge, Thomas
Yale University
Poverty (Vol. 1)

Pogutz, Stefano
Bocconi University
Energy Industries—Hydrogen and Fuel Cells
    (co-authors: Angeloantonio Russo and
    Paolo Migliavacca) (Vol. 2)

Pojasek, Robert B.
Harvard University
Manufacturing Practices (Vol. 2)

Possehl, Gregory L.
University of Pennsylvania
Indus River (Vol. 9)

Possingham, Hugh P.
The University of Queensland
Biodiversity Hotspots (co-authors: Michael Bode, Takuya Iwamura, and Kerrie A. Wilson) (Vol. 5)

Poulsen, Bo
Aalborg University
Fisheries (Vol. 9)

Power, Greg
Arriba Consulting Pty Ltd.
Aluminum (Vol. 4)

Pregitzer, Kurt S.
University of Idaho
Nitrogen Saturation (co-author: Alan F. Talhelm) (Vol. 5)

Price, Martin
Perth College, University of the Highlands and Islands
Mountains (Vol. 4)

Prigge, Amanda
Berkshire Publishing Group
Mexico (co-author: Sterling Evans) (Vol. 8)

Primack, Richard B.
Boston University
Biodiversity (co-author: Elizabeth R. Ellwood) (Vol. 5)

Primavesi, Anne
University of London
Gaia (Vol. 1)

Pritchard, Dave
Scientific & Technical Review Panel, Convention on Wetlands
Convention on Wetlands (Vol. 3)

Proto, Maria
University of Salerno
Ecolabeling (Vol. 2)
Life Cycle Management (LCM) (Vol. 6)

Pyšek, Petr
Institute of Botany Průhonice, Czech Republic
Invasive Species (co-author: David M. Richardson) (Vol. 5)

Q

Quilleré-Majzoub, Fabienne
IODE—University of Rennes 1
Environmental Law—Arab Region (co-author: Tarek Majzoub) (Vol. 3)
Urbanization (Western Asia and Northern Africa) (co-author: Tarek Majzoub) (Vol. 9)

Qvenild, Marte
Norwegian Institute for Nature Research
Svalbard Global Seed Vault (Vol. 9)

R

Radcliffe, Nicholas
Stochastic Solutions Ltd. & Edinburgh University
Systems Thinking (co-authors: Anthony M. H. Clayton and C. Andrea Bruce) (Vol. 6)

Rangarajan, Janani
IIT Madras's Rural Technology and Business Incubator (RTBI)
Information and Communication Technologies (ICT) (co-author: Ashok Jhunjhunwala) (Vol. 7)

Rangarajan, Mahesh
University of Delhi
India (Vol. 7)

Rapport, David J.
EcoHealth Consulting
Ecosystem Health Indicators (co-author:
Mikael Hildén) (Vol. 6)

Raskin, Paul
Tellus Institute
Future (Vol. 1)

Reardon, Mitchell
Nordregio (Nordic Centre for Spatial
Development), Stockholm, Sweden
Stockholm, Sweden (co-author: Peter
Schmitt) (Vol. 9)

Redekop, Benjamin W.
Christopher Newport University
Leadership (Vol. 2)

Reed, Maureen
University of Saskatchewan
Gender Equality (Vol. 8)

Reed, Sue
Landscape architect, Shelburne,
Massachusetts
Design, Landscape (Vol. 2)

Rees, William E.
University of British Columbia
True Cost Economics (Vol. 2)

Rennie, Hamish G.
Lincoln University
New Zealand (co-authors: Tom Brooking
and Eric Pawson) (Vol. 8)

Reuss, Martin
United States Army Corps of Engineers
Dams and Reservoirs (Vol. 4)

Reyes, María Eugenia
Baker & McKenzie, Caracas
Environmental Law—South America
(co-authors: Renata Campetti Amaral,
Gustavo Boruchowicz, Alejandra Bugna,
Alessandro De Franceschi da Cruz,
Antonio Ortuzar Jr., María Victoria
Romero, and Cristina Rueda) (Vol. 3)

Rhodes, Catherine
University of Manchester School of Law
Biotechnology Legislation (Vol. 3)

Rhyne, Stephen K.
K&L Gates LLP
Climate Change Disclosure (Vol. 2)
*Climate Change Disclosure—Legal
Framework* (Vol. 3)

Ricci, Kenneth N.
Scientech: A Curtiss-Wright Flow Control
Company
Energy Industries—Nuclear (Vol. 7)

Richardson, David M.
Stellenbosch University, South Africa
Invasive Species (co-author: Petr Pyšek)
(Vol. 5)

Richter, Alexander
Islandsbanki, Geothermal Energy Team;
ThinkGeoEnergy
Energy Industries—Geothermal (Vol. 2)

Ries, Leslie
University of Maryland
Edge Effects (co-author: William F. Fagan)
(Vol. 5)

Rigby, Kate
Monash University
Language (Vol. 1)

Ripa Juliá, Isabel
Independent scholar, Logroño, Spain
Convention on Biological Diversity (Vol. 3)

Robèrt, Karl-Henrik
Blekinge Institute of Technology
*Framework for Strategic Sustainable
Development (FSSD)* (co-authors: Göran
Broman and George Basile) (Vol. 6)

Roberts, Carolyn
University of Oxford
Dhaka, Bangladesh (co-author: Md. Sarfaraz
Gani Adnan) (Vol. 7)

Robertson, G. Philip
Michigan State University
Long-Term Ecological Research (LTER) (Vol. 6)

Robinson, Curt
Geothermal Resources Council
Geothermal Energy (Vol. 4)

Rocha, Juan C.
Stockholm Resilience Center, Stockholm
University
Regime Shifts (co-authors: Reinette [Oonsie]
Biggs and Garry D. Peterson) (Vol. 5)

Rock, Melissa Y.
Dartmouth College
Beijing, China (Vol. 7)

Rockefeller, Steven
Earth Charter International Council
Earth Charter (Vol. 1)

Rodbell, Phillip
United States Forest Service
Urban Forestry (co-authors: Cecil C.
Konijnendijk and Kjell Nilsson) (Vol. 5)

Roller, Gerhard
University of Applied Sciences
Polluter Pays Principle (Vol. 3)

Rolston, Holmes, III
Colorado State University
Dominion (Vol. 1)
Science, Religion, and Ecology (Vol. 1)

Romero, María Victoria
Baker & McKenzie, Caracas
Environmental Law—South America
(co-authors: Renata Campetti Amaral,
Gustavo Boruchowicz, Alejandra Bugna,
Alessandro De Franceschi da Cruz,
Antonio Ortuzar Jr., María Eugenia
Reyes, and Cristina Rueda) (Vol. 3)

Ros-Tonen, Mirjam A. F.
University of Amsterdam
Forest Products—Non-Timber (Vol. 4)

Rosa, Juan Carlos
StatAid
Human Development Index (HDI)
(co-author: Jana Asher) (Vol. 6)

Rose, Deborah Bird
Macquarie University
Indigenous Traditions—Australia (Vol. 1)

Rose, Justin Gregory
University of South Pacific
Environmental Law—Pacific Island Region
(Vol. 3)

Rosenberg, David
Grove Associates LLC
Data Centers (co-author: Deborah Puretz
Grove) (Vol. 2)

Rosencranz, Armin
Stanford University
Environmental Law—India and Pakistan
(co-author: Dominic J. Nardi Jr.) (Vol. 3)

Rosenthal, Amy
Natural Capital Project at the World
Wildlife Fund
Ecosystem Services (co-authors: Kimberly
Lyon and Emily McKenzie) (Vol. 5)
*Intergovernmental Science-Policy Platform on
Biodiversity and Ecosystem Services
(IPBES)* (Vol. 6)

Rosillo-Calle, Frank
Imperial College London
Bioenergy and Biofuels (Vol. 4)

Rottmann, Emily Yandle
McGuireWoods, LLP
University Indicators (co-author: Daniel S.
Fogel) (Vol. 6)

Rowell, Arden
University of Illinois College of Law
Tort Law (Vol. 3)
Cost-Benefit Analysis (Vol. 6)
Risk Assessment (Vol. 6)

Rueda, Cristina
Baker & McKenzie, Bogotá
Environmental Law—South America
(co-authors: Renata Campetti Amaral,
Gustavo Boruchowicz, Alejandra Bugna,
Alessandro De Franceschi da Cruz,
Antonio Ortuzar Jr., María Eugenia
Reyes, and María Victoria Romero)
(Vol. 3)

Ruffell, James P.
The University of Western Australia
Habitat Fragmentation (co-authors: Raphael
K. Didham and Timm F. Döbert) (Vol. 5)

Russo, Angeloantonio
Parthenope University
Energy Industries—Hydrogen and Fuel Cells
(co-authors: Stefano Pogutz and Paolo
Migliavacca) (Vol. 2)

Russon, Jo-Anna
Queen's University Belfast
Corporate Accountability (Africa) (co-author:
Ralf Barkemeyer) (Vol. 9)

Ryser, Rudolph C.
Center for World Indigenous Studies
*Indigenous Peoples and Traditional
Knowledge* (Vol. 5)

S

Sachs, Noah M.
University of Richmond School of Law
*Registration, Evaluation, Authorisation, and
Restriction of Chemicals* (Vol. 3)

Sanford, A. Whitney
University of Florida
Vegetarianism (Vol. 1)

Santos, Evandro C.
Jackson State University
Curitiba, Brazil (Vol. 8)
Mobility (Vol. 8)
Public Transportation (Vol. 8)
Mobility (Vol. 10)

Sarna, Satyajit
Advocate, Delhi High Court
*Convention for the Prevention of Pollution
From Ships* (Vol. 3)
Convention to Combat Desertification (Vol. 3)

Sarzynski, Andrea
University of Delaware
Carbon Footprint (Vol. 6)

Sassen, Saskia
Columbia University
Cities and the Biosphere (Vol. 10)

Satkiewicz, Patricia J.
Cornell University
Fertilizers (co-author: David Pimentel)
(Vol. 4)
Malnutrition (co-author: David Pimentel)
(Vol. 4)

Savage, Arline
California Polytechnic State University,
San Luis Obispo
Accounting (co-authors: Doug Cerf and
Kate Lancaster) (Vol. 2)

Savage, Victor R.
National University of Singapore
Singapore (Vol. 7)

Sawyer, John William David
Department of Conservation, New
  Zealand
Global Strategy for Plant Conservation
  (Vol. 6)

Sayre, Nathan F.
University of California, Berkeley
Carrying Capacity (Vol. 5)

Schaldach, Rüdiger
University of Kassel, Germany
Land-Use and Land-Cover Change (Vol. 6)

Scheid, Daniel
Duquesne University
Common Good (Vol. 1)

Schmitt, Peter
Nordregio (Nordic Centre for Spatial
  Development), Stockholm, Sweden
Regional Planning (Vol. 6)
Stockholm, Sweden (co-author: Mitchell
  Reardon) (Vol. 9)

Schmitz, Oswald J.
Yale School of Forestry & Environmental
  Studies
Food Webs (co-author: Jennie R. B. Miller)
  (Vol. 5)

Scholtz, Werner
North-West University, South Africa
Environmental Law—Africa, Sub-Saharan
  (co-author: Louis Kotzé) (Vol. 3)
Climate Change Refugees (Africa) (Vol. 9)

Schorr, David B.
Tel Aviv University Faculty of Law
Environmental Law—Israel (Vol. 3)

Schrag, Duane
The Land Institute
Grains (co-author: David Van Tassel) (Vol. 4)

Schwarz, Peter M.
University of North Carolina, Charlotte
Natural Resource Economics (co-author:
  Michael Herron) (Vol. 4)

Schweiker, William
University of Chicago Divinity School
Responsibility (Vol. 1)

Schweitzer, Jennifer A.
University of Tennessee
Community Ecology (co-authors: Joseph K.
  Bailey, Randy K. Bangert, Mark A.
  Genung, and Gina M. Wimp) (Vol. 5)

Seetharaman, Badrinarayanan
National Law School of India University
Energy Industries—Renewables (India)
  (co-author: Sony Pellissery) (Vol. 7)

Sellmann, James D.
University of Guam
Daoism (Vol. 1)
Pacific Island Environmental Philosophy
  (co-author: Robert Andreas) (Vol. 8)

Selman, Paul
University of Sheffield
Landscape Planning, Large-Scale (Vol. 5)

Serkin, Christopher
Brooklyn Law School
Land Use—Regulation and Zoning (Vol. 3)

Settanni, Ettore
University of Bari Aldo Moro, Taranto, Italy
Life Cycle Assessment (LCA) (co-authors:
  Bruno Notarnicola and Giuseppe
  Tassielli) (Vol. 6)
Life Cycle Costing (LCC) (co-authors:
  Bruno Notarnicola and Giuseppe
  Tassielli) (Vol. 6)

Sharma, Charu
City University of Hong Kong
Chernobyl (Vol. 3)

Shaw, Brian J.
The University of Western Australia
Perth, Australia (Vol. 8)

Shearing, Susan
Sydney Law School
Environmental Law—Australia and New Zealand (co-author: Vernon Tava) (Vol. 3)

Sherman, Benjamin H.
Health Ecological & Economic Dimensions of Major Disturbances Program
Marine Ecosystems Health (Vol. 8)

Sherman, Kenneth
National Oceanic and Atmospheric Administration (NOAA)
Large Marine Ecosystem (LME) Management and Assessment (Vol. 5)

Shuman, Michael H.
Business Alliance for Local Living Economies
Local Living Economies (Vol. 2)

Sideris, Lisa
Indiana University
Evolution (Vol. 1)

Sidharta, Deny
Soemadipradja & Taher
Environmental Law—Southeast Asia (co-authors: Sansanee Dhanasarnsombat, James Kho, Koh Kheng-Lian, Lye Lin Heng, Chit Chit Myint, and Dominic J. Nardi Jr.) (Vol. 3)

Silveira, André F. Reynolds Castel-Branco da
University of Cambridge
Pearl River Delta (Vol. 7)

Silver, Timothy
Appalachian State University
Appalachian Mountains (co-authors: the editors) (Vol. 8)

Simanis, Erik
Johnson Graduate School of Management, Cornell University
Base of the Pyramid (co-authors: Mark B. Milstein, Stuart Hart, and Duncan Duke) (Vol. 2)
Poverty (co-authors: Mark B. Milstein, Stuart Hart, and Duncan Duke) (Vol. 2)

Simmons, Frederick
Yale Divinity School
Sin and Evil (Vol. 1)

Sims, Michael D.
Independent scholar, Eugene, Oregon
Waste (Vol. 1)
Silent Spring (Vol. 3)
Waste—Social Aspects (Vol. 10)

Small, Ernest
Agriculture and Agri-Food Canada
Alfalfa (Vol. 4)
Hemp (Vol. 4)

Smil, Vaclav
University of Manitoba
Dung (Vol. 4)
Solar Energy (Vol. 4)
Wind Energy (Vol. 4)

Smith, Charlotte A.
WM Healthcare Solutions, Inc.; PharmEcology Services
Health Care Industry (co-authors: Peter Whitehouse, Jeffrey Zabinski, and Andrew Jameton) (Vol. 2)

Smith, David H.
Yale University
Bioethics (Vol. 1)

Smith, M. Alexander
University of Guelph
Species Barcoding (Vol. 6)

Smith, Polly J.
Utica College
Rural Development—Developed World
(co-authors: Gregory M. Fulkerson and
Alexander R. Thomas) (Vol. 2)
Rural Development—Developing World
(co-authors: Gregory M. Fulkerson and
Alexander R. Thomas) (Vol. 2)

Smith, William K.
Wake Forest University
Boundary Ecotones (Vol. 5)
Volume Introduction (Vol. 5)
Biological Indicators—Ecosystems (Vol. 6)

Smyntyna, Olena V.
Odessa I. I. Mechnikov National University
Ukraine (Vol. 9)

Sohail, M.
WEDC (Water, Engineering and
Development Centre), Loughborough
University
Public–Private Partnerships (co-author: Sue
Cavill) (Vol. 2)
Water Use and Rights (co-author: Sue Cavill)
(Vol. 2)

Sommer, Jan Henning
University of Bonn
Biological Indicators—Genetic (co-author:
Nicolas Gerber) (Vol. 6)

Sonesson, Ulf
Swedish Institute for Food and
Biotechnology (SIK)
Food, Frozen (Vol. 4)

Song Quanbin
Shanghai Bi Ke Clean Energy Technology
Co., Ltd.

Energy Industries—Coal (co-authors: Zhao
Ning, Lian Ming, and Xu Guangwen)
(Vol. 2)
Coal (co-authors: Lian Ming, Zhao Ning,
and Xu Guangwen) (Vol. 4)

Sonnenfeld, David A.
State University of New York College of
Environmental Science and Forestry
Rule of Law (Vol. 7)

Soupir, Michelle Lynn
Iowa State University
Pollution, Nonpoint Source (Vol. 5)

Spangenberg, Joachim
Helmholtz Centre for Environment
Research, Halle, Germany
Agenda 21 (Vol. 6)

Spiering, David J.
Buffalo Museum of Science
Rewilding (Vol. 5)

Spretnak, Charlene
California Institute of Integral Studies
Green Parties (Vol. 1)

Sreedharan, Priya
Energy and Environmental Economics,
Inc.
Utilities Regulation and Energy Efficiency
(co-authors: Ranjit Bharvirkar, Chris
Greacen, Chuenchom Sangarasri
Greacen, Fredrich Kahrl, Mahesh
Patankar, and James H. Williams) (Vol. 7)

Sroufe, Robert P.
Duquesne University
Supply Chain Analysis (Vol. 6)

Starrs, Paul F.
University of Nevada
Ranching (co-author: Lynn Huntsinger)
(Vol. 4)

Stave, Krystyna
University of Nevada, Las Vegas
Las Vegas, United States (co-author: Abby
   Beck) (Vol. 8)

Steiner, Frederick
The University of Texas at Austin
Landscape Architecture (Vol. 5)

Steinfeldt, Michael
University of Bremen
Nanotechnology (Vol. 4)

Stevens, John G.
University of North Carolina Asheville
Greenhouse Gases (Vol. 4)

Stevens, Maggie R.
University of Tennessee
Ecosystem Management (co-authors: Kay E.
   Franzreb, Becky L. Jacobs, and John D.
   Peine) (Vol. 3)

Stevenson, Robert B.
James Cook University, Cairns, Australia
Education, Environmental (co-authors:
   Fiona Mwaniki and Aravella Zachariou)
   (Vol. 9)

Stewart, Emma
Business for Social Responsibility
Ecosystem Services (Vol. 2)

Stewart, Michelle O.
University of Colorado at Boulder
Tibetan Plateau (Vol. 7)

Storvick, Truman
University of Missouri
Energy Industries—Nuclear (Vol. 2)
Carbon Capture and Sequestration (Vol. 4)

Straka, Thomas J.
Clemson University
Forest Management Industry (Vol. 2)

Forest Reserve Act (Vol. 3)
Forest Products—Timber (Vol. 4)
Forest Management (Vol. 8)

Striffler, Steve
University of New Orleans
Labor (Vol. 8)

Subic, Aleksandar
School of Aerospace, Mechanical and
   Manufacturing Engineering, RMIT
   University
Sporting Goods Industry (Vol. 2)

Sumaila, U. Rashid
The University of British Columbia
Fisheries Management (Vol. 5)

Sun, Jinong
Fayetteville State University
Steel Industry (co-author: Wenxian Zhang)
   (Vol. 7)

Sun, Li
Bielefeld University
Rural Development (co-author: Sony
   Pellissery) (Vol. 7)

Sundrum, Albert
Kassel University
Animal Husbandry (Vol. 4)

Sundstrom, Shana M.
Nebraska Cooperative Fish & Wildlife
   Research Unit, University of Nebraska
Resilience (co-authors: Craig R. Allen and
   Ahjond S. Garmestani) (Vol. 5)

Supino, Stefania
Salerno University
Social Life Cycle Assessment (S-LCA) (Vol. 6)

Surendra, Lawrence
University of Mysore
Chennai, India (Vol. 7)

Sutton, Adrienne J.
NOAA Pacific Marine Environmental
  Laboratory
Ocean Acidification—Measurement (Vol. 6)

T

Takahashi Guevara, Bruno
State University of New York (SUNY-ESF)
Lima, Peru (Vol. 8)

Takang, J. Manyitabot
University of Cologne
African Union (AU) (co-author: Caroline
  Muthoni Njuki) (Vol. 9)
International Conflict Resolution (Vol. 9)
Water Use and Rights (Africa) (Vol. 9)

Takano Takenaka Kohei
Research Institute for Humanity and Nature
Genetic Resources (Vol. 7)

Talhelm, Alan F.
University of Idaho
Nitrogen Saturation (co-author: Kurt
  Pregitzer) (Vol. 5)

Tassielli, Giuseppe
University of Bari Aldo Moro, Taranto, Italy
Life Cycle Assessment (LCA) (co-authors:
  Bruno Notarnicola and Ettore Settanni)
  (Vol. 6)
Life Cycle Costing (LCC) (co-authors: Ettore
  Settanni and Bruno Notarnicola) (Vol. 6)

Tava, Vernon
University of Auckland
*Environmental Law—Australia and New
  Zealand* (co-author: Susan Shearing)
  (Vol. 3)

Taylor, Joseph E., III
Simon Fraser University
Columbia River (Vol. 8)

Taylor, Laura
York University
Toronto, Canada (Vol. 8)

Taylor, Prue
University of Auckland
Common Heritage of Mankind Principle
  (Vol. 3)

Techera, Erika J.
Macquarie University
*Convention for the Prohibition of Fishing with
  Long Drift Nets in the South Pacific* (Vol. 3)

Teisl, Mario F.
University of Maine
Ecolabeling (Vol. 3)
Values (co-author: Mark W. Anderson)
  (Vol. 10)

Telesetsky, Anastasia
University of Idaho College of Law
Real Property Law (Vol. 3)
Fisheries (China) (Vol. 7)

Tepley, Alan J.
University of Colorado
Disturbance (co-authors: Juan Paritsis and
  Thomas T. Veblen) (Vol. 5)

Teplyakov, Victor K.
Seoul National University
Pollution, Point Source (Vol. 5)
Novosibirsk, Russia (Vol. 9)

Testa, Mario
University of Salerno
Business Reporting Methods (Vol. 6)

Textiles Intelligence editorial staff
Textiles Industry (Vol. 2)

Therivel, Riki
Levett-Therivel Sustainability Consultants,
  United Kingdom
Strategic Environmental Assessment (SEA)
  (Vol. 6)

Thomas, Alexander R.
State University of New York, College at Oneonta
Rural Development—Developed World (co-authors: Gregory M. Fulkerson and Polly J. Smith) (Vol. 2)
Rural Development—Developing World (co-authors: Gregory M. Fulkerson and Polly J. Smith) (Vol. 2)

Thompson, Anthony
Blekinge Institute of Technology
Natural Step Framework, The (TNSF) (co-author: Richard Blume) (Vol. 2)
Product-Service Systems (PSSs) (Vol. 2)

Thompson, Kirill Ole
National Taiwan University
Traditional Knowledge (China) (Vol. 7)

Thompson, Paul B.
Michigan State University
Agriculture (Vol. 1)

Thrasher, Rachel Denae
Pardee Center for the Study of the Longer-Range Future, Boston University
Fair Trade (Vols. 2, 3)
Free Trade (Vols. 2, 3)
Organization of American States (OAS) (Vol. 8)

Tilbury, Daniella
University of Gloucestershire
Education, Higher (Vol. 10)

Tisdell, Clement Allan
University of Queensland, St. Lucia
Conservation Value (Vol. 4)

Topal, Erkan
Curtin University
Mining (Australia) (co-author: Diarmid Mather) (Vol. 8)

Totman, Conrad
Yale University
Japan (Vol. 7)

Treweek, Jo
Treweek Environmental Consultants, United Kingdom
Ecological Impact Assessment (EcIA) (Vol. 6)

Trexler, Mark C.
Sustainability and Innovation Division, Det Norske Veritas
Climate Change Mitigation (co-author: Laura Kosloff) (Vol. 3)

Tribsch, Andreas
University of Salzburg
Refugia (Vol. 5)

Troster, Lawrence
GreenFaith
Judaism (Vol. 1)

Trumbull, Nathaniel S.
University of Connecticut
St. Petersburg, Russia (Vol. 9)

Tucker, Mary Evelyn
Yale University
Confucianism (Vol. 1)
World Religions and Ecology (Vol. 1)

Turner, Graham M.
CSIRO Ecosystem Sciences
The Limits to Growth (Vol. 6)

Turnock, Stephen
University of Southampton
Energy Industries—Wave and Tidal (Vol. 2)

Tuxill, John
Western Washington University
Comanagement (Vol. 5)

Twigg, Caroline
World Business Council for Sustainable
  Development (WBCSD)
Cement Industry (co-author: Roland
  Hunziker) (Vol. 2)

Tyman, Shannon
University of Oregon
Anthroposophy (Vol. 1)
Biophilia (Vol. 1)

Tyrrell, Ian
University of New South Wales
Australia (Vol. 8)

Tyukodi, Gergely
Corvinus University of Budapest
*International Organization for
  Standardization (ISO)* (co-authors:
  Gyula Vastag and Áron Antal)
  (Vol. 6)

U

Underwood, Jared G.
United States Fish and Wildlife Service
Adaptive Resource Management (ARM)
  (Vol. 5)

Uriarte Ayo, Rafael
Basque Country University
Heavy Metals (Vol. 4)

V

Vaccari, David A.
Stevens Institute of Technology
Phosphorus (Vol. 4)

Vallero, Daniel Alan
Duke University
Waste—Engineering Aspects (Vol. 10)

Vallvé, Frederic
Saint Mary's University
Guano (Vol. 4)

Van der Ryn, Sim
Ecological Design Collaborative
Design and Architecture (Vol. 10)

Van Dyke, Jon M. (1943–2011)
University of Hawaii
International Law (Vol. 3)

Van Horn, Gavin
Southwestern University
Biocentrism (Vol. 1)

van Niekerk, Dewald
North-West University, South Africa
Disaster Risk Management (Vol. 9)

Van Saanen, Marisa B.
Yale Law School
World Bank (Vol. 1)

Van Tassel, David
The Land Institute
Grains (co-author: Duane Schrag) (Vol. 4)

Van Wensveen, Louke
Academia Vitae
Virtues and Vices (Vol. 1)

Van Wieren, Gretel
Yale University
Restoration (Vol. 1)

Van Zyl, Dirk
Norman B. Keevil Institute of Mining
  Engineering, University of British
  Columbia, Vancouver
Mining (co-author: Gagne, David) (Vol. 2)

Vanclay, Frank
University of Groningen
Food, Value-Added (co-author: Anna
  Gralton) (Vol. 4)

Vasey, Daniel E.
Divine Word College
Agriculture (Vol. 2)
Agriculture—Organic and Biodynamic (Vol. 4)
Manure, Animal (Vol. 4)
Manure, Human (Vol. 4)
Volume Introduction (Vol. 4)

Vastag, Gyula
Pannon University & Corvinus University
of Budapest
*International Organization for
Standardization (ISO)* (co-authors:
Gergely Tyukodi and Áron Antal) (Vol. 6)

Veblen, Thomas T.
University of Colorado
Disturbance (co-authors: Alan J. Tepley and
Juan Paritsis) (Vol. 5)
Outbreak Species (co-author: Juan Paritsis)
(Vol. 5)

Vermeer, Eduard B.
International Institute for Asian Studies,
Leiden
China (Vol. 7)

Veteto, James R.
University of North Texas
Ecovillages (co-author: Joshua Lockyer)
(Vol. 8)

Visser, Wayne
CSR International
CSR and CSR 2.0 (Vol. 2)

Viviani-Lima, Juliana Baitz
University of São Paulo
Groundwater Management (co-authors:
Bruno Pirilo Conicelli and Ricardo
Hirata) (Vol. 5)

Voigt, Christina
University of Oslo
*Development, Sustainable—Overview of
Laws and Commissions* (Vol. 3)

Vogiatzakis, Ioannis N.
Open University of Cyprus
Genetic Resources (Vol. 9)

von Hippel, David F.
Nautilus Institute for Security and
Sustainability
Energy Security (East Asia) (co-authors:
Peter Hayes, Fredrich Kahrl, and James
H. Williams) (Vol. 7)

Vrtis, George
Carleton College
Rocky Mountains (Vol. 8)

W

Wachter, Susan M.
University of Pennsylvania
Urbanization (Europe) (co-authors:
Alexander M. Keating and Eugenie L.
Birch) (Vol. 9)

Wackernagel, Mathis
Global Footprint Network
Ecological Footprint Accounting (Vol. 6)

Waddock, Sandra
Carroll School of Management, Boston
College
Stakeholder Theory (Vol. 2)
United Nations Global Compact (Vol. 2)

Wagner, Gernot
Environmental Defense Fund
Energy Industries—Overview of Renewables
(Vol. 2)

Wakild, Emily
Boise State University
Parks and Protected Areas (Vol. 8)

Walker, Sean B.
University of Waterloo
Brownfield Redevelopment (co-author: Keith
Hipel) (Vol. 5)

Wallis, Robert
Richmond the American International
    University in London
Shamanism (Vol. 1)

Walmsley, Andreas
Leeds Metropolitan University
Travel and Tourism Industry (co-author:
    Xavier Font) (Vol. 2)

Wang, Deane
University of Vermont
Nutrient and Biogeochemical Cycling (Vol. 5)

Ward, Evan R.
Brigham Young University
Irrigation (Vol. 5)
Travel and Tourism Industry (Vol. 8)

Ware, Alyn
International Association of Lawyers
    Against Nuclear Arms
*New Zealand Nuclear Free Zone,
    Disarmament, and Arms Control Act* (Vol. 3)

Washington, Sylvia Hood
Northwestern University
Africa, Western (Vol. 9)

Watson, Fiona J.
University of Dundee
United Kingdom and Ireland (Vol. 9)

Watson, Ingrid
University of the Witwatersrand
Mining (Africa) (co-authors: Tracy-Lynn
    Humby and Mavis Hermanus) (Vol. 9)

Wayner, Chad
University of Virginia
Ethics, Natural Law (Vol. 1)
God (co-author: Charles Mathewes) (Vol. 1)

Webster, D. G.
Dartmouth College
Fish (Vol. 4)

Weiner, Douglas R.
University of Arizona
Central Asia (Vol. 9)
Lake Baikal (Vol. 9)
Russia and the Soviet Union (Vol. 9)

Weiss, Anita M.
University of Oregon
Pakistan (co-author: Muhammad Aurang
    Zeb Mughal) (Vol. 9)

Welch, David
International Union for Conservation of
    Nature (IUCN)
Light Pollution and Biological Systems
    (co-authors: R. G. S. Bidwell, Robert
    Dick, and Peter Goering) (Vol. 5)

Wells, Peter
Cardiff Business School
Automobile Industry (Vol. 2)

Wells-Dang, Andrew
Independent scholar, Hoi An, Vietnam
Nongovernmental Organizations (NGOs)
    (Vol. 7)

Wessels, Joshka
Lund University, Sweden
*Water Use and Rights (Middle East and
    North Africa)* (Vol. 9)

Westra, Laura
University of Windsor
Justice, Environmental (Vol. 3)
Refugees, Environmental (Vol. 3)

Wheeler, Stephen M.
University of California, Davis
Development, Urban (Vol. 2)

Whited, Tamara L.
Indiana University of Pennsylvania
France (Vol. 9)

Whitehead, Neil L. (1956–2012)
University of Wisconsin, Madison
Amazonia (Vol. 8)

Whitehouse, Peter
Case Western Reserve University
Health—Public and Environmental
(co-author: Daniel George) (Vol. 2)
Health Care Industry (co-authors: Jeffrey
Zabinski, Andrew Jameton, and
Charlotte A. Smith) (Vol. 2)
Pharmaceutical Industry (co-authors: Daniel
George and Chris Laszlo) (Vol. 2)

Wiek, Arnim
Arizona State University
Transdisciplinary Research (co-author:
Daniel J. Lang) (Vol. 6)

Williams, James H.
Monterey Institute of International Studies
Energy Security (East Asia) (co-authors:
Peter Hayes, Fredrich Kahrl, and David
F. von Hippel) (Vol. 7)
Utilities Regulation and Energy Efficiency
(co-authors: Ranjit Bharvirkar, Fredrich
Kahrl, Chris Greacen, Chuenchom
Sangarasri Greacen, Mahesh Patankar,
and Priya Sreedharan) (Vol. 7)

Wilson, Kerrie A.
The University of Queensland
Biodiversity Hotspots (co-authors: Michael
Bode, Takuya Iwamura, and Hugh P.
Possingham) (Vol. 5)

Wilson, Mark
Northumbria University
Southeast Asia (Vol. 7)

Wimp, Gina M.
Georgetown University
Community Ecology (co-authors: Joseph
K. Bailey, Randy K. Bangert, Mark
A. Genung, and Jennifer A. Schweitzer)
(Vol. 5)

Winter, Miriam Therese
Hartford Seminary
The Universe Story (Vol. 1)

Wirzba, Norman
Duke Divinity School
Agrarianism (Vol. 1)

Wise-West, Tiffany
University of California, Santa Cruz
Water Use and Rights (Vol. 8)

Wisner, Priscilla S.
Montana State University
Performance Metrics (co-author: Marc J.
Epstein) (Vol. 2)

Wissenburg, Marcel
Radboud University Nijmegen
Libertarianism (Vol. 1)

Wolf, Julia
EBS Business School, Germany
Global Reporting Initiative (GRI)
(co-author: Anna Grobecker) (Vol. 6)
Organic and Consumer Labels (Vol. 6)
Shipping and Freight (co-author: Anna
Grobecker) (Vol. 9)
Shipping (co-author: Anna Grobecker)
(Vol. 10)

Wolf, Steven
Imperial College, London; Cornell
University
Wise Use Movement (Vol. 4)

Wolfenbarger, L. LaReesa
University of Nebraska, Omaha
Agriculture—Genetically Engineered Crops
(co-author: John P. McCarty) (Vol. 4)

Worthy, Kenneth
Independent scholar, Berkeley, California
Ecopsychology (Vol. 1)

Wouters, Patricia
University of Dundee
Transboundary Water Law (co-author: Ruby
Moynihan) (Vol. 3)

Wowk, Kateryna M.
Global Ocean Forum
Fishing and Whaling Legislation (co-author:
Duncan E. J. Currie) (Vol. 3)
Ocean Resource Management (Vol. 5)
Marine Preserves (Vol. 8)

Wu, Jianguo
Arizona State University
Green GDP (co-author: Tong Wu) (Vol. 2)

Wu, Tong
Northern Arizona University
Green GDP (co-author: Jianguo Wu) (Vol. 2)

Wynn, Graeme
University of British Columbia
Canada (co-author: Matthew Evenden)
(Vol. 8)

X

Xu Guangwen
Chinese Academy of Sciences
Energy Industries—Coal (co-authors: Zhao
Ning, Song Quanbin, and Lian Ming)
(Vol. 2)
Coal (co-authors: Lian Ming, Song
Quanbin, and Zhao Ning,) (Vol. 4)

Y

Yanarella, Ernest J.
University of Kentucky
Vancouver, Canada (Vol. 8)

York, Richard
University of Oregon
$I = P \times A \times T$ *Equation* (Vol. 6)

Yu Wenxuan
China University of Political Science and
Law
Biodiversity Conservation Legislation (China)
(Vol. 7)
Biosafety Legislation (China) (Vol. 7)

Z

Zabinski, Jeffrey
Case Western Reserve University
Health Care Industry (co-authors: Peter
Whitehouse, Andrew Jameton, and
Charlotte A. Smith) (Vol. 2)

Zachariou, Aravella
Cyprus Pedagogical Institute, Nicosia,
Cyprus
Education, Environmental (co-authors:
Robert B. Stevenson and Fiona
Mwaniki) (Vol. 9)

Zhang, Dongyong
Henan Agricultural University
Corporate Accountability (China) (Vol. 7)

Zhang, Wenxian
Rollins College
Steel Industry (co-author: Jinong Sun) (Vol. 7)

Zhang, Yanli
Stephen F. Austin State University
Best Management Practices (BMPs)
(co-author: Matthew W. McBroom)
(Vol. 5)

Zhao, Fengping
Zhengzhou University
Education, Female (co-author: Leemamol
Mathew) (Vol. 7)

Zhao Ning
Shanghai Bi Ke Clean Energy Technology
Co., Ltd.

Energy Industries—Coal (co-authors: Lian Ming, Song Quanbin, and Xu Guangwen) (Vol. 2)
Coal (co-authors: Lian Ming, Song Quanbin, and Zhao Ning) (Vol. 4)

Zhu, Jieming
National University of Singapore; Tongji University
Property Rights (China) (Vol. 7)

Ziganshina, Dinara
University of Dundee
Environmental Law—Russia and Central Asia (co-authors: Irina Krasnova and Bakhtiyor R. Mukhammadiev) (Vol. 3)

Zimmermann, Niklaus E.
Swiss Federal Research Institute WSL
Biological Indicators—Species (co-author: Peter B. Pearman) (Vol. 6)

Zyglidopoulos, Stelios C.
University of Cambridge
Brent Spar (Vol. 3)

Volume 10 Index

commons, the. *See* "Tragedy of the
      Commons, The"
Community, 57–66
  city planning and, 62
  dangers of, 64
  definition of, 58–59
  disasters and, 64–65
  evolution of, 57–58
  "the good life," 61–62
  individualism and, 63–64
  Jacobs, Jane, 62, 63
  key aspects of, 59–62
  "living locally," 61
  Mumford, Lewis, 62
  public awareness and, 63
  restoration of, 59
  the "share" economy, 63
  "third places" (informal places), 62–63
Crutzen, Paul. *See under* **Anthropocene
      Epoch**

D

Daly, Herman. *See under* **Economics,
      Steady State**
data centers, x
degrowth, xi, 59, 84
Design and Architecture, i, 68–76
  architects and, 74–75
  bio-tecture, 75
  building metabolisms, three strategies for, 72
  Chauvet Caves (southern France), xi, 68
  decarbonizing and dematerialization
        through, 72–73
  early education and, 70
  Gaia hypothesis, 71
  The Great Turning, 68
  Leadership in Energy and Environmental
        Design (LEED) program, 71
  Modernist architecture movement, 69–70
  monumentality and, 73–75
  nature as a model for, 72
  ordinances vs. common sense, 70–71
  Physicalists vs. Vitalists, 69
  regenerative buildings, 71
  rigid instability, 69
drought
  impact on food production, 10, 149, 235
  migration and, 152, 153

E

e-waste, 226
Economics, Steady State, 78–85
  Daly, Herman & Georgescu-Roegen,
        Nicholas, 80–82
  limits-to-growth argument, 79–80
  Malthus, T. Robert, 78, 184
  Mill, John Stuart, 78–79
  neo-Malthusianism, 78, 79
  Resources for the Future (RFF), 79
ecosystem services. *See* payment for ecosystem services
      (PES) *under* **Natural Capital**
education
  Directory of Sustainability Programs, 243–262
  See also **Design and Architecture;
        Education, Higher**
Education, Higher, 86–97
  carbon reduction initiatives, 90
  Greening the Campus movement, 87
  interdisciplinary research approaches, 90
  partnerships and, 91–92
  permaculture and, 92
  specialist courses, 93
Energy Efficiency, 98–106
  "efficiency resource," 98
  indirect benefits of, 102
  market failures, 103–104
  returns on investments, 102
  steps to achieve, 103
  technological innovation of, 101–102
  terminology of, 98–100
  whole systems and, 102

F

Fisheries, 108–115
  heavy metal toxins, 112
  herring, 108–109
  individual transferrable quotas (ITQs), 113
  models of populations, 113
  overfishing, 108, 109–110
  pollution of, 110
  serial depletion of, 110
  shifting baseline syndrome, 109
  subsidies and, 112–113
  trawlers, 109
  trophic levels of fish, 110–111
Food Security, 116–122
  animal consumption and, 119–120
  double and triple cropping, 117–118
  fertilizer use and, 116, 117
  hybrid crops, 116
  Plan B, 121

production in Africa, 117
rise in local food production and organic
    farming, 120
urban gardens, 120
victory gardens, 120
water shortages and, 118–119
water users associations, 118
White Revolution in India, 120
World Food Bank (WFB) (proposed entity), 121
yield increases, 116–118
See also Green Revolution
fossil fuels. *See under* **Mobility**
free trade. *See* free trade agreements (FTAs) *under*
    Global Trade

G

Geoengineering, 124–128
artificial weather, 126
carbon capture and sequestration or storage
    (CCS), 125
solar radiation management (SRM), 125
terraforming, 124
Georgescu-Roegen, Nicholas. *See under* **Economics,**
    Steady State
Global Trade, 129–138
Environmental Kuznets Curve (EKC), 131–132
environmental regulation and innovation,
    133–134
free trade agreements (FTAs), 136
General Agreement on Tariffs and Trade (GATT),
    130, 134, 135
green growth, 130
intellectual property rights, 135–136
pollution haven hypothesis, 132
regulatory race to the bottom, 132–133
Rio Declaration on Environment and
    Development, 130
Rio+20 Conference, 130
scale, composition, and technique effects, 130–131
subsidies and, 135
World Trade Organization (WTO), 129, 130,
    134–135, 136, 137
globalization. *See under* **Migration**
Great Britain. *See* United Kingdom
Green Revolution, 13, 117

H

Haiti, earthquake damage in, 70, 151
health, public, 136, 162, 235, 236
    See also **Population**
    See under **Aging**
HIV/AIDS. *See under* **Population**

Holocene epoch. *See under* **Anthropocene Epoch**
hybrid crops. *See* **Food Security**

I

Industrial Revolution, 20, 46, 189, 234
    See also **Progress**

J

Jacobs, Jane. *See under* **Community**
Japan. *See* Fukushima Daiichi Nuclear Power Plant,
    Japan *under* **Nuclear Power**

K

Kyoto Protocol (KP), 41, 133

L

Leopold, Aldo. *See under* **Waste—Engineering**
    Aspects
Local Solutions to Global Problems, 140–146
carbon dioxide (CO_2), 140
conditional cooperation, 142–143
real-time feedback, 144
successful governance of common resources, 141
See also "Tragedy of the Commons, The"
localism. *See* **Community**

M

Migration, 148–156
environmental refugees, 149, 152
food production and, 151
globalization and, 154–155
long vs. short distance migration causes, 150,
    152, 153
natural disasters and, 151, 153
sea level rise and, 148, 150–151, 153
skilled labor movement, 155
Mobility, 157–164
automobiles, 160
bikeways, 159
fossil fuels and, 161–164
integrated public transportation, 157–158
regional considerations for, 160
transit-oriented development (TOD), 158
urban planning and, 159–160
urban sprawl and, 160, 161–162
walkability of a city, 159
Mumford, Lewis. *See under* **Community**

Master Index for the *Berkshire Encyclopedia of Sustainability*

The following is a combined index of all ten volumes of the *Berkshire Encyclopedia of Sustainability*. Each entry lists the volume(s) and page number(s) where each entry may be found. Please refer to the series page on page VI of this volume for the names of the different volumes of the *Encyclopedia of Sustainability*.

A

Airline Industry, Vol. 2: 17–22, 23, 459–460,
     Vol. 10: 207
   emission issues and, **Vol. 2:** 18–19
   emission reduction regulations, **Vol. 2:** 4
   sustainability measures in, **Vol. 2:** 19, 20, 21
Aitareya Upanishad, **Vol. 1:** 197–198
   See also **Sacred Texts**
Akan people, **Vol. 1:** 210
Akha, **Vol. 1:** 218–219
   cultivation practices and, **Vol. 1:** 218–219
Alaska, United States, **Vol. 1:** 376–377, **Vol. 5:** 101,
     237, 309
Alaska National Interest Lands Act (ANILCA) (1980),
     Vol. 3: 508, **Vol. 4:** 353
Albanese, Catherine, **Vol. 1:** 286
Alfalfa, Vol. 4: 22–24
Algae, Vol. 4: 25–29
algae blooms, **Vol. 5:** 269, 304, 305, 331, 335, 353
   See also **Eutrophication**
algal toxins, **Vol. 5:** 125
Algonquin to Adirondack Conservation Association
     (A2A), **Vol. 5:** 342
Allah, **Vol. 1:** 247, 411
Allahabad, India, **Vol. 1:** 422
Allee effects, **Vol. 5:** 38, 39, 315, 372
allele, **Vol. 5:** 23, 129, 327, **Vol. 6:** 20, 21
   See also DNA
Allen, Will, **Vol. 5:** 392
Alliance of Religions and Conservation (ARC), **Vol. 1:**
     28, 240, 363, 438, 442
allin kawsay (well-being), **Vol. 1:** 235
alloys. *See* **Electronics—Raw Materials; Heavy
     Metals; Rare Earth Elements;** *individual
     mineral articles*
alpine treeline. *See* treelines
Alps. S*ee* Little Ice Age
alternative energy, **Vol. 1:** 64, 172, 291
alternative globalization movement, **Vol. 1:** 415
Aluminum, Vol. 4: 30–35, 94, 261, **Vol. 5:** 182, 268
   recycling, **Vol. 4:** 34, 282, 401, 402, 403, 404, 405, 407
Alzheimer's disease, **Vol. 2:** 270
Amazon basin, **Vol. 5:** 339
Amazon River, Vol. 5: 196, **Vol. 8: 6–9**
   climatic changes, historical, **Vol. 8:** 6–7
   human colonization in, **Vol. 8:** 7–8
   Pleistocene refuge theory, **Vol. 8:** 7
   rubber economy in, **Vol. 8:** 7–8, 43
Amazonia, Vol. 1: 177, 428, 430, **Vol. 5:** 114, 265, 328,
     Vol. 8: 10–13
   cacao cultivation in, **Vol. 4:** 62
   rain forests in, **Vol. 5:** 83, 271, 326, 346

   rubber collection in, **Vol. 4:** 422
   See also rain forests; tropical rain forests
American Clean Energy and Security Act, **Vol. 3:**
     483, 484
American Indians. *See* Native Americans
American Lung Association *State of the Air 2010* report,
     Vol. 3: 42
American Southwest
   cattle grazing and disturbance, **Vol. 5:** 101
   water distribution in, **Vol. 5:** 222
American Unitarian Church, **Vol. 1:** 398
American West
   mining laws in, **Vol. 4:** 330
   national parks in, **Vol. 4:** 353
ammonia
   fertilizers and, **Vol. 4:** 130, 131, 133, 202, 209, 273,
     274, 337, 374
   refrigerants and, **Vol. 4:** 157
Amnesty International, **Vol. 3:** 37
Anabaptists. *See* **Christianity, Anabaptist**
Analects (Confucian text), **Vol. 1:** 76
   See also **Confucianism**
Anastas, Paul T., **Vol. 2:** 58
Andean-Amazonian region, **Vol. 1:** 234
Andean region, **Vol. 1:** 233
Anderson, Ray, **Vol. 2:** xxii, 307, 451
   lifecycle thinking / management, **Vol. 2:** 310
Anderson, Warren, **Vol. 3:** 10
Andes Mountains, Vol. 4: 302, 303, **Vol. 8: 14–16**
   agriculture in, **Vol. 4:** 11–12, 417
   campesinos (peasants and rural farmers), **Vol. 1:** 234,
     Vol. 8: 15, 63
   glaciers in, **Vol. 4:** 181, 182, 183
Angola
   diamonds and, **Vol. 4:** 84, 175, 176
animal feeding operations (AFO), **Vol. 5:** 303, 304
   concentrated animal feeding operation (CAFO),
     Vol. 5: 409
Animal Husbandry, Vol. 4: 36–39
Animal Liberation Front, **Vol. 3:** 144
animal products. *See* **Manure; Non-Timber Forest
     Products**
animal rights
   advocacy, **Vol. 1:** 18–19, 119
   utilitarianism and, **Vol. 1:** 404
Animals, Human Relationships to, Vol. 1: 15–19, 210,
     216, 219, 261, 405, 410–411
   beauty and, **Vol. 1:** 34
   cognition, **Vol. 1:** 250
   factory farming of, **Vol. 1:** 15–16, 350, 405, 411
   hunting, **Vol. 1:** 16, 214
   implications for sustainability and, **Vol. 1:** 17
   liberation of, **Vol. 1:** 270
   as resources, **Vol. 1:** 19

Arctic Environmental Protection Strategy (AEPS),
    Vol. 3: 202, 203
Arctic Human Development Report (AHDR), **Vol. 1:**
    213, **Vol. 3:** 202
Arctic Offshore Oil and Gas Guidelines, **Vol. 3:**
    202, 203
areas to be avoided (ATBAs), **Vol. 3:** 80
areography, **Vol. 5:** 32
Argentina, **Vol. 3:** 311
    biofuel production in, **Vol. 4:** 55, 56
    environmental law in, **Vol. 3:** 259–260
    glaciers in, **Vol. 4:** 182, 183
    ranching in, **Vol. 4:** 389
    See also **Southern Cone**
Argentina v. Uruguay, **Vol. 3:** 310, 466, 470
Arisandi, Prigi, **Vol. 7:** 347
    Ecological Observation and Wetlands Conservation
    (Ecoton), **Vol. 7:** 347
Aristotle, **Vol. 1:** 71, 101, 166, 258, 309, 392, 395
Ariyaratne, A. T., **Vol. 1:** 270
Arizona State University (ASU) School of
    Sustainability, **Vol. 6:** 355
Armed Conflict and the Environment, Vol. 3: 1–5
    court cases and events, **Vol. 3:** 3
    International Committee of the Red Cross (ICRC),
    Vol. 3: 4
    international standards, **Vol. 3:** 2–3
    United Nations Compensation Commission
    (UNCC), **Vol. 3:** 3–4
Arn, **Vol. 1:** 433
Arnold, Ron, **Vol. 1:** 435
    See also **Wise Use Movement**
arsenic, **Vol. 4:** 217, 218
Articles of State Responsibility (2001), **Vol. 3:** 466
ARtificial Intelligence for Ecosystem Services
    (ARIES), **Vol. 5:** 114
artificial lighting, **Vol. 4:** 258–259
artisanal food. *See* **Food, Value-Added**
asana, **Vol. 1:** 200
Ýsatrú, **Vol. 1:** 299
    See also **Paganism and Neopaganism**
asbestos, **Vol. 3:** 74
ascesis, **Vol. 1:** 56
asceticism. *See* **Simplicity and Asceticism**
Asia Pacific Green Network, **Vol. 1:** 195
Asia
    agriculture in, **Vol. 5:** 14, 94
    climate change, **Vol. 5:** 163
    greenhouse gases, **Vol. 5:** 165
    large marine ecosystems, **Vol. 5:** 243
    outbreak species in, **Vol. 5:** 286–287

tropical rain forests in, **Vol. 5:** 172, 330
    See also **Indigenous Traditions, Asia**
assemblage assessment of fisheries, **Vol. 6:** 134
Assemblies of God, **Vol. 1:** 58
assisted migration, **Vol. 5:** 106
Association of Southeast Asian Nations (ASEAN),
    Vol. 7: 18–21, 302
    Agreement on the Conservation of Nature and
    Natural Reserves, **Vol. 3:** 268
    Agreement on Transboundary Haze Pollution
    (AATHP), **Vol. 3:** 268
    ASEAN Wildlife Enforcement Network
    (ASEAN-WEN), **Vol. 7:** 19
    Declaration on Environmental Sustainability,
    Vol. 3: 268
    Declaration on Heritage Parks, **Vol. 3:** 268
    environmental law on, **Vol. 3:** 268–269
Association for Women's Rights in Development
    (AWID), **Vol. 1:** 171
asthma, **Vol. 1:** 269
Asva medha, **Vol. 1:** 197
    See also horse sacrifice
Atlantic Empress, **Vol. 5:** 309
    See also oil spills
Atlantic Ocean
    coastal systems management in, **Vol. 5:** 68
    cod fisheries in, **Vol. 5:** 315, 361
    garbage patches in, **Vol. 5:** 283
    North Atlantic, catch profiles in, **Vol. 5:** 146–147
    shifting baselines in, **Vol. 5:** 363
    warming in, **Vol. 5:** 164
    western Atlantic, predator fish levels in, **Vol. 5:** 154
    See also Benguela Current LME (large marine
    ecosystem); **Oceans and Seas**
Atlantic Treaty System (ATS), **Vol. 3:** 193, 194
atmospheric pollution *See* pollution, atmospheric
atmospheric warming, **Vol. 5:** 41, 42
Auckland, New Zealand, Vol. 8: 25–28
    Auckland Plan, **Vol. 8:** 27
    Māori people, **Vol. 8:** 27
    Transition Towns, **Vol. 8:** 27
    walking school bus (WSB) initiatives, **Vol. 8:** 27
Augustine of Hippo, Saint, **Vol. 1:** 71, 95, 166, 333, 343
Austral realm (Australian tropical region), **Vol. 5:** 34
Australia, Vol. 1: 40, 232, **Vol. 2:** 141, 354, **Vol. 3:** 463,
    Vol. 8: 29–34
    agriculture in, **Vol. 5:** 14, 296
    anthropogenic disturbances in, **Vol. 5:** 100
    Bradfield scheme (inland irrigation project),
    Vol. 8: 33
    catchment management in, **Vol. 5:** 60
    Chaffey brothers (George and William), **Vol. 8:** 30
    climate change, **Vol. 5:** 163
    colonization of, **Vol. 8:** 30–31

Bold entries and page numbers denote encyclopedia articles.

Bold entries and page numbers denote encyclopedia articles.

Bold entries and page numbers denote encyclopedia articles.

buildings, **Vol. 1:** 25–26, 33
   See also Leadership in Energy and Environmental
      Design (LEED) rating program
Buildings and Infrastructure, Vol. 10: 26–34
   building environmental assessment methods
      (BEAMs), **Vol. 10:** 31
   ecovillages, **Vol. 10:** 27
   green architecture, **Vol. 10:** 29
   in Norway, **Vol. 10:** 28
   passive design for buildings, **Vol. 10:** 29–30
   retrofitting of, **Vol. 10:** 28, 29
   suburbia and, **Vol. 10:** 27
buildings, design and operational sustainability,
      Vol. 2: 212
   capital vs. running costs, **Vol. 2:** 215–216
   carbon vs. costs, **Vol. 2:** 214–215
   Energy Performance Directive for Buildings
      (EPDB), **Vol. 2:** 212–213
   energy use, **Vol. 2:** 213
   See also **Building Standards, Green;** Leadership in
      Energy and Environmental Design (LEED)
      rating program
Bullard, Robert, **Vol. 3:** 352
Burkina Faso, **Vol. 3:** 311
Burma. *See* Myanmar (Burma)
Burns, James MacGregor, **Vol. 2:** 306
bus rapid transit (BRT) systems. *See* **Public**
      Transportation
Busan Outcome, **Vol. 6:** 207–208
bush encroachment, **Vol. 3:** 102
Bush, George H. W., **Vol. 3:** 379
Bush, George W., **Vol. 1:** 312, 436, **Vol. 2:** 51, **Vol. 3:**
      358, 379
Bushmeat, Vol. 1: 16, **Vol. 4: 59–60,** 163, 382, 383,
      Vol. 5: 154, 190
Bushveld Complex, South Africa, **Vol. 4:** 379
Business Alliance for Local Living Economies
      (BALLE), **Vol. 2:** 315
   See also **Local Living Economies**
business education. *See* **Education, Business**
Business Reporting Methods, Vol. 6: 37–40
business value creation, **Vol. 2:** 433
   See also **Sustainable Value Creation**
Butz, Earl, **Vol. 1:** 11

C

C2C. *See* **Cradle to Cradle**
Cabecar, **Vol. 1:** 29
Cacao, Vol. 4: 62–63
cadmium, **Vol. 1:** 419, **Vol. 4:** 124, 216, 218, 256, 415, 431

manure and, **Vol. 4:** 278
photovoltaics and, **Vol. 4:** 400, 405
Cairo, Egypt, Vol. 9: 48–53
   development problems, **Vol. 9:** 48–49
   green and brown agendas for sustainable
      development, **Vol. 9:** 50
   recycling in, **Vol. 9:** 51
   Sims, David, **Vol. 9:** 49
Cairo Guidelines, **Vol. 3:** 488
calcium
   fertilizer and, **Vol. 4:** 128, 129, 374, 446
   soil fertility and, **Vol. 4:** 436
California, United States
   almond industry in, **Vol. 4:** 224
   Department of Fish and Game, **Vol. 3:** 422
   Environmental Quality Act, **Vol. 3:** 507
   geysers in, **Vol. 4:** 178, 179
   gold in, **Vol. 4:** 184, 294
   habitat fragmentation in, **Vol. 5:** 154
   species succession in, **Vol. 5:** 381, 383
   water rights in, **Vol. 5:** 221–222
California Interfaith Power and Light, **Vol. 1:** 123
Calvert Cliffs' Coordinating Committee, Inc. v. Atomic
      Energy Commission, **Vol. 3:** 393
Cambodia, **Vol. 3:** 471
Cameron County, Texas, United States (pesticide
      testing), **Vol. 6:** 277–278
Campesino a Campesino movement, **Vol. 5:** 13
campesinos (peasants and rural farmers). *See under* **Andes**
      Mountains
Canada, Vol. 1: 121, **Vol. 2:** 141, 166, **Vol. 3:** 203, 463,
      465, 468, **Vol. 8: 48–52**
   administrative law in, **Vol. 3:** 271–272
   agriculture in, **Vol. 5:** 13
   British North America Act (1867), **Vol. 8:** 50–51
   Charter of Rights and Freedoms, **Vol. 3:** 271
   climate change in, **Vol. 5:** 155
   cod stock depletion, **Vol. 8:** 48–49
   constitutional law in, **Vol. 3:** 270–271
   deforestation in, **Vol. 8:** 48
   Hudson's Bay Company (HBC) and fur trade,
      Vol. 8: 49
   hydraulic fracturing (fracking) laws in, **Vol. 5:** 356
   James Bay Project, **Vol. 1:** 121
   judge-made common law, **Vol. 3:** 272
   Keystone XL pipeline, **Vol. 8:** 50
   nonmetal mining, **Vol. 4:** 299
   recycling, **Vol. 4:** 477
   remediation in, **Vol. 5:** 45
   statute law in, **Vol. 3:** 272
   sulfuric acid production, **Vol. 4:** 447, 448
   sustainability in, **Vol. 3:** 274–275
   tar sand oil extraction, **Vol. 8:** 49–50
   uranium in, **Vol. 4:** 464

Coffee, Vol. 4: 77–79, Vol. 5: 81, 299

Cohen, Nevin, **Vol. 2:** 283

coke (coal residue), **Vol. 4:** 74

Cold War, **Vol. 1:** 239–240, 317–318, 388

    chromium stockpiling and, **Vol. 4:** 7

    nuclear weapon testing and, **Vol. 4:** 465

collaborative decision making, **Vol. 5:** 187

Collective Learning, Vol. 10: 49–56

    agriculture and agrarian civilizations and,
        Vol. 10: 53–55

    competitive exclusion between species, **Vol. 10:** 51

    definition of, **Vol. 10:** 49

    feedback loops, **Vol. 10:** 51, 54

    importance of, **Vol. 10:** 49–51

    modern world and, **Vol. 10:** 55

    networks and, **Vol. 10:** 54–55

    technological change and, **Vol. 10:** 51, 54

collective producer responsibility, **Vol. 3:** 427

College Sustainability Report Card, **Vol. 6:** 367

colleges, **Vol. 1:** 148–149

    See also **Education**

Collier, Paul, **Vol. 2:** 358

Collins, Terry, **Vol. 2:** 58

Collocation Services (CoLo), **Vol. 2:** 92–93

Colombia, environmental law in, **Vol. 3:** 261–262

colonialism, **Vol. 1:** 6, 107, 200, 225, 227, 231

    land-culture vs., **Vol. 1:** 233–234

colony collapse disorder (CCD), **Vol. 4:** 224

Colorado beetle, **Vol. 4:** 251

Colorado River, **Vol. 3:** 468

Coltan, Vol. 4: 80–81, 84

Columbia River, Vol. 3: 468, **Vol. 8: 67–69**

    dam impacts on salmon migration, **Vol. 8:** 68

*The Columbia River Watershed: Caring for Creation and
    the Common Good*, **Vol. 1:** 64

Columbia River Watershed bishops, **Vol. 1:** 64

Columbian Exchange, **Vol. 4:** 148

Comanagement, Vol. 5: 74–77

command-and-control approach, **Vol. 3:** 58

commercial fishing. *See* **Fish; Fisheries**

Commission for Sustainable Development (CSD),
    Vol. 6: 6, 9

    CSD Sustainability Development Indicators (SDI),
        Vol. 6: 7, 8–9

    See also **Development Indicators; Rio Earth
        Summit (UN Conference on Environment
        and Development)**

Commission of the European Communities (CEC),
    Vol. 3: 430–431

Commission on the Limits of the Continental Shelf
    (CLCS), **Vol. 3:** 193, 371

Common Good, Vol. 1: 64, **71–72,** 78, 142, 256, 309

**Common Heritage of Mankind Principle, Vol. 3:
    64–69**

    controversies, **Vol. 3:** 66–67

    Moon Treaty (1979), **Vol. 3:** 66

    revolutionizing law of sea, **Vol. 3:** 64–66

    UNCLOS III, **Vol. 3:** 65–66

Common Pool Resources (CPR), **Vol. 4:** 320

common property resources/common pool resources
    (CPRs), **Vol. 1:** 395–396, **Vol. 7:** 326, 329–330

Commoner, Barry, **Vol. 6:** 194, 195

Commonwealth of Independent States, **Vol. 3:** 255

communication, **Vol. 1:** 216, 263–264

    global, **Vol. 1:** 190

communication technology. *See* **Information and
    Communications Technologies (ICT)**

communicative ethics. *See* **Ethics, Communicative**

communitarianism, **Vol. 1:** 165

Community, Vol. 1: 73–74, 307, **Vol. 10: 57–66**

    city planning and, **Vol. 10:** 62

    dangers of, **Vol. 10:** 64

    definition of, **Vol. 10:** 58–59

    disasters and, **Vol. 10:** 64–65

    evolution of, **Vol. 10:** 57–58

    "the good life," **Vol. 10:** 61–62

    individualism and, **Vol. 10:** 63–64

    key aspects of, **Vol. 10:** 59–62

    "living locally," **Vol. 10:** 61

    public awareness and, **Vol. 10:** 63

    restoration of, **Vol. 10:** 59

    the "share" economy, **Vol. 10:** 63

    "third places" (informal places), **Vol. 10:** 62–63

Community and Stakeholder Input, Vol. 6: 58–61

Community Capital, Vol. 2: 68–72

    alternative currency movement, **Vol. 2:** 69

    civic intelligence and, **Vol. 2:** 72

    community culture and importance of, **Vol. 2:** 69–70

    Cooperative Movement, **Vol. 2:** 68–69

    Credit Unions, **Vol. 2:** 69

    ecological capital and, **Vol. 2:** 71

    role of corporations in, **Vol. 2:** 69

community diversity, **Vol. 1:** 38, 353

Community Ecology, Vol. 5: 78–81, 182, 330

    See also ecological community

community-supported agriculture (CSA), **Vol. 4:** 264

    CSA programs, **Vol. 5:** 391

compact city, **Vol. 2:** 412

compact fluorescent lamps (CFLs), **Vol. 4:** 258

company sustainability reporting (CSR), **Vol. 2:**
    244, 320

    See also corporate social responsibility (CSR)

Compassion in World Farming, **Vol. 1:** 292

complementary and alternative medicine (CAM),
    Vol. 2: 261

Bold entries and page numbers denote encyclopedia articles.

Bold entries and page numbers denote encyclopedia articles.

Cornwall Declaration on Environmental Stewardship, **Vol. 1:** 58–59, 180, 181
Corporate Accountability, Vol. 8: 70–74
  Asia Wage Floor Alliance, **Vol. 8:** 72
  Chentex factory, Nicaragua, **Vol. 8:** 71
  Fair Labor Association (FLA), United States, **Vol. 8:** 71
  Fair Wear Campaign, Australia, **Vol. 8:** 72
Corporate Accountability (Africa), Vol. 9: 74–80
  accountability in sub-Saharan Africa, **Vol. 9:** 75
  different meanings of accountability, **Vol. 9:** 75–75
  environmental impacts and, **Vol. 9:** 77
  extent of accountability, **Vol. 9:** 75–78
  human rights and, **Vol. 9:** 78
  labor standards and, **Vol. 9:** 77–78
  pharmaceutical companies and health issues, **Vol. 9:** 77
  poverty alleviation and, **Vol. 9:** 76–77
  transparency and disclosure issues, **Vol. 9:** 75–76
Corporate Accountability (China), Vol. 7: 74–78
Corporate Citizenship, Vol. 2: xxv, **79–82,** 360, 473–476
corporate compliance, **Vol. 3:** 165
Corporate Ecosystem Services Review (ESR), **Vol. 5:** 114
Corporate Register, **Vol. 3:** 52
corporate responsibility. *See* corporate social responsibility (CSR)
corporate social responsibility (CSR), **Vol. 2:** 69, 87, 360, 473
  See also **CSR and CSR 2.0;** company sustainability reporting (CSR); **Corporate Citizenship**
CorporateRegister.com, **Vol. 2:** 132
corporations, **Vol. 2:** 359, 362
  See also **Corporate Citizenship**
Cosmic Commons, Vol. 1: 83–84
cosmogony, **Vol. 1:** 197
cosmologic gauge, of time, **Vol. 1:** 393
cosmological anthropocentrism, **Vol. 1:** 23
Cosmology, Vol. 1: 85–87, 91, 219
cosmopolitan species, **Vol. 5:** 31
Cosmovisions, **Vol. 1:** 233–234
Cost-Benefit Analysis, Vol. 1: 267, 323, 404–405, **Vol. 5:** 89, **Vol. 6: 68–70**
  See also **Safe Minimum Standard (SMS)**
cost of service (COS) regulation, **Vol. 3:** 481
Costa Rica
  ecosystems services and, **Vol. 5:** 115
  environmental law in, **Vol. 3:** 215
  Organic Act of the Environment, **Vol. 3:** 215
Côte d'Ivoire, **Vol. 1:** 210, **Vol. 3:** 469
Cotonou Agreement (2000), **Vol. 3:** 124
Cotton, Vol. 4: 95–98, 137–139
  See also Bt crops *under* Bacillus thuringiensis (Bt)

cotton, organic. *See* organic cotton
Council of All Beings, Vol. 1: 49, **88,** 371, 384
Council on Environmental Quality (CEQ), **Vol. 3:** 139, 393
country-led initiative (CLI), **Vol. 3:** 492
Court of Justice, European Union, **Vol. 3:** 236
Covenant on Civil and Political Rights, **Vol. 3:** 102
cover crops, **Vol. 5:** 12, 13, 259, 368, 369
cows, **Vol. 1:** 17
  protection of, **Vol. 1:** 410
  See also cattle grazing
Cradle to Cradle, Vol. 1: 25, **Vol. 2:** xxvii, **83–85,** 290, 347, 355
  See also Braungart, Michael; McDonough, William;
cradle to grave. *See* **Life Cycle Assessment (LCA)**
cradle-to-grave approach, **Vol. 1:** 25
created order, **Vol. 1:** 5, 191
Creatio ex nihilo (Creation out of nothing) doctrine, **Vol. 1:** 90
Creation, Vol. 1: 89–90, 255, 426
  Babylonian myth of, **Vol. 1:** 89
  care for, **Vol. 1:** 63, 84
  "Canticle of Creation," **Vol. 1:** 345
  Cycle of Creation, **Vol. 1:** 363–364
  Hebrew story, **Vol. 1:** 89
  Mesopotamian story, **Vol. 1:** 89
  order of, **Vol. 1:** 255
  Priestly account, Creation stories, **Vol. 1:** 89
  as sacrament, **Vol. 1:** 344
  Wemale (Indonesian) myth of, **Vol. 1:** 361
Creation Spirituality, Vol. 1: 91–92
Creation-centered spirituality. *See* **Creation Spirituality**
credit unions, **Vol. 2:** 69
Cree, **Vol. 1:** 214
Creole, **Vol. 1:** 203
Cretaceous-Tertiary extinction, **Vol. 1:** 38
criminal enforcement, **Vol. 3:** 165
  corporate compliance, **Vol. 3:** 165
  criminal intent, **Vol. 3:** 165
  See also **Enforcement**
criminal intent, **Vol. 3:** 165
Criminal Law of the Environment, **Vol. 3:** 262
Critias (Plato), **Vol. 5:** 113
crop protection, through biotechnology, **Vol. 2:** 44–45
crop rotation, **Vol. 5:** 12, 13, 368, 369
croplands, **Vol. 5:** 340, 365, 366, 367
Crowe, Sylvia, **Vol. 5:** 402
Crown Minerals Act of 1991 (New Zealand), **Vol. 3:** 210
cruise lines, **Vol. 2:** 460
Crutzen, Paul. *See undere* **Anthropocene Epoch**
CSAs. *See* community-supported agriculture (CSA)

The Greening of Detroit (nonprofit organization),
Vol. 8: 81
immigrant residents in, **Vol. 8:** 79
public transportation in, **Vol. 8:** 80
Southwest Detroit Environmental Vision (SDEV),
Vol. 8: 81
urban agriculture in, **Vol. 5:** 391
developing countries, **Vol. 1:** 39–40, 152, 164, 189,
310, 320
development, **Vol. 1:** 107
as wealth, **Vol. 1:** 101
See also **Development, Rural—Developed World;**
Development, Rural—Developing World;
Development, Sustainable; Development,
Urban
Development Alternatives with Women for a New Era
(DAWN), **Vol. 1:** 171
Development, Concepts and Considerations, Vol. 1:
100–105
Development Facilitation Act of 1995 (South Africa),
Vol. 3: 185
Development Indicators, Vol. 6: 75–82
Development, Rural—Developed World, Vol. 2:
105–107
agritourism, cultural, and nature tourism,
Vol. 2: 106
sustainable agriculture in, **Vol. 2:** 105
sustainable energy, development of, **Vol. 2:** 106–107
Development, Rural—Developing World, Vol. 2:
108–110
ecotourism, **Vol. 2:** 109
issues pertaining to, **Vol. 2:** 109
role of organizations and aid, **Vol. 2:** 110
sustainable agricultural approaches, **Vol. 2:** 108–109
Development, Sustainable, Vol. 1: 106–109, Vol. 2:
xxv, **111–115**, 338
challenges to, **Vol. 2:** 111–112
climate change and, **Vol. 2:** 112
definition, **Vol. 2:** 111
renewable energy and solar power, **Vol. 2:** 113–114
See also sustainable development
Development, Sustainable—Overview of Laws and
Commissions, Vol. 3: 121–128
legal recognition, **Vol. 3:** 124–127
origins, **Vol. 3:** 121–124
See also **Brundtland Report**
Development, Urban, Vol. 2: 116–120
and environment, **Vol. 2:** 119
green buildings, **Vol. 2:** 119
renewable energy use, **Vol. 2:** 118
transportation issues, **Vol. 2:** 117–118

urbanization and land use, **Vol. 2:** 116–117
welfare and social equity, **Vol. 2:** 120
Deveraux, Kathy, **Vol. 1:** 223
Dewey, John, **Vol. 1:** 321–323
DeWitt, Calvin, **Vol. 1:** 62, 180
Dhaka, Bangladesh, Vol. 7: 82–84
Dharma, **Vol. 1:** 72, 198–199, 260, 349
Diamond, Jared, **Vol. 2:** 72, **Vol. 4:** 233, 238
diamonds, **Vol. 4:** 84–85, 176–177
See also blood diamonds
dichloro-diphenyl-tricholor-ethane (DDT). *See* DDT
dieldrin, **Vol. 3:** 452
Diet and Nutrition, Vol. 9: 89–93
calorie consumption increases, **Vol. 9:** 91
climate change and, **Vol. 9:** 91
Columbian Exchange, **Vol. 9:** 90
diet deficiency in Europe, **Vol. 9:** 91–92
farmer diets, **Vol. 9:** 90
hunter-gatherer diets, **Vol. 9:** 89
iodine deficiency in Central Asia, **Vol. 9:** 92
malnutrition unexpectedly promoting health,
Vol. 9: 91
undernourishment and malnourishment in Africa,
Vol. 9: 90
dinitrogen (N$_2$), **Vol. 4:** 336–337
direct spending, **Vol. 3:** 158
Director Scheme for Water Management and Planning
(France), **Vol. 3:** 496
Directory of Sustainability Programs, **Vol. 10:** 243–264
Disaster Risk Management, Vol. 9: 94–97
climate change and, **Vol. 9:** 95–96
definitions of, **Vol. 9:** 94–95
Hyogo Framework, **Vol. 9:** 95
discounting clock (in environmental economics), **Vol. 5:**
149–150
disease vectors, **Vol. 4:** 250
Dispute Settlement Mechanism, WTO, **Vol. 3:** 331
distributive justice, **Vol. 1:** 49
Disturbance, Vol. 5: 98–102
agriculture and, **Vol. 5:** 12, 368
anthropogenic, **Vol. 5:** 24, 42, 108, 110, 201, 262,
381, 399
natural, **Vol. 5:** 49, 157, 159
resilience against, **Vol. 5:** 336
stressors and, **Vol. 5:** 109–110
species succession and, **Vol. 5:** 380–381
diversity-invasibility hypothesis, **Vol. 5:** 215
divided fall dam, **Vol. 2:** 168
divination, **Vol. 1:** 3, 211
divine liturgy, **Vol. 1:** 343
divine protection, **Vol. 1:** 4, 89
Divine Saying, **Vol. 1:** 244
Division for Sustainable Development (DSD), within
UN system, **Vol. 6:** 7, 8

Bold entries and page numbers denote encyclopedia articles.

DNA, **Vol. 5:** 21, 23, 201, 215, 217, **Vol. 6:** 20, 22, 326–328
See also allele; gene
Dobson, James, **Vol. 1:** 180
Doctrine of the Mean, **Vol. 1:** 77
See also **Confucianism**
Dogon, **Vol. 1:** 211
Doha Development Agenda (DDA), **Vol. 3:** 125, 304
Doha Round of WTO negotiations, **Vol. 3:** 304, 306
Dominican Republic, environmental law in, **Vol. 3:** 217–218
Dominican Republic bishops, **Vol. 1:** 64
Dominion, Vol. 1: 110–111
double-dividend theory, **Vol. 3:** 322
Douglass, Andrew E., **Vol. 6:** 359
Douglass, Gordon K., **Vol. 1:** 11–14
Dow Chemical Company, **Vol. 3:** 8, 9
Dowd, Michael, **Vol. 1:** 168
Draft International Covenant on Environment and Development, **Vol. 3:** 126
Draft Ocean Space Treaty of 1971, **Vol. 3:** 65
Draft Protocol on Security and Sustainable Use of Soils, **Vol. 3:** 459
Dravya, **Vol. 1:** 249
The Dream of the Earth, **Vol. 1:** 64, 344
Dreamings, **Vol. 1:** 207, 222, 230
Driesen, David, **Vol. 2:** 53
drift nets, **Vol. 3:** 72
droughts, **Vol. 3:** 101
    impact on food production, **Vol. 10:** 10, 149, 235
    migration and, **Vol. 10:** 152, 153
Drug Production and Trade, Vol. 4: 111–114
drugs control, biotechnology in, **Vol. 3:** 12
Druidry, **Vol. 1:** 286, 299
drug development, Vol. 2: 45
Dualism, Vol. 1: 112–113, 174
Dubai, United Arab Emirates, Vol. 3: 25, **Vol. 9: 98–100**
Dublin Principles, **Vol. 1:** 246, **Vol. 2:** 479, **Vol. 5:** 60
due care, **Vol. 3:** 364–365
Dung, Vol. 4: 115–116, 246
Dunlop, John, **Vol. 4:** 422
DuPont corporation, **Vol. 1:** 355
Durga, Hindu goddess, **Vol. 1:** 199
Durning, Alan, **Vol. 1:** 95
Durkheim, Émile, **Vol. 2:** 70
Dust Bowl, **Vol. 1:** 13, **Vol. 5:** 49, 366
Dutch elm disease, **Vol. 5:** 395
dwelling, **Vol. 1:** 33, 235, 360
dysprosium, **Vol. 4:** 395
Dzanga-Shanga forest region (Central African Republic), **Vol. 5:** 77

E

e-commerce (environmental commerce), **Vol. 2:** 285
E-Waste, Vol. 1: 419–420, **Vol. 2:** 446, **Vol. 3:** 493, **Vol. 4:** 122, 123, 125, 401, 405, **Vol. 5:** 181–182, **Vol. 7: 86–91,** 213–214, **Vol. 8: 84–89, Vol. 9: 102–107, Vol. 10:** 226
    Africa and, **Vol. 9:** 102
    Australia and, **Vol. 8:** 88
    Electronics TakeBack Coalition (ETBC), **Vol. 8:** 87, **Vol. 9:** 104–105
    European Waste Electrical and Electronic Equipment (WEEE) Directive of 2002, **Vol. 9:** 102, 103, 105
    Guiyu, China, and, **Vol. 9:** 104
    illegal dumping of, **Vol. 9:** 102, 104, 105–106
    Probo Koala scandal, **Vol. 9:** 104
    rare earth elements (REEs), **Vol. 8:** 85–86, **Vol. 9:** 103
    recycling of, **Vol. 8:** 86, 103–104
    See also Bamako Convention of 1991; Basel Action Network (BAN); Basel Convention of 1989; **Waste; Waste—Engineering Aspects; Waste—Social Aspects**
Earth Activist Training, **Vol. 1:** 300
Earth Charter, Vol. 1: 8, 103, 105, 109, **115–117,** 162, 384, 416
Earth Charter Commission, **Vol. 1:** 115–116
Earth Charter Initiative, **Vol. 1:** 116, **Vol. 3:** 126
Earth Charter International (ECI), **Vol. 1:** 117
Earth Council in Costa Rica, **Vol. 1:** 115–116
Earth Day, Vol. 1: 118, **Vol. 1:** 254, **Vol. 5:** 176–177
    See also Ecumenical Earth Day
Earth Day Sunday, **Vol. 1:** 118
Earth First!, **Vol. 1:** 133, 286, 388, **Vol. 3:** 36
Earth Gathas, **Vol. 1:** 48
Earth Liberation Front, **Vol. 3:** 144
Earth Ministry, **Vol. 1:** 292
East Asia, **Vol. 1:** 17, 75–76, 86, 349, 359
    See also **Environmental Law—East Asia; Indigenous traditions, Asia**
Eastern Orthodox Christianity. *See* **Christianity, Eastern Orthodox**
Ecclesia reformata semper reformanda (a reformed church is always reforming), **Vol. 1:** 60
    See also **Christianity, Mainline Protestant**
ECI. *See* Earth Charter International
eco-efficiency, **Vol. 2:** 122, 126, 320, 346
eco-innovation, **Vol. 1:** 389
eco-sanghas, **Vol. 1:** 48
Eco-Terrorism, Vol. 3: 143–146
    at sea, **Vol. 3:** 144–145
    jurisdiction over, **Vol. 3:** 143–144
    Ecoterrorism Prevention Act of 2004, **Vol. 3:** 144
eco-twinning, **Vol. 1:** 363

Ecocentrism, Vol. 1: 35, **119–120**
  ecocentric ethics, **Vol. 1:** 119–120, 160, 440
ecocertification, **Vol. 3:** 133
ecocolonialism, **Vol. 3:** 91
Ecocide, Vol. 1: 121–122
ecocriticism, **Vol. 1:** 264
ecodesign, **Vol. 2:** 97, 288, **Vol. 4:** 108–109, 241
  and energy standards, **Vol. 2:** 98–99
  and extended producer responsibility (EPR),
    Vol. 2: 97
ecofascism, **Vol. 1:** 236
ecofeminism, **Vol. 1:** 161, 171, 173–174
  "Eco-feminist Perspectives: Culture, Nature,
    Theory," **Vol. 1:** 173
ecofeminist theory, **Vol. 3:** 314
ecojustice. *See* **Justice, Environmental**
Ecolabeling, Vol. 2: 122–124, 235, 324, 328, 434, 450,
    Vol. 3: 130–134
  controversies of, **Vol. 3:** 133
  definition, **Vol. 2:** 122, **Vol. 3:** 130–131
  effectiveness of, **Vol. 3:** 133
  International Organization for Standardization and
    labelling types, **Vol. 2:** 123–124, 328
  as a marketing tool, **Vol. 2:** 122
  See also **Ecolabels; Fair Trade; Genetically
    Modified Organisms Legislation**
Ecolabels, Vol. 6: 84–90
  See also **Ecolabeling**
ecolinguistics, **Vol. 1:** 264
ecolo, **Vol. 1:** 195
ecological anthropology, **Vol. 5:** 75
ecological capital, **Vol. 2:** 71
ecological citizenship, **Vol. 1:** 340
Ecological Economics, Vol. 1: 383, 429, **Vol. 2:**
    125–126
ecological-evolutionary theory (EET), **Vol. 1:** 376
Ecological Footprint, Vol. 1: 60–61, 85, 94, **123–124,**
    Vol. 2: xxiii, 262, 367, **Vol. 5:** 265, 315
  ecological footprint online test example, **Vol. 1:** 124
Ecological Footprint Accounting, Vol. 6: 91–97
ecological footprint index, **Vol. 6:** 177
Ecological Forecasting, Vol. 5: xxii, **104–107**
ecological imbalances, **Vol. 1:** 6
Ecological Impact Assessment (EcIA), Vol. 6: 98–102
ecological integrity, **Vol. 1:** 11–12, 14, 22, 115, **Vol. 3:** 513
ecological Kuznets curve (EKC), **Vol. 3:** 136
Ecological Modernization Theory, Vol. 3: 135–137
  critics of, **Vol. 3:** 137
  early thought on, **Vol. 3:** 135–136
ecological overshoot, **Vol. 6:** 91
ecological product compatibility, **Vol. 1:** 122

ecological rationality, **Vol. 3:** 135
ecological refugees, **Vol. 3:** 354
  See also **Refugees, Environmental**
Ecological Restoration, Vol. 5: 108–111, 340, 341
Ecological Society of America (ESA), **Vol. 1:** 323, 356,
    Vol. 5: 187, 188
ecological triage, **Vol. 5:** 106
Ecology, Vol. 1: 35, **125–128**
  as activist movement, **Vol. 1:** 126–127
  invasion ecology, **Vol. 5:** 211
  restoration ecology, **Vol. 5:** 341
  sacred, **Vol. 1:** 300
  See also **Agroecology**
Ecology and Liberation, **Vol. 1:** 64
Ecology, Cultural, Vol. 1: 129–131
  environmental knowledge, **Vol. 1:** 130–131
  methodological challenges and debates, **Vol. 1:** 130
  natural resources politics and environment,
    Vol. 1: 130
  nature–culture dichotomy, **Vol. 1:** 129
  and social organization, **Vol. 1:** 129–130
Ecology, Deep, Vol. 1: 35, 88, 126, **132–135,** 407
  conventional vs. critical, **Vol. 1:** 134
  criticisms, **Vol. 1:** 133–134
  deep ecology movement, **Vol. 7:** 163
  meaning and characteristics, **Vol. 1:** 132–133
  "shallow ecology," **Vol. 1:** 132
  "The Shallow and the Deep, Long-Range Ecology
    Movement"
  See also Naess, Arne
The Ecology of a City and Its People, **Vol. 5:** 187
Ecology of Invasions by Animals and Plants, **Vol. 5:** 212
Ecology of the Night Symposium, **Vol. 3:** 118
Ecology, Political, Vol. 1: 136–137, 306
Ecology, Social, Vol. 1: 134, **138–139**
Ecology Party, **Vol. 1:** 195
economic value creation, **Vol. 2:** 433–434
Economics, Vol. 1: 95, 101, **140–143**
  ecological impacts, **Vol. 1:** 141–142
  free-market, **Vol. 1:** 58, 80, 102, 140, 180, 236,
    302, 435
  historical development, **Vol. 1:** 140–141
  progress, **Vol. 1:** 143
The Economics of Welfare, **Vol. 3:** 318
Economics, Steady State, Vol. 10: 78–85
  limits-to-growth argument, **Vol. 10:** 79–80
  Resources for the Future (RFF), **Vol. 10:** 79
  See also Malthus, T. Robert
economism, **Vol. 1:** 349
economy, redesigning of, **Vol. 2:** 346–347
Ecopsychology, Vol. 1: 44, **144–145,** 299
  psycho-ecology, **Vol. 1:** 144
EcoSikh, **Vol. 1:** 363
ecosophy, **Vol. 1:** 133–134

Education, Higher (Africa), Vol. 9: 118–122
 Chagga home gardens, **Vol. 9:** 121
 enrollment rates, **Vol. 9:** 119
 four pillars of education, **Vol. 9:** 121
 systems-thinking approach, **Vol. 9:** 121
 Youth, Education, Skills and Employment (UN
  Economic Commission report), **Vol. 9:** 119
Edwards Aquifer, **Vol. 4:** 44, 47
Edwards Dam, United States, **Vol. 5:** 87
EEE (environment, economies, efficiency) container
 ships, **Vol. 6:** 315
effluent limitations, **Vol. 3:** 46
 technology-based, **Vol. 3:** 47
 water-quality standards, **Vol. 3:** 46
egalitarianism, **Vol. 1:** 95
 biocentric, **Vol. 1:** 133, 414
Egypt, **Vol. 1:** 94, 429, **Vol. 3:** 471, **Vol. 5:** 221, 223
 Cooperative Agreement on Animal Health between
  Egypt and Algeria, **Vol. 3:** 175
 framework environmental laws, **Vol. 3:** 176
 water quality standards in, **Vol. 3:** 177
 See also United Nations International Conference on
  Population and Development, Cairo
Ehrlich, Paul, **Vol. 6:** 194
El Hinnawi, Essam, **Vol. 3:** 441
El Niño Southern Oscillation (ENSO), **Vol. 4:** 210,
 341, **Vol. 5:** 95, 163, 333, **Vol. 8:** 134–135, 141,
 145, 219
El Salvador, environmental law in, **Vol. 3:** 215–216
electric power plants. *See* power plants
electric utility regulatory system, **Vol. 3:** 480
electricity, **Vol. 1:** 141, 150–151
electronic waste. *See* **E-Waste**
Electronics—Raw Materials, Vol. 4: 122–126
 See also **E-Waste**
Elephant Pepper Development Trust, **Vol. 5:** 136
elephants, African, **Vol. 5:** 227, 228, 300
Elkington, John, **Vol. 2:** xxiii, 122, **Vol. 5:** 177,
 Vol. 6: 362
Ellora, Maharashtra, **Vol. 1:** 251
Elvin, Mark. See *The Retreat of the Elephants: An
 Environmental History of China*
Elwha River, Washington, United States, **Vol. 5:** 88
 See also **Dam Removal**
emerging organic chemicals, emerging issues, **Vol. 3:** 28
Emerson, Ralph Waldo, **Vol. 1:** 398, 429
emission cap, **Vol. 2:** 147
emission credits, **Vol. 2:** 4
emission reduction units (ERUs), **Vol. 3:** 358
emissions (of gases), **Vol. 1:** 68–70, 123, 142, 176,
 266–267, **Vol. 4:** 323

 fertilizer production and, **Vol. 4:** 133–134
 of flourides and flurocarbons, **Vol. 4:** 33–34
 of heavy metals, **Vol. 4:** 217, 219
 incentives, **Vol. 4:** 323–324
 of nitrogen and nitrous oxide (N_2O), **Vol. 4:** 337–338
 See also **Coal;** carbon dioxide; greenhouse gases (GHGs)
emissions trading, **Vol. 3:** 58
end-of-life products and processing. *See* **Recycling**
end-of-pipe technology, **Vol. 5:** 310
end-times, **Vol. 1:** 154, 179
Endangered Species, Vol. 3: 90–91, **Vol. 5:** 28, 37, 39,
 51, 74, 91, 316, 342, **Vol. 7: 118–121**
 Arabian oryx, **Vol. 7:** 120
 critically endangered classification, **Vol. 7:** 119
 extinct classification, **Vol. 7:** 118
 extinct in the wild classification, **Vol. 7:** 118
 extinction issues, **Vol. 7:** 93, 118, 189, 345
 giant panda, **Vol. 7:** 93, 120–121
 Père David's deer, **Vol. 7:** 118–119
 Steller's sea cow, **Vol. 7:** 119–120
 See also **Biodiversity;** Endangered Species Act;
  **Convention on International Trade in
  Endangered Species** of Wild Fauna and Flora
  (CITES); species
Endangered Species Act, Vol. 1: 16, 118, 435, **Vol. 3:**
 139, 140, 507, **151–154,** 170, 273, 393
 authority to purchase land, **Vol. 3:** 152
 enacting, **Vol. 3:** 151–152
 prohibitions, **Vol. 3:** 152–154
 species as, **Vol. 3:** 152
 See also **Convention on International Trade in
  Endangered Species** of Wild Fauna and Flora
  (CITES); species
Endangered Species Conservation Act of 1969,
 Vol. 3: 151
Endangered Species Preservation Act, **Vol. 3:** 151
endemic species, **Vol. 5:** 26–30, 31–32, 34–35, 42, 144,
 213, 228, 326–327
endocrine disruptors (EDs), **Vol. 3:** 28
endrin, **Vol. 3:** 452
Energy, Vol. 1: 150–153
 conservation, **Vol. 1:** 26
 definition of, **Vol. 2:** 148
 future challenges, **Vol. 1:** 152–153
 morality and theology, **Vol. 1:** 151
 nuclear controversy, **Vol. 1:** 152
 power vs., **Vol. 2:** 148
 religious education about, **Vol. 1:** 150–151
 renewable, **Vol. 1:** 26, 149, 389
 See also **Geothermal Energy;** renewable energy;
  Solar Energy; Water Energy; Wind Energy
Energy Charter Treaty (ECT) (1994), **Vol. 3:** 124,
 341, 342
Energy Conservation Incentives, Vol. 3: 155–157

Bold entries and page numbers denote encyclopedia articles.

environmentalism, **Vol. 1:** 129, 323, **Vol. 2:** xxv, 298
  conservation vs., **Vol. 1:** 80–81
  cyborg, **Vol. 1:** 203
  fundamentalist views, **Vol. 1:** 179–180
  neo-Luddite, **Vol. 1:** 388, 389
  promethean, **Vol. 1:** 388, 389
  religious, **Vol. 1:** 127, 150, 152, 178, 373
environmentally related taxes, **Vol. 3:** 318
EPA. *See* United States Environmental Protection
  Agency (US EPA)
Epic of Evolution, **Vol. 1:** 168
Epic of Gilgamesh, **Vol. 1:** 93
Episcopal Power and Light, **Vol. 1:** 151, 292
epistemologies, **Vol. 1:** 357
Equator Principles, Vol. 2: 207–209
  implications of, **Vol. 2:** 209
  origins of, **Vol. 2:** 207–208
  principles of, **Vol. 2:** 208
equilibrial state, **Vol. 5:** 380–381
  See also nonequilibrium
erbium, **Vol. 4:** 396
Eritea, **Vol. 3:** 471
erosion, **Vol. 4:** 436–437, **Vol. 5:** 19, 49–50, 60, 114,
  159, 304–305, 365–369
Eschatology, Vol. 1: 154–156
  modern interpretations, **Vol. 1:** 155–156
  origins, in holy texts, **Vol. 1:** 154–155
Essay on the Principle of Population, **Vol. 5:** 56
  See also Malthus, T. Robert
essentialism, **Vol. 1:** 203
ethanol, **Vol. 4:** 28, 54, 370, 419, 446
ethical consumption, future of, **Vol. 3:** 293
ethics
  anthropocosmic, **Vol. 1:** 440
  biomedical, **Vol. 1:** 42
  ecocentric, **Vol. 1:** 119–120, 160, 440
  See also **Ethics, Communicative; Ethics,**
    Environmental; Ethics, Global; Ethics,
    Natural Law
Ethics, Communicative, Vol. 1: 157–158
Ethics, Environmental, **Vol. 1: 159–163**, 172, 414
  debates, **Vol. 1:** 159–161
Ethics, Global, Vol. 1: 162, **164–165**
Ethics, Natural Law, Vol. 1: 166–167
ethnic minorities, **Vol. 1:** 336
ethnicities, **Vol. 1:** 4
Ethiopia, **Vol. 3:** 471
Eucharist, **Vol. 1:** 348–349
Eudaimonia, **Vol. 1:** 403
Eukaryotes, **Vol. 1:** 38
Euphrates River, **Vol. 1:** 9, 246

Euripides, **Vol. 1:** 348
EuroGreens. *See* Federation of European Green Parties
Europe, **Vol. 1:** 14, 160, 398, **Vol. 2:** 122, 355, 385, 410,
  Vol. 5: 13
  buffers in, **Vol. 5:** 51
  conservation in, **Vol. 5:** 75
  environmental movements in, **Vol. 3:** 315
  invasive species in, **Vol. 5:** 213, 216
  water management in, **Vol. 5:** 60, 193
  waste management in, **Vol. 5:** 411
  See also **European Union (EU)**
European Alps, **Vol. 5:** 288, 328
European Americans, **Vol. 1:** 4
European Atomic Energy Community (EURATOM),
  Vol. 3: 232, 490
European Bank for Reconstruction and Development
  (EBRD), **Vol. 3:** 122
European Centre of Nature Conservation (ECNC),
  Vol. 5: 348
European Coal and Steel Community, **Vol. 3:** 232, 282
European Commission, **Vol. 3:** 285, 293
European Common Policy on Agriculture (PAC),
  Vol. 3: 496
European Community (EC), **Vol. 3:** 232, 492
  Environmental Action Program, **Vol. 3:** 425
European Community Treaty, **Vol. 1:** 267
European Court of Human Rights, **Vol. 3:** 331
European Court of Justice (ECJ), **Vol. 3:** 331, 386,
  463, 492
European Directive on Water (DCE), **Vol. 3:** 496
European Economic Community (EEC), **Vol. 3:** 232,
  233, 488
  Articles 130(r)-130(t), **Vol. 3:** 233
European Enlightenment period, **Vol. 1:** 85, 97, 182,
  349, **Vol. 7:** 8
European Environmental Agency (EEA), **Vol. 2:** 52,
  Vol. 3: 26, 319
European Fair Trade Association (EFTA), **Vol. 3:** 291
  See also **Fair Trade**
European law
  polluter pays principle in, **Vol. 3:** 427–428
European Pathways to the Cultural Landscape
  (EPCL), **Vol. 5:** 403
European Spatial Development Perspective, **Vol. 3:** 367
European Union (EU), Vol. 1: 195, 267, 325–326,
  Vol. 2: 3, 6, 52, 98, 122, 141, 202, 284, 365,
  388, 432, 446, 450, **Vol. 3:** 124, 201, 204, 232,
  457, 462, 463, 488, **Vol. 5:** 59, 61, 154, 411,
  Vol. 9: 128–131
  Action Plan, **Vol. 3:** 293
  Directive on End of Life Vehicles, **Vol. 3:** 449
  ecolabels in, **Vol. 6:** 88, 115
  environmental accounting systems in, **Vol. 6:** 257
  European Union Parliament, **Vol. 1:** 195

---

geothermal heat pumps (GHPs), **Vol. 4:** 178
German Green Party, **Vol. 1:** 195, 310
Germany, Vol. 1: 24, 310, 409, **Vol. 2:** 388, **Vol. 3:** 33,
    282, 469, **Vol. 9: 150–155**
    Christian Democratic Union (CDU) economic
        policies, **Vol. 9:** 152
    environmental law, **Vol. 1:** 326
    Nazis and the environment in, **Vol. 9:** 151–152
    nuclear power in, **Vol. 9:** 153
    pollution in, **Vol. 9:** 154
    renewable energy in, **Vol. 9:** 153
    Vision 2050, **Vol. 9:** 154
Gezira Irrigation Scheme, **Vol. 5:** 306
Ghana, **Vol. 1:** 40, 210–211
ghost nets. *See* discarded nets
Ghost Town Farm blog, **Vol. 5:** 393
gigawatt-hours (GWh), **Vol. 2:** 148–149
gigawatts, **Vol. 2:** 148–149
Gila Wilderness designation, **Vol. 3:** 508
gillnet, **Vol. 3:** 72
Gini coefficient (measure of inequality from 0 to 1),
    Vol. 8: 37, 253, 315
girlcott campaign, **Vol. 3:** 406
glacial ice. *See* **Glaciers**
Glacier Bay, Alaska, United States (national park),
    Vol. 5: 237
Glaciers, Vol. 4: 104, **181–183, Vol. 5:** 163, 166, 195
glass, **Vol. 4:** 439
glasnost policy, **Vol. 3:** 32
Gleick Basic Human Needs Index, **Vol. 3:** 499
Glen Canyon Dam, Arizona, United States, **Vol. 5:** 4
Glines Canyon Dam, Washington, United States,
    Vol. 5: 88
global awareness, **Vol. 1:** 171, 190, 388
Global Biodiversity Outlook (GBO 3), **Vol. 3:** 83
global citizenship, **Vol. 1:** 116, 189
Global Climate Change, Vol. 1: 39, 73, 266, 281,
    Vol. 5: 162–167
    ecological forecasting and, **Vol. 5:** 41, 328
    impacts of, **Vol. 5:** 166, 259, 284, 366–368
    outbreak species and, **Vol. 5:** 287
global communications, **Vol. 1:** 190
Global Earth Observation System of Systems
    (GEOSS), **Vol. 6:** 158, 162–163
Global Ecolabelling Network (GEN), **Vol. 3:** 130, 131
Global Environment Facility (GEF), **Vol. 1:** 277,
    Vol. 3: 103, **Vol. 5:** 240, 242
    See also **Rio Earth Summit (UN Conference on**
    Environment and Development)
Global Environment Outlook (GEO) Reports,
    Vol. 6: 160–164

global environmental citizenship, **Vol. 3:** 36–37
global ethics. *See* **Ethics, Global**
Global Ethics of Cooperation of Religions on Human
    and Environmental Issues statement, **Vol. 1:** 442
Global Exchange, **Vol. 2:** 8
Global Footprint Network, **Vol. 6:** 91–92, 93–94, 95
Global Forum of Spiritual and Parliamentary Leaders,
    Vol. 1: 442
Global Greens Network, **Vol. 1:** 195
Global Health and Safety Initiative (GHSI),
    Vol. 2: 262
global hectares, **Vol. 6:** 92
Global North, **Vol. 1:** 238
    environmental movements in, **Vol. 3:** 315
Global Partnership for Plant Conservation (GPPC),
    Vol. 6: 173, 174
Global Reporting Initiative (GRI), Vol. 2: 2, 6,
    244–247, 365, 454, 455, 464, **Vol. 3:** 49, 52,
    Vol. 6: 9, 39, 40, **165–167,** 362
    framework and categories, **Vol. 2:** 3, 244–245
    guidelines pertaining to, **Vol. 2:** 246
    origins of, **Vol. 2:** 244
    reporting issues, **Vol. 2:** 246
Global South, **Vol. 1:** 107, 161, 430
    environmental movements in, **Vol. 3:** 315
Global Strategy for Plant Conservation, Vol. 6:
    168–175
Global Trade, Vol. 1: 189, 325, **Vol. 10: 129–138**
    Environmental Kuznets Curve (EKC), **Vol. 10:**
        131–132
    environmental regulation and innovation, **Vol. 10:**
        133–134
    free trade agreements (FTAs), **Vol. 10:** 136
    green growth, **Vol. 10:** 130
    intellectual property rights, **Vol. 10:** 135–136
    pollution haven hypothesis, **Vol. 10:** 132
    regulatory race to the bottom, **Vol. 10:** 132–133
    scale, composition, and technique effects, **Vol. 10:**
        130–131
    subsidies and, **Vol. 10:** 135
global warming, **Vol. 1:** 68, 69, 141, 179, 180, 202, 232,
    310, **Vol. 3:** 379–381, 475, **Vol. 6:** 42, 47, 91,
    222, 223
    from fossil fuels, **Vol. 1:** 152
    See also climate change
Global Warming Petition, **Vol. 1:** 180
Global Water Partnership (GWP), **Vol. 5:** 61, 414
Global Witness, **Vol. 4:** 456
Globalization, Vol. 1: 4, 139, **189–190,** 215, 387, 430,
    Vol. 2: 317, 358, 432, 465, 473
    impacts of, **Vol. 4:** 303
glocalization, **Vol. 1:** 306
Gnostic sects, **Vol. 1:** 409
God After Darwin: A Theology of Evolution, **Vol. 1:** 64

Bold entries and page numbers denote encyclopedia articles.

Bold entries and page numbers denote encyclopedia articles.

Bold entries and page numbers denote encyclopedia articles.

ice age, **Vol. 5:** 130, 327
ice cores, **Vol. 4:** 183
Iceland, **Vol. 1:** 213, **Vol. 3:** 203
   See also **Cod Wars (*United Kingdom v. Iceland*)**
   See under **Scandinavia**
Iceland Shelf LME (large marine ecosystem), **Vol. 5:** 244
Icelandic ice cap (Eyjafjallajökull) volcanic eruption,
   Vol. 5: 309
ICLEI-Local Governments for Sustainability,
   Vol. 1: 117
idolatry, **Vol. 1:** 333, 349
Ihsan, **Vol. 1:** 311
illegal, unregulated and unreported (IUU) fishing,
   Vol. 3: 373, **Vol. 5:** 148, 149, 282
Illich, Ivan, **Vol. 1:** 388
illiteracy rates of women, **Vol. 7:** 116, 117, 168
illness. *See* disease complexity *under* **Health, Public**
   and Environmental
Immelt, Jeffrey, **Vol. 2:** xxii
immersive environment, **Vol. 5:** 405
Immigrants and Refugees, Vol. 9: 160–164
   Chinese farmers migrating to Africa, **Vol. 9:** 160
   climate change and, **Vol. 9:** 163
   Europe and, **Vol. 9:** 161, 162
   International Organization for Migration (IOM),
      Vol. 9: 161, 162
   migration between Kenya and Somalia, **Vol. 9:**
      161, 163
   refugee camps, **Vol. 9:** 161, 162–163
   See also "brain drain" of skilled professionals
Implementation Agreement (1994), **Vol. 3:** 67, 372
Implementation Agreement (1995), **Vol. 3:** 372
Inca, **Vol. 1:** 235
incandescent light bulbs, **Vol. 4:** 258
Incentives for Global Health, **Vol. 1:** 318
incineration, **Vol. 4:** 476–477
Income Tax Act (Singapore), **Vol. 3:** 266
An Inconvenient Truth, **Vol. 1:** 108–109, 348
Independent Development Monks' Movement,
   Vol. 7: 346
Index of Biological Integrity (IBI), Vol. 6: 198–201
Index of Biotic Integrity (IBI), **Vol. 6:** 134
   See also **Index of Biological Integrity (IBI)**
Index of Sustainable Economic Welfare (ISEW),
   Vol. 6: 152, 177
India, Vol. 1: 102, 121, 129, 206, 310, 415, 422–423,
   430, 437, **Vol. 2:** 24, **Vol. 3:** 311, 454, 468,
   Vol. 5: 76, 412, **Vol. 7: 196–200**
   agricultural yields in, **Vol. 4:** 411
   Air Act of 1981, **Vol. 3:** 237
   air quality, **Vol. 7:** 4, 23

contemporary environmentalism, **Vol. 1:** 200–201
   forest management in, **Vol. 7:** 199, 286
   gemstone production in, **Vol. 4:** 175
   genetically engineered crops in, **Vol. 4:** 203
   globalization and, **Vol. 1:** 200
   groundwater use in, **Vol. 4:** 44
   manure use in, **Vol. 4:** 115
   Narmada Dam Project, **Vol. 1:** 121, 312
   National Environment Protection Authority,
      Vol. 3: 237
   nonviolence, **Vol. 1:** 293, 440
   nuclear power in, **Vol. 4:** 453
   population statistics of, **Vol. 7:** 197, 297
   political participation of women in, **Vol. 7:** 167
   salt and, **Vol. 4:** 427
   Salt March, **Vol. 1:** 311
   tiger poaching in, **Vol. 4:** 382
   waste shipment law in, **Vol. 3:** 492
   See also **Buddhism; Chipko Movement;**
      Environmental Law—India and Pakistan;
      Hinduism; Indigenous Traditions, Asia;
      Islam; Jainism; *specific subjects/headwords*
Indian Patents Act (1970), **Vol. 7:** 373
Indian Supreme Court, **Vol. 3:** 8, **Vol. 7:** 4, 5, 81
Indic model (economic system), **Vol. 1:** 197
Indicator Species, Vol. 5: 200–203
   biodiversity indicators, **Vol. 5:** 201
   ecological indicators, **Vol. 5:** 200, 201
   environmental indicators, **Vol. 5:** 200
   See also bioindicators
Indigenous and Traditional Resource Management,
   Vol. 4: 232–239
indigenous knowledge (IK), **Vol. 1:** 130, 206–208
   See also **Indigenous Peoples and Traditional**
      Knowledge; *individual* **Indigenous**
      Traditions *entries*
Indigenous Peoples, Vol. 7: 201–205
   conflicts in agriculture (southeast Asia),
      Vol. 7: 203
   definition of, **Vol. 7:** 201
   ethnic minorities (China), **Vol. 7:** 202–203
   International Fund for Agricultural Development
      (IFAD), 1976, **Vol. 7:** 203–204
   Muthanga incident, **Vol. 7:** 202
   Sawit Watch, **Vol. 7:** 203
   Scheduled Tribes (India), **Vol. 7:** 202
Indigenous Peoples and Traditional Knowledge,
   Vol. 5: 204–210
Indigenous and Traditional Peoples, Vol. 1: 18,
   206–208, 209–235, 333, 358, 370, 377
Indigenous Traditions (Africa), Vol. 1: 209–212
   differences and shared values, **Vol. 1:** 209–210
   divination, **Vol. 1:** 211
   festivals, **Vol. 1:** 210–211

Bold entries and page numbers denote encyclopedia articles.

Bold entries and page numbers denote encyclopedia articles.

integrated water resource management, 246
on private property, **Vol. 1:** 331
power of water, **Vol. 1:** 244–245
Sufis, **Vol. 1:** 244, 411
vegetarianism and, **Vol. 1:** 411
water management, **Vol. 1:** 245–246
water as social good, **Vol. 1:** 246
wisdom and, **Vol. 1:** 433
Islamic Public Property, **Vol. 1:** 333
Islamic spirituality, **Vol. 1:** 370
Island, Hershel, **Vol. 1:** 337
ISO. *See* International Organization for
Standardization
Israel, **Vol. 1:** 179, 181, 252–253, 354, 429
See also **Environmental Law—Israel; Judaism;
Jordan River Project**
Israeli environmentalism, **Vol. 1:** 254
IT. *See* **Information and Communications
Technologies (ICT)**
Itai-Itai cadmium disease, **Vol. 3:** 224
Italy, **Vol. 3:** 282
ivory, **Vol. 4:** 382
IWMI Indicator of Relative Water Scarcity,
Vol. 3: 499

J

Jacobs, Jane, **Vol. 2:** 315, 317, **Vol. 8:** 301, **Vol. 10:**
62, 63
Jahwist narrative, **Vol. 1:** 89
Jain Vishva Bharati University (Rajasthan, India),
Vol. 1: 251
Jaina text, **Vol. 1:** 249
Jainism, Vol. 1: 249–251
beliefs, **Vol. 1:** 249–250
environmentalism, **Vol. 1:** 250–251
on possession, **Vol. 1:** 333
vegetarianism and, **Vol. 1:** 410
Jains, **Vol. 1:** 303
Jakarta, Indonesia, Vol. 7: 218–221
air quality, **Vol. 7:** 219–220
bus rapid transit (BRT), **Vol. 7:** 219–220
Dutch settlers in, **Vol. 7:** 218–219
electronic road pricing (ERP) system, **Vol. 7:** 220
flooding in, **Vol. 7:** 219
Green Radio 89.2 FM, **Vol. 7:** 220
Mass Rapid Transit (MRT) Jakarta, **Vol. 7:** 220
Monsoon Vermont (company), **Vol. 7:** 220
Jamaica, environmental law in, **Vol. 3:** 218
James, William, **Vol. 1:** 321
James Bay Project, **Vol. 1:** 121

Japan, Vol. 1: 218, **Vol. 2:** 141, 183, 355, 410,
Vol. 3: 37, 191, 202, **Vol. 5:** 180, 181, 412,
Vol. 7: 222–226
agriculture in, **Vol. 7:** 222–223, 224
e-waste recycling in, **Vol. 7:** 88, 89
fish consumption in, **Vol. 4:** 141, 218
Industrialism, **Vol. 7:** 224
lighting habits in, **Vol. 4:** 259
nuclear tragedies in, **Vol. 4:** 465
pollution (industrial) in, **Vol. 7:** 225
reforestation in, **Vol. 7:** 225
shamanism, **Vol. 1:** 217
view of nature, **Vol. 1:** 361–362
waste management in, **Vol. 4:** 476
See also Basic Law for Establishing a Recycling Based
Society (2000) (Japan); Fukushima Daiichi
Nuclear Power Plant; **Shinto; Kyoto Protocol**
Japanese Ministry of the Environment, **Vol. 5:** 45
Jataka Tales, **Vol. 1:** 17, 410
See also **Buddhism; Vegetarianism**
Jensen, Jens, **Vol. 5:** 233, 234
Jerusalem, **Vol. 1:** 303, 429
Jesus, **Vol. 1:** 18, 55, 259, 332, 398
See also individual Christianity *entries*
Jewish Orthodoxy, **Vol. 1:** 181
See also **Judaism**
Jihad, green, **Vol. 1:** 244
Jincandrasuri II, **Vol. 1:** 250
Jinsilu (Reflections on Things at Hand), **Vol. 1:** 77
Jiva, **Vol. 1:** 249
jobs. *See* **Green-Collar Jobs**
Johannesburg Declaration (JD), **Vol. 3:** 125–126, 457
Johannesburg Earth Summit. *See* World Summit
on Sustainable Development (WSSD),
Johannesburg, 2002
Joint Appeal of Religion and Science for the
Environment, **Vol. 1:** 281
Jordan, **Vol. 1:** 253, **Vol. 3:** 469
Workshop on Water Resources Management in the
Islamic World (Amman), **Vol. 1:** 245–246
See also **Middle East**
Jordan River and Jordan River basin. *See under*
**Transboundary Water Issues; Water Use and
Rights (Middle East and North Africa)**
Jordon River Project, Vol. 1: 252–253
Jubilee, **Vol. 1:** 255, 332
Judaism, Vol. 1: 17, 154, 179, **254–257**, 331–332, 441
environmental writings, **Vol. 1:** 254–255
eschatology, **Vol. 1:** 155
ethical obligations, **Vol. 1:** 255–257
ethical values in, **Vol. 1:** 256
Jubilee, **Vol. 1:** 255, 332
on private property, **Vol. 1:** 331
Orthodox, **Vol. 1:** 179, 181, 333

Bold entries and page numbers denote encyclopedia articles.

Manufacturing Practices, Vol. 2: 320–325
defining sustainability in, **Vol. 2:** 321–322
eco-efficiency, importance of, **Vol. 2:** 320
issues with, **Vol. 2:** 323–324
and resource productivity, **Vol. 2:** 320
role of innovation in, **Vol. 2:** 322–323
Manure, Animal, Vol. 4: 273–276
Manure, Human, Vol. 4: 277–279
Mao Zedong (Mao Tse-tung), **Vol. 1:** 75, **Vol. 7:** xxv, 8,
71, 75, 156, 339
Maoist era, **Vol. 7:** 70, 174
Māori people, **Vol. 1:** 187, 208, **Vol. 5:** 76
See also under **Auckland, New Zealand; New
Zealand**
maquiladora industry, **Vol. 3:** 304
maquiladora program. *See* **North American Free Trade
Agreement (NAFTA)**
marijuana. *See* **Hemp**
Marine Ecosystems Health, Vol. 8: 141–149
anoxia and hypoxia events, **Vol. 8:** 143
biotoxin and exposure events, **Vol. 8:** 143
coral reef bleaching, **Vol. 8:** 144–145
disease events, **Vol. 8:** 145
disturbance predicting, **Vol. 8:** 141–142
mass mortality events, **Vol. 8:** 144
novel and invasive events, **Vol. 8:** 145–146
ocean acidification, **Vol. 8:** 147
oil spills and, **Vol. 8:** 146
physical forcing events, **Vol. 8:** 144–145
trophic disturbances, **Vol. 8:** 143–144
marine energy. *See* **Energy Industries—Wave and
Tidal Energy**
marine environment, **Vol. 3:** 478
contemporary threats to, **Vol. 3:** 374
marine fisheries depletion, **Vol. 4:** 142–143, 349
See also **Fisheries**
Marine Life Protection Act (MLPA) (1999, United
States), **Vol. 3:** 420, 422, **Vol. 5:** 253
marine organisms, calcifying, **Vol. 6:** 264, 265
Marine Preserves, Vol. 8: 150–154
Galapagos Marine Reserve, **Vol. 8:** 152
Great Barrier Reef Marine Park, Australia,
Vol. 8: 152
Gwaii Haanas National Park Reserve, Canada,
Vol. 8: 151
marine protected areas (MPAs), **Vol. 8:** 150, 151, 153
Papahānaumokuākea Marine National Monument
(PMNM), Hawaiian Islands, **Vol. 8:** 151
Seaflower MPA, Colombia, **Vol. 8:** 152
Marine Protected Areas (MPAs), Vol. 3: 422, **Vol. 5:**
252–255, 284

Bold entries and page numbers denote encyclopedia articles.

marine resources, **Vol. 4:** 341, 348–349
marine spatial planning. *See* Ocean Zoning
Market, **Vol. 1:** 46, 101, 141
deregulated, **Vol. 1:** 236
economy, **Vol. 1:** 141–142
free markets, **Vol. 1:** 58, 80, 102, 140, 180, 236,
302, 435
fundamentalism, **Vol. 1:** 178
religions of, **Vol. 1:** 349
subduing, **Vol. 1:** 142
world markets, **Vol. 1:** 215
market-based instruments, **Vol. 3:** 319
market mechanisms
and climate change, **Vol. 3:** 58
Marketing, Vol. 2: 326–331
components of and sustainability in, **Vol. 2:** 327–330
and Green consumer, **Vol. 2:** 326–327
role in business sustainability, **Vol. 2:** 326
sustainability and issues, **Vol. 2:** 330
MARPOL Convention (1973/78). *See* **Convention
for the Prevention of Pollution from Ships
(MARPOL)**
Marrakesh Accords, **Vol. 3:** 358
Marrakesh Agreement (1994), **Vol. 3:** 124
Marranunggu language group, **Vol. 1:** 207
Marsh, George Perkins, **Vol. 1:** 430, **Vol. 3:** 300
See also *Man and Nature*
Marx, Karl, **Vol. 2:** 70
Masakin, **Vol. 1:** 433
masculinity, **Vol. 1:** 112, 134, 161, 174
Masdar City, Abu Dhabi, **Vol. 9:** 33, 98
mass rapid transit (MRT). *See* **Public Transportation**
mass transportation, **Vol. 1:** 152
See also **Public Transportation**
Massachusetts Institute of Technology, **Vol. 1:** 106
**Massachusetts v. Environmental Protection Agency,
Vol. 3:** 42, **379–381**
arguments, **Vol. 3:** 380
background, **Vol. 3:** 379–380
consequences, **Vol. 3:** 380–381
Massey, Doreen, **Vol. 1:** 307
Massey, Marshall, **Vol. 1:** 67
Massim society of Kalauna, **Vol. 1:** 230
Matanza-Riachuelo River Basin, **Vol. 3:** 260
material and energy flow analyses (MFA), **Vol. 4:** 241
Material Flow Analysis (MFA), Vol. 6: 242–248
domestic extraction (DE), **Vol. 6:** 243
domestic material consumption (DMC), **Vol. 6:**
243, 246
domestic processed output (DPO), **Vol. 6:** 243
domestic resource dependency (DE/DMC),
Vol. 6: 243
economy-wide material flow analysis (EMFA),
Vol. 6: 243

N

Nader, Ralph, **Vol. 2:** 86

Naess, Arne, **Vol. 1:** 35, 88, 132–133, 160, 388
  "The Shallow and the Deep, Long-Range Ecology
    Movement," **Vol. 1:** 113, 128, 132, 135, 408
  See also **Ecology, Deep**

NAFTA. *See* **North American Free Trade Agreement
  (NAFTA)**

Nagoya-Kuala Lumpur Supplementary Protocol on
  Liability and Redress to the Cartagena Protocol
  on Biosafety, **Vol. 3:** 83

Nagoya Protocol on Access to Genetic Resources and
  the Fair and Equitable Sharing of Benefits
  Arising from their Utilization, **Vol. 3:** 82, 84

Nairobi Declaration on the African Process for
  Combating Climate Change, **Vol. 3:** 181

Nairobi Declaration on the State of the Worldwide
  Environment (1982), **Vol. 3:** 457

Nairobi, Kenya, Vol. 9: 222–227
  Nairobi Metro 2030 Strategy, **Vol. 9:** 226
  transportation issues, **Vol. 9:** 225
  waste collection issues, **Vol. 9:** 224, 225
  water infrastructure and quality issues, **Vol. 9:** 225

Namibia, **Vol. 3:** 469
  uranium and, **Vol. 4:** 464, 466

NAMMCO Agreement, **Vol. 3:** 203

NAMMCO Commission, **Vol. 3:** 203

nanomaterials (NMs), **Vol. 3:** 389, 390, 391

Nanotechnology, Vol. 1: 390, **Vol. 4:** xxv, **306–311,
  Vol. 7: 260–263**
  China and, **Vol. 7:** 261, 262
  emerging issues, **Vol. 3:** 27–28
  India and, **Vol. 7:** 261, 262
  Taiwan and, **Vol. 7:** 261, 262

Nanotechnology Legislation, Vol. 3: 389–392
  future of regulation, **Vol. 3:** 391–392
  international initiatives, **Vol. 3:** 391
  nano-specific regulation, **Vol. 3:** 391

Narmada Dam Project, **Vol. 1:** 121, 312

National 9/11 Memorial, **Vol. 5:** 234

national action plans (NAPs), **Vol. 3:** 102–103

national ambient air quality standards (NAAQS),
  Vol. 3: 39–41

National Association of Evangelicals (NAE), **Vol. 1:**
  179, 312

National Council of Churches (NCC), **Vol. 1:** 6,
  281, 371
  Eco-Justice Working Group, **Vol. 1:** 26, 292

**National Environmental Accounting, Vol. 6:
  254–259**

National Environmental Policy Act (NEPA) (1968,
  United States), **Vol. 3:** 139, 273, **393–395,
  Vol. 5:** 70, 402
  criticism, **Vol. 3:** 394
  impact assessment, **Vol. 3:** 394–395
  legacy, **Vol. 3:** 393

National Forest System, **Vol. 3:** 300, 301, 302

national forests, United States, **Vol. 3:** 302

National Oceanic and Atmospheric Administration
  (NOAA) (United States), **Vol. 3:** 49, **Vol. 5:** 105,
  240, 242, 243

National Park Service (NPS) (United States), **Vol. 5:**
  75–76, 237, 418

national parks, **Vol. 1:** 16, 39–40, 44, 436, **Vol. 5:**
  74–75, 236–237
  See also IUCN's Protected Area Category II *under*
    International Union for the Conservation
    of Nature (IUCN); National Park Service
    (NPS) (United States); **Parks and Preserves—
    National;** United Kingdom National Park
    Authorities; United States National Park
    Service (NPS); **Wilderness Areas;** Yellowstone
    National Park; Yosemite National Park

National Pollution Survey (China), Vol. 7: 234–268
  air pollution, **Vol. 7:** 265–266
  soil pollution, **Vol. 7:** 266–267
  water pollution, **Vol. 7:** 264–265

**National Religious Partnership for the Environment,
  Vol. 1:** 255, **281,** 292, 442

National People's Congress (NPC), **Vol. 3:** 220–221

National Pollution Discharge Elimination System
  (NPDES) permit, **Vol. 3:** 46, 47

National Wilderness Preservation System (NWPS),
  Vol. 3: 508, 509, 511, **Vol. 5:** 418–419

National Wildlife Federation (NWF), **Vol. 1:** 291,
  Vol. 6: 367

Native Americans, **Vol. 1:** 225, 350, **Vol. 4:** 371
  See also **Indigenous Traditions, North America**

native plants, **Vol. 1:** 101–102

Native science, **Vol. 1:** 207

Natural Capital, Vol. 2: 125, 132, **Vol. 3:** 328,
  Vol. 5: 264–267, 270, **Vol. 10: 166–173**
  economics and, **Vol. 10:** 167
  market prices of, **Vol. 10:** 167
  property rights and, **Vol. 10:** 167–168
  shadow prices of, **Vol. 10:** 170
  United Nations Human Development Index (HDI) and
    gross domestic product (GDP) as measurements
    of, **Vol. 10:** 167, 168, 170, 171–172

Natural Capital Institute, **Vol. 1:** 291

Natural Capital Project, **Vol. 5:** 114

Natural Capitalism, Vol. 2: xxiii, xxv, 132, **345–349**
  and living world, **Vol. 2:** 345
  principles of, **Vol. 2:** 346–348

---

plant conservation, **Vol. 6:** 171

Quota Management System (QMS), **Vol. 8:** 202, 203

sealing and whaling in, **Vol. 8:** 202

Treaty of Waitangi, **Vol. 3:** 209, **Vol. 8:** 200, 202, 204

United States and, stalemate between, **Vol. 3:** 407

Waitangi Tribunal, **Vol. 8:** 202, 204

See also **Environmental Law—Australia and New Zealand**

New Zealand Nuclear Free Zone, Disarmament, and Arms Control Act, Vol. 3: 404–410

legislation and New Zealand-U.S. relations, **Vol. 3:** 407

nuclear dispute, **Vol. 3:** 406–407

New Zealand v. France, **Vol. 3:** 309

Newfoundland, Canada

Grand Banks fishery, **Vol. 6:** 137

Newman, Peter G., **Vol. 2:** 410

Ngarrindjeri peoples, **Vol. 1:** 207

NGOs. *See* **Nongovernmental Organizations (NGOs)**

Nguyen Dinh Xuan (legislator), **Vol. 7:** 347

Nicaragua, environmental law in, **Vol. 3:** 217

Nicaragua v. United States, **Vol. 3:** 3

Nickel, Vol. 4: 334–335

Nigeria, **Vol. 1:** 121, 210–211, 371, **Vol. 3:** 469

night soil. *See* **Manure, Human**

Nihon shoki, **Vol. 1:** 360–361

Nile River, Vol. 3: 471, **Vol. 5:** 193, 223, **Vol. 9:** 48, **228–230**

Nile River Basin Commission, **Vol. 3:** 471

Nile River Basin Framework Agreement (CFA), **Vol. 3:** 471

Nile River Basin Initiative (NBI), **Vol. 3:** 177, 471, **Vol. 9:** 229, 311, 374

NIMBY. *See* "Not in my back yard" (NIMBY)

nitrate, **Vol. 5:** 258, 303, 305, 306

nitrate leaching, **Vol. 5:** 268–269

Nitrogen, Vol. 4: 336–338

denitrification, **Vol. 5:** 258, 259, 269, 274, 306

nitrification, **Vol. 5:** 257, 258, 259

nitrogen cycle, **Vol. 4:** 134, **Vol. 5:** 78, 100, 109, 126, 258, 262, 273, 274

nitrogen fertilizers, **Vol. 4:** 23, 130, 133, 135, 411, **Vol. 5:** 14, 125, 259, 262, 273

nitrogen fixation, **Vol. 4:** 20, 23, 128–129, 130, 135, 337–338, 411, 443, **Vol. 5:** 12, 79, 215, 258, 260, 261, 273, 274, 293, 386

nitrogen loads, **Vol. 4:** 102

nitrogen (N) immobilization, **Vol. 5:** 258

nitrogen (N) mineralization, 78, **Vol. 5:** 258

reactive nitrogen, **Vol. 5:** 130, 268–269

water contamination and, **Vol. 5:** 304–305

See also **Eutrophication**

nitrogen oxide (NO_x), **Vol. 4:** 337–338, **Vol. 5:** 126, 130, 162, 272, 279

Nitrogen Saturation, Vol. 5: 268–269, 271

nitrogen use efficiency (NUE), **Vol. 4:** 135

nitrous oxide (N_2O), **Vol. 1:** 68–69, **Vol. 4:** 133–134, 190, 338, **Vol. 5:** 87, 165, 258, 259, 269, 365, 367, **Vol. 7:** 345

Nixon, Richard, **Vol. 3:** 393

Ping-Pong diplomacy, **Vol. 2:** 360

"No Ordinary Sun" (poem), **Vol. 3:** 405

no-significant harm principle, **Vol. 3:** 470

no-tillage farming, **Vol. 5:** 167, 260, 368–369

nocturnal lighting, **Vol. 3:** 118

noise pollution *See* pollution, noise

Non-Legally Binding Forest Principles, **Vol. 3:** 149

non–Organisation for Economic Co-operation and Development (non-OECD), **Vol. 3:** 490

See also Organisation for Economic Co-operation and Development (OECD)

non-state actors, chemical and waste management, **Vol. 3:** 28–29

nonattachment practice, **Vol. 1:** 332–333

nondualism, **Vol. 1:** 97

nonequilibrium, **Vol. 5:** 316, 380, 381, 384

See also equilibrial state

Nongovernmental Organizations (NGOs), Vol. 1: 28, 106, 115, 142, 172, 234, **Vol. 2:** 8–10, **Vol. 5:** 51, 76, 169, 348, 388, **Vol. 7: 269–272**

business, issues with, and, **Vol. 1:** 9–10

China and, **Vol. 7:** 77, 100, 270–271

ecolabeling and, **Vol. 3:** 131, 132

Friends of Nature, **Vol. 7:** 6, 100, 242

goals of, **Vol. 1:** 8

Green Watershed (Luse Liuyu) (China), **Vol. 7:** 270–271

India and, **Vol. 7:** 270

Narmada dam movement (Narmada Bachao Andolan) (India), **Vol. 7:** 270

See also **Activism–NGOs;** Nature Conservancy; Sierra Club; World Wide Fund for Nature (WWF)

nonhumans

humans, connection between, and, **Vol. 1:** 125–127, 144, 391, 408

interests of, **Vol. 1:** 23, 34–35, 88, 91, 103–104, 112

justice to, **Vol. 1:** 260–261

shamans and, **Vol. 1:** 357–358

nonmodern technology, **Vol. 1:** 386–387

nonpoint source pollution (NPS). *See* **Pollution, Nonpoint Source**

Bold entries and page numbers denote encyclopedia articles.

Nutrient and Biogeochemical Cycling, Vol. 5: 261, 270–274
nutrient cycling, **Vol. 5:** 12, 14, 109
nutrient enrichment, **Vol. 5:** 124, 125
   See also **Eutrophication**
nutrient leaching, **Vol. 5:** 104
nutrient loading, **Vol. 5:** 110, 124, 305
   See also **Eutrophication**

O

Obama, Barack, **Vol. 2:** 138, **Vol. 3:** 323, 379, 380, 409, **Vol. 10:** 178
Obama, Michelle, **Vol. 5:** 390, **Vol. 10:** 120
Obedientia vow, of Benedictine monks, **Vol. 1:** 416
ocean acidification, **Vol. 4:** 208
ocean resources, **Vol. 4:** 348
Ocean Acidification—Management, Vol. 5: 276–281
Ocean Acidification—Measurement, Vol. 6: 264–270
   pH levels, **Vol. 5:** 256, 277, 278, 279, 280
Ocean Resource Management, Vol. 5: 282–285
Ocean Zoning, 417–423
   comprehensive vs. ad hoc zoning, **Vol. 3:** 420
   examples, **Vol. 3:** 421–422
   future directions, **Vol. 3:** 422
   laws, design options for, **Vol. 3:** 419–420
Oceania, Vol. 8: 216–221
   exploitation of resources, **Vol. 8:** 216–217
   fertilizer extraction, **Vol. 8:** 218
   indigenous peoples in, **Vol. 8:** 217
   nuclear radiation in, **Vol. 8:** 219
   World War II's effect on, **Vol. 8:** 218–219
Oceania, indigenous traditions. *See* **Indigenous traditions, Oceania**
Oceans and Seas, Vol. 4: 340–346
Odhiambo, Thomas *See* African Academy of Sciences
Odum, Elisabeth, **Vol. 5:** 293
Odum, Eugene P., **Vol. 5:** 56, 57
Odum, Howard, **Vol. 5:** 293
OECD. *See* Organisation for Economic Co-operation and Development (OECD)
oekology, **Vol. 5:** 186
Office of Health and Human Services, **Vol. 3:** 156
Office of the High Commissioner for Human Rights, **Vol. 2:** 474
Ogallala Aquifer, **Vol. 4:** 41
Ogoni, **Vol. 1:** 121, 371
Ogunleye, Chief Bisi, **Vol. 1:** 172
Ohio, United States, water conservancy districts in, **Vol. 5:** 413
Oikos, **Vol. 1:** 25, 108, 125, 373

oil crisis of 1970, **Vol. 3:** 155
oil (crude)
   environmental impacts of, **Vol. 4:** 47, 323, 332, 342, 357
   production, **Vol. 4:** 67, 68
oil industry. *See* **Energy Industries—Oil**
Oil Pollution Act 1990 (OPA), **Vol. 2:** 191, **Vol. 3:** 47, 89, 288–289
oil refineries, **Vol. 4:** 227
oil sands (bitumen), **Vol. 4:** 487–488
   See also Oil Sands, Alberta, Canada; **Petroleum**
Oil Sands, Alberta, Canada, **Vol. 5:** 47
oil sludge, **Vol. 3:** 75
oil spills, **Vol. 5:** 101, 256, 283, 309
   See also *Atlantic Empress*; Deepwater Horizon (oil platform); *Exxon Valdez* Komi Republic of Russia; Kuwait oil fires; *Torrey Canyon*
oilseeds, **Vol. 4:** 138, 189
Ojibwe, **Vol. 1:** 227–228
   animism and, **Vol. 1:** 287
Oke-Ibadan, **Vol. 1:** 211
Okin, Susan Moller, **Vol. 1:** 259
Old Faithful geyser (Yellowstone National Park, United States), **Vol. 4:** 189
Old Order Amish, **Vol. 1:** 54
Old Order Anabaptists, **Vol. 1:** 55
Old Order communities, **Vol. 1:** 54
Old Order Mennonites, **Vol. 1:** 54
Old Testament, **Vol. 1:** 40, 429
Olmsted, Frederick Law, Sr., **Vol. 5:** 233, 234, 238, 402
Olson, Sigurd, **Vol. 1:** 370
Olumo, **Vol. 1:** 211
On the Origin of Species by Natural Selection, **Vol. 5:** 298
   See also Darwin, Charles
One-Child Policy, Vol. 7: 49, 166, **274–277**
Only One Earth, **Vol. 1:** 106, 108
Ontario, Canada, conservation authorities and water management, **Vol. 5:** 60, 414
Operation Flood. *See* **White Revolution of India**
Operation Pollinator, **Vol. 5:** 116
opinio juris, **Vol. 3:** 111–112
opportunism, **Vol. 1:** 239
optimum sustainable yield (OSY) (of fish) (also called maximum economic yield (MEY), **Vol. 6:** 136, 137, 138
orange roughy (fish), **Vol. 6:** 137
Order and Harmony, Vol. 1: 296–297
ore
   deposits, **Vol. 4:** 289, 290
   processing, **Vol. 4:** 286, 292
   See also individual resources
organic agriculture, **Vol. 5:** 12, 14, 179
Organic and Consumer Labels, Vol. 6: 88–89, 271–274

Bold entries and page numbers denote encyclopedia articles.

solar energy in, **Vol. 8:** 244

sustainability challenges in, **Vol. 6:** 355

urban heat island, **Vol. 6:** 120

water supply issues, **Vol. 8:** 242, 243, 244

phosphate rock, **Vol. 4:** 373–376

Phosphorus, Vol. 4: xxiii, **373–377, Vol. 5:** 126, 269, 305, 306

photovoltaic (PV) technologies, **Vol. 2:** 195–197, **Vol. 4:** 440–441

generations, **Vol. 2:** 197

See also **Energy Industries—Solar**

Phra Prajak Khuttajitto (Buddhist monk), **Vol. 7:** 346

Phyto-Sanitary Convention, **Vol. 3:** 174, 180

Pigou's theory, **Vol. 3:** 319

Pilgrimage, Vol. 1: 251, **303–304,** 422–423, 433

Pima County, Arizona, United States *See* Hillside Development Overlay Zone Ordinance

Pinchot, Gifford, **Vol. 1:** 435, **Vol. 8:** 18, 234, 308

See also **Wise Use Movement**

piracy, **Vol. 3:** 146

See also biopiracy; **Eco-Terrorism**

Place, Vol. 1: 131, **305–308**

definition, **Vol. 1:** 305–307

problem of, **Vol. 1:** 307

sense of, **Vol. 1:** 305

placelessness, **Vol. 1:** 306

planetary common good, **Vol. 1:** 71

plano of Colombia, **Vol. 5:** 388

Plant-Animal Interactions (PAI), **Vol. 5: 298–301**

plant breeding, **Vol. 2:** 43–44

plant cell culture, **Vol. 2:** 45

plastic bag taxes, **Vol. 3:** 320–321

plastics, **Vol. 4:** 123, 143

See also **Petroleum; Recycling**

Platinum Group Metals, Vol. 4: 378–380

Plato, **Vol. 5:** 113, 193

definition for justice, **Vol. 1:** 258

notion of wisdom, **Vol. 1:** 433, 462

platonism, **Vol. 1:** 154

pleasure, **Vol. 1:** 259, 278, 332, 402–403

Plumwood, Val, **Vol. 1:** 173

Poaching, Vol. 4: 381–383

point source pollution (PSP). *See* **Pollution, Point Source.** *See also* **Pollution, Nonpoint Source**

political ecology. *See* **Ecology, Political**

Politics, Vol. 1: 309–312

direct actions and civil disobedience, **Vol. 1:** 310–311

international, **Vol. 1:** 309–310

religion and sustainability and, **Vol. 1:** 311–312

see also **Green Parties;** Libertarians

pollucite. *See* cesium

polluted water, **Vol. 3:** 498

polluter, **Vol. 3:** 426

payment costs, **Vol. 3:** 426–427

Polluter Pays Principle, Vol. 3: 234, **425–429,** 495, **Vol. 9:** 129, 152, 263, 264

contribution to sustainability, **Vol. 3:** 428–429

in European law, **Vol. 3:** 427–428

functions and substance of, **Vol. 3:** 425

in international law, **Vol. 3:** 427

and other environmental principles, **Vol. 3:** 427

pollution, defined, **Vol. 3:** 425–426

pollution, **Vol. 1:** 39, 200, 215, 320, **Vol. 3:** 495, 500

air, **Vol. 5:** 110, 180, 233, 250, 308, 345, 356, 359, 395, 397, 410

atmospheric, **Vol. 5:** 184

definition of, **Vol. 3:** 425–426

land, **Vol. 5:** 308

noise, **Vol. 5:** 309, 310, 345

nuclear, **Vol. 5:** 201, 310

taxes, **Vol. 1:** 266

water, **Vol. 5:** 18, 24, 208, 245, 250, 283, 308, 356, 359, 367

white pollution (plastic), **Vol. 5:** 181

Pollution, Nonpoint Source, Vol. 3: 44, 46, **Vol. 5:** 18–20, 60, **302–307,** 308–309, 310, 365

Pollution, Point Source, Vol. 5: xxii, 19, 60, 61, 302, **308–312**

polyaromatic hydrocarbons (PAHs), **Vol. 5:** 46, 91, 283

polychlorinated biphenyls (PCBs), **Vol. 1:** 419, **Vol. 3:** 74, 75, **Vol. 5:** 87, 258, 259, 283, 284

polyculture crops, **Vol. 5:** 12, 13, 80, 323, 325

See also monoculture crops

Polynesians, **Vol. 1:** 231

polyvinylchloride (PVC), **Vol. 1:** 419

Population, Vol. 1: 313–316, **Vol. 10:** 180–188

contraception and family planning, **Vol. 10:** 180, 183, 185

demography, current situation, **Vol. 1:** 313–314

diversity, **Vol. 1:** 38, 353

fertility rates, **Vol. 10:** 181–182

growth, **Vol. 1:** 12, 107, 148, 165, 179, 200, 314–316, 387, 430

key figures and main issues, **Vol. 1:** 314–316

limits to growth, **Vol. 10:** 181

migration and, **Vol. 10:** 182

policy, and health, **Vol. 1:** 172

population strategies, **Vol. 10:** 184–185

population thinking and theories, **Vol. 10:** 184

women's issues and, **Vol. 10:** 181

population biology, **Vol. 5:** 54, 56

The Population Bomb, **Vol. 3:** 149, **Vol. 5:** 113

See also Ehrlich, Paul

Population Dynamics, Vol. 5: 313–316

population growth
  and water insecurity, **Vol. 3:** 500
Population Indicators, Vol. 6: 282–286
population rate parameters, **Vol. 6:** 133–134
populations
  fish, **Vol. 4:** 102, 142, 349
  food supply and, **Vol. 4:** 20, 131, 151–153, 157, 269
  insect, **Vol. 4:** 16, 360, 361, 362, 363
  maximum sustainable yield (MSY) and, **Vol. 4:** 321
  world population, **Vol. 4:** xxiii, 130, 270, 491, 493
port towns, **Vol. 4:** 342
Porter, Michael, **Vol. 2:** 425
Portugal, **Vol. 3:** 469
Posey, Darrell, **Vol. 4:** 232
positivism, **Vol. 3:** 339
possessions. *See* **Property and Possessions**
post-introduction evolution, **Vol. 5:** 214
potash (potassium oxide [K₂O]), **Vol. 4:** 384–385
Potassium, Vol. 4: 384–386
potatoes, **Vol. 4:** 148
potentially responsible parties (PRP), **Vol. 3:** 165, 166
Poverty, Vol. 1: 4–5, 107, 238–239, 256, 269, **317–320,**
    380, 437, **Vol. 2:** xxiii, xxv, **376–378,** 381
  attributes of, **Vol. 2:** 376–377
  challenges, 319–320
  cities and, **Vol. 10:** 38
  history, **Vol. 1:** 319
  future, **Vol. 2:** 320
  global institutional arrangements, **Vol. 1:** 319–320
  interventions, alleviation and reduction,
      Vol. 2: 377–378
  population and, **Vol. 10:** 184
  See also Third World; wealth
poverty gap ratio (PGR), **Vol. 6:** 75, 77
power plants, **Vol. 1:** 152, **Vol. 4:** 65–66, 68–69, 75,
    179, 465, 487
practical wisdom, **Vol. 1:** 74, 433
pragmatic maxim, **Vol. 1:** 322
Pragmatism, Vol. 1: 161, **321–324,** 382
  environmental pragmatism, **Vol. 1:** 160,
      322–323, 407
  history and philosophy, **Vol. 1:** 321–322
  religious dimension of, **Vol. 1:** 323
  as scientific metaphysics, **Vol. 1:** 322
  sustainability and natural piety, **Vol. 1:** 323–324
pragmatists, **Vol. 1:** 302
Prairie Style of landscape architecture,
    Vol. 5: 233–234
  See also Jensen, Jens
Pranayama, **Vol. 1:** 200
praseodymium, **Vol. 4:** 395
Pratītya-samutpāda, **Vol. 1:** 48
prayer, **Vol. 1:** 257, 334, 37
  See also **Meditation and Prayer**

Precautonary Principle, Vol. 1: 265, 267, **325–326,**
    Vol. 3: 234, **430–433,** 435, 466, 507,
    Vol. 4: 91, **Vol. 6:** 374, **Vol. 9:** 263, **Vol. 10:** 216
  conferences, treaties, and law, **Vol. 3:** 430–431
  outlook for future, **Vol. 3:** 432
  transatlantic divide and international applications,
      Vol. 3: 431–432
  United States, application in, **Vol. 3:** 432
  Wingspread Statement on the Precautionary
      Principle, **Vol. 1:** 326
precipitation, **Vol. 1:** 70, 177
preference utilitarianism, **Vol. 1:** 403
preindustrial period, **Vol. 5:** 165, 276
preservation, **Vol. 1:** 5, 22, 40, 79, 134, 233, 370, 382,
    429–430
  conservation vs., **Vol. 1:** 80
Pressure-State-Response (PSR) model, **Vol. 6:** 104
preventative medicine, **Vol. 2:** 269
prevention principle, **Vol. 3:** 234
Primavesi, Anne, **Vol. 1:** 173, 188
Principle-Based Regulation, 434–435
  debate, **Vol. 3:** 435
  future directions, **Vol. 3:** 435
  origin, evolution, and development, **Vol. 3:** 434–435
principle of proportionality, **Vol. 3:** 426
printed circuit boards, **Vol. 4:** 122–123
prior informed consent (PIC), **Vol. 3:** 75, 489
*Priorities for the Conservation of Mammalian Diversity—
    Has the Panda Had Its Day?,* **Vol. 5:** 64
private land tenure and sustainability, **Vol. 3:** 437–439
private nuisance, **Vol. 3:** 411, 418, 461
private property, **Vol. 3:** 402
  See also property; **Property and Posessions**
private rights, definition of, **Vol. 3:** 411–412
private standards and soft law, fair trade on, **Vol. 3:** 292
privatization, **Vol. 1:** 236, 246, 272
Probo Koala incident, **Vol. 3:** 492–493
Proceedings of the National Academy of Science
    (PNAS), **Vol. 5:** 188
process management, **Vol. 2:** 320
process philosophy, **Vol. 1:** 299
process theology, **Vol. 1:** 328
Process Thought, Vol. 1: 327–330
  major thinkers and ideas, **Vol. 1:** 327–328
  process philosophy, **Vol. 1:** 299
  process theology, **Vol. 1:** 328
  sustainable economics and, **Vol. 1:** 329–330
  sustainability ethics and, **Vol. 1:** 328–329
product and industrial design. *See* **Design, Product and
    Industrial**
product development, **Vol. 2:** 287
product labels. *See* **Ecolabeling; Ecolabels; Organic
    and Consumer Labels**
product liability torts, **Vol. 3:** 462

Product-Service Systems (PSSs), Vol. 2: 379–381
concept of, **Vol. 2:** 380
impact on sustainable business, **Vol. 2:** 379
product stewardship, **Vol. 3:** 427
product sustainability index (PSI), **Vol. 2:** 419
production tax credit (PTC), **Vol. 3:** 158–159
Products Liability Directive, **Vol. 3:** 462
Progress, Vol. 10: 189–192
machine-made products, **Vol. 10:** 190
violence and, **Vol. 10:** 191–192
world's fairs, **Vol. 10:** 191
Project GreenHands, **Vol. 5:** 388
Promethean environmentalism, **Vol. 1:** 388–389
promethium, **Vol. 4:** 395
propagule, **Vol. 5:** 110, 213, 215
property, **Vol. 1:** 103, 140, 278
common property resources, **Vol. 1:** 395–396
distribution of, **Vol. 1:** 332
effect of power on, **Vol. 1:** 333
global scheme, **Vol. 1:** 320
private, **Vol. 1:** 63, 80, 180, 207, 236, 309, 331
rights, **Vol. 1:** 141–142, 272, 435
See also Jubilee
Property and Construction Industry, Vol. 2: xxiv, 382–386
assessment tools, importance of, **Vol. 2:** 384
barriers to sustainability in, **Vol. 2:** 384–385
issues with, **Vol. 2:** 382–383
product innovation and sustainability, **Vol. 2:** 383
service and management, sustainability in, **Vol. 2:** 383
Property and Possessions, Vol. 1: 154, **331–334**
See also The Story of Stuff; **Subsistence**
Property Rights, Vol. 4: 90, 166, 284, 298–299, 499, **Vol. 10: 193–202**
ecological degradation and, **Vol. 10:** 198–199
harm, issues with legal definitions of, **Vol. 10:** 197–198
labor theory, **Vol. 10:** 196
private rights, **Vol. 10:** 195, 196, 199
public property, **Vol. 10:** 199
use-right systems, **Vol. 10:** 195
Property Rights (China), Vol. 7: 293–295
Prophet Muhammad, **Vol. 1:** 243–245, 252, 332, 347, 411, 434
See also **Islam**
A Prosperous Way Down: Principles and Policies, **Vol. 5:** 293
protection principle, **Vol. 3:** 234
protein, **Vol. 4:** 22, 24, 188–189, 190,
See also **Soybeans**

Protestant ethic, **Vol. 1:** 60
Protestantism. *See* **Christianity, Mainline Protestant**
See also **Christianity, Anabaptist; Christianity, Evangelical and Pentecostal; Christianity, Society of Friends / Quakers**
Proto-Green party, **Vol. 1:** 194
Protocol for the Environmental Protection of the Antarctic Territory, **Vol. 3:** 259
Protocol on Energy Efficiency and Related Environmental Aspects (PEEREA), **Vol. 3:** 342, 344
proverbs
African tradition, **Vol. 1:** 210, 434
Hebrew Bible, **Vol. 1:** 432
psychobiologic gauge, of time, **Vol. 1:** 392–393
psycho-ecology. *See* ecopsychology.
public domain forests, protection and preservation of, **Vol. 3:** 300
Public Health, Vol. 7: 296–301
flooding and, **Vol. 7:** 299
natural disasters and, **Vol. 7:** 299
pollution, **Vol. 7:** 298
respiratory diseases, **Vol. 7:** 298
tuberculosis (TB), **Vol. 7:** 298
public nuisance, **Vol. 3:** 414, 461
Public-Private Partnerships, Vol. 2: 392–395, 425, **Vol. 7: 302–304**
AT Biopower, **Vol. 7:** 303
crab condominiums, **Vol. 7:** 304
issues associated with, **Vol. 2:** 394
Landfill Gas and Waste-to-Energy Project, **Vol. 7:** 303
need for, **Vol. 2:** 392, 393
types, **Vol. 2:** 393
Public-Private Partnerships (Africa), Vol. 9: 247–252
Public Transportation, Vol. 2: 387–391, 412, **Vol. 7: 305–310, Vol. 8: 246–250**
bus rapid transit (BRT), **Vol. 7:** 309, **Vol. 8:** 248
China and, **Vol. 7:** 306
environmental benefits, **Vol. 2:** 389
funding for, **Vol. 2:** 388
importance of innovations in, **Vol. 2:** 390
India and, **Vol. 7:** 305–306
as an industry, **Vol. 2:** 387
Pakistan and, **Vol. 7:** 306
rail systems, **Vol. 8:** 248–249
role in sustainability, **Vol. 2:** 388–389
Sri Lanka and, **Vol. 7:** 306
subways, **Vol. 8:** 247
Thailand and, **Vol. 7:** 306
water-based systems, **Vol. 8:** 249
See also transit-oriented development (TOD); *individual city articles*
public trust doctrine, **Vol. 3:** 439–440

Bold entries and page numbers denote encyclopedia articles.

Bold entries and page numbers denote encyclopedia articles.

Steiner, Hillel, **Vol. 1**: 271
Steiner, Rudolf, **Vol. 1**: 14, 24
See also **Anthroposophy**
stevia, **Vol. 5**: 209
Stewardship, Vol. 1: 3, 5, 111, 340, **372–374**
agricultural, **Vol. 1**: 13
criticism and success, **Vol. 1**: 374
environmental, 3 **Vol. 1**: 74
of land, **Vol. 1**: 26, 54
religion, **Vol. 1**: 374
STIRPAT. *See* **I = P × A × T Equation**
stock-flow resources, **Vol. 5**: 264, 265
stock flows, **Vol. 5**: 265
stockholder theory, **Vol. 2**: 424
Stockholm Convention. *See* **Convention on Persistent Organic Pollutants**
Stockholm Declaration on the Human Environment (1972), **Vol. 3**: 102, 121, 122, 149, 212, 234, 278, 279, 457, 466
Stockholm Report, **Vol. 1**: 106, 108, 137, 238
See also United Nations Conference on the Human Environment
Stockholm, Sweden, Vol. 9: 291, **297–302**
Hammarby Sjöstad, **Vol. 9**: 299, 300, 347
public transportation in, **Vol. 9**: 298–299
Regional Planning in Stockholm County sidebar, **Vol. 6**: 297
Stockholm Environment Programme for 2012 to 2015, **Vol. 9**: 299
Stockholm Royal Seaport, **Vol. 9**: 299–300
Stockholm University's Resilience Centre, **Vol. 6**: 369
The Storm Leopard, **Vol. 5**: 134
Stormwater
as pollution, **Vol. 5**: 19
filtering of, **Vol. 5**: 318–320
Stormwater Management, Vol. 5: 235, **377–379**
The Story of Stuff, **Vol. 1**: 350, 352
See also **Property and Possessions**
Strategic Environmental Assessment (SEA), Vol. 6: 329–331
Strengthened Smart Grid plan, **Vol. 3**: 485
stressors
and ecological restoration, **Vol. 5**: 109, 110
strict liability torts, **Vol. 3**: 462–463
Strong, Maurice, **Vol. 1**: 115, 238
strong sustainability, **Vol. 3**: 505, 506–507
See also **Weak vs. Strong Sustainability Debate**
structural sin, **Vol. 1**: 367
Study of Critical Environmental Problems, **Vol. 5**: 113
Sturgeon, Noel, **Vol. 1**: 173
sub–Saharan Africa, **Vol. 4**: 4

submersed aquatic vegetation (SAV), **Vol. 5**: 124
Subsistence, Vol. 1: **376–378**
in anthropology and sociology, **Vol. 1**: 376–377
indigenous peoples and, **Vol. 1**: 377
See also **Property and Possessions**
substantive federal environmental statutes, in United States, **Vol. 3**: 273–274
suburbanization, **Vol. 2**: 410
Succession, Vol. 5: 24, **380–384**
succession model, **Vol. 5**: 380, 381, 384
successional seres, **Vol. 5**: 381
Sudan, **Vol. 3**: 471
suffering, **Vol. 1**: 16, 18, 48, 92, 103–104, 133, 260, 270, 311, 333, 404
Sufis, **Vol. 1**: 244, 411
sugar, **Vol. 4**: 148–149
See also **Sugarcane**
Sugarcane, Vol. 4: **445–446**
Sulfur, Vol. 4: **447–448**, **Vol. 5**: 164, 305
sulfur dioxide (SO_2), **Vol. 5**: 165
desulfurization, **Vol. 7**: 52, 53, 145
See also **Greenhouse Gases (GHGs)**
sulfur dioxide emissions, **Vol. 3**: 42
sulfur taxes, **Vol. 3**: 320, 322
Sumeria, **Vol. 1**: 9, 93, 187, 429
Sun Dance ceremonies, **Vol. 1**: 227
Sundarbans delta, India, **Vol. 7**: 62
sunlight. *See* **Solar Energy**
Superfund Act of 1980 (United States), **Vol. 3**: 321, 375, **Vol. 5**: 411, **Vol. 8**: 311
See also Comprehensive Environmental Response, Compensation, and Liability Act
Superfund sites, **Vol. 6**: 119
superindustrialization, **Vol. 3**: 135
Superintendency of the Environment (Chile), **Vol. 3**: 261
Supplemental Environmental Projects (SEPs), **Vol. 3**: 165
Supply Chain Analysis, Vol. 6: **332–336**
Electrolux, **Vol. 6**: 334
Stony Field Farms, **Vol. 6**: 334
Timberland, **Vol. 6**: 334
Trucost, **Vol. 6**: 335
Supply Chain Management, Vol. 2: **432–436**
lifecycle management, **Vol. 2**: 434
scope and importance, **Vol. 2**: 432–433
sustainable strategies in, **Vol. 2**: 434–435
Supreme Being
African concept, **Vol. 1**: 3, 209–210
surface mining, **Vol. 4**: 74, 292
Sustainability Assessment Questionnaire (SAQ), **Vol. 6**: 367
sustainability ethics, **Vol. 1**: 22–23, 191, 241,

T

tailings (metal), **Vol. 4:** 94, 185–186, 254, 294, 380, 466
Taishang Laojun. *See* Laozi
Taiwan, environmental law in, **Vol. 3:** 226–229
    See under **Energy Industries—Nuclear;**
        Nanotechnology
Taiwan Environmental Protection Administration
        (TEPA), **Vol. 3:** 227, 228
Tajikistan
    air quality management and protection, **Vol. 3:** 256
    energy and environment, **Vol. 3:** 256, 257
    land management and protection, **Vol. 3:** 255
    water management and protection, **Vol. 3:** 255
Talloires Declaration, **Vol. 1:** 148–149
Talmud, **Vol. 1:** 181, 256, 411
    See also **Sacred Texts**
Taniguchi, Norio. *See* **Nanotechnology**
tanker ships, **Vol. 4:** 341, 343
tantalum. *See* **Coltan**
Tanzania, **Vol. 3:** 471
Tao Te Ching. See Daodejing, Classic of the Way and its
    Power
Tapas, **Vol. 1:** 198
Tapped, **Vol. 5:** 180
    See also **Groundwater Management; Home Ecology**
Tapu, **Vol. 1:** 229, 230
Taqwa, **Vol. 1:** 433
tar sands, **Vol. 4:** 370, 487
    See also oil sands (bitumen)
taro. *See* **Root Crops**
Tattvartha Sutra, **Vol. 1:** 249
    See also **Sacred Texts**
Tawhid, **Vol. 1:** 87, 433
tax-free grants, **Vol. 3:** 159
tax incremental financing, **Vol. 5:** 45
tax reduction programs, **Vol. 3:** 158–159
Taxation Indicators, Green, Vol. 6: 350–354
taxon (taxa), **Vol. 5:** 31–32, 35, 202, 203
    See also Linnaean hierarchy
Taylor, Bron, **Vol. 1:** 241, 286
Te Kaha, **Vol. 3:** 407
Tea, Vol. 4: 450–452
Technical Barriers to Trade (TBT) Agreement,
    Vol. 3: 311, 312
technical nutrients, **Vol. 2:** 83
Technological innovation, **Vol. 3:** 20
Technology, Vol. 1: 87, 141, 203–204, **386–390**
    accumulation of technological information within
        species, **Vol. 10:** 50, 51
    biotechnology, **Vol. 1:** 389–390
    care for aging populations and, **Vol. 10:** 7
    challenges, **Vol. 1:** 387

definition, **Vol. 1:** 386
development and sustainability, **Vol. 1:** 387–388
future, **Vol. 1:** 390
history of technological creativity and chages,
    Vol. 10: 19, 45, 52, 54, 58
impact on agriculture, **Vol. 1:** 13
instrumentalism, **Vol. 1:** 386–387
modern, **Vol. 1:** 338, 386–388, 393–394
nanotechnology, **Vol. 1:** 390
nonmodern, **Vol. 1:** 386–387
neo-Luddite environmentalism, **Vol. 1:** 388–389
Promethean environmentalism, **Vol. 1:** 388–389
rebound effects and, **Vol. 10:** 33
See also **Collective Learning; Community;**
    Energy Efficiency; Local Solutions to
    Global Problems; Mobility; Nuclear Power;
    Nanotechnology; Progress
technology, clean. *See* **Investment, CleanTech**
Technosphere, **Vol. 1:** 354, 388
Technozoic era, **Vol. 1:** 400
Telecommunications Industry, Vol. 2: xxiii, **444–448**
    climate change issues due to, **Vol. 2:** 444–445
    and e-waste, **Vol. 2:** 446
    positive impact on environment, **Vol. 2:** 446–447
    raw materials and carbon footprint, **Vol. 2:** 445–446
temperate forests/grasslands, **Vol. 1:** 39, 177
temporal scale, **Vol. 1:** 104
Tennessee Valley Authority (TVA), **Vol. 5:** 87, 414
Tennessee Valley Authority v. Hill, **Vol. 3:** 153
Teologia da Terra, **Vol. 1:** 64
tephra, **Vol. 5:** 309
terbium, **Vol. 4:** 395
territorial waters, **Vol. 3:** 86
Texas, United States
    air pollution in, **Vol. 5:** 357
    hydraulic fracturing (fracking) in, **Vol. 5:** 354–355, 356
    oil drilling in, **Vol. 5:** 19
textiles, **Vol. 4:** 138
Textiles Industry, Vol. 2: 449–453
    ecolabeling in, **Vol. 2:** 450
    effects on environment, **Vol. 2:** 449
    organic cotton and green strategies for,
        Vol. 2: 451–452
Thailand, **Vol. 1:** 48, 216, 218, 311, **Vol. 3:** 471
    environmental law in, **Vol. 3:** 266–267
    See also **Southeast Asia**
    See under **Public Transportation; Utilities**
        Regulation and Energy Efficiency
thaw depth, **Vol. 1:** 70
Theocentrism, Vol. 1: 35, 120, 254, 346, **391**
theory of seed plant invasiveness, **Vol. 5:** 215
thermal pollution, **Vol. 4:** 415
thermodynamic gauge, of time, **Vol. 1:** 392
Third World, **Vol. 1:** 171, 181, 239, 269, 430

Bold entries and page numbers denote encyclopedia articles.

Bold entries and page numbers denote encyclopedia articles.

colonization in Oceania, **Vol. 8:** 314
edge cities, **Vol. 8:** 316
Edge City: Life on the New Frontier, **Vol. 8:** 316
Gini coefficient, **Vol. 8:** 315
Melbourne Principles, **Vol. 8:** 317
railroads and streetcars (impacts of), **Vol. 8:** 315
smart growth, **Vol. 8:** 317
water insecurity and, **Vol. 3:** 500–501
Urbanization (Africa), Vol. 9: 335–341
population data collection issues, **Vol. 9:** 335
public transportation and, **Vol. 9:** 339
rural-to-urban migration, **Vol. 9:** 337, 338
sea-level rise and, **Vol. 9:** 340
Urbanization (Europe), Vol. 9: 342–348
bicycle superhighway in Copenhagen, Denmark,
Vol. 9: 347
Green City Index, **Vol. 9:** 345
See also Industrial Revolution
**Urbanization (Western Asia and Northern Africa),
Vol. 9: 349–354**
aflaj (water infrastructure in Oman), **Vol. 9:** 350–351
codified vs. customary law, **Vol. 9:** 349–350, 351–352
himas (protected areas in Saudi Arabia), **Vol. 9:** 351
urban agriculture in, **Vol. 9:** 349
urine, **Vol. 4:** 273, 277–278
Uruguay, **Vol. 3:** 470
See also **Southern Cone**
US v. Washington (1974), **Vol. 5:** 75
USSR. *See* Russia
Utilitarianism, Vol. 1: 42, 261, **402–405**
act, **Vol. 1:** 259, 403
animal rights and, **Vol. 1:** 404
environment and, **Vol. 1:** 404
hedonistic, **Vol. 1:** 402–403
interest vs. individuals, **Vol. 1:** 405
origins, **Vol. 1:** 402–404
perspective on justice, **Vol. 1:** 259
preference, **Vol. 1:** 403
rule, **Vol. 1:** 403–404
Utilities Regulation, Vol. 3: 480–486
feed-in tariffs, **Vol. 3:** 483
rate regulation, **Vol. 3:** 481
real-time pricing and green pricing, **Vol. 3:** 483–484
renewable electricity standards (RES),
Vol. 3: 482–483
restructuring, **Vol. 3:** 482
**Utilities Regulation and Energy Efficiency,
Vol. 7: 382–386**
Bureau of Energy Efficiency (BEE), **Vol. 7:** 383, 384
China and, **Vol. 7:** 382–383
energy efficiency requirement (EE/DSM Rule),

Vol. 7: 382–383, 386
India and, **Vol. 7:** 383–384
Power Development Plan (PDP), **Vol. 7:** 385
Thailand and, **Vol. 7:** 384–385
Top 1,000 Enterprises Program, **Vol. 7:** 66, 67, 157
Uttarakhand, India, **Vol. 1:** 52
Uzbekistan, **Vol. 3:** 469
agriculture in **Vol. 4:** 7
conflict minerals in, **Vol. 4:** 85
cotton production in, **Vol. 4:** 96
energy and environment, **Vol. 3:** 256
illegal crop eradication and germ warfare, **Vol. 4:** 113
in situ leaching (uranium), **Vol. 4:** 466
land management and protection, **Vol. 3:** 255
water management and protection, **Vol. 3:** 255

V

Vajrayana Buddhists, **Vol. 1:** 410
Valiente, Doreen, **Vol. 1:** 299
Vallentyne, Peter, **Vol. 1:** 271
"The Value of the World's Ecosystem Services and
Natural Capital," **Vol. 5:** 265
Values, Vol. 1: 95, **407–408, Vol. 10: 212–218**
anthropocentric values, communal, **Vol. 10:** 217
anthropocentric values, individual, **Vol. 10:** 215–217
biocentric values, **Vol. 10:** 214–215
in nature, **Vol. 1:** 407–408
Values Party, New Zealand, **Vol. 1:** 194–195
Vancouver, Canada, Vol. 8: 320–322
Canadian Pacific Railway (CPR), **Vol. 8:** 320
film production in, **Vol. 8:** 321
Southeast False Creek brownfield, **Vol. 8:** 321, 322
Variant C, **Vol. 3:** 308, 309
Vasudev, Sadhguru Jaggi. *See* Isha Foundation
Vatican, **Vol. 1:** 63, 83, 315
See also **Christianity, Roman Catholic**
vegetarian society, **Vol. 1:** 409
Vegetarianism, Vol. 1: 11, 17–18, 270, 404, **409–412**
Asian traditions, **Vol. 1:** 17, 250, 251, 333, 363,
409–410
factory farming, religious response to, **Vol. 1:** 411
Venezuela, **Vol. 3:** 469
environmental law in, **Vol. 3:** 262
Venice Declaration, **Vol. 1:** 57
religions and sustainability and, **Vol. 1:** 414
See also **Christianity, Eastern Orthodox;
Christianity, Roman Catholic**
Verhulst, Pierre-François, **Vol. 5:** 56
See also **Carrying Capacity**
vices. *See* **Virtues and Vices**
video displays and monitors, **Vol. 4:** 122, 124
Vienna Convention on the Law of Treaties (VCLT),
Vol. 3: 112, 113

Bold entries and page numbers denote encyclopedia articles.

White, Robin, **Vol. 2:** xxii

White Sea, **Vol. 5:** 363

White's Thesis, Vol. 1: 60, 110, 414, **425–426**

    apologetic response to, **Vol. 1:** 425

    constructive/critical response to, **Vol. 1:** 425–426

    "The Historical Roots of Our Ecological Crisis,"

        Vol. 1: 60, 111, 243, 414, 425, 427

    sympathetic response to, **Vol. 1:** 426

    See also **White, Lynn, Jr.**

Whitehead, Alfred North, **Vol. 1:** 34, 327–329

Whole Foods Market, **Vol. 3:** 292

Wicca, **Vol. 1:** 286, 299

Wilderness, Vol. 1: 4, 22, 285, 388, **428–431**

    biophysical, **Vol. 1:** 430

    conservation, preservation, and restoration,

        Vol. 1: 430–431

    deep ecology and, **Vol. 1:** 133–134

    economic development and social justice,

        Vol. 1: 430

    idea of, **Vol. 1:** 429

    modern ideas of, **Vol. 1:** 429–430

    non-Romantic ideas, **Vol. 1:** 388

    protection, **Vol. 1:** 39, 133–134, 370, 407

    See also **Nature; Parks and Preserves—Wilderness**

        Areas

Wilderness Act (1964, United States), **Vol. 3:** 453,

        508–511, Vol. 5: 418

    controversies, **Vol. 3:** 510

    international impact, **Vol. 3:** 510–511

    purpose of, **Vol. 3:** 509

    wilderness area, defining, **Vol. 3:** 509

    wilderness areas, allowed uses in, **Vol. 3:** 509

Wilderness Areas, Vol. 5: 417–420

    wildfires, **Vol. 5:** 138, 139, 140

    "Wildlands and Human Needs," **Vol. 5:** 76

    See also World Wide Fund for Nature (WWF)

    wildlife law, **Vol. 4:** 381

    wildlife management, **Vol. 5:** 419, 54, 55, 56, 233

Willamette River, **Vol. 5:** 144

Wilson, E. O., **Vol. 3:** 453

Wind Energy, Vol. 4: 496–498

    See also **Energy Industries—Wind**

wind farms, **Vol. 2:** 106–107

Windhoek Treaty, **Vol. 3:** 181, 182

Wingspread Statement on the Precautionary Principle.

    See under **Precautionary Principle**

Wisconsin, United States, **Vol. 5:** 88, 377

Wisdom Traditions, Vol. 1: 432–434

    Abrahamic faiths, **Vol. 1:** 432–433

    practical wisdom, **Vol. 1:** 433–434

Wisdom Christology, **Vol. 1:** 433

---

wise use, **Vol. 3:** 98

    and ecosystem services, **Vol. 3:** 99–100

Wise Use Movement, Vol. 1: 180, **435–436,**

    Vol. 4: 499–500

Wittfogel, Karl, **Vol. 5:** 220

    See also **Irrigation**

Woicke, Peter, **Vol. 2:** 208

wolframite, **Vol. 4:** 85

women, **Vol. 1:** 171–175, 193, 246, 269, 311, 315, 333

    consumer power, **Vol. 1:** 172

    nature and, **Vol. 1:** 173–174

    See also **Feminist Thought**

wood and wood products. *See* **Forest**

    Products—Timber

Woolman, John, **Vol. 1:** 67

Word of Wisdom, **Vol. 1:** 279

Working Party on Nanotechnology (WPN),

    Vol. 3: 28, 391

Workshop on Water Resources Management in the

    Islamic World, Amman, **Vol. 1:** 245–246

World Bank, Vol. 1: 136, 175, 239, 247, 314, 318,

    364, **437–438, Vol. 2:** 208, 359, **Vol. 3:** 280,

    Vol. 5: 206, **Vol. 9: 379–382**

    Keynes, John Maynard, **Vol. 9:** 379, 380

    structural adjustments (of the 1980s–1990s),

        Vol. 9: 380–381

    vote shareholding issues, **Vol. 9:** 380, 381

World Charter for Nature (1982), **Vol. 3:** 145, 457

World Commission on Environment and Development

    (WCED), **Vol. 1:** 7, 46, 106–108, 115, 172,

    184, 240, 265, 309, 381–382, 388, **Vol. 2:** 337,

    Vol. 3: 81, 122, 125, 149, 166

    See also Brundtland Commission; Brundtland

        Report; *Our Common Future;* **Development,**

        Sustainable

World Conservation Strategy (1980), **Vol. 1:** 381,

    Vol. 3: 122

World Conservation Union, **Vol. 1:** 116–117, 381

World Constitutionalism, Vol. 3: 64, **512–514**

    international environmental constitution,

        Vol. 3: 513

    origins and development, **Vol. 3:** 512–513

    resistance to, **Vol. 3:** 513–514

World Convocation on Justice, Peace, and the Integrity

    of Creation (Seoul), **Vol. 1:** 61–62

World Council of Churches (WCC), **Vol. 1:** 57, 60–61,

    152, 238–239, 355, 381, 437, **Vol. 4:** 234

World Energy Council, **Vol. 2:** 189–190

World Health Organization (WHO), **Vol. 2:** 478,

    Vol. 3: 255, 266, 312, 493, **Vol. 7:** 296

    air quality standards, **Vol. 7:** 23, 30, 159, 298

World Heritage Convention, **Vol. 3:** 188–189, 207

World Religions and Ecology, Vol. 1: 439–443

    ethical context, **Vol. 1:** 440